PSYCHOLOGY 91/92

Twenty-First Edition

Editor

Michael G. Walraven
Jackson Community College

Michael G. Walraven is professor of psychology and Dean of Instruction at Jackson Community College. He received a B.A. from the University of Maryland in 1966, an M.A. from Western Michigan University in 1968, and a Ph.D. from Michigan State University in 1974. He is affiliated with the Association for Behavior Analysis and the Michigan Society for Behavioral Medicine and Biofeedback. Within his community he has served as a director and officer of several community-based service agencies, and currently serves as president of Aware, an agency providing shelter, counseling, and advocacy services for victims of domestic violence and sexual assault.

Editor

Hiram E. Fitzgerald
Michigan State University

Hiram E. Fitzgerald is a professor and associate chairperson in the Department of Psychology at Michigan State University. He received a B.A. in 1962 from Lebanon Valley College, and an M.A. in 1964 and a Ph.D. in 1967 from the University of Denver. He is a Fellow of the American Psychological Association, a member of the American Psychological Society, the executive director of the International Association for Infant Mental Health, and the regional vice president of the World Association for Infant Psychiatry and Allied Disciplines.

Cover illustration by Mike Eagle

The Dushkin Publishing Group, Inc.
Sluice Dock, Guilford, Connecticut 06437

The Annual Editions Series

Annual Editions is a series of over fifty volumes designed to provide the reader with convenient, low-cost access to a wide range of current, carefully selected articles from some of the most important magazines, newspapers, and journals published today. Annual Editions are updated on an annual basis through a continuous monitoring of over 200 periodical sources. All Annual Editions have a number of features designed to make them particularly useful, including topic guides, annotated tables of contents, unit overviews, and indexes. For the teacher using Annual Editions in the classroom, an Instructor's Resource Guide with test questions is available for each volume.

VOLUMES AVAILABLE

Africa
Aging
American Government
American History, Pre-Civil War
American History, Post-Civil War
Anthropology
Biology
Business and Management
Business Ethics
Canadian Politics
China
Comparative Politics
Computers in Education
Computers in Business
Computers in Society
Criminal Justice
Drugs, Society, and Behavior
Early Childhood Education
Economics
Educating Exceptional Children
Education
Educational Psychology
Environment
Geography
Global Issues
Health
Human Development
Human Resources
Human Sexuality

Latin America
Macroeconomics
Management
Marketing
Marriage and Family
Microeconomics
Middle East and the Islamic World
Money and Banking
Nutrition
Personal Growth and Behavior
Psychology
Public Administration
Race and Ethnic Relations
Social Problems
Sociology
Soviet Union and Eastern Europe
State and Local Government
Third World
Urban Society
Violence and Terrorism
Western Civilization, Pre-Reformation
Western Civilization, Post-Reformation
Western Europe
World History, Pre-Modern
World History, Modern
World Politics

Library of Congress Cataloging in Publication Data
Main entry under title: Annual Editions: Psychology. 1991/92.
    1. Psychology—Addresses, essays, lectures—Periodicals. I. Walraven, Michael G., *comp.*; Fitzgerald, Hiram E., *comp.* II. Title: Psychology.
ISBN 1–56134–028–6   150'.5   79–180263
BF 149.A58

Twenty-First Edition

Manufactured by The Banta Company, Harrisonburg, Virginia 22801

Editors/ Advisory Board

To the Reader

In publishing ANNUAL EDITIONS we recognize the enormous role played by the magazines, newspapers, and journals of the *public press* in providing current, first-rate educational information in a broad spectrum of interest areas. Within the articles, the best scientists, practitioners, researchers, and commentators draw issues into new perspective as accepted theories and viewpoints are called into account by new events, recent discoveries change old facts, and fresh debate breaks out over important controversies.

Many of the articles resulting from this enormous editorial effort are appropriate for students, researchers, and professionals seeking accurate, current material to help bridge the gap between principles and theories and the real world. These articles, however, become more useful for study when those of lasting value are carefully *collected, organized, indexed,* and *reproduced* in a *low-cost format*, which provides easy and permanent access when the material is needed. That is the role played by *Annual Editions*. Under the direction of each volume's *Editor*, who is an expert in the subject area, and with the guidance of an *Advisory Board*, we seek each year to provide in each *ANNUAL EDITION* a current, well-balanced, carefully selected collection of the best of the public press for your study and enjoyment. We think you'll find this volume useful, and we hope you'll take a moment to let us know what you think.

Psychology means many things to many people. Students select a course in psychology because they want answers to a variety of questions. We want to know how people are motivated, how they think, and how their personalities develop. We are curious about how we learn, how our memories work, what effects certain experiences have on us, how we change as we grow older, why some people respond to life events in maladaptive ways, and how these people can be helped. Psychology attempts to answer all of these questions and more.

But psychology approaches these issues in a specific way: the scientific method. Researchers use carefully defined techniques to discover answers to basic questions, in order that their findings may be combined with the findings of other researchers, to eventually paint a complete picture of that most complex of all living organisms: man himself. These research results are usually published in technical journals written for specialists. It is very difficult for the layperson to keep abreast of new findings; indeed, it is difficult for even the professional psychologist to be current in areas other than her or his specialty.

For these reasons, we find more and more accounts and summaries of psychological research in the popular press. Newspapers and magazines are meeting the need of the average adult to discover and understand the complexities of human behavior. But who can spend the time to search out and sort through the large number of articles? And can the average person accurately distinguish those articles that represent solid findings from those that draw inaccurate or overstated conclusions? *Annual Editions: Psychology 91/92* is designed to meet this requirement by providing an organized selection of accurate, readable, and current articles drawn from a wide range of sources. Most of these articles are written not by psychologists, but by journalists and science writers who recognize the importance of certain areas of research and match their talents to the needs and interests of their readers. A few of these articles are written by psychologists, researchers who are gifted with the ability to describe their work in clear and uncluttered styles, retaining the excitement of original discovery and sharing it with us.

The particular articles selected for this volume were chosen to be representative of current work in psychology, both theoretical and experimental. They were selected because they are accurate in their reporting, and provide examples of the types of psychological research discussed in most introductory psychology courses and textbooks. As in any science, some of the findings discussed in this collection are startling, while others will confirm what we already suspected. Some will invite speculation about social and personal implications; others will demand careful thought about potential misuse or dangerous applications of research findings. You, the reader, will be expected to make the investment of effort and critical judgment needed to answer such questions and concerns, for this is a reflection of the field of psychology itself, and we invite you to join in this exploration.

We hope you will find this collection of articles readable and useful. We suggest that you look at the organization of this book, and compare it to the organization of your textbook and course syllabus or outline. By examining the topic guide, you can identify those articles most appropriate to any particular unit of study in your course. Your instructor may provide some help in this effort. As you read the articles, try to connect their contents with the principles you are learning from your text and classroom lectures and discussions. Some of the articles will help you to better understand a specific area of research, while others are designed to help you connect and integrate information from various research efforts. Both of these strategies are important in learning about psychology or any other science, because it is only through intensive investigation and subsequent integration of the findings of many scientists that we are able to discover and apply new knowledge.

During the course of your reading, please take time to provide us with some feedback to guide the annual revision of this anthology by completing and returning the article rating form in the back of the book. With your help, this collection will be even better next year.

Michael G. Walraven, Ph.D.

Hiram E. Fitzgerald, Ph.D.
Editors

Contents

Unit 1

The Science of Psychology

This article examines psychology as the science of behavior.

Unit 2

Biological Bases of Behavior

Six selections discuss the biological bases of behavior. Topics include brain functions, the biological clock, and the brain's control over the body.

The concepts in bold italics are developed in the article. For further expansion please refer to the Topic Guide, the Index, and the Glossary.

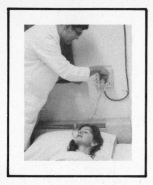

Unit 3

Perceptual Processes

Three articles discuss the impact of senses and dreaming on human perceptual processes.

Unit 4

Learning and Memory

Four selections examine how operant conditioning, positive reinforcement, declarative memory, and procedural memory interact during the learning process.

The concepts in bold italics are developed in the article. For further expansion please refer to the Topic Guide, the Index, and the Glossary.

Unit 5

Cognitive Processes

Four articles examine how social skills, common sense, and intelligence affect human cognitive processes.

Unit 6

Motivation and Emotion

Five articles discuss the influences of stress, mental states, motivation, and emotion on the mental and physical health of the individual.

The concepts in bold italics are developed in the article. For further expansion please refer to the Topic Guide, the Index, and the Glossary.

Unit 7

Development

Four articles consider the importance of experience, discipline, familial support, and physiological aging during the normal human development process.

The concepts in bold italics are developed in the article. For further expansion please refer to the Topic Guide, the Index, and the Glossary.

Unit 8

Personality Processes

Four selections discuss a few of the processes by which personalities are developed. Topics include sex differences, state of mind, cynicism, and change.

Unit 9

Social Processes

Four selections discuss how the individual's social development is affected by genes, stereotypes, prejudice, and self-help.

The concepts in bold italics are developed in the article. For further expansion please refer to the Topic Guide, the Index, and the Glossary.

Unit 10

Psychological Disorders

Four articles examine several psychological disorders. Topics include Alzheimer's disease, unexpected behavior, and the impact of depression on a person's well-being.

Unit 11

Psychological Treatments

Five selections discuss a few psychological treatments, including psychoanalysis, psychotherapy to alleviate depression, and self-care.

The concepts in bold italics are developed in the article. For further expansion please refer to the Topic Guide, the Index, and the Glossary.

Topic Guide

This topic guide suggests how the selections in this book relate to topics of traditional concern to psychology students and professionals. It is useful for locating articles that relate to each other for reading and research. The guide is arranged alphabetically according to topic. Articles may, of course, treat topics that do not appear in the topic guide. In turn, entries in the topic guide do not necessarily constitute a comprehensive listing of all the contents of each selection.

TOPIC AREA	TREATED IN:	TOPIC AREA	TREATED IN:
Abilities	16. New Views of Human Intelligence	Developmentally Appropriate	12. How Kids Learn
Addictions	44. Help Yourself	Disease	20. Emotions
Adoption	5. What a Child Is Given		21. Thinking Well
Ageism	27. Vintage Years		22. Dangerous Thoughts
Alzheimer's Disease	37. Clouded Mind	Dreams	10. What Dreams Are (Really) Made Of
Androgyny	29. Blurring the Lines	Drugs	13. Memory Repair
Anxiety	22. Dangerous Thoughts	Dysthymic Disorder	38. Dysthymic Disorder
	39. Anxiety and Panic	Eidetic Imagery	14. Extraordinary People
Artificial Intelligence	17. Is the Brain's Mind a Computer Program?	Elderly	27. Vintage Years
Attribution	35. Getting Help From Helping	Emotional Development	43. Infants in Need of Psychotherapy?
Authoritarianism	33. Marching in Step	Emotional Problems	44. Help Yourself
Back-to-Basics	12. How Kids Learn	Emotions	19. Face as Window and Machine for Emotions
Behavior	1. Psychology From Standpoint of Generalist		22. Dangerous Thoughts
	35. Getting Help From Helping	Endorphins	7. A Pleasurable Chemistry
	39. Anxiety and Panic		22. Dangerous Thoughts
	44. Help Yourself	Family	36. When Mental Illness Hits Home
Biological Clock	4. Is It One Clock or Several?	Forebrain	8. Are We Led by the Nose?
Brain	3. How the Brain Really Works Its Wonders	Gender Role	29. Blurring the Lines
	6. New Connections	Genetic	28. Why Can't Man Be More Like Woman
	19. Face as Window and Machine for Emotions		32. Are Criminals Made or Born?
	37. Clouded Mind	Genetic Predisposition	36. When Mental Illness Hits Home
Cancer	21. Thinking Well	Health	30. Do Optimists Live Longer?
	31. Health's Character	Heart Disease	31. Health's Character
Cerebral Hemispheres	2. Of One Mind	Hormones	4. Is It One Clock or Several?
			28. Why Can't Man Be More Like Woman
Chemoreceptors	39. Anxiety and Panic	Hostility	33. Marching in Step
Children	25. Shattered Innocence	Humanism	1. Psychology From Standpoint of Generalist
Common Cold	22. Dangerous Thoughts		
Competence	27. Vintage Years	Ideology	35. Getting Help From Helping
Computer Science	3. How the Brain Really Works Its Wonders	Immune Responses	21. Thinking Well
Creativity Training	18. Capturing Your Creativity	Immune System	7. A Pleasurable Chemistry
Criminal	32. Are Criminals Made or Born?		9. No Simple Slumber
			21. Thinking Well
Cultural Values	26. Confident at 11, Confused at 16	Inoculate	20. Emotions
Depression	42. Beating Depression	Intelligence	16. New Views of Human Intelligence

The Science of Psychology

Psychology has been defined as the science of mental activity and behavior. This definition reflects the two parent disciplines from which psychology emerged: philosophy and biology. Historically, philosophy is the elder parent, but current students of psychology are often surprised to discover what a pervasive influence biology and other natural sciences have on the field. Modern scientific psychology traces its heritage as a science to the opening of the first psychological laboratory in Germany in 1879. However, compared to fields such as mathematics, physics, or biology, psychology is still very much an infant science.

Some aspects of modern psychology are particularly biological, such as neuroscience, sensation and perception, behavior genetics, development, and consciousness. Other aspects are more philosophical in perspective, such as humanism and phenomenology. However, as Gregory Kimble points out in the first article, most of psychology's subspecialties share common features, an emphasis on behavior, particularly human behavior, and a belief that behavior can be explained, predicted, and controlled.

It is important to recognize that psychologists work in a great variety of specialties and settings. What they all share, however, is a commitment to pursue knowledge in accordance with scientific methodology. Psychologists are often seen as skeptics; they do not readily accept as valid the assumptions or interpretations of others. They are fond of testing their hunches by actually gathering data to see whether their assumptions and hypotheses are valid.

Any person committed to scientific methodology in the pursuit of knowledge is essentially agreeing to abide by a set of rules that are designed to ensure that findings from one research effort can be replicated by other scientists. The principles of science include the requirement that assumptions be made explicit. These operational definitions enhance communication among scientists, and at the same time keep research on a realistic plane. The experimental method perhaps epitomizes scientific technique. In this procedure, subjects are randomly assigned to conditions, and extraneous variables, which might otherwise influence the data, are controlled. Using this procedure, the scientific investigator can be certain that the conclusions drawn from the data are justified, and can report them with confidence. On the other hand, psychology does not have a single unifying paradigm. Rather, psychologists draw upon a variety of research strategies in their efforts to understand human behavior. Some psychologists use naturalistic methods. Rather than manipulating behavior in the laboratory setting, they are interested in describing behavior as it occurs in nature. Descriptive research is often the first step in the scientific study of a phenomenon. As the comparative psychologist Stanley Ratner often proclaimed, the first step in scientific research is to "know the organism."

Does Gregory Kimble's emphasis on psychology as the science of behavior exclude consciousness, cognition, and volition from its domain as the radical behaviorist would have it? Not at all. Kimble sees each of these aspects of human functioning to be tied to behavior, either as inferences drawn from behavior, or as sources of hypotheses that can be tested by observing and/or manipulating behavior.

Many students respond to certain articles by concluding that psychologists enjoy arguments. We must all recognize that contained in intellectual conflict lie the seeds of new hypotheses, new ideas about the nature of human nature. Learning more about behavior is the goal all psychologists share, and we invite you to share that goal as you plunge into this collection of contemporary readings.

Looking Ahead: Challenge Questions

What is your response to Kimble's assertion that mentalistic concepts, consciousness, and volition are all subject to scientific analysis through the study of behavior?

During the past 25 years, many philosophers of science have attacked the logical empiricist method for its narrow view of the nature of human nature. Does Kimble offer a new twist to such arguments?

Do you think it is possible to reduce the poet's world to that of the science of behavior?

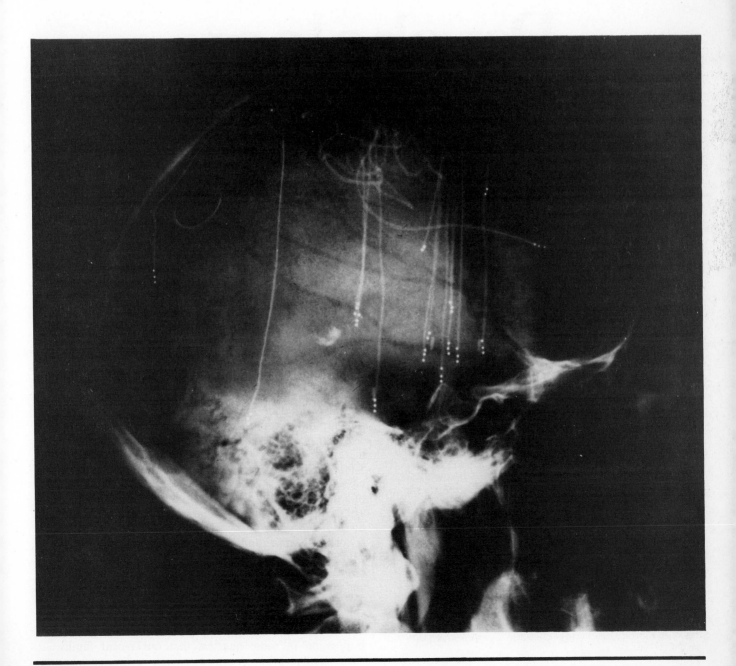

Psychology

From the Standpoint of a Generalist

Gregory A. Kimble
Duke University

ABSTRACT: This article describes the tenets of a liberalized scientific psychology that all psychologists should find acceptable. Such a science is empirical, deterministic, and analytic. Psychology is the science of behavior. Mentalistic concepts are inferences from behavior, and they play a centrally important role. Intuition, common sense, and personal experience provide hypotheses for this science. The elementist–holist controversy disappears with the understanding that the wholes of science differ at different levels of analysis. Free will can be brought within the scope of determinism. Overt behavior is the product of potentials laid down by nature–nurture interactions and conditions of the moment. Behavior is so complexly determined that individual uniqueness is an expected consequence. In this scheme of things, scientific values control

This article is the text of an invited address presented at the APA convention in 1988. I wish to express my thanks to David C. Rubin whose suggestions led to fundamental improvements in the argument. I also want to thank the secretaries at Duke, Lisa Hedgspeth, Sue Kreger, and Patrice LeClerc, for their patience in dealing with a dozen drafts or more of the article.

Correspondence concerning this article should be addressed to Gregory A. Kimble, Department of Psychology, Duke University, Durham, NC 27706.

the science of psychology, and humanistic values control the actions of the psychologists who create this science and apply it. Over the years, the process of change in psychology has been evolutionary rather than revolutionary.

In recent years the question of whether psychology can be a single, general discipline has been the object of considerable discussion and controversy. Although some scholars have been able to see actual (e.g., Matarazzo, 1987) or potential (e.g., Staats, 1981) unity in the field, a greater number (e.g., Furedy & Furedy, 1982; Kendler, 1981; Koch, 1981) have found disunity and chaos. Discussions of this issue sometimes have taken on the quality of a methodological holy war because the disagreements are partly in the realm of values. Psychology is a house divided. One group of psychologists sees the field in terms of scientific values and accepts the concepts of objectivism, elementism, and nomothetic lawfulness. The group opposed sees psychology in terms of humanistic values and accepts the concepts of intuitionism, holism, and idiographic lawfulness. The positions seem irreconcilable, and the war goes on (Kimble, 1984).

Meanwhile, this epistemic jihad has encouraged the impression in some quarters that our recent family

From *American Psychologist*, Vol. 44, No. 3, March 1989, pp. 491-499. Copyright © 1989 by the American Psychological Association. Reprinted by permission.

squabbles are a scientific revolution of the type that Kuhn (1970) referred to as a "paradigm shift." The time has come, however, to put that myth to rest. There has been no revolution in psychology, just a series of tribal wars that have brought a new look to the battlefield. In particular, the concepts, methods and subject matter of both cognitive and humanistic psychology, although very different, have gained legitimacy. As a result, the appearance of psychology now is not at all like what it was less than half a century ago. The major assertion of this article, however, is that the altered appearance of psychology is just a change in surface structure. At a deeper level, the structure of psychology is what it always was. The purpose of this article is to describe that structure in the belief that all psychologists may possibly find it acceptable because it will show that intuition, holism, and idiographic lawfulness are now included in the science of psychology and that this science operates within limits set by human values. In this article, I present a series of assertions that define what I take to be the major commitments and styles of thought that characterize scientific psychology. Each of these assertions is followed by explanatory text.

Determinism, Empiricism, and the Definition of Psychology

Two of the basic tenets of traditional science are those of determinism and empiricism. In psychology, those assumptions decide such fundamental issues as the definition of the field.

1. Behavior is determined by genetic endowment and environmental circumstances. The understanding, prediction and control of behavior are reasonable scientific ambitions.

All psychologists accept these statements but in somewhat different ways. For the purely scientific psychologists, the emphasis is on abstract understanding. *Prediction* and *control* are terms that apply to theory and research. For the applied psychologists, the emphasis is on practical understanding. Prediction and control are concepts related to the goal of improving the lives of people. Although there are some psychologists who regard some human actions as otherwise uncaused voluntary expressions of "free will" (Kimble, 1984), I doubt that such a compromise is necessary.

For some time now it has been clear that voluntary acts are amenable to investigation by the methods of science. In an early article, Kimble and Perlmuter (1970) identified five hallmarks of volition. Voluntary behavior is learned, motivated, planned, attended to, and guided to completion by a comparator process. At one level, this analysis solves the problem of volition by reducing it to accepted scientific concepts. At another level, however, the solution creates problems of its own, because terms like *motivation, attention,* and *comparator process* require objective definition. Without it, they violate the second basic tenet of science, the principle of empiricism.

2. The data of science are the publicly confirmable facts of observation. Psychology is the science of behavior.

Although they are an important part of psychology, inner phenomena like thought, emotion, and ambition are not a part of the basic definition because they are not observable. They are concepts, inferences from behavior. They play a key role in the science of psychology, which I will describe after I develop the required foundation, beginning with a correction of some possible misunderstandings of the definition just presented.

Most important, perhaps, the definition does not exclude personal experience, common sense, or intuition from the science of psychology. Although private, they are important sources of hypotheses for the science. The principle of empiricism does not apply to the discovery of ideas but to the establishment of their validity. How one arrives at an idea has no bearing on its truth. It is its acceptance into science that requires objective evidence. Thus, if a man dreams that he was hiking in the mountains, and your intuition tells you that he had the dream because he unconsciously loves his mother, there is nothing in the tenet of empiricism to prevent your thinking that way. No one should take you very seriously, however, until you produce some type of evidence that the hypothesis is not false. If it turns out that such evidence is logically impossible to obtain, as is true of Marxist theory, "scientific" creationism, and some parts of psychoanalytic theory, the hypothesis is not part of science. Falsifiability is the criterion that marks the boundary line between science and nonscience.

Although personal experience plays the same legitimate role as intuition in psychology, it cannot provide the basic data of the science for reasons that become very clear in cases where the experiences of people differ. Suppose that my experience tells me that learning always is sudden and insightful, that men are more intelligent than women, and that people have dependable traits like honesty and sociability that appear in every situation. Suppose, by contrast, that your experience tells you that learning is always gradual, that women are more intelligent than men, and that traits like honesty and sociability are situation specific. Whose experience (if either) shall we accept as valid? You get the point: We cannot decide without a public test. The only alternatives appear to be (a) the creation of an epistemological elitist class whose personal experiences would define the truth for all the rest of us, or (b) the democratic decision that the experiences of everyone have been created equal. Neither of these alternatives is acceptable to science, however, because both of them violate the criterion of falsifiability.

The great problem with a reliance on common sense as evidence of psychological truths is that these truths are so defective (Kohn, 1988). Some of them are wrong ("Genius is closely related to insanity"). Some of them are contradictory ("Every individual human being is unique" versus "People are about the same the whole world over"). Most of the explanations appeal to essences ("People seek the company of others because they are gregarious by nature"). Probably without exception, the truths of common sense are oversimplifications.

Complexity and Analysis

Almost nothing important in behavior results from a single gene or from a single environmental influence. Behavior and its determinants are both complex. Multiple causes produce multiple psychological effects. Moreover, causes interact, and the influence of any single variable depends on the values of other variables in the situation. The need to unravel the threads of such complex causality has a fundamental implication.

3. Psychology must be analytic. A nonanalyzing science is an inarticulate science. Even to talk about a subject requires that it be analyzed into elements.

All science analyzes. Lewinian field theory (e.g., Lewin, 1931), which psychology now recognizes as possibly the most constructive holistic theory in its history (Jones, 1985), was very analytic. Lewin's fields contained boundaries, barriers, goals, and paths to goals, along with the individual. The individual was full of separate psychic regions, in various states of tension, separated by more or less permeable boundaries. Acted on by attracting and repelling vectors derived from objects with positive and negative valences, the individual moved within the field, sometimes reorganized it, and sometimes left it for the greener pastures of another level of reality. Lewinian theory was holistic in the sense that it treated behavior as dependent on the totality of many interacting variables, but that feature did not distinguish it from any other well-developed theory, for example that of Hull, one of Lewin's great rivals. The important difference between these theories was a difference in the level of analysis.

The products of analysis are the elements of a science. Because all science is analytic, it is also elementistic at some level. Different levels of analysis, and therefore different elements, are appropriate for different purposes. For example, the psycholinguists have been quite convincing on the point that the communicative functions of language involve overarching plans that control the production of sentences. It is impossible to understand the creation of an utterance in terms of strung-together linguistic units. Mistakes in language are another matter. They are only partly understandable in such holistic terms. I still write longhand, and every sentence that I write is the realization of a linguistic plan. The mistakes I make, however—the slips of the pen—almost always occur when some fragment of a word that should come later sneaks forward and occurs too early. The explanation of such linguistic behavior requires the use of elements that are smaller than a word.

In the history of psychology the elementist–holist argument centered on the question of whether the units of perception are attributes of sensations or organized perceptual patterns. The most important thing that has happened to that question is that it has become a question of fact rather than an item of faith. Research has now produced a blueprint of the answer to the question. The peripheral nervous system is equipped to handle only very elementary inputs: primary qualities, intensities, frequencies, durations, and extents of stimulation. By the time these neural messages reach the brain, however, they have given rise to organizations that endow such patterns of stimulation as those produced by phonemes, psychologically primary colors, visual angles, and the human face with the status of perceptual units. These particular organizing processes appear to be inborn, but experience also contributes to the creation of such units. Anyone who has tried the Stroop test (Stroop, 1935) has had a firsthand demonstration of the fact that words (learned organizations of letters) are extremely powerful perceptual units.

Nature–Nurture Interaction

Except in the minds of a few radical nativists and empiricists, the nature–nurture issue has long since been settled. The methods of behavioral genetics give quantitative meaning to the now-accepted statement that heredity and environment both contribute to human psychological characteristics but that they contribute to different degrees for different traits. Social attitudes and values are mostly learned (environmental), whereas height and weight are mostly inherited. Intelligence and introversion are somewhere in between. Whatever the proportions, however, the pattern of joint influence always seems to be the same.

4. For all psychological characteristics, inheritance sets limits on, or creates, a range of potentials for development. Environment determines how near the individual comes to developing the extremes of these potentials.

Inheritance provides different people with the intellect required to become a chess master, with a vulnerability to schizophrenia, or with the physical gifts required to compete in the Olympic Games. Environment determines whether these potential outcomes are realized. Questions about the relative importance of heredity and environment in the determination of such outcomes are questions for research, some of which is now available. For example, coefficients of heritability have been calculated for intelligence, various traits of personality, and the major forms of psychopathology. These coefficients usually ascribe less than half the variance in psychological traits to inheritance. Such data indicate that, although a biological basis for human diversity exists, the most powerful influences are environmental.

Potential Versus Performance

Turning to the short-term dynamics of individual behavior, one encounters a similar pattern. Just as genetic factors put limits on the range of traits a person can develop, these developed traits define the limits of a person's behavior at the moment. Other factors determine whether this behavior reaches the limits of an individual's potential.

5. Individual behavior is the joint product of more or less permanent underlying potentials and more or less temporary internal and external conditions.

Figure 1
Intervening Variable Theorizing

THE GENERAL ADAPTION SYNDROME

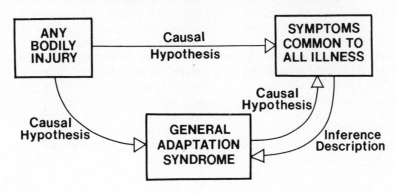

CONCEPTS AND TYPES OF LAWFULNESS

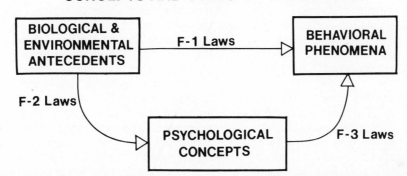

Note. Psychological concepts are conceived as standing logically between independent variables on the left-hand side of the diagram and dependent variables on the right. The upper panel provides a concrete example and shows how inferences and causal hypotheses figure in the creation of intervening variables. The lower panel presents the more general case and shows how Tolman's (1938) F-1, F-2, and F-3 laws fit into the picture.

The distinction between trait- and state-anxiety shows how this idea works. A person may have a long-lasting potential for becoming anxious, a high level of trait-anxiety. The trait will lie dormant, however, until some threat occurs to throw this person into a state of anxiety. The distinctions in psychological theory between availability and accessibility of memories, linguistic competence and linguistic behavior, and sensitivity and bias provide additional examples. One may possess the memory of a certain person's name, but the memory may escape because of an interfering set. A little boy may know that the correct pronunciation of the word is "fish" although the best that he can do is "fis." Given the same sensory evidence, one subject in an experiment may report the presence of a signal and another may not because of their different criteria for making a positive response.

As in the case of nature and nurture, performance can never exceed the limits set by the underlying potential. Suppose that the anxious person described above has the potential to score 130 on an IQ test. In an anxious state, the person's performance may be much lower than that, but never higher. These statements are inherent in the definition of potential.

Mentalistic Concepts

For the radical behaviorists, from Watson (1913) to Skinner (1987), all of this talk about anxiety, criteria, and potentials is offensive because these terms refer to phenomena that are subjective, mentalistic, and unobservable. They are not the raw materials that sciences are made of. In the final analysis, they hold (and I agree) that the only observables available to psychology are the behavior of organisms (responses) and the environmental circumstances (stimuli) in which behavior occurs. Everything else, they say, (but I do not agree) must be excluded if psychology is to be a science. The problem with this radical position is that it sacrifices everything of interest and importance in psychology by its exclusion of mentalistic concepts. Who can possibly care about a psychology that is silent on such topics as thinking, motivation, and volition? What has happened to human experience and the mind in this strangely unpsychological psychology? Do mentalistic concepts have no scientific role at all to play in a behavioristic world of facts? The answers to these questions take us back to a point that came up in connection with the definition of psychology.

6. Mentalistic concepts enter psychology as inferences from behavior. The observations that define them often suggest causes.

For as long as there has been a human species, people have noted that members of the species vary. All languages came to include such terms as "intelligence," "introversion," and "industriousness" to describe such variation. In the history of psychology, applications of this descriptive process have been important. They led Pavlov to the concept of the conditioned reflex, Piaget to the idea of developmental stages, and Selye to a recognition of the General Adaptation Syndrome.

In his very first classes in internal medicine as a young medical student, Selye (1976) was impressed with the fact that patients who were supposed to have different diseases shared many of the same symptoms: "They felt and looked ill, had a coated tongue, complained of more or less diffuse aches and pains in the joints, and of intestinal disturbances with loss of appetite" (p. 15). The symptoms that were supposed to help in differential diagnosis, "were absent or, at least, so inconspicuous that I could not distinguish them" (p. 16). This led Selye to the conception of a "general syndrome of disease," which later on became the "General Adaptation Syndrome" and then "stress." Selye hypothesized that the General Adaptation Syndrome was caused by any form of illness or injury to the body and that it was expressed in the symptoms common to all illness.

Selye was thinking in terms that came to be called "intervening variable theorizing." The construct, General Adaptation Syndrome, intervenes conceptually between a determining independent variable (any bodily injury) and a dependent variable (symptoms common to all illness). Figure 1 presents two diagrams of this kind of theorizing. The upper diagram based on the Selye example shows that processes of inference and hypothesis lead to the identification of psychological concepts and the postulation of possible lawful connections. The lower diagram presents the status of these connections as they were seen by Tolman (1938), the most important advocate of intervening variable theorizing. Tolman identified relationships among variables that are of different kinds, depending on whether the system includes intervening variables. Those that he called F-1 laws describe the direct dependence of behavioral phenomena on their determining antecedents. Those that he called F-2 and F-3 laws enter the picture with the introduction of intervening variables. The F-2 laws relate intervening variables to their antecedents. The F-3 laws describe the dependence of psychological phenomena on the intervening constructs.

The great usefulness of the intervening variable approach is that it provides objectivity for unobservable mentalistic concepts. The F-2 and F-3 laws tie them to observable antecedents and behavioral consequences. This permits entry into psychology of the topics that the radical behaviorists would banish. It allows psychology to deal with such conceptions as "attitude," "plan," and "purpose," which most of us take to be important items in the subject matter of the science.

By now, of course, the cat is out of the bag. The approach that I am recommending is the logical-empiricist method that has received strong criticism from the philosophers of science (e.g., Spector, 1966). Public observability as the criterion of scientific truth is harder to pin down than first thoughts might suggest. What is observable to people with one type of physiology or personal history may not be observable to others. This criticism, however, only leads to another important point of understanding. Before abandoning any significant commitment, it is always a good idea to consider the options that would remain in the absence of what one is planning to give up. In this case, the most frequently offered alternatives are to accept personal experience or linguistic practice as the criterion of truth. These are alternatives that science must reject for reasons presented earlier in this article.

At the same time that we recognize the value of intervening variables, we must also recognize and avoid two abuses to which they are commonly subjected. First, concepts are reified too often. They are captured by the mistaken outlook that Stuart Chase (1938) once called "the tyranny of words." According to that misguided view, if there is a word for it in the dictionary, a corresponding item of physical or psychological reality must exist, and the major task of science is to discover the a priori meanings of these linguistic givens. On the current psychological scene, this foolish assumption gives rise to ill-conceived attempts to decide what motives, intelligence, personality, and cognition "really are." It also legitimates unproductive debates over such questions as whether alcoholism is a disease. Those involved in such disputes never seem to recognize that the controversies are always about definitions and not facts. This first misunderstanding is related to the second one.

Concepts are products of definition. They are merely descriptive and explain nothing. If someone says that a man has hallucinations, withdraws from society, lives in his own world, has extremely unusual associations, and reacts without emotion to imaginary catastrophes because he is schizophrenic, it is important to understand that the word *because* has been misused. The symptomatology defines (diagnoses) schizophrenia. The symptoms and the "cause" are identical. The "explanation" is circular and not an explanation at all.

It may be worth the few sentences that it takes to say that circular definitions are not a scientific sin. Definitions must be circular—by definition. They are verbal equations in which the quantity on the left-hand side of the equals sign must be the same as that on the right. The sin is the offering of definitions as though they were explanations, as one can catch the late-night talk show hosts doing almost any evening on the radio. The following are examples of such statements: "Your eight-year-old son is distractable in school and having trouble reading because he has an attention deficiency disorder"; and "The stock market crash of October 19, 1987, was caused by widespread economic panic." If I could make just one change in what the general public (and some psychologists) understand about psychology, it would be to give them an immunity to such misuses of definitions.

Scientific Structure of Psychology

Figure 2 summarizes much of the previous content of

Figure 2
Summary of the Argument

PSYCHOLOGY WITHOUT CONCEPTS

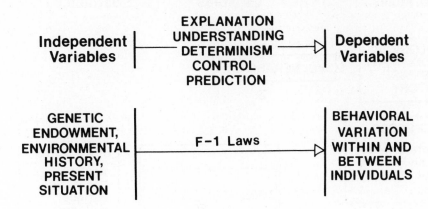

PSYCHOLOGY WITH CONCEPTS

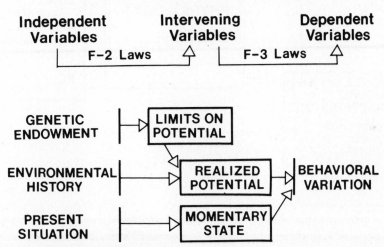

Note. The upper panel reviews the contributions of the empiricistic and deterministic tenets. The lower panel shows how three major classes of independent variables interact to define intervening variables and how the intervening variables interact in the production of behavior.

this article. The top part of the figure, labeled "Psychology Without Concepts," makes two points: (a) Defined in terms of observable dependent variables, psychology is the science of behavior; and (b) this science operates on the assumption that behavior is determined. Explanation, prediction, and control are possible. The bottom part of the figure, labeled "Psychology With Concepts," reviews two further points: (a) In the determination of behavior, nature places limits on potentials for development, and environment determines the extent to which these potentials are realized; and (b) the behavior of an individual at any moment is the joint outcome of realized potential interacting with a temporary state.

In its entirety, Figure 2 is a review of the intervening variable approach and the meaning of Tolman's F-1, F-

2, and F-3 laws. As an aid to the further development of these ideas, I return now to the concept of stress. Figure 3 presents the current situation of this concept in the general framework shown in Figure 2 and in enough detail to support several interpretative points.

First, the collection of independent and dependent variables has become quite large. Moreover, they *are* variables. Each of them has an infinite number of possible values, and people's positions on these many different dimensions are largely uncorrelated. Such complexity surrounds every important psychological concept. It provides a way for bringing common sense and science together on an important point: Individual uniqueness is no problem for psychology.

Figure 3
Current Status of the Concept of Stress

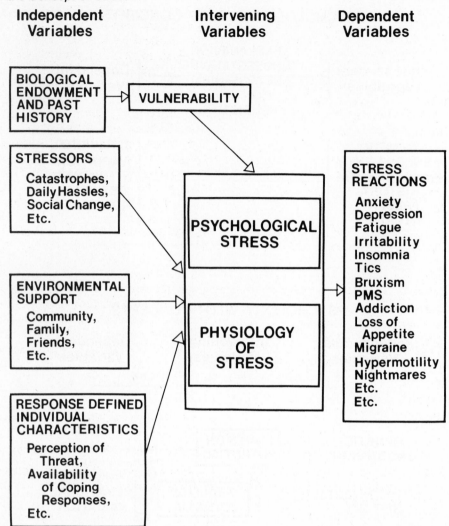

Note. This figure spells out the details and analyzes the argument of Figure 2. This figure is an explication of concepts in Selye (1976).

7. *Every individual is a unique expression of the joint influence of a host of variables. Such uniqueness results from the specific (idiographic) effects on individuals of general (nomothetic) laws.*

The contradictory truths of common sense that "every individual is unique" but that "people are the same the whole world over" are really not contradictory. People are the same in that they represent the outcome of the same laws operating on the same variables. They differ in degree and not in kind. People are unique in that the details of those operations differ from person to person.

Second, in Figure 2, the arrows connecting independent variables to concepts give objective meaning to these concepts. They are the operational definitions of the concepts. They are also Tolman's F-2 laws. The arrows connecting concepts to dependent variables are Tolman's F-3 laws. These F-2 and F-3 arrows identify the criteria of useful intervening variables.

8. *A concept is acceptable to psychology only if it meets both of two criteria. It must be defined operationally and have a relationship to behavior.*

One way in which scientific psychology has become more liberal in recent years is with respect to the requirement for operational definitions of concepts. Although there are still some psychologists who insist on strict and restrictive operational definitions, most of us recognize that our concepts are "open." As knowledge of a concept grows, the number of determining (therefore, defining) variables also increases, as happened with the concept of stress. This state of affairs creates great problems for psychology in the operational realization of its concepts. Such problems do not justify the abandonment of the operational approach, however. "Psychologists must learn to be sophisticated and rigorous in their metathinking about open concepts at the substantive level" (Meehl, 1978, p. 815).

Third, in Figure 3, including "physiology of stress" in the same box as "psychological stress" emphasizes the point that psychological and physiological concepts play identical epistemological roles. The alleged "reality" of physiological concepts may or may not exist. When Mendel proposed the concept of the gene to explain the hereditary transmission of traits, no one had yet observed any corresponding entity. Now we know that genes exist. When Pavlov proposed the concept of cortical irradiation to account for the phenomenon of stimulus generalization, no one had observed a corresponding brain process. So far in the history of psychology, no one has. These examples show that psychological concepts with physiological sounding names differ from other psychological concepts only if the physiological concepts acquire additional meaning through separate operations carried out at the level of physiology. Calling them physiological does not give them physical reality, only surplus meaning. As Donald Hebb (1955) once noted, CNS stands for "conceptual nervous system" until such independent observations have been made.

Finally, the appearance of "response defined individual characteristics" as well as "stressors" on the independent variable side of Figure 3 represents the relevance to the study of stress of both of the two sciences of psychology described by Cronbach (1957). The first science is stimulus–response (S–R) psychology, whose independent variables are situational events. The second science is response–response (R–R) psychology, whose independent variables are the behavior of individuals.

The independent variables of both sciences are independent in the sense that they are the variables from which the scientist makes predictions about behavior. The independent variables of the two sciences differ in that those of stimulus–response psychology can, in principle, be defined without reference to organisms and manipulated directly. Those of response–response psychology lack those properties. Experimental psychology typifies the S–R approach. The effort is to find the laws that relate behavior to environmental variables, for example, amount learned (R) as a function of distribution of practice (S). Psychometric psychology typifies the R–R approach. The effort is to find the laws that relate behavior in one situation to behavior in some other situation, most commonly a test, for example, college grades (R-2) as a function of SAT scores (R-1). The independent variables of R–R psychology sometimes become the dependent variables of S–R psychology. Figure 4 makes this point, using an example based on the concept of intelligence.

Psychological Theory

Networks of the type laid out in Figure 3 represent the present state of theorizing in psychology. They define theoretical concepts, relate these concepts to one another, and identify the laws that connect them to behavior.

9. A psychological theory puts a collection of concepts and their associated laws into a structure that allows the deduction of behavioral consequences. To show that a fact

of behavior is deducible from such a theory is what it means to explain that fact.

This is the method that Hull (1935) sometimes called the "hypothetico-deductive method." Although that designation has gone out of fashion, it is the method that scientists continue to use whenever they argue that their theories lead to specified predictions. Psychology has made recognizable progress in the sophistication with which it uses the method. Theoretical structures are often expressed in terms of formal logic or mathematics. Many of our concepts have acquired legitimate physiological meaning. The basic method remains unchanged, however.

The only alternative to hypothetico-deductive theorizing that I can think of is the radical empiricistic approach, sometimes advocated by the Skinnerians. This alternative would rule out intervening variables, replacing them with an assemblage of F-1 laws like those identified at the top of Figure 2. In this view, theory would arise (if at all) inductively as the individual laws accumulated. Knowledge would provide its own theoretical organization.

One problem with this extreme view is that theory-free investigation is impossible. The choice of empirical questions to study and the selection of dependent and independent variables always entail theoretical assumptions. A second problem is that this approach encourages the delusion that facts somehow give unaided rise to scientific theories. In actuality, theories are creative products

---

Figure 4
Psychology's Two Scientific Disciplines

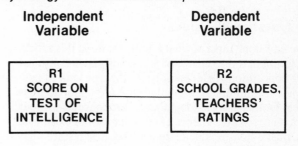

RESPONSE–RESPONSE PSYCHOLOGY

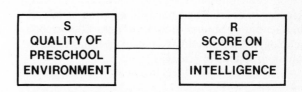

STIMULUS–RESPONSE PSYCHOLOGY

Note. The psychometric (R–R) and experimental (S–R) sciences of psychology differ in their choice of independent variables. The first uses previous behavior to predict performance, and the second uses stimulus events for that purpose. Depending on their functions, performance measures such as scores on tests can be independent variables (upper panel) or dependent variables (lower panel). Neither of the disciplines is more important than the other (Cronbach, 1957).

of scientific minds. Finally, for many of us the most unattractive aspect of the radical empiricistic view is that it takes the joy out of science. The process of making predictions, testing them, and finding out that they are right is the most exciting part of science. The radical empiricistic approach would rob the scientist of this excitement. In addition, that approach would leave the scientist unable to see the forest through the impenetrable tangle of F-1 trees. For all of those reasons it seems unlikely that theorizing will soon go out of style.

Because behavior is so complex and because it is amenable to treatment at so many different levels, an essentially unlimited array of theories is possible. Is there any way to choose among them? Obviously there is. The best theory is the one that survives the fires of logical and empirical testing. An evolutionary metaphor appears to be applicable. Scientific progress will be most rapid when a large pool of theoretical variants exists along with heavy selective pressure in the form of criticism and empirical tests. In the ideal scientific world, psychologists could preach and publish whatever they wanted to, no matter how unpopular, unorthodox, or unlikely to be correct. Physiological, mathematical, behavioristic, and humanistic theories would all participate in the struggle for survival. Freely published criticism would quickly lead to the extinction of the most maladaptive theoretical mutations. Empirical investigations would decide the fate of all the rest. The theories that survived and continued to evolve would be those that were best able to generate and validate behavioral deductions. The great diversity in psychology means that there is a niche for many different theoretical species.

The Question of Values

I have now done most of what I set out to do in this article in showing that the science of psychology is not inimical to the conceptions that characterize the new look in psychology. Intuition and common sense are major sources of ideas for this science. Mental states are concepts without which an acceptable science of behavior cannot exist. The elementism–holism issue disappears because research has shown that what is whole and what is elementary depends on the level of analysis. Human uniqueness is a factual consequence of the complexity of the determination of behavior. Idiographic and nomothetic lawfulness both make their contributions. Every type of theorizing is allowed its day in court. This leaves the question of values. Should scientific or humanistic values control the science of psychology? What should psychology be doing to solve the human problems of our age?

10. The values that govern the science of psychology are scientific values. Humanistic values govern the behavior of psychological scientists and of psychologists who apply the knowledge gained by science.

As a science, psychology is dedicated to discovering facts about behavior and creating theories to explain these facts. In this abstract conception, questions of human values do not arise. The scientific value system requires only that psychology discover the most dependable facts and produce the best theories that it can. Reality is more complex than that, however, because the science of psychology deals with living organisms. Research may require deprivation, concealment, deception, threat, punishment, or the invasion of privacy, and such procedures put scientific values into conflict with human values. For every psychological investigation this conflict raises a question: Is it worth it? Do the potential benefits to science and eventually to animal and human lives justify the costs to be extracted here and now? Psychology has wrestled with this issue for years, and guidelines now exist that protect the welfare of animal and human participants in psychological research. In these guidelines, humanistic values take precedence and form the basis for decisions regarding the acceptability of scientific research. In psychology today most research is in conformity with these codes of ethics.

The ethical acceptability of psychological research does not mean that it will answer the great moral questions of our age or decide which social policy is best. Such questions include the right to bear arms versus handgun control, bans on dirty books versus freedom of literary expression, the public's right to know versus the individual's right to privacy, retribution versus rehabilitation as the aim of criminal codes, affirmative action versus traditional indexes of merit, a verdict of "not guilty by reason of insanity" versus one of "guilty but insane," and freedom of choice versus right to life. Much of what scientific psychology knows is relevant to these important questions, but it cannot supply the answers. They must come from decisions that are made beyond the reach of science, in the court of human values.

The distinction that is implied here is one that should be guarded jealously. If psychology is to have a future as a science, it must obey the scientific rules. These rules define the limits of scientific authority. Science gains its strength and credibility by operating within these limits and understanding that, in other realms, it has no special power or status. Already in its short history, psychology has made important scientific contributions. The credibility acquired by reason of those accomplishments must not be mistaken for moral authority, however. It is a misuse of the credibility of psychology to use it as a basis to promote social prejudices or political goals, and the use of our status as psychologists for such purposes is an even worse misuse. The potential cost of these misuses is loss of the very credibility and status that allowed the misuse in the first place (Gould, 1987).

REFERENCES

Chase, S. (1938). *The tyranny of words.* New York: Harcourt, Brace.
Cronbach, L. J. (1957). Two disciplines of scientific psychology. *American Psychologist, 12,* 671–684.
Furedy, J. J., & Furedy, C. (1982). Socratic versus sophistic strains in the teaching of undergraduate psychology: Implicit conflicts made explicit. *Teaching of Psychology, 9,* 14–20.
Gould, S. J. (1987). William Jennings Bryan's last campaign. *Natural History, 96*(11), 16–26.
Hebb, D. O. (1955). Drives and the C. N. S. (conceptual nervous system). *Psychological Review, 62,* 243–254.

Hull, C. L. (1935). The conflicting psychologies of learning—A way out. *Psychological Review, 42,* 491–516.

Jones, E. E. (1985). History of social psychology. In G. A. Kimble & K. Schlesinger (Eds.), *Topics in the history of psychology* (Vol. 2, pp. 371–407). Hillsdale, NJ: Erlbaum.

Kendler, H. H. (1981). *Psychology: A science in conflict.* New York: Oxford University Press.

Kimble, G. A. (1984). Psychology's two cultures. *American Psychologist, 39,* 833–839.

Kimble, G. A., & Perlmuter, L. C. (1970). The problem of volition. *Psychological Review, 77,* 361–384.

Koch, S. (1981). The nature and limits of psychological knowledge. *American Psychologist, 36,* 257–269.

Kohn, A. (1988, April). You know what they say. *Psychology Today,* pp. 36–41.

Kuhn, T. S. (1970). *The structure of scientific revolutions.* Chicago: University of Chicago Press.

Lewin, K. (1931). Environmental forces in child behavior and development. In C. Murchison (Ed.), *A handbook of child psychology* (pp. 94–127). Worcester, MA: Clark University Press.

Matarazzo, J. D. (1987). There is only one psychology, no specialties, but many applications. *American Psychologist, 42,* 893–903.

Meehl, P. E. (1978). Theoretical risks and tabular asterisks: Sir Karl, Sir Ronald and the slow progress of soft psychology. *Journal of Consulting and Clinical Psychology, 46,* 806–834.

Selye, H. (1976). *The stress of life.* New York: McGraw-Hill.

Skinner, B. F. (1987). Whatever happened to psychology as the science of behavior? *American Psychologist, 42,* 780–786.

Spector, M. (1966). Theory and observation (I). *British Journal of the Philosophy of Science, 17,* 1–20.

Staats, A. W. (1981). Paradigmatic behaviorism, unified theory, unified theory construction methods, and the zeitgeist of separatism. *American Psychologist, 36,* 239–256.

Stroop, J. R. (1935). Studies of interference in serial verbal reactions. *Journal of Experimental Psychology, 18,* 643–662.

Tolman, E. C. (1938). The determiners of behavior at a choice point. *Psychological Review, 45,* 1–41.

Watson, J. B. (1913). Psychology as a behaviorist views it. *Psychological Review, 20,* 158–177.

Biological Bases of Behavior

Historically, philosophical questions regarding the nature of human nature and human functions gave way to a scientific methodology promoted by biology. It is to be expected, then, that the biological sciences provide a major source of methodology for psychological inquiry. As psychologists work to uncover the biological correlates of behavior, they also encounter issues of control over behavior. Many of these issues are both scientific and ethical; for example, it is possible to alter the brain to remove aggressive tendencies, but should such procedures be developed for use on humans? On the other hand, if it is discovered that a type of brain disorder can be held responsible for a particular human behavior, should an individual not be punished for that behavior?

Much of what we know about human brain/behavior relationships has been learned from two major sources. Animal studies involving manipulation, stimulation, or destruction of certain parts of the brain, and the observation of the effects of these changes on behavior, have helped us to understand much of the brain's workings. We have also learned much from the observation and testing of humans whose brains were defective at birth, or damaged in accidents or by disease at some time after birth.

The articles in this section were selected to represent the breadth of research efforts and strategies, as well as to represent the state of our knowledge of the biological correlates of human behavior.

In the first article, Wendy Heller allows us to share the excitement of new discoveries about the contribution each hemisphere of the brain makes to the individual's integrated functioning. Although each cerebral hemisphere is highly specialized, human function is much more the result of interhemispheric integration than popularly believed. The second article extends our understanding of brain function by proposing a comprehensive theory of brain organization and operation, based on rather complex neural networks.

The presence of biological cycles has been known for many years, and the search for the control circuits or biological "clocks" has been a long one. Now, as the next article shows, we are zeroing in on at least one clock. Are there more? And how do they work? Part of the answer to such questions may come from the National Institutes of Health Human Genome Project, the most ambitious attempt to date to unravel the genetic instructions coded in deoxyribonucleic acid (DNA).

A human being begins life with a full set of genetically coded species characteristics that provide the substrate for bio-psycho-social function, including behavior. However, as Deborah Franklin points out, behavior is a function of genotype-environment interaction—an interaction that begins prenatally and includes interaction with the organism's internal biochemical environment. Interestingly enough, as geneticists come ever closer to mapping the human genome, behavior geneticists provide stronger and stronger evidence that environmental events play a critical role in structuring how the individual's genotype will be expressed.

How chemistry affects organization of polygenetic characteristics and/or functional organization is another mystery that awaits unraveling. Studies of hormonal action and brain endorphins have provided intriguing insights about the chemical messengers by which the brain controls the peripheral body, as well as insights into how the brain is influenced by the chemical agents that it secretes. For several years, scientists have sought out the mysterious opiate-like substances which permit severely wounded soldiers and athletes to feel no pain from their injuries. As the last article in this section reflects, we now have detailed evidence about endorphins and their effects on daily functions and systems, including the immune system.

Looking Ahead: Challenge Questions

As we learn more about the distinctive special functions of each hemisphere of the brain, how has our approach to the research changed? If interhemispheric integration is the basis of optimal human performance, should we be challenging popular notions related to "right-brain" and "left-brain" learners?

How can theories of the organization of the functioning brain help us to develop new research strategies? What types of questions can such theories raise? How can we investigate them?

How does knowledge of biological rhythms and their effects on our moods assist us in understanding daily behavior? Does such knowledge provide "excuses" for mood states (premenstrual syndrome, for example), or does it enrich our understanding of the intricate relationships between biology and behavior?

If manipulation of genetic material can lead to prevention of genetic disease, might not similar manipulations be used to genetically engineer intelligence, personality, and social behavior? What individual or societal factors would constrain attempts to explicitly practice selective breeding or attempts at genetic manipulation in order to produce "superior" human beings?

If the production of endorphins can accomplish so much in pain relief and support of the immune system, should we teach people how to stimulate endorphin secretion? How could we best do that?

OF ONE MIND

Second Thoughts About the Brain's Dual Nature

WENDY HELLER

WENDY HELLER *is an assistant professor of psychiatry at the University of Chicago. She specializes in the study of brain mechanisms underlying emotion.*

CALL HER F.R. Her birth was difficult, and the surgical instruments that helped bring her into the world also broke her arm and inflicted a deep tear over her left eye. When she was two she suffered her first epileptic seizure—an electrical storm in her brain, probably touched off by a knot of neural tissue damaged at birth. Now, at the age of twenty-six, she is stricken as often as several times a day. She loses consciousness and falls to the ground; her body convulses powerfully and then goes limp. Drugs to control the seizures have little effect, and the illness restricts F.R.—a cheerful, bright young woman—to bookkeeping and helping with chores on her family's poultry farm. As a last resort, her physician refers her to a neurosurgeon in Rochester, New York, who has treated several similar cases.

The neurosurgeon, William P. Van Wagenen, suggests surgery to cut the corpus callosum—the band of fibers spanning the deep crevice between the two hemispheres of the brain. The surgery is meant to create a firebreak down the midline of the brain, preventing the electrical disturbance in one hemisphere from kindling a seizure in the other as well. F.R., desperate for help, agrees to the operation; it is performed early in 1939.

The procedure goes well, and it somewhat reduces the frequency of the seizures. Indeed, such surgery, pioneered in Rochester around the time of the Second World War and refined in California in the 1950s and early 1960s, could in some cases be remarkably effective. Although anticonvulsant drugs and other surgical procedures that eliminate the focus of the seizure generally suffice, the operation is still available as a last resort. It also has another dimension of significance, albeit one that was not grasped immediately: F.R. and others like her acquired a strange duality. By severing the corpus callosum, the surgery removed the main communication channel between the two hemispheres of the brain, splitting it into two largely independent entities.

At the time of F.R.'s operation it was thought the right hemisphere contributed little to higher brain function, though it was known that the right brain controls movement and sensation on the left side of the body. In the 1860s the French neurologist Paul Broca had established that a patch of cortex in the left hemisphere controls speech; later investigators had filled out a picture of the left hemisphere as the seat of language—speech, reading and writing—in right-handed people and the majority of left-handers. Language is distinctively human, and with time the reputation of the left hemisphere grew; neu-

This article is reprinted by permission of *The Sciences*, May/June 1990, pp. 38-44. Individual subscriptions are $18.00 per year. Write to The Sciences, 2 East 63rd Street, New York, NY 10021 or call 1-800-THE-NYAS.

rologists came to view it as the substrate of most of the higher functions, including consciousness and motivation.

A few workers, notably the late–nineteenth century British neurologist John Hughlings Jackson, had argued that the right hemisphere also had specializations. Patients with damage only to the right side of the brain, for example, often had trouble comprehending complex patterns. Still, by the early twentieth century most neurologists had come to view the right hemisphere as subsidiary at best. With this modest assessment of the role of the right hemisphere came doubts that the corpus callosum played any important part in brain functioning. Some investigators even suggested, half seriously, that the fibers served merely an architectural function, as a kind of scaffolding holding the hemispheres in place. Many people believed the corpus callosum could be severed with impunity.

That view seemed to receive definitive confirmation in the early 1940s with the work of the Rochester neuropsychologist Andrew J. Akelaitis, who was investigating the function of the corpus callosum. Akelaitis asked to examine thirty of Van Wagenen's split-brain patients, including F.R. He reported that once they recovered from the operation, they showed few traces of the extensive surgery—no impairment in reading, speech or the ability to answer questions and no loss of movement or sensation.

In a 1944 paper Akelaitis noted only a single anomaly, in F.R. and one other subject. In trying to carry out simple tasks the two patients seemed strangely at odds with themselves. While dressing herself, F.R. "would put her stocking on with her right hand and pull it off with her left and repeat this performance several times"; after washing the dishes she "would dry the cleaned dishes and then put them back into the pan to be washed again, realizing during the act or shortly afterwards that it was an absurd action." Since these oddities affected only two of the thirty patients and, in both cases, eventually disappeared, Akelaitis believed they were unrelated to the surgery.

His conclusions reinforced the view that the right brain was insignificant. Yet within a few decades Akelaitis's successors in the study of the split brain would overturn that view with one that was equally extreme. By the 1970s the fortunes of the right brain had been reversed so completely that, at least in the popular press, *it* had become the exclusive seat of such valued human capacities as creativity, intuition and emotion. A new caricature of the division of labor within the brain had replaced the old one; a new antithesis had crowded out the old thesis, and the time was ripe for synthesis. Now that synthesis is emerging. Recent studies of split-brain patients as well as of other subjects, including people with normal brains, are suggesting a richer and more complex picture of brain lateralization, in which both hemispheres retain distinct functions, but neither deserves pride of place.

BEFORE ANYONE COULD APPLY studies of split-brain patients to the question of the functional differences between the hemispheres, a clear understanding of how consciousness is organized in the split brain had to emerge. A major step toward that understanding came in the 1950s from Roger W. Sperry and several colleagues, who carried out studies of the split brain, first at the University of Chicago and then at the California Institute of Technology, that ultimately led to Sperry's 1981 Nobel Prize.

Sperry was uncomfortable with Akelaitis's conclusion that disconnecting the two halves of the brain had no effect on behavior. The human corpus callosum is massive by neuroanatomical standards; it is made up of roughly 200 million axons, the tiny filaments that carry nerve signals. The idea that this broad highway could be closed off without affecting function seemed implausible.

Sperry, who was working with Ronald E. Myers of the University of Chicago, began by studying cats. To isolate the brain hemispheres, the investigators not only cut the corpus callosum in some of the animals but also disconnected part of the wiring of the visual system. In cats, as in humans, each eye sends information to both brain hemispheres. Information from the right side of each retina flows to the visual cortex in the right hemisphere; information from the left side flows to the visual cortex in the left hemisphere. By cutting the optic chiasm, where half the fibers from each eye are routed to the opposite hemisphere, the workers prevented the hemispheres from sharing information from the same eye.

Once each eye was connected exclusively to one brain hemisphere, the workers administered visual tests to demonstrate the isolation of the hemispheres. They covered one eye and trained each cat to move a lever in response to an image flashed before the exposed eye. Ordinarily cats that have learned to respond to a stimulus seen with one eye can quickly adapt to responding when the other eye is signaled instead. But the split-brain cats could not make the shift; it was as if the side of the brain wired to the other eye knew nothing about the task the first hemisphere had mastered. A cat that had learned the task via its right eye (right hemisphere) had to learn the routine all over again for the left eye (left hemisphere).

Sperry's demonstration of a "disconnection syndrome" in split-brain cats quickly inspired a similar finding in a human patient by Norman Geschwind, a neurologist at the Harvard Medical School, and his colleague Edith Kaplan. Of course Geschwind and Kaplan could not alter the wiring of their patient's visual system to gain exclusive access to one hemisphere or the other, and so they based their tests on another faculty largely confined to one side of the brain: speech.

The patient (who suffered not from epilepsy but from brain abnormalities that had affected the corpus callosum) displayed an intriguing pattern of handicaps. When asked to make a simple movement, he responded readily with his right hand but had trouble responding with his left. Yet if the command was delivered nonverbally—in the form of a demonstration—his left hand proved perfectly competent. In another test, the patient was asked to close his eyes before grasping a simply shaped object, such as a hammer. He could say what he felt only if he used his right hand; if he was allowed to respond afterward by picking the same object out of a collection, however, he was just as accurate when the object had been placed in his left hand.

The implication of these behavioral patterns was clear: the right side of the patient's brain (which controlled the left side of his body) seemed to be isolated from the left side of his brain, with its mechanisms for producing and understanding speech. The patient, Geschwind and Kaplan wrote, "appears to behave as if there were 2 nearly isolated half-brains, functioning almost independently."

How could such dramatic deficits have escaped Akelaitis's eye? It may be that in the patients he examined the surgery had not completely severed the corpus callosum, and so some communication between the hemispheres had been retained. It is also possible that Akelaitis was misled by the fact that in many respects split-brain patients appear entirely normal; the peculiar split consciousness emerges only in tests designed to address just one side of the brain or the other—and perhaps in such fleeting behavioral anomalies as the ones Akelaitis described for F.R.

AT ABOUT THE TIME Geschwind and Kaplan were exploring the effects of disconnection in their patient, two California neurosurgeons, Joseph E. Bogen and Philip J. Vogel, were picking up where Van Wagenen had left off. They treated a number of patients with severe epilepsy by cutting the corpus callosum and other, smaller links between the hemispheres. Many of their patients became subjects for Sperry, who could thereby continue his study of the split-brain syndrome in human beings. Sperry and his students at CalTech confirmed the existence of the split-brain syndrome in human patients and then turned to the obvious next question: How do the functions of the isolated hemispheres compare?

The Sperry group explored the responses of each half-brain to visual images. To channel each image to just one hemisphere—even though each eye is wired to both—they relied on a tachistoscope (from the Greek *tachys*, meaning swift), a device for flashing images onto a screen. Each split-brain patient was asked to fix his gaze on a bright spot in the center of the screen while images were flashed to the left or the right of the spot more quickly than his gaze could shift. In that way the workers ensured that each image fell on just one side of the retinas and so was conveyed to just one brain hemisphere.

As Geschwind's report had suggested, the disconnected right hemisphere of such patients was not at all stupid. In a typical case, a split-brain patient sits in front of the screen with his eyes fixed on the dot in the middle. A picture of a spoon is flashed to the right of the dot, and the patient is asked what he sees. "A spoon," he replies, as expected: the right side of the visual field falls on the left side of the retinas and is channeled to the left brain, with its powers of speech. When a picture of a spoon is flashed to the left of the dot and the subject is asked what he sees, he cannot respond. Yet when the subject is allowed to answer by reaching under the screen and selecting the same object from an array of possibilities on a concealed shelf, he chooses correctly.

Split-brain patients—or more precisely their right hemispheres—succeeded even at a more difficult task: picking not the same object as the one displayed (a cigarette, say) but a related one (an ashtray). In tests of this kind the right hemisphere was altogether the equal of the left hemisphere in its ability to reason and remember, except that it was mute. The articulate left hemisphere,

meanwhile, unaware of what was being shown to the right hemisphere, often spun what Sperry and his colleagues called confabulations. When the image of a spoon appeared in the left visual field and a subject was asked to identify it orally, he might say, quite confidently, "a pencil." Often the confabulation was roughly plausible, as in this case. Perhaps the left hemisphere knew that the object had to be small enough for one hand to pick up; perhaps some sketchy information about the object—that it was long and thin, for example—had leaked from the right hemisphere to the left through unsevered connections deep in the brain.

THE RIGHT HEMISPHERE turned out to be more than a mute left hemisphere, however. Years before, Hughlings Jackson and a few other workers had suggested that the right hemisphere might play a large role in the recognition of faces and in other tasks that demand the comprehension of a spatial pattern or image. Those claims, made at a time of left-brain ascendancy, had had little impact. Now Sperry and his students confirmed and extended them: the right brain, they found, is at home with spatial relations. It is much better than the left brain at integrating many parts into a visual whole and at mentally manipulating images in space.

In one study, carried out by Sperry's student Robert D. Nebes, split-brain subjects felt a complex three-dimensional shape with the left hand or the right and decided whether it could be assembled from a set of scattered pieces displayed on a screen. The left hand—the right brain—proved far better at the task than the right. In another study the left hand also proved far better than the right hand at drawing a cube, even though most of the split-brain subjects were right-handed.

What is more, when both brain hemispheres confront the same spatial task, the right hemisphere takes control of the person's response. To give the hemispheres a chance to compete for control of a spatial task, Jerre Levy, Colwyn Trevarthen and Sperry developed what they called chimeric stimuli—images made by cutting two patterns or illustrations in half and then pasting together the disparate halves. The workers positioned each chimeric stimulus on the tachistoscope screen so that the halves fell on different sides of the subject's visual field.

In one study each chimeric stimulus combined the halves of two faces that were familiar to the patient, and the patient could either name the face he saw or point to it on a separate display showing a range of possible responses. The subjects overwhelmingly pointed to a complete version of the half-face that had been perceived by the right hemisphere. If instead they had to name the face, they named the half-face that had appeared before their left hemispheres—and made more mistakes.

Other tests suggested that the strategy adopted by the right hemisphere for such spatial tasks is fundamentally different from that of the left hemisphere, not just a more adept variant. Laura Franco and Sperry studied the ability of their subjects to match a displayed object by feel alone, choosing from an array of possibilities on a hidden shelf. The left hand (the right hemisphere) consistently did better than the right hand, but the disparity was smallest when the object was geometrically simple and increased as the object became more free-form. The right hemisphere, it seemed, is skilled at grasping a general form—the gestalt—of an object. The left hemisphere is more successful at apprehending objects that can readily be analyzed into simpler features, easy to count or name: corners, edges, indentations.

Thus Sperry and his colleagues had rescued the right hemisphere from obscurity. Later work, including some of my own, showed that along with its superiority in spatial processing, the right hemisphere has a special role in emotion: it is responsible for interpreting the emotional content of gestures, facial expressions and scenes. People who have suffered certain kinds of damage to the right brain, it turns out, often have trouble telling the difference between a whoop of laughter and a yelp of pain.

In the 1970s popular opinion completed the elevation of the right brain. The laboratory finding that the right brain is better at spatial tasks, such as drawing and mentally representing complex shapes, metamorphosed into the popular notion that the right hemisphere is the seat of creativity. Whereas forty years before, the left hemisphere had been seen as the repository of all things human, now the right hemisphere became the shrine at which followers of imagination and intuition laid their offerings. Educators sought new teaching methods aimed at students' right brains instead of their verbal, analytic left brains. Psychology shelves in bookstores began filling with titles such as *Right-brain Sex* and *Unleashing Your Right Brain*. The left brain had become the right brain's colorless, pedantic companion.

Notwithstanding the popular excesses and oversimplifications, the same studies that had uncovered the right hemisphere's specialized skills had also hinted that things are not quite so simple. Levy and Trevarthen's work with chimeric images, for example, had indicated that even though the right brain is better at recognizing faces, the left brain can sometimes cope with the task. A rare disorder of recognition known as prosopagnosia underscores the point. When stroke or other disease damages a specific region of tissue at the back of the brain, the victim may become unable to recognize even the face of a family member or a close friend. The handicap is exquisitely specific: the prosopagnosic remains able to recognize the same person by voice, to describe a face in terms of specific features (blue eyes, a furrowed brow) and to recognize everyday objects.

Joseph Bogen, one of the California neurosurgeons, has argued that right-sided damage to the critical brain region is the most important factor in the development of prosopagnosia. But even in cases of right-sided damage, the prosopagnosia is not always permanent, provided the corresponding region in the left hemisphere is intact. Eventually the left hemisphere seems to activate some rusty face-recognition strategies of its own—strategies that are probably based more on specific features than on the overall impression of a face. The victim's ability to recognize other people may slowly return.

Justine Sergent of the Montreal Neurological Institute has pursued research on face recognition by the left hemisphere. In one study, Sergent and a colleague presented normal subjects with images of familiar faces that had been blurred to varying degrees, obliterating detail but leaving the overall pattern of the face unchanged. The workers used a tachistoscope to flash the images to each subject's left or right hemisphere. Even though these subjects had intact brains, in which information could flow from one hemisphere to the other, their ability to identify a face differed depending on which hemisphere had the first glimpse of the face. In this study the left hemisphere actually proved more adept than the right at identifying familiar faces when the image was sharp, but the right hemisphere did better when the image was blurry. Evidently the left brain depends on fine detail for face recognition, whereas the right brain can make do with the general pattern.

Other research supports the idea that the hemispheres collaborate routinely, even on tasks that were once thought to be the sole purview of one side of the brain. Since the nineteenth century the neurological mechanisms underlying speech production have been known to reside in the left hemisphere for nearly all right-handed people. Yet the right hemisphere too has a role in modulating speech and shaping its understanding.

Sperry's split-brain experiments had suggested that the right brain has at least rudimentary language ability; in those tests, after all, the right brain as well as the left responded to spoken commands. More specifically, the right brain seems to govern prosody—the variations in intonation that are often crucial for signaling distinctions in meaning or emotional content. The evidence comes from patients with damage to one side of the brain. The loss of certain regions of the right hemisphere seems to impair the ability to modulate speech so as to make its meaning clear—to ask "What's that in the road ahead?" instead of "What's that in the road, a head?" or to give the statement "My mother is coming to visit" the right emotional inflection. By the same token, the loss impairs the victim's sensitivity to intonation in other people's speech.

Reading too would seem to be a straightforward language task, with the left hemisphere its natural territory. Yet, though left-hemisphere damage can severely hamper reading, right-hemisphere damage can affect the process in subtler ways. Howard Gardner of the Boston University School of Medicine has shown that the right hemisphere adds depth—layers and metalayers of meaning—to the left hemisphere's interpretation of reading material. Right brain–damaged patients have trouble understanding puns and double entendres, proverbs, metaphors and tongue-in-cheek comments. They may not grasp the plot of a story, understand the characters' interrelationships or get the main idea.

Fundamentally these patients fail to submerge the details of a story in the interests of perceiving the larger whole. Gardner and his colleagues dramatically demonstrated this failure by comparing the story comprehension of patients who had one-sided brain damage with that of control subjects who had normal brains. Each subject was asked to read stories that included nonsensical elements—for example, a sentence telling that a farmer, on finding his lazy hired man asleep in a haystack, gave him a raise. The investigators then tested the subjects' recall and understanding of each story. Left-brain patients and the normal controls either left out the nonsensical detail or "normalized" it: they misremembered it so that it became compatible with the larger meaning of the story.

People with right-brain damage, in contrast, remembered each aberrant detail extremely well, but they often missed the point of the story. Rather than sacrifice the details to make sense of the larger picture, as the other subjects had, they sacrificed the larger picture to fit in the details. They tended to offer irrelevant or implausible explanations of the nonsensical content: the farmer gave the hired man a raise "to encourage him to work harder." On the basis of these observations, Gardner and his colleagues have suggested that the right brain incorporates a "plausibility metric," which gauges the relative verity of information, screening out what is nonsense.

Recently workers have been looking for direct evidence of collaboration between the hemispheres. One kind of evidence comes from measurements of blood flow, which increases in busy parts of the brain just as it does in hardworking muscles. Such studies have suggested that success in certain difficult cognitive tasks requires activity in many areas of both hemispheres. Marie Banich of the University of Illinois made a similar finding by sending information via the tachistoscope to one or both hemispheres in normal subjects. She found that on relatively complex tasks—comparing an uppercase letter with a lowercase one and deciding whether they represent the same sound, for instance—subjects do better when the information is shared between the hemispheres than when it is all delivered to one hemisphere. On difficult tasks, then, it behooves the hemispheres to work together.

Tasks demanding creativity may be the hardest of all, and yet the notion that the right hemisphere alone is the "creative" one is the heart of the right-brain mystique. Studies of brain-damaged people suggest, however, that creativity depends not on the right or the left hemisphere exclusively but on the frontal lobes of both hemispheres. To be sure, the two halves of the brain seem to make different contributions to the creative act. Neuropsychologists try to gauge creative ability through such tests as design fluency, in which a person is asked to sketch as many designs as possible in a fixed period, and verbal fluency, in which the goal is to generate as many words as possible. These tests show that damage to the right frontal lobe impairs design fluency the most, and damage to the left frontal lobe has the largest effect on verbal fluency.

Even so, there is no sharp division of labor. In May 1988 I was co-curator of a Chicago art exhibit accompanying a symposium called "Art and the Brain." The artists whose work was featured had suffered various brain injuries and diseases, many of them affecting the right hemisphere. Yet prominent art critics judged the creative expression to be at an extraordinarily high level. Such expressiveness in spite of right-brain damage suggests that the left hemisphere makes its own contribution to drawing. Indeed, case studies suggest it supplies the ability to reproduce detail faithfully, whereas the right hemisphere oversees spatial relations and the broad outline of the image.

One might compare the frontal lobes to a working artist who constantly switches from one to another of the various tools provided by the hemispheric specializations. The same pooling of the hemispheric resources, I believe, underlies cognition in general. Higher functioning—and especially achievement of the highest order—emerges from an interplay of left and right brain, of verbal and spatial, analytic and synthetic, accomplished through constant communication across the corpus callosum.

This picture only deepens the mystery of the split-brain syndrome. How could F.R. and most of her successors have appeared roughly normal when this collaboration was blocked—when speech was severed from the plausibility metric and feature analysis severed from the perception of spatial relations? The new understanding also sets a program for future research: to describe the interaction between the hemispheres and how it leads to the unified mind, functioning at its highest potential.

How the brain really works its wonders

A new model of the brain is beginning to explain how it can do things the most powerful computers cannot—recognize faces, recall distant memories, make intuitive leaps. The key: Intricate networks that link together the brain's billions of nerve cells

"Imagine a block of wax. . . ." So wrote the Greek philosopher Plato more than 2,000 years ago to describe memory. Since then, scholars have invoked clocks, telephone switchboards, computers—and even a cow's stomach—in equally futile attempts to explain the mysterious workings of the brain.

But an explosion of recent findings in brain science—aided by new computer programs that can simulate brain cells in action—is now revealing that the brain is far more intricate than any mechanical device imaginable. For the first time, brain researchers are beginning to explain how the brain can call up distant memories from a vast storehouse of recollections and instantly recognize faces, odors and other complex patterns—tasks that even the most powerful electronic computers stumble over.

"For physicists, the most exciting time was during the birth of quantum mechanics earlier this century," says Christof Koch, a brain researcher at the California Institute of Technology. "We are seeing the same excitement now in neuroscience—we are beginning to get an understanding of how the brain really works."

Scientists are now coming to regard the brain as far from some kind of orderly, computerlike machine that methodically plods through calculations step by step. Instead, the new image of our "engine of thought" is more like a beehive or a busy marketplace, a seething swarm of densely interconnected nerve cells—called neurons—that are continually sending electrochemical signals back and forth to each other and altering their lines of communication with every new experience. It is in this vast network of neurons that our thoughts, memories and perceptions are generated in a cellular version of a New England town meeting.

This new view of the brain has burst into every corner of science where researchers think about thinking. Brain scientists are hoping that a comprehensive new theory of how the mind works will lead to ways to control afflictions such as epilepsy and Alzheimer's disease. Computer researchers are looking at how the brain computes in an attempt to give robots eyesight, hearing and memory and to build brainlike machines that can learn by themselves. The new model of the mind even has philosophers dusting off hoary questions about the nature of rationality and consciousness.

A meeting of minds

The revolution in understanding the brain has come about because of a marriage of two widely different fields—neurobiology and computer science—that would have been impossible a decade ago. For years, computer researchers attempting to create machines with humanlike intelligence all but ignored the complex details of the brain's anatomy. Instead, they tried to understand the mind at the more theoretical level of psychology—that is, in terms of the brain's behavior.

Neuroscientists, meanwhile, were focusing on the brain's biology, using microscopic probes to sample electrical pulses from the 100 billion neurons that make up the brain and trying to unravel the chemistry of how those neurons communicate with one another. Many neuroscientists, however, are now beginning to realize that the brain is far more than the sum of its parts. "Suppose you wanted to know how a computer worked," says Koch. "You could sample the signals at all the transistors, and you could crush some up and see what they're made of, but when you were finished you still wouldn't know how the computer operated. For

that, you need an understanding of how all the components work together."

With the recent development of inexpensive, powerful computers and the expansion of knowledge about the details of the brain's anatomy, researchers are finally teaming up with computer scientists to simulate the way neurons might join together in the vast networks that make up our mind. No one is suggesting this new approach will explain, neuron by neuron, how we fall in love or laugh at the Marx Brothers. Nor is it yet clear whether different types of neural networks are responsible for producing all the remarkable things the brain can do. But researchers are beginning to see the outlines of the brain's remarkable organization, which allows it to learn new skills, remember old events, see and hear and adapt itself to new situations.

Laboratory models of the brain—called neural networks—consist of a dozen to several hundred artificial neurons whose actions are simulated on a conventional digital computer, just as modern computers can simulate the way millions of particles of air flow around a fighter jet's wings. Just as a single neuron in the brain is connected to as many as 10,000 other neurons, each artificial neuron in a neural network is connected to many others, so that all the neurons can send signals to each other. Simple rules that mimic how actual neurons alter their communication pathways in the brain are programed into the simulations as well.

The result is a device that shares some properties with the real thing but is far easier for scientists to take apart, examine and run experiments on. "These things aren't toys," says Richard Granger, a brain researcher at the University of California at Irvine who uses neural networks to model how the brain processes smell. "These are from real brain. We put data from the lab into our model, and then we run our model to get predictions that we go back and test in the lab."

Researchers are creating neural networks that show how the brain makes general categories of odors such as cheese or fruit and distinguishes between specific odors such as Swiss or cheddar. Others are modeling the way a casual mention of a particular place or event can evoke a memory of a long-lost friend, how the brain organizes incoming signals from the eyes to give us vision and how neurons rearrange their connections to restore operations after a damaging stroke or in response to a new task.

The models are also giving researchers new insights into the dynamic process by which the brain does all these things. A neuron takes a million times longer to send a signal than a typical computer switch, yet the brain can recognize a familiar face in less than a second—a feat beyond the ability of the most powerful computers. The brain achieves this speed because, unlike the step-by-step computer, its billions of neurons can all attack the problem simultaneously.

This massive collection of neurons acting all at once makes decisions more in the manner of a New England town meeting than of a highly structured bureaucracy. The brain's freewheeling, collective style of processing information may explain why it has trouble doing mathematical computations that are easily done by a $5 calculator. But it may also be what gives the brain its enormous flexibility and the power to match patterns that are similar but not exact, draw scattered bits of visual data into a cohesive picture and make intuitive leaps.

Consider what the brain must do to recognize a smell, for example. It's unlikely that one barbecued-rib dinner will smell exactly like another or that the strength of the odor will be the same each time it is encountered. But a neural network doesn't simply check if the pattern of nerve signals coming from the ribs exactly matches any of the patterns stored in memory: Comparing patterns one by one would take far too long.

Instead, the network goes through a process analogous to a group of people debating evidence. Neurons that are highly activated by the odor signal strongly to other neurons, which in turn activate—or in some cases deactivate—others in the group, and those neurons will influence still others and feed back to the original senders. As the neurons signal back and forth, varying their levels of activity, the group as a whole evolves toward a pattern that most closely matches one in memory, a pattern that reflects

fundamental similarities among the many variations of how barbecued ribs smell.

Completing thoughts

This type of interactive process may be what allows the brain to recognize patterns that are slightly different or incomplete as nonetheless belonging to the same overall group. We are able to recognize all the different kinds of things we sit on as types of chairs, for example, even though we might have a hard time writing down exactly what it is about them that qualifies them as such. Likewise, small bits of a memory can trigger the whole memory, even if some of the incoming information is faulty: If someone asks if you have read the latest issue of *U.S. News & Global Report,* you still know which magazine he is talking about.

This kind of memory is possible because, just as some members of a town meeting outshout others, some neurons in a network have stronger communications pathways to their neighbors. These "rabble-rousing" neurons can have a strong influence on the way other neurons behave, and so even when only a few of them are activated, they can nudge the network in the right direction.

By simulating these processes in the lab, researchers are gaining surprising insights into how neural networks—and thus perhaps the brain itself—can perform these tasks. Granger and his colleague at the University of California at Irvine, neuroscientist Gary Lynch, used data from their lab experiments on neurons in a rat's olfactory system to create a neural-network simulation of smell recognition. The 500-neuron network was presented with groups of simulated odors, each containing variations of a general pattern such as cheese or flowers.

At first, the network responded with a unique pattern of activity for each odor. But as it processed more and more odors that were similar, those neurons that were repeatedly activated became stronger and stronger, eventually dampening the activity of other neurons that were less active. Eventually, these highly activated neurons became representatives of each category of smells: After a half-dozen samplings of the group, says Granger, the artificial brain circuit responded with the same pattern of neurons on the first sniff of any of several smells within one category. On subsequent sniffs, however, the neural network did something totally unexpected. The old pattern disappeared, and new neurons fired, creating a different pattern for each particular smell. "We're thrilled with it," says Granger. "With the first sniff, it recognizes the overall pattern and says: 'It's a cheese.' With the next sniffs, it distinguishes the pattern and says: 'It's Jarlsberg.'"

Studies of actual brain tissue are continually refining the ground rules that scientists program into these models—thus making them more realistic. One recently confirmed rule—that two neurons communicate more strongly if both have been active at the same time—has been incorporated into many neural network simulations. Often, such simple rules are enough to produce the striking result that a network will organize itself to perform a task such as smell recognition when given repeated stimuli.

Biological studies have also given some exciting confirmation that neural network models are on the right track. Recent experiments with neural networks that model vision in monkeys have also shown a surprising match with the actual biology of the brain. They may also explain how the growing brain of a fetus lays down its neural circuitry. Nearly two decades ago, Harvard University brain researchers Torsten Wiesel and David Hubel discovered that a monkey's brain has neurons that respond to very specific types of visual scenes such as spots of light or dark bars set at different angles. Yet these neurons are developed before birth—and before any light signals can influence the way they are organized.

Ralph Linsker, at the IBM Thomas J. Watson Research Center in Yorktown Heights, N.Y., has created a neural-network model of the brain's visual system that shows how the brain might be able to wire itself up spontaneously to do such tasks. Linsker's network consists of several sheets of neurons arranged in layers, with groups of neurons in one sheet connected to various individual neurons in the sheet above it. To make his network evolve, Linsker uses the same neuroscientific rules that govern how synapses in the brain increase their communication strength when the neurons they connect to are active at the same time.

Linsker starts his model off with random connections between neurons and feeds in a random pattern of stimulation to the neurons at the bottom layer. Just as with Granger's smell model, the network's simple reinforcement rules cause the neurons to organize themselves into groups for specific tasks. By the time the input pattern has worked its way up through the network, the neurons in the top layer have formed into specialized clusters that respond the most when bars of light with specific orientations are presented—just like the specialized neurons in the monkey's brain.

The network organizes itself because each neuron in one layer gets information from a committee of neurons in the layer below it. Those neurons that "vote" with the majority get reinforced while lone dissenters lose their influence. "As the group develops a consensus," explains Linsker, "the mavericks get kicked out."

New connections

New studies have shown that, even though much of the brain's wiring is laid down in the womb, the connections between neurons can also be rearranged during adulthood. It is likely, in fact, that your brain has made subtle changes in its wiring since you began reading this article. More-substantial rearrangements are believed to occur in stroke victims who lose and then regain control of a limb. Michael Merzenich of the University of California at San Francisco first mapped the specific areas in a monkey's brain that were activated when different fingers on the monkey's hand were touched, then trained the monkey to use one finger predominantly in a task that earned it food. When Merzenich remapped the touch-activated areas of the monkey's brain, he found that the area responding to signals from that finger had expanded by nearly 600 percent. Merzenich found a similar rearrangement of processing areas when he simulated brain damage caused by a stroke.

Researchers Leif Finkel and Gerald M. Edelman of Rockefeller University were able to duplicate these overall phenomena in a neural network when they applied a simple rule to the behavior of small groups of neurons. Groups of neurons were set up to "compete" for connections to the sensory nerves. The researchers found that when they gave one group an excessive input—analogous to training the monkey to use a particular finger—that patch grew in size. When that input was stopped, the patch grew smaller.

Working in concert

The biggest impact of neural networks may be in helping researchers explore how the brain does sophisticated information processing. Even though scientists can record signals from the individual neurons in the brain that might be involved in such a task as tracking an object with the eyes, they still don't know how the brain puts those millions of signals together to perform the computation. But because a neural network can adapt its connections in response to its experiences, it can be trained to learn sophisticated

brainlike tasks—and then researchers can examine the artificial brain in detail to get clues to how a real brain might be doing it.

In one study, for example, a neural network helped researchers explain how the brain is able to judge the position of an object from signals sent by neurons connected to the eyes. Brain scientists Richard Andersen of the Massachusetts Institute of Technology and David Zipser of the University of California at San Diego trained a neural network to do the task by giving it data recorded from a monkey's neurons as the animal tracked an object moving in front of it. Since the researchers already knew the position of the object that the nerve signals corresponded to, they were able to "train" the network to do the task: They gave the network a series of recorded input signals and let the network adjust itself until it consistently was able to give the right answer. The researchers then examined the network to reveal the complex calculations it uses to forge all the data into the correct answer.

These experiments suggest that some extremely complex feats of perception can, at least in theory, be explained by the interaction of many neurons, each of which performs a seemingly quite simple task. Terrence Sejnowski of Johns Hopkins University, for example, created a neural network that learned to judge how much a spherical object was curved by the way a beam of light cast a shadow on it. Much to his surprise, Sejnowski found that even though the network was trained to compute the object's shape from its shading, individual neurons within the network actually responded with the most activity when he later tested the network not with curved surfaces but with bars of light. In fact, the neurons responded just like the specialized neurons in the monkey's brain discovered years ago by Hubel and Wiesel—neurons that had long been assumed to be involved in helping the brain detect the straight edges of objects, not their curvature. "My network doesn't prove that those cells in the monkey's brain are actually there to compute curvature and not edges," says Sejnowski. "But it does mean that you can't make quick assumptions about what the entire brain is doing simply by sampling what individual neurons are doing. You need to look at

the system as a whole." Several neuroscientists, inspired by Sejnowski's study, plan to investigate whether such curvature-computing cells actually exist in the brain.

The ability of neural networks to learn to simulate these brainlike tasks has also inspired researchers who are interested in creating machines that act more like real brains. While conventional computers can perform powerful feats of number crunching, they are dismal failures at doing more-brainlike operations such as seeing, hearing, and understanding speech—things we usually take for granted but that are extremely complex computationally. "The things that distinguish us from monkeys—playing chess, for example—are easy for computers to do," says Caltech's Koch. "But when it comes to doing things we share with the animal kingdom, computers are awful. In computing vision or movement, for example, no computer comes even close to matching the abilities of a fly." Engineers at the National Aeronautics and Space Administration, the Defense Department and computer companies around the world are all busily scrambling to find the best ways to implement neural networks on computer chips.

It may be a long time, however, before anybody is able to build a machine that actually works like a brain. After all, nature has had a 7-million-year head start on engineers, and researchers have never encountered anything as complex and ingeniously designed as the 3-pound lump of tissue inside your skull.

Meanwhile, the first steps at understanding how the brain really works have already been taken. Many brain researchers now believe that the bigger mysteries of how we make choices and use language—or why some memories last forever while others fade—will inevitably yield their secrets. Even the nature of the brain's creativity, attention and consciousness may someday be revealed. "Basically, the brain is a neural network —however complicated," says Andersen. "It will take time, but we will solve it."

by William F. Allman

Is It One Clock, or Several, that Cycle Us Through Life?

Susan Cunningham

Staff Writer

As regular as the rising and the setting sun, every person's day is marked by cycles of the body. The most obvious, of course, is the inexorable rhythm of sleeping and waking. But there are many other organic functions in humans, as well as in animals, plants and lower organisms, that also follow 24-hour cycles.

Our body temperature is highest at noon, and dips by as much as one degree at its lowest point in the early morning. Blood sugar level, urine excretion, pulse and heart rates, plasma cortisol concentration and secretions of adrenal and most other hormones all follow daily patterns as well.

Hormones are released intermittently in varying amounts into the bloodstream; in the case of cortisol and growth hormone, the levels may vary by as much as 100 percent within a 24-hour period. In some animals, eating, drinking and other activities are regulated by internal clocks and occur at the same time each day.

The rhythms help explain why we are hungry, lively, tired, sleepy or irritable at certain times in the day. They help explain why women often go into labor in the small hours of the morning and why we work more efficiently at certain times of the day.

Greater knowledge about how these rhythms function and interact can help us explain and cope with the discomfiting feelings that accompany jet lag and shift work. They may eventually guide us in choosing the best time of day to administer a drug. If rhythm disorders are at the root of some depressive and manic-depressive illnesses, we may someday be able to treat them with new, even non-chemical, behavioral techniques.

But it has only been within the past 20 years that science has thoroughly discredited the still popularly entrenched idea that the cycles are regulated by light or some other change in the environment outside of the body. Daily rhythms are driven and synchronized by at least one self-sustaining biological clock within each organism. Today, at an accelerating speed, neuroscientists are discovering the nature and function of these internal timing mechanisms in most living things.

Daily rhythms are described as circadian. The word comes from combining the Latin *circa* (about) and *dies* (day). There are shorter and longer cycles which also seem to be governed by internal clocks, but even less is known about their physiological bases. Such rhythms as heart beat and electrical activity in the brain, which follow cycles of less than 24 hours, are called ultradian. Longer cycles, such as menstrual and estrous cycles, hibernation and seasonal gains and losses of weight are described as infradian.

With a series of experiments beginning in the 1950s, Colin Pittendrigh and Jurgen Aschoff demonstrated that external cues didn't control circadian rhythms.

Pittendrigh disproved the theory that circadian rhythms were learned by raising fruit flies in constant environmental conditions. Even when they weren't exposed to a 24-hour light-dark cycle, the flies still exhibited 24-hour rhythms.

Aschoff isolated people from normal temperature, light and sound cues in underground caverns outside Munich for as long as months at a time. He concluded that humans have spontaneous or "free-running" periods of activity and rest each day, although the entire cycle doesn't naturally take place over 24 hours. The most common cycle is about 25 hours. So, even though a person freed from environmental cues generally continues to sleep about eight hours, he or she rises an hour later each day.

Environmental changes don't control circadian rhythms, but in normal living, light, darkness, temperature, mealtimes and other environmental and social cues play an integral role in conveying information to which the internal clocks respond. In humans, these external cues reset the "hands" of the clock back an hour each day. Much circadian research today concentrates on the physical and biochemical mechanisms that underlie this resetting and resynchronization, which neuroscientists call entrainment.

Race for the Clock

Launching the race in the 1960s to identify a biological clock, Curt Richter ruled out many parts of the brain as possible pacemakers by a literal process of elimination. He removed, in turn, the adrenals, gonads, pituitary, thyroid and pineal glands of rats. He also gave them shock therapy, induced alcoholic stupors and convulsions and made lesions in various parts of their brains.

Nothing permanently disrupted the circadian rhythmicity of the rats' feeding, drinking and activity until he made lesions in the hypothalamus, the tiny structure deep in the forebrain between brainstem and cerebral hemispheres.

Subsequent research using lesions narrowed the site to the anterior portion of the hypothalamus. In 1972, two groups of researchers made lesions in a cluster of tiny neurons within the anterior hypothalamus of rats and independently discovered that they had destroyed the rats' daily rhythms of water drinking, physical activity and adrenal corticosterone secretion. The results were rapidly duplicated in hamsters, cats, squirrels and, in 1981, in the first nonhuman primates, rhesus monkeys.

The clusters are called the superchiasmatic nuclei (SCN). The nuclei, consisting of thousands of neurons, are each about 5 to 15 microns in diameter and sit on either side of the optic recess of the third ventricle, a fluid-filled space in the midline of the brain. A micron is one-thousandth of a millimeter. The SCN of hamsters, rats, monkeys and humans resemble each other in their general features and, from what little we know, appear to function similarly. From front to back, the SCN in humans are only two to three microns long.

Throughout the 1970s and early 1980s, the number of rhythms that were shown to be regulated by the SCN mounted. Today, we know that the SCN regulate sleeping and waking, heart and pulse rates, and the secretion of thyroid-stimulating hormone, testosterone, prolactin, thyrotropin, growth hormone and pineal N-acetyl-transferase. Pineal A-acetyltransferase is the enzyme controlling production of melatonin, the chief hormone of the pineal gland. Melatonin, in turn, inhibits sex hormone secretions.

Scientists already knew that estrous and menstrual cycles were regulated by biological clocks. But only

now are they finding that they are linked to SCN, the daily clock. Newborn rats with SCN lesions fail to develop estrous cycles, and adult female rats with SCN lesions cease ovulating.

Irving Zucker, a psychologist at the University of California in Berkeley and one of the discoverers in 1972 of SCN function, has suggested that the lesions interfere with either the release or the transport of lutenizing hormone-releasing hormone (LHRH) to the pituitary. LHRH, in turn, influences the secretion of other hormones that trigger ovulation.

Most theories about which human functions are regulated by the SCN are extrapolations from data on monkeys. "Some of it is okay. None of it is great. It's reasonable to imagine that it applies to humans," commented Michael Menaker, a University of Oregon neuroscientist.

One rare clinical case offered further validation that the SCN function in humans similar to the way it does in animals.

An autopsy on a woman revealed that she had a tumor in her left ventricle that had virtually destroyed her SCN. Before she died, she had been troubled with excessive sleepiness. However, as is the case with SCN-lesioned animals, she could be easily roused. A tumor in another part of the brain would have caused a much deeper, coma-like sleep.

How Many Clocks?

Early discoveries about the regulatory power of SCN led many people to the conclusion that they were *the* biological clock. The current debate is not over whether SCN are an important clock—indisputably they are—but whether there are others, whether they are subsidiaries of the SCN or autonomous and whether they must be coordinated by the SCN or can take over the regulation of a rhythm when SCN are destroyed.

Tom Wehr, a psychiatrist conducting research on sleep cycles at NIMH, believes that SCN are the master clock in mammals and said "it's not fashionable now" to believe there are multiple clocks. On the other hand, Frank Sulzman, a neuroscientist at the State University of New York in Binghamton, is convinced that SCN are not the single oscillator, "at least not in primates."

As evidence he points to experiments that have shown that, when SCN are destroyed, the rhythms of core body temperature, plasma cortisol, urine potassium excretion and REM (rapid eye movement) sleep are not affected.

Sulzman concedes, however, that most of these experiments are controversial. As is frequently the case in neuroscience, researchers question whether the lesions done in the laboratory were complete. Even having a few SCN cells remain might be sufficient to generate a rhythm.

Another problem is the possibility that entraining agents, such as the light-dark cycle, can mask the effects of a clock. For example, an animal whose SCN has been destroyed often may continue its regular sleeping and activity rhythms. Damage to the clock is revealed only when the entraining agent is removed and the rhythm falls apart.

The strongest evidence for a second oscillator are frequently duplicated experiments showing the persistence of drinking and body temperature rhythms after the destruction of SCN.

In these experiments, SCN does destroy the usual temporal drinking patterns in the sense that drinking gradually becomes spread throughout the day. But the rodents and monkeys still drink the same amount in a 24-hour period as they did before the SCN lesions. One explanation is that there is at least one other, perhaps weaker, secondary oscillator which drives drinking behavior while the SCN coordinates it. In short, SCN may organize the *timing* of drinking behavior.

Numerous experiments have shown that body temperature rhythms likewise persist after the SCN are destroyed. Psychologist Evelyn Satinoff and her colleagues at the University of Illinois in Champaign-Urbana recently completed several years of experiments which showed that lesions in rats' SCN had no effect on the rhythms of body temperature. (The work has led her to believe that rhythms of adrenocorticotropic hormone also are controlled by a separate mechanism.)

Making lesions in the medial preoptic region, another part of the hypothalamus, Satinoff was able to disrupt but not destroy temperature rhythms in rats. Although the medial preoptic area must be intimately involved in regulating body temperature, Satinoff doesn't suggest that it or any other area of the brain is the single regulator for body temperature.

"I don't happen to believe we'll ever find enough data [for a temperature oscillator]. I think it's much more complicated than that . . . [and includes] peripheral blood flow and activity and all those things that make body temperature."

Different areas of the brain may have evolved separately to control the peak, trough, phase, amplitude, period and shape of the waves that measure temperature and other body rhythms, she suggested.

"It's perfectly reasonable to imagine there are other oscillators," said Menaker, "and they could be almost anywhere. There's no reason to exclude any part of the nervous system."

Some amphibians have an autonomous clock in their eyes. In lizards, birds and many vertebrates, although not in mammals, the pineal gland also seems to operate as an independent clock. Removed from animals and cultured, it continues to produce the hormone melatonin in the same rhythm it did within the organism.

"There may be a loop in which the SCN and the pineal are connected by nerves in one direction and hormones in the other, and they may be both oscillating," he speculates.

As scientists zero in on what makes SCN (and the other oscillators in plants and organisms such as fungi) oscillate, they are finding that individual cells oscillate on 24-hour cycles. "Any collection of cells might oscillate," Menaker said.

Satinoff and Menaker agree that the neuroscience of circadian rhythmicity is still in its infancy, that the body of solid research is still very small, and that the mechanisms of the clock are much more complex than anyone anticipated 13 years ago, when the functions of SCN were first discovered. "Everything starts with a nice simple story and then it gets a lot more complicated," commented Satinoff.

Because cycles of light and darkness seem to be such strong entraining agents in most animals, the next great search has been for the pathway or pathways by which light reaches the SCN. Some animals have photoreceptors in several parts of their brains. In adult mammals, however, the only site for light reception is the retina. Information it receives is transmitted neurochemically to the brain via the optic tracts.

Injecting the retina of rats with a radioactive chemical, Robert Y. Moore of the State University of New York at Stony Brook discovered in the early 1970s a bundle of nerve fibers that extended from the optic chiasm and terminated exclusively in the SCN. Neuroscientists thought initially that this pathway, the retinohypothalamic tract (RHT), was the means by which all rhythms were entrained by light.

Now, because of experiments in which other pathways were destroyed, "what's clear is that it is sufficient for entrainment, but it's equally clear that it's not the only pathway involved," explained Benjamin Rusak, a psychology professor at Dalhousie University in Nova Scotia.

Some of the newest research has established the importance of the pathway that runs from the optic chiasm to a thin wedge of cells between the dorsal and ventral geniculates in the hypothalamus. Newly recognized as a distinct structure, it is called the intergeniculate leaflet.

Rusak's colleague, Mary Harrington, and Gary Pickard of the University of Oregon recently have found that destroying the intergeniculate leaflet in rats produces advances and delays in rhythms. Other work has traced neuropeptide-Y (one of the chemical messengers of the nervous system) from the leaflet to the SCN.

At this point, Rusak said, there are many threads of information that have yet to be sewn together.

"The implications are that, when one does intergeniculate leaflet lesions, one could be producing indirect changes in the projections to the SCN." The functioning of the SCN may be damaged, he added, or the impact may be quite the opposite and the SCN may grow and change in response to the RHT being strengthened.

Even harder to trace than the incoming pathways to the SCN are the very fine outgoing fibers which convey temporal information from the SCN to the various parts of the body. But neural connections have been documented to several areas of the hypothalamus and the central nervous system, including the pituitary, pineal and brainstem areas.

Entrainment

Using noninvasive procedures, other kinds of experiments on how SCN interpret light information seems to offer more immediate applications for human health. Both Menaker and Sulzman are studying how pulses of light shift sleeping and other rhythms.

Menaker has found that two brief pulses of light per day, spaced 10 hours apart, will stimulate the growth of gonads in male hamsters otherwise kept totally in the dark. In natural conditions, their gonads begin to grow in the spring just prior to their breeding season. Unlikely as it may seem, the pulses of light seem to mimic the onset of spring. If the pulses are spaced only nine hours apart, mimicking the shorter days of winter, the gonads do not grow.

"It's not the amount of light, it's something about the time between when the light goes on and off," Menaker explained. "So you can represent the whole day just by starting and stopping it. The clock is involved in that measurement, and we're not sure how."

Sulzman is studying how the pulses of light shift circadian rhythms. The lower the species, the stronger the response.

He has found that a 10-minute pulse of light can permanently cause a 12-hour shift in the rhythms of fungi and fruit flies. With rodents, a 15-minute pulse of light can cause all rhythms to advance or be set backward by two hours. Collecting data on monkeys, Sulzman is now painstakingly plotting out which times are most sensitive to light and which set rhythms either forward or backward.

The work could someday help humans with rhythm disorders. A circadian rhythm disorder may be responsible, for example, for chronic insomnia. At the National Institute of Mental Health, Wehr and colleagues have had some success in advancing rhythms with sleep deprivation techniques. NIMH researchers are also treating people who suffer from "winter depression" by exposing them to intense light twice a day.

"The hypothesis is that, during the short days during the winter, the SCN is not getting enough light. So they have an inappropriate phase relationship to the world," Sulzman said.

Manic Depression

Because of the cyclicity of its symptoms, manic-depressive illness is a particularly attractive candidate as a circadian rhythm disorder. One exciting theory, Rusak noted, is that the mechanism that generates the rhythm abnormalities might be identical to the one that generates the abnormal symptoms of behavior and mood.

One reason that lithium is a successful treatment for many manic-depressives, according to Wehr, is that it may slow down the circadian clock by lengthening the phase of a rhythm. But manic-depressives and others with affective disorders may not just have abnormally fast clocks.

The problem might be a lack of synchronization among all their rhythms. It's possible that lithium may lengthen not only the period of an abnormal rhythm, but also lengthen rhythms that were normal. The hope is that drugs could be developed to act only on the abnormal disorders.

People with affective disorders have been reported to have abnormal hormone levels and the drugs with which they are treated can alter them. To Rusak, that treatment points to the importance of obtaining hormone samples many times throughout the day to chart an individual's peaks and troughs.

"The detection of abnormal *rhythms* of endocrine activity is as important a goal as the detection of abnormal levels," according to Rusak. A person that appears to have a low level of cortisol, for example, may in fact have shorter or longer phases—a different rhythm—than a normal control subject. Rusak conceded, however, that there are good reasons why such procedures have not been undertaken on humans: they would be very invasive with no guarantee of a benefit.

Franz Halberg is probably the leading proponent of a circadian approach to treating psychological and medical problems. Director of the chronobiology laboratories at the University of Minnesota, he coined the term "chronobiology" to describe the study of temporal relationships between metabolic, hormonal and neuronal processes. He believes not only that depressed people have clear abnormalities in their rhythms, but "you can also find differences in individuals at high or low risk for depression."

Halberg has also conducted experiments in which he administered chemotherapeutic drugs to cancerous animals. One of the problems with such drugs, of course, is that they may not only kill a tumor but also the patient. As many as 74 percent of rats died when a drug was administered at one time a day, while only 15 percent died at another. The synthesis of DNA in the bone marrow follows circadian cycles, and one theory is that the drug is most toxic to the animals at the beginning of the DNA synthesis phase.

Despite the clear implications in his work for the treatment of cancer patients, Halberg does not know of any drugs being developed with chronobiologic principles in mind. The same indifference has been shown by companies whose employees could benefit from findings that relate to coping with jet lag and shift work.

Scientists who conduct basic research on new fields traditionally face the question of the value of their work in improving the human condition. But those uncovering the physiology of circadian rhythms do not doubt that important applications will someday exist.

"Thirty years ago," noted Menaker, "when the structure of nucleic acid was first understood, it was completely unknown what benefits to mankind would come out of knowing the mechanisms of heredity. Certainly no one thought we could engineer plants with all the amino acids necessary to support animal life."

He recalled what Michael Faraday said when asked about the usefulness of his new invention, the electric motor. Replied Faraday, "What good is a baby?"

WHAT A CHILD IS GIVEN

We have long accepted that chromosomes form our physical selves. Now, scientists say they also provide a blueprint for personality.

Deborah Franklin

Deborah Franklin, who lives in San Francisco, is a staff writer at Hippocrates magazine.

On the August morning in 1971 when Marietta Spencer first met the birth family of her adopted son, Paul, she was prepared to be nervous. In the four years that she had worked as a social worker for the Children's Home Society of Minnesota, in St. Paul, Spencer had arranged and guided many such meetings. She had seen firsthand the fears and confusion stirred up when strangers, joined at the heart by adoption, examine the potent ties among them. But what Spencer wasn't prepared for, as she and Paul and the rest of the family spent a day swapping stories with a score of her son's birth relatives in their home in northern Germany, was how familiar all these strangers would seem.

It was more than physical appearance, she decided, though Paul's tall, slight build, blue eyes and narrow smile were echoed throughout the birth family, who had not seen the boy since they had arranged for his adoption 17 years earlier. It had more to do with the way one of the birth mother's brothers tossed a pillow up atop a bookcase to punctuate a joke, and with the jokes themselves—no slapstick here, only very dry, occasional one-liners. The conversational tone was familiar, too—mostly quiet and spare of excess emotion.

Like Paul, a gifted pianist, they reserved their passion for music; three of the birth mother's brothers had played for years in the local orchestra. In this German family of the woman who had died soon after giving birth to Paul, Spencer saw striking reflections of her son's personality.

"I felt such a tremendous sense of relief, as I realized, of course, this is Paul, here are the roots of who he is," she recalls.

For Paul, the encounter sparked a friendship that he pursued, returning again to visit the family on his own. For Spencer, it hammered home a lesson that scientific studies of the last 20 years have validated: A newborn child is not a formless bit of clay waiting to be shaped by parents or anybody else.

Rather, the core of many behaviors and most personality traits—the determinants of whether we're shy or extroverted, even the kinds of jokes we find funny and the kinds of people we like—seem largely embedded in the coils of chromosomes that our parents pass to us at conception. The question today is no longer whether genetics influence personality, but rather how much, and in what ways?

The answers, emerging in the last few years primarily from long-term studies of twins and adopted children, bring increasing clarity to the nature/nurture debate: While environmental forces *can* help shape temperament, it is apparently equally true that genes can dictate an individual's response to those environmental forces.

The cumulative evidence also suggests that it's not full-blown personality traits that are inherited, but rather predilections. And, in an interesting turnabout, that information has already begun to change the process of adoption itself. At many adoption agencies, a child is no longer passed from one family to another like a closely held secret. Instead, birth parents fill out lengthy questionnaires that probe not only their medical histories, but also their interests, talents and goals; that information is presented to the adoptive parents as a part of the child's birthright.

Spencer is unsentimental about the value of this information.

"A genetic history—psychological as well as medical—is something like a child's washing instructions," she ways. "When you buy a sweater, you want to know all about its fabric content. How much more important is it to know everything you can about the care and feeding of the child you are about to nuture?"

Not long ago, such views were scandalous. James Watson, Francis Crick and Maurice Wilkins were awarded a 1962 Nobel Prize for puzzling out the structure of the human genetic code, and the medical discoveries that their work has spawned—genetic clues to Tay-Sachs disease, sickle-cell anemia and hemophilia, for example—have been universally heralded. But the notion that psychological traits and behavioral disorders may also be genetically rooted has had more difficulty escaping the pall of Nazi experiments in eugenics during World War II.

Irving Gottesman, a psychologist at the University of Virginia, has studied genetic influences in intelligence, criminality and mental illness for 30 years and has some chilling memories. "At one point, I was invited to speak at the University of Texas," he says. "When I arrived, there were flyers all over campus with the title of my talk and a large swastika, implying that my work was somehow fascist." Gottesman, who is Jewish and lost several members of his family in the Holocaust, was both unnerved and outraged.

"That was the moment I first realized that it's important to say not only what I believe but what I don't believe," he says, "and to explain not only what the results of my studies mean, but also what they don't mean."

Many political activists of the 1960's and 70's, wary that genetic theories might ultimately be used to justify social inequality, attacked anyone who suggested that it wasn't within the DNA of each person to be a mathematical genius, a concert pianist or a gifted statesman. "Potential" was the buzzword; any mention of limits was deemed reactionary. It was all right to talk to your veterinarian about a sweet-tempered pup, but heaven forbid you should suggest that your child had an inherent nature. Still, even then, in a few psychology departments scattered around the world, researchers were stubbornly chipping away at the idea that every aspect of personality is learned.

It is within the family that the alchemy of nurture and nature works its strongest magic, and it is by studying families—of twins and adopted children—that behavioral geneticists have best succeeded in untangling those forces. Thomas J. Bouchard at the University of Minnesota heads one of the most dramatic of such studies.

Since 1979, Bouchard has specialized in the examination of adult identical and fraternal twins who were separated soon after their birth and reared in separate families, separate worlds. To date, he has found about 100 twin pairs—60 of them identical—and has brought each to his laboratory for a week of tests.

These days, when newspapers carry stories every other week of scientists closing in on the gene that causes one or another illness, such as cystic fibrosis or Huntington's disease, it is tempting to think of all genetic research in terms of test tubes and bits of chopped-up DNA. But those aren't a behavioral geneticist's tools. Bouchard does take many physical measurements—of heart rhythms, brainwave patterns and motor skills, for example—but most of his tests are done with pencil and paper.

He finds that identical twins reared in completely different families and communities answer the 15,000 questions he asks in remarkably similar ways. In fact, in questions that reveal traits as diverse as leadership ability, traditionalism or irritability, for example, they respond just as identical twins would who grew up in the same family. When measuring traditionalism—a composite trait that includes showing respect for authority, endorsing strict child-rearing practices and valuing the esteem of the community—the similarities between twins reared in different families were striking.

What elevates these findings above the level of what Mark Twain, borrowing from Disraeli, disparaged as "lies, damned lies, and statistics," is that these are very well-controlled statistics. By focusing on identical twins reared apart, Bouchard has found individuals who have all of their genes—and perhaps only their genes—in common. The clincher is that he and his colleagues run the same battery of tests on three other types of twins: identical pairs raised in the same families, fraternal twins reared together and fraternal twins reared apart.

Remember that identical twins arise from the fertilization of a single egg that splits in half shortly after conception, while fraternal twins are the product of *two* fertilized eggs. Identical twins have in common all their genes; fraternal twins, on average, half. By comparing the degree of similarity among twins in each of

---

Adoptions lend insight—what do we get from nature and what from nurture?

---

these four categories, Bouchard is able to look trait by trait and see how much each is influenced by genetics. In measuring I.Q., for example, Bouchard found that identical twins reared apart were more similar than fraternal twins reared together.

Internationally, there are two other major, ongoing studies of identical twins reared apart—one in Sweden, the other in Finland—encompassing more than 7,000 pairs of twins all told. Together with earlier, smaller studies, this research has allowed behavioral geneticists to begin to speak confidently about the influence of genes on a number of human characteristics.

Though the debate over the value of intelligence quotient tests continues, for example, there is ample evidence that whatever it is they measure is in large part inherited. Studies of some 100,000 children and adults internationally suggest that genes are 50 percent to 70 percent responsible for an individual's I.Q. "That,s not to say that you can't reduce anybody's I.Q. to zero if you hit them over the head hard enough," says John C. Loehlin, a behavioral geneticist at the University of Texas at Austin. Physical or psychological abuse, malnutrition or even a lack of intellectual stimulation can act as environmental bludgeons to native intelligence. However, Loehlin adds, "The idea that, if raised in the same environment, we would all have the same I.Q. has pretty much been laid to rest."

The findings are trickiest to understand where what we call personality is concerned. Research of the last decade shows that genetics are as influential as environment on characteristics as varied as extraversion, motivation for achievement, leadership, conscientiousness and conservatism. But whether some traits are more genetically controlled than others is much harder to tease apart. Like Bouchard and others, Robert Plomin, a developmental psychologist at Pennsylvania State University, is trying to do just that in a study of nearly 700 pairs of Swedish twins.

"The interesting question today," says Plomin, "is, 'Are there any traits that *aren't* significantly affected by genetics?' " He thinks he has found one: agreeableness, or as he calls it, "niceness"—whether a person is more trusting, sympathetic and cooperative, or cynical, callous and antagonistic. "We found that where a person tends to fall on that scale is much more influenced by environment—mostly early environment—that by genes," Plomin says, "and as a parent, I find that very reassuring."

The same studies continue to shed light on behavioral disorders such as alcoholism—a particularly complicated area of inquiry, since research shows that "situational" alcoholism caused by environmental factors such as war and unemployment skews the findings.

Men appear to be much more susceptible to the disorder than women; an alcoholic father is a strong indicator of a possible problem in a son. Conventional wisdom holds that about 25 percent of the male relatives of alcoholics are problem drinkers themselves, as compared with less than 5 percent of the general population. Perhaps the best evidence for a genetic link comes from a 1987 adoption study in Sweden, which found that the adopted sons of alcoholic birth fathers were four times more likely to grow up to be alcoholic than were members of a control group. A smaller study of adopted daughters of alcoholic birth mothers found they were three times more likely to have the disorder.

Recent adoption and twin studies also suggest that there's a genetic link to most—but not all—forms of schizophrenia. The likelihood that a child or sibling of someone with schizophrenia will develop the disorder is about 12 percent—12 times higher than the risk for everyone else—and if one identical twin has schizophrenia, the other has a 50 percent chance of developing the illness. Researchers suspect that a constellation of genes, working in combination with environmental forces, triggers the disease.

Both adoptive and twin studies confirm that clinical depression, particularly the bipolar manic-depressive variety, has a strong genetic component. According to one of the largest studies, in Denmark in 1977, if one identical twin suffers from bipolar manic depression, the other has a 79 percent likelihood of having the same disorder. Among fraternal twins, that correlation is only 19 percent.

The genetic study of criminality has replaced the study of I.Q. as the most controversial area of behavioral genetics. It is also one of the most speculative. In the mid-1960's, a theory was put forward, based on several studies of felons, that men with an extra Y choromosome were more aggressive than the average male. But further research disproved the finding. More recent adoption and twin studies, says Gottesman, indicate that if there *is* a genetic component to criminal behavior, it is slight.

MARIETTA SPENCER'S SECOND-FLOOR OFFICE AT THE CHILdren's Home Society overlooks a shaded avenue on the residential fringe of St. Paul. On her way upstairs after lunch one afternoon last spring, she walked through the examining room, where a nurse gently prodded and poked a line-up of infants, waiting for adoption, who had been brought to the society by their foster mothers for routine check-ups. Spencer paused to play with a strikingly serious 3-month-old girl. After getting a smile from the child, she moved on.

"Even at this age, children have such obviously different temperaments," Spencer said. "Every child comes into the world with a genetic history. You can't expect them to let go of that, like so much baggage, just because they've been adopted into a new family."

These views were confirmed in the mid-1970's, Spencer said, when "people who had been adopted as children were coming back to us for more information. Some wanted to meet their birth parents, but many just wanted to know more about them, as a way of knowing more about themselves." Even if sympathetic, most adoption workers at the time had little information to offer. Disorders like depression, schizophrenia and alcoholism carried a much stronger social stigma then, and were commonly thought to be either failures of character or environmentally induced. Rather, the emphasis was on integrating the child into the new family as quickly as possible, and for some families that even meant denying the child was adopted.

To help the adopted learn more about their backgrounds, Spencer assembled a team of social workers whose main job was and continues to be detective

---

Twins, raised apart and together, form the basis for the new findings.

---

work; they've answered 1,600 requests for information since 1977. They locate birth parents wherever possible, discreetly contact them and—if and when the individuals are willing—fill in the history of the adopted child.

"Anything that might be even partially inherited, and provide useful information for the adopted person, we'll ask about," Spencer says. She steps into her office and pulls open a file drawer filled with folders detailing the lives of her clients.

One particularly thick file belongs to Robert Morse. He and his family weren't much interested in questions of personality when they sought Spencer's help eight years ago; they were afraid for the boy's life. Though apparently healthy when adopted soon after birth, Morse, now 21, nearly died at age 5 from a bout with Crohn's disease, an intestinal disorder that kept him from absorbing nutrients from food. He recovered, but went on to develop arthritis at 12. The pain was so intense that at times he couldn't walk.

"I was starting to feel like a time bomb," Morse remembers, "wondering what was going to happen to me next." While hospitalized, he had plenty to wonder about. Without any medical history to work from, doctors were forced to perform painful test after painful test to come up with a definitive diagnosis of juvenile chronic arthritis, which has sometimes been associated with Crohn's disease.

"They asked if we had any illness like this in the family," Morse recalls. "All we knew from my records was that my birth mother was of Swedish extraction and allergic to hollyhocks.

Spencer, whose agency had arranged the adoption, had more information, which eventually led her to Sally Boyum, a 39-year-old whose avocation is acting. In 1967, on the day of her fiancé's funeral—he had drowned in a boating accident—Boyum had discovered she was pregnant. Grief-stricken, she arranged for an adoption. Though she didn't think to mention it at the time of the adoption—"Both Jim and I had always been so healthy"—there was a history of Crohn's disease and intestinal illness in her family. Several of her close relatives, Boyum would later learn, had bone abnormalities and the same type of arthritis as Morse.

"At first I didn't want to meet with Sally, and she didn't push it," Morse says. "I had the medical information, and that was enough." But after a few weeks of gentle encouragement from his parents, he changed his mind.

"Apparently Jim—my birth father—was a terrible tease, and so am I," Morse says. "Both my folks have a good sense of humor, but teasing—calling up on the phone and pretending to be someone else, for example—tha's a kind of joking that I do, but they don't." The list goes on. "At school, or in the fraternity, I've always been a coalition-builder—it's one of the things I do best," says Morse, "and that's a role that Sally plays too." Then there's acting—a love of playing to the crowd that for Sally Boyum is also a passion.

One piece of information, Morse says, has changed his life: Many members of both sides of the family struggled with alcoholism. "Like a lot of kids in college, I used to go out and drink a lot on the weekends," he says. "Now I know that's a danger for me, and I've stopped."

MARY ANNE MAISER, WHO SUPERVISES SOCIAL WORKERS at the Children's Home Society, works in an office dotted with photographs of her three daughters, the oldest of whom, Laura, is adopted. "At the time my husband and I adopted Laura, social workers were taught—and taught clients—that each baby is a tabula rasa," Maiser says. "But by the time Laura was a year old, I knew something was wrong." She was an extremely difficult child, even alienated.

Over the years, the family sought help from a therapist. It wasn't until age 17 that Laura was diagnosed with bipolar disorder, or manic-depressive illness. Around that time, after two years of trying, Maiser was able to get more information about Laura's birth family; she had been adopted through a different agency in another state. The agency revealed that within months of Laura's adoption, her biological father had been hospitalized. "You can guess the diagnosis,: Maiser says. "Bipolar disorder and schizophrenia."

If she had been given the information earlier, would it have made a difference? Maiser's voice gets tight and her mouth forms a resolute line. "Laura had so much pain and went undiagnosed for so long," she says. "She didn't just need family therapy, she needed lithium."

Despite such testimonials, some people still argue that wrapping an adopted child in genetic history does more damage than good. Laura had only about a 15 percent chance of inheriting her biological father's illness. If the disorder had never appeared, might not the label itself have twisted her life?

Marietta Spencer dismisses such objections: "Everyone I have ever worked with has said it is always better to know the history than not to know. Because, believe me, it's the parents who *don't* know who imagine the worst if they have a child who seems to be troubled."

For his part, Plomin thinks it's at least as important to tell adoptive parents that the birth father was an alcoholic as to alert them to their child's tiny risk of inheriting a rare disease. "Even if you have a genetic vulnerability," he points out, "you don't become an alcoholic unless you drink a lot over a long period. If you have the genetic history ahead of time, and you see the symptoms developing, you may be more likely to get help early."

If adoption agencies are going to do everything they can to maximize the chances of harmony in a family, should they perhaps go one step further and take temperamental factors into account when "matching" a child to new parents?

Spencer, while stressing that genetic history isn't the *only* factor to consider in an adoption, thinks it shouldn't be ignored. "Adoption, like marriage, is a process of family building, and empathy is very important," she says.

While Spencer might have a point, Plomin says, accurately predicting whether family members will be sympathetic or antagonistic to each other—in essence, predicting the chemistry of relationships—is much more difficult than she imagines. And even if adoption workers could give long, detailed personality tests to both sets of parents, they would still be a long way from predicting the baby's temperament.

Moreover, Plomin cautions, the current infatuation with genetic influences has obscured the very real importance of environment in human development. "More and more, I find myself standing up before funding committees and the public to say, 'Hey, wait a minute everybody, hold on. It's not *all* genetic.'"

In fact, Plomin's most recent research suggests that the influences of genes and the environment may be intractably intertwined. He asked participants in the Swedish twin study, who were an average of 59 years old, to fill out questionnaires about their parents, siblings and childhood experiences. The questions were phrased so as to get at the respondents' perceptions of their families—how cohesive, or emotionally demonstrative the families were, for example, or how much stress parents had placed on achievement, organization, discipline or culture.

The results were striking: identical twins reared in different families described their early childhood environments as remarkably similar—almost as similar as if they had been raised in the same family. Fraternal twins, on the other hand, even when raised in the same family, described that family very differently.

"You can interpret the finding in one of two ways," Plomin says. "Maybe, because of their identical genes, identical twins perceive their environment in a quite similar way—sort of like looking at the world through the same shade of gray- or rose-colored glasses. But it

In matters of human development, 'It's not all genetic,' as one researcher stresses. 'The trait develops via the environment,' says another.

is also possible—and we think quite likely—that their parents and others respond to them similarly because of genetically influenced quirks of personality that they share."

Bouchard is finding much the same thing in his study; . . . He cites the example of one pair of identical twins from Britain, now middle-aged, who were separated soon after birth. One was adopted by a working-class family with little time or money for books. The other grew up exposed to a rich library as the daughter of a university professor. "From early childhood, both women loved to read," Bouchard says. "One had only to walk out into the living room and pull books off the shelf. The other went every week to the library and came home with a huge stack. Though one had to work a little harder at it than the other, they both ended up creating functionally similar environments."

However, "if one of those women had been raised in a family with *no* access to libraries, she would have been dramatically different from her sister," he explains. "The trait develops via the environment."

If the behavioral geneticists are right, then those who fear the tyranny of biological determinism can rest a little easier. Genes aren't the sole ingredient of the personality soup, they are merely the well-seasoned stock. That message should be liberating for all parents—and children.

N E W
CONNECTIONS

When it's time to make changes in your life,

what role does your brain play?

SANDRA BLAKESLEE

Sandra Blakeslee *of Los Angeles writes on science and health for* The New York Times *and is coauthor of* Second Chances.

Suppose you are contemplating a major change in your life. You want to redefine a relationship, stop smoking, lose weight, go back to school or switch careers. You go to the bookstore, read up on the appropriate changes, and now you know which strategies are supposed to work.

But there's one aspect of personal change you probably won't find in the self-help books. It has to do with your brain and the vast network of interconnecting cells that account for everything you do, think, feel, remember and believe. When you set out to alter course, what are you up against? How did your brain get to be the way it is in the first place? What is the biological basis for the behavior or thought patterns you want to change?

Recent brain research has begun to explain why it's so much easier to buy those how-to books than make enduring changes in our lives. To some degree, the adult brain is designed to be set in its ways. If the brain changed with every whim, we'd be mental chameleons, unable to make commitments, hold onto values or stick with difficult tasks.

Fortunately, however, the adult brain is also designed to accommodate change. The possibility for change—both original growth and the reworking of established pathways—is built into the physical and chemical structure of the human nervous system. We learn and adapt.

Researchers have found that the human brain undergoes three distinctly different stages of development. Before you are born, the processes are largely biological and preprogrammed. Then from birth to your early 20s, your brain is fundamentally shaped by

You can't
think
away a
habit.

experience and the emotions that surround those events. Finally, in adulthood your brain is more or less set—but not in concrete. Change is still possible; it's just more subtle and may require extra effort.

To appreciate what your brain must go through to learn something new or steer a fresh course, it helps to understand how it evolved into an orchestrated array of billions of cells with trillions of connections. In an intricate dance of nature and nurture, genes and environment interact to shape each of us into a unique human being. As we mature, biological choices are made: We hone the skills that will mark our adult lives—but lose the potential for others.

BIRTH: MASSIVE CELL DEATH

Your brain begins as a small group of cells that proliferate explosively. Midway through gestation, this proliferation ends, and the neurons—the nerve cells that send and receive the messages that compose all your thoughts and actions—begin a second great expansion. The cell axons—long, thin projections with which neurons communicate—travel all over the brain, seeking out the receiving stations of other neurons.

Once an axon finds a compatible target, it releases a chemical neurotransmitter across the synapse (the tiny gap between cells), thus establishing a communication link. Eventually, neurons make countless such connections, building up complex circuits. Late in gestation, the brain is wired and ready for the next major phase—massive cell death.

That the brain loses billions of cells right before birth may seem startling. But nature doesn't want to risk coming up short; it overproduces and then prunes the excess. This pruning continues until the emerging brain builds up its essential functional networks. It's now ready to face the world.

GROWING UP: NETWORKING

Soon after birth, another growth phase begins. Surviving neurons sprout additional axons and set about making enormous numbers of new synaptic connections. The brain's wiring gets increasingly complicated, building vast neural networks that may or may not be useful later in childhood. The neocortex—the outer part of the brain devoted to higher mental processes—actually thickens in the first three years of life as this explosive growth continues. At the same time, the growing brain begins interacting with its environment to solidify important circuits.

By age three, the healthy brain achieves three-quarters of its adult weight, and the number of synaptic connections reaches its maximum. And once again, it's time for another massive pruning—this time directed by experience.

University of Chicago studies show that right after the toddler years, the number of connections begins to decline and keeps dropping until it finally stabilizes in the early adult years. Positron emission tomography (PET) scans of infants and children also show the metabolic activity of the brain's cortex reaches a maximum—about double the adult level—around age three, says Dr. Harry Chugani, an associate professor of pediatrics and neurology at UCLA. It stays high until around age nine and then slows until it stabilizes in young adulthood.

These observations strongly suggest that between the toddler years and young adulthood, experience literally sculpts the brain. Although growth is an essential element in brain maturation, the dominant theme is loss. Many researchers believe that synaptic connections not recruited early in life—say, by age nine or 10—are slowly eliminated as you mature.

Language capacity is thought to represent this kind of process. Little children are equipped with a brain that allows them to learn to speak any language flawlessly—be it the complex tones of Mandarin Chinese or the odd clicks of the !Kung bushmen. If English is your native tongue, you learned to pronounce the incredibly difficult (for most of the world) American "r." As you learned English, your brain recruited synaptic circuits dedicated to replicating the sound system of your mother tongue. Had you been consistently exposed to two or three languages in early childhood, you could have spoken each with native fluency, because your brain would have recruited special circuits for each.

But after age nine, this ability starts to decline. Unused synaptic circuits, scientists theorize, begin to die off. Although many children acquire second languages in later childhood—and speak them fluently—linguists can almost invariably tell that the second language isn't the native tongue. Similarly, if you had musical talent and your parents had waited until you were 10 or 11 before bringing you to a master teacher to be trained for a concert career, the teacher probably would have told them it was too late—no matter how talented you were.

On the other hand, the loss of unused synapses has benefits. As child psychologists have noted, children acquire new cognitive powers as they grow older. In some ways, the more children lose, the more they seem to gain. The stages of development described by psychologist Jean Piaget may, in fact, mirror stages of brain maturation driven by synaptic pruning.

According to Piaget, from 12 to young adulthood—a time of massive pruning—children lose some versatility but gain the ability to focus. They master logical thought and manipulate abstract ideas; they begin to think about astronomy and infinity, when just a few years before they couldn't fathom how far it was to Grandma's house. They also begin to solidify basic beliefs about the world. Researchers at the University of Michigan have found that the political beliefs people adopt in their late teens and early 20s tend to endure for life. Many of our basic attitudes are similarly ingrained.

When it comes to laying down learning and memory circuits, researchers are finding that emotions play a critical role—and may make learned patterns difficult to change in later life. When a memory is formed, neurons undergo structural changes that affect the strength of synaptic connections. Much of what you remember depends on your emotional state—fear, excitement, surprise—at the time, your alertness and the nature of the event itself, says Dr. Larry R. Squire, professor of psychiatry at the University of California in San Diego.

Trivial events are best forgotten. But if the event is important, your brain modulates its storage through neurotransmitters and hormones associated with specific emotional states. Adrenaline, for example, can indirectly strengthen the connection between neurons in a memory trace. This would explain why emotional responses are so difficult to change as we get older. Emotional patterns established in the early years—habits, phobias or simply ways of relating to people—have left strong memory traces in our brains that are hard to alter.

ADULTHOOD: CHANGING COURSE

For about 20 years, nature and nurture conspire to create a brain uniquely yours—a brain shaped by a singular set of experiences, memories and emotions. When you become an adult, it's time to settle down, neurologically speaking. But even though your brain is mature, a lifetime of experience still to come will continue to modify your nervous system and make further change possible. Animal evidence supports this idea, Squire says. For example, rats housed in enriched environments up to old age develop brains with especially dense synaptic connections and thick cortical regions, compared with animals confined in empty cages.

The details of how the human brain maintains its plasticity are still unknown. But the repertoire of our neural connections is probably never complete, says Dr. Dale Purves, professor of neurobiology at Washington University in St. Louis. New connections are apparently constructed, and old ones removed, throughout the adult years.

What exactly happens to the adult nervous system when we want to make a change or break a habit? "Our understanding of the process is very sketchy," Squire says. New learning must entail structural change in the neurons and synapses. But instead of a whole new pathway being formed, he says, the existing pathways may be re-shaped. To form a new habit, you might alter an old pathway, instead of laying down an entirely new one. Rather than disappearing, the old pathway would simply weaken.

This idea makes sense, Squire continues, because memory formation is such a dynamic process. As time passes, depending on their relevance to your life, certain memories fade. When you forget or "unlearn," a memory circuit is progressively weakened. At the same time, other memories are strengthened as their traces become more highly organized and strongly connected.

Old memory traces can also be reactivated to your advantage. Though unused circuits can fade away, they probably never disappear. Say you studied calculus in high school but have not used it since. If your son or daughter should need help 20 years later, you can reread the calculus text and rapidly regain your knowledge by reactivating the pathways.

Clearly, with a little effort adults are capable of change. It's still possible to learn a language, take up the guitar, or adopt new roles in life. But change is less facile than it was in childhood. As we acquire new skills and abilities and lay down fresh synaptic pathways, we must practice, practice, practice. We can learn just about anything. It just takes a little longer.

The change must come through experience. You can't think away a habit. It has to be *actively eliminated* through new behavior that modifies old circuits or establishes alternative pathways.

This is one reason it's so difficult to make changes in adulthood. When, for example, you decide to lose weight, it's not simply a matter of putting less food on your plate. All the visual and olfactory cues that give rise to strong emotions about food must be rewired. Genes also play a role, Squire adds.

If you have invested powerful emotions in a relationship you now want to change, you can't simply wish for change to happen. You must work at establishing a new set of emotional responses to that person, which will override the earlier feelings. As everyone knows, this is one of life's most difficult tasks.

Whether you take advantage of the fact or not, the adult brain remains extremely flexible into old age. Although some of our abilities decline, we compensate. We make lists to shore up a shaky memory. But neurobiologists have shown that we can continue to lay down new synaptic networks well into our 80s or 90s. Being human means we are endowed with superior ability to learn, grow and even alter course. In other words, we change.

A Pleasurable Chemistry

Endorphins, the body's natural narcotics, aren't something we have to run after.
They're everywhere.

Janet L. Hopson

Janet L. Hopson, who lives in Oakland, California, gets endorphin highs by contributing to Psychology Today.

Welcome aboard the biochemical bandwagon of the 1980s. The magical, morphine-like brain chemicals called endorphins are getting a lot of play. First we heard they were responsible for runner's high and several other cheap thrills. Now we're hearing that they play a role in almost every human experience from birth to death, including much that is pleasurable, painful and lusty along the way.

Consider the following: crying, laughing, thrills from music, acupuncture, placebos, stress, depression, chili peppers, compulsive gambling, aerobics, trauma, masochism, massage, labor and delivery, appetite, immunity, near-death experiences, playing with pets. Each, it is claimed, is somehow involved with endorphins. Serious endorphin researchers pooh-pooh many or most of these claims but, skeptics notwithstanding, the field has clearly sprinted a long way past runner's high.

Endorphin research had its start in the early 1970s with the unexpected discovery of opiate receptors in the brain. If we have these receptors, researchers reasoned, then it is likely that the body produces some sort of opiate- or morphine-like chemicals. And that's exactly what was found, a set of relatively small biochemicals dubbed "opioid peptides" or "endorphins" (short for "endogenous morphines") that plug into the receptors. In other words, these palliative peptides are sloshing around in our brains, spines and bloodstreams, apparently acting just like morphine. In fact, morphine's long list of narcotic effects was used as a treasure map for where scientists might hunt out natural opiates in the body. Morphine slows the pulse and depresses breathing, so they searched in the heart and lungs. Morphine deadens pain, so they looked in the central and peripheral nervous systems. It disturbs digestion and elimination, so they explored the gut. It savages the sex drive, so they probed the reproductive and endocrine systems. It triggers euphoria, so they scrutinized mood.

Nearly everywhere researchers looked, endorphins or their receptors were present. But what were they doing: transmitting nerve impulses, alleviating pain, triggering hormone release, doing several of these things simultaneously or disintegrating at high speed and doing nothing at all? In the past decade, a trickle of scientific papers has become a tidal wave, but still no one seems entirely certain of what, collectively, the endorphins are doing to us or for us at any given time.

Researchers do have modern-day sextants for their search, including drugs such as naloxone and naltrexone. These drugs, known as opiate blockers, pop into the endorphin receptors and block the peptides' normal activity, giving researchers some idea of what their natural roles might be. Whatever endorphins are doing, however, it must be fairly subtle. As one researcher points out, people injected with opiate blockers may feel a little more pain or a little less "high," but no one gasps for breath, suffers a seizure or collapses in a coma.

Subtle or not, endorphins are there, and researchers are beginning to get answers to questions about how they touch our daily lives—pain, exercise, appetite, reproduction and emotions.

•ANSWERS ON ANALGESIA: A man falls off a ladder, takes one look at his right hand—now cantilevered at a sickening angle—and knows he has a broken bone. Surprisingly, he feels little pain or anxiety until hours later, when he's home from the emergency room. This physiological grace period, which closely resembles a sojourn on morphine, is a common survival mechanism in the animal world, and researchers are confident that brain opiates are responsible for such cases of natural pain relief. The question is how do they work and, more to the point, how can we make them work for us?

The answers aren't in, but researchers have located a pain control system in the periaquaductal gray (PAG), a tiny region in the center of the brain, and interestingly, it produces opioid peptides. While no one fully understands how this center operates, physicians can now jolt it with electric current to lessen chronic pain.

One day in 1976, as Navy veteran Dennis Hough was working at a hospital's psychiatric unit, a disturbed patient snapped Hough's back and ruptured three of his vertebral discs. Five years later, after two failed back operations, Hough was bedridden with constant shooting pains in his legs, back and shoulders and was depressed to the point of suicide. Doctors were just then pioneering a technique of implanting platinum electrodes in the PAG, and Hough soon underwent the skull drilling and emplacement. He remembers it as "the most barbaric thing I've ever experienced, including my tour of duty in Vietnam," but the results were worth the ordeal; For the past seven years, Hough has been able to stimulate his brain's own endorphins four times a day by producing a radio signal from a transmitter on his belt. The procedure is delicate—too much current and his eyes flutter, too little and the pain returns in less than six hours. But it works dependably, and Hough not only holds down an office job now but is engaged to be married.

Researchers would obviously like to find an easier way to stimulate the brain's own painkillers, and while they have yet to find it, workers in many labs are actively developing new drugs and treatments. Some physicians have tried direct spinal injections of endorphins to alleviate postoperative pain. And even the most cynical now seem to agree that acupuncture works its magic by somehow triggering the release of endorphins. There may, however, be an even easier path to pain relief: the power of the mind.

Several years ago, neurobiologist Jon Levine, at the University of California, San Francisco, discovered that the placebo effect (relief) based on no known action other than the patient's belief in a treatment) can itself be blocked by naloxone and must therefore be based on endorphins. Just last year Levine was able to quantify the effects: One shot of placebo can equal the relief of 6 to 8 milligrams of morphine, a low but fairly typical dose.

Another line of research suggests that endorphins may be involved in self-inflicted injury—a surprisingly common veterinary and medical complaint and one that, in many cases, can also be prevented with naloxone. Paul Millard Hardy, a behavioral neurologist at Boston's New England Medical Center, believes that animals may boost endorphin levels through self-inflicted pain and then "get caught in a self-reinforcing positive feedback loop." He thinks something similar may occur in compulsive daredevils and in some cases of deliberate self-injury. One young woman he studied had injected pesticide into her own veins by spraying Raid into an intravenous needle. This appalling act, she told Hardy, "made her feel better, calmer and almost high."

Hardy also thinks endorphin release might explain why some autistic children constantly injure themselves by banging their heads. Because exercise is believed to be an alternate route to endorphin release, Hardy and physician Kiyo Kitahara set up a twice-a-day exercise program for a group of autistic children. He qualifies the evidence as "very anecdotal at this point" but calls the results "phenomenal."

•RUNNER'S HIGH, RUNNER'S CALM: For most people, "endorphins" are synonymous with "runner's high," a feeling of well-being that comes after an aerobic workout. Many people claim to have experienced this "high," and remarkable incidents are legion. Take, for example, San Francisco runner Don Paul, who placed 10th in the 1979 San Francisco Marathon and wound up with his ankle in a cast the next day. Paul had run the 26 miles only vaguely aware of what turned out to be a serious stress fracture. Observers on the sidelines had to tell him he was "listing badly to one side for the last six miles." He now runs 90 miles per week in preparation for the U.S. men's Olympic marathon trial and says that when he trains at the level, he feels "constantly great. Wonderful."

Is runner's high a real phenomenon based on endorphins? And can those brain opiates result in "exercise addiction"? Or, as many skeptics hold, are the effects on mood largely psychological? Most studies with humans have found rising levels of endorphins in the blood during exercise.

However, says exercise physiologist Peter Farrell of Pennsylvania State University, "when we look at animal studies, we don't see a concurrent increase in the brain." Most circulating peptides fail to cross into the brain, he explains, so explaining moods like runner's high based on endorphin levels in the blood is questionable. Adds placebo expert Jon Levine, "Looking for mood changes based on the circulating blood is like putting a voltmeter to the outside of a computer and saying 'Now I know how it works.' " Nevertheless, Farrell exercises religiously: "I'm not going to waste my lifetime sitting around getting sclerotic just because something's not proven yet."

Murray Allen, a physician and kinesiologist at Canada's Simon Fraser University, is far more convinced about the endorphin connection. He recently conducted his own study correlating positive moods and exercise—moods that could be blocked by infusing the runner with naloxone. Allen thinks these moods are "Mother Nature's way of rewarding us for staying fit" but insists that aerobic exercisers don't get "high." Opioid peptides "slow down and inhibit excess activity in the brain," he says. "Many researchers have been chasing after psychedelic, excitable responses." The actual effect, he says, is "runner's calm" and extremes leading to exhaustion usually negate it.

In a very similar experiment last year, a research team at Georgia State University found the mood-endorphin link more elusive. Team member and psychologist Wade Silverman of Atlanta explains that only those people who experience "runner's high" on the track also noticed it in the lab. Older people and those who ran fewer, not more, miles per week were also more likely to show a "high" on the test. "People who run a lot—50 miles per week or more—are often drudges, masochists, running junkies," says Silverman. "They don't really enjoy it. It hurts." For optimum benefits. Silverman recommends running no more than three miles per day four times a week.

Silverman and Lewis Maharam, a sports medicine internist at Manhattan's New York Infirmary/Beekman Downtown Hospital, both agree that powerful psychological factors—including heightened sense of self-esteem and self-discipline—contribute to the "high" in those who exercise moderately. Maharam would still like to isolate and quantify the role of endorphins, however, so he could help patients "harness the high." He would like to give people "proper exercise prescriptions," he says, "to stimulate the greatest enjoyment and benefit from exercise. If we could encourage the 'high' early on, maybe we could get people to want to keep exercising from the start."

The questions surrounding exercise, mood and circulating endorphins remain. But even if opioids released into the bloodstream from, say, the adrenal glands don't enter the brain and give a "high" or a "calm," several studies show that endorphins in the blood do bolster the immune system's activity. One way or the other, regular moderate exercise seems destined to make us happy.

•APPETITE CLOCKS AND BLOCKS: Few things in life are more basic to survival and yet more pleasurable than eating good food—and where survival and pleasure intersect, can the endorphins be far behind? To keep from starving, an animal needs to know when, what and how much to eat, and researchers immediately suspected that opioid peptides might help control appetite and satiety. People, after all, have long claimed that specific foods such as chili peppers or sweets give them a "high." And those unmistakably "high" on morphine or heroin experience constipation, cravings and other gastrointestinal glitches.

Indeed, investigators quickly located opiate receptors in the alimentary tract and found a region of the rat's hypothalamus that—when injected with tiny amounts of beta endorphin—will trigger noshing of particular nutrients. Even a satiated rat will dig heartily into fats, proteins or sweets when injected with the peptide. Neurobiologist Sarah Leibowitz and her colleagues at Rockefeller University produced this result and also found that opiate blockers would prevent the snack attack—strong evidence that endorphins help regulate appetite. The opiates "probably enhance the hedonic, pleasurable, rewarding properties" of fats, proteins and sweets—foods that can help satiate an animal far longer than carbohydrates so it can survive extended periods without eating.

Intriguingly, rats crave carbohydrates at the beginning of their 12-hour activity cycles, but they like fats, proteins or sweets before retiring—a hint that endorphins control not just the nature but the timing of appetites. Leibowitz suspects that endorphins also help control cravings in response to stress and starva-

tion, and that disturbed endorphin systems may, in part, underlie obesity and eating disorders. Obese people given opiate blockers, for example, tend to eat less; bulimics often gorge on fat-rich foods; both bulimics and anorexics often have abnormal levels of endorphins; and in anorexics, food deprivation enhances the release of opiates in the brain. This brain opiate reward, some speculate, may reinforce the anorexic's self-starvation much as self-injury seems to be rewarding to an autistic child.

Researchers such as Leibowitz are hoping to learn enough about the chemistry of appetite to fashion a binge-blocking drug as well as more effective behavioral approaches to over- or undereating. In the meantime, people who try boosting their own endorphins through exercise, mirth or music may notice a vexing increase in their taste for fattening treats.

•PUBERTY, PREGNANCY AND PEPTIDES: Evolution has equipped animals with two great appetites—the hunger for food to prevent short-term disintegration and the hunger for sex and reproduction to prevent longer-term genetic oblivion. While some endorphin researchers were studying opioids and food hunger, others began searching for a sex role—and they found it.

Once again, drug addiction pointed the way: Users of morphine and heroin often complain of impotence and frigidity that fade when they kick their habits. Could natural opioids have some biochemical dampening effect on reproduction? Yes, says Theodore Cicero of Washington University Medical School. Endorphins, he says, "play an integral role—probably the dominant role—in regulating reproductive hormone cycles."

This formerly small corner of endorphin research has "exploded into a huge area of neurobiology," Cicero says, and researchers now think the opioid peptides help fine-tune many—perhaps all—of the nervous and hormonal pathways that together keep the body operating normally.

Cicero and his colleagues have tracked the byzantine biochemical loops through which endorphins, the brain, the body's master gland (the pituitary), the master's master (the hypothalamus) and the gonads exchange signals to ensure that an adult animal can reproduce when times are good but not when the environment is hostile. Cicero's work helped show that beta endorphin rules the hypothalamus and thus, indirectly, the pituitary and gonads.

The Washington University group also sees "a perfect parallel" between the brain's ability to produce endorphins and the onset of puberty: As the opioid system matures, so does the body sexually. A juvenile rat with endorphins blocked by naloxone undergoes puberty earlier; a young rat given opiates matures far later than normal and its offspring can have disturbed hormonal systems. Cicero calls the results "frightening" and adds, "there couldn't possibly be a worse time for a person to take drugs than during late childhood or adolescence."

Endorphins play a critical role in a later reproductive phase, as well: pregnancy and labor. Women in their third trimester sometimes notice that the pain and pressure of, say, a blood pressure cuff, is far less pronounced than before or after pregnancy. Alan Gintzler and his colleagues at the State University of New York Health Science Center in Brooklyn found that opioid peptides produced inside the spinal cord probably muffle pain and perhaps elevate mood to help a woman deal with the increasing physical stress of pregnancy. Endorphin activity builds throughout pregnancy and reaches a peak just before and during labor. Some have speculated that the tenfold drop from peak endorphin levels within 24 hours of delivery may greatly contribute to postpartum depression.

•CHILLS, THRILLS, LAUGHTER AND TEARS: Just as the effects of morphine go beyond the physical, claims for the opioid peptides extend to purely esthetic and emotional, with speculation falling on everything from the pleasure of playing with pets and the transcendence of near-death experiences to shivers over sonatas and the feeling of well-being that comes with a rousing laugh or a good cry.

Avram Goldstein of Stanford University, a pioneer in peptide research, recently collected a group of volunteers who get a spine-tingling thrill from their favorite music and gave them either a placebo or an opiate blocker during a listening session. Their shivers declined with the blocker—tantalizing evidence that endorphins mediate rapture, even though the mechanics are anyone's guess.

Former *Saturday Review* editor Norman Cousins may have spawned a different supposition about endorphins and emotion when he literally laughed himself out of the sometimes fatal disease ankylosing spondylitis. He found that 10 minutes of belly laughing before bed gave him two hours of painfree sleep. Before long, someone credited endorphins with the effect, and by now the claim is commonplace. For example, Matt Weinstein, a humor consultant from Berkeley, California, frequently mentions a possible link between endorphins, laughter and health in his lectures on humor in the workplace. His company's motto: If you take yourself too seriously, there's an excellent chance you may end up seriously ill.

Weinstein agrees with laughter researcher William Fry, a psychiatrist at Stanford's medical school, that evidence is currently circumstantial. Fry tried to confirm the laughter-endorphin link experimentally, but the most accurate way to assess it would be to tap the cerebrospinal fluid. That, Fry says, "is not only a difficult procedure but it's not conducive to laughter" and could result in a fountain of spinal fluid gushing out with the first good guffaw. Confirmation clearly awaits a less ghoulish methodology. But in the meantime, Fry is convinced that mirth and playfulness can diminish fear, anger and depression. At the very least, he says, laughter is a good aerobic exercise that ventilates the lungs and leaves the muscles relaxed. Fry advises patients to take their own humor inventory, then amass a library of books, tapes and gags that dependably trigger hilarity.

Another William Frey, this one at the University of Minnesota, studies the role of tears in emotion, stress and health. "The physiology of the brain when we experience a change in emotional state from sad to angry to happy or vice versa is an absolutely unexplored frontier," Frey says. And emotional tears are a fascinating guidepost because "they are unique to human beings and are our natural excretory response to strong emotion." Since all other bodily fluids are involved in removing something, he reasons, logic dictates that tears wash something away, too. Frey correctly predicted that tears would contain the three biochemicals that build up during stress: leucine-enkephalin, an endorphin, and the hormones prolactin and ACTH. These biochemicals are found in both emotional tears and tears from chopping onions, a different sort of stress.

Frey is uncertain whether tears simply carry off excess endorphins that collect in the stressed brain or whether those peptides have some activity in the tear ducts, eyes, nose or throat. Regardless, he cites evidence that people with ulcers and colitis tend to cry less than the average, and he concludes that a person who feels like crying "should go ahead and do it! I can't think of any other physical excretory process that humans alone can do, so why suppress it and its possibly healthful effects?"

All in all, the accumulated evidence suggests that if you want to use your endorphins, you should live the unfettered natural life. Laugh! Cry! Thrill to music! Reach puberty. Get pregnant. Get aerobic. Get hungry, Eat! Lest this sound like a song from *Fiddler on the Roof*, however, remember that stress or injury may be even quicker ways to pump out home-brew opioids. The bottom line is this: Endorphins are so fundamental to normal physiological functioning that we don't have to seek them out at all. We probably surf life's pleasures and pains on a wave of endorphins already.

Test yourself by imagining the following: the sound of chalk squeaking across a blackboard; a pink rose sparkling with dew; embracing your favorite movie star; chocolate-mocha mousse cake; smashing your thumb with a hammer. If any of these thoughts sent the tiniest tingle down your spine, then you have have just proved the point.

Perceptual Processes

The study of sensation and perception is one of the oldest specialty areas in experimental psychology. Much of the work that occurred in Wundt's original psychological laboratory, and other labs around the world for several decades, had to do with sensation and perception. Indeed, psychology owes much of its early development as a science to the debates that arose over how to define and measure perceptual processes.

For many years it was popular to consider sensation and perception as two distinct processes. Sensation was defined in passive terms as the simple event of some stimulus energy (sound waves, light, atmospheric pressure, etc.) impinging on the body or on a specific sense organ, which then reflexively transmitted appropriate information to the central nervous system. Both passivity and simple reflexes were stressed. Perception, on the other hand, was defined as an integrative and interpretive process that the higher centers of the brain supposedly accomplished based on the sensory information and available memories for similar events. This dichotomy of sensation and perception is no longer widely accepted. The revolution came in the mid-1960s when James Gibson published a then-radical treatise (*The Senses Considered as Perceptual Systems*, Boston: Houghton Mifflin, 1966). According to this new view, perceptual processes included all the sensory events, which were now seen as directed by a searching central nervous system. Also, this view provided the thesis that certain perceptual patterns, such as recognition of some types of events and objects, may be species-specific. This is, all humans, independent of learning histories, should share some perceptual repertoires.

The first article concerns a sensory system only recently receiving significant focused attention: olfaction. Careful behavioral analyses of the conduct of other mammals suggest strong influences of olfactory stimuli, and it appears likely that for humans olfaction is a much more powerful sensory modality than has previously been recognized. But how can we generalize from studies of other animals to humans? And how can we conduct specific olfactory studies with humans when the dependent measures include mate selection?

One of the most puzzling human experiences is sleep, which each of us appears to need, although in varying amounts. James Krueger takes us on a fascinating historical tour of notions about what sleep is and why we need it, and then provides a dynamic review of his own work on the nature of sleep.

The third article in this section deals with dreaming, a perceptual event without a clearly identified sensory source. Dreams have fascinated people, including psychologists, since ancient times. Freud referred to dreams as the "royal road to the unconscious," because he believed that dreams concealed hidden representations of a person's unconscious motives and fears. More recent research, and theories based on this research, refute Freud's arguments and raise new ones. In this way, science goes forward. However, we are left with the question: What is the real purpose of dreaming? Could such an elaborate event have been an accident of nature?

Looking Ahead: Challenge Questions

If olfactory stimuli can trigger significant behavioral sequences in humans, and if these triggering stimuli can be learned or imprinted very early in life, to what extent are individuals personally responsible for these later behaviors? Should parents be informed about this research, and if so, what recommendations should they consider relative to the olfactory stimulation of their infants?

Aside from providing some rest and respite from work, what purposes could sleep have? How can we differentiate the chemical and the neural benefits of sleep? Can we easily learn to get by with significantly less sleep?

Much dream research is based on EEG patterns. Are we sure that we are measuring dreaming? Is it really possible that dreams do not mean anything? If so, why are they often so troubling?

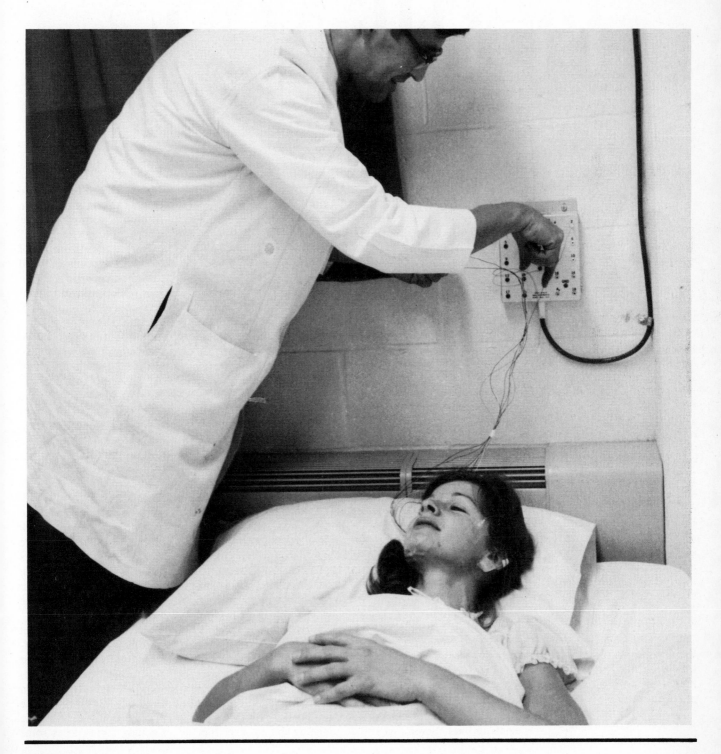

ARE WE LED BY THE NOSE?

T E R E N C E   M O N M A N E Y

Terence Monmaney writes about health for Newsweek.

On a rainy October night in Chicago 11 years ago, 33-year-old mathematician David Griffin* stepped off a curb and into the path of a Dodge van. He was on his usual after-dinner walk, although he was perhaps feeling an unusual need for it—the buffet supper of turkey and potatoes and fixings had not fully agreed with him.

Griffin considered himself something of an epicure, with an ability to taste and smell that was the functional equivalent of perfect pitch. Impressed once, for instance, by the exotic flavor of some broiled fish he had eaten in a restaurant in Pisa, he divined the secret recipe and re-created the dish, down to the basting of lime juice, rosemary, and mustard.

The van was moving about five miles an hour when it hit him. He cracked his skull on the pavement. His recovery

*This is not his real name, but all the details of his case are true.

What a rat smells in the womb is what it seeks

in a mate. What mammals smelled 100 million years

ago may have led to the human forebrain.

---

was good, and during the eight days he spent in the hospital he did not have any remarkable symptoms. True, he noticed that the hospital food was terribly bland and yet very salty, but that was clearly just a sign of his good taste. It appeared he would suffer no deep or lasting injury. The day after returning home he poured his father a snifter of pear brandy—sweet, ethereal, redolent of fruit ripening in a sun-washed orchard—and discovered he could smell absolutely nothing. "I was devastated," he says.

The doctors said that if he still couldn't smell anything after six months to a year, he probably never would. The blow, they explained, apparently tore nerves connecting his brain and nose. Griffin's taste buds worked fine, so at least he sensed the salty, bitter, sour, and sweet ingredients in food. Seven years

went by. His condition unchanged, Griffin sued the van's driver and won a modest settlement.

These days—well, he has resigned himself to an odorless existence, rationalizing that it certainly could be worse. Yet he has learned it is a hazardous as well as a hollow way of life.

Shortly after the accident his apartment building caught fire; he awoke to the shouts of neighbors, not to the smell of smoke that might have alerted him sooner. He cannot detect leaking gas. He has been poisoned by spoiled food. But Griffin says he suffers a more profound loss: deprived now of the rush of memory that an odor can let loose, he feels cut off from moments in his own past. "Think about rotting leaves or a campfire or a roast or a Christmas tree—I enjoyed those smells so much. I miss not being able to experience

them again and be reminded of other times. A dimension of my life is missing. I feel empty, in a sort of limbo."

Approximately one out of every 15 victims of head trauma wakes up in a permanently odorless world. Accidents are the leading cause of anosmia (loss of smell) in people Griffin's age. Influenza, brain tumors, allergies, and the uncertain effects of old age are other reasons some 2 million people in the United States can't smell anything. No surveys have charted what these people miss most, but it's safe to say their lives lack spice.

At least three quarters of the flavors in food and drink are not tastes but aromas. The volatile essences of black pepper or blue cheese are breathed into passageways originating at the back of the mouth and delivered to olfactory nerve endings high in the nasal cavities.

Sex without smells is not quite the same either, according to Robert Henkin, former director of the Center for Sensory Disorders, Georgetown University. He says about one in four people with little or no smelling ability loses some

Between your eyes, just below the forebrain, some 20 million
olfactory nerves hang from the roof of each nasal cavity; their wispy cilia
bathed in mucus, swaying in the currents like sea grass.

sex drive. This is hardly the loss suffered by a male golden hamster with such a disability—remove that part of his brain devoted to olfaction and he'll give up mating entirely. But it suggests how our lives are enriched by olfactory signals, however unconsciously we tune them in.

The mysterious way smells refresh memories fascinates novelists as well as neuroscientists. Proust said the aroma of lime-flower tea and madeleines launched his monumental *Remembrances of Things Past*. Kipling, in his poem "Lichtenberg," wrote that the pungence of rain-soaked acacia meant home. That smell should be the most nostalgic sense seems logical. Compared with sights, sounds, and touch, odors are messages that last; the smell of burned gunpowder lingers long after the firecracker has sparkled and popped.

Unlike some other animals, we don't much rely on our noses to get around anymore, although some curious new experiments suggest we could if we were so inclined. Researchers at the Monell Chemical Senses Center in Philadelphia have shown that humans can smell the difference between two mice that are identical except for a small set of genes on one chromosome. People can in fact distinguish the urine of these two mice. If we close our eyes and lower our noses, we might not only find the urine-marked trails mice leave but tell one mouse's route from another's.

But we don't often track odors— we just keep track of them. The close tie between odors and

memory is more than happy coincidence; without it, odors would be meaningless. You can't identify an odor you've never experienced any more than you can recognize a face you've never seen.

The most primitive and evocative of the senses, smell is also the most intimate. Odors give you away. Everyone knows you can't hide alcohol on the breath. The urine of children with the genetic disease phenylketonuria is mousy. Intimate, too, is the very act of smelling. You have to inhale the stimulus, bring it inside, before you know what to make of it. "Touch seems to reside in the object touched..." Helen Keller wrote, "and odor seems to reside not in the object smelt, but in the organ."

The smelling organ turns out to be a lot more complicated than scientists imagined it would be: Chemicals flowing into some hollow tubes and reacting with a bunch of nerves—what could be simpler? But there are two strange things about olfactory nerves. For one, they constantly replace themselves, the only nerves we have capable of rebirth. One by one they die after a month or so, and new nerves sprout from cells in the nasal lining, growing thin filaments that seek the brain like seedlings pushing toward sunlight.

The reason olfactory nerves probably need to renew themselves is the other strange thing. Protected merely by a film of mucus, they are the only nerve endings out in the open. In the nose, in other words, the brain directly confronts and tries to sort out the world.

Michael Shipley, a neurobiologist at the University

of Cincinnati College of Medicine, is one of the new breed of olfaction researchers trying to get to the brain through the nose. "I've got a hunch if we can come close to understanding how the brain keeps track of odors," he says, "we'll be a long way toward understanding how it processes other kinds of information."

Between your eyes, just below the forebrain, some 20 million olfactory nerves hang from the roof of each nasal cavity, their wispy cilia bathed in mucus, swaying in the currents like sea grass. Just here, where olfactory nerves greet odorants dissolved in mucus, researchers have for decades drawn a blank. What nobody understands is what everybody wants to know: Why do things smell the way they do?

Solving the problem would be easier if all odors could be broken down into a few elements, as visible light can be separated into its spectral colors. The retina can faithfully reproduce a scene, in color, by means of a few sensory cell types, such as those dedicated to picking up red, green, or blue. But there is no odor spectrum. Olfactory nerves must recognize each odorant individually.

Many scientists imagine that olfactory receptors work like other receptors—like, say, the specialized protein on a muscle cell that receives the hormone insulin in the way a lock admits a key, and passes along insulin's message to break down more glucose. One problem with this idea, though, is that it doesn't account for the smell of a new car. While it's conceivable that olfactory nerves have evolved receptors for

natural odorants, surely humans haven't had time to evolve receptors devoted specifically to smelling the vinyl odors in a new car's interior. Around 10,500 chemical compounds are invented or discovered each week, and many are smelly.

Another idea, publicized by physician-essayist Lewis Thomas a decade ago, suggests that the immune and smelling systems, both dedicated to recognizing new, foreign substances, perform that task in much the same way. Recently, researchers at the Johns Hopkins Medical School offered some support for the theory. They discovered a protein in the nasal linings of cows that binds specifically to six different types of smelly chemicals, including pyrazines, which give scent to bell peppers. This pyrazine-binding protein, they say, looks and behaves somewhat like a disease-fighting antibody protein. From this bit of evidence it would appear that our smelling and immune systems literally come to grips with the outside by tailoring a protein to fit new materials encountered.

This theory of made-to-odor receptors represents a promising new approach, but it probably won't tell the whole story even if it holds up. Neurobiologist Robert Gesteland of the University of Cincinnati College of Medicine says, "Since these nerve cells are sitting out there in the fluid, accessible to the world—anything that gets into the fluid in your nose is certainly going to get to those

Boys and girls both start smelling right away. We're generally outfitted to smell days before birth, so it is possible to get a whiff of the world in the womb. Perhaps from spicy amniotic fluid we begin to acquire a taste for garlic.

cells—probably a few different receptor mechanisms have evolved. And no experiment so far favors one mechanism over another."

Seeing, touching, hearing—the neurons controlling these senses are relatively "hard wired," a fact of life the brain seems to have taken advantage of. It keeps track of stimuli by sending them down dedicated circuits. A dot of light on the retina, for instance, sets off an impulse through the optic nerve that activates brain cells corresponding to just that point on the retina.

Gordon Shepherd, a Yale University neuroscientist, believes olfaction works in a manner something like that of the other senses, despite its obvious differences. In his view, an odorant first stimulates particular receptors, which then transmit a signal to neurons dedicated to that odor in the olfactory bulbs, two matchstick-size brain structures above the nasal cavities. Those cells relay the news to brain centers involved, ultimately, in behavior appropriate to that odor. When researchers in Shepherd's lab analyzed the olfactory bulbs of newborn rats, they found that certain odors—especially those associated with the mother rat's nipples—were processed by a particular patch of cells on the bulbs, the makings of a kind of olfactory circuit. One stimulus, one circuit, one response—presented with the odor, the newborn suckles.

Walter Freeman, a neurophysiologist at the University of California, Berkeley, doesn't believe in olfactory circuits. He measures brain waves emanating from the olfactory bulb of a rabbit while it sniffs an odor. When a rabbit is presented with an odor for the first time, according to Freeman's studies, its olfactory bulbs give off brain waves in fairly disordered fashion. After several exposures to an odor, a pattern emerges, and thereafter that odor prompts that pattern of neuronal activity—the sign of recognition.

The essence of Freeman's view is that olfactory neurons—and perhaps all neurons devoted to the senses—are not hard wired to perform single tasks but are creative; given a stimulus, they improvise a song of brain waves to go with it, and later sing the theme whenever cued. When Freeman speaks of neurons in action, he refers not to circuits but to ensembles.

Freeman's and Shepherd's views of olfactory-signal processing may simply be different versions of the same reality. It is too early to tell. But it's important to know, because the stakes are high: an understanding of the means by which the brain turns stimulus into sensation. Many olfaction researchers believe that even those who study vision and hearing (the so-called higher senses) and touch will have to turn to olfaction for inspiration. Ultimately, sensory biologists are in pursuit of the answer to the same question: How does a particular clump of neurons in the brain generate the awareness of an F-sharp, say, or a 1983 chardonnay?

Richard Doty is in a glistening steel room showing off his olfactometer. Fluorescent lights shine through chrome grids in the ceiling, and the walls and floors are paneled with stainless steel. The room, in a University of Pennsylvania hospital, is as odorproof as can be.

The olfactometer is a closet-size machine connected by steel piping to a thing on a table that looks like a glass octopus with 11 tentacles. You put your nostril over the tip of a tentacle and the machine serves up a precisely measured wisp of, say, phenylethyl alcohol, an essence of rose. Then you indicate whether or not you detect it. In this way Doty measures smelling thresholds.

From the looks of this room you might get the idea that olfaction research is so advanced that the only task remaining is to add more decimal places to existing data. Yet smelling isn't such a precise experience. Your sensitivity to phenylethyl alcohols depends on your health, your allergies, whether you're tired or rested, whether you smelled it an hour ago, the humidity, the elevation above sea level, your age, and your sex.

So, the exquisite high-tech instruments so impressive to funding agencies won't necessarily solve the mysteries of human smelling. Consider Doty's low-tech success. He recently settled two much-debated questions—does smelling ability decline with age, and are men or women better smellers?—using a $20 scratch-and-sniff test.

It comes in a letter-size envelope and consists of 40 scratch-and-sniff patches: bubble gum, paint thinner, menthol, cherry, leather, skunk, pizza. Next to each patch are the words, "This odor smells most like," followed by four choices. One is correct. At his lawyer's request, David Griffin, the mathematician struck by a van, took the test twice, and the scores helped convince the judge of Griffin's anosmia. He scored 9 and 8 out of 40. A score of 35 or better is considered normal. By now the researchers have administered the University of Pennsylvania Smell Identification Test to more than 5,000 people—males and females, white and black Americans, Korean-Americans, native Japanese (they had trouble recognizing cherry), some 50 five-year-olds, and many over 90.

Doty and his coworkers discovered that smelling power does fade late in life and that the sense is sharpest around middle age: The average score for 20- to 50-year-olds was 37. The average for 75-year-olds was 30. What's more, a quarter of the people between 65 and 80, and half of those over 80, appear anosmic. As the researchers concluded, "it is not surprising that many elderly persons complain that food lacks flavor and that the elderly account for a disproportionate number of accidental gas poisoning cases each year."

In a study published last May, these investigators showed that patients with Alzheimer's disease are unusually likely to have smelling deficits. Of 25 men and women diagnosed with Alzheimer's, all but 2 scored lower on the test than age-matched control subjects without the degenerative disease. "It's interesting that in a disease like Alzheimer's, where memory loss is a major dysfunction, there is also a problem with olfaction," Doty says. Researchers at Stanford and other universities have also demonstrated that memory and smelling often fade together in Alzheimer's patients. Olfaction may even sometimes disappear before other problems become evident, Doty says. Scratching and sniffing could turn out to be an effective and inexpensive screening tool for the disease.

Digging deeper into the test results, Doty found that at every age, women scored better on the smelling test than men, in all ethnic groups tested so far. At peak performance, by those subjects around middle age, the differences were slight—a point or less, on average. At the extremes it was more dramatic. Five-year-old boys scored an average of 27, while girls of the same age scored 34. At the other end, 65-year-old men averaged 33, compared with the 36 scored by 65-year-old women.

Doty can't explain the sex differences, but he may have ruled out one popular theory. Researchers who previously said women are superior smellers often gave credit to ovarian hormones like estrogen. After all, pregnant women, who are besieged by hormones, are considered especially acute smellers. But, Doty asks, if ovarian hormones are the key, why are five-year-old girls, years shy of puberty, better smellers than five-year-old boys?

Whatever their differences, boys and girls both start smelling right away. We're born with a set of olfactory nerves and bulbs already in working order. We're generally outfitted to smell days before birth, so it is possible we get a whiff of the world in the womb. Researchers have even suggested, and not entirely in jest, that from spicy

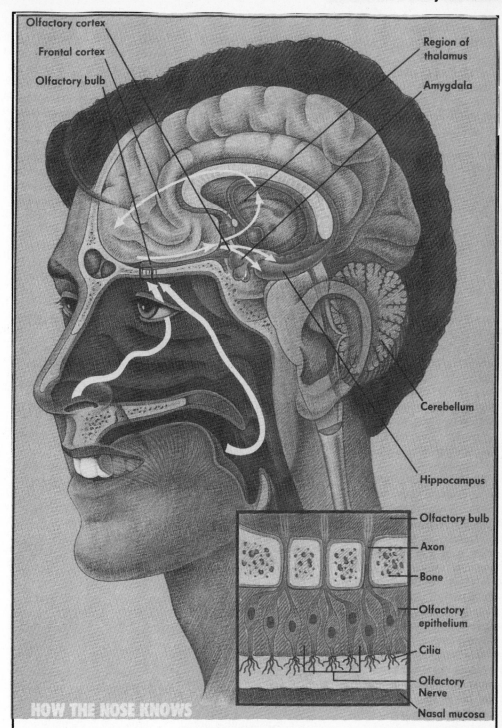

ILLUSTRATION BY MICHAEL REINGOLD

HOW THE NOSE KNOWS

Aromas enter the nasal cavities through the nose and the back of the mouth, swirl around, and flow up to the top, where they encounter the mucus-bathed cilia of millions of tiny olfactory nerve cells. The aromatic molecules react with specific nerve receptors and send signals to the olfactory bulbs. That is where the signal begins to be interpreted; you become aware that you've smelled something, but you still can't identify what it is. The message is then relayed to the olfactory cortex, which puts a label on the odor ("The sea!"). From there it travels down two pathways: to the thalamus and cerebral cortex, where, for example, smell and sight are compared ("I smell the sea, but I'm in the Midwest. Why?"), and to the amygdala and hippocampus, structures that handle emotion and memory. It is there that an experience associated with a smell can be recalled ("The seaside cottage of childhood summers...").

amniotic fluid we might begin to acquire a taste for garlic, or cigarettes.

Rats, anyway, learn a thing or two about their mothers in utero, according to experiments done at Johns Hopkins by psychologists Elliot Blass and Patricia Pedersen, who now works in Shepherd's lab at Yale. A rat pup, born deaf and blind, smells the way to its mother's nipples, homing in on the already familiar odor of amniotic fluid on her underside. They found that if they injected a pregnant rat with citral, a lemon scent, a few days before she gave birth, the pups would prefer citral-rinsed nipples to their own mother's.

Blass and psychologist Thomas Fillion, of Yale, completed further experiments showing how odors shape behavior. Again the experiments were done on rats, and again the researchers can't say what the findings mean for the rest of us. But you have to wonder. They say odors that rats experience while suckling can be a sexual turn-on later in life.

Each experiment began with a litter of pups that were suckled by mothers whose nipples and genitals were painted with citral. After weaning, the male pups were isolated from both citral odors and females until they reached sexual maturity, at about 100 days. Then the rats were introduced to a female in heat—either a normal female or one with citral-scented genitals.

Blass and Fillion found that males exposed to citral while suckling were more eager to mate with citral-scented females and finished mating more quickly—an average of five minutes, or 30 percent, faster than when mating with normal females. "These findings," the researchers concluded, "suggest that, at least for this mammal, the degree to which

a feminine feature is sexually arousing to adult males can be established in the context of suckling."

That's exciting to the male rat, apparently, is not any particular odor—fragrance of lemon furniture polish will do—but the sensation associated with it. "There's a learning process going on," Fillion says. "My intuition is that suckling is such a powerful experience, and the arousal provided by it is so powerful, it's an ideal time and place for any mammal to learn an important sensory cue." Far from coldly objectifying rat sex, Blass and Fillion have revealed its poignance, showing it is in part a rat's pursuit of infantile satisfactions.

No equivalent studies have been done on humans, but research does show that babies experience and recognize maternal odors while suckling. The first such study was done a decade ago at the University of California, San Francisco, by Michael Russell, then a graduate student. A two-day-old infant, he showed, would not respond to a cotton pad worn for three hours in its mother's bra. Yet most six-week-olds tested did begin suckling if they smelled a cotton pad worn by their mothers, although they didn't respond to a pad worn in the bra of an unfamiliar lactating woman. Writing in *Nature*, Russell also noted that most infants were obviously attracted to their mother's scent and often repulsed by a stranger's. Russell concluded: "The existence of olfactory maternal attraction suggests that humans have a pheromonal system and that it operates at a very early age."

A pheromone is a substance that is produced by an organism and that elicits a

specific and unlearned response in another member of the same species. At least that's how researchers defined it in 1959, after collecting several examples of chemicals that insects use to communicate—ant trail markers, queen-bee anointments, and so forth. By the mid-1970s there was an increased interest in human pheromones, and Russell's study was considered by many as support for the substances' existence.

But critics say Russell never ruled out the possibility that the infants were merely recognizing ordinary odors, even traces of their own saliva. What Russell called "olfactory maternal attraction," they said, was simply the infant's recognition, after learning, of their mothers' body odor.

The strongest case for a human pheromone involves menstrual synchrony. Psychologist Martha McClintock wasn't the first to notice that when women live together in close quarters for months at a time, their menstrual cycles begin to coincide. But her 1970 study of women in a college dormitory documented synchrony so thoroughly that the phenomenon is now widely known as the McClintock effect. And she made the crucial observation that many of the dormitory residents adopted the rhythms of a certain few women—perhaps, she said, because they broadcast a chemical signal, a pheromone, that the other women heeded.

Skeptics have said women achieve menstrual synchrony because they eat, study, wash, vacation, talk, and stay up all night together; shared stresses and joys regulate their cycles, not chemical messages. Still, late last year, researchers at the Monell Chemical Senses Center and the University of Penn-

sylvania offered the firmest evidence yet that pheromones mediate the McClintock effect. George Preti and Winnifred Cutler exposed 10 women with normal cycles to underarm sweat from other women. The subjects were daubed under the nose every few days with the female sweat. After three months, the subjects' cycles began to coincide with sweat-donors' cycles—evidence, the researchers say, that a pheromone in sweat mediates menstrual synchrony (other women, controls, were daubed with alcohol and showed no significant change). "Pheromone effects are real in human beings," Preti grandly told the *Washington Post*, "and the anecdotal evidence suggests they even occur here in the United States, where we're all deodorized and perfumized."

Maybe so. But Doty doesn't believe that humans, like moths, have automatic or built-in responses to certain odors or pheromones; instead, he says, we interpret odors much as we do visual or auditory signals: "If I'm walking down the street and see a woman with beautiful blond hair and I get sort of excited—you don't say blond hair is a *visualmone*. Our idea of what is attractive depends on styles we grow up with, what we see on TV, what society values. In some cultures blond hair is unattractive. The same thing occurs in the sense of smell. Smelling is just a way of extracting information from chemicals in the environment. The *meaning* that information may have is affected by locale and learning and memory, by the context of the experience."

That is partly what makes the smell of smoke pleasant at a barbeque, not so welcome in a movie theater. Even a rat can learn that an odor's message depends on

Researchers at the Monell Chemical Senses Center have shown that humans can smell the difference between two mice that are identical except for a small set of genes on one chromosome.

the context. Trained to anticipate a rewarding sip of water after smelling the banana odor of amyl acetate, a rat will quickly learn to avoid amyl acetate if the "reward" is changed to an electric shock. A silkworm moth is less flexible. It is difficult to imagine training the moth not to respond to bombykol, a mating pheromone secreted by females that males can detect from miles away.

Psychologist William Cain's experiments at the Pierce Foundation at Yale spell out how important the context is. Cain asked a dozen undergraduates to identify by smell alone 80 familiar things, such as baby powder, burned toast, shoe polish, and popcorn. The samples were kept in opaque jars and the students, eyes closed, sniffed them through cloth. They could identify fewer than half. "They knew the smell was familiar," says Cain. "They just couldn't always name it."

I t happens all the time. You've smelled it before, you like it—but what is the spice in that dish, what is it about that perfume? Cain, Shipley, and others believe

odors often leave us dumb because brain centers concerned with language are not richly connected to the olfactory cortex.

For most of us, as Cain's study suggests, smelling is somehow remote from the higher cognitive functions. You cannot really conjure up an odor in the way you can imagine a face or voice. Nor can you manipulate that image as you can rotate an imaginary cube, for example, or put words in someone's mouth. And while odors evoke memories, the opposite is not generally true.

That's because there are different brain structures for detecting and remembering odors, according to Gary Lynch, a neurobiologist at the University of California, Irvine. After the olfactory bulbs receive and sort a signal, they relay it to several places—to the olfactory cortex (to make you aware you smell something), and from there to centers involved in memory (most importantly the hippocampus, which connects to higher visual centers). Although information flows from olfactory bulbs to hippocampus to visual cortex, prompting a memory, visual information can't make it back to odor-sensing areas of the olfactory cortex.

Kipling saw this memory lane as a one-way street in "Lichtenberg." After reaching town and its smell of wattle, or acacia, a cascade of memories—"the picnics and brass-bands"—is let loose, courtesy of hippocampal connection:

"It all came over me in one
    act
Quick as a shot through the
    brain—
With the smell of the wattle
    round Lichtenberg,
Riding in, in the rain."

Lynch believes that the kind of memory we use to store facts began to emerge in some primitive mammal 100 million years ago, as a means of keeping track of odors. It was only a matter of time before a more advanced smeller made a breakthrough, rousing the image corresponding to an odor—"mother," say—without actually smelling her. In this evolutionary view, the collections of neurons originally designed to process olfactory information gave rise to higher forms of memory and cognition; the human forebrain, seat of art making and history writing and joke telling, is basically a souped-up smelling machine.

You can take this as an insult to your intelligence or a

celebration of your nose. But the more neuroscientists learn about smelling, the more it looks right for this sophisticated new role. Olfactory nerves in flux, receptors arising to each smelly occasion, bulbs creating patterns of neuronal activity for each odorant, memory linking the sensation of odor with whatever happens to be around—you'd expect this sort of creativity of the sense that introduced learning and memory into the world.

Brainy snobs, our noses up in the air, we don't follow odor trails anymore. We work in skyscrapers where the windows don't open, drive around in climate-controlled cars, hide behind "five-day deodorant protection," gobble up processed cheese. We are starting to act like birds, too high up and fast-moving to heed earthly chemical signals.

Even as our lives become more rarefied, the orphan sense, as Lynch calls it, is turning into one of the premier problems in biology. "Olfaction has always been in the back shed of neuroscience," Walter Freeman says. "The reason is largely emotional, I think. It has always been thought of as primitive. It's not glamorous. Olfaction is—it's *smells*."

NO SIMPLE SLUMBER

Exploring the Enigma of Sleep

JAMES M. KRUEGER

JAMES M. KRUEGER is a professor of physiology at the University of Tennessee Medical School, in Memphis.

DURING THE SECOND ACT of Shakespeare's *Macbeth*, the usurping thane of Cawdor whispers to his wife that he has "done the deed"—that, according to their plan, he has murdered the sleeping King Duncan and thus has cleared his own path to the throne of Scotland. Though the remorseless Lady Macbeth implores her husband to "consider it not so deeply," regicide does not sit well with him. Guilt-ridden, he raves:

> Methought I heard a voice cry "Sleep no more!
> Macbeth does murder sleep"—the innocent sleep,
> Sleep that knits up the ravelled sleave of care,
> The death of each day's life, sore labor's bath,
> Balm of hurt minds, great Nature's second course,
> Chief nourisher in life's feast.

Throughout the play, Shakespeare portrays sleep's contradictory nature—at once soothing and haunting, restorative and tormenting (as in one of the more famous scenes, when Lady Macbeth, at last wracked by guilt, sleepwalks, rubbing her hands together, as if to wash the blood from them, and crying aloud: "Out, damned spot!"). Sleep in *Macbeth* is also a time of death, whether the death "of each day's life" or the murder of a king. Shakespeare was neither the first nor the last to link slumber and mortality; his reference to sleep as "death's counterfeit" echoes both Homer, who, in *The Iliad*, called sleep and death "twin brothers," and Ovid, who wrote, in *The Amores*, "What else is sleep but the image of chill death?" After Shakespeare, the seventeenth-century author and physician Thomas Browne mused, in his *Religio Medici*, that "sleepe... is that death by which we may be literally said to die daily." And, not quite two hundred years later, in *Queen Mab*, Shelley remarked, "How wonderful is Death,/Death and his brother Sleep!"

Intimations of mortality notwithstanding, it is common wisdom that sleep is, in fact, the "chief nourisher in life's feast"—the possessor of some essential, recuperative power. And, indeed, a good night's rest has for centuries been a cornerstone of preventive medicine—an observation based largely on the subjective experience that most people feel better when they have slept eight hours than when they have slept substantially less. There have been exceptions, of course. Thomas Edison is said to have resented sleep's hold and to have trained himself to get by on three or four hours of sleep a night—with the help of a midday nap. Similarly, Salvador Dali claimed to have cheated long-term sleep with short-term napping: He liked to doze off holding a spoon above a tin plate. At the moment the spoon slipped from his grasp and struck the plate, the surrealist would awaken, a new man.

But whether we view sleep as benign or malevolent, it draws each of us helplessly into its arms; the average person spends one-third of his existence (which, over the course of a normal life span, amounts to about twenty-five years) asleep. Yet, until recently, science understood surprisingly little about sleep's physiological cause and effects. There has been no shortage of theories—some involving the brain, some the circulation, and others a combination of both—but on the whole, sleep remains largely the same enigma described two hundred years ago by Samuel Johnson (who regularly slept until noon): "No searcher has yet found either the efficient or final cause; or can tell by what power the mind and body are thus chained down in irresistible stupefaction; or what benefits the animal receives from this alternate suspension of its active powers."

Still, a growing body of research is coloring in some of the blank spaces in our picture of sleep. Fittingly, considering the centuries of mystery that have shrouded it, sleep is no simple matter. Rather, as recent studies indicate, it results from a complicated series of biochemical reactions involving many parts of the brain, various kinds of cells, and the immune system.

Some twenty-four hundred years ago, Hippocrates advised that a patient "should follow our natural habit and spend the day awake and the night asleep. If this habit be disturbed, it is not so good.... It is worst of all when he sleeps neither night nor day." Several times in writings attributed to the Greek physician, sleeplessness (as well as too much sleep) is cited as a sign that something is amiss. Noting the cooling of the limbs experienced by sleepers, Hippocrates concluded that sleep is caused by the retreat of blood and warmth into the body's inner regions. A century or so later, Aristotle proposed another hypothesis, based on humoralism, a medical doctrine that arose in Greece in the late sixth century B.C. and held sway for more than two thousand years.

The Greeks believed that each person's physical and emotional well-being depended upon maintaining a balance between four fluids, called humors, circulating throughout the body: blood, phlegm, black bile, and yellow bile. One of the factors thought to influence this equilibrium was the ingestion of food, a notion Aristotle seized on as an explanation for sleep. Sleep, he suggested, results from "the evaporation attendant upon the process of nutrition. The matter evaporated must be driven onwards to a certain point, then turn back, and change its current to and fro, like a tide-race in a narrow strait." In other words, vapors, emanating from food digesting in the stomach, were transported through the body via the humors, causing sleepiness. This, Aristotle posited, "explains why fits of drowsiness are especially apt to come on after meals."

Scant research was done on the subject during the two millennia after Aristotle, though a sensible routine of bed rest was acknowledged as crucial to a healthy, productive life. Maimonides, the twelfth-century Jewish physician and philosopher, recommended that a person sleep eight hours a night, "not... on his face nor on his back but on his side; at the beginning of the night, on the left side and at the end of the night on the right side," and that "he should not go to sleep shortly after eating but should wait approximately three or four hours after a meal." Four hundred years later, in *A Dyetary of Helth*, the English physician Andrew Boorde reflected a concern for psychological, as well as physical, influences on sleep when he offered this exhortation: "To bedwarde be you mery, or have mery company aboute you, so that, to bedwarde, no anger nor hevynes, sorrowe, nor pencyfulnes, do trouble or disquyet you."

During the nineteenth century, humoralism reasserted itself, with some variations (to this day, any theory that attributes sleep to the circulation, or lack thereof, of some substance in blood is referred to as humoral). The circulation of blood, which the ancients considered the most important humor, then lay at the foundation of two popular—albeit diametrically opposed—hypotheses of sleep. According to one, the cardiovascular system brings on sleep by flooding the brain with blood. The second theory suggested that, on the contrary, cerebral anemia—a *lack* of blood in the brain—induces slumber. Proponents of this view believed that, during sleep, blood is rerouted away from the brain, to other organs. The prominence of two such antithetical notions made for quite a dilemma among insomniacs: whereas some physicians prescribed sleeping without pillows, to help draw blood back to the anemic cerebrum, others advised using as many cushions as possible, to divert blood from the congested brain.

Then, in the early twentieth century, René Legendre and Henri Piéron helped fuel a new idea: that during waking hours, the brain produces a variety of substances that combine to cause sleep. The two French physiologists conducted experiments involving pairs of dogs; one of each pair was made to stay awake for as long as two weeks, while the other was allowed to maintain its usual sleeping regimen. When the researchers injected cerebrospinal fluid from the sleep-deprived dogs into those that were well rested, the recipients fell into a deep, unusually long slumber.

Legendre and Piéron concluded that a sleep substance —which they dubbed hypnotoxin—was present in the cerebrospinal fluid and had accumulated in large quantities over the extended period during which the donor dogs had been awake. They were unable to isolate the substance, however, and by the 1920s a new line of inquiry— actually a variety of hypotheses generally classified as neural theories—had gained ascendancy, boosted, in no small measure, by the Russian physiologist Ivan Petrovich Pavlov.

At bottom, all neural theories hold that sleep results not from substances circulating in bodily fluids but from some characteristic change in the patterns of electrical impulses traveling between neurons in the brain. The most popular of these schemes was Pavlov's, according to which sleep originates in the cerebral cortex, the brain's furrowed outer layer. Once each day, Pavlov postulated, cortical neurons, exhausted as a result of overstimulation during wakefulness, become inhibited; then the inhibition spreads to other neurons, and sleep ensues. (Within the past twenty years, Pavlov's theory has been disproved: experiments have shown that laboratory animals sleep even after their cerebral cortices have been removed. Similarly, anencephalic babies, born without cerebral cortices, have sleep–wake cycles.)

Whereas Pavlov concentrated on cortical neurons, other investigators probed beneath the cerebral cortex, in search of an area deep within the brain geared specifically to regulating sleep. Recently, it became clear that there are, in fact, several such areas, including two clusters of neurons (the reticular formation network and the raphe nuclei) located in the brainstem and some parts of the hypothalamus (the small structure, tucked inside the base of the forebrain, that regulates the pituitary gland, along with hunger, thirst, and sexual appetite). It is just as apparent, however, that no one brain site is necessary for at least some sleep to occur: in laboratory animals, sleep continues, albeit impaired, even after any one of these areas is destroyed. Thus, the concept of a single sleep center is gradually being abandoned.

3. PERCEPTUAL PROCESSES

As some scientists groped in vain for clues to the cause of sleep, others made extraordinary progress in different areas of sleep research. Until fifty years ago, it had been assumed that sleep was a homogeneous, unified state, during which the brain is all but inactive. This notion was radically revised upon the development, during the thirties, of the electroencephalograph, the machine that charts the brain's electrical activity by recording rhythmic bursts of voltage oscillations (brain waves). It was then that researchers discovered that sleepers pass through two major stages, as well as a number of transitional phases.

The first stage of sleep was detected in 1935, by the physiologists Alfred L. Loomis, E. Newton Harvey, and Garret Hobart. It is characterized by high-amplitude brain waves of low frequency, during which the sleeper lies still and appears to be in his most restful state, and so came to be called slow-wave sleep. The second stage, discovered in 1952 by Nathaniel Kleitman, a physiologist at the University of Chicago, and his student Eugene Aserinsky, is marked by agitated high-frequency brain waves resembling those experienced during wakefulness; irregular heart rate, respiration, and blood pressure; muscular twitching; and the flurries of frenetic eye movement from which the stage derives its name, REM (rapid eye movement) sleep.

It is now known that sleep begins as a brief light slumber, lasting perhaps ten minutes, during which blood pressure, breathing, and body temperature ease into decline. This phase culminates in the first major sleep stage: deep slow-wave sleep. About an hour and a half later, there is a transition back to light slumber, followed by a shift to REM sleep. Over the course of eight hours, this cycle recurs four or five times; all told, about one-quarter of a night's sleep is spent in REM sleep, and the rest in slow-wave sleep and the transitional phases, all of which scientists group under the umbrella NREM (nonrapid eye movement) sleep.

Although advances in electroencephalopathy illuminated much about how we sleep, they said little about why. Only in the past two decades have scientists renewed the search for the cause—the somnogenic agent, or group of agents, that interacts with sleep centers in the brain to propel us from the structured, goal-directed, often stressful state of wakefulness to the less encumbered repose with which most of us bridge our days.

In the late sixties, John Pappenheimer, a physiologist at the Harvard Medical School, ushered in the modern era of sleep research with a series of studies on goats. Pappenheimer kept the animals awake for one or two days, after which—as did Legendre and Piéron, in their work with dogs—he extracted samples of their cerebrospinal fluid. Within the fluid was a substance that, when injected into rats that had been allowed to sleep normally, proved to be somnogenic.

After several years, Pappenheimer identified the substance as a peptide (a compound containing amino acids, the molecular building blocks of proteins), and in view of its marked sleep-producing ability, he named the compound factor S. Subsequently, other researchers confirmed his work, but because cerebrospinal fluid is available only in limited quantities—as opposed to, say, urine, which is more easily obtained—further characterizing of factor S has moved at a crawl. (We probably never will know whether Pappenheimer's peptide is the same as the mysterious hypnotoxin named by Legendre and Piéron in 1907.)

By 1980, however, Pappenheimer, Manfred Karnovsky, and I had observed that somnogenic substances similar—indeed, very likely identical—to the peptide found in goats are present in the brain tissues of sleep-deprived rabbits and in the urine of humans. These compounds have been further characterized as muramyl peptides, a class of glycopeptides (substances containing sugars as well as amino acids) contained in bacterial cell walls. When injected into laboratory rabbits, the muramyl peptides exert a potent effect: as little as one-billionth of a gram induces deep slow-wave sleep for several hours. Normally, rabbits spend about forty-five percent of their time in slow-wave sleep during daylight hours, but after an injection of muramyl peptides, this percentage jumps to about seventy.

All laboratory animals so far tested have responded to muramyl peptides by increasing the length and number of their sleep episodes. At the same time, their EEG readings have shown slow brain waves of very high amplitude, which are thought to indicate unusually deep slow-wave sleep similar to that which follows prolonged wakefulness. For reasons still unresolved, the effects of muramyl peptides on REM sleep vary from species to species.

Once it became clear that muramyl peptides are somnogenic, the task was to determine exactly how they induce sleep. One particularly intriguing possibility—that there is some link between sleep and the body's immune system—could justify centuries of medical wisdom. In the early seventies, scientists had discovered that muramyl peptides are immune adjuvants: they enhance the production of antibodies in the immune system and, therefore, are potentially valuable components of vaccines. Specifically, muramyl peptides stimulate the manufacture of lymphokines (including interleukin 1, tumor necrosis factor, and interferon)—chemicals involved in immune cell activation and proliferation. (In recent years, several research teams have discovered that one of these substances, interleukin 1, is not only a product of the immune system but also a constituent of the central nervous system.)

The search for a connection between sleep and the body's defenses against disease led us to ask whether lymphokines alter sleep. In fact, all three lymphokines tested—interferon, tumor necrosis factor, and interleukin 1—greatly enhanced slow-wave sleep in rabbits. What's more, the somnogenic effects of these substances were in many ways identical to those of muramyl peptides. But there was a crucial difference: the onset of sleep was much more rapid after the injection of lymphokines than after an injection of muramyl peptides, suggesting that lymphokine release occurs late in the sleep-activation process —that muramyl peptides exert their somnogenic powers only after some intermediate step that involves lymphokine production.

One of the ways in which lymphokines contribute to the immune response is by stimulating the production of prostaglandins—a family of compounds derived from fatty acids, some of which regulate the activities of macrophages, the immune cells that devour bacteria and viruses. Last year, the Japanese biochemist Osamu Hayaishi demonstrated that both muramyl peptides and lymphokines trigger the output of prostaglandin D2—which he had earlier shown to be somnogenic. Hayaishi's findings thus suggest that at least three biochemical events, involving both the immune system and the central nervous system, are associated with sleep: muramyl peptides induce an increase in the manufacture of lymphokines, which, in turn, give rise to prostaglandins.

That such key elements of the immune system as muramyl peptides and lymphokines are somnogenic seems to explain, at least in part, the sleepiness that often overpowers us when we are in the throes of an infectious disease. And because muramyl peptides are key components of bacteria, scientists have begun to suspect that the compounds also play a role in everyday sleep.

Bacteria, of course, are far more than couriers of disease: they contribute in a number of ways to mammalian physiological processes and have established symbiotic relationships with many forms of life. For example, in the rumen, one of the four stomach cavities in cattle and other cud-chewing animals, an ensemble of bacterial strains is essential to the breakdown of complex carbohydrates, which the animals' bodies otherwise would be unable to metabolize. Human skin harbors thriving colonies of the microorganisms, and most of us carry about a kilogram of bacteria in our intestinal tracts, where they help synthesize vitamin K and from which many of them pass through the intestinal wall.

As bacteria enter the body, they are devoured by macrophages, and as a by-product of this processs, muramyl peptides are released. That the macrophages' activity is continuous suggests that muramyl peptides influence not only the excess sleep that often accompanies the body's immune response to infection but also everyday sleep, as a result of the normal metabolism of microbes.

During the past several years, our understanding of these biochemical relationships has broadened considerably, in large part because of the discovery of close ties between the immune response, the endocrine network (the glands involved in hormone secretion), and the brain. Studies of their elaborate interactions have made it possible to sketch a rudimentary sleep-activation system, incorporating thirty chemicals that interact in various ways, working with—and sometimes against—one another, to both promote and inhibit sleep.

Consider, by way of illustration, some of the metabolic events set in motion when a muramyl peptide stimulates the production of interleukin 1, a key actor in this complex biochemical system of checks and balances. Interleukin 1 triggers an increase in the release of somatotropin—also known as growth hormone. (Exactly how this occurs is uncertain. One theory is that interleukin 1 stimulates the hypothalamus to secrete growth hormone–releasing factor, which regulates somatotropin release.) Somatotropin fosters the development of bone and muscle, aids in protein synthesis and tissue regeneration, and in humans is tightly coupled with sleep: most of the body's supply of the hormone is produced during slow-wave sleep. Moreover, somatotropin both enhances REM sleep, and, in large doses, inhibits NREM sleep. As it accumulates in the bloodstream, the hormone eventually suppresses the very substance that triggers its own synthesis, growth hormone–releasing factor—one of many examples of feedback (inherent self-regulatory "on–off switches") that appear to maintain a balance between the various sleep-inducing and sleep-preventing processes.

Another possible feedback loop underscores the synergism between the brain, the endocrine system, and the immune response that drives the sleep-activation network: Interleukin 1 signals the hypothalamus to secrete corticotropin-releasing factor, which stimulates the pituitary gland to secrete adrenocorticotropin hormone. Adrenocorticotropin, in turn, signals the adrenal gland to produce hormones called glucocorticoids. All the substances produced in this chain reaction—hypothalamic corticotropin–releasing factor, pituitary corticotropin hormone, and adrenal glucocorticoids—inhibit sleep, possibly via a feedback loop that reduces the synthesis of interleukin 1.

Though it is clear that most, if not all, sleep substances are involved in similar biochemical cascades, the timing of these events, and their impact on sleep, remain to be seen. We have yet to learn, for example, why certain of these chemicals promote both NREM and REM sleep in some doses but elicit contradictory results in others. Or why the effects of some substances seem to vary widely from species to species. Or exactly how many as yet unidentified sleep substances are circulating in our bodies. Indeed, at times it seems that for every layer of complexity we strip from sleep countless more lie still concealed. Certainly, to answer Samuel Johnson (and a great many other thinkers), a labyrinth of causes—at once hopelessly tangled yet remarkably synchronized—confine us to the "irresistible stupefaction" without which no mammal has been known to survive.

What
DREAMS
Are (Really) Made Of

The psychiatrist and neuroscientist Allan Hobson suggests replacing the traditional Freudian view—that dreams stem from unacceptable, hidden wishes and fears—with a more commonsense theory. Dreams, he says, are caused by spontaneous electrochemical signals in the brain, and their meaning is transparent, not obscure

EDWARD DOLNICK

Edward Dolnick is a contributing editor of In Health, *formerly called* Hippocrates.

I N THE SPRING OF 1900, SHORTLY AFTER THE PUBLICAtion of *The Interpretation of Dreams*, Sigmund Freud wrote a letter to a friend. "Do you suppose," he asked, "that someday one will read on a marble tablet on this house: 'Here, on July 24, 1895, the secret of the dream revealed itself to Dr. Sigm. Freud'?"

Freud's faith in his theory never wavered. Nine years later he told an American lecture audience that "the interpretation of dreams is in fact the royal road to a knowledge of the unconscious. It is the securest foundation of psychoanalysis and the field in which every worker must acquire his convictions and seek his training."

Two decades after that, looking back on *The Interpretation of Dreams* in his old age, Freud still felt pride of authorship. "It contains," he wrote, "even according to my present-day judgement, the most valuable of all the discoveries it has been my good fortune to make. Insight such as this falls to one's lot but once in a lifetime."

The world has echoed that verdict. Virtually all scholars of psychoanalysis agree with Freud that his dream book was his most important work. Perhaps more significant, Freud's dream theory has become an inescapable part of modern culture. Even people who reject much of Freudian theory as dubious or bizarre, who would never give credence to talk of Electra complexes or penis envy, make an exception for dreams.

We all accept, as a commonplace, that dreams bubble up from a troubled subconscious, that they represent hidden and mysterious wishes, and that they require deciphering. In both popular culture and high culture these notions are generally accepted without argument. As Walt Disney's Cinderella put it, "A dream is a wish your heart makes when you're fast asleep." Move from Hollywood to Harvard and the view doesn't change much. In a discussion of a book called *Dream Time,* Sven Birkerts, a Cambridge-based literary critic, notes in passing, "Ah, but we are all now children of Freud. We know that nothing in dreams is really accidental."

In 1977 Freud's dream theory was finally commemorated with the plaque he had hoped for. In that same year, by coincidence, a campaign began that would enlist all the tools of modern neuroscience in an effort to dethrone Freud and to vanquish the cult of the dream.

Chief among the would-be debunkers is a Harvard psychiatrist and neuroscientist named Allan Hobson. In a steady series of books and lectures and research papers and debates he has argued that the psychoanalytic theory of dreams is a museum piece, as outdated as theories of possession by demons. Not surprisingly, he has an alternative theory.

Hobson is fifty-seven, trim, and a bit above medium height, with wispy white hair and a long, thin nose, which was rearranged by muggers a couple of decades ago. He is an animated man, a good talker, whose voice rises and whose delivery speeds up as he works his way to a punch line. He made his reputation as a scientist, but his fascination with dreams has led him into diverse realms.

On one wall of his lab hangs a fan letter from Federico Fellini. Hobson is a film buff who has spent time on the set with Fellini and written an essay on Bergman's dream imagery. Now, on a winter morning in his office at the Massachusetts Mental Health Center, a facility affiliated with Harvard Medical School, he is recounting a dream from the previous night.

Hobson was talking with a woman at what seemed to be a reunion of his medical school class. What was strange, what made the dream "dreamy," was that he couldn't quite place her. "Only eight women were in my class, and I know them all," he says. "Some of the data suggested classmate A, but the woman's actual appearance was closer to that of classmate B, though not precisely."

What is the psychological significance of that confusion? Hobson's voice grows loud and indignant. "That was the best I could do. It's the best that my mind could do under the circumstances." He pauses for breath and adds a soupçon of incredulity to the mix, his voice now almost a squeak. "It's not my *mother*, or somebody else that's stuck in there dressed like my medical school classmates. My mind, or brain-mind, was making the best of a bad job. It was trying to fit the thing together into some whole meaning, and it didn't work."

That picture of the dreamer as a kind of sorcerer's apprentice, racing madly to keep up with a flood of imagery, is central to Hobson's theory. Every night, he says, the dreaming brain automatically generates a barrage of signals that we do our best to assemble into a coherent story. The imagery itself has no "message," but the mind, waking or dreaming, cannot help investing its world with meaning. "I walk out this door," Hobson says, swinging his chair around his tiny office, "and I see the coatrack standing there. It's got *my* coat on it, *my* hat, but when I look at it, I see a person."

He snorts in derision at his own gullibility. "It's happened fifty times. I fill in, I project. I know that it happens, but I look around startled. That's clear evidence that in the waking state I'm taking bits of form and filling in the holes. And that's what happens in dreams."

This view stands conventional thinking about dreaming on its head. Dreams are caused by electrochemical signals darting helter-skelter around the brain, like untied balloons released in a room. The familiar expression "I had a dream" should probably be reversed: "A dream had me."

Why Dreams Are Bizarre

LIKE THE ANONYMOUS NOVELIST WHOM NOEL Coward described as "every other inch a gentleman," Allan Hobson is intermittently a modest fellow. His theory is bold—it aims to supplant

Freud, after all—but many of his claims for it are surprisingly limited.

To begin with, Hobson has restricted his attention to the formal properties of dreams, the features that all dreams share. He wants to know why dreams are bizarre, why they are vivid, and why they are hard to remember. The specifics of a given dream—why I dreamed of my grandfather last night—lie outside his reach.

The theory is not a ploy to dismiss dreams. Hobson is inordinately fond of them and has kept a dream journal off and on since 1973. One night recently I heard a family friend who had come to Hobson's house for dinner proffer a dream the way a guest of another household might present a bottle of wine or a dessert.

Hobson does not deny that dreams have meaning. They are revealing, he says, much as interpretations of Rorschach inkblots can be. The particular narrative that a dreamer fashions from randomly generated signals does reflect his preoccupations and hopes and fears.

The dispute isn't over whether dreams have a meaning but over where their meaning lies. Hobson's dreamer reveals himself by what he *adds* to a jumble of apparently unrelated elements. Freud's view was just the opposite. The unconscious, he said, teems with secret, forbidden wishes that we cannot bear to acknowledge. To guard our sleep, a censor disguises and *subtracts* information from our dreams so that we can endure them. Dreams seem strange and full of gaps and scene shifts because the censor has gotten to the newsstand ahead of us, tearing out incriminating pages, blacking out key sentences, disguising photographs.

Hobson concedes that we all walk around with painful memories that we do our best to banish. But he emphatically rejects Freud's view that those repressed memories are the cause of dreams. Instead, he says, dreams are caused by the brain's spontaneous self-activation while we sleep.

On the most general level, Hobson and Freud are in accord. Like Freud, Hobson believes that dreams are psychologically significant. Like Freud, Hobson rejects the dismissive view of one of Freud's scientifically minded predecessors that the dreaming brain is analogous to "the ten fingers of a man who knows nothing of music wandering over the keys of the piano."

But on the specific nature of dreams Hobson has little use for Freud. Dreams are not obscure but transparent; they are not censored but unedited; dreaming is not triggered by daily events that resurrect buried memories but is a process as automatic as breathing. Most important, the characteristic strangeness of dreams is not a result of the dreamer's inability to face up to unpleasant memories. The explanation, according to Hobson, is simply that the dreaming brain is working under adverse conditions, deprived of any access to information from the outside world while laboring to fashion a tale from a cascade of internally generated signals.

Hobson's and Freud's shared belief that dreams are meaningful has ancient roots. The Bible tells of Pharaoh's dream of seven lean cattle following and then devouring seven fat cattle and Joseph's interpretation that the dream forecast seven years of famine following seven years of plenty.

That view of dreams as hidden prophesies endures in popular culture. The accompanying view, that dreams are messages from gods or angels, has lost its hold. Dreams are indeed messages, we still believe, but thanks to Freud we now look inward to find their source. Freud was not the first intellectual to champion dreams, but, especially among scientists, he was in a minority. In the opinion of most scientists of his day, dreams were mental froth. And even among the psychologists and writers whose views of dreams anticipated Freud, no one had produced a theory with the scope and detail of *The Interpretation of Dreams*.

Freud's theory was that the dream we recall, the "manifest" dream, is only a distorted version of the true dream, the "latent" dream. This latent dream contains the unacceptable wish that instigated the dream in the first place. The point of the nearly 500 pages of *The Interpretation of Dreams* is to explain how the two forms of the dream are related, and how the latent dream can be uncovered.

Hobson's theory is far less ornate. Where a physiological explanation is at hand, he says, a psychological explanation is unnecessary. "The nonsensical features of dreams are not a psychological defense," Hobson insists, "any more than the disoriented ramblings of a patient with Alzheimer's disease are."

Such barbs are aimed at Freud, but Hobson isn't a doctrinaire follower of any therapeutic school. "The scientific evidence is very strong in favor of the idea that it is therapists, and not therapies, that help people," he says. "There's very little evidence that one school or one technique is better than another. The only exception is behavior therapy, which is probably the treatment of choice for phobias."

In some ways, though, Hobson's view of dreaming is similar to Jung's. Hobson doesn't have much use for Jung's archetypical symbols, but he does follow Jung in seeing dreaming as creative rather than neurotic. And he agrees with Jung that dreams are undisguised.

The meaning, he says, is right out on the surface, shouting to the rooftops. "When I'm up for promotion or tenure and there's a really unbelievable administrative botch of the whole thing," he says, "I have *five years* of dreams where I'm missing trains, missing boats, I don't have my papers, my dossier's not in order."

He has rattled off that list of calamities at tobacco-auctioneer speed and now can hardly sit still. "*This is a transparent reflection of my concern about my credentials,*" he roars. "*No problem!* It's not a disguise of my fear of failure or my anxiety that I'm going to succeed. My anxiety is, I'm afraid either those bureaucrats won't get my records straight or they'll say no promotion."

To venture more-elaborate explanations, Hobson says, is a kind of showing off, an entertaining but empty display of intellectual ingenuity. This is a point Hobson circles back to repeatedly, sometimes sounding as enamored of "plain talk and common sense" as a Fourth of July orator praising the homespun wisdom of the American people.

That is an odd stance for a scientist to take (common sense surely tells us that, say, the earth is flat), and in his more considered moments Hobson instead invokes one of the patron saints of science, William of Occam. That fourteenth-century philosopher spelled out the doctrine now known as Occam's razor, which says that a simple explanation that fits the facts is preferable to a complex one. Never introduce more than is required for an explanation, Occam declared, or, in Hobson's free translation, "Given two alternative theories, one of which is straightforward and the other convoluted, you pays your money and you takes your choice."

Hobson wields Occam's razor with the flair and self-righteousness of a knight of old brandishing his sword. Does Freud say that we dream because at night, when our defenses are down, lurid thoughts escape from the dungeon of the unconscious? *Whhsssst!* cuts the razor. We dream because the sleeping brain automatically sparks itself into life every ninety minutes or so. Does Freud say that dreams are bizarre because we censor and disguise their true message? *Whhsssst!* Dreams are bizarre because they're constructed from random bits and pieces. Does Freud say that we forget dreams largely because even in censored form they're too painful to acknowledge? *Whhsssst!* We forget them because the dreaming brain happens to be deprived of certain chemicals that are essential for storing memories.

The Origins of Hobson's Theory

THE SCIENCE UNDERLYING HOBSON'S THEORY of dreaming stems from a discovery by a most unlikely Archimedes, a ne'er-do-well graduate student named Eugene Aserinsky. In 1952 Aserinsky was studying physiology at the University of Chicago. In the dozen years before that he had tried college but left without a degree, begun dental school but dropped out, served in the Army, and been a social worker. He had never earned even a bachelor's degree. Now he was, in his words, a "stray cat" whom a kindly professor had taken in, and he was working on a "nonsensical idea" that no one else was interested in.

For no very clear reason Aserinsky wanted to know how a person's eyes move while he is asleep. The best way to tackle the problem, he decided, was to observe a sleeper for a full night. The most convenient research subject available was his eight-year-old son, Armond.

Aserinsky found an ancient, broken-down electroencephalograph machine, abandoned in a university basement. His plan was to tape electrodes near Armond's eyes and use the electroencephalograph, a machine akin to a lie detector, to record any eye movements.

For week after frustrating week the machine malfunctioned. "It would break down with one ailment and I would fix that, and it would break down with something else," Aserinsky recalls. Throughout this period the pens attached to the EEG would occasionally interrupt their slow, wavy tracing of Armond's eye movements and begin marking spiky peaks and valleys.

The interruptions seemed to show that the brain was occasionally as active in sleeping as in waking. That didn't make sense, and Aserinsky figured he still hadn't fixed his machine. Scientists thought of the sleeping brain as like a house late at night, the day's hubbub of activity replaced by the quiet hum of rest. We wake refreshed, conventional wisdom had it, because the brain has had a break from work. Aserinsky's research adviser was one of the leading proponents of this view. Either Aserinsky had made a startling discovery or his machine was still broken, and he didn't know which.

He phoned the manufacturers. They couldn't help. He managed to reach the scientist who was the reigning authority on the EEG, and this man advised Aserinsky to abandon the project. "If I had a suicidal nature, this would have been the time," Aserinsky says. Even today, safe in retirement, his tone as he tells the story recalls the panicky young man he was. "I was married, I had a child, I'd been in universities for twelve years with no degree to show for it. I'd already spent a couple of years horsing around on this. I was absolutely finished."

Finally he saw the solution. He could record the movements of each eye independently. Eyes move in tandem, and if the pens did too, that would suggest that the spiky patterns probably weren't caused by mechanical problems. This strategy of double-checking the machine turned out to be an old idea, but, Aserinsky says, "it saved my life."

Episodes of rapid eye movement, Aserinsky was soon convinced, came periodically throughout the night. "Well, it was a pretty quick jump to think of dreaming," Aserinsky says. "But that wasn't an idea I readily accepted. As a physiologist, I was more interested in blood and guts than in behavior."

Aserinsky now recruited a number of volunteers; he woke them up when their eyes began twitching and they reported that they had indeed been dreaming. His adviser asked for a demonstration but, wary of cheating, turned down Aserinsky's offer to recruit a volunteer and insisted that his own daughter be the test subject. She fell asleep. Soon after, her father's theory that the sleeping brain is resting was "totally demolished," Aserinsky says. "It doesn't exist anymore, except in the Annals of Peculiar Notions."

In the following years discoveries about rapid-eye-movement sleep tumbled out of laboratories around the world. Wake someone up during REM sleep and about 80 percent of the time he or she will report vivid, elaborate, hallucinatory dreams; wake the person during one of the bursts of particularly intense eye movement that punctuate REM sleep and the odds rise to 95 percent. But if the sleeper isn't wakened, the dream will almost certainly be lost. Dreams melt quickly: 95 percent of what we dream,

perhaps 99 percent, is never remembered.

REM sleep begins some ninety minutes after we fall asleep. The brain begins running at full speed, blood pressure rises, breathing quickens, and the heart beats faster. Muscles become totally relaxed and unresponsive, though eyes and extremities may twitch. The dreamer is floating free in a self-created universe, his churning brain trying to keep its bearings without any cues from the outside world.

Episodes of REM-sleep are separated by calmer, deeper periods of sleep. We may dream during these hiatuses, but such dreams are rarer than REM-sleep ones and tend to be briefer and less bizarre. And every ninety minutes we automatically shift back into REM sleep.

We pass through four or five such dream episodes a night. They grow longer as the night goes on, and total about two hours. Because bed partners tend to fall asleep at roughly the same time and to wake each other by jostling or snoring, their pathways to REM sleep are roughly synchronized. "It may be biologically trivial but it is nonetheless charming," Hobson says, that "by sleeping together, couples increase the chances of dreaming together."

REM sleep has been found in all mammals studied to date except the spiny anteater, and, to a limited extent, in birds and some reptiles. (Any cat or dog owner watching his pet's twitching eyes and paws could have anticipated Aserinsky's discovery.) A newborn baby spends about eight hours a day in REM sleep. And before birth, at about thirty weeks after conception, the developing infant appears to spend almost all its time in REM sleep.

Just what infants (let alone animals) could be dreaming about is unclear. David Foulkes, a psychologist at Emory University, in Atlanta, has done the best work on the dreams of children. By monitoring children in a sleep lab and waking them at intervals, he found that children aged three to seven rarely reported that they'd been dreaming. After the age of seven children seem to dream about as often as adults.

The nature of dreams, as well as their frequency, changes with age. The earliest dreams are brief and almost devoid of action—a child might dream of herself asleep in a bathtub. At age five, six, or seven dreams become much longer but the dreamer still figures only rarely as an active participant in the dreams. By age eight or nine children's dreams begin to become as complex and lengthy as adult ones.

Any of the REM-sleep discoveries could have called Freud's dream theory into question. If dreams are caused by wishes, as Freud proposed, why should those wishes come every ninety minutes? If dreams are caused by repressed sexual desires, what unmentionable fantasies is a newborn baby entertaining? What of Fido asleep in front of the fireplace?

The challenge to Freud is not so much that the sleeping brain turns out to be active (his hardworking censor fits nicely with that finding) as that it is active at recurrent, predictable intervals. We dream with clockwork regularity. That poses no problem for physiology, which has long focused on explaining the body's rhythms. For psychology, however, and especially for a theory that dreams reflect individual and idiosyncratic hopes and fears, that regularity is a major mystery.

But the scientific assault on Freud waited another generation. The fortress, apparently, was strong, and didn't have to be abandoned just because of some sniper fire from the physiologists' camp. What was needed, in addition to criticism of Freud, was a scientifically based theory that could serve as an alternative to Freudian ideas.

Developing one was the mission that Allan Hobson saw for himself. The confrontational style that was required came naturally. He says, "One of the most important things that has happened to me is that I went to school in England when I was nineteen and was exposed to formal debate."

He absorbed the lessons well. To this day he can address a single listener in tones more appropriate to a prosecutor making a closing argument to a jury. After summarizing a critic's charges, he will say, "I submit to you that that is absurd." "What is most objectionable," he will cry, as he conjures up a flock of dream-interpreting psychoanalysts, "is that they do it under the mantle of science when it's not science at all. That is a lie."

Hobson seems genuinely fond of confrontation. "Some people count their blessings with the number of enemies they have," one of his colleagues observes, "and I think Allan is like that." But, surprisingly, he is on good terms with most of these "enemies." The sparring is serious, but Hobson seems not to take it personally. "He's the best psychologist working on dreams," he says of one researcher, and adds in the next breath, "He thinks my theory is bunk, just totally useless."

To the debater's combativeness Hobson adds a showman's flair. In 1977 he helped design an art exhibit *cum* science experiment that drew 10,500 visitors. The main attraction of the Dreamstage show was a volunteer sleeping behind a one-way mirror while hooked up to gadgets that continuously monitored his brain waves, eye position, and muscle tone. An audience sat in a darkened adjacent room watching colored lights paint those waves of information along the walls. At the same time, a synthesizer converted the waves into music, in effect a kind of improvised jazz composed by the sleeper. When he rolled over or began dreaming, the music grew louder and faster, and crowds of visitors scurried to the one-way mirror to see what was happening.

The Assault Begins

THIS ATTACK ON FREUD BEGAN IN 1977, WHEN Hobson and his longtime collaborator, Robert McCarley, a psychiatrist who teaches at Harvard, published two papers on dreaming in the *American Journal of Psychiatry*. The articles, written in dry and rigorous prose, were explicitly intended as assaults on psychoanalysis. "I would admit to having created some heat where light might have been more useful," Hobson says, "but I can tell you, they weren't paying any attention until I turned the heat up a bit." Hobson and McCarley caught the eye of the psychiatric community. The articles generated more letters to the editor than any papers the journal had ever before published. Most were from outraged analysts, who perceived correctly that Hobson and McCarley were deeply skeptical of the theories that guided their profession.

The two articles amounted to a one-two punch. First came a critique of Freud's "antique neurobiology." Freud's dream theory, Hobson and McCarley argued, was based on the brain science of the 1890s, which is now universally agreed to be obsolete. Since those biological ideas had proved false, a psychology built on them must also be mistaken.

The first decade of Freud's career was devoted to neurobiology and neurology. Freud produced a spate of technical papers on such topics as the nerve cells of crayfish. In 1895, at the age of thirty-eight, he began an ambitious essay now known as the "Project for a Scientific Psychology." Memory, cognition, dreaming, and more were all to be explained biologically, in terms of the activity of brain cells. "The intention," Freud announced, "is to furnish a psychology that shall be a natural science."

That goal was never achieved. After a few months of frenzied work in 1895, Freud left the "Project" unfinished. Abandoning neuroscience, he turned his efforts to psychology. His theory of dreams, Freud later said, was based on a lengthy, painful self-analysis in the mid-1890s rather than on any theory of how the brain works. By probing his own emotions and earliest memories with ruthless honesty, psychoanalytic history has it, Freud unearthed such prizes as the Oedipus complex, the stages of sexual development, and the source of "accidental" slips of the tongue. His most important tool was free association, mainly with respect to the material from dreams. Hobson and McCarley didn't buy it. The self-analysis story, they insisted, was a myth. Freud's dream theory was simply a translation of the "Project" into a form that concealed its origins in neurobiology.

The second paper described Hobson and McCarley's own theory. In the years since it was written, Hobson has continued to refine his model. (McCarley, still a friend and ally, has gone his own way.) The fullest account appears in Hobson's 1988 book *The Dreaming Brain*.

Dreaming is so familiar that we tend to overlook its strangeness. In Hobson's summary,

> We see things, but the lights are out; we imagine running, flying, or dancing the tango, but are paralyzed; we explain the bizarre proceedings to our full satisfaction, but the logic by which we do so is as bizarre as the proceedings; we have intense emotional involvement in the action, but we forget the whole business as soon as it is over. What is going on?

That question, like What is time?, is easy to ask but maddeningly hard to answer. The brain, estimated to contain between 20 billion and 100 billion nerve cells, is one of the most complicated regions in the universe. The brain's nerve cells communicate in chemical messages called neurotransmitters, and each nerve cell, or neuron, is in simultaneous communication with upwards of 10,000 others. Each cell sends between two and a hundred messages every second, ceaselessly, day and night.

By a process that no one claims to understand, this electrified mound of gray-white Jell-O–like matter somehow becomes conscious. Brain becomes mind. But a daunting chasm separates the two. Physiologists assess one side of the territory, psychologists and therapists the other.

Hobson has a more ambitious (some would say ludicrously ambitious) goal. He want to travel back and forth across the body-mind chasm, using dreams as the bridge. Formidable as that task would seem to be, the strategy is straightforward, because the discovery of REM sleep provides a physiological handle on a psychological state. But the human brain is difficult to study experimentally. So research into the workings of the brain must detour by way of animal subjects.

Most of what sleep physiologists know about the living brain they've learned from cats. That may sound like a peculiar choice for research intended to explain the mystery of thought, but it is a practical one. Cat and human brains are roughly similar in design, and for a student of sleep a better subject would be hard to find.

A generation or so ago new tools were developed that provide more-detailed pictures of the brain at work than EEGs could offer. These are microelectrodes that record not electrical activity in general but the activity of single cells in particular. The tiny probes revealed that many neurons in the visual areas of the brain fire at least as often in REM sleep as they do in waking.

That was a surprise. When a wide-awake cat eyes the world, its visual cortex lights up with activity. Let that cat fall asleep, eyes shut tight in a black room, and the same cells will light up just as intensely. The brain interprets its own internally generated signals as if they had come from outside.

Similarly, brain cells that have to do with physical activity fire as intensely in REM sleep as in waking. "As far as the neurons are concerned," Hobson says, "the brain is both seeing and moving in REM sleep."

None of this was known in Freud's day. For Freud, for example, the question of why dreams are so intensely visual was a tricky one. Dreams represent a regression to infancy, he argued, and therefore a return to a mental life dominated by imagery rather than thought. For Hobson, matters are simpler. Dreams are visual because the dreaming brain is bombarded by internally generated signals that make it think it is seeing. (And sensations of taste and smell and pain are rare in dreams because the appropriate regions of the brain aren't as effectively activated.)

Why do dreamers find themselves trying to run but unable to move? Freud suggested that we are stalemated because our conscious wishes and our unconscious de-sires are in conflict. Hobson refers instead to physiological studies showing that in REM sleep we are effectively paralyzed. Though our dreams are full of effortless movement, things often go wrong when we try to exert our will and move voluntarily. Then a stalemate does occur, in the best Freudian tradition, but it is between the mind giving the command "Run!" and muscles that are blocked from acting. The dreamer *can't* move, so he can't flee the dragon chasing him.

Much of Hobson's research has sought answers to a different layer of questions. He, and many others, wanted to find the brain cells that trigger REM sleep. The search focused on the brainstem, a structure atop the spinal column that regulates such "primitive" functions as body temperature and appetite. A French researcher named Michel Jouvet had already homed in on a region of the brainstem called the pons, in 1962. But which cells in the pons were the crucial ones?

Like most questions in neurophysiology, this one was difficult to answer. When you probe with microelectrodes, a tiny miss can land you in a region of cells with a role entirely different from that of the target cells. Moreover, the components of the brain are interconnected in a bewilderingly complex fashion. To test a theory that certain brain cells are essential to REM sleep, for instance, you might try destroying them. But, in the glum words of one neuroscientist, "when you make a hole, you're going to cut down all the telephone wire that goes through that area as well as the telephone pole."

In 1973 Hobson made an accidental discovery, a "thrilling" find that he calls "the highlight of my scientific career." While looking for cells that fired only in REM sleep, he found a cell that *stopped* firing in REM sleep. Though this was the opposite of what he had sought, Hobson kept watching. When REM sleep ended, the cell began firing. When REM sleep resumed, the cell stopped again.

Hobson's microelectrode had missed its target by a millimeter. His mistake had taken him to a region of the brainstem called the locus ceruleus. Other laboratories made similar findings, locating additional populations of so-called REM-off cells elsewhere in the brainstem, and a new picture of the dreaming brain emerged.

The idea is that the brainstem contains clusters of cells that trigger REM sleep and other clusters of cells that turn REM sleep off. Whether we are dreaming or not depends on which group of cells has the upper hand. Hobson has described this cellular interplay as "a sort of continuous war whose effects spread from the brain stem throughout the brain, taking the mind hostage. This battle for the mind occurs regularly—and silently—every night in our sleep. And the only outward sign may be the fleeting recollection of a dream as we read the morning newspaper!"

The war is regulated by a curious clock that operates in ninety-minute cycles. Hobson's colleague McCarley developed a theory about its workings after studying the problems of Canadian fur trappers in the 1800s.

Trappers sold fur pelts from lynx and snowshoe hares, but because the lynx preyed on the hares, the populations of the two species fluctuated in balance. When the hare population was large, the lynx population grew large. Eventually, more and more predators meant fewer and fewer hares. Less food for the predators meant, eventually, fewer predators, which meant more hares and thus, eventually, more predators. And so on and on, the two populations rising and falling in cycles, the timing of which depended chiefly on the reproduction rates of the lynx and hares.

All that had been worked out in detail by nineteenth-century mathematicians. The pleasant surprise for Mc-Carley was that he could use essentially the same model to explain the periodic onset of dreaming. Instead of lynx and hares, he had cells that turn on in REM sleep and cells that turn off in REM sleep. Moreover, the two populations of brain cells functionally silence each other. Just as prey and predators compete for territory, the two populations of cells compete for control of the mind. In slow oscillations repeated through the night, first one group holds sway and we sleep deeply, and then the other takes over and we move into REM sleep, and dream.

The model is appealingly tidy, not least because it has several testable consequences. The cells that turn on REM sleep seem to do so by releasing a neurotransmitter called acetylcholine, which is broken down by an enzyme in the brain. If you inject a substance that mimics acetylcholine into the brainstem, you should increase REM sleep. If you block the enzyme that breaks down acetylcholine, you should also increase REM sleep.

And so you do. The model has a flip side, too, that can equally well be tested. The brain cells that turn off REM sleep release their own neurotransmitters. Like playground monitors whose job is to keep rowdy children quiet, these substances tamp down the activity of the cells they come in contact with. Enhance the effect of *these* neurotransmitters and you should see less REM sleep. Break them down—blindfold the playground monitor—and you should see more REM sleep.

That is what Hobson predicts, but the results of tests of this half of his model aren't in yet. In any event, REM sleep in cats, which is what is being studied in these experiments, is not dreaming in human beings. And experiments with people have to be oblique, for reasons relating to ethics. In 1978, however, researchers at the National Institute of Mental Health devised a way to test Hobson's model on human beings. A substance that imitates acetylcholine was given to volunteers intravenously, while they slept. As expected, they quickly entered a long, intense phase of REM sleep. More tellingly, when they were awakened, they reported that they had been dreaming. For the first time, dreams had been triggered artificially.

Hobson's Critics Have Their Say

HOBSON'S THEORY OF DREAMING HAS SOMETHING to offend everyone. His many scientific critics say that it is premature. The great majority of them concede that the research itself is careful and solid, but they insist that not enough is known about the brain to justify theories of how and why we dream.

Hobson is happy to concede that his theory of dreaming is far from proved. "I agree it's incomplete," he says. "It's very important to admit that. But I'd also say that you have to make a distinction between the specific burdens of a dream theory and a general theory of consciousness. If you're interested in why dreams are bizarre, my theory has to interest you. If you want it to solve the whole mind-body question at a single stroke and create a completely detailed theory of human consciousness, you're going to be disappointed."

"In one generation we've got a rough blueprint of a theory," Hobson continues. "What do you want? Let's go on and build a house. That's going to take a while, probably on the order of hundreds of years. But the door is open to establishing a physical theory of consciousness."

That's daring and vision if you like Hobson, grandstanding if you don't. He concedes that his manner has provoked some of his peers. In one notorious instance, involving a dispute over the properties of a particular group of brain cells, Hobson took years to acknowledge that his critics had been right and he had been wrong.

The skepticism has lingered. "He's extraordinarily clever, one of the most creative people in the field," one critic who wishes to remain anonymous acknowledges, "but if you really look into the details of what he says, you say, 'This isn't true, and that's not true,' and the whole thing just falls apart."

Hobson is unruffled by such charges. "If you're bold and ambitious," he says, "you can expect a lot of people not to like that." He points out that he has proposed a conceptual model for thinking about dreaming, and he notes (correctly) that even most of his detractors, while criticizing him on details, accept the framework he has suggested. "Allan's an unusual scientist, in that he does propose fairly general theories," says Robert Moore, the chairman of the neurology department at the State University of New York at Stony Brook. "I think people who say he's a flimflam artist are the ones who aren't smart enough to do that kind of thing themselves."

But Hobson's scientific critics can also muster substantive objections. Over the years, Hobson has modified his model of the dreaming brain significantly. He argued originally, for example, that one particular localized group of cells triggered REM sleep, but he now maintains that the trigger is distributed in multiple locations. Even McCarley, Hobson's collaborator of sixteen years, has reservations about this approach.

And some predictions implicit in the model haven't panned out. Several distinct groups of cells that turn off in REM sleep have been identified, for example. According to Hobson, those cells secrete neurotransmitters that block REM sleep. Destroy the cells, therefore, and you would expect to disrupt the REM-sleep cycle. But when such cell groups were destroyed in laboratory animals, the REM-sleep cycle continued.

Is that because the system is redundant? This is Hobson's explanation, and he points out that no one has destroyed all the cells at once. Or is Hobson simply wrong?

"I think that to be useful a scientific theory has to be fairly specific, to go out on a limb and make predictions that could be refuted," says Jerome Siegel, a physiologist at the University of California-Los Angeles and a longtime rival of Hobson's. "His initial version of the theory did make predictions, and they were refuted. Now his theory seems to have evolved to the point where it makes fewer predictions and the predictions are too vague to refute."

Such charges may sound as if they could be resolved simply, by weighing facts impartially. But in the end, the quarrel over Hobson's model of the dreaming brain comes down to the kind of judgment call we are all familiar with. Hobson looks at his theory and sees a trusty old car that might need an oil change or a new set of spark plugs. His scientific rivals look at the same car and see a patched-together jalopy that has outlived its usefulness.

Much as he perturbs some of his fellow physiologists, the harshest attacks on Hobson come from outside science. For traditional psychoanalysts, Hobson's approach was doomed from the start, because of his refusal to use their methods. "I can't convince anybody that there are microbes in this world unless I apply a light microscope," says Theodore Shapiro, the editor of the *Journal of the American Psychoanalytic Association*. "I can't tell you anything about the ultrastructure of cells unless I apply an electron microscope. How can Hobson say anything about the insights to be derived from dreams if he doesn't apply the psychoanalytic method?"

The New Dream Interpreters

LATELY HOBSON HAS BEEN STIRRING UP A NEW group. These are therapists who hold no brief for Freud but are devoted students of dreams. They dislike Hobson's theory because they feel that it denigrates dreaming. Their opposition is significant, for while these are lean days for psychoanalysis, the dream business is booming. Anyone interested in the meaning of dreams may choose among fifty or more psychology and self-help books. Dozens of colleges and universities around the country, including such unlikely schools as Notre Dame and the Stanford School of Business, offer courses on working with dreams.

The new dream interpreters don't follow an explicit party line, but they tend to share several beliefs. Dreams can be triggered by any emotional concern, they maintain, and are not the result of repressed wishes alone. Dreams needn't have to do with sex. Dreams don't employ or reflect a universal symbolism. Dreams use symbols as metaphors to convey meaning rather than as disguises to obscure it.

Hobson has no quarrel with those ideas. Nonetheless, he rails against what he calls "the dream-cult people." Doffing his scientist's lab coat in favor of his psychiatrist's tweed jacket, he mounts his attack. "I've never had an experience in therapy of feeling that a dream was a turning point of treatment," he says, "or a revelation of a truth not otherwise suspected or known, or anything else of that nature. And I have had successful therapies where dreams were almost never discussed. I'd *rather* talk about dreams. I think they're fun. I think that a full view of human experience includes them. And sometimes I'd have to grant that I learned something important from them. But is the dream *uniquely* valuable, *uniquely* informative? I would have to say a qualified no. I am just not sure it's all that useful."

That is heresy to the dream groups, who have pruned and trimmed the Freudian garden but who continue to huddle under the familiar old tree at its center. Freud's approach to dream interpretation was off-target, they say, but his basic insight was valid: dreams *are* a royal road to the unconscious, messages to ourselves that convey truths we might otherwise miss. Perhaps the best-known dream psychologist, Gayle Delaney, has built her entire career around that belief. Delaney knows and likes Hobson, and she shares his anti-Freudianism, but she insists that dreams are invaluable in therapy. "Doing psychology without using dreams, she says, is like doing orthopedics without using x-rays."

Skeptics look at Delaney and never get past her celebrity: she has written a best seller on dreams, and she was the host of a radio show on which people phoned in their dreams. And she lives and works in San Francisco. But she resents those who would dismiss her as "a California touchy-feely." Not many minutes had passed in our conversation before she pointed out that she "graduated with highest honors from Princeton."

Delaney has heard people tell her tens of thousands of dreams over the years. Dreamers have characteristic styles, she says. She believes that dreams use symbols and metaphors unique to each dreamer to convey important messages with an uncanny compactness. She repeats the dream of a woman named Barbara as an example: "I was in a pool swimming with my eight-year-old son on my back. I would swim under the water while my son's head would stay above it. I did this in several short bursts, while my husband was supposed to take a picture of us in this position. But somehow he wasn't getting the picture taken. I was beginning to feel as if I was going to drown if he didn't get it soon. Each time I surfaced, I asked him, 'Did you get the picture?' Each time his answer was 'Not yet.'"

To Delaney, the message was blatant. The dreamer felt she was drowning under her child-care responsibilities, and her husband didn't get the picture. Did the dream reveal anything that Barbara didn't already know? "Dreams take you to a point where you can feel things that you don't allow yourself to feel or think while you're awake," Delaney says. "I would agree that at some level you know it—dreams don't come out of the ether and tell you what God wants for you. Our dreams tell us what we should know but don't let ourselves know."

Hobson bristles at such talk. He thinks this business of "approaching the dream in hushed tones" is cultishness. If the function of dreaming is to convey information, how do we explain that ninety-nine messages in every hundred are lost before they are delivered?

A therapist can learn about a client in any number of ways that have nothing to do with dreaming, Hobson says. Inkblots or free association or simply asking someone what he did the day before would serve equally well. "I do most of my therapy without any special recourse to dreams," Hobson says. "I don't feel I need to do that to find out what's going on. And I rarely find out from discussing dreams what I didn't already know."

Here therapists and psychoanalysts of all persuasions join forces to tackle Hobson. By focusing so much of his attention on the bizarreness of dreams, they say, Hobson dismisses them too glibly. Listen to foreigners telling stories, one analyst says, and if you don't bother to learn their language, their tales will sound like gibberish. "Dreaming is involuntary poetry," another analyst says—and sometimes understanding poetry is hard work.

Undoubtedly, these therapists continue, we have some conscious knowledge of our hopes and fears. But Hobson is missing the point if he thinks that dreams simply restate in symbolic or ornate language truths that we already grasp.

"The point of Freud's work on dreams," says Mardi Horowitz, a professor of psychiatry at the University of California–San Francisco, "was that we tend to be consciously aware of our more proximal wishes, which are to solve our workaday problems, but we tend to be only dimly aware of why it's so imperative that we solve those problems. Perhaps we have to solve our problems or we'll be unloved, or some thought like that. Freud was presenting the idea that the deepest and most unrecognized wishes—unconscious wishes—might sometimes be found in dreams."

Faced with such challenges from psychotherapists, Hobson retreats just long enough to slip back into his lab coat. There's nothing wrong with therapists' interpreting dreams, he says. Their interpretations may even be right. "But the burden of proof is on them to show either that their knowledge is richer or that their results are better," he says.

Above all, they should make clear that their interpretations lack a foundation in science. "I'd have no quarrel if they'd tell patients, 'This isn't based on science; it's more like interpreting literary texts.' I say to them, 'Stand up and be counted. Don't say you're a doctor if you're an artist.'"

Dreams as Neurotic Symptoms

DESPITE THE INTENSITY OF HIS ANTI-FREUDIAN critique, Hobson's approach to dreaming is in a sense an homage to Freud. Freud made dreams a subject worthy of serious study, after centuries in which they had been brushed aside as the stuff of fortune-tellers. And both Hobson and Freud, in their efforts to explain the bizarre discontinuities and images of dreams, have taken for granted that these are the central and obvious issue to explore.

In addition, the scientific approach to psychology, which Hobson follows, is the one with which Freud himself began. Freud's early attempt to establish psychology on a solid scientific foundation, his "Project for a Scientific Psychology," was a major effort. "[It] does not precisely read like an early draft of psychoanalytic theory," notes the historian and Freud partisan Peter Gay, "but Freud's ideas on the drives, on repression and defense, on the mental economy with its contending forces of energies, and on the human animal as the wishing animal, are all adumbrated here."

James Strachey, a translator of Freud and the editor of the standard English-language edition of his works, wrote, "The Project's invisible ghost haunts the whole series of Freud's theoretical writings to the very end." Throughout his life Freud clung to the hope that someday science would vindicate his early attempts to ground psychology in physiology.

Now Allan Hobson has stepped forward, proclaimed himself the voice of modern science, and announced that Freud had it all wrong. The role is an odd one for Hobson. As a college student, he was a "Freud idolater" who read and reread everything Freud wrote. His college honors thesis was on Freud and Dostoevsky. Even today Hobson happily acknowledges, "Freud is brilliant. And the dream theory is wonderful, it's compelling and beautifully written and developed, and it's rich."

Freud's ambition extended far beyond interpreting the dreams of individual patients. His real goal was a theory of the mind. The key to such a synthesis was a crucial analogy: dreams are caused by the festering of unacceptable wishes, just as neuroses are caused by the repressing of unacceptable emotions or memories.

"Freud regarded dreams as if they were neurotic symptoms," writes Anthony Storr, a British psychiatrist sympathetic to Freud. "Since normal people dream, Freud's theory of dreams supported the idea that neurotic and normal cannot be sharply distinguished, and paved the way for establishing psycho-analysis as a general theory of the mind which applied to everyone."

Hobson's charge that this revolutionary theory of the mind is in fact based on Freud's abandoned "Project for a Scientific Psychology" is a serious one, since, as noted, everyone today agrees that the 1890s neurobiology of the "Project" is worthless. Freud and his contemporaries thought of the brain as a "passive reflex" machine that could act only in response to messages from outside. A dream was triggered by an event from daily life—say, a run-in with the boss—that somehow unearthed and activated a hidden wish from long ago. That is in sharp contrast with today's picture of a self-activating brain that can both create and cancel its own energy.

Brain cells are now known to be of two types, excitatory and inhibitory. Excitatory cells transmit electrochemical impulses that increase the activity of the cells they contact; inhibitory cells decrease that activity. In Freud's day only excitatory cells were known. "This meant," one scientist explains, "that once you got a notion in your head, it was doomed to run around in there forever until you finally decided to do something about it. Or, alternatively, until *it* found a way to trick you into unconsciously expressing it in some unintended action—like the famous 'Freudian slip.'"

Similarly, it was thought that repressed wishes would boil and bubble endlessly in the cauldron of the unconscious, until they managed to emerge, suitably disguised, as dreams. In essence, Hobson argues that Freud's dream theory came into being in a somewhat comparable way: the brain-based picture of the mind that he labored over in the "Project" never panned out, but eventually it emerged, suitably translated into psychological terms, as *The Interpretation of Dreams*.

But, oddly, this feature of Hobson's argument seems not to faze the analytic community. "It never dawns on psychoanalysts," says Frank Sulloway, a historian of science and a revisionist Freud scholar, "that if Freud was wrong about the general properties of dreams, he might also have been wrong about the interpretation of specific dreams. If you say that the whole dream theory is based on outmoded biology, they say, 'We'll give you that and keep everything else.' It's as if they lived in a building and someone said, 'The first floor's about to collapse,' and they said, 'We don't care; we live on the tenth floor.'"

Even on the tenth floor signs of trouble are visible. Significant numbers of strict Freudian analysts are still treating patients, but psychoanalysis has been in decline since the 1960s. Hundreds of alternate forms of psychotherapy have sprung up, the psychoanalytic-training institutes are hard pressed for students, and the leading psychiatric journals have cut down on their psychoanalytically based articles. "It's almost dead," says Robert Moore, the Stony Brook neurologist. "I know of no institution looking for a chief of psychiatry that's looking for a psychoanalyst."

The decline of psychoanalysis is due largely to the rise of biology. Depression, manic depression, schizophrenia, and other mental illnesses seem to be yielding some of their secrets to neurobiology. With support from the National Institute of Mental Health, Congress has declared the 1990s the "decade of the brain."

Freud's dream-analysis technique, in particular, has fallen out of favor with some psychoanalysts. Despite Freud's insistence that dream interpretation is "the securest foundation of psychoanalysis," contemporary analysts seem to believe that following the weaving course of a patient's free associations to each dream element takes too long and is too much trouble. Freud's approach to dreams in therapy may eventually suffer the cruelest of all fates—to be deemed not wrong but irrelevant.

Nevertheless, the decline of Freud within the therapeutic community seems not to have significantly affected his reputation in the rest of the academic world, where his standing is as high as it ever was. Many debunking books and articles have appeared, most of them the work of historians or philosophers, but they have not had lasting impact. They are published, they win prizes and respectful audiences, and then their message is forgotten.

Great numbers of literary critics, social scientists, and historians continue to march to a Freudian drummer. Every day sees the publication of a new psychobiography of someone or other, or a new psychoanalytically based work of literary scholarship. On campus, at least, Auden's words remain apt: Freud is "no more a person now but a whole climate of opinion."

Dreams as Creative Opportunities

AS INTELLECTUAL FASHIONS CHANGE, DREAMING falls in and out of favor. It remains as mysterious as ever. For two hours in every twenty-four, for six years in an average lifetime, we are mad as hatters. Why? What is dreaming for?

Dreaming seems to be important. We can't decide to dream or not to dream, and if some sleep researcher prevents us from dreaming one night, we make up for it the next.

Hobson, in many ways an optimistic man, has devised a much sunnier answer than Freud did to the question Why dream? "Instead of seeing the dream process as some sort of laundry for kinky thoughts," he says, "I see it as a resourceful artist producing all kinds of wonderful new solutions."

In this view, dreaming is a virtual parody of scientific thinking, in which every idea can be considered, even outlandish notions can be pursued, and anything is possible. And, indeed, numerous problems have been solved in dreams. Robert Louis Stevenson dreamed the plot of *The Strange Case of Dr. Jekyll and Mr. Hyde*. Elias Howe claimed that the crucial idea for his sewing machine came to him in a dream, after years of struggle. In all his failed models the needle's eye was in the middle of the shaft. One night Howe dreamed he had been captured by a tribe of savages who carried spears with eye-shaped holes near the tip.

At least one dreamer earned a Nobel Prize. Otto Loewi, a German-born physiologist and pharmacologist, wanted to know how nerves send signals. Do they simply transmit electricity, like tiny wires, or do they also send chemical signals? Loewi was studying frogs, trying to learn why stimulating the vagus nerve causes the heart to slow. Unlike his peers, he believed that chemicals were somehow involved, but he couldn't think how to prove he was right.

On Easter Sunday of 1920 the answer came to him in a dream. Loewi woke up, scrawled it down, and fell back asleep. In the morning he couldn't read his writing and he couldn't remember his dream.

"The next night, at three o'clock, the idea returned," he wrote later. "I got up immediately, went to the laboratory, and performed the experiment." Loewi's inspiration was to stimulate the vagus nerve of one frog, thus slowing its heart, and then to transfer blood from that frog's heart to a second frog. When the second heart slowed too, Loewi had proved that the vagus nerve acted by releasing a chemical. The chemical turned out to be acetylcholine, the very substance that is now known to be the neurotransmitter that triggered Loewi's dream in the first place.

Hobson likes such stories, but he is wary of them too. "Nobody ever tells you about all the cockamamie ideas that didn't work," he says. "You don't hear about the guy who went off for ten years and worked on this crazy idea that occurred to him in a dream. In fact, you don't even know whether two days later it would have occurred to him at breakfast." He laughs, but then turns crabby. "You never hear anybody raise those questions!" he shouts. "Because, again, that's the dream mystique. You want to believe this thing's wonderful."

In fact, the notion of problem-solving in dreams is one that therapists of all sorts rush to embrace. The idea rests on the commonsensical premise that we work to make sense of our lives while we're awake and the process continues while we're asleep.

Perhaps the best-known advocate of this view is Rosalind Cartwright, the chairman of the psychology department at Rush University, in Chicago. The function of dreaming, she says, is to give the mind a chance to sort uninterrupted through emotional issues that we are too preoccupied to untangle during our waking lives. The process goes on automatically, whether or not we can recall our dreams later.

"In dreaming, you update the program of who you are every night," Cartwright says. "If nothing much has changed in your life, you get a night off to play or be creative or tell jokes to yourself, or you just have a dull night of nothing much going on. But when you're going through crises, you need to revise who you are, and you have to update that program in a dramatically new way."

To test her theory, Cartwright has spent several years studying men and women who are going through divorces and are depressed. She has found that their dreams differ in key ways from those of people who are happily married. For people whose lives are going along smoothly, the first dream of the night is typically brief and dull: "I went shopping." In Cartwright's reading, the dream hasn't much work to do. For most of the depressed subjects in her studies, however, the first dream comes much sooner than it does for others, lasts much longer, and is far more complicated.

And the dreams are terrible, endless and masochistic rehashes of mistakes made and opportunities lost. One of the supposed benefits of anti-depressant medications, in fact, is that they suppress dreaming. But with a nudge from therapy sessions during the day, dreams change during the course of the night. Dreamers become more angry and less depressed. "When they do that," Cartwright says, "they recover. It's a predictor that dreaming has gone into high gear, has stirred up the feelings to be worked through. When I see those people at follow-up, they're no longer depressed."

Hobson is almost visibly ambivalent about such stories. On the one hand, he is perfectly happy to concede that dreaming has a constructive, creative side. It fits with his theory that the dreamer fashions a plot from whatever materials happen to be at hand, and it furnishes ammunition against "the peculiar modern, psychoanalytic tendency to view even the normal as somehow neurotic."

On the other hand, as a good scientist, Hobson is fearful of venturing too far into speculative talk of "purpose." And to talk about the purpose of dreaming is to pile intangible on intangible. He is more comfortable speculating about the purpose of REM sleep.

For example, we spend more time in REM sleep as infants in the womb than we ever will again. Why? Hobson suggests that infants prior to birth are literally "making up their minds," working on tasks that are somehow essential to cognitive development.

Some experiments with adults also seem to link REM sleep and intellectual work. Volunteers deprived of REM sleep by experimenters have more trouble solving complicated puzzles than do people deprived of non-REM sleep. And people trying to assimilate new information—students of a foreign language, for example—show an increase in REM sleep.

But because REM sleep is distributed so widely throughout the animal kingdom, no such explanation is adequate. Both opossums and moles spend substantial amounts of time in REM sleep, for instance, and neither species is noted for perspicacity.

The hardheaded scientific attitude is to dismiss dreams altogether. All mammals undergo REM sleep, the argument runs, human beings in particular have powerful minds, and the combination yields the strange experiences we call dreams. Dreaming isn't *for* anything; it just happens. Occasionally Hobson talks in this vein, speculating that "dreaming is just the noise the brain makes while it automatically sorts and files," but more often he takes a softer line.

He prefers to think of REM sleep as a time when the brain refreshes and readjusts itself, a notion that explains why we have so much trouble remembering our dreams. The explanation is based on a striking observation: the brain cells that turn off in REM sleep release neurotransmitters that are crucial to attention, learning, and memory.

"You have these systems firing all day long like a metronome," Hobson says, "with zillions and zillions of packets of neurotransmitter being bled out over the day, and your attention sort of runs down. At a certain point the sleep system kicks in, you go to bed, and before you know it these neuronal systems are shut down. Your metabolic rate doesn't go to zero—you continue to manufacture enzymes and neurotransmitters, and all the packets just get filled up again. You wake up in the morning and you say, 'God, I feel good. I feel sharp.' "

The brain is ready for another day's work, but the night's dreams are lost, because the dreamer was deprived of the very substances necessary to lay down memories. Hobson's explanation of REM sleep has still another facet. The dreaming brain also carries out what he calls an "active maintenance" program to test its own circuitry. While the dreamer is barely connected with the outside world, dreaming provides a chance "to run through your repertoire of instinctive behaviors with the clutch pressed in, to make sure they're still working in the proper way."

For Hobson, such armchair speculation is an intellectual version of sport. Ask him a question or give him an analogy to consider and he engages his whole body in the attempt to find an answer. He twists in his chair, throws his arms out, and casts his eyes around to address invisible listeners in every corner of the room. He starts an explanation headed one way, sees a grinning tackler lying in wait, and cuts back in the opposite direction. Sometimes he arrives far downfield, visibly proud of himself. Occasionally he doubles back and forth so often that when he

finally runs out of steam he has made hardly any progress.

The picture is far from that of the stereotype of the scientist as a bloodless logic machine. Indeed, the romantic accusation that science banishes beauty by dissecting it might better be directed at Freud than at Hobson.

In a curious way, the two men have exchanged roles. Hobson, the neurophysiologist, who might be expected to play the level-headed spokesman for the hard sciences, has devised a theory of dreams that leaves a great deal of room for chance. Dreams are unpredictable and improvised, he argues. The dreamer's own interpretation can be as valid as a therapist's. Freud, the psychologist, who might have emphasized the variety of human experience, proposed a rigidly determinist, reductionist theory of dreams. Every feature of a dream, no matter how trivial, is deeply significant. Every dream, "invariably and indisputably," has the same cause. Dreams can be interpreted only by following the psychoanalytic method.

The years between the two theories saw the most extensive scientific progress the world has ever known. One might have expected steady progress in revealing the dream in its true guise. But the science of dreaming has brought a different, more humbling message: the dream was undisguised all along. Like Poe's purloined letter, it lay hidden in plain sight.

Freud's dream interpretations were brilliant, so brilliant that in the end he outsmarted himself. It now appears that his rival Carl Jung came nearer the mark. "I was never able to agree with Freud that the dream is a 'façade' behind which its meaning lies hidden—a meaning already known but maliciously, so to speak, withheld from consciousness," Jung wrote. "To me dreams are a part of nature, which harbors no intention to deceive, but expresses something as best it can, just as a plant grows or an animal seeks its food as best it can."

Learning and Memory

Over the past hundred years, experimental psychology has enlarged its scope and intensified its efforts to understand the nature of behavior, particularly the behavior of humans. From a simple beginning focused on the subjective correlates of physical sensations, the experimental approach to understanding behavior has grown to the point where, today, the technology developed in earlier efforts to control variables now suggests new variables to study. In still other areas, topics and issues formerly the province of philosophy are proving to be gold mines for experimental investigation.

If we attempted to encapsulate the field of experimental psychology today, we would have to describe it as the study of any aspect of behavior by scientific techniques. At the core of this empirical search for the most basic principles of a behavioral science is the study of learning and memory. Historically, learning was equated with conditioning, both respondent and operant. Today we also appreciate the importance of observation, imitation, and expectancy. We are also beginning to appreciate learning as a characteristic ability of all species. Are animals uniquely equipped to learn? Are some animals, perhaps humans, particularly designed to adapt to change, to modify their behavior, and to maintain and transmit (teach) these changes symbolically? In the unit's first article, the late B. F. Skinner articulates basic principles that seem endemic to humans and some other animals, but applies them to a distinctly human class of behavior, namely, verbal behavior. This article provides us with an opportunity to learn some direct applications of operant principles in our lives. And the principles, of course, can be as easily applied to other classes of behavior.

The study of basic learning and memory processes is an important venture in its own right. However, application of such knowledge is an equally important research goal. What kind of instructional environment is most beneficial for learning? Understanding the basic processes involved in learning does not necessarily mean that we understand how learners learn best. One approach to instruction, "back-to-basics," emphasizes repetition, drill, and sustained attention in a highly structured classroom setting. Another approach, "open education," emphasizes self-pacing and exploration in an unstructured setting. In the next article, Barbara Kantrowitz and Pat Wingert review evidence suggesting that children learn best when the learning environment is based on the concept of "developmentally appropriate practice." This approach, firmly grounded in the knowledge gained from scientific studies of child development, stresses matching educational programs to the child's developmental level. Implementing "developmentally appropriate practice" in American schools, however, will require extensive retraining of teachers and more parental involvement in the education of children.

If learning has been the prime paradigm of experimental psychology, memory has been the second. Indeed, the study of learning, by definition, implies the presence of memory. For many years experimental psychology was characterized by competition in the search for the actual mechanism of memory, which was conceptualized as consisting of real changes in some part of the body, particularly the brain. As Sandra Blakeslee points out in the next article, neuroscientists and cognitive psychologists have intensified this search while simultaneously addressing age-related impairments in long-term, primary, and secondary memory. One aspect of this research focuses on the use of drugs, mental imagery, and mnemonic strategies to improve memory, or, at least, to counter the effects of age-related memory impairments. Our understanding of memory may also be greatly aided by studies of individuals with extraordinary memory abilities. In the final article, Darold Treffert discusses how the study of savant syndrome may enhance our knowledge of normal brain function, creativity, the relation between aging and memory, and the link between memory and emotion.

Looking Ahead: Challenge Questions

How is human learning similar to the patterns of learning demonstrated by other animals? If we manipulate consequences of our own behavior, and shape that behavior in the way we want, are we developing or weakening our self-control? What can we learn about ourselves this way?

Is "developmentally appropriate practice" the solution to the crisis in American education, or is it simply the latest fad? Even if it were demonstrated to be the best learning environment for children, what other social and cultural problems would have to be solved in order to give developmentally appropriate practice a fair chance to make a difference in the public school system?

As we discover more of the chemical details of memory storage, what safeguards will be needed to prevent unethical and/or criminal attempts to alter (improve or im-

pair) memory chemically? Is this another research area where beneficial discoveries will be offset by potentially harmful abuses of scientific knowledge? How will we learn about long-term effects of drug interventions before it is too late to counter their possible detrimental side effects?

If facts and skills are encoded differently, what implications does this have for educational efforts that teach facts but assume students will "naturally" be able to translate those facts into skills?

How can the study of individuals with unusual talents superimposed on mental illness or intellectual deficiencies aid in our understanding of "normal" behavior and skill acquisition? Are there any examples in the history of psychology where such a strategy has paid off?

HOW TO DISCOVER WHAT YOU HAVE TO SAY— A TALK TO STUDENTS

B. F. Skinner
Harvard University

My title will serve as an outline. It begins with "How to," and this is a "How to" talk. It is about a problem we all face, and the solution I propose is an example about verbal self-management, using my *Verbal Behavior* (1957) as the basis of a technology. At issue is how we can manage our own verbal behavior more effectively. (I may note in passing that psycholinguistics, a very different kind of analysis, largely structural and developmental, has given rise to no comparable technology, in part because it so often devotes itself to the listener rather than the speaker.)

Verbal behavior begins almost always in spoken form. Even when we write, we usually speak first, either overtly or covertly. What goes down on paper is then a kind of self-dictation. I am concerned here only with written behavior and even so with only a special kind, the kind of writing at the heart of a paper, a thesis, or a book in a field such as the analysis of behavior. What such writing is "about" is hard to say—indeed, that is just the problem. Certain complex circumstances call for verbal action. You have a sheet of paper and a pen; what happens next? How do you arrive at the best possible account?

Do I mean how are you to "think" about those circumstances, to "have ideas" about them? Yes, if those terms are properly defined. In the last chapter of *Verbal Behavior,* I argue that thinking is simply behaving, and it may not be too misleading to say that verbal responses do not express ideas but are the ideas themselves. They are what "occur to us" as we consider a set of circumstances. If I have forgotten the key to my house and "it occurs to me" to look under the mat, it is not an idea that has occurred to me but the behavior of looking, and it occurs because under similar circumstances I have found a key under the mat. What

verbal responses "express" are not preverbal ideas but the past history and present circumstances of the speaker. But how are we to arrive at the most effective expression? How can we behave verbally in a way that is most relevant to a problem at hand?

It is hard to give a "how to" talk without posing as an authority. I hasten to say that I know that I could write better than I do, but I also know that I could write worse. Over the years I believe I have analyzed my verbal behavior to my advantage. What distresses me is that I should have done so so late. Possibly some of what I have learned may help you at an earlier age.

The next word in my title is "discover." If it suggests that verbal behavior lurks inside us waiting to be uncovered, it is a bad term. We do not really "search our memory" for forgotten names. Verbal behavior, like all behavior, is not inside the speaker or writer before it appears. True, I have argued that most behavior is *emitted* rather than elicited as in a reflex, but we also say that light is emitted from a hot filament, although it was not *in* the filament in the form of light. Perhaps a better title would have been "How to Succeed in Saying What You Have to Say." ("How to Say It" suggests style-book advice.)

A first step is to put yourself in the best possible condition for behaving verbally. La Mettrie thought he had supporting evidence for his contention that man was a machine in the fact that he could not think clearly when he was ill. (Freud on the other hand said that he could write only when experiencing a certain discomfort.) Certainly many writers have testified to the importance of diet, exercise, and rest. Descartes, one of the heros of psychology, said that he slept ten hours every night and "never employed more than a few hours a year at those thoughts which engage the understanding . . . I

First appeared in *The Behavior Analyst*, 1981, 4, 1-7, No. 1 (Spring), published by the Society for the Advancement of Behavior Analysis.

have consecrated all the rest of my life to relaxation and rest.'' Good physical condition is relevant to all kinds of effective behavior but particularly to that subtle form we call verbal.

Imagine that you are to play a piano concerto tomorrow night with a symphony orchestra. What will you do between now and then? You will get to bed early for a good night's rest. Tomorrow morning you may practice a little but not too much. During the day you will eat lightly, take a nap, and in other ways try to put yourself in the best possible condition for your performance in the evening.

Thinking effectively about a complex set of circumstances is more demanding than playing a piano, yet how often do you prepare yourself to do so in a similar way? Too often you sit down to think after everything else has been done. You are encouraged to do so by the cognitive metaphor of thinking as the expression of ideas. The ideas are there; the writer is simply a reporter.

What about drugs? Alcohol? Tobacco? Marijuana? There are authentic cases of their productive effects in poetry and fiction, but very little in serious thinking. Tactitus said that the Germans made their decisions when drunk but acted upon them when sober, and Herodotus said the same of the Persians. In other words, it may be possible to solve an intellectual problem when drunk or stoned, but only if the solution is reviewed soberly. In spite of much talk of expanded consciousness, good examples of the advantages of drugs are still lacking.

So much for the condition of your body. Equally important are the conditions in which the behavior occurs. A convenient place is important. It should have all the facilities needed for the execution of writing. Pens, typewriters, recorders, files, books, a comfortable desk and chair. It should be a pleasant place and smell good. Your clothing should be comfortable. Since the place is to take control of a particular kind of behavior, you should do nothing else there at any time.

It is helpful to write always at the same time of day. Scheduled obligations often raise problems, but an hour or two can almost always be found in the early morning—when the telephone never rings and no one knocks at the door. And it is important that you write something,

regardless of quantity, every day. As the Romans put it, *Nulla dies sine linea*—No day without a line. (They were speaking of lines drawn by artists, but the rule applies as well to the writer.)

As a result of all this, the setting almost automatically evokes verbal behavior. No warmup is needed. A circadian rhythm develops which is extremely powerful. At a certain time every day, you will be highly disposed to engage in serious verbal behavior. You will find evidence of this when traveling to other time zones, when a strong tendency to engage in serious verbal behavior appears at the usual time, though it is now a different time by the clock.

It may be a mistake to try to do too much at first. Such a situation only slowly acquires control. It is enough to begin with short sessions, perhaps 15 minutes a day. And do not look for instant quality. Stendhal once remarked, ''If when I was young I had been willing to talk about wanting to be a writer, some sensible person might have said to me: 'Write for two hours every day, genius or not.' That would have saved ten years of my life, stupidly wasted in waiting to become a genius.''

How should you spend the rest of the day? Usually you will have little choice, for other demands must be met. But there is usually some leisure time, and a fundamental rule is not to try to do more writing. You may tease out a few more words, but you will pay the price the next morning. The Greeks spoke of eutrapelia—the productive use of leisure. A little experimentation will reveal the kinds of diversion which maximize your subsequent productivity.

There is an exception to the rule against writing elsewhere. Verbal behavior may occur to you at other times of day, and it is important to put it down in lasting form. A notebook or a pocket recorder is a kind of portable study. Something you see, hear, or read sets off something relevant, and you must catch it on the wing. Jotting down a brief reminder to develop the point later is seldom enough, because the conditions under which it occurred to you are the best conditions for writing a further account. A longer note written at the time will often develop into something that would be lost if the writing were postponed. The first thing that occurs to you may not be the most important response with respect to a given situation, and writing a note gives other verbal behavior a chance to emerge.

As notes accumulate they can be classified and rearranged, and they will supply some of the most important materials for your papers or books. One of the most widely reprinted and translated papers of mine, "Freedom and the Control of Men" (Skinner, 1955-56), was first written almost entirely in the form of notes. When I was asked for a paper on that theme, I found that it was practically written. Notes which are left over can of course be published in a notebook, as I have recently found (Skinner, 1980).

The metaphor of discovery redeems itself at this point. When you construct the best possible conditions for the production of verbal behavior and have provided for catching occasional verbal responses on the wing, you are often *surprised* by what turns up. There is no way in which you can see all of your verbal behavior before you emit it.

I am not talking about how to *find* something to say. The easiest way to do that is to collect experiences, as by moving about in the world and by reading and listening to what others say. A college education is largely a process of collecting in that sense. And so, of course, is exploration, research, and a full exposure to daily life. Nor am I talking about the production of ideas through the permutations and combinations of other material. A very different kind of idea is generated, for example, by playing with contradictions or antinomies. The young Marx was addicted: ". . . The world's becoming philosophical is at the same time philosophy's becoming worldly, . . ." "That the rational is real is proved even in the contradiction of irrational reality that is at all points the opposite of what it proclaims, and proclaims the opposite of what it is." "History has long enough been resolved into superstition, but now we can resolve superstition into history." I daresay Marx thought he was discovering something worth saying, and the verbal play suggests profoundity, but it is a dangerous practice.

The next word is "You." Who is the you who has something to say? You are, of course, a member of the human species, absolutely unique genetically unless you have an identical twin. You also have a personal history which is absolutely unique. Your identity depends upon the coherence of that history. More than one history in one lifetime leads to multiple selves, no one of which can be said to be the real you. The writer of fiction profits from the multiplicity of selves in the invention of character.

We also display different selves when we are fresh or fatigued, loving or angry, and so on. But it is still meaningful to ask what *you* have to say about a given topic *as an individual*. The you that you discover is the you that exists over a period of time. By reviewing what you have already written, going over notes, reworking a manuscript, you keep your verbal behavior fresh in (not your mind!) your history, and you are then most likely to say all that you have to say with respect to a given situation or topic.

Obviously, it will not be simply what you have read or heard. It is easy to get books out of the books of other people, but they will not be your books.

The last three words of my title are "Have to Say," and they have at least three meanings.

The first is the verbal behavior I have just identified—the thing we refer to when we ask a person "What do you have to say to that?" We are simply asking "What is your verbal behavior with respect to that?"

A second meaning is what you *have* to say in the sense of *must* say. It is usually easy to distinguish between the things we want to do and those we have to do to avoid the consequences of not doing them, where "have to" refers to aversive control. A familiar example is the pause in conversation which must be filled and which leads, too often, to verbal behavior about trivia—the weather, the latest news, what someone is wearing. It is also the occasion for hasty and ungrammatical speech, or nonsense, or revealing slips. Much the same aversive pressure is felt in completing an hour's lecture when one has prematurely exhausted one's notes, or finishing a paper on time. It is then that we tend to borrow the verbal behavior of others and resort to clichés and phrases or sentences which simply stall for time ("It is interesting to note that . . .," "Let us now turn to . . .").

The results are not always bad. Many famous writers have worked mostly under aversive pressure. Balzac wrote only when he needed money, Dostoevski only in return for advances he had received. Aversive control may keep you at work, but what you write will be traceable to other variables if it is any good. Moreover, it is under such conditions that writers report that writing is hell, and if you write primarily to avoid the consequences of not writing, you may find it hard to resist other forms of escape—stopping to get a cup of coffee, needlessly rereading something already written, sharpening pencils, calling it a day.

There may be an aversive element in maintaining the schedule which builds a circadian rhythm. It is not always easy to get up at five o'clock in the morning and start writing. Even though you make the space in which you work so attractive that it reinforces your behavior in going to it, some aversive control may be needed. But other variables must take over if anything worthwhile is written. Positive reinforcement may be as irresistible as negative, but it is more likely to lead you to say what you have to say effectively.

The great generalized reinforcer, money, is usually poorly contingent upon behavior at your desk. It controls too effectively when a writer begins to write only the kinds of things which have sold well. Prestige and fame are also long deferred consequences inadequately contingent upon the production of sentences, but progress toward the completion of a book which may lead to money or prestige and fame may help if it is made clear. Some kind of record of the number of words or pages you write may act as a reinforcing consequence. For years, an electric clock on my desk ran only when the light was on, and I added a point to a cumulative record whenever the clock completed twelve hours. The slope of the curve showed me how much time I was spending each day (and how damaging it was to go off on a speaking tour!). A simple calculation reinforces that reinforcer. Suppose you are at your desk two hours a day and produce on the average 50 words per hour. That is not much, but it is about 35,000 words a year, and a book every two or three years—which I myself have found reinforcing enough.

Other immediate consequences are more effective in discovering what you have to say. Saying something for the first time that surprises you, clearing up a confusing point, enjoying what you have written as you read it over—these are the things which, in the long run, are most likely to produce verbal behavior which is your own. The best reason for liking what you have written is that it says what *you* have to say.

Your audience as a source of reinforcers is not to be overlooked. As Pascal put it, "There are those who speak well and write badly. The occasion, the audience fires them and draws from them more than they find in themselves without this heat." Writing often suffers when it is not directed toward a particular kind of reader. Just as in writing a letter to a close friend you may find a picture helpful or at least a warm salutation at the head of the letter, so some visible sign of an audience may help. Reading what someone else has said about you sometimes strengthens behavior, since one is seldom at a loss for words in a warm discussion. I once used E. G. Boring's *Physical Dimensions of Consciousness* as an instrument of self-management. I disagreed so violently with the author's position that after reading a page or two I would find my verbal behavior very strong. And one day when I was lecturing to a class but was not speaking well, I noticed that a student had brought his parents. My behavior changed dramatically under the influence of that new audience. Searching for good audiences may be worthwhile.

Just as those who write for money may begin to write things that sell rather than what they have to say as individuals, so an audience may have too strong an effect. I once gave what was supposed to be the same lecture to 15 audiences. I used a good many slides which served as an outline, but I began to abbreviate or drop comments which did not seem to arouse interest and retain everything which brought a clean-cut response or a laugh. Near the end of the series, I had to struggle to say anything worthwhile.

That verbal behavior is sustained by the prevailing contingencies is shown by the fact that writing exhibits many effects of scheduling. Fixed-ratio reinforcement often produces a "snowball effect:" The closer one comes to finishing a piece of work, the easier it is to work on it (where "easy" means that one works without moving to escape or without "forcing oneself" to remain at work). Writing papers, articles, or stories one after the other "for a living" tends to be on a ratio schedule, and the "post-reinforcement pause" takes the form of abulia, or "not being able to get started on something new."

There are many reasons why you may stop writing or "find it difficult" to go on. When something is not going well, when you are not saying anything important, when matters remain as confusing as ever, extinction sets in. You may continue, but only because aversive consequences take over. Punishment in the form of frequent criticism decreases production, a point not recognized by teachers of composition who spend most of their time pointing to the faults in their students' work (Vargas, 1978).

Satiation also weakens behavior. Many novelists never tell a story before they write it. Just as you cannot tell the same story to the same company a second time (or at least with the same effect!), so you are less likely to get a novel written if you have already told the plot. Enforced silence is a useful practice. Satiation also sets in when one writes more or less to the same effect again and again.

There is also a kind of subject-matter fatigue. One starts to write in excellent condition but eventually becomes "sick of the subject." One solution is to work on two subjects at the same time. It is easier to write short sections of two papers during a session than to spend the whole session on one.

A third sense of "have to say" is the heart of the matter. In a paper called "On 'Having' a Poem" (Skinner, 1972), I compared a poet with a mother. Although the mother bears the child and we call it her child, she is not responsible for any of its features. She gave it half its genes, but she got those from her parents. I argued that the same thing could be said of the poet. Critics who trace the origins and influences of a poem seem to agree, at least to the extent that they can account for features of a poem by pointing to the verbal or non-verbal history of the poet. Samuel Butler's comment that "A hen is simply an egg's way of making another egg" holds for the human egg as well and

for the poet. A poet is a literary tradition's way of making more of a literary tradition. (Much the same thing could be said of the scholar. A psychologist is just psychology's way of making more psychology.)

But the mother does make a contribution: She nourishes, protects, and in the end gives birth to the baby, and so does the poet and so does the scholar. There is a process of verbal gestation. Your history as a writer lacks the structure and coherence of the behavior which eventually emerges from it. Sentences and paragraphs are not lurking inside you waiting to be born. You possess some behavior in the form of prefabricated sentences, and may often do little more than utter them as such, possibly with minor changes, but that is not discovering what you have to say.

A new situation may strengthen dozens—possibly hundreds—of verbal responses which have never before been strengthened together at the same time. They may lack organization. Relations among them may be unclear. They will have little effect on the reader who has not had the same history and is not confronted by the same situation. They must therefore be ordered and interrelated in an effective way. That is what you do as you compose sentences, paragraphs, and at last a book. Only then will your verbal behavior lead to successful action by your readers or to a less active but still behavioral "understanding" of what you are saying.

Verbal Behavior (Skinner, 1957) takes up these stages in order. The first half describes the kinds of verbal operants produced by different contingencies of reinforcement. Although these are more than structures because they have probabilities of reinforcement, they are not assertion. The second half describes how they are fashioned into effective verbal discourse as they are asserted, qualified, denied, and so on, in such a way that the reader responds effectively. The writer thus generates sentences as effective sequences of the material emerging upon a given occasion.

I have found the following rules helpful in discovering what one has to say in this sense.

Rule 1. Stay out of prose as long as possible. The verbal behavior evoked by the setting you are writing about does not yet exist in the form of sentences, and if you start by composing sentences, much will be irrelevant to the final product. By composing too early you introduce a certain amount of trash which must later be thrown away. The important parts of what you have to say are more easily manipulated if they have not yet become parts of sentences.

Rule 2. Indicate valid relations among responses by constructing an outline. Very large sheets of paper (say, 22″ by 34″) are helpful. Your final verbal product (sentence, paragraph, chapter, book) must be linear—with a bit of branching—but the variables contributing to your behavior are arranged in many dimensions. Numbering the parts of a composition decimally is helpful in making cross-references and temporary indices and in noting connections among parts. As bits of verbal behavior are moved about, valid arrangements will appear and sentences will begin to emerge. It is then time to "go into prose."

Rule 3. Construct the first prose draft without looking too closely at style. "Full speed ahead, and damn the stylebook." (How hard that will be depends upon the extent to which aversive control has been used in teaching you to write.) When what you have to say about a given state of affairs exists at last in prose, rewrite as you please, removing unnecessary words, articulating sentences with better connectives, making new rearrangements which seem necessary, and so on. At this stage, some advice on style is helpful. I myself read Follett's *Modern American Usage* straight through every two or three years.

There is an old distinction between ecstatic and euplastic composition. There have been times when ecstatic verbal behavior (impulsive, unreasoned) was particularly admired, because it seemed more genuine, less contrived. In poetry and some forms of fiction it may be particularly effective. But in writing about a complex subject matter, it is too much to expect that adequate statements will appear fully formed. Neither phylogenically nor ontogenically has verbal behavior evolved to the point at which a complex combination of personal history and a current situation will give rise to a passage having an appropriate effect upon the reader. Only the most skillful "euplastic" (reasoned) management of verbal behavior will suffice.

Possibly I am confessing some special need for crutches. No doubt other people arrive more quickly at effective statements. They do not need to work so hard to say important things. I myself did not need to work so hard when I was younger. I am simply telling you how I succeed in saying what I have to say. Of course I wish I had more to say and that I had said it better, and I wish I could tell you more clearly what I have learned about saying it. But it would be impossible to tell you all you need to know. No two people are alike; your personal histories will lead you to respond in different ways. You will have to work out your own rules. As in any application of a behavioral analysis, the secret of successful verbal self-management is an understanding of what verbal behavior is all about.

REFERENCES

Follett, Wilson. *Modern American Usage,* New York, 1966.

Skinner, B. F. Freedom and the control of men. *American Scholar,* Winter 1955-56.

Skinner, B. F. *Verbal Behavior.* New York, 1957.

Skinner, B. F. On "having" a poem. *Saturday Review,* July 15, 1972. Reprinted in *Cumulative Record.* New York, 1972.

Skinner, B. F. *Notebooks.* Englewood Cliffs, N. J., 1980.

Vargas, J. S. A behavioral approach to the teaching of composition. *Behavior Analyst,* 1978, *1,* 16-24.

How Kids Learn

BARBARA KANTROWITZ & PAT WINGERT

Ages 5 through 8 are wonder years. That's when children begin learning to study, to reason, to cooperate. We can put them in desks and drill them all day. Or we can keep them moving, touching, exploring. The experts favor a hands-on approach, but changing the way schools teach isn't easy. The stakes are high and parents can help.

With Howard Manly in Atlanta and bureau reports

It's time for number games in Janet Gill's kindergarten class at the Greenbrook School in South Brunswick, N.J. With hardly any prodding from their teacher, 23 five- and six-year-olds pull out geometric puzzles, playing cards and counting equipment from the shelves lining the room. At one round table, a group of youngsters fits together brightly colored wooden shapes. One little girl forms a hexagon out of triangles. The others, obviously impressed, gather round to count up how many parts are needed to make the whole.

After about half an hour, the children get ready for story time. They pack up their counting equipment and settle in a circle around Gill. She holds up a giant book about a zany character called Mrs. Wishy-washy who insists on giving farm animals a bath. The children recite the whimsical lines along with Gill, obviously enjoying one of their favorite tales. (The hallway is lined with drawings depicting the children's own interpretation of the book; they've taken a few literary liberties, like substituting unicorns and dinosaurs for cows and pigs.) After the first reading, Gill asks for volunteers to act out the various parts in the book. Lots of hands shoot up. Gill picks out four children and

they play their parts enthusiastically. There isn't a bored face in the room.

This isn't reading, writing and arithmetic the way most people remember it. Like a growing number of public- and private-school educators, the principals and teachers in South Brunswick believe that children between the ages of 5 and 8 have to be taught differently from older children. They recognize that young children learn best through active, hands-on teaching methods like games and dramatic play. They know that children in this age group develop at varying rates and schools have to allow for these differences. They also believe that youngsters' social growth is as essential as their academic achievement. Says Joan Warren, a teacher consultant in South Brunswick: "Our programs are designed to fit the child instead of making the child fit the school."

Educators call this kind of teaching "developmentally appropriate practice"—a curriculum based on what scientists know about how young children learn. These ideas have been slowly emerging through research conducted over the last century, particularly in the past 30 years. Some of the tenets have appeared

The Lives and Times of Children

Each youngster proceeds at his own pace, but the learning curve of a child is fairly predictable. Their drive to learn is awesome, and careful adults can nourish it. The biggest mistake is pushing a child too hard, too soon.

● Infants and Toddlers

They're born to learn. The first important lesson is trust, and they learn that from their relationships with their parents or other caring adults. Later, babies will begin to explore the world around them and experiment with independence. As they mature, infants slowly develop gross motor (sitting, crawling, walking) and fine motor (picking up tiny objects) skills. Generally, they remain egocentric and are unable to share or wait their turn. New skills are perfected through repetition, such as the babbling that leads to speaking.

■ 18 months to 3 years

Usually toilet training becomes the prime learning activity. Children tend to concentrate on language development and large-muscle control through activities like climbing on jungle gyms. Attention spans lengthen enough to listen to uncomplicated stories and carry on conversations. Vocabulary expands to about 200 words. They enjoy playing with one other child, or a small group, for short periods, and learn that others have feelings too. They continue to look to parents for encouragement and protection, while beginning to accept limits on their behavior.

▲ 3-year-olds

Generally, they're interested in doing things for themselves and trying to keep up with older children. Their ability to quietly listen to stories and music remains limited. They begin telling stories and jokes. Physical growth slows, but large-muscle development continues as children run, jump and ride tricycles. They begin to deal with cause and effect; it's time to plant seeds and watch them grow.

● 4-year-olds

They develop better small motor skills, such as cutting with scissors, painting, working with puzzles and building things.

They can master colors, sizes and shapes. They should be read to and should be encouraged to watch others write; let them scribble on paper but try to keep them away from walls.

■ 5-year-olds

They begin to understand counting as a one-to-one correlation. Improved memories make it easier for them to recognize meaningful words, and with sharper fine motor skills, some children will be able to write their own names.

▲ Both 4s and 5s

Both groups learn best by interacting with people and concrete objects and by trying to solve real problems. They can learn from stories and books, but only in ways that relate to their own experience. Socially, these children are increasingly interested in activities outside their immediate family. They can play in groups for longer periods, learning lessons in cooperation and negotiation. Physically, large-muscle development continues, and skills such as balancing emerge.

● 6-year-olds

Interest in their peers continues to increase, and they become acutely aware of comparisons between themselves and others. It's a taste of adolescence: does the group accept them? Speech is usually well developed, and children are able to joke and tease. They have a strong sense of true and false and are eager for clear rules and definitions. However, they have a difficult time differentiating between minor and major infractions. Generally, children this age are more mature mentally than physically and unable to sit still for long periods. They learn better by firsthand experiences. Learning by doing also encourages children's "disposition" to use the knowledge and skills they're acquiring.

■ 7- to 8-year-olds

During this period, children begin developing the ability to think about and solve problems in their heads, but some will continue to rely on fingers and toes to help them find the right answer. Not until they're 11 are most kids capable of thinking purely symbolically; they still use real objects to give the symbols—such as numbers—meaning. At this stage they listen better and engage in give and take. Generally, physical growth continues to slow, while athletic abilities improve—children are able to hit a softball, skip rope or balance on a beam. Sitting for long periods is still more tiring than running and jumping.

under other names—progressivism in the 1920s, open education in the 1970s. But they've never been the norm. Now, educators say that may be about to change. "The entire early-childhood profession has amassed itself in unison behind these principles," says Yale education professor Sharon Lynn Kagan. In the last few years, many of the major education organizations in the country—including the National Association for the Education of Young Children and the National Association of State Boards of Education—have endorsed remarkably similar plans for revamping kindergarten through third grade.

Bolstered by opinions from the experts, individual states are beginning to take action. Both California and New York have appointed task forces to recommend changes for the earliest grades. And scores of individual school districts like South Brunswick, figuring that young minds are a terrible thing to waste, are pushing ahead on their own.

The evidence gathered from research in child development is so compelling that even groups like the Council for Basic Education, for years a major supporter of the traditional format, have revised their thinking. "The idea of putting small children in front of workbooks and asking them to sit at their desks all day is a nightmare vision," says Patte Barth, associate editor of Basic Education, the council's newsletter.

At this point, there's no way of knowing how soon change will come or how widespread it will be. However, there's a growing recognition of the importance of the early grades. For the past few years, most of the public's attention has focused on older children, especially teenagers. "That's a Band-Aid kind of approach," says Anne Dillman, a member of the New Jersey State Board of Education. "When the product doesn't come out right, you try and fix it at the end. But we really have to start at the beginning." Demographics have contributed to the sense of urgency. The baby boomlet has replaced the baby-bust generation of the 1970s. More kids in elementary school means more parents asking if there's a better way to teach. And researchers say there is a better way. "We've made remarkable breakthroughs in understanding the development of children, the development of learning and the climate that enhances that," says Ernest Boyer of The Carnegie Foundation for the Advancement of Teaching. But, he adds, too often, "what we know in theory and what we're doing in the classroom are very different."

The early grades pose special challenges because that's when children's attitudes toward school and learning are shaped, says Tufts University psychologist David Elkind. As youngsters move from home or preschool into the larger, more competitive world of elementary school, they begin to make judgments about their own abilities. If they feel inadequate, they may give up. Intellectually, they're also in transition, moving from the intensely physical exploration habits of infancy and toddlerhood to more abstract reasoning. Children are born wanting to learn. A baby can spend hours studying his hands; a toddler is fascinated by watching sand pour through a sieve. What looks like play to an adult is actually the work of childhood, developing an understanding of the world. Studies show that the most effective way to teach young kids is to capitalize on their natural inclination to learn through play.

But in the 1980s, many schools have tried to do just the opposite, pressure instead of challenge. The "back to basics" movement meant that teaching methods intended for high school students were imposed on first graders. The lesson of the day was more: more homework, more tests, more discipline. Children should be behind their desks, not roaming around the room. Teachers should be at the head of the classrooms, drilling knowledge into their charges. Much of this was a reaction against the trend toward open education in the '70s. Based on the British system, it allowed children to develop at their own pace within a highly structured classroom. But too many teachers and principals who tried open education thought that it meant simply tearing down classroom walls and letting children do whatever they wanted. The results were often disastrous. "Because it was done wrong, there was a backlash against it," says Sue Bredekamp of the National Association for the Education of Young Children.

At the same time, parents, too, were demanding more from their elementary schools. By the mid-1980s, the majority of 3- and 4-year-olds were attending some form of pre-school. And their parents expected these classroom veterans to be reading by the second semester of kindergarten. But the truth is that many 5-year-olds aren't ready for reading—or most of the other academic tasks that come easily to older children—no matter how many years of school they've completed. "We're confusing the numbers of years children have been in school with brain development," says Martha Denckla, a professor of neurology and pediatrics at Johns Hopkins University. "Just because a child goes to day care at age 3 doesn't mean the human brain mutates into an older brain. A 5-year-old's brain is still a 5-year-old's brain."

As part of the return to basics, parents and districts demanded hard evidence that their children were learning. And some communities took extreme measures. In 1985 Georgia became the first state to require 6-year-olds to pass a standardized test before entering first grade. More than two dozen other states proposed similar legislation. In the beginning Georgia's move was hailed as a "pioneering" effort to get kids off to a good start. Instead, concedes state school superintendent Werner Rogers, "We got off on the wrong foot." Five-year-olds who used to spend their days finger-painting or singing were hunched over ditto sheets, preparing for the big exam. "We would have to spend a month just teaching kids how to take the test," says Beth Hunnings, a kindergarten teacher in suburban Atlanta. This year Georgia altered the tests in favor of a more flexible evaluation; other states have changed their minds as well.

The intense, early pressure has taken an early toll. Kindergartners are struggling with homework. First graders are taking spelling tests before they even understand how to read. Second graders feel like failures. "During this critical period," says David Elkind in his book "Miseducation," "the child's bud-

In Japan, First Grade Isn't a Boot Camp

Japanese students have the highest math and science test scores in the world. More than 90 percent graduate from high school. Illiteracy is virtually nonexistent in Japan. Most Americans attribute this success to a rigid system that sets youngsters on a lock-step march from cradle to college. In fact, the early years of Japanese schooling are anything but a boot camp; the atmosphere is warm and nurturing. From kindergarten through third grade, the goal is not only academic but also social—teaching kids to be part of a group so they can be good citizens as well as good students. "Getting along with others is not just a means for keeping the peace in the classroom but something which is a valued end in itself," says American researcher Merry White, author of "The Japanese Educational Challenge."

Lessons in living and working together grow naturally out of the Japanese culture. Starting in kindergarten, youngsters learn to work in teams, with brighter students often helping slower ones. All children are told they can succeed if they persist and work hard. Japanese teachers are expected to be extremely patient with young children. They go over lessons step by step and repeat instructions as often as necessary. "The key is not to scold [children] for small mistakes," says Yukio Ueda, principal of

Mita Elementary School in Tokyo. Instead, he says, teachers concentrate on praising and encouraging their young charges.

As a result, the classrooms are relaxed and cheerful, even when they're filled with rows of desks. On one recent afternoon a class of second graders at Ueda's school was working on an art project. Their assignment was to build a roof with poles made of rolled-up newspapers. The children worked in small groups, occasionally asking their teacher for help. The room was filled with the sound of eager youngsters chatting about how to get the job done. In another second-grade class, the subject was math. Maniko Inoue, the teacher, suggested a number game to practice multiplication. After a few minutes of playing it, one boy stood up and proposed changing the rules just a bit to make it more fun. Inoue listened carefully and then asked if the other students agreed. They cheered, "Yes, yes," and the game continued according to the new rules.

Academics are far from neglected in the early grades. The Education Ministry sets curriculum standards and goals for each school year. For example, third graders by the end of the year are supposed to be able to read and write 508 characters (out of some 2,000 considered essential to basic literacy). Teachers have time for play and lessons: Japanese children attend school for 240 days, compared with about 180 in the United States.

Mothers' role: Not all the teaching goes on in the classroom. Parents, especially mothers, play a key role in education. Although most kindergartens do not teach writing or numbers in any systematic way, more than 80 percent of Japanese children learn to read or write to some extent before they enter school. "It is as if mothers had their own built-in curriculum," says Shigefumi Nagano, a director of the National Institute for Educational Research. "The first game they teach is to count numbers up to 10."

For all their success in the early grades, the Japanese are worried they're not doing well enough. After a recent national curriculum review, officials were alarmed by what Education Minister Takeo Nishioka described as excessive "bullying and misconduct" among children—the result, according to some Japanese, of too much emphasis on material values. So three years from now, first and second graders will no longer be studying social studies and science. Instead, children will spend more time learning how to be good citizens. That's "back to basics"—Japanese style.

BARBARA KANTROWITZ *with* HIDEKO TAKAYAMA *in Tokyo*

---

ding sense of competence is frequently under attack, not only from inappropriate instructional practices . . . but also from the hundred and one feelings of hurt, frustration and rejection that mark a child's entrance into the world of schooling, competition and peer-group involvement." Adults under similar stress can rationalize setbacks or put them in perspective based on previous experiences; young children have none of these defenses. Schools that demand too much too soon are setting kids off on the road to failure.

It doesn't have to be this way. Most experts on child development and early-childhood education believe that young children learn much more readily if the teaching methods meet their special needs:

Differences in thinking: The most important ingredient of the nontraditional approach is hands-on learning. Research begun by Swiss psychologist Jean Piaget indicates that somewhere between the ages of 6 and 9, children begin to think abstractly instead of concretely. Younger children learn much more by touching and

seeing and smelling and tasting than by just listening. In other words, 6-year-olds can easily understand addition and subtraction if they have actual objects to count instead of a series of numbers written on a blackboard. Lectures don't help. Kids learn to reason and communicate by engaging in conversation. Yet most teachers still talk at, not with, their pupils.

Physical activity: When they get to be 10 or 11, children can sit still for sustained periods. But until they are physically ready for long periods of inactivity, they need to be active in the classroom. "A young child has to make a conscious effort to sit still," says Denckla. "A large chunk of children can't do it for very long. It's a very energy-consuming activity for them." Small children actually get more tired if they have to sit still and listen to a teacher talk than if they're allowed to move around in the classroom. The frontal lobe, the part of the brain that applies the brakes to children's natural energy and curiosity, is still immature in 6- to 9-year-olds, Denckla says. As the lobe develops, so does what Denckla describes as "boredom tolerance." Simply put, learning by doing is much less boring to young children.

Language development: In this age group, experts say language development should not be broken down into isolated skills—reading, writing and speaking. Children first learn to reason and to express themselves by talking. They can dictate stories to a teacher before they actually read or write. Later, their first attempts at composition do not need to be letter perfect; the important thing is that they learn to communicate ideas. But in many classrooms, grammar and spelling have become more important than content. While mastering the technical aspects of writing is essential as a child gets older, educators warn against emphasizing form over content in the early grades. Books should also be interesting to kids—not just words strung together solely for the purpose of pedag-

ogy. Psychologist Katherine Nelson of the City University of New York says that her extensive laboratory and observational work indicates that kids can learn language—speaking, writing or reading—only if it is presented in a way that makes sense to them. But many teachers still use texts that are so boring they'd put anybody to sleep.

Socialization: A youngster's social development has a profound effect on his academic progress. Kids who have trouble getting along with their classmates can end up behind academically as well and have a higher incidence of dropping out. In the early grades especially, experts say youngsters should be encouraged to work in groups rather than individually so that teachers can spot children who may be having problems making friends. "When children work on a project," says University of Illinois education professor Lillian Katz, "they learn to work together, to disagree, to speculate,

The early years of a child's education are indeed wonder years. They begin learning to socialize, to study, and to reason. More and more education experts are favoring a hands-on approach to introducing young children to the mysteries of their surroundings.

to take turns and de-escalate tensions. These skills can't be learned through lecture. We all know people who have wonderful technical skills but don't have any social skills. Relationships should be the first 'R'."

Feelings of competence and self-esteem: At this age, children are also learning to judge themselves in relation to others. For most children, school marks the first time that their goals are not set by an internal clock but by the outside world. Just as the 1-year-old struggles to walk, 6-year-olds are struggling to meet adult expectations. Young kids don't know how to distinguish between effort and ability, says Tynette Hills, coordinator of early-childhood education for the state of New Jersey. If they try hard to do something and fail, they may conclude that they will never be able to accomplish a particular task. The effects of obvious methods of comparison, such as posting grades, can be serious. Says Hills: "A child who has had his confidence really damaged needs a rescue operation."

Rates of growth: Between the ages of 5 and 9, there's a wide range of development for children of normal intelligence. "What's appropriate for one child may not be appropriate for another," says Dr. Perry Dyke, a member of the California State Board of Education. "We've got to have the teachers and the staff reach children at whatever level they may be at . . . That takes very sophisticated teaching." A child's pace is almost impossible to predict beforehand. Some kids learn to read on their own by kindergarten; others are still struggling to decode words two or three years later. But by the beginning of the fourth grade, children with very different histories often read on the same level. Sometimes, there's a sudden "spurt" of learning, much like a growth spurt, and a child who has been behind all year will catch up in just a few weeks. Ernest Boyer and others think that multigrade classrooms, where two or three grades are mixed, are a good solution to this problem—and a way to avoid the "tracking" that can hurt a child's self-esteem. In an ungraded classroom, for example, an older child who is having problems in a particular area can practice by tutoring younger kids.

Putting these principles into practice has never been easy. Forty years ago Milwaukee abolished report cards and started sending home ungraded evaluations for kindergarten through third grade. "If anything was developmentally appropriate, those ungraded classes were," says Millie Hoffman, a curriculum specialist with the Milwaukee schools. When the back-to-basics movement geared up nationally in the early 1980s, the city bowed to pressure. Parents started demanding letter grades on report cards. A traditional, direct-teaching approach was introduced into the school system after some students began getting low scores on standardized tests. The school board ordered basal readers with controlled vocabularies and contrived stories. Milwaukee kindergarten teachers were so up-

A Primer for Parents

When visiting a school, trust your eyes. What you see is what your child is going to get.

● Teachers should talk to small groups of children or individual youngsters; they shouldn't just lecture.

■ Children should be working on projects, active experiments and play; they shouldn't be at their desks all day filling in workbooks.

▲ Children should be dictating and writing their own stories or reading real books.

● The classroom layout should have reading and art areas and space for children to work in groups.

■ Children should create freehand artwork, not just color or paste together adult drawings.

▲ Most importantly, watch the children's faces. Are they intellectually engaged, eager and happy? If they look bored or scared, they probably are.

set by these changes that they convinced the board that their students didn't need most of the standardized tests and the workbooks that go along with the readers.

Some schools have been able to keep the progressive format. Olive School in Arlington Heights, Ill., has had a nontraditional curriculum for 22 years. "We've been able to do it because parents are involved, the teachers really care and the children do well," says principal Mary Stitt. "We feel confident that we know what's best for kids." Teachers say they spend a lot of time educating parents about the teaching methods. "Parents always think school should be the way it was for them," says first-grade teacher Cathy Sauer. "As if everything else can change and progress but education is supposed to stay the same. I find that parents want their children to like school, to get along with other children and to be good thinkers. When they see that happening, they become convinced."

Parental involvement is especially important when schools switch from a traditional to a new format. Four years ago, Anne Norford, principal of the Brownsville Elementary School in Albemarle County, Va., began to convert her school. Parents volunteer regularly and that helps. But the transition has not been completely smooth. Several teachers refused to switch over to the more active format. Most of them have since left the school, Norford says. There's no question that some teachers have trouble implementing the developmentally appropriate approach. "Our teachers are not all trained for it," says Yale's Kagan. "It takes a lot of savvy and skill." A successful child-centered classroom seems to function effortlessly as youngsters move from activity to activity. But there's a lot of planning behind it—and that's the responsibility of the individual teacher. "One of the biggest problems," says Norford, "is trying to come up with a program that every teacher can do—not just the cadre of single people who are willing to work 90 hours a week." Teachers also have to participate actively in classroom activities and give up the automatic mantle of authority that comes from standing at the blackboard.

Teachers do better when they're involved in the planning and decision making. When the South Brunswick, N.J., schools decided in the early 1980s to change to a new format, the district spent several years studying a variety of curricula. Teachers participated in that research. A laboratory school was set up in the summer so that teachers could test materials. "We had the support of the teachers because teachers were part of the process," says teacher consultant Joan Warren.

One residue of the back-to-basics movement is the demand for accountability. Children who are taught in nontraditional classrooms can score slightly lower on commonly used standardized tests. That's because most current tests are geared to the old ways. Children are usually quizzed on specific skills, such as vocabulary or addition, not on the concepts behind those skills. "The standardized tests usually call for one-word answers," says Carolyn Topping, principal of Mesa Elementary School in Boulder, Colo. "There may be three words in a row, two of which are misspelled and the child is asked to circle the correctly spelled word. But the tests never ask, 'Does the child know how to write a paragraph?'"

Even if the tests were revised to reflect different kinds of knowledge, there are serious questions about the reliability of tests on young children. The results can vary widely, depending on many factors—a child's mood, his ability to manipulate a pencil (a difficult skill for many kids), his reaction to the person administering the test. "I'm appalled at all the testing we're doing of small children," says Vanderbilt University professor Chester Finn, a former assistant secretary of education under the Reagan administration. He favors regular informal reviews and teacher evaluations to make sure a student understands an idea before moving on to the next level of difficulty.

Tests are the simplest method of judging the effectiveness of a classroom—if not always the most accurate. But there are other ways to tell if children are learning. If youngsters are excited by what they are doing, they're probably laughing and talking to one another and to their teacher. That communication is part of the learning process. "People think that school has to be either free play or all worksheets," says Illinois professor Katz. "The truth is that neither is enough. There has to be a balance between spontaneous play and teacher-directed work." And, she adds, "you have to have the other component. Your class has to have intellectual life."

Katz, author of "Engaging Children's Minds," describes two different elementary-school classes she visited recently. In one, children spent the entire morning making identical pictures of traffic lights. There was no attempt to relate the pictures to anything else the class was doing. In the other class, youngsters were investigating a school bus. They wrote to the district and asked if they could have a bus parked in their lot for a few days. They studied it, figured out what all the parts were for and talked about traffic rules. Then, in the classroom, they built their own bus out of cardboard. They had fun, but they also practiced writing, problem solving, even a little arithmetic. Says Katz: "When the class had their parents' night, the teacher was ready with reports on how each child was doing. But all the parents wanted to see was the bus because their children had been coming home and talking about it for weeks." That's the kind of education kids deserve. Anything less should get an "F."

Memory Repair

Sandra Blakeslee

Sandra Blakeslee writes on science and medicine for The Times.

The 68-year-old congressman was frantic. Long proud of his ability to remember the names, the children's names and even the birthdays of important constituents, he now made embarrassing mistakes. His memory clearly wasn't what it used to be. Devastated, he sought help at a memory clinic near Washington. Could these memory lapses be reversed? Was his career in jeopardy? God forbid, was he in the early stages of Alzheimer's disease?

Highly educated people in demanding jobs tend to panic when they feel their memories slipping. Psychologist Thomas H. Crook, founder and director of the Memory Assessment Clinics, headquartered in Bethesda, Md., says, "We've had doctors, lawyers, business executives and other active people come to us for help. They are acutely aware of these deficits, and they're terrified."

Recent research is helping to calm such fears. While it's true that most people in their 50's and 60's begin to experience a decline in their ability to remember things, it is now known that this decline is rarely a sign of neurological disorders such as Alzheimer's disease. In a majority of cases, memory loss is a result of normal changes in the brain, as well as psychological changes that typically come with aging. The good news is that, for most people, there are ways of rejuvenating memory.

More than a dozen drugs have been shown to improve memory in animals, including primates. Clinical trials with human volunteers are now under way, and results are expected in a few years. But for now, there's only one proven method for reversing memory loss: training. Just as physical exercise counteracts the effects of aging on the body, mental exercises help keep the memory relatively fit. Studies have shown that these techniques are extremely effective if a person is sufficiently motivated.

Without such intervention, people in their mid-60's score 30 to 40 percent lower on a number of memory tests than people in their mid-20's. "It's not that your memory is slower," Crook says. It is genuinely impaired. Even the sharp-witted octogenarian whose memory seems unaffected by age is, by comparison to his or her earlier self, less able to remember.

Many people who have trouble remembering things jump to the conclusion that they have Alzheimer's, a disease which slowly saps the memory, eventually leading to severe confusion and disorientation. But epidemiological studies have shown that people between the ages of 65 and 75 have only a 2 percent chance of developing the disease. That means 98 out of 100 people who at age 65 find themselves forgetting names, shopping lists and facts in magazine articles have normal, healthy brains.

Neuroscientists now view learning and memory as a dynamic process that sculpts and resculpts the connections between nerve cells, called neurons, in the brain. Every time a memory is laid down, some of these cells undergo molecular changes that either strengthen or weaken their connections with other neurons. When a person forgets something, it most likely means that some of the connections have been weakened or broken.

Most people develop memory loss with age. But psychologists find these problems are often correctable.

This pattern can be applied to the three basic types of memory: long-term, primary and secondary. Long-term memory (called remote memory by scientists) involves information that is likely to be retained for a lifetime. Big events like a car crash or the birth of a child are indelibly traced into one's neural circuitry.

Primary memory involves information—a string of numbers like a phone number, for example—that is held only briefly in our focus of attention. Our ability to repeat a phone number immediately after hearing it seldom declines with age.

But secondary memory—the ability to retain information beyond the span of a few moments—is vulnerable. Secondary memory is what "allows you to remember where you parked your car," says Raymond T. Bartus, senior vice president of research and development at Cortex Pharmaceuticals, an Irvine, Calif., company that is developing memory-restoring drugs. "But you certainly don't need to remember every place you ever parked your car." So the memory is stored just long enough—minutes, hours or days—to be useful, and is then forgotten.

People in their 60's don't perform as well as younger people on just about every test of secondary memory ever designed, says David Arenberg, a psychologist at the National Institute on Aging. In one test, for example, people are shown a list of 12 words and after five minutes are asked which words they can remember. Sixty-year-olds simply do not do as well as 30-year-olds. Moreover, participants in an ongoing institute study show a steady decline when they are retested every six years.

A panel of experts at the National Institutes of Health has given this phenomenon a name: age-associated memory impairment. Many insights into its causes have come from major advances in the neurosciences in the past decade.

In terms of neurochemistry, age-associated memory impairment and the early stages of Alzheimer's disease are virtually indistinguishable. It may turn out that dementias like Alzheimer's are exaggerated forms of natural aging, but why the process runs amok in some people and is relatively benign in others is unknown. Nor do scientists know why age affects secondary memory more than other kinds of memory.

AT ONE TIME, SCIENTISTS BELIEVED THAT MEMORY LOSS was caused by the death of an estimated 100,000 neurons each day. But better techniques for counting neurons have overturned that notion. It now appears that although some neurons do die in areas of the brain important for memory, the loss is more on the order of 100 cells per day. Over the course of five or six decades, these deaths mount up, so cell loss could account for some of the memory decline that comes with aging, explains Larry R. Squire, a neuroscientist at the San Diego Veterans Administration Medical Center. But perhaps a more important factor is that many neurons shrink or atrophy with age. According to one theory, this happens because of a decline in the production of substances called growth factors, which nourish neurons. Although these cells still function, they maintain fewer connections with other neurons.

Another theory points to chemical changes. Chemicals called neurotransmitters shuttle back and forth between neurons at nerve endings, enabling the neurons to communicate. Changes in the levels of these neurotransmitters may be partly responsible for the memory loss associated with age. Experiments have supported this hypothesis. Researchers were able to induce in 25-year-olds the kinds of memory lapses often experienced by 65-year-olds by giving the younger people drugs that inhibit the action of cholinergic compounds, a class of neurotransmitters that are important for memory. When the drugs wore off, their memories returned to normal.

Some prescription drugs that many older people take can have a similar deleterious effect. Here, the solution is straightforward: change the patient's drug regimen.

Scientists reason that if chemical changes in the brain contribute to memory loss, then chemicals, in the form of drugs, may be able to counteract it. More than 20 drugs for improving memory are now available in Europe, but they have not been tested under America's rigorous standards. Only one drug, Hydergine, has so far been approved in the United States.

Nevertheless, there is reason for optimism. Experiments have shown that the memories of healthy old monkeys can be improved with drugs. Other experiments have demonstrated that humans experience the same kinds of memory loss as monkeys. It is reasonable to believe that if such problems can be reversed in monkeys, they may also be reversible in humans.

WHEN THOMAS CROOK FOUNDED THE MEMORY ASSESSMENT Clinics in 1985, one of his goals was to test various drugs that were believed to have the power to restore memory. He was, however, faced with a problem: Few healthy people had ever been tested for memory function, so there were no criteria, or baselines, for distinguishing between the memory loss caused by disease and the normal forgetfulness caused by aging. It was important to make such a distinction so the drugs could be tested with precision. Crook surmised that some drugs might benefit people whose memories were impaired by disease but not people experiencing normal memory loss, and vice versa. To determine which drugs were effective for which conditions, he first had to establish baselines.

But the available tests of memory function were outdated and irrelevant to problems in everyday life. So Crook and his colleagues developed several new tests. They are administered by a computerized system employing a video screen and a laser disk, which stores visual images in much the same way a compact disk stores sounds. Thousands of volunteers have taken the tests, which evaluate the ability to solve such everyday memory problems as finding misplaced items and remembering names. The results of these tests have shed light on normal and abnormal memory loss. For example, according to Crook, people suffering from normal memory loss tend to misplace objects, but they rarely get lost when retracing their steps along a familiar route. Losing one's way in familiar territory can be a sign of Alzheimer's. Once baselines were established, the clinics began testing a number of memory-enhancing drugs.

Several drugs prescribed for high blood pressure seem to improve memory as a side effect, and they are being tested in people with normal blood pressure. Also under study are substances called phospholipids, which are believed to help neurons absorb chemicals important for memory. Raymond Bartus of Cortex reports that some cholinergic compounds have also shown promise in the laboratory. But these studies are still in the early stages, so it will probably be years before any new memory drugs receive Government approval. And both Crook and Bartus caution that no drug will be a panacea. In order to combat memory loss effectively, the psychological dimensions of the problem must be addressed as well.

The normal aging process leads many people to adopt a defeatist attitude. They become "convinced that their memory is going down the tubes and nothing can be done," says Marjorie E. Lachman, a psychologist at Brandeis University. A young person who loses his car keys thinks, "I wish I'd paid attention," or he turns to his wife and says, "Did you take my keys?" It is not a salient event. An older person is more likely to interpret the loss of keys as significant. He or she thinks, "I'm losing my memory." These feelings can become a self-fulfilling prophecy. They can also lead to depression, which is believed to contribute to memory loss.

Many older people become less active, both physically and mentally. As a result, they find themselves less stimulated by their environment. According to Dr. Jerome Yesavage, a psychiatrist at Stanford University, such stimulation may be an important factor in keeping the brain fit, and the lack of it may affect the biochemical processes involved in memory. In this view, memory is like a muscle: it atrophies if it's not exercised.

But the solution to these problems does not begin with memory exercises, which require great motivation. A person must first develop self-confidence, says Lachman. (And if he or she is depressed, that must be treated.) In trying to help people with age-associated memory impairment, she uses behavioral therapy to counteract negative stereotypes. She tries to get her patients to realize that "although there are memory changes in later life, one can compensate and one can control one's memory by trying hard and paying attention."

ONE SET OF EXERCISES FOR IMPROVING MEMORY RELIES ON mental imagery. The idea is to associate a person's name with something concrete. For example, if you meet a person with a prominent nose whose name is Bill, you might link the name with the image of a dollar bill stuck to his big nose. The next time you see him, the image should come to mind and you will remember his name. Dr. Yesavage has tested the technique on Stanford undergraduates. "Within 15 minutes they can remember names like crazy," he says.

Older people, however, find it more difficult. To help them along, Thomas Crook and Robin L. West, a psychologist at the University of Florida in Gainesville, have produced a videotape "that is the memory equivalent of a Jane Fonda workout," Crook says. Here's a sample exercise from the tape. A person's face appears on the video screen, in this case a woman named Joan who has big brown eyes. You're told to exaggerate her eyes in your mind. Then the eyes on the screen become enlarged. In step two, you are asked to imagine a picture that corresponds to the person's name. The image for some names, like Penny, is obvious. In Joan's case, you're told to conjure up the image of a phone. Then you're told to imagine the image superimposed on the face on the screen. And the video brings this to life: a phone appears over Joan's big brown eyes. This technique is repeated with images of other people. Over time, as you build up a library of images, the technique becomes easier. Eric, for example, can be a Viking hat; Sherry a wine bottle.

Another memory-improving technique, called the loci method, is helpful in remembering lists. Employed by Roman orators centuries ago, it doesn't require a computer or a videotape. Say it's a shopping list that you want to remember. First, you visualize landmarks along a familiar route through a house, an apartment or a room. For a house the landmarks might be mailbox, front door, hallway and so on, up to about 20 places. For a single room they might be doorway, desk, bed and so on.

Once the landmarks have been established, you mentally place a grocery item in each location. The bread might go in the mailbox, the milk near the front door, the raisins in the hallway. When it's time to recall the list of groceries, you "walk" along the route and remember each item as it is encountered. The task is easy because you don't have to think about the order of the items and because the associations often provide striking images—a loaf of bread stuffed into the mailbox, or raisins strewn along the hallway. Using this method, lists can be stored in the memory for about 24 hours.

Other tricks are helpful in remembering numbers. Say you need to remember "Flight 216." You could use memorable mental images for the numbers: two could be twins, one could be a pole and six a six-pack of beer. Flight 216 then becomes a mental image of twins hanging from a pole drinking a six-pack. Or rhymes and images can be used in conjunction: two and shoe, one and sun, six and sticks. Flight 216 becomes an image of a shoe sitting in the hot sun near a pile of sticks.

Of course, the key to using memory-enhancing techniques successfully is motivation. Often the knowledge that memory loss is generally reversible is enough to get people to give it their best effort.

The elderly Congressman certainly had enough motivation: he believed that his career was on the line, and nothing motivates a politician more than the thought of being retired back to the district. With the help of techniques learned at Thomas Crook's clinic, the Congressman now can remember names and faces as well as he ever did.

Extraordinary People

Understanding the remarkable abilities of the "idiot savant" could help us unlock deep secrets about our own minds.

Darold Treffert, M.D.

Darold Treffert, M.D., a psychiatrist, has been director of several Wisconsin psychiatric hospitals, and has studied savants for the last twenty-six years. He lectures frequently on the subject throughout the country.

LESLIE HAS NEVER HAD any formal musical training. Yet upon hearing Tchaikovsky's Piano Concerto no. 1 for the first time when he was a teenager, he played it back on the piano flawlessly and without hesitation. He can do the same with any other piece of music, no matter how long or complex. Yet he cannot hold a utensil to eat and can only repeat in monotone that which is spoken to him. Leslie is blind, is severely mentally handicapped, and has cerebral palsy.

George and his identical twin brother, Charles, can rattle off all the years in which your birthday fell on a Thursday. They can also tell you, within a span of forty thousand years backward or forward, the day of the week on which any date you choose fell, or will fall. In their spare time George and Charles swap twenty-digit prime numbers for amusement. Yet they cannot add simple figures or even tell you what a formula is, let alone write one out.

Kenneth is thirty-eight years old but has a mental age of eleven. His entire conversational vocabulary consists of fifty-eight words. Yet he can give the population of every city and town in the United States that has a population of over five

thousand; the names, number of rooms, and locations of two thousand leading hotels in America; the distance from each city and town to the largest city in its state; statistics concerning three thousand mountains and rivers; and the dates and essential facts of over two thousand leading inventions and discoveries.

All of these people are examples of the fascinating phenomenon called the *idiot savant,* a term coined by J. Langdon Down of London some one hundred years ago, when the word *idiot* did not have the negative, comical implication it now carries. At that time, *idiot* was an accepted medical and psychological term referring to a specific level of intellectual functioning—an IQ level of less than twenty-five. The word *savant* was derived from a French word meaning "to know" or "man of learning." The observation that persons with severe mental handicap displayed advanced levels of learning, albeit in very narrow ranges, led to the once descriptive, still colorful juxtaposition of the two words.

Understandably, some people object to the term *idiot savant* because the word *idiot* now gives the condition a connotation that is neither deserved nor fair. Therefore, the terms *savant* and *Savant Syndrome* will be used hereafter

in referring to these remarkable people and the astonishing phenomenon they represent.

Savant syndrome is a condition in which persons with major mental illness or major intellectual handicap have spectacular islands of ability and brilliance that stand in stark, startling contrast to their handicaps. In some savants—those I call *talented savants*—the skills are remarkable simply in contrast to the handicap, but in other, more rare savants—those I call *prodigious*—the abilities and skills would be remarkable even if seen in normal people.

Until now, the scientific articles and media presentations describing the several hundred savants discovered during this past century have been isolated, anecdotal accounts of single individuals and their extraordinary stories. But there is much more to Savant Syndrome than interesting stories. Among these remarkable people, diverse as they may at first appear, is a commonality that deserves study, for in the future it may provide a key to better understanding not only how *they*—handicapped but with uncommon talent—function, but also how *we*—without handicap but with common talent—function as well. Of particular promise is what Savant Syndrome might tell us about memory (and thus conditions such as Alzheimer's disease), the nature of creativity, and the elusive relationship between memory and emotion.

At present, the significance of Savant Syndrome lies in our inability to explain it. The savants stand as a clear reminder of our ignorance about ourselves, for no model of brain function—particularly memory—could be complete unless it included and accounted for this remarkable condition.

When confronted by Savant Syndrome, so many questions leap up: How can extremely handicapped persons possess these islands of genius? What do they have in common? Why, with all the skills in the human repertoire, do the skills of the savant always fall in such narrow ranges and include such rare talents as calendar calculating?

Why is phenomenal memory seen in all the savants, no matter what exceptional individual skills they exhibit? Is the savant's memory qualitatively different from normal memory? Is their genius a direct result of their deficiencies, or do the two factors coexist coincidentally?

What can we learn about this spectacular dysfunction of mind and memory that might provide clues to normal mind and memory? Might the existence of these geniuses among us suggest that some such genius lies within each of us, waiting to be tapped?

The time has come to take the savants out of the "Gee Whiz" category and learn what we can about them, and from them—not just about memory and brain function, but about human potential as well.

I MET MY FIRST SAVANT on July 1, 1959. I was twenty-six years old and had just completed a residency in psychiatry at University Hospital in Madison, Wisconsin.

My first professional assignment was to develop and direct a thirty-bed Children's Unit at Winnebago State Hospital near Oshkosh, Wisconsin. As I walked onto the unit that first day, I noticed David. He stood there with a device he had fashioned out of cardboard and pencils that held a rolled-up paper scroll on which perhaps a hundred names were neatly written. As David turned the pencil on which the scroll had been wound, each name came into view, one at a time, through an opening in the cardboard that had been placed over the scroll. The device looked just like the window on the front of a bus where the destinations are listed and changed as the bus

route changes. And that's just what it was. The names on David's homemade scroll were the names of streets—Capitol Drive, State Street, Lincoln Avenue. David had memorized the bus system of Milwaukee. If you gave him the number of a bus and the time of day, he could tell you at which corner the bus was then stopping.

David was a very disturbed boy. His violent temper and his severe behavioral problems necessitated continuous hospitalization. His overall functioning was at a very low level—except for this one peculiar area of exceptional ability. He would have made a great cab dispatcher.

There were other savants on this unit. Billy could make free throws. Could he ever make free throws! He was like a baseball pitching machine, except he used a basketball. He always stood in exactly the same place at the free-throw line, with his feet in exactly the same position and his body in the same stance. For every shot his arm motions were identical, as were the arcs of the ball. He never missed. He showed no emotion, no overcorrection or undercorrection. There was nothing to correct. He was a basketball robot. Unfortunately, he had the same robot-like approach to everything. His mutism and his inability to communicate were evidence of his profound emotional and behavioral disturbance, which required his hospitalization on a long-term basis.

Then there was Tony. Unlike Billy, Tony did use language and, in fact, was a voracious reader. But he, too, had a serious behavioral condition that caused him to make vicious attacks against himself, and sometimes toward others. Tony knew history. He delighted each day in approaching visitors or staff—including new young doctors like me—asking them the significance of that particular date in history. Usually he elicited no answer, or just a few wild guesses, and so Tony would begin spouting off a long list of events that occurred throughout history on that day, much like the radio announcer on the morning show that I listened to on my way to work. Except that the announcer read his information

from an almanac. Tony, it seemed, *was* an almanac.

There were other cases on the unit similar to those of David, Billy, and Tony. I was struck by the islands of intelligence, even genius, that existed in what otherwise was a sea of severe handicap and disability. I soon became fascinated by this paradox of ability and disability, and began my research studying its appearance in patients with Early Infantile Autism, a form of childhood schizophrenia marked by withdrawal. My work eventually put me in touch with researchers throughout the world who were working in related fields. But it also left me with some lingering questions regarding Savant Syndrome—questions that remained unanswered for years.

AFTER TWO YEARS developments in my career forced me to put aside my work with Savant Syndrome until 1979, when I left Winnebago to begin a private practice and run a 150-bed community mental health center in the nearby community of Fond du Lac. Though I had mentally filed away the data on the autistic children I had seen fifteen years earlier on the Children's Unit—and on the savant skills present in some of them—the phenomenon continued to intrigue me.

I didn't see many autistic children in my Fond du Lac practice. What I did see, though, were a number of adult patients on whom I was conducting sodium amytal (truth serum) interviews as a means of enhancing their recall of buried memories and hidden traumas. In those interviews, patients remembered—in extraordinarily minute detail—a whole variety of experiences they thought they had forgotten. It was a demonstration of memory powers that, like Savant Syndrome, seemed to redefine human potential.

In some instances an entire journey down a particular street on a particular night would be recalled with exquisite attention to particulars—changing traffic lights, street signs, and passing cars. Both the patients and I were often startled by the voluminous amount of material that was in storage but unavailable in an everyday waking state. It was as if some

Some researchers have suggested that such extraordinary talents might be acquired from a shared field of knowledge similar to psychologist Carl Jung's "collective unconscious."

sort of tape recorder were running all the time, recording all of our experiences. The memories were there. What was missing was access and recall.

Simultaneously, reports were cropping up in scientific literature about neurosurgical studies of brain mapping, especially concerning the use of tiny electrical probes to determine epileptogenic foci—the seizure trigger—in the exposed cortex of patients who suffered certain kinds of seizures. The brain itself has no pain fibers within it; the pain fibers are in the surrounding capsule of the brain, the dura mater. Once the dura is numbed with a local anesthetic, the patient can remain awake while the surgeon uses a tiny electrical probe to find the site where certain kinds of seizures are triggered. This site then can be surgically removed and some seizure disorders corrected. In the random search for these foci, the probe hits a variety of spots on the cortex, and when it does, memories flood the patient's consciousness.

These memories, long forgotten by our conscious minds, are the kind of "random" recollections we often experience in our dreams: the fifth birthday party, including all the guests present; a day in class twenty years earlier; a walk on a particular path on a particular day, complete with the accompanying aromas and sound. If we were to remember such dream memories upon awakening, we would dismiss them, wondering, Where did that come from? But we know their origin in these instances: The probe had activated a circuit or pathway not ordinarily available to us.

I filed away these accounts, too, along with my observations of the savants I had known, as I continued to be busy with many other things.

Then, in June 1980, I met Leslie Lemke.

THE DEPARTMENT of social services had invited May Lemke and her remarkable foster son, Leslie—then twenty-eight—to give a concert honoring the foster parents of the county. I did not attend, but a short time afterward, in the wake of the publicity that followed, I became intrigued and decided to visit Leslie and his foster parents at their small cottage on Lake Pewaukee.

When I arrived, Leslie was sitting in a chair in his music room, a converted porch. He sat motionless and silent, but he seemed contented and at ease. He echoed my name when May told him who I was. Then he sat motionless and mute once again. May could hardly wait for him to play for me. She was so proud. Despite his blindness he walked unaided,

feeling his way, from the chair to the piano.

Then he played. I don't recall what the song was, but I do recall what I felt—astonishment, fascination, and inspiration. I still have the same reaction, many years and many tunes later, whenever I see and hear Leslie play. Here was someone with a triple handicap—blindness, retardation, and cerebral palsy—playing, for his audience of three, a concert worthy of an audience of a thousand. Though he had had no formal training, piece after piece poured forth: hymns, concertos, arias, popular songs, and imitations of singers. Some pieces he sang; some he just played. Some of the lyrics were in English, some in German, and some in Greek.

Leslie is the most remarkable savant I have ever met, read about, or studied. He was born prematurely in Milwaukee on January 31, 1952, and his mother immediately gave him up for adoption. He spent the first months of his life at Milwaukee County Children's Home. There it was noticed that the baby did not open his eyes, which were swollen and hard and had cloudy corneas. The doctors diagnosed his condition as retrolental fibroplasia, a disorder often seen in premature infants in which the retina proliferates wildly and sometimes, as in this case, blocks drainage in the eye, creating childhood glaucoma or a condition called *buphthalmos*. When Leslie was four months old, his left eye had to be removed. Six weeks later his right eye also was removed because of the glaucoma and because his doctors feared that the eye would burst. That was the source of Leslie's blindness.

Soon thereafter, at age six months, this frail and pathetic baby was given to the care of a remarkable woman. May Lemke was then fifty-two. She had been a nurse/governess and had developed a reputation for the extraordinary skill and love she showed in caring for children, handicapped or well. May received a call from the Social Services Department of Milwaukee County and, without a moment's hesitation, took on the role of foster mother, tutor, therapist, mentor, model, cheerleader, and inspiration to this blind, palsied, and intellectually handicapped little boy.

When Leslie was seven years old, May bought him a piano. She would play and sing for her foster son, running his fingers up and down the keyboard so he could identify the notes. By age eight Leslie could play the piano as well as a number of other instruments, including bongo drums, ukulele, concertina, xylo-

phone, and accordion. By nine Leslie had learned to play the chord organ. Medical notes indicate that, at age ten, Leslie still was not conversant, with the exception of repetition and imitation. He required help in dressing himself. He could not feed himself anything that required the use of utensils.

One evening, when Leslie was about fourteen, he watched a movie on television called *Sincerely Yours*, starring Dorothy Malone and Basil Rathbone. May and her husband, Joe, watched it, too, but then went to bed. At about three o'clock in the morning, May awoke, thinking that Joe had left the television on. She went to the living room to check. There sat Leslie. He had crawled over to the piano and was playing Tchaikovsky's Piano Concerto no. 1—the theme song to *Sincerely Yours*—vigorously and flawlessly. Leslie had heard it one time. That was sufficient. He played it through from beginning to end.

To this day, if you ask Leslie to play that piece, you get not only the song, but the entire television introduction, mimicked exactly as he heard it in true echolalic fashion: "Tonight's movie is *Sincerely Yours*, starring Dorothy Malone and Basil Rathbone. As he falls in love with the beautiful black-haired woman . . . [In the background are heard the beautiful strains of Tchaikovsky's Piano Concerto no. 1.] And now, *The Sunday Night Movie* is proud to present . . ." Usually, there is no stopping Leslie once he begins. He's like a jukebox: You put in your quarter and you hear the whole song. Until recently, the *Sincerely Yours* recitation and lengthy piece were virtually unstoppable. (That was a real hazard during Leslie's live television appearances, where time was so very limited.) Leslie now can be persuaded to stop, or at least to bring the piece to an end more quickly, with a gentle tap on the shoulder from Mary Parker, May's daughter, who acts as Leslie's guardian and caretaker now that May is frail.

Leslie was twenty-two years old when, in 1974, he gave his first public concert, at the Waukesha County Fair, a few miles from his home. He played and sang his hymns and did his Louis Armstrong and Tiny Tim imitations. He was a smash hit. He was "incredible," the newspaper said. As would happen at all of his concerts to follow, the audience members at the Waukesha County Fair shook their heads in astonishment and wiped tears from their eyes as he closed the concert with "Everything Is Beautiful."

Leslie recently completed a tour that included twenty-six cities in Japan. His repertoire now features thousands of pieces and is continually expanding. He is gradually becoming more polished in his presentations, more spontaneous in his conversations, and more sociable in his interaction. He appears to love what he is doing, is remarkably good at it, and seems to enjoy the appreciation and applause of his audiences, whether large or small, prestigious or ordinary, young or old. He has not yet reached his limits.

My personal familiarity with Leslie and his remarkable family made me a popular interview subject whenever the media turned to the topic of savants. These exposures put me in touch with a wide variety of researchers and scientists around the world who shared an interest in this condition. They in turn brought many new cases to my attention, cases I never would have known about were it not for this sudden attention to and curiosity about the puzzling paradox of being backward and brilliant at the same time.

THE OVERRIDING QUESTION for any researcher in this field is all too obvious: How do they do it? How does someone like Leslie Lemke, a person of clear deficiency, achieve such greatness in one limited area? I have found that there are about as many theories attempting to answer this question as there have been investigators. Many of the theories stem from the study of a single case, so-called "undemocratic" research that often provides useful information but also is rather idiosyncratic and limited. Among the recent research, I have found no single finding or theory that could explain all savants. But several theories could explain aspects of the syndrome and are worth exploring.

Eidetic imagery. Some researchers link Savant Syndrome to this fairly rare phenomenon in which a person continues to "see" an object as an afterimage for as long as forty seconds after it has been taken away. The retained image is intensely vivid and absolutely accurate. The term also is used by some to describe what popularly is known as photographic memory (whereby the afterimage can be recalled later and viewed as if it were a photograph). While some studies have found a higher number of "eidekers" among savants than among non-savants, other studies have not documented this difference. At any rate, eidetic imagery is not uniformly present in all savants and thus could not serve as a universal explanation for the condition.

Heredity. Could the savant be the product of two coincidentally inherited genes—one for retardation and the other for special abilities? While some investigators have found higher incidences of special skills in the families of savants, others have not. Thus, like eidetic imagery, heredity cannot serve as the sole explanation.

Sensory deprivation. Other researchers have postulated that Savant Syndrome may be a consequence of social isolation or biologically impaired sensory input. While social isolation does apply to some savants—those in deprived institutional settings, for example—many others come from stimulating environments where they received a great deal of personal attention. There are similar problems with the theory that the syndrome results from some biological form of sensory deprivation such as blindness or deafness. While some sensorily deprived individuals do develop savant skills, most do not.

Impaired ability to think abstractly. Under this theory, organic brain damage reduces the savant's ability to think abstractly, and the savant compensates by developing and refining concrete abilities as well as a vivid memory. While this is an accurate characterization of many savants, it is only a description— not an explanation—of the syndrome.

Compensation for defects and reinforcement from praise. There is no doubt that the praise that savants receive for their unusual skills can compensate for feelings of inferiority and aid in their development of relationships. Yet these same dynamics are factors for many developmentally disabled people, and only a few achieve the performance level of the savant. There must be specific and unique factors that separate the savant from the rest of the mentally handicapped.

Right brain/left brain localization and other organic factors. While not an absolute rule, the left brain hemisphere generally is responsible for skills that require intellect, cognition and logic, such as reading and speaking. The right hemisphere deals with abilities that are more intuitive and nonverbal, such as painting, sculpting, and playing music. In general, skills most often seen in savants are those associated with right hemisphere function, and those lacking tend to be left-hemisphere-related. Could Savant Syndrome result from damage to the left hemisphere of the brain?

One case lending impetus to this last theory involves a normal nine-year-old boy who suffered a gunshot wound very precisely confined to the left side of the brain, leaving him deaf, mute, and paralyzed on the right side. Following that injury, the boy developed a savant-like ability to troubleshoot and repair mechanical devices, presumably resulting from increased function in his undamaged right hemisphere.

Unfortunately, there has been very little research to confirm left brain damage in savants. It is interesting to note, however, that in two of the three reported cases where CAT scans (detailed x-rays of the brain) were performed on savants, there was clear evidence of such left brain damage. The other reported CAT scan—on a very high-functioning autistic savant with mathematical skills—showed an undamaged left brain.

No doubt some savants do have left brain damage as we generally think of it—trauma or injury before, during, or after birth. Yet, in the case of the identical twins George and Charles, both of whom had identical calculating skills, it seems most unlikely that both of them would have incurred such an injury in exactly the same area of the brain to give them their identical abilities. Their case argues for genetic or behavioral factors as well—or perhaps for some other process affecting the left brain.

FURTHER INSIGHT into the damaged-left-brain theory is provided by the 1987 findings of Harvard neurologists Norman Geschwind and Albert Galaburda, who studied right brain/left brain development and cerebral dominance. The doctors note that, from conception onward, the left brain is larger than the right and that it completes its growth and development later than the right brain in utero, leaving it vulnerable for a longer period of time to a variety of prenatal influences and injury. One such influence is the male sex hormone testosterone, which in the male fetus reaches levels that have been shown to impair neural cell development in some instances. This testosterone effect could therefore produce the type of left brain "damage" postulated for the savant.

Such damage—coming before birth at a time when the brain is still developing— would result in right brain cells being recruited for what would ordinarily be left brain circuits. A "pathology of superiority" of the right brain would then develop, along with a preponderance of right-brain-type skills—the kind of skills seen in the savant.

According to Geschwind and Galaburda, testosterone-caused damage would account as well for the correspondingly high male-to-female ratios seen in savants and in other "left brain" disorders such as dyslexia, delayed speech, autism, stuttering, and hyperactivity. It correlates as well with the higher incidence of left-handedness in males.

Further implications can be drawn from the fact that a striking number of savants were born prematurely. The phenomenon of massive brain cell death in humans just before birth is well established and commonly accepted. There are many more brain cells in the fetus than can possibly make connections, and those unconnected neural cells are simply discarded late in the pregnancy.

Geschwind and Galaburda point out that when left brain injury occurs early in pregnancy—as postulated by the testosterone theory—there is still a large reservoir of spare right brain neurons available to accommodate a neuronal shift to the right hemisphere. Indeed, the right brain actually becomes enlarged compared to the left. Could the savant's premature birth prevent the normal brain-cell die-off and provide a large reservoir of right brain cells that, when recruited, produce the extraordinary right brain skills seen in the savant?

Another body of research that could be of importance in understanding the savant is the work of Mortimer Mishkin, M.D., and others at the National Institute of Mental Health. Mishkin outlined two types of memory, each with its own distinct pathways: cognitive or associative memory, in which facts or stimuli first are consciously recognized, then sorted, stored, and later recalled; and habit memory, more a system of conditioned reflexes, such as that used when driving a complex daily route to work while thinking about other things. It is the latter that more accurately characterizes savant memory—the "memory without consciousness" described over and over again in savant literature. Mishkin points to data suggesting two different neurological pathways, or circuits, for these two different kinds of memory. In the savant, it appears that habit memory pathways compensate for damaged cognitive memory circuits.

Clearly, the one quality or trait that all savants have in common, irrespective of their particular skills, is phenomenal memory. It is memory of a specific type: literal, vivid, reflex-like, unconscious, devoid of emotion, tremendously deep but impressively narrow. This is in dramatic contrast to memory in the rest of us, which tends to be much more conscious, highly associative, more abstract,

less literal and precise, emotion-laden, and tremendously wide-ranging in subject matter but conspicuously limited in depth. Savants' unique memory function and circuitry distinguishes them from non-savants and points to the most fruitful area of further study.

Indeed, recent findings from new x-ray studies of the brain and autopsy data suggest that, in addition to the savant's left hemisphere damage, there is corresponding damage in lower brain areas, including those that control memory circuitry. This could explain the characteristic appearance in the savant of both right brain skills and an over developed reliance on habit memory.

Combining the various theories and new research, then, the talented savant emerges as an individual whose left-brain function has been disrupted as a result of some brain injury—perhaps sex-linked—occurring before, during, or after birth that leads to a compensatory increase in right brain function. The left brain damage is coupled with lower brain damage as well, causing a reliance on habit memory circuitry. These two factors somehow combine to produce the savant's characteristic cluster of abilities. Constant repetition and practice then refine these circuits, resulting in conspicuous talent within an exceedingly narrow range.

This scenario would account for the talented savants—those whose skills are remarkable simply in contrast to their obvious mental handicaps. However, in order to explain the prodigious savants, we must take into account some inherited factors as well. The prodigious savant's access to the vast rules of mathematics, art, or music could not be learned by practice alone. Some researchers have suggested that such extraordinary talents might be acquired from a shared field of knowledge similar to psychologist Carl Jung's "collective unconscious," or that these skills could reflect knowledge gained in so-called "past lives." These are explanations that no one can confirm or refute, but they are nevertheless explanations held by some.

Clearly, in both varieties of savant, intense concentration, practice, compensatory drives, and reinforcement play major roles in developing and polishing the skills made possible by this idiosyncratic brain function. But there is another factor as well: the deep care and concern that families or other caregivers have for the savants—not just for what they can do but for who they are; not just for what is missing but for all that remains. By radiating so much love,

encouragement, and praise, they serve to reinforce and motivate in ways that are truly touching and inspirational.

UNTIL RECENTLY, almost all of the technical advances in the study of the brain have allowed us to better and more precisely view brain *structure*: Are all the parts there? Now, for the first time, new technology, such as the positron emission tomography (PET) scan and similar devices, allows researchers to better study brain *function*, the actual way the brain works. Such new technology for studying the brain, coupled with new knowledge about the brain, has far-reaching implications for understanding savants—and thus ourselves.

For starters, the savant's "memory without consciousness"—Leslie's exact mimicry of an overheard German song or a random conversation, for example—can be studied in detail. Surely this distinct memory—so deep but so narrow, so vast but so emotionless—arises from circuitry far different from our ordinary memory, which is shallow and limited but far more flexible, associative, and creative.

By allowing us to better understand memory circuitry, savants may help us counteract the disruption of memory pathways by conditions such as Alzheimer's disease. Such brain repair might take any one of several forms: pharmacologic (with memory-enhancing drugs), neurologic (with brain cells recruited from unaffected areas and rerouted over new pathways), electrical (with brain-pacing devices such as those now used to treat certain types of epilepsy and to pace the electrical system of the heart), or neurosurgical (with brain grafts and neuronal transplants such as those now used in the treatment of Parkinson's disease).

Almost everything we have learned about health we have learned from the study of disease. Thus, from the research on Alzheimer's disease may come applications for expanding and enhancing normal memory. Each of us has tremendous numbers of memories—literally a lifetime's worth—stored in an organ to which we have relatively poor access. In our dreams, under hypnosis, or in sodium amytal interviews, some of this stored data cascades forth. And, as mentioned earlier, when neurosurgeons touch the cortex of a patient's brain with a tiny electrical probe, it also triggers thousands of memories of which the patient is unaware.

It seems "lost" memories have not disappeared; they have simply been misfiled, making them difficult to find. Normal memory enhancement, whether pharmocologic, electrical, or by some other method, promises to someday allow us to tap that tremendous reservoir of data we all possess but cannot now access.

The link between memory and creativity is another area in which studying savants may lead us to better understand ourselves. Their tremendous skills aside, savants almost exclusively echo and mimic—there is little or no creativity involved in what they do. Adding improvisation to existing music—as striking as that is—is still not the same as creating a new musical idea. Alonzo Clemons, a sculpting savant, can recreate fantastically what he sees but cannot do free-form sculpting. This is not to detract from such remarkable skills. It is simply to say that they differ from the creative process, and that difference warrants further study.

Savants, as a group, also demonstrate an unusual emotional flatness. Again, this trade-off is a mixed blessing. While they may miss some of the peaks of normal human emotion, they seem to be spared the valleys. While they may not shout at a ball game or weep at a movie, they also seem to be free of performance jitters or bouts of deep despair or cynicism. They may never feel ecstasy, but neither will they feel despondency. With further study, this emotional detachment may provide clues to the normal interplay of memory and emotion.

Indeed, we can learn a great deal about human potential from the jarring contradiction—the magnificent coexistence of deficiency and superiority—that is Savant Syndrome. We can learn that handicap need not necessarily blur hope and that stereotyping and labeling serve only to obscure—in a pernicious manner—an individual's strengths. We can learn the difference between paucity of emotion and purity of emotion. From the families, teachers, and therapists of the savant, we can learn that in dealing with people who have problems—even severe ones—it is not enough to care *for* those people: We must care *about* them as well. We can learn that there is a difference between sharing the spirit and shaping the spirit. We can learn how to work with a differently shaped soul—to understand, to actualize, and to appreciate it—while still respecting its uniqueness.

In short, a complete understanding of human experience requires that we include and account for Savant Syndrome. Until then, we will be able only to marvel at people such as Leslie Lemke, Alonzo Clemons, or the calendar calculator named George who can compute twenty-digit prime numbers but cannot add two plus two. "It's fantastic I can do that," he says.

For now, it truly is.

Cognitive Processes

Cognitive psychology has grown faster than most other specialties in the past 20 years, responding to new computer technology as well as the growth of psycholinguistics. For contemporary students, these two sources of theoretical and experimental pressure on cognitive psychology have almost totally eclipsed the earlier organismic theories, with the exception of Piaget's theory of cognitive development. Within cognitive psychology we find a growing range of topics. In this section, we will focus on two major areas: intelligence and creativity.

In the area of intelligence, one persistent problem has been the difficulty of defining just what intelligence is. David Wechsler, author of several of the most popular intelligence tests in current clinical use, defines intelligence as the global capacity of the individual to act purposefully, to think rationally, and to deal effectively with the environment. Other psychologists have proposed more complex definitions. But the problem arises when we try to develop tests that validly and reliably measure such concepts. Indeed, Edward Boring once suggested that we define intelligence as whatever it is that intelligence tests measure!

One point that most psychologists now agree on is that intelligence is a concept, not a "thing." Thus, it is more correct to talk about intelligent behaviors than to adhere to the view that intelligence exists as a unitary trait that can be measured. From this point of view, one's ability to score high on an "intelligence test" reflects a form of intelligent behavior, just as one's ability to perform intricate ballet movements reflects a different form of intelligent behavior.

The newer information-processing view holds that, first, intelligence must be understood as a series of activities, most of which are covert; then, each activity must be measured individually. Recently, the information-processing perspective has generated more interest and controversy about the possibility of creating a computer program that would simulate human mental operations.

The unit's first three articles reflect and extend these themes. In the first article, Jean Mandler reviews research suggesting that from as early as the first days of life, infants use perceptual analysis—the ability to recognize similarities and differences—to structure their cognitive understanding of environmental events. Evidence that challenges Piaget's theory of sensorimotor intelligence continues to accumulate as researchers discover more about the infant's sophisticated information processing skills. The next article focuses on Howard Gardner's theory of multiple intelligences. Gardner argues against the idea that there is a singular general factor underlying intelligence. In contrast, he proposes that there are many kinds of intelligence, and individuals who excel in one type may not necessarily excel at another. In the third article, John Searle tackles research on artificial intelligence by asserting that simulation programs do not provide evidence that computers can think. Searle notes that the human brain evolved to perform a highly specialized function, namely, that of producing mental operations. Although computer programs manipulate symbols, they cannot independently attach meaning to symbols. Conversely, the human brain evolved to produce minds that have both syntactic (symbol) and semantic (meaning) properties.

Just as intelligence is difficult to define, so too is creativity. Indeed, there was a time when psychologists defined the two almost synonymously. There was a circularity to such definitions: highly creative people are so because they have high intelligence. However, in such comparisons intelligence generally was defined by the score one achieved on IQ tests—tests that do not measure one's ability to generate novel ideas, to paint the unusual, to write a book, or to arrive at innovative solutions to complex problems. Can one teach others to be creative? The last article in this unit answers with a resounding yes. Interestingly enough, the impetus for this new interest in creativity has been supplied by the business world.

Looking Ahead: Challenge Questions

Why do all traditional attempts to define and measure intelligence fall short? What benefits do the new models provide for the theorist and for the researcher?

Is Gardner's seven-facet measure of intelligence simply an example of accommodation to critics who claimed that intelligence did not correlate well with common sense or wisdom? Is Gardner tapping into intelligence, or is he simply providing a convenient way of cataloging human abilities and talents? What characteristics must a behavior have in order to be defined as intelligent? If intelligence

is not a unitary concept, and if it can be affected by one's self-concept and/or attitudes, does it have a place in modern psychology? Why does the academic world continue to use such measures as the ACT and SAT as criteria for admission to college?

If computer technology continues to advance as rapidly in the next 25 years as it did in the past 25 years, do you think Searle would be writing the same article? If computers eventually are able to attribute meaning to the symbols contained in their programs, what might they think about their creators?

Think of an individual you consider to be high in creativity. Which of that individual's characteristics lead you to your conclusion? Do you agree with the thesis that creativity (your friend's characteristics) can be taught? Why is the business world so interested in enhancing creativity in the work force? Do you think this will succeed?

A New Perspective on Cognitive Development in Infancy

Jean M. Mandler

Jean Mandler received her Ph.D. from Harvard in 1956. She is currently professor of psychology and cognitive science at the University of California, San Diego. Her interests are cognition and cognitive development, with emphasis on the representation of knowledge. She has done research on how our knowledge of stories, events, and scenes is organized and the way in which such organization affects remembering. In recent years her research has concentrated on conceptual development in infancy and early childhood. Preparation of this article was supported by an NSF grant. Address: Department of Cognitive Science D-015, University of California, San Diego, La Jolla, CA 92093.

Over the past decade something of a revolution has been taking place in our understanding of cognitive development during infancy. For many years one theory dominated the field—that of the Swiss psychologist Jean Piaget. Piaget's views on infancy were so widely known and respected that to many psychologists at least one aspect of development seemed certain: human infants go through a protracted period during which they cannot yet think. They can learn to recognize things and to smile at them, to crawl and to manipulate objects, but they do not yet have concepts or ideas. This period, which Piaget called the sensorimotor stage of development, was said to last until one-and-a-half to two years of age. Only near the end of this stage do infants learn how to represent the world in a symbolic, conceptual manner, and thus advance from infancy into early childhood.

Piaget formulated this view of infancy primarily by observing the development of his own three children—few laboratory techniques were available at the time. More recently, experimental methods have been devised to study infants, and a large body of research has been accumulating. Much of the new work suggests that the theory of a sensori-

motor stage of development will have to be substantially modified or perhaps even abandoned (Fig. 1). The present article provides a brief overview of Piaget's theory of sensorimotor development, a summary of recent data that are difficult to reconcile with that theory, and an outline of an alternative view of early mental development.

In Piaget's (1951, 1952, 1954) theory, the first stage of development is said to consist of sensorimotor (perceptual and motor) functioning in an

Recent research suggests that infants have the ability to conceptualize much earlier than we thought

organism that has not yet acquired a representational (conceptual) capacity. The only knowledge infants have is what things look and sound like and how to move themselves around and manipulate objects. This kind of sensorimotor knowledge is often termed procedural or implicit knowledge, and is contrasted with explicit, factual (conceptual) knowledge (e.g., Cohen and Squire 1980; Schacter 1987; Mandler 1988). Factual knowledge is the kind of knowledge one can think about or recall; it is usually considered to be symbolic and propositional. Some factual information may be stored in the form of images, but these are also symbolic, in the sense that they are constructed from both propositional and spatial knowledge. Sensorimotor knowledge, on the other hand, is subsymbolic knowledge; it is knowing *how* to recognize something or use a motor skill, but it does not require explicitly knowing *that* something is the case. It is the

kind of knowledge we build into robots in order to make them recognize and manipulate objects in their environment, and it is also the kind of knowledge we ascribe to lower organisms, which function quite well without the ability to conceptualize facts. It is the kind of knowledge that tends to remain undisturbed in amnesic patients, even when their memory for facts and their personal past is severely impaired.

In the case of babies, the restriction of functioning to sensorimotor processing implies that they can neither think about absent objects nor recall the past. According to Piaget, they lack the capacity even to form an image of things they have seen before; a fortiori, they have no capacity to imagine what will happen tomorrow. Thus, the absence of a symbolic capacity does not mean just that infants cannot understand language or reason; it means that they cannot remember what they did this morning or imagine their mother if she is not present. It is, in short, a most un-Proustian life, not thought about, only lived (Mandler 1983).

According to Piaget, to be able to think about the world requires first that perceptual-motor schemas of objects and relations among them be formed. Then, symbols must be created to stand for these schemas. Several aspects of Piaget's formulation account for the slow course of both these developments. First, on the basis of his observations Piaget assumed that the sensory modalities are unconnected at birth, each delivering separate types of information. Thus, he thought that one of the major tasks of the first half of the sensorimotor stage is to construct schemas integrating the information from initially disconnected sights, sounds, and touches. Until this integration is

From *American Scientist*, Vol. 78, No. 3, May/June 1990, pp. 236-243. Reprinted by permission of *American Scientist*, journal of Sigma Xi, The Scientific Research Society.

accomplished, stable sensorimotor schemas of three-dimensional, solid, sound-producing, textured objects cannot be formed and hence cannot be thought about.

In addition, babies must learn about the causal interrelatedness of objects and the fact that objects continue to exist when not being perceived. Piaget thought that these notions were among the major accomplishments of the second half of the sensorimotor stage. He suggested that they derive from manual activity—for example, repeated covering and uncovering, poking, pushing, and dropping objects while observ-

represent bottles in their absence.

All the anticipatory behavior that Piaget observed throughout the first 18 months was accounted for in similar terms. Signs of anticipation of future events became more wideranging and complex but did not seem to require the use of images or other symbols to represent what was about to happen. Rather, Piaget assumed that an established sensorimotor schema set up a kind of imageless expectation of the next event, followed by recognition when the event took place. He used strict criteria for the presence of imagery—for example, verbal recall of the past

Figure 1. According to the Swiss psychologist Jean Piaget, babies like the author's 8-month-old grandson shown here have learned to recognize people, and their smile is a sign of that recognition. However, Piaget believed that babies have not yet learned to think at such an early age and thus cannot recall even the most familiar people in their lives when those people are not present. Recent research suggests that this view may be mistaken and that babies such as this one are already forming concepts about people and things in their environment.

William James described the perceptual world of the infant as a "blooming, buzzing confusion"

---

ing the results. Handling objects leads to understanding them; it allows the integration of perceptual and motor information that gives objects substantiality, permanence, and unique identities separate from the self. Since motor control over the hands is slow to develop, to the extent that conceptual understanding requires physical interaction with objects, it is necessarily a late development. Much of the first year of life, then, is spent accomplishing the coordination of the various sources of perceptual and motor information required to form the sensorimotor object schemas that will then be available to be conceptualized.

According to Piaget, the development of the symbolic function is itself a protracted process. In addition to constructing sensorimotor schemas of objects and relations, which form the basic content or meaning of what is to be thought about, symbols to refer to these meanings must be formed. Piaget assumed that the latter development has its precursors in the expectancies involved in conditioning. For example, the sight of a bottle can serve as a signal that milk will follow, and babies soon learn to make anticipatory sucking movements. This process, essentially the same as that involved in Pavlovian conditioning, does not imply a symbolic function; there is no indication that the baby can use such signals to

(which implies the ability to represent absent events to oneself) or rapid problem-solving without trial and error. Neither of these can be ascribed merely to running off a practiced sensorimotor schema, but they require instead some representation of information not perceptually present.

Piaget did not observe recall or covert problem-solving until the end of the sensorimotor period. One might think that the fact that infants begin to acquire language during the latter part of the first year would be difficult to reconcile with a lack of symbolic capacity. However, Piaget characterized early words as imitative schemas, no different in kind from other motor schemas displayed in the presence of familiar situations.

Imitation, in fact, plays an important role in this account, because it provides the source of the development of imagery. Piaget assumed that images are not formed merely from looking at or hearing something, but arise only when what is being perceived is also analyzed. The attempt to imitate the actions of others provides the stimulus for such analysis to take place. Although infants begin to imitate early, it was not until near the end of the first year or beyond that Piaget found his children able to imitate novel actions or actions involving parts of their bodies they could not see themselves, such as blinking or sticking out their

tongues. He took this difficulty as evidence that they could not form an image of something complex or unobserved until detailed analysis of it had taken place; it is presumably during this analysis that imagery is constructed. Piaget's study of imitation suggested that such analysis, and therefore the formation of imagery, was a late development in infancy. To complete the process of symbol formation, then, the anticipatory mechanisms of sensorimotor schemas become speeded up and appear as images of what will occur, thus allowing genuine representation. Finally, by some mechanism left unspecified, these newly created images can be used to represent the world independent of ongoing sensorimotor activity.

All these developments—constructing sensorimotor schemas, establishing a coherent world of objects and events suitable to form the content of ideas, learning to imitate and to form images that can be used to stand for things—are completed in the second half of the second year, and result in the child's at last being able to develop a conceptual system of ideas. Images can now be used to recall the past and to imagine the future, and even perceptually present objects can begin to be interpreted conceptually as well as by means of motor interactions with them. With the onset of thought, an infant is well on the way to becoming fully human.

This theory of the sensorimotor foundations of thought has come under attack from two sources. One is experimental work suggesting that a stable and differentiated perceptual world is established much earlier in infancy than Piaget realized. The other is recent work suggesting that recall and other forms of symbolic activity (presumably mediated by imagery) occur by at least the second half of the first year. I will discuss each of these findings in turn.

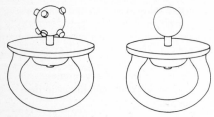

Figure 2. The old idea that the senses are unconnected at birth and are gradually integrated through experience is contradicted by an experiment using bumpy and smooth pacifiers to study the visual recognition of an object that has been experienced only tactilely. A one-month-old infant is habituated to one of the two kinds of pacifiers in its mouth without being allowed to see it. The pacifier is then removed, and the infant is shown both kinds of pacifiers. Infants look longer at the nipple they felt in their mouth. (After Meltzoff and Borton 1979.)

Perceptual development

The notion that the senses are unconnected at birth and that they become integrated only through experience is an old idea that was popularized by William James's (1890) description of the perceptual world of the infant as a "blooming, buzzing confusion." Recent work, however, suggests that either the senses are interrelated at birth or the learning involved in their integration is extremely rapid. There is evidence for integration of auditory and visual information as well as of vision and touch in the first months of life. What follows is a small sample of the research findings.

From birth, infants turn their heads to look at the source of a sound (Wertheimer 1961; Mendelson and Haith 1976). This does not mean that they have any particular expectations of what they will see when they hear a given sound, but it does indicate a mechanism that would enable rapid learning. By four months, if one presents two films of complex events not seen before and accompanied by a single sound track, infants prefer to look at the film that matches the sound (Spelke 1979). Perhaps even more surprising, when infants are presented with two films, each showing only a speaker's face, they will choose the correct film, even when the synchrony between both films and the soundtrack is identical (Kuhl and Meltzoff 1988). In addition, one-month-olds can recognize visually presented objects that they have only felt in their mouths (Fig. 2; Meltzoff and Borton 1979; Walker-Andrews and Gibson 1986). Such data suggest either that the output of each sensory transducer consists in part of the same amodal pattern of information or that some central processing of two similar patterns of information is accomplished. In either case, the data strongly support the view that there is more order and coherence in early perceptual experience than Piaget or James realized.

In addition to sensory coordination, a good deal of information about the nature of objects is provided by the visual system alone, information to which young infants have been shown to be sensitive. For example, it used to be thought that infants have difficulty separating objects from a background, but it ap-

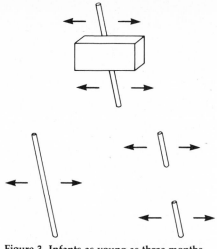

Figure 3. Infants as young as three months can use the perception of relative movement to determine object boundaries. They are habituated to the display shown at the top, which represents a rod moving back and forth behind a block of wood. Then they are tested with the two displays on the bottom: the rod moving as it did before, but with no block in front, or the two pieces of the rod that were visible behind the block, also moving as they did before. Infants tend to continue to habituate to the whole moving rod—that is, they cease to look at it, indicating that it is familiar to them. They prefer to look at the broken rod, indicating that they consider it something new. If the same experiment is done with a stationary rod behind a block, infants exhibit no preference when presented with a whole stationary rod or a broken stationary rod. (After Kellman and Spelke 1983.)

pears that such confusion is a rare event, not the norm. Infants may not "see" that a cup is separable from a saucer without picking it up, but in general they do not have difficulty determining the boundaries of objects. They use information from motion to parse objects from the perceptual surround long before they are able to manipulate them manually. At an age as young as three months, they can use the relative motion of objects against both stationary and moving backgrounds to determine the objects' boundaries (Fig. 3; Kellman and Spelke 1983; Spelke 1988). Even stationary objects are seen as separate if they are spatially separated, whether in a plane or in depth. Infants also use motion to determine object identity, treating an object that moves behind a screen and then reappears as one object rather than two (Spelke and Kestenbaum 1986).

Other work by Spelke and by

Baillargeon (Baillargeon et al. 1985; Baillargeon 1987a; Spelke 1988) shows that infants as young as four months expect objects to be substantial, in the sense that the objects cannot move through other objects nor other objects through them (Fig. 4), and permanent, in the sense that the objects are assumed to continue to exist when hidden. Finally, there is evidence that by six months infants perceive causal relations among moving objects (Leslie 1988) in a fashion that seems to be qualitatively the same as that of adults (Michotte 1963).

From this extensive research program, we can conclude that objects are seen as bounded, unitary, solid, and separate from the background, perhaps from birth but certainly by three to four months of age. Such young infants obviously still have a great deal to learn about objects, but the world must appear both stable and orderly to them, and thus capable of being conceptualized.

Conceptual development

It is easier to study what infants see than what they are thinking about. Nevertheless, there are a few ways to assess whether or not infants are thinking. One way is to look for symbolic activity, such as using a gesture to refer to something else. Piaget (1952) himself called attention to a phenomenon he called motor recognition. For example, he observed his six-month-old daughter make a gesture on catching sight of a familiar toy in a new location. She was accustomed to kicking at the toy in her crib, and when she saw it across the room she made a brief, abbreviated kicking motion. Piaget did not consider this true symbolic activity, because it was a motor movement, not a purely mental act; nevertheless, he suggested that his daughter was referring to, or classifying, the toy by means of her action. In a similar vein, infants whose parents use sign language have been observed to begin to use conventional signs at around six to seven months (Prinz and Prinz 1979; Bonvillian et al. 1983; see Mandler 1988 for discussion).

Another type of evidence of conceptual functioning is recall of absent objects or events. Indeed, Piaget accepted recall as irrefutable evidence

of conceptual representation, since there is no way to account for recreating information that is not perceptually present by means of sensorimotor schemas alone; imagery or other symbolic means of representation must be involved. Typically we associate recall with verbal recreation of the past, and this, as Piaget observed, is not usually found until 18 months or older. But recall need not be verbal—and indeed is usually not when we think about past events—so that in principle it is possible in preverbal infants.

One needs to see a baby do something like find a hidden object after a delay or imitate a previously observed event. Until recently, only diary studies provided evidence of recall in the second half of the first year—for example, finding an object hidden in an unfamiliar location after

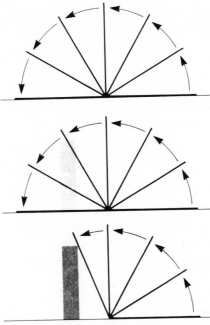

Figure 4. Shown here is a procedure used to demonstrate four- and five-month-olds' memory for the location of a hidden object. At the top is a screen moving through a 180° rotation, to which infants viewing from the right are habituated by repetition. Following habituation, a box is placed behind the screen, and the infants see two test events: an impossible *(middle)* and a possible event *(bottom)*. In the impossible event, the screen continues to rotate 180°, moving "magically" through the hidden box (which the experimenter has surreptitiously removed). In the possible event, the screen rotates only to the point where it would hit the box. The infants' surprise at the impossible event demonstrates that they remember an object they cannot see. (After Baillargeon 1987a.)

a 24-hour delay (Ashmead and Perlmutter 1980). Now, however, similar phenomena are beginning to be demonstrated in the laboratory. Meltzoff (1988) showed that nine-month-olds could imitate actions that they had seen performed 24 hours earlier. Each action consisted of an unusual gesture with a novel object—for example, pushing a recessed button in a box (which produced a beeping sound)—and the infants were limited to watching the experimenter carry it out; thus, when they later imitated the action, they could not be merely running off a practiced motor schema in response to seeing the object again. Control subjects, who had been shown the objects but not the actions performed on them, made the correct responses much less frequently. We have replicated this phenomenon with 11-month-olds (McDonough and Mandler 1989).

Because of the difficulties that young infants have manipulating objects, it is not obvious that this technique can be used with infants younger than about eight months. One suspects, however, that if ninemonth-olds can recall several novel events after a 24-hour delay, somewhat younger infants can probably recall similar events after shorter delays.

There is a small amount of data from a procedure that does not require a motor response and that, although using quite short delays, suggests recall-like processes. Baillargeon's experiments on object permanence, mentioned earlier, use a technique that requires infants to remember that an object is hidden behind a screen. For example, she has shown that infants are surprised when a screen appears to move backward through an object they have just seen hidden behind it (see Fig. 4). In her experiments with four- and five-month-olds, the infants had to remember for only about 8 to 12 seconds that there was an object behind the screen (Baillargeon et al. 1985; Baillargeon 1987a). However, in more recent work with eight-month-olds, Baillargeon and her colleagues have been successful with a delay of 70 seconds (Fig. 5; Baillargeon et al. 1989). This kind of performance seems to require a representational capacity not attributable to sensorimotor schemas. Not only is an absent

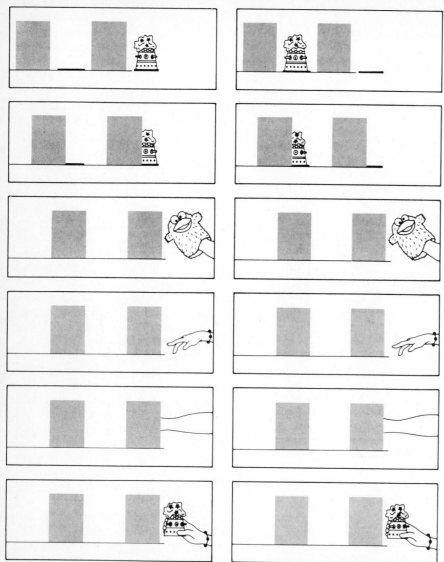

Figure 5. Another procedure involving possible *(left)* and impossible events *(right)* elicits meaningful responses from eight-month-old infants after a delay of 70 seconds. Moving from top to bottom, an object is hidden respectively behind the right or left of two screens; puppets and hand tiptoes are used to keep infants attentive during the delay period; the experimenter reaches behind the right screen and brings the hidden object into view from behind it. (The object was placed there surreptitiously as part of the impossible event.) Surprise at the impossible event indicates memory of the place where the object was hidden. The apparent recall suggests a kind of conceptual functioning that goes beyond the sensorimotor functioning described by Piaget. (After Baillargeon et al. 1989.)

object being represented, but the information is rather precise—for example, Baillargeon (1987b) found that infants remembered not only that an object was hidden but where it was located and how tall it was.

Where do concepts come from?

The data described above indicate that the theory of an exclusively sensorimotor stage of development, in which babies cannot yet represent the world conceptually, is in need of considerable revision. There does not

appear to be a protracted period during which infants have no conception of objects or events and cannot represent them in their absence. A great deal of information is available to and used by infants from an early age, even before they have developed the motor coordination enabling manual exploration that Piaget thought was crucial to conceptual development.

Indeed, a good deal of evidence suggests that we have tended to confuse infants' motor incompetence with conceptual incompetence. Piaget was particularly influenced in his theorizing by the difficulties that

children as old as a year have finding a hidden object, especially when it is hidden in more than one location a number of times in succession. The phenomena he demonstrated have been replicated many times, but it now appears that much of the difficulty infants have in such situations is due not to a lack of understanding of object permanence but to other factors. For example, repeatedly hiding an object in different locations can be confusing and leads to perseverative responding to the same place (see Diamond 1985; Mandler 1988, in press).

If a conceptual system of knowledge has begun to be formed by at least six months and perhaps earlier, where does it come from? Piaget's theory of a transformation of well-developed action schemas into conceptual thought cannot account for conceptual knowledge occurring before the action schemas themselves have developed. On the other hand, perceptual schemas about objects and events develop early. What is needed, then, is some mechanism for transforming these schemas into concepts, or ideas, about what is being perceived, preferably a mechanism that can operate as soon as perceptual schemas are formed.

Little has been written about this problem. One approach is to assume that even young infants are capable of redescribing perceptual information in a conceptual format. I have suggested a mechanism that might accomplish this (Mandler 1988): perceptual analysis, a process by which one perception is actively compared to another and similarities or differences between them are noted. (Such analysis, like other sorts of concept formation, requires some kind of vocabulary; this aspect, still little understood, is discussed below.) The simplest case of perceptual analysis occurs when two simultaneously presented objects are compared, or a single object is compared to an already established representation (i.e., one notes similarities or differences between what one is looking at and what one recalls about it). It is the process by which we discover that sugar bowls have two handles and teacups only one, or that a friend wears glasses. Unless we have engaged in this kind of analysis (or someone has told us), the information will not be accessible for us to think about. Much of the time, of course, we do not make such comparisons, which is why we often can recall few details of even recent experiences.

Although it is analytic, perceptual analysis consists primarily of simplification. Our perceptual system regularly processes vast amounts of information that never become accessible to thought. For example, we make use of a great deal of complex information every time we recognize a face: proportions, contours, subtle shading, relationships among various facial features, and so on. Yet little of this information is available to our thought processes. Few people are aware of the proportions of the human face—it is not something they have ever conceptualized. Even fewer know how they determine whether a face is male or female (this categorization depends on subtle differences in proportions). For the most part we do not even have words to describe the nuances that our perceptual apparatus uses instantly and effortlessly to make such a perceptual categorization.

For us to be able to think about such matters, the information must be reduced and simplified into a conceptual format. One way this redescription is done is via language; someone (perhaps an artist who has already carried out the relevant analytic process) conceptualizes aspects of a face for us. The other way is to look at a face and analyze it ourselves, such as noting that the ears are at the same level as the eyes. The analysis is often couched in linguistic form, but it need not be. Images can be used, but these, in spite of having spatial properties, have a major conceptual component (e.g., Kosslyn 1983).

An infant, of course, does not have the benefit of language, the means by which older people acquire much of their factual knowledge. So if infants are to transform perceptual schemas into thoughts, they must be able to analyze the perceptual information they receive. The perceptual system itself cannot decide that only animate creatures move by themselves or that containers must have bottoms if they are to hold things, and so forth. These are facts visually observed, but they are highly simpli-

fied versions of the information available to be conceptualized.

The notion of perceptual analysis is similar to the process that Piaget theorized as being responsible for the creation of images. He thought that this kind of analysis does not even begin until around eight or nine months and does not result in imagery until later still. However, he had no evidence that image formation is such a late-developing process, and his own description of his children's imitative performance as early as three or four months strongly suggests that the process of perceptual analysis had begun. For example, he observed imitation of clapping hands at that time, a performance that would seem to require a good deal of analysis, considering the difference between what infants see and what they must do. In many places in his account of early imitation, Piaget

noted that the infants watched him carefully, studying both their own and his actions. Other developmental psychologists have commented on the same phenomenon. For example, Werner and Kaplan (1963) noted that infants begin ''contemplating'' objects at between three and five months. Ruff (1986) has documented intense examination of objects at six months (the earliest age she studied).

To investigate contemplation or analysis of objects experimentally is not easy. A possible measure is the number of times an infant looks back and forth between two objects that are presented simultaneously. Janowsky (1985), for example, showed that this measure increased significantly between four and eight months. At four months infants tend to look first at one object and then the other; at eight months they switch back and forth between the two a

Infants whose parents use sign language have been observed to begin to use conventional signs at around six to seven months

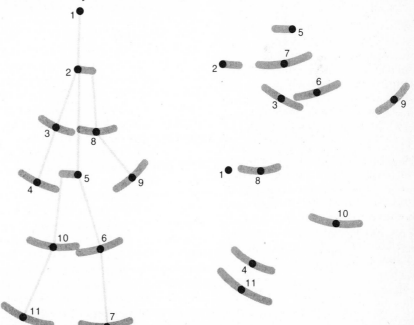

Figure 6. An equally subtle ability is involved in this demonstration of three-month-olds' responses to biological as opposed to nonbiological motion. The infants watch videotapes of computer-generated displays. On the left is a display of 11 point-lights moving as if attached to the head and major joints of a person walking. The motion vectors drawn through each point represent the perceived motions of the display; the lines connecting points, like the numbers and vectors, are not visible to the infants. The display on the right is identical to the normal walker except that the relative locations of the point-lights are scrambled. Correspondingly numbered points in the two displays undergo identical motions. Infants show greater interest in the scrambled display, indicating that they consider it novel. (After Bertenthal et al. 1987.)

good many times. Fox and his colleagues (1979) have reported a similar phenomenon. Interestingly, Janowsky found that the differences in looking back and forth are not associated with differences in total looking time, the rate at which infants habituate to objects (cease to look at them), or accuracy of recognition. So the looking back and forth must serve some other function. I would suggest that it is a comparison process, by which one object is being contrasted with the other.

A vocabulary for concepts

Assuming that perceptual analysis can lead to concept formation, it is still necessary to formulate the vocabulary in which the resulting concepts are couched. But here we face one of the major stumbling blocks in psychological theory: the problem of specifying conceptual primitives (see Smith and Medin 1981). Perhaps because of its difficulty, it has been largely ignored by developmental psychologists, in spite of the fact that any theory of conceptual development must resolve the issue of what the earliest concepts are like, no matter when they may first be formed. Leslie (1988) has offered an analysis of the primitives involved in early causal concepts, and people working on language acquisition have speculated about semantic primitives. For example, Slobin (1985) points out that children must already have concepts of objects and events, as well as relational notions about them, in order for language to be acquired. Since language comprehension begins at around nine to ten months (and perhaps earlier for sign language), some kind of conceptual system must be well established by that time. But we have almost no information as to its character.

Help may come from recent studies by cognitive linguists (e.g., Fauconnier 1985; Johnson 1987; Lakoff 1987). Although the primary goal of these theorists is to understand how language works, their analyses of the root concepts expressed in language may be of use in our search for babies' earliest concepts. For example, Lakoff and Johnson have proposed that image schemas—notions derived from spatial structure, such

as trajectory, up-down, container, part-whole, end-of-path, and link—form the foundation of the conceptualizing capacity. These authors suggest that image schemas are derived from preconceptual perceptual structures, forming the core of many of our concepts of objects and events and of their metaphorical extensions to abstract realms. They demonstrate in great detail how many of our most complex concepts are grounded in such primitive notions. I would characterize image schemas as simplified redescriptions of sensorimotor schemas, noting that they seem to be reasonably within the capacity of infant conceptualization.

The potential usefulness of image schemas as conceptual primitives can be illustrated by the example of the container schema. According to Johnson and Lakoff, the structural elements of this image schema are "interior," "boundary," and "exterior." It has a bodily basis likely to be appreciated by quite young infants, and a perceptual basis that seems to require minimal redescription of the object schemas described earlier. It also has a simple binary logic—either in or not-in; if A is in B and B is in C, then A is in C—that may or may not be the sensorimotor basis of the Boolean logic of classes, as Lakoff suggests, but is certainly a characteristic of concepts as opposed to percepts. (The conceptual system tends to reduce the continuous information delivered by the perceptual system to a small number of discrete values.)

The use of such an image schema might be responsible for the better performance nine-month-old infants show on hiding tasks when a container is used rather than cloths or screens (Freeman et al. 1980). Current work by Baillargeon (pers. com.) suggests that at approximately the same age infants are surprised when containers without bottoms appear to hold things. Of course, these are only fragments of the kind of information needed to document the development of the idea of a container, but

they indicate how we might go about tracking the early establishment of simple concepts.

A more complex concept that may also be acquired relatively early in infancy is that of animacy. Consider some possible sources for such a concept. We know that infants differentiate biological from nonbiological motion as early as three months (Fig. 6; Bertenthal et al. 1987). This perceptual differentiation, although an excellent source of information, does not constitute a concept by itself; it is an accomplishment similar to categorizing male and female faces, which infants have learned to do by six months (Fagan and Singer 1979). As discussed earlier, such perceptual categorization is not accessible for purposes of conceptual thought unless it has been redescribed in conceptual terms. An infant needs to conceptualize some differences between categories of moving objects, such as noting that one type starts up on its own and (sometimes) responds to the infant's signals, whereas the other type does not. An image schema of a notion such as beginning-of-path could be used to redescribe the perceptual information involved in initiation of motion. A link schema (whose elements are two entities and some kind of path between them) could be used to describe the observation of responsivity to self. From such simple foundations might arise a primitive concept of animal, a concept that we have reason to believe is present in some form by at least the end of the first year of life (Golinkoff and Halperin 1983; Mandler and Bauer 1988).

These are some examples of how a conceptual system might emerge from a combination of perceptual input and some relatively simple redescriptions of that input. I have suggested that a mechanism of perceptual analysis could enable such redescription, with the terms of the redescription being derived from spatial structure. The mechanism would not require an extended period of

A good deal of evidence suggests that we have tended to confuse infants' motor incompetence with conceptual incompetence

exclusively sensorimotor functioning but would allow conceptualization of the world to begin early in infancy. The data I have summarized indicate that babies do indeed begin to think earlier than we thought. Therefore, it seems safe to assume that they either are born with or acquire early in life the capacity to form concepts, rather than to assume that conceptual functioning can occur only as an outcome of a lengthy sensorimotor stage.

References

Ashmead, D. H., and M. Perlmutter. 1980. Infant memory in everyday life. In *New Directions for Child Development: Children's Memory*, vol. 10, ed. M. Perlmutter, pp. 1–16. Jossey-Bass.

Baillargeon, R. 1987a. Object permanence in 3.5- and 4.5-month-old infants. *Devel. Psychol.* 23:655–64.

———. 1987b. Young infants' reasoning about the physical and spatial properties of a hidden object. *Cognitive Devel.* 2:179–200.

Baillargeon, R., J. De Vos, and M. Graber. 1989. Location memory in 8-month-old infants in a nonsearch AB task: Further evidence. *Cognitive Devel.* 4:345–67.

Baillargeon, R., E. S. Spelke, and S. Wasserman. 1985. Object permanence in five-month-old infants. *Cognition* 20:191–208.

Bertenthal, B. I., D. R. Proffitt, S. J. Kramer, and N. B. Spetner. 1987. Infants' encoding of kinetic displays varying in relative coherence. *Devel. Psychol.* 23:171–78.

Bonvillian, J. D., M. D. Orlansky, and L. L. Novack. 1983. Developmental milestones: Sign language and motor development. *Child Devel.* 54:1435–45.

Cohen, N. J., and L. R. Squire. 1980. Preserved learning and retention of pattern-analyzing skills in amnesia: Dissociation of knowing how and knowing that. *Science* 210:207–10.

Diamond, A. 1985. The development of the ability to use recall to guide action, as indicated by infants' performance on AB. *Child Devel.* 56:868–83.

Fagan, J. F., III, and L. T. Singer. 1979. The role of simple feature differences in infant recognition of faces. *Infant Behav. Devel.* 2:39–46.

Fauconnier, G. 1985. *Mental Spaces.* MIT Press.

Fox, N., J. Kagan, and S. Weiskopf. 1979. The growth of memory during infancy. *Genetic Psychol. Mono.* 99:91–130.

Freeman, N. H., S. Lloyd, and C. G. Sinha. 1980. Infant search tasks reveal early concepts of containment and canonical usage of objects. *Cognition* 8:243–62.

Golinkoff, R. M., and M. S. Halperin. 1983. The concept of animal: One infant's view. *Infant Behav. Devel.* 6:229–33.

James, W. 1890. *The Principles of Psychology.* Holt.

Janowsky, J. S. 1985. Cognitive development and reorganization after early brain injury. Ph.D. diss., Cornell Univ.

Johnson, M. 1987. *The Body in the Mind: The Bodily Basis of Meaning, Imagination, and Reason.* Univ. of Chicago Press.

Kellman, P. J., and E. S. Spelke. 1983. Perception of partly occluded objects in infancy. *Cognitive Psychol.* 15:483–524.

Kosslyn, S. M. 1983. *Ghosts in the Mind's Machine: Creating and Using Images in the Brain.* Norton.

Kuhl, P. K., and A. N. Meltzoff. 1988. Speech as an intermodal object of perception. In *Perceptual Development in Infancy: The Minnesota Symposia on Child Psychology*, vol. 20, ed. A. Yonas, pp. 235–66. Erlbaum.

Lakoff, G. 1987. *Women, Fire, and Dangerous Things: What Categories Reveal about the Mind.* Univ. of Chicago Press.

Leslie, A. 1988. The necessity of illusion: Perception and thought in infancy. In *Thought without Language*, ed. L. Weiskrantz, pp. 185–210. Clarendon Press.

Mandler, J. M. 1983. Representation. In *Cognitive Development*, ed. J. H. Flavell and E. M. Markman, pp. 420–94. Vol. 3 of *Manual of Child Psychology*, ed. P. Mussen. Wiley.

———. 1988. How to build a baby: On the development of an accessible representational system. *Cognitive Devel.* 3:113–36.

———. In press. Recall of events by preverbal children. In *The Development and Neural Bases of Higher Cognitive Functions*, ed. A. Diamond. New York Academy of Sciences Press.

Mandler, J. M., and P. J. Bauer. 1988. The cradle of categorization: Is the basic level basic? *Cognitive Devel.* 3:247–64.

McDonough, L., and J. M. Mandler. 1989. Immediate and deferred imitation with 11-month-olds: A comparison between familiar and novel actions. Poster presented at meeting of the Society for Research in Child Development, Kansas City.

Meltzoff, A. N. 1988. Infant imitation and memory: Nine-month-olds in immediate and deferred tests. *Child Devel.* 59:217–25.

Meltzoff, A. N., and R. W. Borton. 1979. Intermodal matching by human neonates. *Nature* 282:403–04.

Mendelson, M. J., and M. M. Haith. 1976. The relation between audition and vision in the newborn. *Monographs of the Society for Research in Child Development*, no. 41, serial no. 167.

Michotte, A. 1963. *The Perception of Causality.* Methuen.

Piaget, J. 1951. *Play, Dreams and Imitation in Childhood*, trans. C. Gattegno and F. M. Hodgson. Norton.

———. 1952. *The Origins of Intelligence in Children*, trans. M. Cook. International Universities Press.

———. 1954. *The Construction of Reality in the Child*, trans. M. Cook. Basic Books.

Prinz, P. M., and E. A. Prinz. 1979. Simultaneous acquisition of ASL and spoken English (in a hearing child of a deaf mother and hearing father). Phase I: Early lexical development. *Sign Lang. Stud.* 25:283–96.

Ruff, H. A. 1986. Components of attention during infants' manipulative exploration. *Child Devel.* 57:105–14.

Schacter, D. L. 1987. Implicit memory: History and current status. *J. Exper. Psychol.: Learning, Memory, Cognition* 13:501–18.

Slobin, D. I. 1985. Crosslinguistic evidence for the language-making capacity. In *The Crosslinguistic Study of Language Acquisition*, vol. 2, ed. D. I. Slobin, pp. 1157–1256. Erlbaum.

Smith, E. E., and D. L. Medin. 1981. *Categories and Concepts.* Harvard Univ. Press.

Spelke, E. S. 1979. Perceiving bimodally specified events in infancy. *Devel. Psychol.* 15:626–36.

———. 1988. The origins of physical knowledge. In *Thought without Language*, ed. L. Weiskrantz, pp. 168–84. Clarendon Press.

Spelke, E. S., and R. Kestenbaum. 1986. Les origines du concept d'objet. *Psychologie française* 31:67–72.

Walker-Andrews, A. S., and E. J. Gibson. 1986. What develops in bimodal perception? In *Advances in Infancy Research*, vol. 4, ed. L. P. Lipsitt and C. Rovee-Collier, pp. 171–81. Ablex.

Werner, H., and B. Kaplan. 1963. *Symbol Formation.* Wiley.

Wertheimer, M. 1961. Psychomotor coordination of auditory and visual space at birth. *Science* 134:1692.

New Views of Human Intelligence

A far broader range of important skills and abilities emerges.

Marie Winn

Marie Winn, author of "The Plug-In Drug," writes regularly about child development.

Intelligence—the dark secret of American social science and education—is coming out of the closet. Once intelligence was perceived as a narrow group of mental abilities, those measurable by an I.Q. test. But according to that view great groups of the population turned out to be not very smart or educable. Since these groups were generally composed of poor minorities, nobody liked to talk about intelligence very much—it seemed somehow un-American. In recent years a new definition of intelligence has been gaining acceptance, one which includes a far greater range of mental abilities among the components of human cognition. This conceptual change foreshadows the most far-reaching social and educational consequences.

The idea that intelligence is a single *thing*, a kind of brain power that can be measured by a test the way electric power may be measured by a galvanometer, has informed thinking in the academic and research world for much of this century. Although French psychologist Alfred Binet, creator of the first extensively used intelligence test in 1905, saw intelligence as the exercise of a variety of mental facilities, his disciple Charles Spearman, an English psychologist, added a principle that soon became widely accepted: there is a single factor common to all these diverse functions. He called this factor "general intelligence" and symbolized it with a lower-case g. All cognitive activity, Spearman proposed, required access to that g factor.

While there was always dispute, sometimes violent disagreement, about whether this factor is basically innate or more or less susceptible to environmental influence, psychologists after Spearman continued to believe in the g factor and worked to create new and better tests to measure it. In 1912 William Stern, a German psychologist, invented the concept of the intelligence quotient, which divided the "mental age" of a person (as discovered through a test) by the chronological age, thereby coming up with a fraction. Four years later, when Stanford University psychologist Lewis Madison Terman came up with an American version of Binet's test that came to be known as the Stanford-Binet—he multiplied the final result by 100, to avoid the fraction—the stage was set for large-scale intelligence testing throughout America.

Yet a curious and strangely neglected fact about I.Q. tests serves to cast doubt on their reliability as a measure of intelligence: while these scores do predict success in school fairly well, there is little correlation between how people score on I.Q. tests and their later success in life. The numbers of people with undistinguished childhood I.Q. scores who excel in later life, as well as the numbers of certified "geniuses" who come to naught, are legion. Clearly, what the standard I.Q. test measures is but a small part of the complex conglomeration of elements that make up human intelligence, a part that may not have much to do with those cognitive abilities that allow people to function successfully in various walks of life.

Today the g factor concept of intelligence no longer dominates scientific discussion. In its place is a far more pluralistic view. According to John L. Horn, a psychologist at the University of Southern California, "What we see as intelligence, and tend to regard as a whole, is in fact a mosaic of many distinct units." Robert J. Sternberg, a psychologist at Yale, has constructed a "triarchic" theory of human intelligence, which focuses on such areas as common sense and insight. J. P. Guilford, a California psychologist, classified intellectual acts into 120 categories, while one researcher at a recent meeting of psychologists suggested that humans might have 800,000 intellectual abilities.

By far the most intuitively satisfying of the current approaches is Howard Gardner's theory of multiple intelligences, or M.I. theory. Gardner, a psychologist and recipient of a MacArthur Foundation "genius" award, runs a research institution at Harvard's Graduate School of Education named Project Zero, which is also a fertile testing ground for many of his ideas. Using data from such diverse sources as neurology, anthropology, psychology and pathology, Gardner has come up with seven areas of intellectual competence — intelligences, he calls them — that are relatively independent of one another. A summary of the seven areas, the "end-states" or careers they might lead to and a prominent person proposed by Gardner to exemplify each type of intelligence, follows:

1. Linguistic: sensitivity to the meaning and order of words; poet, translator (T. S. Eliot).

2. Logical-mathematical: the ability to handle chains of reasoning and to recognize patterns and order; mathematician, scientist (Einstein).

3. Musical: sensitivity to pitch, melody, rhythm and tone; composer, singer (Stravinsky).

4. Bodily-kinesthetic: the ability to use the body skillfully and handle objects adroitly; athlete, dancer, surgeon (Martha Graham).

5. Spatial: the ability to perceive the

world accurately and to re-create or transform aspects of that world; sculptor, architect, surveyor (Picasso).

6. Interpersonal: the ability to understand people and relationships; politician, salesman, religious leader (Gandhi).

7. Intrapersonal: access to one's emotional life as a means to understand oneself and others; therapist, social worker (Freud).

In his highly regarded book "Frames of Mind" Gardner goes beyond the theoretical by providing physiological evidence that each of the seven intelligences exists as a discrete entity. It is this body of material, based on his own research in neuropsychology at the Boston Veterans Administration Medical Center, that lends the theory its strongest credence.

Gardner provides numerous examples of patients who have lost all language abilities as a result of damage to the speech centers in the left hemisphere of the brain, who nevertheless retain the ability to be musicians, visual artists, even engineers. Most musical abilities appear to be located in the right hemisphere, and thus injuries to the right frontal and temporal lobes cause difficulties in distinguishing tones. He points out that lesions in certain areas of the left hemisphere dramatically affect logical and mathematical abilities.

To buttress his claim for a separate bodily-kinesthetic intelligence, Gardner describes patients whose linguistic and logical capacities have been devastated, but who show little or no difficulty in carrying out complicated motor activities. He cites numerous case histories of patients with right hemisphere injuries who have difficulties with spatial representation and other visual tasks; meanwhile, their linguistic abilities remain intact.

Even for the elusive personal intelligences, there is supporting neurological data. While a lobotomy causes little damage to those intellectual abilities measured on an I.Q. test, the ruinous impact of this surgical procedure on various aspects of the personality is well known.

"I started out thinking that intelligence would break down according to the senses — visual, auditory and so on," Gardner said in a recent interview, "but my study convinced me it didn't work that way. My methodological principle is to look at the mind through a lot of lenses — development, breakdown, cross-cultural material, evolutionary data. And these different lenses all support the existence of multiple intelligences."

Since the publication of "Frames of Mind" in 1983, Gardner's theory has attracted extraordinary attention from both the academic world and the education establishment. A symposium on M.I. theory held last year at the University of South Carolina was attended by scholars from across the country. Educational journals regularly feature articles on Gardner's ideas. But the most unexpected testing ground for his theoretical work materialized in the fall of 1985, when eight Indiana school teachers approached Gardner with an audacious plan: to start a public school based on the theory of multiple intelligences.

ON SEPTEMBER 8, 1987, 150 students arrived at a nondescript building in downtown Indianapolis to take part in a unique educational experiment: a school devised to develop the wide gamut of intelligences identified in Gardner's M.I. theory. What made this theory so attractive to the eight founding teachers was Gardner's belief that while everyone is born with certain strengths and weaknesses in each of the cognitive areas, all people are capable of developing greater proficiency in *all* of them.

The Key School, as it was named, covers a rigorous curriculum devoted to the three R's. This is required by Indiana law, which also mandates periodic standardized testing of all students in these subjects. In a traditional school, that would pretty much sum it up. But at the Key School the daily schedule of every child also includes music, art and physical education — four times the exposure children usually get to these subjects. And every day there is instruction in Spanish and computers. (Federal "magnet" funds have allowed the school to hire eight additional teachers.) A detailed report card evaluates each child in the seven intelligences and provides a far more precise profile of his or her abilities than a conventional report card.

In Room 25 one day last winter, 22 highly concentrated little violinists are eagerly honing their musical intelligence to the tune (or somewhere vaguely near it) of "Frosty the Snowman." In Room 15 teacher Beverly Hoeltke is on the floor, surrounded by a noisy but disciplined group of first, second and third graders exercising their logical-mathematical intelligence. By moving small blocks into circles of varying sizes they are discovering the deeper connections between addition and multiplication: four plus four ends up with the same result as four times two.

In Room 17 Carol Forbes is demonstrating the difference between a small triangle and a large circle — in Spanish — a lesson that combines exercise in both the linguistic and spatial intelligences. In the gym a noisy bunch of kids are playing backboard dodgeball, little realizing, as they gleefully try to bean one another with a large ball, that they are developing their bodily-kinesthetic intelligence.

Intelligences run amok in Room 10, where a two-month-long schoolwide effort has produced a spectacular re-creation of a tropical rain forest. Wildly colorful papier-mâché birds of paradise, parrots and butterflies stare down from the forest canopy at pumas and various primates, which in turn gaze down upon the exotic denizens of the forest floor.

In addition to this splendid manifestation of spatial intelligence, there are charts, graphs and carefully researched reports pinned to the wall giving information on creatures as diverse as tuataras, golden eagles and toucans, demonstrating that the linguistic and logical-mathematical intelligences have not been neglected. The cooperative nature of the project attests to the involvement of the two personal intelligences. Meanwhile, a high level of musical intelligence is revealed in the taped background music, a composition called "Train in the Tropical Forest" written and performed by three upper-graders. It is a remarkable work, filled with unconventional sound effects reminiscent of the composer George Crumb.

It is hard to remember that this is not a special school for gifted children, but one whose racially and ethnically diverse population is chosen entirely by lottery, with more than a third of the students qualifying for free or reduced-price school lunch.

In its third year of operation, the Key School shows every sign of being a runaway success. Scores on standardized tests show that the two intelligences most valued in our educational system are thriving. Only five children in the entire school failed to reach the acceptable level mandated by the school district. Principal Patricia Bolaños also reports: "The test scores reveal that we are diminishing the gap between the achievement lev-

A narrow idea of intelligence misleads some children into thinking they are stupid.

els of our black students and our white students, and it certainly is not because the achievement levels of the white students are diminishing."

Parental enthusiasm, always a litmus test of a school's well-being, is high. "I can't say enough good things about the Key School," says Marilyn Altom, mother of Crystal, who graduated last year, and Alexandra, a second grader. Art teacher Kathy Ann Calwell says: "Crystal Altom was a child who definitely could have been lost in the cracks. She wasn't good in spelling or math or any of the academic areas. But she just flowered, right before our eyes. And in the process of growing confident about her art and music and theater, the other areas got stronger."

IN RECENT YEARS HOWARD Gardner's attention has moved from establishing the multiple intelligences to the more practical area of testing. With David Henry Feldman, a psychologist at Tufts University, he is involved in Project Spectrum, an assessment program that measures a far greater range of abilities than I.Q. tests do. Indeed, it has been designed to touch on all of the seven intelligences. Spectrum evaluates a child's skills over a period of time in the familiar environment of the classroom, and gives a written report on his or her strengths and weaknesses. It is already in use at the Healey School in Somerville, Mass.

The Educational Testing Service, the very institution that administers some of the nation's most widely used standardized tests, has begun to acknowledge the need for change. Drew H. Gitomer, a research scientist at E.T.S., says: "There's a growing recognition that the traditional assessments don't accomplish all that can be done and in certain ways work against educational objectives." E.T.S. is collaborating with Gardner on another alternative assessment program, Arts Propel, which is developing new ways to evaluate children's work in the arts in a number of Pittsburgh public schools.

As the education establishment faces the need for reform, Gardner's ideas are frequently cited. The Education Commission of the States, which serves as a policy resource for the nation's governors, finds his work a promising model. Rexford Brown, the commission's director of communications, says: "Gardner's work has been important in attacking the monolithic notion of intelligence that has undergirded much of our thinking. We are beginning to see that education is not meant merely to sort out a few children and make them leaders, but to develop the latent talents of the entire population in diverse ways."

Gardner's ideas are not without their critics. Sandra Scarr, a professor of psychology at the University of Virginia, looks on M.I. theory as an example of "faulty optimism that leads to dead ends in both theory and practice." She calls it a "lumper theory in which everything good in human behavior is called intelligence."

Robert Sternberg of Yale observes that a person deficient in some of Gardner's cognitive areas, musical intelligence, for example, is not thereby mentally impaired in the way a person lacking in verbal or reasoning skills would be. Sternberg describes Gardner's theory as "a theory of talents, not one of intelligences." He explains: "An ability is a component of intelligence when we cannot get along without it, and a talent when we are not noticeably handicapped by its absence."

Nor is everyone in the education establishment sanguine about Gardner's influence. Chester E. Finn, chairman of the board of governors of the National Assessment of Educational Progress, a Federal testing program, sees this influence as both "good and bad." "The good part," he says, "is the perception that people who aren't very good at one thing can be very good at another and that there are multiple ways of evaluating performance of any given task.

"But his ideas can be turned to ill effect," he continues. "You hear people saying it's all right if kids don't get the right answer as long as they're creative in their approach. But is that good? I firmly believe that every young American ought to have some idea of who Thomas Jefferson and Abraham Lincoln are, and I don't care whether their greatest strength is playing the ukelele or skating backward on the ice."

In his latest book, "To Open Minds," Howard Gardner defends himself against such critics, and expresses a respect for tradition and basic skill development together with the encouragement of creativity in the classroom. As he concluded an interview in his office at Project Zero, he emphasized the value of a more humanistic view of intelligence. "I believe that as long as we have a narrow definition of intelligence — a very scholastic definition — most kids are going to think they're stupid, and they're going to miss the fact that they may have a lot of abilities that could be important vocationally and avocationally. Enlarging the concept of intelligence, and realizing that people may not have the school intelligence but may have other equally important ones — I think that would be an enormously valuable thing to happen."

Gardner pauses and then adds with a smile, "M.I. theory is not the last word. I'm trying to shake things up and pluralize things a bit. To think that there *is* a last word is what's wrong with most intelligence theorists."

Is the Brain's Mind a Computer Program?

No. A program merely manipulates symbols, whereas a brain attaches meaning to them

John R. Searle

John R. Searle is professor of philosophy at the University of California, Berkeley. He received his B.A., M.A. and D.Phil. from the University of Oxford, where he was a Rhodes scholar. He wishes to thank Stuart Dreyfus, Stevan Harnad, Elizabeth Lloyd and Irvin Rock for their comments and suggestions.

Can a machine think? Can a machine have conscious thoughts in exactly the same sense that you and I have? If by "machine" one means a physical system capable of performing certain functions (and what else can one mean?), then humans are machines of a special biological kind, and humans can think, and so of course machines can think. And, for all we know, it might be possible to produce a thinking machine out of different materials altogether—say, out of silicon chips or vacuum tubes. Maybe it will turn out to be impossible, but we certainly do not know that yet.

In recent decades, however, the question of whether a machine can think has been given a different interpretation entirely. The question that has been posed in its place is, Could a machine think just by virtue of implementing a computer program? Is the program by itself constitutive of thinking? This is a completely different question because it is not about the physical, causal properties of actual or possible physical systems but rather about the abstract, computational properties of formal computer programs that can be implemented in any sort of substance at all, provided only that the substance is able to carry the program.

A fair number of researchers in artificial intelligence (AI) believe the answer to the second question is yes; that is, they believe that by designing the right programs with the right inputs and outputs, they are literally creating minds. They believe furthermore that they have a scientific test for determining success or failure: the Turing test devised by Alan M. Turing, the founding father of artificial intelligence. The Turing test, as currently understood, is simply this: if a computer can perform in such a way that an expert cannot distinguish its performance from that of a human who has a certain cognitive ability—say, the ability to do addition or to understand Chinese—then the computer also has that ability. So the goal is to design programs that will simulate human cognition in such a way as to pass the Turing test. What is more, such a program would not merely be a model of the mind; it would literally be a mind, in the same sense that a human mind is a mind.

By no means does every worker in artificial intelligence accept so extreme a view. A more cautious approach is to think of computer models as being useful in studying the mind in the same way that they are useful in studying the weather, economics or molecular biology. To distinguish these two approaches, I call the first strong AI and the second weak AI. It is important to see just how bold an approach strong AI is. Strong AI claims that thinking is merely the manipulation of formal symbols, and that is exactly what the computer does: manipulate formal symbols. This view is often summarized by saying, "The mind is to the brain as the program is to the hardware."

Strong AI is unusual among theories of the mind in at least two respects: it can be stated clearly, and it admits of a simple and decisive refutation. The refutation is one that any person can try for himself or herself. Here is how it goes. Consider a language you don't understand. In my case, I do not understand Chinese. To me Chinese writing looks like so many meaningless squiggles. Now suppose I am placed in a room containing baskets full of Chinese symbols. Suppose also that I am given a rule book in English for matching Chinese symbols with other Chinese symbols. The rules identify the symbols entirely by their shapes and do not require that I understand any of them. The rules might say such things as, "Take a squiggle-squiggle sign from basket number one and put it next to a squoggle-squoggle sign from basket number two."

Imagine that people outside the room who understand Chinese hand in small bunches of symbols and that in response I manipulate the symbols according to the rule book and hand back more small bunches of symbols. Now, the rule book is the "computer program." The people who wrote it are "programmers," and I am the "computer." The baskets full of symbols are the "data base," the small bunches that are handed in to me are "questions" and the bunches I then hand out are "answers."

Now suppose that the rule book is written in such a way that my "answers" to the "questions" are indistinguishable from those of a native Chinese speaker. For example, the people outside might hand me some symbols that unknown to me mean, "What's your favorite color?" and I might after going through the rules give back symbols that, also unknown to me, mean, "My favorite is blue, but I also like green a lot." I satisfy the Turing test for understanding Chinese. All the same, I am totally ignorant of Chinese. And there is no way I could come to understand Chinese in the system as described, since there is no way that I can learn the meanings of any of the symbols. Like a computer, I manipulate symbols, but I attach no meaning to the symbols.

The point of the thought experi-

From *Scientific American*, January 1990, pp. 26-31. Copyright © 1990 by Scientific American, Inc. Reprinted with permission.

ment is this: if I do not understand Chinese solely on the basis of running a computer program for understanding Chinese, then neither does any other digital computer solely on that basis. Digital computers merely manipulate formal symbols according to rules in the program.

What goes for Chinese goes for other forms of cognition as well. Just manipulating the symbols is not by itself enough to guarantee cognition, perception, understanding, thinking and so forth. And since computers, qua computers, are symbol-manipulating devices, merely running the computer program is not enough to guarantee cognition.

This simple argument is decisive against the claims of strong AI. The first premise of the argument simply states the formal character of a computer program. Programs are defined in terms of symbol manipulations, and the symbols are purely formal, or "syntactic." The formal character of the program, by the way, is what makes computers so powerful. The same program can be run on an indefinite variety of hardwares, and one hardware system can run an indefinite range of computer programs. Let me abbreviate this "axiom" as

Axiom 1. *Computer programs are formal (syntactic).*

This point is so crucial that it is worth explaining in more detail. A digital computer processes information by first encoding it in the symbolism that the computer uses and then manipulating the symbols through a set of precisely stated rules. These rules constitute the program. For example, in Turing's early theory of computers, the symbols were simply 0's and 1's, and the rules of the program said such things as, "Print a 0 on the tape, move one square to the left and erase a 1." The astonishing thing about computers is that any information that can be stated in a language can be encoded in such a system, and any information-processing task that can be solved by explicit rules can be programmed.

Two further points are important. First, symbols and programs are purely abstract notions: they have no essential physical properties to define them and can be implemented in any physical medium whatsoever. The 0's and 1's, qua symbols, have no essential physical properties and a fortiori have no physical, causal properties. I emphasize this point because it is tempting to identify computers with some specific technology—say,

silicon chips—and to think that the issues are about the physics of silicon chips or to think that syntax identifies some physical phenomenon that might have as yet unknown causal powers, in the way that actual physical phenomena such as electromagnetic radiation or hydrogen atoms have physical, causal properties. The second point is that symbols are manipulated without reference to any meanings. The symbols of the program can stand for anything the programmer or user wants. In this sense the program has syntax but no semantics.

The next axiom is just a reminder of the obvious fact that thoughts, perceptions, understandings and so forth have a mental content. By virtue of their content they can be about objects and states of affairs in the world. If the content involves language, there will be syntax in addition to semantics, but linguistic understanding requires at least a semantic framework. If, for example, I am thinking about the last presidential election, certain words will go through my mind, but the words are about the election only because I attach specific meanings to these words, in accordance with my knowledge of English. In this respect they are unlike Chinese symbols for me. Let me abbreviate this axiom as

Axiom 2. *Human minds have mental contents (semantics).*

Now let me add the point that the Chinese room demonstrated. Having the symbols by themselves—just having the syntax—is not sufficient for having the semantics. Merely manipulating symbols is not enough to guarantee knowledge of what they mean. I shall abbreviate this as

Axiom 3. *Syntax by itself is neither constitutive of nor sufficient for semantics.*

At one level this principle is true by definition. One might, of course, define the terms syntax and semantics differently. The point is that there is a distinction between formal elements, which have no intrinsic meaning or content, and those phenomena that have intrinsic content. From these premises it follows that

Conclusion 1. *Programs are neither constitutive of nor sufficient for minds.*

And that is just another way of saying that strong AI is false.

It is important to see what is proved and not proved by this argument.

First, I have not tried to prove that "a computer cannot think." Since anything that can be simulated computationally can be described as a computer, and since our brains can at some

levels be simulated, it follows trivially that our brains are computers and they can certainly think. But from the fact that a system can be simulated by symbol manipulation and the fact that it is thinking, it does not follow that thinking is equivalent to formal symbol manipulation.

Second, I have not tried to show that only biologically based systems like our brains can think. Right now those are the only systems we know for a fact can think, but we might find other systems in the universe that can produce conscious thoughts, and we might even come to be able to create thinking systems artificially. I regard this issue as up for grabs.

Third, strong AI's thesis is not that, for all we know, computers with the right programs might be thinking, that they might have some as yet undetected psychological properties; rather it is that they must be thinking because that is all there is to thinking.

Fourth, I have tried to refute strong AI so defined. I have tried to demonstrate that the program by itself is not constitutive of thinking because the program is purely a matter of formal symbol manipulation—and we know independently that symbol manipulations by themselves are not sufficient to guarantee the presence of meanings. That is the principle on which the Chinese room argument works.

I emphasize these points here partly because it seems to me the Churchlands [see "Could a Machine Think?" by Paul M. Churchland and Patricia Smith Churchland, page 32] have not quite understood the issues. They think that strong AI is claiming that computers might turn out to think and that I am denying this possibility on commonsense grounds. But that is not the claim of strong AI, and my argument against it has nothing to do with common sense.

I will have more to say about their objections later. Meanwhile I should point out that, contrary to what the Churchlands suggest, the Chinese room argument also refutes any strong-AI claims made for the new parallel technologies that are inspired by and modeled on neural networks. Unlike the traditional von Neumann computer, which proceeds in a step-by-step fashion, these systems have many computational elements that operate in parallel and interact with one another according to rules inspired by neurobiology. Although the results are still modest, these "parallel distributed processing," or "connectionist," models raise useful questions about how complex, parallel network systems like those in brains might actually function in the production of intelligent behavior.

The parallel, "brainlike" character of the processing, however, is irrelevant to the purely computational aspects of the process. Any function that can be computed on a parallel machine can also be computed on a serial machine. Indeed, because parallel machines are still rare, connectionist programs are usually run on traditional serial machines. Parallel processing, then, does not afford a way around the Chinese room argument.

What is more, the connectionist system is subject even on its own terms to a variant of the objection presented by the original Chinese room argument. Imagine that instead of a Chinese room, I have a Chinese gym: a hall containing many monolingual, English-speaking men. These men would carry out the same operations as the nodes and synapses in a connectionist architecture as described by the Churchlands, and the outcome would be the same as having one man manipulate symbols according to a rule book. No one in the gym speaks a word of Chinese, and there is no way for the system as a whole to learn the meanings of any Chinese words. Yet with appropriate adjustments, the system could give the correct answers to Chinese questions.

There are, as I suggested earlier, interesting properties of connectionist nets that enable them to simulate brain processes more accurately than traditional serial architecture does. But the advantages of parallel architecture for weak AI are quite irrelevant to the issues between the Chinese room argument and strong AI.

The Churchlands miss this point when they say that a big enough Chinese gym might have higher-level mental features that emerge from the size and complexity of the system, just as whole brains have mental features that are not had by individual neurons. That is, of course, a possibility, but it has nothing to do with computation. Computationally, serial and parallel systems are equivalent: any computation that can be done in parallel can be done in serial. If the man in the Chinese room is computationally equivalent to both, then if he does not understand Chinese solely by virtue of doing the computations, neither do they. The Churchlands are correct in saying that the original Chinese rocm argument was designed with traditional AI in mind but wrong in thinking

that connectionism is immune to the argument. It applies to any computational system. You can't get semantically loaded thought contents from formal computations alone, whether they are done in serial or in parallel; that is why the Chinese room argument refutes strong AI in any form.

Many people who are impressed by this argument are nonetheless puzzled about the differences between people and computers. If humans are, at least in a trivial sense, computers, and if humans have a semantics, then why couldn't we give semantics to other computers? Why couldn't we program a Vax or a Cray so that it too would have thoughts and feelings? Or why couldn't some new computer technology overcome the gulf between form and content, between syntax and semantics? What, in fact, are the differences between animal brains and computer systems that enable the Chinese room argument to work against computers but not against brains?

The most obvious difference is that the processes that define something as a computer—computational processes—are completely independent of any reference to a specific type of hardware implementation. One could in principle make a computer out of old beer cans strung together with wires and powered by windmills.

But when it comes to brains, although science is largely ignorant of how brains function to produce mental states, one is struck by the extreme specificity of the anatomy and the physiology. Where some understanding exists of how brain processes produce mental phenomena—for example, pain, thirst, vision, smell—it is clear that specific neurobiological processes are involved. Thirst, at least of certain kinds, is caused by certain types of neuron firings in the hypothalamus, which in turn are caused by the action of a specific peptide, angiotensin II. The causation is from the "bottom up" in the sense that lower-level neuronal processes cause higher-level mental phenomena. Indeed, as far as we know, every "mental" event, ranging from feelings of thirst to thoughts of mathematical theorems and memories of childhood, is caused by specific neurons firing in specific neural architectures.

But why should this specificity matter? After all, neuron firings could be simulated on computers that had a completely different physics and chemistry from that of the brain. The

answer is that the brain does not merely instantiate a formal pattern or program (it does that, too), but it also *causes* mental events by virtue of specific neurobiological processes. Brains are specific biological organs, and their specific biochemical properties enable them to cause consciousness and other sorts of mental phenomena. Computer simulations of brain processes provide models of the formal aspects of these processes. But the simulation should not be confused with duplication. The computational model of mental processes is no more real than the computational model of any other natural phenomenon.

One can imagine a computer simulation of the action of peptides in the hypothalamus that is accurate down to the last synapse. But equally one can imagine a computer simulation of the oxidation of hydrocarbons in a car engine or the action of digestive processes in a stomach when it is digesting pizza. And the simulation is no more the real thing in the case of the brain than it is in the case of the car or the stomach. Barring miracles, you could not run your car by doing a computer simulation of the oxidation of gasoline, and you could not digest pizza by running the program that simulates such digestion. It seems obvious that a simulation of cognition will similarly not produce the effects of the neurobiology of cognition.

All mental phenomena, then, are caused by neurophysiological processes in the brain. Hence,

Axiom 4. *Brains cause minds.*

In conjunction with my earlier derivation, I immediately derive, trivially,

Conclusion 2. *Any other system capable of causing minds would have to have causal powers (at least) equivalent to those of brains.*

This is like saying that if an electrical engine is to be able to run a car as fast as a gas engine, it must have (at least) an equivalent power output. This conclusion says nothing about the mechanisms. As a matter of fact, cognition is a biological phenomenon: mental states and processes are caused by brain processes. This does not imply that only a biological system could think, but it does imply that any alternative system, whether made of silicon, beer cans or whatever, would have to have the relevant causal capacities equivalent to those of brains. So now I can derive

Conclusion 3. *Any artifact that produced mental phenomena, any artificial brain, would have to be able to duplicate the specific causal powers of brains, and it could not do that just by running a formal program.*

Furthermore, I can derive an important conclusion about human brains:

Conclusion 4. *The way that human brains actually produce mental phenomena cannot be solely by virtue of running a computer program.*

I first presented the Chinese room parable in the pages of *Behavioral and Brain Sciences* in 1980, where it appeared, as is the practice of the journal, along with peer commentary, in this case, 26 commentaries. Frankly, I think the point it makes is rather obvious, but to my surprise the publication was followed by a further flood of objections that—more surprisingly—continues to the present day. The Chinese room argument clearly touched some sensitive nerve.

The thesis of strong AI is that any system whatsoever—whether it is made of beer cans, silicon chips or toilet paper—not only might have thoughts and feelings but *must* have thoughts and feelings, provided only that it implements the right program, with the right inputs and outputs. Now, that is a profoundly antibiological view, and one would think that people in AI would be glad to abandon it. Many of them, especially the younger generation, agree with me, but I am amazed at the number and vehemence of the defenders. Here are some of the common objections.

a. In the Chinese room you really do understand Chinese, even though you don't know it. It is, after all, possible to understand something without knowing that one understands it.

b. You don't understand Chinese, but there is an (unconscious) subsystem in you that does. It is, after all, possible to have unconscious mental states, and there is no reason why your understanding of Chinese should not be wholly unconscious.

c. You don't understand Chinese, but the whole room does. You are like a single neuron in the brain, and just as such a single neuron by itself cannot understand but only contributes to the understanding of the whole system, you don't understand, but the whole system does.

d. Semantics doesn't exist anyway; there is only syntax. It is a kind of prescientific illusion to suppose that there exist in the brain some mysterious "mental contents," "thought processes" or "semantics." All that exists in the brain is the same sort of syntactic symbol manipulation that goes on in computers. Nothing more.

e. You are not really running the computer program—you only think you are. Once you have a conscious agent going through the steps of the program, it ceases to be a case of implementing a program at all.

f. Computers would have semantics and not just syntax if their inputs and outputs were put in appropriate causal relation to the rest of the world. Imagine that we put the computer into a robot, attached television cameras to the robot's head, installed transducers connecting the television messages to the computer and had the computer output operate the robot's arms and legs. Then the whole system would have a semantics.

g. If the program simulated the operation of the brain of a Chinese speaker, then it would understand Chinese. Suppose that we simulated the brain of a Chinese person at the level of neurons. Then surely such a system would understand Chinese as well as any Chinese person's brain.

And so on.

All of these arguments share a common feature: they are all inadequate because they fail to come to grips with the actual Chinese room argument. That argument rests on the distinction between the formal symbol manipulation that is done by the computer and the mental contents biologically produced by the brain, a distinction I have abbreviated—I hope not misleadingly—as the distinction between syntax and semantics. I will not repeat my answers to all of these objections, but it will help to clarify the issues if I explain the weaknesses of the most widely held objection, argument c—what I call the systems reply. (The brain simulator reply, argument g, is another popular one, but I have already addressed that one in the previous section.)

The systems reply asserts that of course *you* don't understand Chinese but the whole system—you, the room, the rule book, the bushel baskets full of symbols—does. When I first heard this explanation, I asked one of its proponents, "Do you mean the room understands Chinese?" His answer was yes. It is a daring move, but aside from its implausibility, it will not work on purely logical grounds. The point of the original argument was that symbol shuffling by itself does not give any access to the meanings of the symbols. But this is as much true of the whole room as it is of the person inside. One can see this point by extending

the thought experiment. Imagine that I memorize the contents of the baskets and the rule book, and I do all the calculations in my head. You can even imagine that I work out in the open. There is nothing in the "system" that is not in me, and since I don't understand Chinese, neither does the system.

The Churchlands in their companion piece produce a variant of the systems reply by imagining an amusing analogy. Suppose that someone said that light could not be electromagnetic because if you shake a bar magnet in a dark room, the system still will not give off visible light. Now, the Churchlands ask, is not the Chinese room argument just like that? Does it not merely say that if you shake Chinese symbols in a semantically dark room, they will not give off the light of Chinese understanding? But just as later investigation showed that light was entirely constituted by electromagnetic radiation, could not later investigation also show that semantics are entirely constituted of syntax? Is this not a question for further scientific investigation?

Arguments from analogy are notoriously weak, because before one can make the argument work, one has to establish that the two cases are truly analogous. And here I think they are not. The account of light in terms of electromagnetic radiation is a causal story right down to the ground. It is a causal account of the physics of electromagnetic radiation. But the analogy with formal symbols fails because formal symbols have no physical, causal powers. The only power that symbols have, qua symbols, is the power to cause the next step in the program when the machine is running. And there is no question of waiting on further research to reveal the physical, causal properties of 0's and 1's. The only relevant properties of 0's and 1's are abstract computational properties, and they are already well known.

The Churchlands complain that I am "begging the question" when I say that uninterpreted formal symbols are not identical to mental contents. Well, I certainly did not spend much time arguing for it, because I take it as a logical truth. As with any logical truth, one can quickly see that it is true, because one gets inconsistencies if one tries to imagine the converse. So let us try it. Suppose that in the Chinese room some undetectable Chinese thinking really is going on. What exactly is supposed to make the manipulation of the syntactic elements into specifically Chinese thought contents? Well, after all, I am assuming that the programmers were Chinese speakers, programming the system to process Chinese information.

Fine. But now imagine that as I am sitting in the Chinese room shuffling the Chinese symbols, I get bored with just shuffling the—to me—meaningless symbols. So, suppose that I decide to interpret the symbols as standing for moves in a chess game. Which semantics is the system giving off now? Is it giving off a Chinese semantics or a chess semantics, or both simultaneously? Suppose there is a third person looking in through the window, and she decides that the symbol manipulations can all be interpreted as stock-market predictions. And so on. There is no limit to the number of semantic interpretations that can be assigned to the symbols because, to repeat, the symbols are purely formal. They have no intrinsic semantics.

Is there any way to rescue the Churchlands' analogy from incoherence? I said above that formal symbols do not have causal properties. But of course the program will always be implemented in some hardware or another, and the hardware will have specific physical, causal powers. And any real computer will give off various phenomena. My computers, for example, give off heat, and they make a humming noise and sometimes crunching sounds. So is there some logically compelling reason why they could not also give off consciousness? No. Scientifically, the idea is out of the question, but it is not something the Chinese room argument is supposed to refute, and it is not something that an adherent of strong AI would wish to defend, because any such giving off would have to derive from the physical features of the implementing medium. But the basic premise of strong AI is that the physical features of the implementing medium are totally irrelevant. What matters are programs, and programs are purely formal.

The Churchlands' analogy between syntax and electromagnetism, then, is confronted with a dilemma; either the syntax is construed purely formally in terms of its abstract mathematical properties, or it is not. If it is, then the analogy breaks down, because syntax so construed has no physical powers and hence no physical, causal powers.

If, on the other hand, one is supposed to think in terms of the physics of the implementing medium, then there is indeed an analogy, but it is not one that is relevant to strong AI.

Because the points I have been making are rather obvious—syntax is not the same as semantics, brain processes cause mental phenomena—the question arises, How did we get into this mess? How could anyone have supposed that a computer simulation of a mental process must be the real thing? After all, the whole point of models is that they contain only certain features of the modeled domain and leave out the rest. No one expects to get wet in a pool filled with Ping-Pong-ball models of water molecules. So why would anyone think a computer model of thought processes would actually think?

Part of the answer is that people have inherited a residue of behaviorist psychological theories of the past generation. The Turing test enshrines the temptation to think that if something behaves as if it had certain mental processes, then it must actually have those mental processes. And this is part of the behaviorists' mistaken assumption that in order to be scientific, psychology must confine its study to externally observable behavior. Paradoxically, this residual behaviorism is tied to a residual dualism. Nobody thinks that a computer simulation of digestion would actually digest anything, but where cognition is concerned, people are willing to believe in such a miracle because they fail to recognize that the mind is just as much a biological phenomenon as digestion. The mind, they suppose, is something formal and abstract, not a part of the wet and slimy stuff in our heads. The polemical literature in AI usually contains attacks on something the authors call dualism, but what they fail to see is that they themselves display dualism in a strong form, for unless one accepts the idea that the mind is completely independent of the brain or of any other physically specific system, one could not possibly hope to create minds just by designing programs.

Historically, scientific developments in the West that have treated humans as just a part of the ordinary physical, biological order have often been op-

posed by various rearguard actions. Copernicus and Galileo were opposed because they denied that the earth was the center of the universe; Darwin was opposed because he claimed that humans had descended from the lower animals. It is best to see strong AI as one of the last gasps of this antiscientific tradition, for it denies that there is anything essentially physical and biological about the human mind. The mind according to strong AI is independent of the brain. It is a computer program and as such has no essential connection to any specific hardware.

Many people who have doubts about the psychological significance of AI think that computers might be able to understand Chinese and think about numbers but cannot do the crucially human things, namely—and then follows their favorite human specialty—falling in love, having a sense of humor, feeling the angst of postindustrial society under late capitalism, or whatever. But workers in AI complain—correctly—that this is a case of moving the goalposts. As soon as an AI simulation succeeds, it ceases to be of psychological importance. In this debate both sides fail to see the distinction between simulation and duplication. As far as simulation is concerned, there is no difficulty in programming my computer so that it prints out, "I love you, Suzy"; "Ha ha"; or "I am suffering the angst of postindustrial society under late capitalism." The important point is that simulation is not the same as duplication, and that fact holds as much import for thinking about arithmetic as it does for feeling angst. The point is not that the computer gets only to the 40-yard line and not all the way to the goal line. The computer doesn't even get started. It is not playing that game.

FURTHER READING

MIND DESIGN: PHILOSOPHY, PSYCHOLOGY, ARTIFICIAL INTELLIGENCE. Edited by John Haugeland. The MIT Press, 1980.
MINDS, BRAINS, AND PROGRAMS. John Searle in *Behavioral and Brain Sciences*, Vol. 3, No. 3, pages 417-458; 1980.
MINDS, BRAINS, AND SCIENCE. John R. Searle. Harvard University Press, 1984.
MINDS, MACHINES AND SEARLE. Stevan Harnad in *Journal of Experimental and Theoretical Artificial Intelligence*, Vol. 1, No. 1, pages 5-25; 1989.

Capturing Your Creativity

Steve Kaplan

Steve Kaplan is a free-lance writer living in St. Paul, Minnesota, and a contributing editor of St. Paul Magazine.

Many creative people approach their own creativity much as the Supreme Court approaches pornography: They cannot define it, but they can recognize it when they see it. However, the last few decades have witnessed the rise of a group of creative people who believe that creativity is a skill that can be learned, exercised, and developed by people of all ages and occupations.

This concept has been warmly welcomed by people who would like to think more creatively. But nowhere has the teaching of creativity been more openly embraced and supported than in the business world. The creative edge can often mean the difference between a failed product and a resounding success. Take, for example, the case of the forgotten adhesive and the creative chorister.

Art Fry, a researcher for 3M, sings every Sunday in his choir at North Presbyterian Church in St. Paul, Minnesota. Fry marked the pages of his hymnal in the time-honored way—with scraps of paper. Often, though, the paper would fall out of place without his noticing. He'd get up to sing only to find the marker gone, leaving him scrambling to find his place.

"I don't know if it was a dull sermon or divine inspiration," says Fry, "but one morning during services my mind began to wander and suddenly I thought of an adhesive that had been discovered several years earlier by another 3M scientist." That scientist had been attempting to find a strong adhesive product but instead had discovered an unusually weak one: It was strong enough to hold but could be easily removed. The product was considered a failure and was relegated to descriptions in the back pages of dusty files. In a burst of creativity, Fry realized that the failed adhesive would be ideal as a "temporary, permanent" bookmark.

By the time he took the idea to work with him the next morning, he had already made the mental leap to using the adhesive for notepaper. In a moment of inspiration Fry had created Post-its, the most successful new product 3M has had in the past decade.

With stakes so high, it's little wonder that business and education have taken a serious interest in the matter of creativity training.

In the early 1970s, studies began to suggest that creativity was not some special and mysterious force but a faculty inherent in all human beings. That great gift, though, begins to fade as children become socialized and learn to see the world as everyone around them does. Tests have shown that a child's creativity plummets 90 percent between the ages of five and seven. By the time they're forty, most adults are about 2 percent as creative as they were at five.

But some of what has been lost can be recovered. In 1975 psychologists began experimenting with creativity training, with overwhelmingly positive results. Since that time, creativity training has become a growing business in the United States. Much of this training is aimed at the business community, which has both the will to use it and the money to seek it out. The techniques taught by creativity trainers, though, work as well for homemakers and salesmen as they do for researchers and chief executive officers.

Creativity training comes in all shapes and packages. There are creativity purveyors who specialize in group process, in individual training, in product positioning and naming, and a hundred other specialized areas. Below, three successful creativity trainers share some of the methods they use to jog their clients' imaginative faculties. What works for their clients is bound to work for you.

Al Fahden: Pumping irony

"Creating is quite easy," says Al Fahden, creativity teacher, "if we can just get our clinging minds out of the way." The mind, Fahden says, wants to cling to order, to things as they have been in the past. We program our minds, like a computer, to do a particular task; thereafter, the mind looks for a replicable pattern to use. "But when we decide to go another way," he says, "the mind clings, it fights back, it doesn't want to change. It's been said that the mind is a much better slave than it is a master. But if that is so, we're going to be stuck doing the same things again and again."

To find a way out of this dilemma, Fahden has developed a relatively simple three-point system that he believes can turn everyone into a creative person. "The theory itself is very simple," Fahden says.

"I'll say it the way that Niels Bohr, the Danish physicist, said it, and that is that the opposite of truth is not necessarily a falsehood, but often an even greater truth. And this is what I have observed as well. That there is some kind of unity in opposites in every great idea. Using this, I've tried to find a structure for creativity. I've read just about everything you can read about creativity, and they give you everything but a structure, the basic tool. I offer the tool."

Fahden's tool is a three-part process that involves discovering a paradigm and its opposite, then creating a new truth that comes from resolving the first two steps.

"The paradigm," he says, "is reality, or the fact. The important thing here is that facts should be more properly understood, as widely held beliefs. Generally, the reason that we're not creative is that we're stuck in our paradigms. So the first thing I try to do is get people to become aware of their paradigms. We often use selling refrigerators to Eskimos as an example of this process. Most people assume that Eskimos have no use for a refrigerator. But that's because of their assumptions about Eskimos. They're working with Eskimo paradigms of north, igloos, blubber, and parkas, and refrigerator paradigms of cold, insulated, white, and food, among others.

"The second part of the process is to take a paradigm's opposite and put it into a concept statement that creates a contradiction. For example, some opposites of the Eskimo paradigms might be south, condos, pizza, and T-shirts. Some refrigerator opposites would be hot, open, black, and nonfood. Making contradiction statements from these, we would get such things as Eskimos live in the south and refrigerators keep things hot."

The third step of the process is resolving the contradiction, or finding a group of people for whom the statement is true or a way in which the statement is true. In this example, it could be that an Eskimo couple decides to move to Phoenix and live in a condo. Then they might want a refrigerator. Or a refrigerator shipped to the northern wilderness could be used for its insulating properties to keep your food from freezing.

"The irony," says Fahden, "is that there is no right answer, only the most elegant solution. Using this system will help to reach the contradiction, and from there the mind will take over and resolve it, thus getting an abundance of ideas with no anxiety."

Fahden says his three-part process can be used to approach virtually any problem in a creative fashion. He began thinking about creativity after he took charge of a large advertising agency. He tried to recruit all the creative hotshots he knew around town, but none of them would join his agency. He was left with an agency to run and no great creative talent to run it. "All I had working there were beginners," Fahden says, "so I realized I'd better come up with a way to train them or I was in big trouble."

It was that challenge that led Fahden into the creativity theory he now teaches at seminars across the country under the name of "Pumping Irony." Fahden has written a book about his creativity theories, tentatively titled *Aha*, which he expects to publish within the next year.

Paul Maccabee: Make bagels, not war

Anyone can solve a problem by throwing money at it, but it takes a special kind of person to solve his problem using bagels; ten thousand bagels, to be precise. That's the solution that Paul Maccabee, a madman-with-a-method at Mona, Meyer & McGrath Public Relations agency, came up with when commissioned by the owner of a small delicatessen in St. Paul, Minnesota, to solve a parking problem.

It seems that when the property upon which the delicatessen sat was bought by a Texan, he abolished all the barriers that had traditionally delineated parking reserved for deli customers only. Parkers from nearby office buildings cut into customer parking for the restaurant, and the store owner's business began to decline. Instead of suing him, Maccabee designed a program to heighten the landlord's awareness of the problem by blitzing him with free bagels.

Thousands of the deli's customers signed a petition, and the owner was encouraged by Maccabee to send the petition plus ten thousand bagels to the property owner. Not only did the "bagel blitz" campaign save the deli's parking, and possibly the restaurant itself, but because of Maccabee's calls to major newspapers, it earned press attention across the country (including bits in the *Wall Street Journal* and *U.S.A. Today*). Maccabee even had the nerve to write a song rhyming "bagel" with "Hegel" ("Danny's no philosopher, / He's no Nietzsche, Kant, or Hegel, / He's just a little guy with chutzpah, / Who wants to bake a better bagel").

Paul Maccabee is obviously a creative guy, and he owes that, he says, to what he calls the Pasteur theory of creativity.

"I base it," he says, "on Louis Pasteur's comment 'Chance favors the prepared mind.' That means when I begin a campaign, I try to pack my mind with all the possible information about my subject. Then I have to rely on the images that are in my head and everything I've learned about culture and society in the past. That's why the education of a creative person is so important.

"One very famous copywriter goes to see abstract art to jog his creativity . . . then his mind interacts with the abstract forms and he can reach into his subconscious and get what he needs. But to make that method work, you have to have something in your subconscious when you finally do get there."

Maccabee lectures on creativity in advertising and offers the following guidelines:

1. There are no rules for creativity.

2. Avoid any formal education in advertising or public relations. If you must go to school, try studying magic, juggling, improvisational theater, or whatever. Read about the lives of creative people. Reading about Harry Houdini has helped me much more than reading Lee Iacocca could.

3. Creativity is not pretty. You

have to go through a lot of failure before you come to your success. A truly creative person doesn't care if he comes up with a hundred names that are stupid and silly before he finds the right one. Even dare to come up with ideas that are dangerous.

4. Know what to discard as well as what to create. You have to know when to let go of an idea but also when to hold onto it in the face of disagreement. *Casablanca* was originally titled *Everybody Goes to Rick's*. On the other hand, the executives at the movie studio that produced the movie we know as *Star Wars* urged George Lucas to change the title. But Lucas held his ground.

5. Get excited and obsessed. I find that when creative people are excited about a problem, they don't sleep, they eat lousy food, they're totally obsessed with the creative process and the problem they're working on at the moment. As an example, architect Eero Saarinen was assigned to redesign the TWA terminal at JFK Airport in New York. He studied the problem completely but was stumped for a solution. Then one morning he began staring at the grapefruit in front of him at breakfast. He flipped the fruit over and carved into it the revolutionary shape that was to shake the design world.

6. Be curious. Nothing escapes the view of creative people. Louis Pasteur used to drive his friends crazy because when he'd eat dinner, he'd examine their hands and the tablecloth, and if there was a crumb of bread, he'd study it to see its shape.

7. Pay attention. Over and over you'll hear creative people say "I see things other people can see but I think things other people don't think." Consider Bob Chesebrough, a traveling inventor who noticed how Texas oilmen would wipe the gooey "rod wax" off their oil pumps into wounds as salve. This rod wax was a throwaway by-product of the oil. Chesebrough packaged the odorless substance, and now it's sold across the world as Vaseline.

8. Go to sleep. Sleep has creative properties. Thomas Edison would literally doze off for hours at a time

Serendipity, the Mother of Invention

James Schlatter, a chemist with G.D. Searle & Company, was heating a combination of amino acids when he accidentally spilled some on his fingers. A few moments later, trying to pick up a piece of paper, Schlatter licked his fingers and noticed a very sweet taste. The chemist wasn't looking for an artificial sweetener, but good luck—and his own clear observations—dropped the discovery into his lap. He eventually traced the sweet taste back to his mixture of amino acids, which resulted in the discovery of aspartame, an artificial sweetener that Searle has marketed since 1982 under the names "NutraSweet" and "Equal." The company, which wasn't even in the food business at the time, now makes almost a billion dollars a year from aspartame.

Other creative ideas that were born from haphazard observations include:

● *The circular saw.* Sister Tabatha Babbett, a Shaker, was sitting at her spinning wheel early in the nineteenth century, watching two men sawing a board. She wondered why the men couldn't put the blades of a saw on a wheel such as the one she was working on, thus making their work a lot easier. The men listened to her idea, and the circular saw was born.

● *Teflon.* Chemist Roy J. Plunkett was experimenting with gases in 1938 while looking for alternate refrigerant materials when he noticed that one of the gases he had stored had turned into a waxy, white solid. He tested the strange solid and found it to be extremely slippery, unaffected by extreme temperatures, and resistant to most chemicals. Today Teflon is used not only for kitchenware, but in space suits, automobiles, fabrics, and even to insulate subway cables.

● *Slinkys.* Lots of sailors saw the torsion springs of boats during World War I, but naval engineer Richard James saw the springs fall off a table and bounce and thought they would make a good children's toy. He obtained a patent on the device and began producing the toys with his wife. Toy stores were not interested in buying the strange item, so the Jameses demonstrated them directly to children at Gimbel's Philadelphia store in 1945. Their entire stock of four hundred was sold out in an hour and a half. Since that day, tens of millions of Slinkys have been sold across the world.

● *Scotchgard.* After a 3M laboratory assistant spilled a fluid being developed for aircraft use on her sneaker in 1956, she noticed that the spotted area remained cleaner than the rest of the shoe. She brought her observation to the attention of 3M chemists Patsy Sherman and Samuel Smith, who immediately recognized the potential in such a product. Smith and Sherman eventually developed Scotchgard out of that observation. Today, Scotchgard protects carpets, furniture, clothing and, in other formulations, has more than twenty-five additional applications in home and industry.

while inventing. Elias Howe, the inventor of the sewing machine, was trying to solve the problem of how the machine could be threaded properly. He thought and thought about it and, exhausted, finally fell asleep. While asleep he began to have a nightmare. He was being chased by cannibals who had spears shaped like sewing needles. He tripped and fell; the cannibals were upon him. They lifted their spears and were about to plunge them into him when he looked up and noticed

that there, at the tip of the spear, was the exact kind of eye necessary for his sewing machine. He woke up, grabbed a pen and sketched it out, and his problem was solved.

9. Stop trying so hard. King Gillette was a frustrated inventor who obsessively went through the alphabet looking to jog his mind to find a product he could produce to make him rich. When he finally gave up and went to his bathroom to shave, he thought of the idea of the disposable safety razor.

Fred Meyer: Mine your subconscious

"What creativity is all about," says Fred Meyer, "is delving into the data banks we all have in our heads. In your head is your life experience, your career, your education, but also the time somebody beat up on you when you were in fourth grade, and so on. It's all there and available to tap into, if you can find it. Being able to touch the subconscious data bank is a big part of what creativity is all about."

Meyer runs a business that helps corporate executives reach their subconscious data banks. Executives who come to him may spend anywhere from a few hours to an entire weekend brainstorming new product ideas, product names, manufacturing improvements, or whatever is important to the client. The rules at such sessions are minimal: no ties, shoes off, and no negativity. Out of such sessions have come scores of new products, including Dial's Pure & Natural Soap and General Mills' Brownie Sundaes. A one-day session of General Mills executives responsible for Granola bar production resulted in ideas that reduced production costs by almost a million dollars a year.

Meyer believes that how people get along with each other is vital to the creative process. He calls himself a "process consultant" and is as concerned with the way a group interacts as he is with fostering creativity inside that group. Negativity and fear of speaking up are, to his mind, among the great destroyers of creativity.

"A business that has a problem to discuss," he says, "will call a business meeting, with three levels of management sitting around the table. Imagine that you're a junior there. Everyone is wearing a suit and tie and looking very stiff. You don't dare open your mouth unless you've got a very carefully thought-out position that you know is going to make you look sensible and smart. Here, though, we offer an entirely different situation. We're trying to tap into intuition and hunches and strange new ways of thinking about things and so we encourage people to speculate. About the only thing not allowed in this room is negative criticism."

Meyer has discovered a number of methods to tap into the subconscious data banks of his clients and release their creativity. Among the methods he uses are:

THE EXCURSION. "We may be examining a problem," Meyer explains, "and this is where we say 'Let's forget about this right now and go off and do something else.' If we're working at how to make better flashlights, we'll take the conversation way out to, say, the sex life of clams, or something like that. After we've talked about that for a while we'll say 'O.K., this is what we know about clams, now how does that relate back to making a better flashlight?' I promise you this is going to result in some new ways of thinking about flashlights. You've tapped into some data to bring to the problem that you wouldn't logically bring to it. This process is forcing an incubation artificially."

ATTRIBUTE TWISTING. The first step in this process is to take the attributes of the item in question and list them. If you were dealing with a flashlight, its attributes might be that it has a length, batteries inside, and a switch; it furnishes light; it wears down, and anything else you can think of about a flashlight that is true. Meyer then has his participants match each attribute with an arbitrary choice of two long lists of words that he has labeled "MAKE IT" and "CHANGE." Under the former list are words such as the following: flexible, flicker, zigzag, vacillate, portable, copy, and self-destruct. Meyer says it doesn't actually matter which words are chosen for which list, as the intent is to force new ideas. Participants attempt to make the arbitrary match of word and attribute somehow make sense. Matching, for example, the attribute "batteries inside" with the CHANGE IT word "portable" could lead to imagining a flashlight that could be telescoped from large to small when the batteries were removed.

ROLE-PLAYING. Meyer has some participants enter method acting role-playing games. He may assign such roles as a bag lady in New York, a kid who lives on a ranch in North Dakota, and an over-the-road truck driver. He'll then ask the players to get themselves into the feelings and value systems of their roles, what those lives are like, what kinds of problems those people have and, as much as possible, to step into their shoes. When the players have the role down completely, he'll ask them for ways they can help think about the product or problem in question—for example, the ways in which flashlights might be helpful in their (assumed) lives.

FREE ASSOCIATION. Pure Freudian-type word associations are used to jog the mind into illogical connections.

FANTASY TRIP. After putting participants through relaxation exercises, Meyer may take them on an imagination-provoking fantasy. For instance, "We'll walk them across a field," he says, "and up a hill, and on top of the hill is a big old white house. The doors of the house are open, and we'll walk in the door and turn to the room at the left: Then the participants are encouraged to relate what their experience of the imaginative journey has been."

What all of these exercises are designed to do is move into what Meyer calls "approximate thought," which, he explains, lies somewhere near metaphorical thinking and between rational thought, and the other extreme —hypnotism, meditation, and hallucination. "If we use the same kind of analytical thinking that most of us have been trained to do," Meyer says, "we're not apt to get any ideas that are very new. But if we get up into metaphorical and associative thinking, strange new ways of thinking about problems, we've got a better chance of finding an original approach and answer."

Motivation and Emotion

Some of the earliest work in animal research examined the role of motivation in determining behavior patterns. This work led to the general view that motivation resulted from the deprivation of some desired or needed stimulus event. For example, rats being trained to lever-press under a variety of circumstances were first deprived of food for 23 hours and then reinforced with small food pellets to reward lever-pressing. Unfortunately, the same type of reasoning that guided such research (that is, the emphasis on deprivation patterns), also heavily influenced theories of personality development such as Freud's. Fortunately, more recent theories have taken on a more positive tone.

One very important part of motivation is emotion; people often report making decisions or taking action based on their feelings. Yet the actions that give rise to both the experience of emotional arousal and the expression of that state to others are not yet clearly understood. In the first article in this section, Robert Zajonc revisits some very old theories about emotion, and then proposes, as a result of his own research, a bold and novel approach to understanding the experience of emotions—particularly to the categorization of the experiences as positive or aversive. Whether his tentative theory is correct or not, it is certain to stimulate lively debate and significant research.

The experience of emotion is often very powerful; some people report emotional arousal at levels above their ability to manage. Another way to express this is to argue that high levels of emotional arousal are stressful. Since the mechanisms of emotional response and arousal are well known in their physiology, it is reasonable to wonder whether such high levels of arousal cause changes in the body that may be damaging.

Gina Maranto's article details the impact of emotions on the body: the resulting weakening of defenses against disease is an important part of the picture. More crucial, however, is the question of whether we can adapt to such experiences. Can we be protected against such dangers?

The next two articles focus and extend Maranto's ideas. In "Thinking Well," Nicholas Hall and Allan Goldstein connect the sensitivity and vigor of the immune system to experiences. In fact, animals (including humans) can be conditioned (taught) to alter their immune responses. We can learn to be less or more healthy! In "Dangerous Thoughts," Bernard Dixon extends the level of analysis to the molecular, focusing on neuropeptides. At the same time, he provides an evolutionary basis for understanding the rise in incidence of certain diseases and disorders over generations: increasing levels of stress have systematically weakened natural defenses.

Looking Ahead: Challenge Questions

What practical consequences of Zajonc's new theory of emotions can you envision? If he is correct, how can his work help us to understand the emotional displays of others? Similarly, can we take practical steps to improve the tone and quality of our own emotional experiences?

What types of experiences should young children have to inoculate them against the stresses of elementary school? What types of inoculating experiences would help college students deal with the stresses they face?

If diseases such as cancer may be linked to attitudes, what attitudes will foster the most healthy and vigorous immune responses? Can these attitudes exist comfortably in a social setting without increasing the risk of aggression toward others?

What proof do we have that the links between chemical agents in the body and susceptibility to disease are in fact cause and effect? To be healthy, must we change our lifestyles?

Unit 6

The Face as Window and Machine for the Emotions

Do we smile because we are happy? Or, are we happy because we smile? New studies suggest that both may be true.

Robert Zajonc

Robert Zajonc is the Charles Cooley Distinguished Professor of Social Sciences and director of the Institute for Social Research. He presented the 1989–90 LS&A Distinguished Senior Faculty Lectures, from which this article was prepared.

Emotions are fundamental psychological processes that participate in nearly all aspects of our behavior. Because emotions are the essential ingredients of reinforcement, they are basic to learning and conditioning: a behavior that removes an organism from danger or results in a positive outcome will be repeated. Emotions are also basic to perception and cognition: we attend to what is significant, and what is significant *is* so because of its relation to emotion.

All emotional experiences involve a sudden and vigorous change in the nervous system; we are *always* in a state of emotion, and what we know of emotion is simply a change from one state to another. Some stimuli, such as strong sensory events, are intrinsically capable of evoking emotional reactions. But *any* stimulus can become emotional under particular circumstances: the harmless ticking of a clock is felt as a real threat if we believe it is connected to a bomb fuse.

The bodily manifestation of emotion can be noted in muscular action in the face and other parts of the body, in posture and movement, in modulation of voice patterns, in breathing patterns, and certainly in language. The subjective aspect of emotion is feeling. But where does feeling come from and what is its nature? What is *it* that we feel when we feel sad or angry? For we do feel *something*, since *to feel* is a transitive verb.

The traditional view of the relationship between feeling and expression holds that expression of emotion is the manifestation of an internal subjective state, the externalization of the feeling. The 19th-century psychologist William James had a more radical view. He described the process as the other way around. According to James,

> the more rational statement is that we feel sorry because we cry, angry because we strike, afraid because we tremble, and not that we cry, strike, tremble, because we are sorry, angry, or fearful, as the case may be.

Can both views be correct? My research suggests that the answer to this question may be Yes. We are now learning that the face can display our internal states *and* can itself cause changes in our feelings. How and why it does both is the subject of this article.

The face as a window of the emotions

Psychologists inherited from philosophers the assumption of a mind-body dualism, a dualism that persists in some form to this day. Aristotle's classic remark is unambiguous:

> Mental character is . . . conditioned by the state of the body; and contrariwise the body is influenced by the affections of the soul.

Significant parallels between animals and humans imply the existence of cross-cultural uniformity in emotional expressions. Darwin was the first to undertake a systematic study of this. His classic book is called *The Expression of Emotions in Man and Animals*. He may also have been the first to use the mail questionnaire. He sent a large number of letters to military men, government officials, missionaries, and his friends who lived in distant parts of the British Empire, asking them in a series of very clear questions if the people in those areas expressed grief by weeping, joy by laughing, and so on. The results of his survey led him to accept the proposition of cross-cultural universality of emotional expression.

My colleagues at the Survey Research Center, however, would dismiss Darwin's research, not only because it was unrepresentative, but because it gave more answers about the observers than about those they observed: they could describe what they saw, but they could not judge what the people they were observing actually felt. In fact,

From *LSAmagazine* (University of Michigan), Vol. 14, No. 1, Fall 1990, pp. 17-21. Reprinted by permission of the author.

recent cross-cultural comparisons indicate that while there are several uniformities, there are also considerable differences. It now seems that although there is a good deal of agreement among Americans, Brazilians, Chileans, Argentineans, and Japanese in the facial configuration expressing *happiness* (agreement ranges between 95 and 100 percent), there is much less agreement about the expression that might stand for *fear*.

Different cultures clearly have different display rules. If you grew up in Italy, you are more likely to let your face readily manifest your internal states than if you went to an English public school. Clearly, Darwin exaggerated the universality of emotional expression, but there is, nevertheless, considerable uniformity among what appear to be facial *manifestations* of emotion.

The face is a very special organ, the major instrument of social interaction. Its muscles are capable of countless expressive configurations, all having meaning for others. Observe people in conversation, and you will note that the important thing is not the exchange of knowledge, but the *dance of emotions*, with each participant displaying emotion so as to evoke a particular emotion in the other; the exchange of pure cognitions occurs rarely.

Because of its crucial role in the display of emotion, the face is also a very special perceptual object. It is readily accessible to perception and is very easy to identify and remember. Faces presented for only 150 milliseconds can be judged quite reliably for attractiveness. In fact, specialized cells in the brain have been discovered—in the temporal sulcus—that respond only to faces. These cells do not respond to hands; they do not respond to feet, nor to any other parts of the body, and they do not respond to items of clothing or to flowers. They respond only to faces.

A common supposition is that the eyes are the window of the soul and thus best communicate emotion. St. Jerome (A.D. 342–420) said that "the face is the mirror of the mind, and eyes, without speaking, confess the secrets of the heart." Not so: in an experiment many years ago, photographs of happy and sad faces were cut in half horizontally and the halves exchanged (fig.1). It is obvious from this experiment that the bottom of the face dominates the expression. When you put a sad mouth on smiling eyes, you get a sad countenance; when you

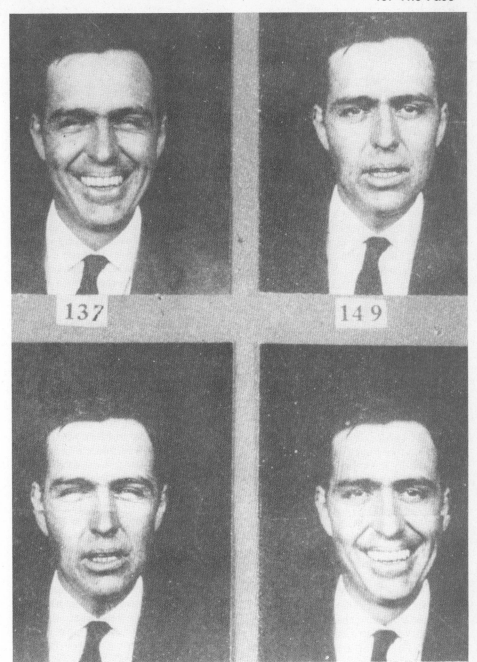

Fig.1. Are the eyes the window of the soul? When photographs of happy and sad faces are cut in half and the halves exchanged, it is obvious that the bottom half of the face dominates the expression.

put a smiling mouth on sad eyes, you get a happy countenance.

Why *are* particular facial expressions associated with particular emotions? Why do we contract the major zygomatic muscle when we are happy? Why don't we pucker instead? This is the question that motivated Darwin's study.

Darwin proposed that emotional expression was an adaptive process that evolved by natural selection. When one bird screeches in distress, other birds are alerted and can be saved from a predator. When an attacker bears its teeth, the attacked animal might leave the territory without a fight, thus preserving both. However, although Darwin began his famous book by asking why particular facial actions accompany particular emotional states, he never came up with an answer; he simply ended with the assertion that the evidence he reviewed proved once again that man descended from lower animal forms.

The next important figure in the debate is William James, who, as noted earlier, turned previous conceptions of emotion and expression upside down. James wrote:

My theory . . . is that the bodily changes follow directly the perception of the exciting fact, and that our feelings of the same changes as they occur *is* the emotion. . . . Common sense says, we lose our fortune, are sorry and weep; we meet a bear, are frightened and run; we are insulted by a rival, are angry and strike. . . . The hypothesis here to be defended says that this order of sequence is incorrect.

When James spoke of "bodily changes," he meant mainly "visceral changes," but he also included respiratory, cutaneous, and circulatory effects as sources for feedback that produces the subjective feeling. Note that this sequence is totally inconsistent with Darwin's idea of emotional expression arising from selective pressures. One can communicate an internal state by outward gesture *only* if that state has already been felt. If the internal state is to *follow* the gesture—the crying, the striking, the trembling—it would be quite difficult to explain the adaptive value of particular expressions.

Of course, James was immediately attacked by several people, whose experiments indicated that the sequence he described did not adequately explain emotion. However, I propose that although James was wrong in his belief that visceral changes are necessary as the basis for our feelings, he may have been right in disputing the traditional classical sequence. Our research suggests that feelings are in fact controlled by hypothalamic temperature, and that the face can cause changes in our feeling states because it can act to control temperature in the area of the brain that is crucially implicated in emotion: the hypothalamus.

The face as a machine of the emotions

"*Expression* of emotions" is the commonly accepted phrase; but note that the very word "expression" is in itself a theory, in that it implies that an internal state is manifested externally. By using this word we commit ourselves to a theory that feelings have to precede a related outward action, as well as to the idea that internal states seek externalization—hence the word *suppression*. But if, as I suggested, the face can *cause* internal changes as well as register them, these terms are somewhat misleading. More neutral terms would be

facial action or *facial efference*.

I was compelled to come to the conclusion that facial action can precede and even *cause* feelings, on the basis of our recent studies, which were stimulated by a book written in 1907 by Israel Waynbaum, a Russian immigrant to France who wrote only one book, and that one hardly known.

Waynbaum, a physician, argued that facial gestures in general, and emotional gestures in particular, have regulatory and restorative functions for the vascular system of the head. He observed first, that all emotional experiences produce a considerable disequilibrium of the vascular process. Second, he noted the curious fact that the main carotid artery is divided at the neck into two arteries, the internal, which supplies the brain, and the external, which supplies the face and skull.

Waynbaum conjectured that this strange configuration exists to allow the facial branch of the artery to act as a safety valve. The muscles of the face could, he thought, press against facial arteries and thus shunt blood away from the brain in case of oversupply and allow greater inflow when the supply is insufficient. In other words, he thought of the facial muscles as tourniquets.

Waynbaum's theory makes better sense than Darwin's in explaining several kinds of facial efference. Darwin argued that we blush because blood rushes to those parts of the body that are under intense scrutiny of others. Those more sensitive to this scrutiny will blush more easily than others; therefore women and children blush more readily than men—an interesting idea, but it isn't obvious what adaptive value such behavior would have. Waynbaum, on the contrary, suggested that blushing results when there is danger of blood flooding the brain. In these cases, blood is shunted away to the face, which becomes flushed. We blush when we are embarrassed and cannot run or hide. Energy is mobilized for flight or fight; blood surges up, but the energy cannot be released, and the face takes it up to prevent congestion to the brain.

It is not surprising that, based on turn-of-the-century physiology, several of Waynbaum's assumptions are questionable and others are outright wrong. Because arterial flow can be controlled directly by vasodilators and vasoconstriction, it is unlikely to be much affected by muscular action of the face.

Nevertheless, much of Waynbaum's thinking can be useful. Facial muscles might not have a significant effect on arteries, but they can affect venous flow. More importantly, by interfering with or facilitating the cooling process of the brain, facial action might alter the temperature of blood entering the brain. Facial action can produce changes in brain blood temperature, which, in turn, has significant hedonic consequences. Such a process may in turn have subjective effects through its impact on the neurochemical activity in the brain. For example, if a certain action of facial muscles results in changing the temperature in a particular brain region that is active in releasing norepinephrine, then norepinephrine might be either partially blocked or released, with subsequent calming or excitation effects. If the action releases serotonin, the action will be an antidepressant. (The absence of serotonin is associated with depressive states.)

To be sure, the conjecture that changes in brain temperature can influence brain neurochemicals associated with subjective emotional states still needs empirical documentation, but it is consistent with the fact that *all* biochemical processes are affected by temperature. Cooling of the brain is a crucial physiological function. The brain is an organ that cannot tolerate temperature variations as readily as other organs, and its cooling relies heavily on heat exchange, whereby venous blood, cooled by evaporation, exchanges heat with the arterial blood entering the brain. In addition, brain temperature is controlled by the temperature of venous blood that reaches the cavernous sinus, a venous configuration enveloping the internal carotid just before the latter enters the brain (fig.2).

The cooling function of the cavernous sinus has been verified by experiments with animals. The near panic felt by people whose nasal airways must be packed and the great discomfort experienced by anyone with extreme nasal congestion suggest that nose breathing serves another function besides air intake. In each of these cases the cooling action of the cavernous sinus is severely restricted. It seems likely, therefore, that the cooling action of the cavernous sinus has an important influence on the subjective state of an individual.

I must say here that we really don't know exactly how the cavernous sinus does its job, but we do know that the temperature of the blood before it enters the brain is about .3°C warmer than after it has passed through the cavernous sinus.

To summarize:

1. Subjective feeling states—feeling good and feeling bad—are the result of neurochemical activity of the brain.

2. Neurochemical activity that is implicated in emotion is temperature-sensitive.

3. Therefore, changes in brain temperature can modulate neurochemical activity of the brain and will be experienced as changes in feeling states.

4. The metabolic activity of the brain produces considerable amounts of heat, and the brain, therefore, requires continuous cooling.

5. Hypothalamic cooling depends on the temperature of the arterial blood supplying it.

6. The temperature of the arterial blood that supplies the brain is cooled by the cavernous sinus, a venous structure that surrounds the internal carotid artery.

7. Facial veins, including those from the nasal airways, drain into the cavernous sinus, or they can drain into the external jugular vein, and they carry cooled blood, which cools the internal carotid artery.

8. Both breathing patterns and facial muscular action control the temperature and the flow in the veins that empty into the cavernous sinus.

9. Because the metabolic activity of the brain requires continuous cooling, the absence of cooling is felt as discomfort and negative affect, whereas increased cooling is felt as pleasurable and positive affect.

This, then, is a process that connects subjective feeling states in the emotions to bodily processes—a form of resolution to the mind-body problem. In recent experimental work we examined the connections between facial expressions and feeling states. We wanted to learn whether facial action alone, without accompanying emotional excitation, can change subjective states. Can facial action have hedonic consequences?

Look at the expressions on the faces in figures 3 and 4. One's first impression is that they are indications of a felt emotion. In fact, the subject is saying "cheese" (fig.3) and "für" (fig.4). A number of experiments have now shown that the expressions accompanying phonetic actions that resemble positive emotional expressions (such as saying "cheese") generate lower temperatures and positive affect, while those accompanying phonetic actions that resemble

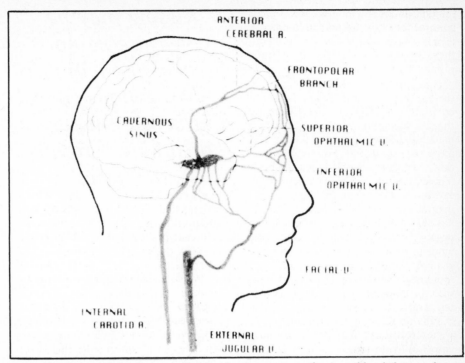

Fig.2. Brain temperature is controlled by the temperature of venous blood that reaches the cavernous sinus, a venous configuration enveloping the internal carotid just before the latter enters the brain.

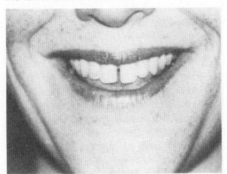

Fig.3. Person saying "cheese."

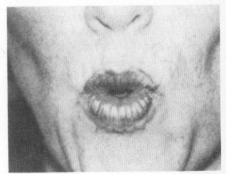

Fig.4. Person saying "für."

negative emotional expressions (saying the German "für") generate higher temperatures and negative affect. In one study, German subjects read stories containing many instances of the German umlaut (the phoneme $ü$ [ue]), which requires action the opposite of a smile; they also read stories that did not contain many umlauts. When they read the stories with the many $ü$'s, their forehead temperatures were elevated and the concurrent feelings were negative; in contrast, when they read the other stories, temperatures remained normal and feelings neutral.

Further experiments invited subjects to breathe what they supposed were subtle odors and to indicate whether the odors were pleasant or unpleasant. In fact, the air they breathed was either slightly heated or slightly cooled. The result was that the subjects' forehead

temperatures went down with cooled air and up with warm air. More important, these changes were correlated with positive and negative feelings. Experiments with animals substantiated these findings.

The varied roles of sneezing, sucking, and smiling

If the vascular theory of hedonic states makes any sense, it is reasonable to suppose that universality of emotional facial action evolved not because it served a communicative function, as Darwin argued, but because it was a useful regulator of brain temperature. As an added attraction, it also became an emotional language. Viewed in this light, the smile is similar to a sneeze, which is a regulatory process and tells us something about the internal state of the sneezer. The sneeze is present in humans and many animals and is cross-cultural, but it is not an emotional expression; we don't sneeze to inform those around us of a difficulty in our respiratory system.

Another line of research is exploring the link between brain temperature and emotion in a different way. It turns out that the metaphors "hothead," "boiling mad," and "cool as a cucumber" are not altogether accidental. Forehead temperature, which is very diagnostic of brain temperature, is higher for a person expressing anger than for one with a neutral expression. Extensive research has also shown that aggression and negative affect occur more readily when ambient temperature is high. In one example, students gave an instructor more negative ratings under conditions of high temperature than in moderate temperature.

Why do we scratch our heads when we are confused? Why do we rub our chins? Why do some people bite their

Kissing may be pleasurable not because the mouth is an erogenous zone, but because it forces breathing through the nose.

fingernails, or pens or pencils? Why do people chew gum? My answer to these questions is that these movements may help cool brain blood by moving cooled blood to the cavernous sinus more efficiently.

Thumb-sucking may be a prime example of this. Sucking is a powerful unlearned action that is very hard to extinguish, even after the reinforcement and obvious incentives are long gone. Why? Sucking is an activity that forces

nasal breathing—deep nasal breathing that can cool the brain quite efficiently—and it is not unlikely that this releases endorphins, for it seems to have a pacifying effect. Cooling of the brain is particularly important for infants, whose brain produces 80 percent of body heat. So, there are two reasons for sucking: sucking for milk, which is indeed a reflex that is probably a result of natural selection pressures; and sucking that results in cooling of the brain and brings a different kind of satisfaction.

Kissing, too, may be pleasurable not because the mouth is an erogenous zone, as Freud suggested, but because it forces breathing through the nose. Likewise with screaming and cringing: they have an effect on venous blood flow, which changes brain temperature and perhaps releases endogenous opiates that act as analgesics. Weight lifters scream not to communicate the effort they are making, but to relieve the pain.

EMOTIONS: HOW THEY AFFECT YOUR BODY

GINA MARANTO

Gina Maranto is a staff writer for Discover.

> *Be cheerful while you are alive.*
> —Ptahhotep

Authors of maxims over the millennia have suggested, as did this 24th-century B.C. Egyptian vizier, that life is borne more easily with a smile—even a wan half-smile—than a grimace. That philosophy has survived to the 20th century, which has seen countless practices, both plausible and bizarre, from psychosomatic medicine to biofeedback to hypnosis, proclaiming the relationship between emotions and health, and touting the power of the mind to thwart disease. But only in the past few years have researchers confirmed experimentally that the psyche can actually affect the body.

DEPRESSION AND THE PHYSICAL STATE

Even before solid evidence was in hand, long-range studies of people revealed a tantalizing connection between such psychological states as depression, pessimism, loneliness, and anxiety on the one hand with cancer, heart disease, and other wasting or potentially fatal ailments. The link is now fairly well established. For instance, a National Academy of Sciences panel announced in September that grief over the death of a family member may substantially raise the risk, especially among men, of contracting an infectious disease or of dying of a heart attack or stroke. And although experiments with human subjects are still far from conclusive, a variety of experiments with animals have now proved that higher functions of the brain can influence the physical state. These discoveries suggest that what a person feels, and how he perceives himself and his place in the world, are critical to his physical well-being.

Many researchers—including immunologists, physiologists, psychiatrists, psychologists, and neurobiologists—who have explored the murky boundary between mind and body now suspect that certain negative psychological states, brought on by adversity or a chemical imbalance, actually cause the immune system to falter. Says John Liebeskind, a UCLA psychologist, "I'm fascinated by the possibility that the brain can exert control over the immune system, that our welfare might be determined by our training." Some biologists go so far as to claim that psychological therapy that teaches people how to feel in control of their lives might in some measure "inoculate" against disease and act as a valuable supplement to conventional medical care.

Because evidence buttressing such claims has been hard to come by, most researchers warn against overenthusiastic interpretations of the findings. Nonetheless, they view the new field—whether it goes by the name of psychoneuroimmunology or simply behavioral medicine—as the hottest and most promising area of medical research today. Says Carl Eisdorfer, president of Montefiore Hospital in New York, "One of the great and terribly exciting mysteries is how cognition, or mental activities, relates to physiology."

Detailing that relationship will take years. No one yet knows, for instance, whether each individual emotion sparks a distinct bodily response, or even precisely what emotions are. But, says Paul Ekman, a psychologist at the University of California at San Francisco, "there are now the first glimmerings of hope that researchers can define the role that all the universal emotions—fear, happiness, anger, disgust—play in health."

Reprinted from *Current*, February 1985, pp. 3–5. Originally appeared in *Discover*, November 1984, pp. 35–38. Gina Maranto/© Discover 1984, Family Media, Inc.

EARLY RESEARCH The course of the investigation thus far has been a twisted one. Having only primitive knowledge of the workings of the brain and the complex mechanisms the body uses to maintain its equilibrium, early researchers into psychosomatics (from the Greek for mind and body) studied not specific emotions but the effects of the broad group of phenomena that they defined as stressful. These included any stimulus that seemed extreme enough to provoke a physiological response—for example electric shock, loud noise, cold, starvation, surgery, or fear.

MODERN EXPERIMENTS

Early in this century, the American physiologist Walter Cannon sketched the broad outlines of the body's response to this kind of stress. In a series of experiments he showed that several organs and glands were involved in the response, including the hypothalamus in the brain, the pituitary gland directly beneath, and the adrenal glands atop the kidneys. During the 1930s, the Austrian-born doctor Hans Selye proved that under stress this interconnected system and the sympathetic nervous system primed the heart and muscles for action, for fighting or fleeing; hence the name fight-or-flight response.

These findings soon filtered into the popular press, where they appeared in slightly modified form as the maxims "Stress is bad for you," and "Stress causes disease." But no scientific data then, or now, have actually ever supported either contention. "Stress does not actually cause disease," Eisdorfer says. "What it may do is predispose you to illness or promote a latent disease."

Getting the hard data to support this view required that scientists perform an arduous series of distinctly unglamorous experiments. In the mid-1960s Martin Seligman and Steven Maier at the University of Pennsylvania found that rats given electrical shocks they could not escape became passive. They called the phenomenon "learned helplessness." Then, in the late 1970s, Seligman and colleagues determined that learned helplessness increased a rat's susceptibility to disease. When rats were injected with tumor-causing cells and subjected to inescapable shock, a high percentage of them developed tumors. Rats that could escape the shock by moving to another part of their cage, as well as those given no shock, tended to reject the tumor cells. Recently, Mark Laudenslager, a psychologist at the University of Denver, confirmed that inescapable shock dulls the response of T-lymphocytes—key cells in recognizing bodily invaders—to chemicals that normally cause them to divide rapidly.

Other teams of researchers, working both independently and in concert, helped prove that stress directly interfered with the body's defenses by crippling lymphocytes and other white blood cells, leaving the way open for disease. Then a team of investigators in John Liebeskind's psychology lab at UCLA showed in 1982 that two different kinds of shock triggered two different reactions in a rat's brain. Intermittent shocks of a certain intensity caused it to release endorphins and enkaphalins, the powerful, opiate-like chemicals normally involved in dampening pain. Continuous shock of the same intensity did not prompt this reaction. Following up on this work, Yehuda Shavit, then a graduate student in the lab, showed conclusively that the opiate shock harmed the body.

Shavit suspects that opiates wreak havoc with the immune system by latching on to white blood cells called natural killer cells, which hunt out and kill certain tumor cells. Laden with opiates, the killer calls may falter and be less successful in their vigil against cancers. Or the opiates may boost the release of some hormones that, in the test tube at least, slow the activity of killer cells.

Why should the brain's reaction to terrifying or inescapable situations harm the immune system? Some researchers suggest that the difference may be one of degree: only stresses extreme enough to provoke the release of opiates may lower resistance. Says Laudenslager, "I don't think we would be here today if every time we had a minor pain our immune system went down." In fact, other scientists think that small periodic doses of stress may actually have some benefit: they may help an animal learn how to deal with its environment more rapidly than it otherwise would.

Still other investigators believe that the brain and the immune system may sometimes be at odds, that, ordinarily, merely adopting a positive attitude toward problems or difficulties may prevent the tilt in body chemistry that harms immunity. "One of the things we now know," says Carl Eisdorfer, "is that if you create a way of dealing with the event mentally, it decreases your chance of being negatively affected."

THE SIGNIFICANCE OF PERCEPTIONS

Several recent studies support that contention. September's National Academy report notes that a sizable fraction of Americans whose spouses die (800,000 annually) sink into depression for as long as three years. This mental agony has a bodily counterpart: depressed activity of the immune system's lymphocytes. For men in poor health, especially those with few friends or relatives, the NAS panel concluded, the result can be a fatal illness. A report released by the Health Insurance Plan of Greater New

York in August showed that of more than 2,000 men who had suffered one heart attack, those who were loners and under a great deal of stress on the job or at home had four times the risk of having a second, fatal attack than men who were sociable and under little stress. (In addition, the study contradicted the theory that hard-driving, so-called type A people are most likely to succumb to heart attacks, because few of the victims fitted that profile.) The researchers hypothesize that hormones released during stress may have made the hearts of the high-risk men vulnerable to fibrillation.

The fact that individuals show such a varied degree to resilience to disease has suggested that dumping all seemingly negative events under the category "stress" is sloppy and unscientific. "Using the overarching term stress smears all results," Seligman says. He recommends that events be categorized according to a person's perception of them: good or bad, controllable or uncontrollable, predictable or unpredictable, intense or mild. Laudenslager offers an example: the death of a spouse will be viewed differently, depending on the context. "If the police come to your house in the middle of the night to tell you your husband is dead, that's a totally unpredictable, uncontrollable event. That's going to hit you very differently from watching your spouse dying of a painful form of cancer. Then, you might actually prefer to see him taken out of his misery."

Ekman thinks researchers also need to define more precisely just what qualifies as an emotion. In a provocative report last year, he and his colleague Robert Levenson concluded that simply moving the facial muscles to create the masks of anger, fear, or other emotions, or re-creating the feeling mentally, can have profound physiological effects: increasing the heartbeat, raising body temperature, and producing other distinct shifts in the autonomic nervous system, the network of nerves that carries signals directly from the brain to the heart muscle, smooth muscles, and glands.

These findings, Ekman contends, offer strong evidence that each emotion wreaks its own unique changes on the autonomic nervous system. Yet, he says, because normal emotions are fleeting, they are unlikely to provoke health problems. The villains, he suggests, are psychological states of longer duration—emotions that have run amuck. He breaks these states into four categories: emotions, moods, emotional traits, and emotional disorders, each lasting for a longer period than the one before. Sadness, for example, is an emotion; feeling blue is a mood; melancholy is a trait; and depression is the disorder. Only traits and disorders, Ekman thinks, can have long-term health consequences. "Emotions have evolved because they are useful to the species," he says, "and it's possible that moods have as well. But when a whole personality is organized with anger as its salient emotion, it may cause health problems."

IMMUNE SYSTEM

Before behavioral medicine investigators can track the way in which the mind can harm or help the body, they may need to devise new and better procedures for assessing the strength of the immune system. In addition, they need to have a better understanding of how the entire immune system works. Doing more experiments will require more financing, which could be a problem; government and private agencies are reluctant to provide money for research that crosses scientific disciplines. But the researchers remain hopeful. "We always work by half measures in science," says Eisdorfer. "At least people from various disciplines are talking about the issues now."

"We're beginning to discover the anatomical connections between the brain and the body," says Yehuda Shavit. "Now we just have to show how the whole thing works." Indeed, Jonas Salk, developer of the first polio vaccine, thinks that the time may be right for a major clinical study of the effects of emotional states on the body. The study would take years, might cost millions, and would involve an enormous cast: dozens of scientists from various disciplines and as many as 4,000 children would would be monitored over a period of years. But if the project could show that children who consciously attempted to view themselves as creatures in control of their lives thrived and stayed healthier than their peers, it would be worth the investment. "The people who do such a study," says Salk, "will be the poets of biology."

THINKING WELL

The Chemical Links Between Emotions and Health

Nicholas R. Hall and

Allan L. Goldstein

Nicholas R. Hall, with training in psychology, neuroendocrinology, and immunology, is associate professor, and Allan L. Goldstein is professor and chairman, in the department of biochemistry at the George Washington University School of Medicine, in Washington, D.C.

In 1977, a twenty-eight-year-old Philippine-American woman, feeling weak and complaining of pain in her joints, visited a clinic in Longview, Washington. A physician there ordered blood and urine tests and, based on their results, concluded that the woman was suffering from systemic lupus erythematosus, a disease in which the body's immune system attacks healthy organs with all the ferocity it usually reserves for life-threatening intruders. After various drugs failed to restore her health, the woman sought the advice of another physician, who examined samples of her kidney tissue, confirmed the original diagnosis, and recommended that she follow an aggressive therapeutic regimen using drugs that would dampen the immune system's misguided assault. Instead, the patient decided to return to her native village, in a remote part of the Philippines, where she was treated according to local custom: a witch doctor removed the curse that had been placed on her by a former suitor. Three weeks later, back in the United States, she showed none of the symptoms she had earlier displayed, and two years afterward she gave birth to a healthy girl.

Had this case been reported in one of the nation's tabloids (indeed, it bears all the earmarks of such a sensational story), it might have escaped serious attention. But it was published in *The Journal of the American Medical Association*, in 1981. Significantly, neither the author—Richard Kirkpatrick, of Saint John's Hospital, in Longview—nor, by implication, the journal disputed the basic facts: a serious form of autoimmune disease had been swiftly and, by all indications, permanently reversed. Rather than attempt to explain the transformation, Kirkpatrick concluded his report with a question: By what means did an Asian medicine man cure the woman and, moreover, prevent the medical complications that invariably accompany a precipitous withdrawal from the sort of drug treatment she had been receiving?

The idea that mental states—the target, presumably, of the witch doctor's treatment—influence the body's susceptibility to and recovery from disease has a long and hallowed history. As early as the second century A.D., the Greek physician Galen asserted that cancer struck more frequently in melancholy than in sanguine women. And the belief that disease is a consequence of psychic or spiritual imbalance governed the practice of medicine in both Asia and Europe until the rise, after the seventeenth century, of modern science and its mechanistic view of physiology. But from that point onward, the role of behavior in human disease became a concern proper to none but the superstitious; attempts to empirically investigate the relationship were almost unheard of. Only within the past thirty years, and in particular during the past ten, has the systematic study of this ancient concept been broadly regarded as a legitimate aim of serious medical research.

Scientists have known since the 1950s that the immune systems of laboratory animals can be influenced by behavior. One of the modern pioneers in the field, Robert Ader, of the University of Rochester School of Medicine and Dentistry, has shown that, using the methods of classical conditioning—in this case, by associating the taste of a sweetener with the effects of an immunosuppressive drug—rats can be taught to suppress their own immune responses. And numerous other investigators have demonstrated that when rats and mice are subjected to acute stress—for example, by being confined for short periods of time in crowded living quarters—they become increasingly susceptible to disease.

But in recent years, Marvin Stein and his colleagues, of the Mount Sinai School of Medicine, in New York City, have documented a similar impairment in humans, particularly among men whose wives had recently died. Stein found that during the first few months of bereavement the ability of the widowers' lymphocytes (small white blood cells that spearhead the immune response) to react to intruders sharply diminished. He has also discovered a hampered immune response in people hospitalized for severe depression. In a study done in 1984, Stein documented in such patients not only an ebbing of lymphocyte activity but also a decline in the number of certain kinds of lymphocytes circulating in their bloodstreams.

Less established are the effects on the immune system of positive mental states. Indeed, until quite recently, the data have been largely anecdotal. When, in 1976, Norman Cousins, then editor of *Saturday Review*, described how he overcame ankylosing spondylitis, a chronic, progressive disease of the spine, through the use of vitamin C and laughter (and the buoyant, affirmative frame of mind it produced), there existed no empirical evidence beyond the sheer fact of his restored health to support his claims. As many critics were quick to note, information about the influence of behavior on health was scant and equivocal and, besides, spontaneous remissions of ankylosing spondylitis, inexplicable as they may be, were known to occur.

Since Cousins's recovery, however, a number of rigorously controlled studies have provided evidence of a strong link between behavioral therapy and patient prognosis. In one of the most notable, conducted from 1974 to 1984 at King's College Hospital Medical School, in London, a strong correlation was found between the mental attitudes of women with breast cancer and life expectancy. Of the women who displayed aggressive determination to conquer their disease, seventy percent were still alive ten years after their mastectomies; but among those who had felt fatalistic or hopeless, only twenty-five percent survived. And in our own two-year-long investigation, with Stephen Hersh, Lucy Waletzky, and Barry Gruber, we evaluated the effects of a behavioral approach to disease by measuring certain physiological dimensions of immune responsiveness in cancer patients. Among other things, the therapy consisted of relaxation techniques and guided exercises in which patients imagined that feeble cancer cells were crushed by stalwarts of the immune system. The preliminary results of this investigation show that behavioral therapy amplified the immune system's response to disease; in physiological terms, it accelerated the rate at which lymphocytes mobilized to attack foreign bodies and possibly increased their own numbers. This pilot study, if its results are confirmed by further research, will have provided the first thoroughly empirical confirmation of a correlation between mental states and immunity that as recently as five years ago the medical community viewed as a mixture of pseudoscientific hocus-pocus, self-delusion, and dumb luck.

But for all its novelty and importance, documenting a correspondence between behavioral events and the body's response to disease no more constitutes a satisfactory understanding of immune processes than an observed association between eating and tissue growth constitutes an understanding of digestion and absorption. By what means does stress disturb the functions of lymphocytes? Or, to return to the woman with systemic lupus erythematosus, which physiological systems did the witch doctor engage to relieve her of autoimmune disease? If, as a growing body of evidence suggests, mental states can both retard and enhance the body's ability to fight illness, there must exist a functional pathway that links the organ most closely associated with emotions and ideas—the brain—to the organs and tissues that collectively make up the immune system. In fact, two such pathways—one biochemical, the other anatomical—have been discovered.

THE FIRST LINE OF DEFENSE against viruses and bacteria that invade the body is the phagocyte, or cell-eater. When the skin is breached, by means of a wound or a lesion, swarms of these scavenging white blood cells descend upon the scene and devour the trans-gressors one by one until the phagocytes literally eat themselves to death.

Though indispensable, phagocytes make up only the most elementary part of the immune response. In humans, as well as in other mammals, a second type of defense also comes into play, one whose chief distinctions are its abilities to recognize particular invaders (phagocytes are indiscriminate in their appetites) and to tailor highly specific chemical counterattacks. The basic functional units of this immunity are the lymphocytes, so named because of the clear fluid in which they are stored and conveyed.

Like all white blood cells, lymphocytes derive from bone marrow; but whereas some remain in the marrow until they reach full maturity, and are therefore designated B cells, others, early in their development, migrate to the thymus—the master gland of the immune system—and for that reason are called T cells. Both types of lymphocytes circulate through the bloodstream before lodging in such lymphoid tissues as the spleen, the tonsils, and the adenoids, where they remain inactive until confronted with any of thousands of antigens, or foreign substances—organic waste, toxins, viruses, and bacteria.

In the presence of a particular antigen, B cells synthesize and release proteins, called antibodies, that are designed specifically to destroy that antigen. T cells also respond to individual antigens, though not by producing antibodies but by performing a variety of special immunological support tasks. Some, called helper T cells, release lymphokines, chemicals that assist B cells in producing antibodies. Others, killer T cells, attack antigens directly, with lethal substances of their own manufacture. Still others, known as suppressor T cells, help protect the body's tissues from being ravaged by its own immune response, by preventing B cells from making antibodies when they are no longer needed (a breakdown of this function is implicated in such autoimmune diseases as systemic lupus erythematosus).

Other chemical mediators of the immune response that are released by T cells and macrophages (a type of phagocyte) include histamine, which dilates blood vessels in preparation for the arrival of legions of lymphocytes; complement proteins, which, by inflaming the afflicted area, create an inhospitable thermal environment for foreign tissues; and prostaglandins and leukotrienes, substances that help start and stop the activities of macrophages and T cells. This complex arrangement lends to the immune system the flexibility it requires to strategically orchestrate its responses to countless new and varied microorganisms that invade the microenvironment of the body.

IN THE 1960s, investigators discovered that in test tubes certain immune functions of lymphocytes transpired spontaneously, suggesting that the immune system, for the most part, functions independently of the rest of the body; that the behavior of lymphocytes is governed solely by the number and kinds of antigens encountered—a system of self-contained biochemical reflexes. But subsequent research, much of it done in the past few years, has disclosed that not only is the immune system heavily influenced by other bodily processes—in particular, by those of the central nervous system, via the endocrine network (the glands that secrete hormones into the bloodstream), and the autonomic nervous system—but it is also impossible to separate the day-to-day functions of the immune system from those processes.

The best-documented influence occurs along a biochemical pathway that links the part of the brain located beneath the cerebral hemispheres—the hypothalamus—with the thymus gland, where the T cells mature, by means of two endocrine organs—the pituitary and adrenal glands. Outlining the cascade of biochemical exchanges that occur along this hypothalamic-pituitary-adrenal axis illuminates well the subtle but infrangible ways in which the brain and the immune system are knit together. In stressful conditions, the hypothalamus produces a chemical called corticotropin-releasing factor, which induces the pituitary to secrete adrenocorticotropic hormone. This hormone, in turn, stimulates the adrenal glands to release steroid hormones (glucocorticoids) into the bloodstream. It happens that T cells are acutely sensitive to glucocorticoids. This is especially true of nascent T cells, which represent about ninety percent of all T cells present in the thymus at any time. Abnormally elevated glucocorticoid levels will either damage or destroy these cells or prematurely induce their migration from the thymus to other immune tissues. The resultant shrinkage of the thymus is so pronounced that the gland has been called a barometer of stress and its weight used as an indirect way to assay the release of adrenal glucocorticoids. Left on their own, the adrenal glands secrete glucocorticoids in a daily tidal rhythm, and the point at which lymphocytes respond most aggressively to antigens has been correlated with the interval during which the level of circulating glucocorticoids falls to its lowest point.

In short, the biochemistry of the hypothalamic-pituitary-adrenal axis is far more complex than anyone ever dreamed. Not only are the participating hormones diverse, including even such agents as those that regulate reproduction and growth, but they produce different effects from one circumstance to another as well. Glucocorticoids, for instance, are biphasic: in high concentrations they mute the immune response, whereas in small amounts they have been shown to activate it. Complicating the issue further is the disparity between the consequences of acute and chronic stress. Whereas acute stress causes immunosuppression, chronic stress sometimes enhances the immune response. Thus, stress-induced modulation of the immune system involves a matrix of factors, any or all of which may be at work in the response of a single lymphocyte.

AT THE TOP of the hypothalamic-pituitary-adrenal axis, shuttling electrical impulses across the gaps that separate nerve cells in the brain, are the neurotransmitters. These compounds—in particular, serotonin, acetylcholine, and norepinephrine—regulate the secretion of corticotropin-releasing factor from the hypothalamus, thereby triggering the serpentine chain of events that arouse or pacify the immune response. The same neurotransmitters are now being implicated in the control of the immune system via a second, anatomical pathway—the autonomic nervous system.

The autonomic nervous system is to the central nervous system what an automatic pilot is to a pilot; in some sense the autonomic system can be overridden, but it typically operates on its own, regulating the involuntary actions of the heart, the stomach, the lungs, and other organs through a pervasive network of nerve fibers. Only in the past two years have we learned that branches of this network, chiefly the norepinephrine and acetylcholine circuits, are rooted deep within the body's lymphatic tissues as well. In ground-breaking work at the State University of New York at Stony Brook, Karen Bulloch demonstrated that signature patterns of autonomic nerve fibers radiate into the thymic tissues of reptiles, birds, and mammals, including humans, and that the acetylcholine portions of these circuits appear to originate within the brain stem and the spinal cord. No less striking is the discovery, by David Felten, of the University of Rochester, of a similarly unique mesh of nerves in the spleen, bone marrow, and lymph nodes, as well as in the thymus. These neural fibers follow blood vessels into the glands and radiate into fields profuse with T cells, where they likely manipulate lymphocyte processes. All the biological equipment required for such direct intervention is at hand: adrenaline, norepinephrine, and acetylcholine receptors have been identified on the surfaces of lymphocytes.

The discovery that autonomic nerves interlace lymph tissues has recast our view of the immune system. As a whole, it now seems to resemble an endocrine gland, and, like all endocrine tissue, possesses a direct anatomical link to the brain. Though it remains to be seen whether messages carried by that anatomical link flow in both directions—as they do with the endocrine glands—there now is ample reason to believe that such two-way communication takes place by means of the hypothalamic-pituitary-adrenal axis. Since the substances that exert this influence—adrenocorticotropic hormone and beta-endorphin, an internally manufactured opiate; lymphokines and cytokines, the chemical products of macrophages; and the hormonelike thymosins, which are synthesized in the thymus—originate within the immune system itself, they might be called immunotransmitters.

Unknown until recently, immunotransmitters are now turning up everywhere in the body. Here is a partial list of the disparate phenomena under review: Eric Smith and J. Edwin Blalock, of the University of Texas Medical Branch at Galveston, have reported that adrenocorticotropic hormone and beta-endorphin, once thought to have been released only by the pituitary and the brain, are also secreted by lymphocytes. This suggests that many cells of the immune system act as separate, minuscule glands, dispensing agents that modulate the immune response as they migrate throughout the body. According to a 1984 study by James Krueger and his colleagues, of the University of Health Sciences-Chicago Medical School, the cytokine interleukin-1 (also called T-cell activating factor) induces deep sleep and hyperthermia. Both effects accelerate disease recovery and can thus be regarded as elements of the body's sequence of defensive tactics. And in still another confirmation of the action of immunotransmitters, Hugo Besedovsky, of the Swiss Research Institute, has shown that the firing rates of neurons in the brain can be altered by lymphokines similar to those that assist in the fight against viruses.

But it is the family of substances that originate in the thymus—the thymosins—that best demonstrate how the immune system may influence the central nervous system. When injected into the cavities of the brain, thymosin beta four stimulates the pituitary, via the hypothalamus, to release luteinizing hormone, which helps regulate other endocrine glands. Further, adrenocorticotropic hormone and beta endorphin are released by isolated pituitary cells when cultured in the presence of another group of thymic hormones—thymosin fraction five. But most important, it has been shown that immunotransmitters can exercise a direct influence on a neurotransmitter. Hugo Besedovsky has found that the amount of norepinephrine, the neurotransmitter that suppresses the secretion of corticotropin-releasing factor by the hypothalamus, in the brains of rats drops significantly after administration of a preparation that contains thymosin and lymphokines. If the same holds true for humans, it may be that the thymosins can themselves stimulate the hypothalamus by way of a neurotransmitter and thereby set in motion the chain of chemical reactions associated with the hypothalamic-pituitary-adrenal axis.

The precise function of thymosins and other immunotransmitters in the body's defense against viruses and bacteria has yet to be explained, but they most likely modulate the immune response and therefore constitute the final stage of a feedback loop between the central nervous system and the immune system's lymphatic tissues. The concept of a self-correcting functional circuit that ties the brain to the pituitary, adrenal, and thymus glands has been proposed by many investigators. But missing from this hypothetical circuit has been evidence of chemically defined molecular signals between the thymus and the pituitary, by which the brain adjusts immune responses and the immune system alters nerve cell activity. That link is now known to include such immunotransmitters as thymosin.

CLINICAL PRACTICE cannot long remain unaffected by this research. The discovery of pathways that bind the brain and the immune system rescues the behavioral approach to disease from the shadowy practices of witch doctors and places it squarely within the rational tradition of Western medicine. Aware now of the complex physiological basis for behavioral modification of the immune response, physicians can spend less time fielding criticism and more time exploring which types of therapy are of the greatest benefit. We are witnessing the birth of a new integrative science, psychoneuroimmunology, which *begins* with the premise that neither the brain nor the immune system can be excluded from any scheme that proposes to account for the onset and course of human disease.

Regrettably, much of the present debate is preoccupied with the results of behavioral approaches to the treatment of the most intractable, least understood diseases. Consider the argument that unfolded in the pages of *The New England Journal of Medicine* during 1985. In the journal's June 13 issue, Barrie R. Cassileth and her colleagues, of the University of Pennsylvania Cancer Center, reported that in a study of three hundred fifty-nine cancer patients no correlation could be found between behavioral factors and progression of the illness. The same issue included an editorial in which Marcia Angell, a physician and deputy editor of the journal, cited Cassileth's findings to support the view that the contribution of mental states to the cause and cure of disease is insignificant.

If they accomplished nothing else, the responses, to both the study and the editorial, published in the journal's November 21 issue, called attention to the difficulties facing anyone attempting to unravel the relationship between illness and what one writer called the "dynamic richness and variety of human experience." Most of the correspondents had found (or, at least, acknowledged) evidence for the contribution of mental states to human health, but none could agree as to how such states might affect the myriad immunological factors that come into play during the course of a malignant disease.

Unquestionably, much more research regarding the behavioral approach to illnesses such as cancer has to be done. But in the meantime, the most immediately realizable applications of behavioral medicine lie elsewhere. The first, and, in the long run, the most valuable, clinical spinoffs of psychoneuroimmunology will be in disease prevention—initially, in the development of ways to manage stress. As we study further the relationship between behavior and the biochemistry of immunity, the aim should not be to replace the witch doctor with a Western equivalent so much as to reduce the need for both.

DANGEROUS THOUGHTS

How we think and feel can make us sick.

BERNARD DIXON

Bernard Dixon is a contributing editor of Science 86.

UNTIL RECENTLY, Ellen hadn't seen a physician in years. When other people got a bug, she was the one who invariably stayed healthy. But then her luck seemed to change. First she caught a bad cold in January, then had a bout of flu in February, followed by a nasty cough that still lingers. What an infuriating coincidence that these ailments hit as her career was faltering—months of unemployment following companywide layoffs.

But is it a coincidence? Intuition may suggest that we have fewer colds when we are content with our lives, more when we are under stress. That the mind can influence the body's vulnerability to infection in an insidious but potent way is a perennial theme of folklore and literature. Now even scientists are beginning to take that idea seriously. An alliance of psychiatrists, immunologists, neuroscientists, and microbiologists, specialists who rarely look beyond their own disciplines, are beginning to work together in a field so new that it goes under a variety of names, including behavioral immunology, psychoimmunology, and neuroimmunomodulation. Behind these polysyllables lies the challenge of understanding the chemical and anatomical connections between mind and body and eventually,

perhaps, even preventing psychosomatic illness.

Just 10 years ago, most specialists in communicable disease would have scoffed at any suggestion that the mind can influence the body in this way. Textbooks portrayed infection as the simple, predictable outcome whenever a disease causing microbe encountered a susceptible host. Various factors such as old age, malnutrition, and overwork could make a disease more severe. But there was no place for the fanciful notion that elation, depression, contentment, or stress could affect the course of disease.

Today, that once-conventional wisdom is being revised by scientists around the world. Playing a major role in these investigations are researchers at England's Medical Research Council Common Cold Unit near Salisbury. Their work shows that even this relatively trivial infection is affected by the psyche. And the lessons learned may apply to more serious diseases, including cancer.

For nearly four decades now, volunteers at the Common Cold Unit have helped test the efficacy of new antiviral drugs and have proven that colds are caused by rhinoviruses and a few related viruses. In 1975 psychologist Richard

Totman at Nuffield College, Oxford, and Wallace Craig and Sylvia Reed of the Common Cold Unit conducted the first psychological experiments. The scientists infected 48 healthy volunteers by dribbling down their nostrils drops containing two common cold viruses. The researchers then offered 23 of their subjects the chance to take a new "drug," actually a placebo, that would presumably prevent colds. The investigators warned these subjects that if they accepted this treatment, they would have to have their gastric juices sampled with a stomach tube. The scientists had no intention of doing this; the warning was simply a ruse to put the volunteers under stress. The other half of the group was neither offered the drug nor cautioned about the stomach tube. Totman and his colleagues theorized that the 23 offered the placebo would experience either mild anxiety or regret, depending on the decision they made. This might cause them to allay their state of mind by justifying to themselves their decision—as a theory called cognitive dissonance predicts—which would result in greater bodily resistance and milder colds.

The experts were wrong. When an independent physician assessed the volun-

IT'S JUST AN OLD WIVES' TALE

For some researchers, the idea that an individual's attitude can cause or cure disease is nothing more than an old wives' tale. Doctors have been treating the body and mind as separate entities for decades, and many see no reason for change.

In a highly controversial editorial in the prestigious *New England Journal of Medicine*, senior deputy editor and pathologist Marcia Angell said that the media have sold the public a bill of goods on the connection between mental state and disease. She notes that popular literature is full of "heal thyself" incantations, such as Norman Cousins's laughter-and-vitamin-C remedy for disease and Carl and Stephanie Simonton's program, which teaches cancer patients to imagine their healthy white blood cells gobbling up tumors. Angell fears that regimens like these may instill enormous guilt in patients who succumb to illness despite all their attempts to maintain positive attitudes.

She also fears that many studies done under the banner of psychoimmunology suffer from serious flaws in design, analysis, or interpretation. "We have let our standards slip a bit," she says, "because we are too ready to accept our mental state as a major and direct cause or cure of disease." In a notable study of recently widowed spouses published in 1959, for example, Arthur Kraus of the Maryland Department of Health and Abraham Lilienfeld of Johns Hopkins University found a high death rate among the survivors. Angell says, "Although the authors were cautious in their interpretation, others have been quick to ascribe the findings to grief rather than to, say, a change in diet or other habits." She cautions both researchers and the public not to jump to conclusions from meager experimental findings.

Suggesting that there is little evidence for linking stress and disease, Angell writes, "The known physiologic effects of stress on the adrenal glands are often overinterpreted so that it is a short leap to a view of stress as a cause of one disease or another."

Supporting Angell's views is James Melby, chief endocrinologist at Boston University. Melby suggests that researchers sometimes put the cart before the horse—a lymphocyte disorder might cause a debilitating depression, rather than the other way around, for instance—but he notes that such ideas have not yet been tested experimentally.

Not all psychoimmunology research shows a correlation between mental state and illness. In a study published in 1985, Barrie R. Cassileth and her colleagues at the University of Pennsylvania determined that neither positive attitudes nor feelings of depression or hopelessness had significant effects on the survival rate of 359 patients with advanced cancers. Cassileth concedes, however, that a good outlook may improve the quality of a patient's life.

In another study, published in March 1985, Robert B. Case, a cardiologist at St. Luke's-Roosevelt Hospital Center in New York, found no relation between the much-publicized type A behavior and heart disease.

Despite these studies and Angell's persuasive editorial, most researchers in the field of psychoimmunology remain firm believers in the mind-body connection. But they agree they have little in the way of proof. "A lot of the mechanisms for mind-and-body interaction are just being put into place. It is very difficult to do a totally conclusive experiment," says Michael Ruff of the National Institutes of Health in Bethesda, Maryland. But Ruff believes that "emotions and feelings are fundamentally biochemical in nature" and thus could affect the immune system both directly and indirectly.

Neurobiologist Novera Herbert Spector at NIH agrees with Angell on one point only—that patients should not be made to feel guilty about their illnesses. But, he says, popular conceptions that the mind influences the body are not necessarily inaccurate: "The public is sometimes ahead of the medical community." Laughter and a cheerful spirit, he says, are useful in creating a relaxed environment in the body for the immune system to function better.

Angell is not convinced. "Laughter is a worthy end in itself, not as a means or a medicine toward curing disease. That is not science."

—*Beth Py*

---

teers' symptoms, he found that the 23 offered the choice had cold symptoms that were significantly more severe than those given no option. Apparently anxiety generated by contemplating something unpleasant or refusing to help a worthy cause had a tangible influence on the course of the illness.

Totman's group also made some intriguing observations about the way stress affects people outside the laboratory. Volunteers were interviewed by a psychologist, received rhinoviruses, caught colds, and were monitored. Individuals who during the previous six months had experienced a stressful event, such as death of a loved one, divorce, or a layoff, developed worse colds than the others, and introverts had more severe colds than extroverts. Not only were the introverts' symptoms worse than those of their peers, their nasal secretions contained more rhinovirus, confirming that their illnesses were worse.

The Common Cold Unit is now trying to find out how stress affects people with

In one landmark study, 15 men showed depressed immunity after their wives died of breast cancer.

strong social networks compared with their more introverted colleagues.

But how could an individual's mental state encourage or thwart the development of a cold? Research at several centers in the United States supports the most plausible explanation—that psychological stress impairs the effectiveness of the immune system, which has the dual role of recognizing and eliminating microbes from outside the body as well as cancer cells originating within.

The first line of defense of the immune system is the white blood cells called lymphocytes. These include B cells, which manufacture antibodies against microbes; helper T cells, which aid the B cells in making the right kind of antibodies; and killer T cells, which wipe out invading organisms if they have been exposed to them before. Another kind of lymphocyte, the natural killer cell, has received a lot of attention lately for its ability to detect and destroy harmful cells, including malignant ones, even if it hasn't encountered the invaders previously. Together with scavenging white blood cells that gobble up dead cells and debris, the various types of lymphocytes work in complex, coordinated ways to police the body's tissues.

Researchers can measure the efficiency of the immune system by measuring how well a patient's lymphocytes respond to foreign substances. For instance, they can grow the patient's lymphocytes in glassware and expose them to substances called mitogens, which mimic the behavior of microorganisms by stimulating the white cells to divide. Since a rapid increase in the number of white cells is a crucial early stage in the defense against invasion, patients whose white cells don't proliferate may have malfunctioning immune systems.

But most researchers are cautious

about generalizing from the results obtained from a single technique of this sort, since the immune system has complicated backups to keep us healthy even when our lymphocytes aren't proliferating. Nevertheless, reports of stress reducing the efficiency of the immune system have been accumulating on such a scale—and with such variety—that it is becoming difficult to resist the conclusion that anxiety increases our vulnerability to disease.

In one landmark study, for example, Steven Schleifer and his colleagues at Mt. Sinai School of Medicine in New York sought help from spouses of women with advanced breast cancer. They persuaded 15 men to give blood samples every six to eight weeks during their wives' illnesses and for up to 14 months after the women died. While none of the men showed depressed lymphoctye response while their wives were ill, their white cell response was significantly lowered as early as two weeks after their wives died and for up to 14 months later. Schleifer believes he has shown, contrary to earlier studies, that it was bereavement, not the experience of the spouses' illness, that lowered immunity.

Prompted by his observations of the bereaved widowers, Schleifer wondered if serious, debilitating depression would also show up as weakened immunity. When he took blood samples from 18 depressed patients at Mt. Sinai and the Bronx Veterans Administration Hospital, he found their lymphocytes were significantly less responsive to mitogens than those of healthy individuals from the general population matched for age, sex, and race.

We sometimes think humans are uniquely vulnerable to anxiety, but stress seems to affect the immune defenses of lower animals too. In one experiment, for example, behavioral immunologist Mark Laudenslager and colleagues at the University of Denver gave mild electric shocks to 24 rats. Half the animals could switch off the current by turning a wheel in their enclosure, while the other half could not. The rats in the two groups were paired so that each time one rat turned the wheel it protected both itself and its helpless partner from the shock. Laudenslager found that the immune response was depressed below normal in the helpless rats but not in those that could turn off the electricity. What he has demonstrated, he believes, is that lack of control over an event, not the

Scavenging white cells may serve as free-floating nerve cells able to communicate with the brain.

experience itself, is what weakens the immune system.

Other researchers agree. Jay Weiss, a psychologist at Duke University School of Medicine, has shown that animals who are allowed to control unpleasant stimuli don't develop sleep disturbances, ulcers, or changes in brain chemistry typical of stressed rats. But if the animals are confronted with situations they have no control over, they later behave passively when faced with experiences they can control. Such findings reinforce psychiatrists' suspicions that the experience or perception of helplessness is one of the most harmful factors in depression.

One of the most startling examples of how the mind can alter the immune response was discovered by chance. In 1975 psychologist Robert Ader at the University of Rochester School of Medicine and Dentistry conditioned mice to avoid saccharin by simultaneously feeding them the sweetener and injecting them with a drug that while suppressing their immune systems caused stomach upsets. Associating the saccharin with the stomach pains, the mice quickly learned to avoid the sweetener. In order to extinguish the taste aversion, Ader reexposed the animals to saccharin, this time without the drug, and was astonished to find that those rodents that had received the highest amounts of sweetener during their earlier conditioning died. He could only speculate that he had so successfully conditioned the rats that saccharin alone now served to weaken their immune systems enough to kill them.

If you can depress the immune system by conditioning, it stands to reason you can boost it in the same way. Novera Herbert Spector at the National Institute of Neurological and Communicative Disorders and Stroke in Bethesda, Maryland, recently directed a team at the University of Alabama, Birmingham, which confirmed that hypothesis. The researchers injected mice with a chemical that enhances natural killer cell activity while simultaneously exposing the rodents to the odor of camphor, which has no detectable effect on the immune system. After nine sessions, mice exposed to the camphor alone showed a large increase in natural killer cell activity.

What mechanism could account for these connections between the psyche and the immune system? One well-known link is the adrenal glands, which the brain alerts to produce adrenaline and other hormones that prepare the body to cope with danger or stress. But adrenal hormones cannot be the only link between mind and body. Research by a group under Neal Miller, professor emeritus of psychology at the Rockefeller University in New York City, has shown that even rats whose adrenal glands have been removed suffer depressed immunity after being exposed to electric shocks.

Anxiety, it seems, can trigger the release of many other hormones, including testosterone, insulin, and possibly even growth hormone. In addition, stress stimulates secretion of chemicals called neuropeptides, which influence mood and emotions. One class of neuropeptides known as endorphins kills pain and causes euphoria. Endorphins have another interesting characteristic: they fit snugly into receptors on lymphocytes, suggesting a direct route through which the mind could influence immunity.

This idea is borne out in the lab, where one of the natural pain-killers, beta-endorphin, can impair the response of lymphocytes in test tubes. Evidence from cancer studies shows that chemicals blocking the normal functions of endorphins can slow the growth of tumors. And other work suggests that tumor cells may be attracted to certain neuropeptides, providing a route for cancer to spread all over the body.

Neuropeptides are turning out to be extraordinarily versatile in their interaction with the immune system. At the National Institutes of Health in Bethesda, Maryland, Michael Ruff has found neuropeptides that attract scavenging white cells called macrophages to the site of injured or damaged tissue. There the macrophages regulate and activate other immune cells as well as gobble up bacteria and debris. What is even more surprising, however, is that the macrophages themselves actually release neuropeptides. This has led Ruff to speculate that these scavenging white cells may also serve as free-floating nerve cells able to communicate with the brain.

But why should that two-way communication sometimes have the effect of allowing stress to upset the body's defenses? One answer may lie in evolution. When early man was attacked by a saber-toothed tiger, for example, it may have been more important from a survival standpoint for his immune system to turn off briefly. In its zeal to get rid of foreign matter and damaged tissue, a revved-up immune system can also attack healthy tissue. Shutting down the immune system for a short time would avert any damage to the body's healthy tissues and would cause no harm, since it takes a while for infection to set in. As soon as the danger had passed, the immune system was able to rebound—perhaps stronger than before—and go about its main business of fighting invading organisms. But the kind of stress we modern humans suffer is of a different kind: it is rarely life threatening and often lasts a long time, weakening our immune defenses for long periods and making us vulnerable to infections and cancer.

The immune system is extraordinarily complex, and the mind is even more so. As Nicholas Hall of George Washington University School of Medicine says, "We're putting together two kinds of black boxes and trying to make sense of what happens."

In the process, researchers are wrestling with three issues of scientific and social import. First, what can be done to protect people at vulnerable times in their lives from a potentially catastrophic failure of their immune defenses? Second, should counseling and psychological support become as important as traditional therapeutic measures in the treatment of disease? And finally, what are the corresponding benefits to health of the positive emotions of hope, affection, love, mirth, and joy?

MANAGING STRESS AND LIVING LONGER

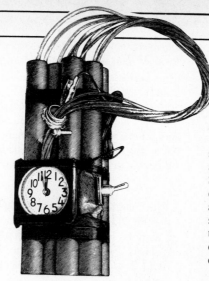

"Every person is born with a genetically predetermined amount of stress-coping energy. . . . When it is depleted, death occurs."

Jerome Murray

Dr. Murray, a clinical psychologist, lecturer, and consultant from Santa Rosa, Calif., is author of From Uptight to All Right.

WARNING! Even though you rigorously follow a stress management program, stress still could be ravaging you and shortening your life. This is true because most people's definition of stress management is erroneous.

To the average person, it means learning to relax and enjoy life, taking time to mellow out in comfortable, stress-free environments, exercising regularly, and a healthy diet. Many, believing themselves to be engaged in pursuing greater health and self-fulfillment, energetically practice relaxation techniques, yoga, meditation, and biofeedback. They play tennis every weekend, jog faithfully, watch their cholesterol intake, and take pride in their enlightened lifestyle.

Millions of dollars are spent annually on gym memberships, exercycles, and other means of improving cardiovascular efficiency. Multimillion-dollar industries have been created to service these enthusiasts' need for clothing and shoes.

The problem is one of timing. Much of the damage attributable to stress has occurred before these stress management efforts even have begun. Permitting yourself to be bombarded by stressors during the day and trying to undo the damage evenings and weekends is the classic "too little, too late." Living a hectic and frenzied life compounded by pressure and frustration and punctuated by periodic attempts to relax and exercise is a parody of stress management. More accurately, it is an endeavor to manage *dis*tress, not stress.

While managing distress effectively is not to be decried, it is analogous to fighting a fire. Even with sophisticated apparatus, the best strategy is to avoid the conflagration in the first place. This means learning to prevent stress from becoming distress, expanding the range of one's coping skills, and not allowing stressors to continue unabated.

Even though distress management techniques have their place, they frequently are nothing more than expensive padlocks to put on a barn already empty of horses. The elimination of stress isn't the answer either. True stress management is distress *prevention.*

In an experiment to find out what would happen in a stress-free environment, subjects were placed in a deprivation tank, where they floated in water warmed to body temperature. The drug curare was used to paralyze muscle movement. Eyes were blindfolded, ears were plugged, and there was nothing to smell or taste, or sensations to which the subjects had to adjust. After a period of relaxation, they began to hallucinate and have delusional thoughts—they became psychotic. Lacking stimulation, the brain produced its own. The marvelous mechanisms of brain and body require stimulation to function. The issue is, how much, how frequent, and how long?

Stress is the body's non-specific response to stressors such as frustrations, conflicts, and pressures. In more general terms, they are known as adjustment demands. Every adjustment we make in life takes its toll in stress.

Yet, stressors, as the deprivation tank illustrates, can not and should not be avoided. They are essential to mental and physical health. Without the stress of learning, there would be no education. Without the stress of exercise, bodies would be flabby and unable to perform.

Stressors are inevitable and even necessary. They serve to condition our minds and bodies, enabling greater performance. Stressors can stimulate growth and confidence and actually assist in keeping us alive. The problem occurs when the stressors exceed our coping ability or continue too long. When that happens, stress becomes distress, and that is the issue of concern.

There are two human conditions having the greatest potential for producing distress—impotence and isolation. When they are experienced, the human organism is at its most vulnerable to stress.

Resist the impulse to jump to conclusions—this type of impotence refers to a psychological state in which we feel a demand to act, but lack the authority or ability.

If you took psychology in college, you may remember studying the "executive monkey" experiment, conducted at the Walter Reed Army Institute of Research. Two monkeys were strapped upright in a plastic box permitting limited movement, a console in front of each of them with a light and a button. The light was turned on 10 seconds before the monkeys received a jarring shock to their feet. The button would prevent the shock if it was pushed within the 10-second grace period. The monkeys learned this fact faster than most graduate students.

The researchers then added an inventive twist. They disconnected a wire to one of the buttons, reconnecting it to the other. Now, one monkey controlled the shock for both. Being responsible for another and having decision-making power, he was dubbed the executive monkey. After 23 days of this pressure, the executive monkey expired. A post-mortem revealed the beginning of atherosclerosis, incipient renal failure, and a perforated duodenal ulcer. The surviving non-executive monkey was sacrificed to the cause of science and found to be without physiological abnormality.

The moral was supposed to be that executives were prone to stress-related diseases because they have responsibility for others. At first examination, that interpretation had face validity, and overstressed executives sympathized with the deduction. It duly was printed in most general psychology textbooks and taught to undergraduates.

However, that conclusion was not supported by attempted replications. Every other attempt to duplicate the original results failed. Each time, it was the monkey whose button didn't work that developed ulcers. He knew he was going to get shocked, but was helpless to prevent it. This state is identified as responsibility without authority, better known in corporations as mid-level management.

The most devastating type of stress is not heavy responsibility—it is having a sense of responsibility without the power to do anything about it. Responsibility won't kill you as long as your buttons work, but feeling responsible for something over which you have no authority will send you to an early grave.

To avoid the distressful consequences of feeling impotent, limit your sense of responsibility to those areas over which you have authority. Parents who agonize over the behavior of children whose age precludes parental authority suffer from impotence. Employees who feel stymied in their careers because of the perceived inadequacies of their supervisors are making themselves impotent. Anyone who laments the quality of his or her life because of inability to control the actions of another suffers from distress. In effect, they are saying to others, "I am powerless to improve the quality of my life unless you change." That produces a feeling of impotence and heightened vulnerability to stress.

This does not suggest that attempts to influence the lives of others are inconsequential. Sometimes, efforts to influence others succeed, causing them to change in ways that enhance the complexion of your life. However, don't be misled—influence is not authority. If others do not respond positively to your efforts to modify their behavior, don't make yourself impotent by persisting in your efforts. Keep the responsibility where the authority is. Ask yourself: "What can I do to live a more successful life even though this other person is not cooperating with my pursuit of happiness?"

That is the only effective question to ask. It focuses the issue on what *you* do—not what others do or don't do. By concentrating on the authority you have to enrich your own life, you will minimize feelings of impotence. This reduces susceptibility to distress and has another important benefit—you'll be happier and more productive.

Isolation

There is ample evidence that vulnerability to stress is intensified by the lack of close, bonded relationships. Social research confirms that we derive something from attachments that, in effect, serve to immunize us from stress. This "need for nearness" is manifested in strivings to feel wanted, needed, and valued. It is met by establishing intimate social bonds and involves the feeling of belonging and being loved. Even the need for self-esteem is an expression of the necessity for nearness. When we feel good about ourselves, it strengthens our confidence that we are worthy of belonging.

Historically, marriage and family have been the prime source for meeting nearness needs. In this age of anxiety, when tranquilizers are the most frequently prescribed medicine, it is not surprising that these institutions are less secure than ever before. Broken families seem to be the rule, not the exception. Sadly, family and marriage do not offer the stability and support they once did.

Actuarial statistics reveal that married people live longer than single people. We simply don't do as well alone as we do when we have intimacy. As the divorce rate escalates, so does vulnerability to stress.

Increasingly, health specialists are adopting the attitude that disrupted social bonds affect the body's immune system, increasing susceptibility to disease. The California Department of Mental Health found the following correlation between social ties and health:

● People who isolate themselves from others face two to four times the risk of premature death.

● Terminal cancer strikes isolated people more often than those with bonded relationships.

● The rates of mental hospitalization are five to 10 times greater for separated, divorced, and widowed persons than for married people.

● Pregnant women under stress and without supportive relationships have three times the number of complications than expectant mothers with intimate ties who are equally stressed.

● Women who can confide in a close friend are much less likely to become depressed.

Moreover, studies indicate the mortality rate of widowers is 40-60% higher during the first six months of bereavement. If remarriage occurs, mortality rates return to normal.

The health risk vulnerability of people lacking committed social bonds is dramatized further by a study examining death rates for smokers and non-smokers. Not surprisingly, those who smoke have higher death rates than people who don't. The most revealing statistic is that, in both smoking and non-smoking populations, single, widowed, and divorced men had the highest rates. Divorced men who smoked had the highest rates of all. Being alone is bad enough; feeling unwanted is worse. If the loss of established relationships increases stress vulnerability, creating loving, committed relationships is the best safeguard against it.

Several microcosmic population groups have been found with high percentages of centenarians. Efforts to discover the secret of their long lives have been inconclusive.

The first, in the U.S.S.R. area of Georgia, led physically active lives, which led to the acceptance of cardiovascular fitness as the explanation. This conjecture was weakened by the discovery of a similar group in India that had a high percentage of its populace living past 100 years of age despite being extremely sedentary in lifestyle. Eventually, the revelation of their high-fiber diet led to its attribution as the genesis of their longevity. In still another community in the Peruvian Andes, the aged not only weren't active, their diet was primarily home-made beer.

Further reflection on these populations reveals only one common tie—in every instance, the communities valued and respected their elders. There were no mandatory retirement age or convalescent homes. There was no segregation by age at all. The older members of each group were involved in community activities, including meaningful work, and were valued for their experience and knowledge. They felt needed, wanted, and loved.

Every person is born with a genetically predetermined amount of stress-coping energy. Using this energy exacts a physiological toll known as aging. When it is depleted, death occurs. The most rapid depletion occurs in conditions of distress.

Think of yourself as a vehicle and the stress-coping energy as gas in your car. The size of your gas tank, set at birth, and how well your engine is tuned determine how much mileage your vehicle will get. Many people treat their lives just like cars. They "run out of gas" long before they should because they don't take care of their "engine" or "drive" sensibly. While you can't change the size of your gas tank, you can do two things to maximize your mileage—keep your engine tuned and don't take any unnecessary trips.

The next time you impotently rage at the "idiot" going 40 in the fast lane, ask yourself: Is it worth it? It could cost you seconds of your life. Do you really want to waste your finite stress-coping energy on someone you don't even know?

Permitting the feeling of responsibility without a corresponding authority to act is like revving the car's engine with the brakes on. It may sound impressive, but it's a waste of gas.

The next time you decide to "write off" any of the people in your life because they have offended you, ask yourself: Can I afford it? Do you really want to lose the potential support and nourishment represented by that relationship? Doesn't it make more sense to salvage it?

As important as diet and exercise are to "tuning up your engine," they are not as crucial as avoiding the feeling of isolation. Making and maintaining loving relationships is the single most important way to stress-proof your personality. Minimizing feelings of impotence and isolation are the philosophical heart of stress management.

Development

Philosophical principles that give definition to developmental psychology have their roots in the evolutionary biology of Darwin, Wallace, and Spencer, and in the embryology of Preyer. Both James Mark Baldwin and G. Stanley Hall, the two most influential developmental psychologists of the early twentieth century, were influenced by questions about phylogeny (species' adaptation) and ontogeny (individual adaptation or fittingness). Baldwin challenged the assertion that species changes (phylogeny) precede individual organism changes (ontogeny). Instead, Baldwin argued that ontogeny precedes phylogeny. Thus, from the outset, developmental psychology has focused on the forces that guide and direct development. Early theorists like Arnold Gesell stressed maturation as the guiding force in development. Other theorists argued that the guiding forces of development were to be found in the environment. Contemporary developmentalists generally accept some version of the epigenetic principle that asserts that development is an emergent process of active, dynamic, reciprocal, and systemic change. This systems perspective forces one to think about the historical, social, cultural, interpersonal, and intrapersonal forces that shape the developmental process, and it explicitly endorses heredity-environment interactionism.

In the past few years we have all been made aware that the sexual abuse of children is more common than was previously known. Alfie Kohn's article not only details some of the serious consequences of this abuse, but also suggests some appropriate interventions.

Some researchers argue that much of the storm and stress attributed to adolescence is a myth, created from an overemphasis on adolescent fads and rebelliousness and an underemphasis on obedience, conformity, and cooperation. Focusing on the negative aspects of adolescent behavior may create a set of expectations that the adolescent then strives to achieve. Moreover, for some adolescents the transition to adulthood is marked by despair, loneliness, and interpersonal conflict. The pressures of peer group, school, and family may produce conformity, or may lead to rebellion or withdrawal from friends, parents, or society at large. These pressures may peak as the adolescent prepares to separate from the family and assume the independence and responsibilities of adulthood. In the next article, Francine Prose reviews Carol Gilligan's studies of girls' transition from preadolescence to adolescence. Gilligan argues that socialization and moral development differs for boys and girls, leading boys to emphasize justice in their moral decision-making and girls to emphasize care and relationships. Moreover, Gilligan finds that cultural values and socialization practices have a particularly negative effect on adolescent girls' self-esteem, self-confidence, and feelings of competence.

Old age has long been considered either a problem in itself, or at best, a time in which many problems arise. As the number of elderly Americans rises rapidly, descriptions of them as a group are also changing. Jack Horn and Jeff Meer suggest strongly that these trends are progressive; what will aging be like in another 100 years?

Looking Ahead: Challenge Questions

What historical factors created the myth that adolescence was a time of storm and stress? Is it actually a myth? What cultural values and/or child-rearing practices are responsible for the changes from preadolescence to adolescence that Gilligan observes in girls? How might parents counter such factors to provide greater continuity in personality development for girls? Do sex differences in moral reasoning provide a balance necessary for successful human social behavior? How would human interactions differ if both boys and girls stressed the principle of justice in their moral reasoning?

If Horn and Meer are correct in their observations about successful aging, what advice would you give a 20-year-old to help prepare him or her to be 70? To what extent are these strategies for successful aging dependent on the personality of the individual applying them?

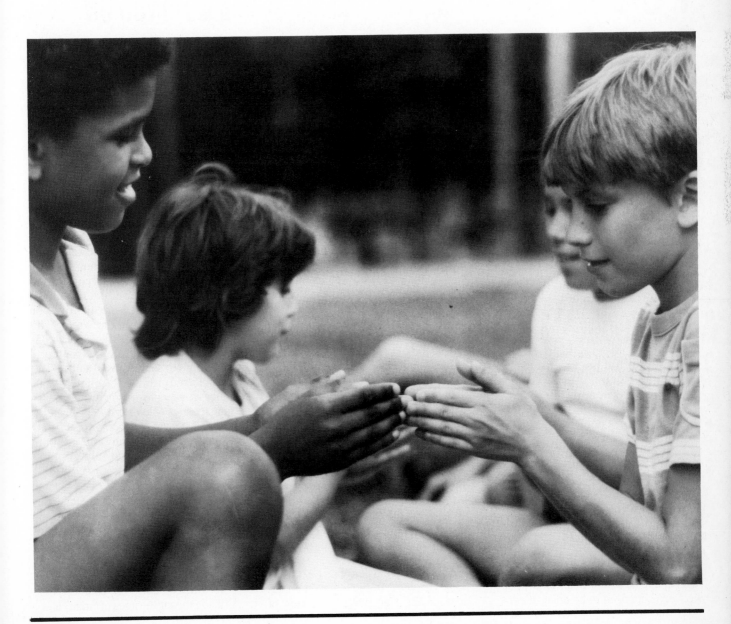

DON'T ACT YOUR AGE!

Life stages no longer

roll forward in a

cruel numbers game

Carol Tavris, Ph.D.

Carol Tavris *is a social psychologist and writer, and author of* Anger: The Misunderstood Emotion.

A friend of mine has just had her first baby. Not news, exactly. It's not even news that she's 45 years old. The news is it's not news that a 45-year-old woman has just had her first baby.

Another friend, age 32, has decided to abandon the pursuit of matrimony and remodel her kitchen instead. The news is that her parents and friends don't think she's weird. They're giving her a Not-Wedding party.

It used to be that all of us knew what we were supposed to be doing at cer-

tain ages. The "feminine clock" dictated that women married in their early 20s, had a couple of kids by 30 (formerly the baby deadline), maybe went back to work in their 40s, came down with the empty nest blues in their 50s, and faded into grandmotherhood in their 60s. The "masculine clock" ticked along as men marched up the career ladder, registering their promotions and salaries with notches at each decade.

Nowadays, many women are following the masculine clock; many men are resetting their schedules; and huge numbers of both sexes have stopped telling time altogether. This development is both good news and bad.

The good news is that people are no longer expected to march in lock step through the decades of life, making changes on schedule. "No one is doing things on time anymore," says Dr. Nancy Schlossberg, an adult development expert at the University of Maryland, and the author of the forthcoming *Overwhelmed: Coping with Life's Ups and Downs* (Lexington Books). "Our lives are much too irregular and unpredictable. In my classes I've seen women who were first-time mothers at 43 and those who had their first baby at 17. I just met a woman who is newly married—at age 65. She quit her job, and with her husband is traveling around on their yacht writing articles. You can bet she won't be having an age-65 retirement crisis. She's having too much fun."

The bad news is that without timetables, many people are confused about what they're "supposed" to be doing in their 20s, 30s, 40s and beyond. They have confused *age* (a biological matter) with *stage* (a social matter). Women ask: "When is the best time to have children—before or after I've started working?" Men want to know: "Since I can't make up my mind about marriage, work, children and buying a dog, is it possible I'm having a midlife crisis even though I'm only 32?"

Although confusion can be unsettling, I prefer it to the imposed phoniness of the "life stage" theories of

personal development. Actually, I date my dislike of stage theories to my childhood. My parents used to keep Gesell's *The First Five Years of Life* and *The Child From Five to Ten* on the highest shelf of their library (right next to Rabelais), and I *knew* they were consulting these volumes at regular intervals to check on my progress. I was

NO ONE IS DOING THINGS ON TIME ANYMORE.

indignant. For one thing, a 9¾-year-old person finds it humiliating to be lumped with six-year-olds. For another, I was sure I wasn't measuring up, though what I was supposed to be measuring up to I never knew.

I survived Gesell's stages only to find myself, as a college student in the '60s, assigned to read Erik Erikson's theory of the eight stages of man. Every few years in childhood, and then every 10 years or so after, Erikson said, people have a special psychological crisis to resolve and overcome.

The infant must learn to trust, or will forever mistrust the world. The toddler must develop a sense of autonomy and independence, without succumbing to shame and doubt. The school-aged child must acquire competence at schoolwork, or will risk lifelong feelings of inferiority. Teenagers, naturally, must overcome the famous "identity crisis," or they will wallow in "role confusion" and aimlessness. Once you have your identity, you must learn to share it; if you don't master this "intimacy crisis," you might become lonely and isolated. To Erikson, you're never home free. Older adults face the crises of stagnation versus generativity, and, in old age, "ego integrity" versus despair.

It turned out, of course, that Erikson meant the ages of "man" liter-

From *American Health*, July/August 1989, pp. 50-52, 54, 56, 58. Copyright © 1989 by Carol Tavris and American Health Partners.

ally, but none of us knew that in those days. We female students all protested that our stages were out of order—but that was just further evidence, our instructor said, of how deviant, peculiar and irritating women are. Erikson's theory, he said, was a brilliant expansion of Freud's stage theory (which stopped at puberty). If women didn't fit, it was their own damned fault.

In the 1970s, stage theory struck again with an eruption of popular books. (Stage theories recur in predictable stages.) Journalist Gail Sheehy published *Passages: Predictable Crises of Adult Life* (no one asked how a crisis, by definition a "turning point" or "a condition of instability," could be predictable). Harvard psychiatrist George Vaillant, now at Dartmouth, studied privileged Harvard (male) students, and concluded that men go through orderly stages even if their lives differ. Yale psychiatrist Daniel J. Levinson, in *The Seasons of a Man's Life*, argued that the phases of life unfold in a natural sequence, like the four seasons. This book had nothing to say about women's seasons, possibly because women were continuing to irritate academics by doing things unseasonably.

By this time I was really annoyed. I wasn't having any of my crises in the right order. I hadn't married when I was supposed to, which put my intimacy and generativity crises on hold; leaving my job created an identity crisis at 32, far too late. My work-linked sense of competence, having reached a high of +9, now plunged to -2, and I was supposed to have resolved *that* one at around age seven.

I had only to look around to realize I was not alone. All sorts of social changes were detonating around me. Women who had been homebodies for 35 years were running off to start businesses, much to the annoyance of their husbands, who were quitting their businesses to take lute lessons. People who expected to marry didn't. People who expected to stay married didn't. Women who expected never to work were working. Men who expected never to care about babies were cooing over their own. Expectations were out the window altogether.

LIFE AS A FAN

Eventually, stages no longer mat-

EXPERTS CAN'T AGREE ON WHERE TO LOCATE "MIDLIFE."

tered, either. Psychological theories—which follow what people actually do—have had to change to keep up with the diversity of modern life. In recent years, researchers have discovered a few things that, once and for all, should drive a stake through the idea of fixed, universal life stages:

The psychology and biology of aging are not the same thing. Many of the problems of "old age" stem from psychological, not physical, losses. They would afflict most people at any age who were deprived of family, close friends, meaningful activity, intellectual stimulation and control over what happens to them. Today we've learned to distinguish the biology of normal aging from the decline caused by illness: Conditions once thought inevitable— osteoporosis, senility, excessive wrinkling, depression—can result from poor nutrition, overmedication, lack of exercise, cell damage or disease. For example, only 15% of people over 65 suffer serious mental impairment, and half of those cases are due to Alzheimer's disease.

These findings have played havoc with the basic definition of "old." It used to be 50. Then it was 60, then 70. Today there are so many vibrant octogenarians that "old" is getting even older. Researchers can't even agree on where to locate "midlife" (30 to 50? 40 to 60? 35 to 65?), let alone what problems constitute a midlife crisis.

Although children progress through biologically determined "stages," adults don't. Children go through a stage of babbling before they talk; they crawl before they walk; they wail before they

can say, "Can we discuss this calmly, Mom?" These developments are governed by maturational and biological changes dictated by genes. But as children mature, genes become less of a driving force on their development, and the environment has greater impact.

Bernice Neugarten, a professor of behavioral science at the University of Chicago, observes that the better metaphor for life is a fan, rather than stages. When you open a fan, you can see all its diverse pieces linked at a common point of origin. As people age, their qualities and experiences likewise "fan out," which is why, she says, you find greater diversity in a group of 70-year-olds than in a passel of seven-year-olds.

The variety and richness of adult life can't be crammed into tidy "stages" anymore. Stage theorists such as Erikson assumed that growth is fixed (by some biological program or internal clock), progressive (you grow from a lower stage to a higher one), one-way (you grow up, not down; become more competent, not less), cumulative (reflecting your resolution of previous stages), and irreversible (once you gain a skill, there's no losing it).

Yet it has proven impossible to squash the great variety of adult experience into a fixed pattern, and there is no evidence to support the idea of neat stages that occur in five- or 10-year intervals. Why must you master an "identity crisis" before you learn to love? Don't issues of competence and inferiority recur throughout life? Why is the need for "generativity" relevant only to 30-year-olds?

EVENTS AND NONEVENTS

For all these reasons, new approaches to adult development emphasize not how old people are, but what they are doing. Likewise, new studies find that *having* a child has stronger psychological effects on mothers than the age at which they have the baby. (New mothers of any age feel more nurturing and less competent.) Entering the work force has a strong positive effect on your self-esteem and ambition, regardless of when you start working. Men facing retirement confront similar issues at 40, 50 or 60. Divorced people have certain

THE NEW APPROACH: NOT HOW OLD YOU ARE, BUT WHAT YOU ARE DOING.

common problems, whether they split at 30 or 50.

In their book *Lifeprints* (McGraw-Hill), Wellesley College psychologists Grace Baruch and Rosalind Barnett and writer Caryl Rivers surveyed 300 women, ages 35 to 55. They found that the differences among the women depended on what they were doing, not on their age. A career woman of 40, for example, has more in common with a career woman of 30 than with an unemployed woman her age.

At the heart of *Lifeprints* is the heretical notion that "there is no one lifeprint that insures all women a perpetual sense of well-being—nor one that guarantees misery, for that matter. American women today are finding satisfying lives in any number of role patterns. Most involve trade-offs at different points in the life cycle."

Instead of looking for the decade landmarks or the "crises" in life, the *transitions* approach emphasizes the importance of shifting from one role or situation to another. What matters are the events that happen (or fail to happen) and cause us to change in some way. Maryland's Schlossberg describes four kinds of transitions:

▪ **Anticipated** transitions are the events you plan for, expect and rehearse: going to school, getting married, starting a job, getting promoted, having a child, retiring at 65. These are the (previously) common milestones of adult life, and because they're predictable, they cause the least difficulty.

▪ **Unanticipated** transitions are the things that happen when you aren't prepared: flunking out of school, being fired, having a baby after being told you can't, being forced to retire early. Because these events are bolts from the blue, they can leave you reeling.

▪ **Nonevent** transitions are the changes you expect to happen that

don't: You don't get married; you can't have children; you aren't promoted; you planned to retire but need to keep working for the income. The challenge here is knowing when to accept these ongoing events as specific transitions and learning to live with them.

▪ **Chronic Hassle** transitions are the situations that may eventually require you to change or take action, but rumble along uncomfortably for a long stretch: You aren't getting along with your spouse; your mother gets a chronic illness and needs constant care; you have to deal with discrimination at work; your child keeps getting into trouble.

There are no rules: An anticipated change for one person (having a baby) might be unanticipated for another. An upsetting "nonevent" transition for one person (not getting married) can be a planned decision for another and thus not a transition at all. And even unexpected good news—you recover despite a hopeless diagnosis—can require adjustment. This approach acknowledges that nonevents and chronic situations cause us to change just as surely as dramatic events do, though perhaps less consciously.

Seeing our lives in terms of these transitions, says Schlossberg, frees us from the old stereotypes that say we "should" be doing one thing or another at a certain time in our lives. But it also helps us understand why we can sail through changes we thought would be traumatic—only to be torpedoed by transitions expected to be a breeze. Our reactions have little to do with an internal clock, and everything to do with expectations, goals and, most of all, what else is happening to us.

For example, says Schlossberg, people have very different reactions to "significant" birthdays. For some, 30 is the killer; for others it's 50. For an aunt of mine, who breezed through decade markers without a snivel, 70

was traumatic. "To determine why a birthday marker creates a crisis," says Schlossberg, "I'd ask what was going on in the person's life, not their age. How old were they when their last parent died? How is their work going? Have they lost a loved one?" If they see a birthday as closing down options, then the event can feel negative, she adds.

"All of us carry along a set of psychological needs that are important throughout our lives, not just at one particular age or stage," says Schlossberg. "We need to feel we *belong* to a family, group or community, for example. Changing jobs, marriages or cities often leaves people feeling temporarily left out.

"We also need to feel we matter to others, that we count. At some phases of life, people are burdened by mattering too much to too many people. Many women in their 30s must care for children, husbands and parents, to say nothing of working at their paid jobs. At other phases, people suffer from a sense of mattering too little."

In addition to belonging and "mattering," says Schlossberg, people need to feel they have a reasonable amount of control over their lives; they need to feel competent at what they do; they need identity—a strong sense of who they are; and they need close attachments and commitments that give their lives meaning.

These themes, says Schlossberg, reflect our common humanity, uniting men and women, old and young. A freshman in college and a newly retired man may both temporarily feel marginal, "out of things." A teenager and her grandmother may both feel they don't "matter" to enough other people, and be lonely as a result. A man may feel he has control over his life until he's injured in a car accident. A woman's identity changes when she goes back to school in midlife. A newly divorced woman of 30 and a recently laid-off auto worker of 40 may both feel inadequate and incompetent. When people lose the commitments that give their lives meaning, they feel adrift.

"By understanding that these emotional feelings are a normal response to what is going on in your life, and not an inevitable crisis that occurs at 23 or 34, or whatever," says Schlossberg, "people can diagnose their problems more accurately—and more important, take steps to fix them." If you say, "No wonder I'm miserable; I'm having my Age 30 Decade Panic," there's nothing to do but live through it—getting more panicked when you're still miserable at age 36½.

But if you can say, "No wonder I'm miserable—I don't feel competent at work, I don't feel I matter to enough people, I feel like a stranger in this neighborhood," then more constructive possibilities present themselves. You can learn new skills, join new groups, start a neighborhood cleanup committee, and quit whining about being 30.

None of this means that age doesn't matter, as my 83-year-old mother

A WOMAN'S IDENTITY CHANGES WHEN SHE GOES BACK TO SCHOOL.

would be the first to tell you. She mutters a lot about irritating pains, wrinkles, forgetfulness and getting shorter. But mostly my mother is too busy to complain, what with her paralegal counseling, fund-raising, organizing programs for shut-in older women, traveling around the world, and socializing. She knows she belongs; she matters to many; she has countless commitments; she knows who she is.

And yet the transitions approach reminds us that adult concerns aren't settled, once and for all, at some critical stage or age. It would be nice if we could acquire a sense of competence in grammar school and keep it forever, if we had only one identity crisis per lifetime, if we always belonged. But adult development is more complicated than that, and also more interesting. As developmental psychologist Leonard Pearlin once said, "There is not one process of aging, but many; there is not one life course, but many courses; there is no one sequence of stages, but many." The variety is as rich as the diversity of human experience.

Let's celebrate the variety—and leave stages to children, geologists, rocket launches and actors.

Shattered Innocence

CHILDHOOD SEXUAL ABUSE IS YIELDING ITS DARK SECRETS TO THE COLD LIGHT OF RESEARCH.

Alfie Kohn

Alfie Kohn is the author of No Contest: The Case Against Competition, *published by Houghton Mifflin.*

No one would claim today that child sexual abuse happens in only one family in a million. Yet that preposterous estimate, based on statistics from 1930, was published in a psychiatric textbook as recently as 1975. Sensational newspaper headlines about day-care center scandals seem to appear almost daily and, together with feminist protests against sexist exploitation, these reports have greatly increased public awareness of what we now know is a widespread problem.

Even so, the most recent scientific findings about child sexual abuse—how often it happens and how it affects victims in the short and long term—have received comparatively little attention. These findings suggest that as many as 40 million people, about one in six Americans, may have been sexually victimized as children. As many as a quarter of these people may be suffering from a variety of psychological problems, ranging from guilt and poor self-esteem to sexual difficulties and a tendency to raise children who are themselves abused.

The startling figure of 40 million is derived from several studies indicating that 25 to 35 percent of all women and 10 to 16 percent of all men in this country experienced some form of abuse as children, ranging from sexual fondling to intercourse. In August 1985, *The Los Angeles Times* published the results of a national telephone poll of 2,627 randomly selected adults. Overall, 22 percent of respondents (27 percent of the women and 16 percent of the men) confided that they had experienced as children what they now identify as sexual abuse.

Some victims of abuse may be reluctant to tell a stranger on the telephone about something as traumatic and embarrassing as sexual abuse, which suggests that even the *Times* poll may have understated the problem. When sociologist Diana Russell of Mills College sent trained interviewers around San Francisco to interview 930 randomly selected women face-to-face, she found that 357, or 38 percent, reported at least one instance of having been sexually abused in childhood. When the definition of abuse was widened to include sexual advances that never reached the stage of physical contact, more than half of those interviewed said they had had such an experience before the age of 18.

Confirming the *Times* and Russell studies is a carefully designed Gallup Poll of more than 2,000 men and women from 210 Canadian communities. The results, published in 1984, show that 22 percent of the respondents were sexually abused as children. As

with Russell's study, that number increases dramatically, to 39 percent, when noncontact abuse is included.

John Briere, a postdoctoral fellow at Harbor-University of California, Los Angeles Medical Center, has reviewed dozens of studies of child abuse in addition to conducting several of his own. "It is probable," he says, "that at least a quarter to a third of adult women and perhaps half as many men have been sexually victimized as children."

One reason these numbers are so surprising, and the reason estimates of one family in a million could be taken seriously for so long, is that many children who are sexually abused understandably keep this painful experience to themselves. In the *Times* poll, one-third of those who said they had been victimized also reported that they had never before told anyone. Many therapists still do not bother to ask their clients whether abuse has taken place, even when there is good reason to suspect that it has.

Studies demonstrate that most child sexual abuse happens to those between the ages of 9 and 12 (although abuse of 2- and 3-year-olds is by no means unusual), that the abuser is almost always a man and that he is typically known to the child—often a relative. In many cases, the abuse is not limited to a single episode, nor does the abuser usually use force. No race, ethnic group or economic class is immune.

All children do not react identically to sexual abuse. But most therapists would agree that certain kinds of behavior and feelings occur regularly among victims. The immediate effects of sexual abuse include sleeping and eating disturbances, anger, withdrawal and guilt. The children typically appear to be either afraid or anxious.

Two additional signs show up so frequently that experts rely upon them as indicators of possible abuse when they occur together. The first is sexual

abuse, it is far more difficult to draw a definitive connection between such abuse and later psychological problems. "We can't say every child who is abused has this or that consequence, and we are nowhere near producing a validated profile of a child-abuse victim," says Maria Sauzier, a psychiatrist who used to direct the Family Crisis Program for Sexually Abused Children at the New England Medical Center in Boston. In fact, some experts emphasize that many sexual abuse victims emerge relatively unscathed as adults. Indeed, David

der," people whose relationships, emotions and sense of self are all unstable and who often become inappropriately angry or injure themselves. "Not all borderlines have been sexually abused, but many have been," Briere says.

Briere, working with graduate student Marsha Runtz, has also noticed that some female abuse victims "space out" or feel as if they are outside of their own bodies at times. And he has observed that these women sometimes have physical complaints without any apparent medical cause. Briere points out that these two tendencies, known as "dissociation" and "somatization," add up to something very much like hysteria, as Freud used the term.

Other therapists believe the label Post-Traumatic Stress Disorder (PTSD), which has most often been applied to veterans of combat, may also be an appropriate diagnosis for some of those who have been abused. Symptoms of the disorder include flashbacks to the traumatic events, recurrent dreams about them, a feeling of estrangement from others and a general sense of numbness. "It feels to me like the fit is very direct to what we see with [victims of] child sexual abuse," says Christine Courtois, a psychologist from Washington, D.C. "Many victims ... experience the symptoms of acute PTSD." She describes an 18-year-old client, abused by her father for nine years, who carved the words "help me" in her arm. In the course of dealing with what had happened, she would sometimes pass out, an occasional response to extreme trauma.

*A*T LEAST 25 PERCENT OF ALL WOMEN AND 10 PERCENT OF ALL MEN IN THIS COUNTRY EXPERIENCED SOME ABUSE AS CHILDREN, RANGING FROM SEXUAL FONDLING TO INTERCOURSE.

preoccupation: excessive or public masturbation and an unusual interest in sexual organs, sex play and nudity. According to William Friedrich, associate professor of psychology at the Mayo Medical School in Rochester, Minnesota, "What seems to happen is the socialization process toward propriety goes awry in these kids."

The second sign consists of a host of physical complaints or problems, such as rashes, vomiting and headaches, all without medical explanation. Once it is discovered that children have been abused, a check of their medical records often reveals years of such mysterious ailments, says psychologist Pamela Langelier, director of the Vermont Family Forensic Institute in South Burlington, Vermont. Langelier emphasizes that children who have been sexually abused should be reassessed every few years because they may develop new problems each time they reach a different developmental stage. "Sometimes it looks like the kids have recovered," she says, "and then at puberty the issues come back again."

While there are clear patterns in the immediate effects of child sexual

Finkelhor, associate director of the Family Violence Research Program at the University of New Hampshire, has warned his colleagues against "exaggerating the degree and inevitability of the long-term negative effects of sexual abuse." For example, Finkelhor and others point out that studies of disturbed, atypical groups, such as prostitutes, runaways and drug addicts, often find that they show higher rates of childhood sexual abuse than in the general population. Yet according to the estimate of Chris Bagley, a professor of social welfare at the University of Calgary, "At least 50 percent of women who were abused do not suffer long-term ill effects."

If 50 percent survive abuse without problems, of course it follows that 50 percent do not. And Bagley, in fact, has conducted a study indicating that a quarter of all women who are sexually abused develop serious psychological problems as a result. Given the epidemic proportions of sexual abuse, that means that millions are suffering.

Briere, for example, has found a significant degree of overlap between abuse victims and those who suffer from "borderline personality disor-

Even when no such serious psychological problems develop, those who were sexually abused often display a pattern of personal and social problems. Abused individuals in psychotherapy have more difficulties with sexuality and relationships than do others in psychotherapy, for instance. And women who have been victimized often have difficulty becoming sexually aroused. Ironically, others engage in sex compulsively.

Abused women often feel isolated, remain distrustful of men and see themselves as unattractive. "Some [victims] become phobic about intimacy. They can't be touched," says Gail Ericson, a social worker at the Branford Counseling Center in Connecticut. "These women feel rotten about themselves—especially their bodies." As a group, adults who were sexually abused as children consistently have lower self-esteem than others. Other studies have found abuse victims to be more anxious, depressed and guilt-ridden.

Might there be a connection between the high incidence of child sexual abuse among girls and the fact that women tend, in general, to score lower on measures of self-esteem than men? Bagley believes that this disparity may simply reflect the fact that in our society, more women are abused: Seven of ten victims are girls, so any random sampling of men and women will pick up more abused women than men,

those in Russell's survey who had been abused as children reported that they were later victims of rape or attempted rape. Abuse victims "don't know how to take care of themselves," Courtois says. "They're easy targets for somebody, waiting for victimization to happen." This may be due to poor self-image, lack of assertiveness or the feeling that they deserve to be punished.

Women, of course, are not to blame for being victims. "In a society that raises males to behave in a predatory fashion toward females, undermining a young girl's defenses is likely to be exceedingly perilous for her," Russell says, since childhood abuse "could

that the prognosis is particularly bad for those who have been abused by more than one person. Counselor Claire Walsh, director of the Sexual Assault Recovery Service at the University of Florida, has paid special attention to this subgroup. She studied 30 women who were in psychotherapy and who had been abused by their fathers, 18 of whom had also been abused by at least one other person. Walsh found a different psychological profile for those who had been molested by more than one person, which included more anxiety, fear and flashbacks. She also believes that PTSD may show up more often when there is more than one abuser.

Another important variable is the age of the abuser. Russell found that victims are most traumatized if their abuser was between the ages of 26 and 50.

Victims seem to experience more serious problems if force is used during the abuse and if the abuser is a close relative, but evidence for these claims is not conclusive.

SINCE GIRLS IN OUR SOCIETY ARE ABUSED MORE COMMONLY THAN BOYS, PERHAPS IT'S UNDERSTANDABLE THAT WOMEN, AS A GROUP, HAVE LOWER SELF-ESTEEM THAN MEN.

---

perhaps enough of a difference to account for the gender gap in self-esteem.

In one study, Bagley discovered that half of all women with psychological problems had been abused. "The reason for the higher rate [of psychopathology] for women is the higher rate of sexual abuse in women," he says. Other researchers might not support so sweeping a conclusion, but Bagley points to a study of his that showed that nonabused men and women have comparable self-esteem.

One of the most disturbing findings about child abuse is its strong intergenerational pattern: Boys who are abused are far more likely to turn into offenders, molesting the next generation of children; girls are more likely to produce children who are abused. Two of five abused children in a study conducted by Sauzier, psychologist Beverly Gomes-Schwartz and psychiatrist Jonathan Horowitz had mothers who were themselves abused.

In addition, victimization can lead to revictimization. Nearly two-thirds of

have stripped away some of [her] potential ability to protect" herself.

Men who were abused, meanwhile, are likely to be confused about their sexual identity, deeply ashamed, unwilling to report the experience and apt to respond aggressively. Says Jack Rusinoff, a counselor in Minneapolis who works with male victims, "I have one 5-year-old boy who's already on the road to being an abuser." This boy, like many others, has displayed sexual aggression, even at this age. Langelier, who has seen more than 200 victims over the last three years, notes that her young male clients are sometimes caught reaching for others' genitals or "making demands for sexual stimulation."

Is there any indication, given this variation in psychological outcome, why one case of childhood sexual abuse leads to serious adult problems while another does not? So far, only two characteristics of abuse have consistently been linked with major difficulties later on. For one, studies by Bagley, Briere and others have shown

Obviously, large gaps remain in the research on the long-term effects of child sexual abuse. This is not very surprising given how new the field is. Most of the studies reported here have been conducted since 1980, and the five scholarly journals devoted to the subject have all been launched within the last two years. Only in 1986 was the groundwork finally laid for an American professional society dealing with sexual child abuse.

There is no question that the field already has produced striking findings. "We now clearly know that sexual abuse is a major risk factor for a lot of later mental-health problems," Finkelhor says. "What we don't yet know is who is most susceptible to these problems, how other experiences interact with abuse or what can be done."

Finkelhor adds that research on child sexual abuse "should teach all social scientists and mental-health practitioners some humility. Despite several generations of clinical expertise and knowledge of childhood development, it was only very recently that we came to see how incredibly widespread this childhood trauma is.

"It may make us realize that there are other things about childhood that we don't have a clear perspective on as well," he says.

CONFIDENT AT 11, CONFUSED AT 16

*Harvard Professor Carol Gilligan
tracks the psychological development
of girls as they enter adolescence.*

Francine Prose

*Francine Prose is a novelist and critic. Her most recent book
is a collection of stories, "Women and Children First."*

The atmosphere in Carol Gilligan's office at the Harvard Graduate School of Education could hardly be less like my own days as a Harvard graduate student—those seminars mired in torpor from which students were periodically roused by revivifying jolts of pedagogical bad temper. Professor Gilligan's faculty and student colleagues at the Project on the Psychology of Women and the Development of Girls seem relaxed and almost unaccountably buoyant as they gather around the conference table on a rainy Cambridge morning to describe their current work. Indeed the only face in the room that seems less than fully engaged is that of Virginia Woolf, gazing wistfully into the distance from a photograph on the wall.

Perhaps one reason for the group's collective good humor is that Gilligan and her associates see their mission as extending beyond abstract clinical research. As the title of their latest work, "Strengthening Healthy Resistance and Courage in Girls," suggests, they're seeking ways to intervene in the developmental process actively, to help girls weather the crises occasioned by adolescence.

Now the results of a major phase in this project have appeared in a new book. "Making Connections: The Relational Worlds of Adolescent Girls at Emma Willard School" draws on data collected during a five-year study of students at a private girls' school in Troy, N.Y. Gilligan decided to focus on Willard after she was approached by the school's former principal, the late Robert C. Parker. "The school had a question," she says. " 'How can we make intelligent decisions about girls' education without knowing about their psychological development?' " In the Dodge Study, as it's officially known—funds were provided by the Geraldine Rockefeller Dodge Foundation—extensive interviews and sentence completion tests were used to explore girls' attitudes toward friendship and leadership, sexual morality, politics and violence.

What interviewers kept hearing as they questioned their subjects was that many girls, around the age of 11, go through what Gilligan and her colleagues have come to call a "moment of resistance"—that is, a sharp and particular clarity of vision, an almost perfect confidence in what they know and see, a belief in their integrity and in their highly complex responsibilities toward the world. "Eleven-year-olds are not for sale," says Gilligan.

"I looked at girls at four different age groups, from 7 and 8 years old up to 15 and 16," says Lyn Mikel Brown, just appointed at the Harvard ed school faculty. "And the younger girls had a real sense of outspokenness, of claiming their own sense of authority in the world, being very honest about relationships and the things that hurt them." Responding to the sentence completion tests, the younger girls came up with what Annie Rogers, another member of the faculty, calls "outrageously wonderful statements. One of them was, 'What gets me in trouble is—chewing gum and not tucking my shirt in,' and then, in parentheses, 'but it's usually worth it.' "

But as they get older the girls seem to undergo a kind of crisis in response to adolescence and to the strictures and demands of the culture which, in Gilligan's view, sends a particular message to women: "Keep quiet and notice the absence of women and say nothing." Or as a graduate student, Elizabeth Debold, says: "Girls don't see themselves being what the culture is about. And that has to give them some kind of double vision."

"And by 15 or 16," says Gilligan, "that resistance has gone underground. They start saying, 'I don't know. I don't know. I don't know.' They start not knowing what they had known."

This observation may cause many women to feel an almost eerie shiver of recognition, and inspire them to rethink that period in their lives. It will also be interesting to monitor the responses from psychologists and feminist theorists, for "Making Connections" may well oblige traditional psychology to formulate a more accurate theory of female adolescence (an area that's been virtually ignored until now). Ideally, parents, teachers and therapists who work with girls have begun to find ways to prevent them from "going underground."

In a prologue to "Making Connections," Gilligan provides an overview of the larger issues raised by her book (in effect a collection of essays written individually and collectively by Dodge study team members):

"Each essay originated with a question that arose or became clarified in the experience of the research. No attempt has been made to unify these essays or arrive at a central thesis, beyond a common intention to listen for the ways in which girls orchestrate themes of connection and separation and concerns about care and justice in speaking about themselves, about their relationships, and about their experiences of conflict."

The researchers drew on a broad and various sample of the student population at Willard, an elite school with a substantial number of pupils on scholarship. In one-on-one interviews, teams of researchers asked the same girls at different ages questions like: "How would you describe yourself to yourself? Who is someone you admire? Could you describe a situation in which you had to make a decision and you weren't sure what was the right thing to do?" In addition, girls were given the Washington University Sentence Completion Test, asked to finish 37 sentences such as "A woman should always—"; "Rules are—"; "What gets me into trouble is—"; "My conscience bothers me if—", and so on.

For the chapter "Unfairness and Not Listening," Gilligan asked 34 girls to describe a situation they felt was unfair. ("The fact that the United States backs counterrevolutionaries in Nicaragua, that's unfair. . . . The United States was built on a revolution.") In "Competencies and Visions," 22 student leaders and 26 "nonleaders" were asked questions about authority and power—such as "What does leadership mean to you?" Writing on "Racial Identity Formation and Transformation," Janie Victoria Ward, a Simmons College faculty member, interviewed seven minority girls over a four-year period and asked them to describe what it means to be a black woman—how that view had changed over time, and how they expected it to develop. (" 'It means it's going to be hard,' was a prediction echoed by all.")

Gilligan's discovery of a crisis in female adolescence is thought-provoking and intriguing, but hardly, it would seem, incendiary—until one realizes how small a spark it takes to kindle a conflagration in the academic psychology establishment. Since the 1982 publication of her first book, "In a Different Voice: Psychological Theory and Women's Development,"

Carol Gilligan's work has generated heated debate in a field in which it is still thought fairly radical to suggest that women's development might be fundamentally different from men's.

The controversial nature of her research has provoked intense hostility on the part of academics, but it has also made her the object of almost cult-like veneration. "In a Different Voice" has sold more than 360,000 copies to date. Asked how they came to work with Carol Gilligan, research associates and doctoral candidates tell stories reminiscent of novitiate accounts of being guided to study with this or that perfect master; Lyn Mikel Brown half ironically credits "divine intervention." But though Gilligan—one of the notably few tenured women at Harvard—has clearly "established the voice" of the project since it was founded in 1983, one senses none of the toadying and subtle intimidation typical of academic life. "It's not just Carol's work," says a graduate student, Deb Tolman. "It's our work."

Born in 1936, Carol Gilligan grew up in Manhattan, attended Swarthmore College and received her doctorate in clinical psychology from Harvard for a thesis called "Responses to Temptation in Analysis of Motives," in which she demonstrated that young children who had been read stories about Andrew Carnegie and the robber barons were more likely to cheat than those who had been read narratives in which groups of children were shown acting honorably and loyally.

After she received her doctorate, Carol Gilligan left Harvard in some disaffection. "The things that attracted me to psychology—the complex renderings of relationships and feelings and the moments when peoples' lives go this way or that way—were not to be found in the academic world." She married Jim Gilligan—now a psychiatrist currently writing a book about violence in our culture—and had three sons, the oldest of whom is 28.

During the 1960's and early 70's, Gilligan was active in the peace and civil rights movements, worked as a dancer with an interracial modern dance company in Cleveland, then moved back to New England and began teaching part time at Harvard as a section leader in Erik Erikson's course on the life cycle. She is now a professor of education. Much about her still suggests the former dancer, the early-60's Cambridge bohemian, the long-haired, willowy young women one used to see marching with backpacks and baby strollers behind banners bearing the logo of Another Mother for Peace.

The germ of "In a Different Voice," the book that established Gilligan's reputation, was an essay she wrote in 1975, "sitting at my kitchen table" in the hope of "putting to rest certain things that had been bothering me since high school and all through graduate school"—questions mostly about the role of gender in psychological development and maturation. Among the issues that Gilligan raised—and that even her severest critics acknowledge as a valid and important aspect of her work—is that very few of the landmark psychological studies had included women. The models of the "healthy" and desirable life cycle had all been based on the lives of men.

Using data generated by three research studies (one involved 25 Harvard students, another drew its subjects from women considering abortion, and the third involved 144 males and females at nine separate points in the life cycle), "In a Different Voice" posited the existence of two contrapuntal interior moral voices. One of these voices attends to abstract principles such as justice; the other (Gilligan often chooses metaphors from music) is scored in the more dulcet key of human connection and care—that is, this second voice asks how a moral decision will hurt or help the people involved.

"The occasion for this observation," Gilligan wrote, "was the selection of a sample of women for a study of the relation between judgment and action in a situation of moral conflict and choice." What she discovered was that the ethical distinctions women made were different from those of men: "It was then that I began to notice the recurrent problems in interpreting women's development and to connect these problems to the repeated exclusion of women from the critical theory-building studies of psychological research."

One "recurrent problem" Gilligan identified was that previous studies—based largely on male subjects—interpreted the ability to reason from abstract principles as a sign of having reached the highest plane of moral development. But when women were tested (confronted with classical ethics dilemmas—should a poor man whose wife is dying steal the drugs she needs, etc.), many of them apparently failed to reach the "higher" level of putting justice first, and so in the language of the profession were classified as "low stage respondents."

What Gilligan suggested was that the second moral voice (which she termed the "care voice" as opposed to the "justice voice") was not fundamentally inferior and less highly evolved, but simply different—more concerned with human relationships than with abstract principles. This corrective was understandably cheering to many female psychologists and graduate students who had been dismayed to find themselves and their sex viewed as morally undeveloped.

Gilligan's essay circulated among colleagues and friends, then appeared in Harvard Education Review and, finally, in an expanded version, in the 1982 book that brought Gilligan national attention—a development in her life that has not been entirely positive. Visibility has embroiled her in time-consuming and distracting controversy but has in practical ways enabled her to continue pursuing the questions that drove her to write that first draft at the kitchen table.

Now, as she sits drinking coffee in the sunny kitchen of her airy pre-Civil War Cambridge house, her strong-boned face goes visibly slack with fatigue as she discusses the controversy that greeted "In a Different Voice." "In 1985, I was invited to participate in a symposium at a meeting, in Toronto, of the Society for Research in Child Development. I looked on the program and I saw that the symposium 'In a Different Voice' was scheduled in the ballroom. There must have been 2,000 people in the room, every senior person in the field, many of them defenders of the *ancien régime*.

"I was on a panel with three women criticizing me. And Eleanor Maccoby"—a professor emeritus of psychology at Stanford—"began by telling a joke. She said that a male colleague had just stopped her in the hall and asked 'Are you going to the shootout at the O.K. Corral?' "

Certainly it is a barometer of the rarefied air breathed in some academic circles that one of the most hotly debated questions at that panel was: *Are* there gender distinctions beyond the obvious reproductive functions? However logical it might seem to the casual observer that profound differences in male and female life experience might foster different ways of perceiving the world, this possibility has been vehemently contested in academia; the first volleys of that high-minded shootout continue to echo in the pages of scholarly journals. Yet even those who share Gilligan's beliefs that male/female differences do exist often disagree with her analysis of what those differences are.

Linda Kerber, May Brodbeck Professor in the Liberal Arts and professor of history at the University of Iowa, was one of the contributors to an interdisciplinary forum that appeared in "Signs: Journal of Women in Culture and Society." Like many of Gilligan's critics, Kerber was disturbed by Gilligan's apparent reinforcement of the stereotypical view of women as more nurturant, nicer, less likely to be moved by the harsh voice of justice than by the kinder promptings of care. Gilligan's focus on the "care voice" in women, says Kerber, recalls the "romantic sentimentalism of old voices in the women's movement, with their notions of women as more peaceable than men."

Kerber also complains that Gilligan's work ignores certain realities of economics and race, the possibility that one's social and moral attitudes have less to do with gender than with power. "Marginality is the real issue," Kerber insists. "Women become critics of society because they're on the fringes of society."

Gilligan professes astonishment that she has been so consistently misread. The project's work, she points out, has included several studies designed to examine moral development across a wide sampling of economic and ethnic groups. One study, directed by Janie Victoria Ward, has focused on racial identity and psychological development among black and white girls and boys in Roxbury, South Boston, and Charlestown, asking the same questions about self-description, moral crisis and relationships that the more privileged research subjects had been asked. "Care kids work hard to resist violence and to find ways to prevent violence," says Ward. "At 11, they know when it's time to intervene."

In another study, Jill McLean Taylor and Deb Tolman have been following groups of minority students considered at risk for early pregnancy or dropping out, using the same method of clinical interviews and sentence completion tests. One of their hypotheses is that leaving school constitutes, for many of these students, a form of moral resistance. Tolman says: "They're holding on to a vision of the world that is very true for them, compared to what they're learning at school, which in terms of their experience is patently ridiculous."

As for the accusation that she makes rigid and artificial distinctions between men and women, Gilligan says, "It's so far from my life and experience to think I could line up 'caring' women vs. 'just' men." As proof of her belief that both voices exist in both sexes, she cites the fact that "In a Different Voice" begins with a section of dialogue from Chekhov, who was of course exquisitely capable of writing from both male and female points of view. "What am I showing women doing?" she says, referring to the fact that some of her critical data on moral choice came from a study of women deciding whether to terminate pregnancy—an act that by definition contradicts the stereotype of the nurturant female. "I'm showing them having abortions. 'Care' isn't simply a matter of being 'the nice girl' or 'the perfect woman'—it's about being responsible to oneself as well as to others."

It may be that Gilligan has expected her readers to meet her rather more than halfway, to intuit a new definition of "care" from her idiosyncratic usage of it and grasp from a reference to Chekhov that her notions of male/female difference aren't as ironclad as they may appear. "There's so much argument between Gilligan and her critics about what she said, what she meant, what she intended," suggests Linda Kerber. "It must go back to her failure to find words to accurately express her thoughts."

Unhappily, the problems of clarity that marred "In a Different Voice" haven't been entirely eradicated in "Making Connections." While some of the essays are admirably lucid, others are obscured by murky academic psychologese, complete with less than helpful and almost self-parodic appendices and charts. But for the most part, Gilligan's new book is more straightforward than her first one. By concentrating on girls, the project's new studies avoid the muddle of gender comparisons and the issue of whether boys experience a similar "moment of resistance." Gilligan and her colleagues are simply telling us how girls sound at two proximate but radically dissimilar stages of growing up.

In explaining this difference, project members often refer to one of their interview subjects, a 12-year-old named Tanya who was a classic "resister." On behalf of a homesick younger cousin, Tanya bravely challenged a summer camp rule against campers calling home—she believed and acted upon her conviction that "people are more important than rules." By 15, however, Tanya seemed to have lost some of that uncompromising moral purity, and told an interviewer of having signed "love" to a letter she wrote to someone she did not love. What emerges from talks with Gilligan and her associates is their disbelief and dismay at repeatedly seeing a morally articulate preadolescent transformed into an apologetic, hesitant teen-ager who prefaces every opinion with "this may sound mediocre but. . . ." These teen-agers' syntax "is like a sailboat tacking," says Gilligan. "One sentence goes this way. Another sentence goes that way."

The source of the change, in Gilligan's view, is that, during adolescence, girls come up against "the wall of Western culture," and begin to see that their clear-sightedness may be dangerous and seditious; in consequence they learn to hide and protect what they know—not only to censor themselves but "to think in ways that differ from what they really think."

Perhaps Gilligan's most radical challenge to traditional developmental psychology is her emphasis on collectivity—in contrast to "individuation," the establishment of an autonomous self that has until now been seen to mark the highest stage of personality development. The practical benefits of encouraging young people's talent for collaboration are already being felt at schools like Emma Willard, where, in the aftermath of the Dodge Study, teachers and administrators have redoubled their commitment to listen to what girls really have to say. Many Emma Willard students, says Acting Principal Trudy Hanmer, had been "very bright, very articulate, very verbal sixth graders who somehow had changed. They'd got quiet." Consequently the school "demands participation from everyone, until girls who were quiet as freshmen are, by their sophomore or junior year, saying 'I have an opinion that counts.'" Hanmer describes a dramatic rise in the quiz scores of geography students who were organized into map study groups and told that their grades would be the average of all the group members' scores. Relieved of the necessity to compete with their peers, the girls achieved "extraordinarily high grades. Almost everyone got a perfect score."

In the search for more active ways of "strengthening healthy resistance and courage in girls," Gilligan and her colleagues took a group of 11-year-olds from the Atrium School in Watertown, Mass., a suburb of Boston, on a week-long outing last summer during which they wrote, drew and did theater work designed to help the girls function as a group and, as Annie Rogers says, "talk about things they wouldn't ordinarily talk about and bring their voices right out into the public.

"And it worked wonderfully. It did just what we wanted it to do. The kids had to direct and listen to one another, they wrote some beautiful pieces and did some really interesting drawings and formed a community among themselves." These girls will be the subject of follow-up studies for three years, and this year another "Sixth Grade Writing and Outing Club"—its members drawn from Cambridge public schools—will visit the Boston Museum of Fine Arts and Old Sturbridge Village. The girls will also keep journals—in order, says Gilligan, "to amplify their voices for themselves" before these voices can be quieted or silenced.

Carol Gilligan often speaks of her most recent work as "very new" and "very fragile," and again one hears a weariness creep into her voice, as if she is anticipating in advance all the objections that will be raised—debates she fears will resemble those that greeted "In a Different Voice." One can imagine the discussions of whether 11-year-olds are really more or less morally advanced than their older sisters, or what sorts of resistance boys go through when, like the supreme resister, J. D. Salinger's Holden Caulfield, they attempt to hold out against "the phoniness" of adult society. These debates could continue to obscure the real diffi-culties experienced by women (and men) who, as children, learned to doubt what they know.

Exploring what Freud called "the dark continent" of female psychology, Carol Gilligan describes feeling "like a 19th-century naturalist," and she and her colleagues seem to share a Darwinian sense of mission to excavate the hidden chambers of a common buried past. One can't help noting an extraordinary degree of personal commitment, an appreciation of the connections between their own lives and those of the girls they are studying. "For me," says Gilligan's colleague Elizabeth Debold, "the issues that we're dealing with are issues about my life."

Hearing Carol Gilligan describe the joy and physical freedom of playing tag at the beach with the Sixth Grade Outing Club, one is moved by an almost spooky sense that what she and her colleagues are unearthing is that moment in their own pasts during which they "went underground." "The thing that's so powerful about studying girls," Gilligan says, "is that it takes you back. You remember how you moved in the world, how your body felt when you were 11. You remember how you were with your friends, how your life was— what it was like."

The Vintage Years

THE GROWING NUMBER OF HEALTHY, VIGOROUS OLDER PEOPLE HAS HELPED OVERCOME SOME STEREOTYPES ABOUT AGING. FOR MANY, THE BEST IS YET TO COME.

Jack C. Horn and Jeff Meer

*Jack C. Horn is a senior editor and Jeff Meer is
an assistant editor at the magazine.*

Our society is getting older, but the old are getting younger. As Sylvia Herz told an American Psychological Association (APA) symposium on aging last year, the activities and attitudes of a 70-year-old today "are equivalent to those of a 50-year-old's a decade or two ago."

Our notions of what it means to be old are beginning to catch up with this reality. During the past several decades, three major changes have altered the way we view the years after 65:

• The financial, physical and mental health of older people has improved, making the prospect of a long life something to treasure, not fear.

• The population of older people has grown dramatically, rising from 18 million in 1965 to 28 million today. People older than 65 compose 12 percent of the population, a percentage that is expected to rise to more than 20 percent by the year 2030.

• Researchers have gained a much better understanding of aging and the lives of older people, helping to sort out the inevitable results of biological aging from the effects of illness or social and environmental problems. No one has yet found the fountain of youth, or of immortality. But research has revealed that aging itself is not the thief we once thought it was; healthy older people can maintain and enjoy most of their physical and mental abilities, and even improve in some areas.

Because of better medical care, improved diet and increasing interest in physical fitness, more people are reaching the ages of 65, 75 and older in excellent health. Their functional age—a combination of physical, psychological and social factors that affect their attitudes toward life and the roles they play in the world—is much younger than their chronological age.

Their economic health is better, too, by almost every measure. Over the last three decades, for example, the number of men and women 65 and older who live below the poverty line has dropped steadily from 35 percent in 1959 to 12 percent in 1984, the last year for which figures are available.

On the upper end of the economic scale, many of our biggest companies are headed by what once would have been called senior citizens, and many more of them serve as directors of leading companies. Even on a more modest economic level, a good portion of the United States' retired older people form a new leisure class, one with money to spend and the time to enjoy it. Obviously not all of America's older people share this prosperity. Economic hardship is particularly prevalent among minorities. But as a group, our older people are doing better than ever.

In two other areas of power, politics and the law, people in their 60s and 70s have always played important roles. A higher percentage of people from 65 to 74 register and vote than in any other group. With today's increasing vigor and numbers, their power is likely to increase still further. It is perhaps no coincidence that our current President is the oldest ever.

Changing attitudes, personal and social, are a major reason for the increasing importance of older people in our society. As psychologist

Bernice Neugarten points out, there is no longer a particular age at which someone starts to work or attends school, marries and has children, retires or starts a business. Increasing numbers of older men and women are enrolled in colleges, universities and other institutions of learning. According to the Center for Education Statistics, for example, the number of people 65 and older enrolled in adult education of all kinds increased from 765,000 to 866,000 from 1981 to 1984. Gerontologist Barbara Ober says that this growing interest in education is much more than a way to pass the time. "Older people make excellent students, maybe even better students than the majority of 19- and 20-year-olds. One advantage is that they have settled a lot of the social and sexual issues that preoccupy their younger classmates."

Older people today are not only healthier and more active; they are also increasingly more numerous. "Squaring the pyramid" is how some demographers describe this change in our population structure. It has always been thought of as a pyramid, a broad base of newborns supporting successively smaller tiers of older people as they died from disease, accidents, poor nutrition, war and other causes.

Today, the population structure is becoming more rectangular, as fewer people die during the earlier stages of life. The Census Bureau predicts that by 2030 the structure will be an almost perfect rectangle up to the age of 70.

The aging of America has been going on at least since 1800, when half the people in the country were younger than 16 years old, but two factors have accelerated the trend tremendously. First, the number of old people has increased rapidly. Since 1950 the number of Americans 65 and older has more than doubled to some 28 million—more than the entire current population of Canada. Within the same period, the number of individuals older than 85 has quadrupled to about 2.6 million (see "The Oldest Old," this article).

Second, the boom in old people has been paired with a bust in the proportion of youngsters due to a declining birth rate. Today, fewer than one American in four is younger than 16. This drop-off has been steady, with the single exception of the post-World War II baby boom, which added 76 million children to the country between 1945 and 1964. As these baby boomers reach the age of 65, starting in 2010, they are expected to increase the proportion of the population 65 and older from its current 12 percent to 21 percent by 2030.

The growing presence of healthy, vigorous older people has helped overcome some of the stereotypes about aging and the elderly. Research has also played a major part by replacing myths with facts. While there were some studies of aging before World War II, scientific

*B*Y THE YEAR 2030 MORE THAN 20 PERCENT OF THE POPULATION IS EXPECTED TO BE 65 OR OLDER.

interest increased dramatically during the 1950s and kept growing.

Important early studies of aging included three started in the mid or late 1950s: the Human Aging Study, conducted by the National Institute of Mental Health (NIMH); the Duke Longitudinal Studies, done by the Center for the Study of Aging and Human Development at Duke University; and the Baltimore Longitudinal Study of Aging, conducted by the Gerontological Institute in Baltimore, now part of the National Institute on Aging (NIA). All three took a multidisciplinary approach to the study of normal aging: what changes take place, how people adapt to them, how biological, genetic, social, psychological and environmental characteristics relate to longevity and what can be done to promote successful aging.

These pioneering studies and hundreds of later ones have benefited from growing federal support. White House Conferences on Aging in 1961 and 1971 helped focus attention on the subject. By 1965 Congress had enacted Medicare and the Older Americans Act. During the 1970s Congress authorized the establishment of the NIA as part of the National Institutes of Health and NIMH created a special center to support research on the mental health of older people.

All these efforts have produced a tremendous growth in our knowledge of aging. In the first (1971) edition of the *Handbook of the Psychology of Aging,* it was estimated that as much had been published on the subject in the previous 15 years as in all the years before then. In the second edition, published in 1985, psychologists James Birren and Walter Cunningham wrote that the "period for this rate of doubling has now decreased to 10 years...the volume of published research has increased to the almost unmanageable total of over a thousand articles a year."

Psychologist Clifford Swenson of Purdue

University explained some of the powerful incentives for this tremendous increase: "I study the topic partly to discover more effective ways of helping old people cope with their problems, but also to load my own armamentarium against that inevitable day. For that is one aspect of aging and its problems that makes it different from the other problems psychologists study: We may not all be schizophrenic or neurotic or overweight, but there is only one alternative to old age and most of us try to avoid that alternative."

One popular misconception disputed by recent research is the idea that aging means inevitable physical and sexual failure. Some changes occur, of course. Reflexes slow, hearing and eyesight dim, stamina decreases. This *primary aging* is a gradual process that begins early in life and affects all body systems.

But many of the problems we associate with old age are *secondary aging*—the results not of age but of disease, abuse and disuse—factors often under our own control. More and more older people are healthy, vigorous men and women who lead enjoyable, active lives. National surveys by the Institute for Social Research and others show that life generally seems less troublesome and freer to older people than it does to younger adults.

In a review of what researchers have learned about subjective well-being—happiness, life satisfaction, positive emotions—University of Illinois psychologist Ed Diener reported that "Most results show a slow rise in satisfaction with age. . .young persons appear to experience higher levels of joy but older persons tend to judge their lives in more positive ways."

Money is often mentioned as the key to a happy retirement, but psychologist Daniel Ogilvie of Rutgers University has found another, much more important, factor. Once we have a certain minimum amount of money, his research shows, life satisfaction depends mainly on how much time we spend doing things we find meaningful. Ogilvie believes retirement-planning workshops and seminars should spend more time helping people decide how to use their skills and interests after they retire.

A thought that comes through clearly when researchers talk about physical and mental fitness is "use it or lose it." People rust out faster from disuse than they wear out from overuse. This advice applies equally to sexual activity. While every study from the time of Kinsey to the present shows that sexual interest and activity diminish with age, the drop varies greatly among individuals. Psychologist Marion Perlmutter and writer Elizabeth Hall have reported that one of the best predictors of continued sexual intercourse "is early sexual activity and past sexual enjoyment and frequency. People who have never had much pleasure from sexu-

WHILE THE OLD AND THE YOUNG MAY BE EQUALLY COMPETENT, THEY ARE DIFFERENTLY COMPETENT.

ality may regard their age as a good excuse for giving up sex."

They also point out that changing times affect sexual activity. As today's younger adults bring their more liberal sexual attitudes with them into old age, the level of sexual activity among older men and women may rise.

The idea that mental abilities decline steadily with age has also been challenged by many recent and not-so-recent findings (see "The Reason of Age," *Psychology Today*, June 1986). In brief, age doesn't damage abilities as much as was once believed, and in some areas we actually gain; we learn to compensate through experience for much of what we do lose; and we can restore some losses through training.

For years, older people didn't do as well as younger people on most tests used to measure mental ability. But psychologist Leonard Poon of the University of Georgia believes that researchers are now taking a new, more appropriate approach to measurement. "Instead of looking at older people's ability to do abstract tasks that have little or no relationship to what they do every day, today's researchers are examining real-life issues."

Psychologist Gisela Labouvie-Vief of Wayne State University has been measuring how people approach everyday problems in logic. She notes that older adults have usually done poorly on such tests, mostly because they fail to think logically all the time. But Labouvie-Vief argues that this is not because they have forgotten how to think logically but because they use a more complex approach unknown to younger thinkers. "The [older] thinker operates within a kind of double reality which is both formal and informal, both logical and psychological," she says.

In other studies, Labouvie-Vief has found that when older people were asked to give concise summaries of fables they read, they did so. But when they were simply asked to recall as much of the fable as possible, they concentrat-

THE OLDEST OLD: THE YEARS AFTER 85

"Every man desires to live long, but no man would be old," or so Jonathan Swift believed. Some people get their wish to live long and become what are termed the "oldest old," those 85 and older. During the past 22 years, this group has increased by 165 percent to 2.5 million and now represents more than 1 percent of the population.

Who are these people and what are their lives like? One of the first to study them intensively is gerontologist Charles Longino of the University of Miami, who uses 1980 census data to examine their lives for the American Association of Retired People.

He found, not surprisingly, that nearly 70 percent are women. Of these, 82 percent are widowed, compared with 44 percent of the men. Because of the conditions that existed when they were growing up, the oldest old are poorly educated compared with young people today, most of whom finish high school. The average person now 85 years and older only completed the eighth grade.

Only one-quarter of these older citizens are in hospitals or institutions such as nursing homes, and more than half live in their own homes. Just 30 percent live by themselves. More than a third live with a spouse or with their children. There are certainly those who aren't doing well—one in six have incomes below the poverty level—but many more are relatively well-off. The mean household income for the group, Longino says, was more than $20,000 in 1985.

What of the quality of life? "In studying this group, we have to be aware of youth creep," he says. "The old are getting younger all the time." This feeling is confirmed by a report released late last year by the National Institute on Aging. The NIA report included three studies of people older than 65 conducted in two counties in Iowa, in East Boston, Massachusetts, and in New Haven, Connecticut. There are large regional differences between the groups, of course, and they aren't a cross-section of older people in the nation as a whole. But in all three places, most of those older than 85 seem to be leading fulfilling lives.

Most socialize in a variety of ways. In Iowa, more than half say they go to religious services at least once a week and the same percentage say they belong to some type of professional, social, church-related or recreational group. More than three-quarters see at least one or two children once a month and almost that many see other close relatives that often.

As you would expect, many of the oldest old suffer from disabilities and serious health problems. At least a quarter of those who responded have been in a hospital overnight in the past year and at least 8 percent have had heart attacks or have diabetes. In Iowa and New Haven, more than 13 percent of the oldest old had cancer, while in East Boston the rate was lower (between 7 percent and 8 percent). Significant numbers of the oldest old have suffered serious injury from falls. Other common health problems for this group are high blood pressure and urinary incontinence. However, epidemiologist Adrian Ostfeld, who directed the survey in New Haven, notes that "most of the disability was temporary."

Longino has found that almost 10 percent of the oldest old live alone with a disability that prevents them from using public transportation. This means that they are "isolated from the daily hands-on care of others," he says. "Even so, there are a surprising number of the oldest old who don't need much in the way of medical care. They're the survivors.

"I think we have to agree that the oldest old is, as a group, remarkably diverse," Longino says. "Just as it is unfair to say that those older than 85 are all miserable, it's not fair to say that they all lead wonderful lives, either."
                                                    —*Jeff Meer*

ed on the metaphorical, moral or social meaning of the text. They didn't try to duplicate the fable's exact words, the way younger people did. As psychologists Nancy Datan, Dean Rodeheaver and Fergus Hughes of the University of Wisconsin have described their findings, "while [some people assume] that old and young are equally competent, we might better assume that they are differently competent."

John Horn, director of the Adult Development and Aging program at the University of Southern California, suggests that studies of Alzheimer's disease, a devastating progressive mental deterioration experienced by an estimated 5 percent to 15 percent of those older than 65, may eventually help explain some of the differences in thinking abilities of older people. "Alzheimer's, in some ways, may represent the normal process of aging, only speeded up," he says. (To see how your ideas about Alzheimer's square with the facts, see "Alzheimer's Quiz" and "Alzheimer's Answers," this article.)

Generalities are always suspect, but one generalization about old age seems solid: It is a different experience for men and women. Longevity is one important reason. Women in the United States live seven to eight years longer, on the average, than do men. This simple fact has many ramifications, as sociologist Gunhild Hagestad explained in *Our Aging Society*.

For one thing, since the world of the very old is disproportionately a world of women, men and women spend their later years differently. "Most older women are widows living alone; most older men live with their wives...among individuals over the age of 75, two-thirds of the men are living with a spouse, while less than one-fifth of the women are."

The difference in longevity also means that among older people, remarriage is a male prerogative. After 65, for example, men remarry at a rate eight times that of women. This is partly a matter of the scarcity of men and partly a matter of culture—even late in life, men tend to marry younger women. It is also a matter of education and finances, which, Hagestad explains, "operate quite differently in shaping remarriage probabilities among men and women. The more resources the woman has available (measured in education and income), the less likely she is to remarry. For men, the trend is reversed."

The economic situations of elderly men and women also differ considerably. Lou Glasse, president of the Older Women's League in Washington, D.C., points out that most of these women were housewives who worked at paid jobs sporadically, if at all. "That means their Social Security benefits are lower than men's, they are not likely to have pensions and they are less likely to have been able to save the kind of money that would protect them from poverty during their older years."

Although we often think of elderly men and women as living in nursing homes or retirement communities, the facts are quite different. Only about 5 percent are in nursing homes and perhaps an equal number live in some kind of age-segregated housing. Most people older than 65 live in their own houses or apartments.

We also think of older people as living alone. According to the Census Bureau, this is true of 15 percent of the men and 41 percent of the women. Earlier this year, a survey done by Louis Harris & Associates revealed that 28 percent of elderly people living alone have annual incomes below $5,100, the federal poverty line. Despite this, they were four times as likely to give financial help to their children as to receive it from them.

In addition, fewer than 1 percent of the old people said they would prefer living with their children. Psychiatrist Robert N. Butler, chairman of the Commonwealth Fund's Commission

AMONG OLDER PEOPLE TODAY, REMARRIAGE IS STILL LARGELY A MALE PREROGATIVE, DUE TO THE SEX DIFFERENCE IN LONGEVITY.

on Elderly People Living Alone, which sponsored the report, noted that these findings dispute the "popular portrait of an elderly, dependent parent financially draining their middle-aged children."

There is often another kind of drain, however, one of time and effort. The Travelers Insurance Company recently surveyed more than 700 of its employees on this issue. Of those at least 30 years old, 28 percent said they directly care for an older relative in some way—taking that person to the doctor, making telephone calls, handling finances or running errands—for an average of 10 hours a week. Women, who are more often caregivers, spent an average of 16 hours, and men five hours, per week. One group, 8 percent of the sample, spent a heroic 35 hours per week, the equivalent of a second job, providing such care. "That adds up to an awful lot of time away from other things," psychologist Beal Lowe says, "and the stresses these people face are enormous."

Lowe, working with Sherman-Lank Communications in Kensington, Maryland, has formed "Caring for Caregivers," a group of professionals devoted to providing services, information and support to those who care for older relatives. "It can be a great shock to some people who have planned the perfect retirement," he says, "only to realize that your chronically ill mother suddenly needs daily attention."

Researchers who have studied the housing needs of older people predictably disagree on many things, but most agree on two points: We need a variety of individual and group living arrangements to meet the varying interests, income and abilities of people older than 65; and the arrangements should be flexible enough that the elderly can stay in the same locale as their needs and abilities change. Many studies have documented the fact that moving itself can be stressful and even fatal to old people, particularly if they have little or no influence over when and where they move.

This matter of control is important, but more complicated than it seemed at first. Psychologist Judith Rodin and others have demonstrated that people in nursing homes are happier, more alert and live longer if they are allowed to take responsibility for their lives in some way, even in something as simple as choosing a plant for their room, taking care of a bird feeder, selecting the night to attend a movie.

Rodin warns that while control is generally beneficial, the effect depends on the individuals involved. For some, personal control brings with it demands in the form of time, effort and the risk of failure. They may blame themselves if they get sick or something else goes wrong. The challenge, Rodin wrote, is to "provide but not impose opportunities. . . . The need for self-determination, it must be remembered, also calls for the opportunity to choose not to exercise control. . . ."

An ancient Greek myth tells how the Goddess of Dawn fell in love with a mortal and convinced Jupiter to grant him immortality. Unfortunately, she forgot to have youth included in the deal, so he gradually grew older and older. "At length," the story concludes, "he lost the power of using his limbs, and then she shut him up in his chamber, whence his feeble voice might at times be heard. Finally she turned him into a grasshopper."

The fears and misunderstandings of age expressed in this 3,000-year-old myth persist today, despite all the positive things we have learned in recent years about life after 65. We don't turn older people into grasshoppers or shut them out of sight, but too often we move them firmly out of the mainstream of life.

In a speech at the celebration of Harvard

> *If I had known when I was 21 that I should be as happy as I am now, I should have been sincerely shocked. They promised me wormwood and the funeral raven.*
>
> —Christopher Isherwood, letter at age 70.

University's 350th anniversary last September, political scientist Robert Binstock decried what he called The Spectre of the Aging Society: "the economic burdens of population aging; moral dilemmas posed by the allocation of health resources on the basis of age; labor market competition between older and younger workers within the contexts of age discrimination laws; seniority practices, rapid technologi-

ALZHEIMER'S QUIZ

Alzheimer's disease, named for German neurologist Alois Alzheimer, is much in the news these days. But how much do you really know about the disorder? Political scientist Neal B. Cutler of the Andrus Gerontology Center gave the following questions to a 1,500-person cross section of people older than 45 in the United States in November 1985. To compare your answers with theirs and with the correct answers, turn to the next page.

	True	False	Don't know
1. Alzheimer's disease can be contagious.	___	___	___
2. A person will almost certainly get Alzheimer's if they just live long enough.	___	___	___
3. Alzheimer's disease is a form of insanity.	___	___	___
4. Alzheimer's disease is a normal part of getting older, like gray hair or wrinkles.	___	___	___
5. There is no cure for Alzheimer's disease at present.	___	___	___
6. A person who has Alzheimer's disease will experience both mental and physical decline.	___	___	___
7. The primary symptom of Alzheimer's disease is memory loss.	___	___	___
8. Among persons older than age 75, forgetfulness most likely indicates the beginning of Alzheimer's disease.	___	___	___
9. When the husband or wife of an older person dies, the surviving spouse may suffer from a kind of depression that looks like Alzheimer's disease.	___	___	___
10. Stuttering is an inevitable part of Alzheimer's disease.	___	___	___
11. An older man is more likely to develop Alzheimer's disease than an older woman.	___	___	___
12. Alzheimer's disease is usually fatal.	___	___	___
13. The vast majority of persons suffering from Alzheimer's disease live in nursing homes.	___	___	___
14. Aluminum has been identified as a significant cause of Alzheimer's disease.	___	___	___
15. Alzheimer's disease can be diagnosed by a blood test.	___	___	___
16. Nursing-home expenses for Alzheimer's disease patients are covered by Medicare.	___	___	___
17. Medicine taken for high blood pressure can cause symptoms that look like Alzheimer's disease.	___	___	___

Alzheimer's Answers — National Sample

	True	False	Don't know
1. False. There is no evidence that Alzheimer's is contagious, but given the concern and confusion about AIDS, it is encouraging that nearly everyone knows this fact about Alzheimer's.	3%	83%	14%
2. False. Alzheimer's is associated with old age, but it is a disease and not the inevitable consequence of aging.	9	80	11
3. False. Alzheimer's is a disease of the brain, but it is not a form of insanity. The fact that most people understand the distinction contrasts with the results of public-opinion studies concerning epilepsy that were done 35 years ago. At that time, almost half of the public thought that epilepsy, another disease of the brain, was a form of insanity.	7	78	15
4. False. Again, most of the public knows that Alzheimer's is not an inevitable part of aging.	10	77	13
5. True. Despite announcements of "breakthroughs," biomedical research is in the early laboratory and experimental stages and there is no known cure for the disease.	75	8	17
6. True. Memory and cognitive decline are characteristic of the earlier stages of Alzheimer's disease, but physical decline follows in the later stages.	74	10	16
7. True. Most people know that this is the earliest sign of Alzheimer's disease.	62	19	19
8. False. Most people also know that while Alzheimer's produces memory loss, memory loss may have some other cause.	16	61	23
9. True. This question, like number 8, measures how well people recognize that other problems can mirror Alzheimer's symptoms. This is crucial because many of these other problems are treatable. In particular, depression can cause disorientation that looks like Alzheimer's.	49	20	30
10. False. Stuttering has never been linked to Alzheimer's. The question was designed to measure how willing people were to attribute virtually anything to a devastating disease.	12	46	42
11. False. Apart from age, research has not uncovered any reliable demographic or ethnic patterns. While there are more older women than men, both sexes are equally likely to get Alzheimer's.	15	45	40
12. True. Alzheimer's produces mental and physical decline that is eventually fatal, although the progression varies greatly among individuals.	40	33	27
13. False. The early and middle stages of the disease usually do not require institutional care. Only a small percentage of those with the disease live in nursing homes.	37	40	23
14. False. There is no evidence that using aluminum cooking utensils, pots or foil causes Alzheimer's, although aluminum compounds have been found in the brain tissue of many Alzheimer's patients. They may simply be side effects of the disease.	8	25	66
15. False. At present there is no definitive blood test that can determine with certainty that a patient has Alzheimer's disease. Accurate diagnosis is possible only upon autopsy. Recent studies suggest that genetic or blood testing may be able to identify Alzheimer's, but more research with humans is needed.	12	24	64
16. False. Medicare generally pays only for short-term nursing-home care subsequent to hospitalization and not for long-term care. Medicaid can pay for long-term nursing-home care, but since it is a state-directed program for the medically indigent, coverage for Alzheimer's patients depends upon state regulations and on the income of the patient and family.	16	23	61
17. True. As mentioned earlier, many medical problems have Alzheimer's-like symptoms and most of these other causes are treatable. Considering how much medicine older people take, it is unfortunate that so few people know that medications such as those used to treat high blood pressure can cause these symptoms.	20	19	61

cal change; and a politics of conflict between age groups."

Binstock, a professor at Case Western Reserve School of Medicine, pointed out that these inaccurate perceptions express an underlying ageism, "the attribution of these same characteristics and status to an artificially homogenized group labeled 'the aged.'"

Ironically, much ageism is based on compassion rather than ill will. To protect older workers from layoffs, for example, unions fought hard for job security based on seniority. To win it, they accepted mandatory retirement, a limitation that now penalizes older workers and deprives our society of their experience.

A few companies have taken special steps to utilize this valuable pool of older workers. The Travelers companies, for example, set up a job

GREAT EXPECTATIONS

SOURCE: U.S. NATIONAL CENTER FOR HEALTH STATISTICS

If you were born in 1920 and are a . . .

	. . .white man	. .white woman
your life expectancy was . . .		
at birth	*54.4 years*	*55.6 years*
at age 40	*71.7*	*77.1*
at age 62	*78.5*	*83.2*

If you were born in 1940 and are a . . .

	. . .white man	. . .white woman
your life expectancy was . . .		
at birth	*62.1 years*	*66.6 years*
at age 20	*70.3*	*76.3*
at age 42	*74.7*	*80.7*

If you were born in 1960 and are a . . .

	. . .white man	. . .white woman
your life expectancy was . . .		
at birth	*67.4 years*	*74.1 years*
at age 22	*73.2*	*80.0*

bank that is open to its own retired employees as well as those of other companies. According to Howard E. Johnson, a senior vice president, the company employs about 175 formerly retired men and women a week. He estimates that the program is saving Travelers $1 million a year in temporary-hire fees alone.

While mandatory retirement is only one example of ageism, it is particularly important because we usually think of contributions to society in economic terms. Malcolm H. Morrison, an authority on retirement and age discrimination in employment for the Social Security Administration, points out that once the idea of retirement at a certain fixed age was accepted, "the old became defined as a dependent group in society, a group whose members could not and should not work, and who needed economic and social assistance that the younger working population was obligated to provide."

We need to replace this stereotype with the more realistic understanding that older people are and should be productive members of society, capable of assuming greater responsibility for themselves and others. What researchers have learned about the strengths and abilities of older people should help us turn this ideal of an active, useful life after 65 into a working reality.

Personality Processes

The psychological study of personality has included two major thrusts. The first thrust has focused on the search for the commonalities of human life and development. Its major question would be: How are humans affected by specific events or activities? Personality theories are based on the assumption that given events, if they are important, will affect almost all people in similar ways, or that the processes by which events affect people are common across events and people. Most psychological research into personality variables has also made this assumption. Failures to replicate a research project are often the first clues that differences in individual responses require further investigation.

While some psychologists have focused on personality-related effects that are presumed to be universal among humans, others have devoted their efforts to discovering the bases on which individuals differ in their responses to environmental events. In the beginning, this specialty was called genetic psychology, since most people assumed that individual differences resulted from differences in genetic inheritance. By the 1950s, the term genetic psychology had given way to the more current term: the psychology of individual differences.

Does this mean that genetic variables are no longer the key to understanding individual differences? Not at all. For a time, psychologists took up the philosophical debate over whether genetic or environmental factors were more important in determining behaviors. Even today, behavior geneticists compute the heritability coefficients for a number of personality and behavioral traits, including intelligence. This is an expression of the degree to which differences in a given trait can be attributed to differences in inherited capacity or ability. Most psychologists, however, accept the principle that both genetic and environmental determinants are important in any area of behavior. These researchers are devoting more of their efforts to discovering how the two sources of influence interact to produce the unique individual.

Some of the most intriguing individual differences are those attributed to sex. That males and females differ biologically is hardly argued. Females generally have higher survival rates at all ages, and outlive males by about seven years. They seem more resistant to mild infections, able to withstand greater variability in temperature, and have, pound for pound, superior musculature. They also suffer less frequently from serious emotional and mental problems. But how do we know that these differences are the result of genetic or genital sex, and not the result of the way the sexes are treated? For example, we know that mothers talk more than twice as much to baby girls as they do to baby boys, and baby boys are held more tightly, jostled more vigorously, and moved through space more rapidly than baby girls. Could these early differences in handling account for later behavioral differences?

Another area of contention about sex differences is their statistical versus pragmatic significance. Suppose we find that there is a difference between males and females, and the difference is statistically significant—that is, reliable. How will we know whether the difference is due to genetic or social factors, and how will we be able to discern whether the difference has interpersonal implications? The first article in this section, "Why Can't a Man Be More Like a Woman . . . and Vice Versa," begins to answer some of these questions. If you read this article critically, however, you will find that it raises as many questions as it answers. This is truly the nature of research into individual differences.

The second article extends some of the issues raised in the first article, particularly those involving gender roles and gender-specific behaviors in a multicultural way. Historically, those who reject their gender roles (gender dysphoria), transsexuals in the extreme case, have complained that the roles are too confining. In recent years, the focus on androgyny has suggested that each of us embodies characteristics that our culture defines as masculine and feminine, and many experts have contended that it is healthy to express the positive characteristics of both gender roles. After reading the second article, do you agree?

Perhaps the most devastating experience one can have is the feeling of helplessness. Martin Seligman, who developed the best current paradigm of learned helplessness (the basis for human depression) has turned his attention to a more positive viewpoint. As Nan Silver tells us, optimism may cause us to live longer.

It has become almost a truism that certain personality traits are associated with increased likelihood of certain diseases. In the final article in this section, the highly regarded researcher Hans Eysenck explains how he has been conducting experiments to determine whether those traits can be changed, and if so, whether the change is for the better.

Looking Ahead: Challenge Questions

How can evidence of genetic or hormonal causes for sex differences be used to reduce discrimination on the basis of sex or gender? Could the same evidence be used by others to increase discrimination? How can evidence for genetic or hormonal causes for sexual orientation be interpreted? Would those with less prevalent sexual orientations have fewer problems with this interpretation than those whose sexual orientations represent the majority?

If androgyny were more common and more people were comfortable rejecting social gender roles, would the incidence of transsexualism likely increase or decrease?

Is optimism really related to health and longevity? If it is desirable, how can optimism be developed?

If a person exhibits personality traits associated with fatal illnesses, what can be done to change both the traits and the likelihood of becoming ill?

WHY CAN'T A MAN BE MORE LIKE A WOMAN . . . AND VICE VERSA

Male and female brains aren't the same. Does this mean that sexual differences are biologically determined?

Kathryn Phillips

For a year Marie-Christine De Lacoste waited for phone calls from the Southwestern Medical Center Forensics Institute telling her that one more undamaged brain was available after autopsy. With each call she would hurry to the morgue and collect another brain. Eventually the Columbia University graduate student had a cache of 14, nine from men and five from women, most of them shooting victims. De Lacoste's study in the early Eighties would change her life. It would also alter the way scientists thought about sex differences in the brain. De Lacoste took each new brain to her lab at the University of Texas Southwestern Medical Center, where she was a research assistant. There, using a combination of cameras, old-fashioned metric rulers, and computers, she measured each brain's corpus callosum. This thick, boomerang-shaped band of fibers connects the brain's hemispheres and is the massive midline conduit for processing and relaying information between the two cerebral halves. De Lacoste suspected she would find a significant difference in callosum size between the men and women. And she did. Her research was the first study of the human corpus callosum showing a possible anatomical basis for sexual differences in intellect, skills, and behavior.

The publication of her paper caused an uproar, and De Lacoste became a "branded" woman. Overnight the popular press trumpeted that science had determined that one sex's brainpower was superior to the other's (although there was considerable confusion about which sex that was). "I'd say the paper really hurt my career as opposed to enhancing it," comments De Lacoste, now at Yale Medical School. At meetings she was known before she was introduced, based solely on that paper, and not always favorably. "It generated quite a stir and I was very young. It made me an 'infamous' neuroscientist."

De Lacoste had not merely entered a field of research but strode into a mine field of contentious debate. "That stuff is hokey," says Anne Fausto-Sterling, a Brown University biologist and prominent critic of the brain research. "The evidence that there are differences is so fragmentary and so weak, it ought to stop there." Critics fear that simply by publishing their data, these neuroscientists may have handed society a means to justify sexual discrimination.

"I was giving a seminar at an Eastern university," recalls De Lacoste, "and this man stood up and said, 'How dare you do work in this area when the politics are such?'" Yet each time the debate seemed nearly suppressed, another study would appear indicating that differences may not stop at the neck but reach into the brain itself, affecting how the average man and woman think. Brain differences, in fact, may explain some—not all—of the differences featured in the disputations about which sex is better at what.

Current theory—and battleground—propounds that boys seem to excel in math and computational skills, whereas girls are superior in language, spoken and written. Motor coordination tests give women the edge in executing fine finger and hand movements, and in overall agility. But men tend to have faster reaction times. Male supremacy appears greatest in tasks involving spatial visualization—the ability to see, manipulate, and compute the position of a real or abstract figure in the mind's eye.

Although the typical cognitive profile of women may be different from that of men, there is a huge overlap. Many women do better than men on some spatial tests, and vice versa. "In large groups, if you look at the mean score or the tendency, that's where you see the difference," says Sandra Witelson, professor of psychiatry at McMaster University in Hamilton, Ontario. "But this doesn't mean that you know the cognitive skills of an individual." That is, you can't predict sexwise who will do better on real-life tasks such as running a company or an experiment. Still, when men and women perform equally on a test in a lab environment, there are indications that their brains go about it in different ways.

In the last decade neurobiologists have reported structural differences in at least two regions of the human brian. One is the corpus callosum, the mind's big "telephone" cable, connecting as it does hundreds of millions of neurons between the two hemispheres. The other is the hypothalamus, the master controller for the integration of many basic behavioral patterns—from temperature regulation and appetite to sex drives—involving brain and endocrine functions. Neuroendocrine research also strongly indicates that nervous system differences begin as sex hormones bathe the developing fetus in the womb. Hormonal differences continuing throughout childhood—and perhaps even through adult life—affect brain activity and guide performance. Other studies suggest that men and women may process the same information differently and yet come to the same or similar conclusions. Nonetheless with every significant new finding comes the researcher's caveat: "No one knows for sure what this means in terms of behavior, but I think. . . ."

CORPUS CALLOSUM: LEFT BRAIN, RIGHT BRAIN

In her pioneering research De Lacoste studied the splenium. Shaped like a light bulb, the splenium, which composes the back fifth of the corpus callosum, is a pathway connecting the visual areas of both hemispheres as well as associational areas that serve complex cognitive functions. She discovered that the splenium's surface area and width were greater in women than men, relative to brain weight. She speculated that the larger splenium probably meant women and men have different interhemispheric connections.

De Lacoste's findings are in line with a prominent theory that goes back at least to the famous "split-brain" work of Nobel laureate Roger Sperry and still dominates thinking on brain differences. Male brains with fewer connections across the corpus callosum are more lateralized than those of females. This increased lateralization, so the theory goes, allows for greater right-brain performance—visuospatial skills. Women, with their theoretically increased *bi* lateralization, excel at verbal skills because, with more cross-communication, they have decreased focus on the right hemisphere.

Even before De Lacoste stated gathering brains from the Dallas morgue, Witelson patiently collected data for a ten-year study correlating people's hand preference—right- or left-handed—with anatomical measurements in their brains. Hand preference is a behavioral index of, or "window" into, the wiring of the brain. Witelson figured she would find a structural difference between left- and right-handers, since they have differing patterns of brain lateralization. Among right-handers, the left side of the brain controls language ad motor skills, and the right side controls spatial perception. Among left-handers, there is more bilateral representation of these functions. Also, in psychological tests left-handers appear to have more bilateral function. Since the corpus callosum is the great communicator between hemispheres, Witelson thought she might see the differences there.

Running into the usual problem—how to do behavioral anatomy in living

---

Differences in language processing in women suggest something more global—that women recruit areas of the brain that enable them to use more strategies than men.

---

humans—she devised an unusual solution. Cancer patients who were seriously ill and wanted to make a contribution to science were asked to participate in a study. They were given psych tests, and they agreed to donate their brains to her lab when they died. With the psychological tests, Witelson determined whether each patient was consistently right-, left-, or mixed-handed. By the end of ten years, she had collected test data and brains from 50 people—35 women and 15 men.

What she found surprised her. She discovered that among men, the isthmus, a segment linking the mid-portions of the two cortices, was larger in the left- or mixed-handed men than in the right-handed men. She had anticipated this. However, she found there was no difference among women in isthmus size based on handedness. Furthermore the isthmus was larger in women across the board. "I did not suspect—there would be no reason to predict—this difference between men and women," Witelson says. "The idea was that the callosum might be bigger for left- than right-handers, not specifically for men but for everyone."

The significance of a larger isthmus? "One possibility is a greater total number of fibers," Witelson says, "or the fibers could be thicker. It will take closer studies to find the answers." A greater number of or thicker fibers could be an anatomical basis for more communication between the hemispheres. "Remember a headline when our report was published?" she muses. "SUBTLE SEX DIFFERENCES FOUND?" It is 'subtle' in the sense that it is complex but not subtle in the sense that it's more elusive, harder to find, or smaller."

Witelson found the variation in isthmus size to be strongly related to hand preference—but only in her male subjects. There was almost no correlation with the handedness measure in women. "The variation in women is not associated with handedness, and it is in men. That means the neurobiological substrate of handedness in women, which obviously must exist, must be mediated by different brain structures than it is in men. That's a big sex difference," says Witelson.

Although men and women do a lot of things similarly, if not identically, they may be doing them with different parts of the brain. This could relate to differences in verbal and spatial skills, she thinks, because they are controlled by the temporal and parietal lobes of the cortex, and these regions send their fibers through the isthmus. "If one part of a package is different, there could be a domino effect. There must be other parts that are different as well." Do Witelson's findings mean one sex is better able to process information than the other? "The key: Different is different. It's so easy to fall into the words *better or worse*. What's better, an apple or an orange?"

THE LANGUAGE MAKER

Cecile Naylor, a neuropsychologist at The Bowman Gray School of Medicine in Winston-Salem, North Carolina, stumbled upon dramatic sex differences almost accidentally as she was studying people with learning disabilities. As part of her study she recruited a control group of 30 men and 30 women "unhindered" by neurological problems. She gave them an oral spelling test that required them to identify whether a word was exactly four letters long. To take the test, each person lay flat on a table, wearing what Naylor describes as "basically a revised motorcycle helmet." The helmet contained devices that measured blood flow through the cortex.

She found no essential difference in how well the men and women scored on the spelling test. An analysis of blood flow, however, showed sex differences in brain activity during the test. In men the patterns of blood flow showed that the most intense brain activity seemed to occur "in a tight linkage" between two areas known to be involved in language and verbal communication: Wernicke's area in the left temporal lobe and Broca's area in the left frontal lobe adjacent to the motor cortex region controlling muscles of the face, jaw, tongue, and throat. The two areas are connected by a thick band of fibers. The standard model for language holds that language making and comprehension arise in Wernicke's area and then travel via the pathway to Broca's, where they call up the program that causes the phrases to be spoken.

In women, though, she found no such intense coupling between the two areas. Instead Wernicke's was actively engaged with two other areas, one behind it in the left temporal lobe. Wernicke's was also linked to its "mirror" area in the *right* temporal lobe. Without further research, Naylor is loath to say what these startling differences mean, but she will speculate a little. "The area behind Wernicke's lies between the primary visual and auditory regions," she says, "so one might ague that women have an additional imaging function" during the language process. The area opposite Wernicke's in the right hemi-

> ❝Some of these early behaviors, such as playing with Lincoln Logs, may lead to changes in cognitive function—you might develop better visual–spatial skills.❞

sphere is involved in the emotional comprehension and expression aspect of language. If this region is engaged in women, then it is not farfetched to think that during language processes a typical woman brings a richer, more expanded emotional component into play than most men do.

In men, as language impulses move toward speech, only Broca's area is engaged. In women, Naylor found, "almost every area of the cortex, left and right hemisphere, has some unique relationship with Broca's during the task, as if there were many independent things going on between Broca's and lots of different regions." Is it almost as if a woman's brain is "ablaze" during language processing? "Well," Naylor responds carefully, "it suggest something more global—that women are recruiting areas of the brain that enable them to use more strategies than men."

The male arrangement follows the classical model of language function "as a unit independent from the rest of the brain," she says, adding that most language-area studies have been made with men. The classical model may be classic for only about 50 percent of the human population. Naylor's work may also explain why, according to some studies, women recover faster than men from certain types of strokes attacking the core language regions.

THE MASTER CONTROLLER

Sex differences have also been located deep within the hypothalamus, the small structure that orchestrates many vital functions. In 1978 UCLA's Roger Gorski discovered what became known as the sexually dimorphic nucleus (SDN) in the preoptic area of the male rat. This area, located in the front part of the hypothalamus and believed to help direct sexual behavior, was five times larger in males. Investigators began hunting for a similar area in humans.

In 1985 Dick Swaab, a Dutch neuroscientist, reported that he had found two areas in the human hypothalamus that showed sex differences. One was the superchiasmatic nucleus (SCN), a group of neurons that acts as a built-in clock, controlling circadian rhythms and, in women, ovulation. Swaab saw that in women the SCN has a more elongated shape. "Because there's a difference in shape, the nucleus can make different contacts, and that way it might have a different function," he says. "But we haven't got a clue about the difference in function at this point."

Swaab also looked at the preoptic area, pinpointing a cell group he believes is similar to the one Gorski investigated in rats. Swaab found it was twice as large in men and had about twice as many neurons as the women's cell group. And last year a team led by Gorski reported a sex difference in two regions of the human preoptic area. The UCLA scientists stopped short of describing the cell groups as analogous

to those of the rat. "We don't know if either of these [Swaab's or UCLA's] is the same cell group as the rodent SDN, but they would be candidates for it," says Melissa Hines, a neuroscientist then on Gorski's team. Hines speculates that hormone regulation might be a function of the cell groups. They might also be involved in male sexual behavior, although just how, too, is still unknown.

Swaab noted in one rat study that the size of the SDN appears to be related to the male rat's "libido." "For instance, there's a correlation between the number of mounts and the size of the SDN." The bigger the nucleus, the more the mounts. Implications for men? Again unknown. Scientists in this field exercise caution in making rat-to-man leaps. In their sexual behavior humans have overcome, to a greater degree than rats at least, the tyranny of their hormones. Yet Swaab's and Gorski's research has encouraged animal investigators by providing "evidence that the human brain has sex differences very much like those seen in rats and lower animals," says Bruce McEwen, a leading Rockefeller University neuroscientist.

SEA OF LOVE

Based on animal models scientists are increasingly convinced, furthermore, that prenatal hormone exposure in humans may govern some brain anatomy and behavioral differences between the sexes. For the last several years, Hines has conducted human studies to test this idea. In 1975 she began her graduate work on physical aggression and its causes. But her interest soon turned from the problem of aggression to the question of hormonal influence on behavioral development.

Now on the UCLA faculty, Hines has studied two special groups: women whose mothers took diethylstilbestrol (DES), an estrogen, or "female" hormone, during pregnancy; and girls who had congenital adrenal hyperplasia (CAH), a genetic disorder resulting in excessive production of androgens, or "male" hormones. In animal studies DES had been shown to masculinize female reproductive systems and behavior. "We think of estrogen as a female hormone. But during development, at least in the rat, testosterone is converted into estradiol [an estrogen] before it masculinizes certain brain cells. By giving DES, you're mimicking what would occur with testosterone," Hines says. "So that's why DES masculinizes."

Hines wanted to know if DES might masculinize human female brains. So she gave dichotic listening tests to DES women and their sisters who had not been exposed to DES. In the tests, different words are presented simultaneously to each ear. Because of the brain's circuitry, the word going in the right ear is recorded by the left hemisphere, and the word going into the left ear recorded by the right hemisphere.

"Because their left hemisphere is dominant in language, most people have what is called a right-ear advantage," Hines explains. "They're better at recognizing the syllables from the right ear." And there's a sex difference: Men typically are more right eared than women, because, as the theory goes, women tend to be more bilateral. Hines found that in the 25 DES women she studied, there was a bigger right-ear advantage than in their unexposed sisters. The women performed more like men, suggesting a subtle masculinizing from the early hormone exposure.

More recently Hines and psychologist Sheri Berenbaum studied CAH girls, ages two and a half to eight, to see if their prenatal exposure to excess androgens had masculinized their behavior. The scientists created a playroom with toys classified as female-type toys, male-type toys, and neutral toys. Then one by one the children—including CAH girls, their unaffected female cousins and sisters, and unaffected boys—were placed in the room and observed. "We found that more often than the other girls and about as often as the control boys, the androgenized girls played with cars, trucks, Lincoln Logs, and other male-type toys, and less with dolls," Hines says.

"I was quite surprised," she admits, "because you don't think of there being a brain region governing toy preferences." The result suggests that prenatal exposure to androgens helped create a brain that thinks more like a typical male than a typical female brain. But Hines says the research is still incomplete. "There may be other steps in the pathway between the hormone and the preference for the truck over the doll. I'm looking at that now. And of course these could be early behaviors, such as playing with Lincoln Logs, that subsequently lead to changes in cognitive function—you might develop better visual-spatial skills."

Barbara Lippe, chief of pediatric endocrinology at UCLA Medical School, is skeptical of suggestions, based on studies of hormonally abnormal people, that prenatal hormonal exposure has masculinized or feminized brain function or behavior. "The problem is that 'abnormal' experiences in the womb are more often than not coupled with abnormal hormonal levels postnatally, and it's difficult to separate them out," she says. CAH girls may also have unusual genitalia that affect the way the child is treated. "So it's a difficult model to use."

SEXUAL ORIENTATION

If early hormonal exposure can shape your brain and behavior, can it also explain sexual orientation—who turns you on? Could it answer the riddle of why some people are homosexual and others heterosexual? Witelson believes this may be a factor. In testing this, she and her colleagues found that in a group of lesbians there were nearly twice as many left-handers as in the general population. A group of gay men, too, showed a trend toward greater-than-average left-handedness.

❛The way the brain develops anatomically, then functionally, has a large hormonal component. One thing it develops is sexual orientation. It's one of many variations within each genetic sex.❜

"We don't think the increased left-handedness can be explained by learned or socially induced factors," she says. "In contrast, because left-handedness is well documented to be related to a typical pattern of brain organization, we feel there must be a neurobiological factor to homosexuality."

Witelson suspects that in women "higher levels of masculinizing hormones in utero lead to the increased left-handedness and the homosexual orientation." In men, the process may work a little differently. "We'd guess fewer androgens in utero leads to increased left-handedness and homosexual orientation." It doesn't mean, though, that "every left-handed person is homosexual or every homosexual left-handed, but as a group there's an atypical pattern of cerebral dominance [right brain] compared to the general population." It does suggest, however, that sexual orientation may develop differently in men and women.

Shelton E. Hendricks, a University of Nebraska psychologist who studies sexual orientation, says Witelson's research, while interesting, is weakened by her choice of populations to compare with the homosexual groups. She used a general population collected by another scientist in 1970 in Britain to compare with an Eighties homosexual population in Canada. "The rate of left-handedness varies with the population," Hendricks says, and factors such as time, place, age, ethnicity, and cultural pressures can affect that rate.

Witelson has also found evidence of differences in thinking patterns between homosexual and heterosexual populations, suggesting that the differences between the two groups—on average—may extend beyond the issue of what turns them on. Last year Witelson's group reported that in spatial tests, gay men performed somewhat less well than heterosexual men and better than heterosexual women—who typically do less well on spatial tests than heterosexual men. In verbal tests, the gay men again fell between the heterosexual men and women. This month at the Society for Neuroscience's meeting, Witelson and Cheryl McCormick will report how lesbians fared on the same spatial and verbal tests.

"The difference in the pattern of skills suggests something different in the organ of thought, the brain," she says. She predicts that difference may be found in the anatomy of the corpus callosum. "Unfortunately, we don't have MRIs of the brains of people we tested. This might provide further evidence of a neurobiological basis to sexual orientation and might be convincing to those strongly biased to a solely environmental theory."

Witelson hopes such findings could improve the way homosexuals are understood by society. "Our results suggest that homosexual orientation is not unnatural for homosexuals," she says. "It's as natural for them as heterosexual orientation is for heterosexuals. The way the brain develops anatomically, then functionally, has a large early hormonal component. One of the things the brain develops is sexual orientation. This is one of many variations within each genetic sex."

Hormonal changes throughout life may affect thinking as well. Canadian psychologists Doreen Kimura and Elizabeth Hampson found that during different stages of their menstrual cycle 150 women performed differently on various tests. The difference appeared to be controlled by shifts in estrogen levels. When estrogen levels were high, just before ovulation, women performed as much as 10 percent better on such items as tongue twisters, a test of motor and verbal dexterity—or, as Kimura puts it, "the articulatory, complex manual, verbal fluency, and some perceptual speed tests, on which women are often superior to men." Tests of spatial ability showed the reverse effect "in that they were depressed for women in the high-estrogen phase." In the low-estrogen phase marking the beginning of the cycle, though, the women performed better than usual on spatial perception tests, such as picking a shape out of a complex pattern. They might complete 40 spatial tasks in three minutes on low-estrogen days and only 35 on high-estrogen days.

Scientists are going to discover that sex hormones have a pervasive influence not only on the development of the brain but on aging and on various stages of life.

"I'm not at all surprised by Kimura's findings," says Gorski. "They fit with everything we've seen. If anything, her work is an updating of [American pioneer endocrinologist] Charles Sawyer's. More than thirty years ago he showed that female sex hormones altered the level of excitability in the brain stem in rabbits. This leads to changes in firing rates elsewhere, higher in the brain. The speed and quality of how we think, move, and speak could well be affected by hormones."

Men, too, experience daily fluctuations in their sex steroids. Testosterone is higher in the morning than in the evening. How these changes affect thinking skills is unknown. But recent reports indicate testosterone levels correlate surprisingly well with certain behavioral traits, such as dominance and power seeking. Testosterone levels in individuals are also influenced by environment and can vary with changing personal environmental situations.

There is also growing evidence that steroids alter connectivity between various parts of the brain throughout life. Neurons can remodel their synapses—develop new or retract old ones. It's conceivable that women make new neuronal connections when estrogen is rising and, in the postovulatory phase at the end of the cycle, lose them. "I'm in the obstetrics and gynecology department at Yale," says De Lacoste, "because the department has a long-standing interest in the role of estrogen in synaptic remodeling. This is an ideal environment to find out in what ways steroids influence how neurons live or die by synaptic remodeling. I think scientists are going to find that sex hormones have a pervasive influence not only on brain development but on aging and various stages throughout life. They aren't at all there just for your preovulatory surge or stuff like that."

Even with mounting data on sex differences, the controversy goes on. "On average, women and men perform differently. But when it comes to trying to assign causes or reasons, that's where [the scientists] get into trouble," says Ruth Hubbard, a retired Harvard biologist who has written extensively about women and biology. "In most societies men and women live very different lives, and so we develop very different capabilities. We don't know how to translate anatomical sex differences into behavioral difference."

Hines thinks much of the criticism is based on faulty logic. "The thought is that if women are demonstrated to be different from men, and it is linked to biological factors, then it will be used to justify social inequities. It's assumed that if women are different, they'll be devalued for it. Unfortunately, this has been true historically, but it doesn't have to be true." Still, she is concerned that neurobiology may be twisted to justify discrimination. "I've seen research, not mine but others', misused—you know, quoted as justifying why men are more likely to be engineers. That's a giant leap from actual knowledge. It's a big step from seeing relatively subtle hormonal contributions to behavior to seeing the average woman make substantially less money than the average man, or seeing the vast majority of heads of state and CEOs being male."

Yet while critics worry that women may become objects of increased op-pression because of sex differences in the brain, most of the prominent researchers in the field are women. Hines suspects there is just a natural interest in the field among women because women are most often the victims of sex stereotypes. Witelson says, "The sexes are different and it does no good to assume they're not. We're not going to help equal opportunity and equal recognition when we assume both are equally good in all aspects, when it may well be that there are certain things each sex is somewhat better at." And many women biologists say the findings will have a positive impact.

Indeed, sex research is uncovering variations in the way brain cells are programmed to respond to chemical signals such as neurotransmitters and circulating hormones. In animal studies investigators have found that male as well as female neurons have receptors for estrogens. "Those receptors in the male and female brain are pretty similar; both have the same number and distribution," says McEwen. "But if you then look at what estrogens and progesterones, another female hormone group, *do* to male and female brains, you'll find that the male is not always responding in the same way as the female brain. It's at that level you can begin to see how the program of the cell has become different."

This is basic chemical information scientists will obtain only after identifying sex differences in the brain. The knowledge could lead to drugs targeted more accurately to each sex. "If we're going to give women the equivalent medical treatment as men," says Jean Hamilton, a psychiatrist at the University of Texas Southwestern Medical School, "we'd better find out about sex differences where they exist. Someday men and women may be treated differently for conditions such as Alzheimer's disease and epilepsy, and the treatments will be more effective because they are different."

Finally, the value of the research is not just for understanding why men and women differ, says Hines, "but also for understanding basic processes of brain and behavioral development." Yet the added bonus would be that the ancient question about the sexes could be permanently replaced by a simple declaration: Vive la différence.

BLURRING THE LINES: ANDROGYNY ON TRIAL

Don Monkerud

One day Linda received a phone call from Laura, a friend for five years. Linda and Laura regularly met for coffee, exchanged dinner invitations, and chatted in the powder room at the local church. "I've been living a lie," Laura confessed. "I'm a man who had a sex change operation. I'm going to stop taking hormones and become a man again. You can call me Walter."

Today stories of a man or woman cross-dressing or being "trapped" in an unwanted body are not that uncommon. In Laura's case the confusion was overwhelming. Although he was a successful national operations manager at a Japanese automobile company in California and was married with two children, Walter had never felt particularly comfortable as a businessman. So when his wife accepted his cross-dressing after work, he began to change and ventured onto a gender roller coaster.

He had breast implants inserted and removed seven times. When doctors told him he could end his gender confusion with a sex change operation, Walter wrote a check for the operation and went for a walk. He came back two hours later, tore the check up, and went home. Two years later he had the operation. His wife left. His children won't speak to him. He lost his job. "If surgery is the solution, what's the problem?" he asks today.

Walter feels victimized by society's expectation of what it means to be a man. He found that being a woman was even worse. After his operation he felt confident he'd be able to continue his career. But it didn't happen. When Laura applied for upper-level positions, employers discovering her sex change wouldn't hire her. When she applied for a low-level position, employers claimed she was overqualified.

Once Laura took a position as a clerk and was quickly promoted to secretary for a vice-president. But her boss, demanding that Laura serve coffee and be acquiescent, got irritated when she refused, and wanted her fired. People treated her "with disrespect" and her income plummeted.

Depressed and very lonely, Laura stopped taking estrogen. Walter took charge and let his beard grow back in. "It's a lot easier finding a job as Walter than as Laura," he says. He'd like to change into a man, but it's a $40,000 series of operations to graft skin from his leg to build a new penis. Walter thinks he'll buy a house first so he can be financially secure before he undergoes the operation.

On one level Walter is a candidate for intensive psychotherapy. On another level his dilemma is a more intense reflection of what many experience as they assume sex roles in a world of changing expectations. Sex-appropriate behavior is still prescribed for men and women in a society that increasingly merges economic and social responsibilities and styles. Yet the cracks in gender identity are shattering the stereotypes. Pop figures like Prince and Michael Jackson play off the confusion. Madonna wears men's suits and occasionally grabs her crotch. Since 1979 between 7,000 and 12,000 sex change operations have been performed in the United States, according to the Henry Benjamin International Gender Dysphoria Association of Palo Alto, California. Fifty percent are of the female-to-male variety.

On the street, gender bending expresses itself in fashion. Men and boys are wearing earrings and hair of any length; women don boxer shorts. Behaviorally, women practice assertive techniques and men try to be nurturing. Legally, it manifests itself in litigation over equal pay for equal work and a father's time off for childbirth. The possibilities for expressing one's sexual identity today are multifaceted and novel to the human race. So how will the concepts of masculine and feminine be defined? What will replace conventional sex-defined behavior in the future?

With such questions in mind, I recently went to a Stanford University conference on androgyny, sponsored by the Institute for Research on Women and Gender at Stanford as well as the French consulate and the Goethe Institut in San Francisco. Conversing in English, French, and German and some-

times switching in mid-paragraph, the researchers articulated their positions on modernity, cross-cultural variations on androgyny, experiments in sex changes, and gynandry, or the female equivalent of androgyny.

Much of the talk was theoretical and academic. But sexist or not, I couldn't help noticing how differently the women from various cultures presented themselves. Yes, it was the sort of observation that could get me torn to ribbons in such a sex-stereotype-sensitive group. Still, it was as if the Germans and the French staked out positions jettisoning patriarchy but returning to aspects of femininity, while the Americans opted for gender amorphousness. Well, Europeans are more style conscious than Americans. But on the whole, the French and German female participants wore more makeup and jewelry, a greater variety of hairstyles—they played with their femininity. The Americans seemed plainer, with short hair, little makeup or jewelry. They wore clothes the French women probably wouldn't wear around the house on a rainy day. The Americans took a more austere, intellectual approach to the gender dilemma.

"One thing is for sure," stated Anna Kuhn, from the University of California, Davis, as if to underscore the American stance. "Until we redefine behavior in terms of human, rather than masculine and feminine, we are locked in a dance of death." In a swirl of clothes, the professor of German, who has made extensive studies of the role of women in Weimar and Nazi Germany, elaborated: A male-centered vision perpetuates the world as a battleground, a place to conquer and struggle. Women are "the other," and men continually attempt to dominate them, hence the war between the sexes. Until we drop stereotypical ideas of gender, she says, neither men nor women will be free to develop as self-sufficient individuals.

Few investigators of human behavior leave gender-related issues out of their analysis. The term *gender* became acceptable in the Seventies to signify an individual's personal, legal, and social status without reference to one's genetic

Reprinted by permission from *Omni*, October 1990, pp. 81-84, 86, 111. Copyright © 1990, Omni Publications International, Ltd.

sex. "Gender was introduced to assert that the sexes are not merely biological entities, or even primarily biological entities," explains Nancy Chodorow, professor of sociology at Berkeley, "and to make the case for gender as constructed culturally, socially, economically, politically." Gender, then, may be in the mind of the beholder.

Most gender studies still revolve around the problem of nature or nurture—biology versus learned behavior. Children's studies, particularly those looking at differences in verbal and math skills in boys and girls, attempt to distinguish the influences of environment or genetics. Many more observe children's play habits. Eleanor Maccoby, a Stanford psychologist and pioneer in children's research, saw striking differences. Four-and-a-half-year-old nursery-school children played with same-sex playmates three times as much as they did with cross-sex playmates in mixed groups. At six and a half, they were 11 times more likely to play with children of the same sex.

Yet Maccoby found considerable variation on any given day in the children's degree of playmate choice. She discovered that socialization affected sex-typed attitudes more, perhaps, than how masculine or feminine the child appeared. "The connection between individual personalities and preference for same-sex playmates is weak at best," she says. "Socialization occurs when children are presented with activities based on gender; for example, they classify sports and occupations by whether or not men or women practice them." This process begins at a young age. Maccoby maintains that some gender activities are biological universals, such as women giving birth. Others exist in a gray area with both biological and social elements affecting behavior, and some, like men driving trucks or women being secretaries, are completely arbitrary and can change over time.

"Children," says Maccoby, "make inferences from culture-wide information. As is well-known, once the stereotypes have been formed, they tend to become self-perpetuating and resistant to change—even on the basis of information that destroys the stereotype."

How reliable are studies claiming either biology or environment is the shaping force of gender? "Examples of studies proving environment's effect are hard to find," says neuropsychologist Sandra Witelson of McMaster University in Ontario. "There are many showing little girls playing with dolls and boys with trucks. It is common to say this is because parents buy dolls for girls and reinforce this, and buy trucks for boys and

reinforce that. But the real question is, What shaped the parents' choice of toys for their children in the first place? It's possible that a sex difference in the child's response to various toys may influence the parents' behavior."

If you thought the idea that women belong in the kitchen went out with hand-cranked phonographs, here's Michael Levin, professor of philosophy at City College of New York. Levin asserts there's a deep and abiding difference between the sexes and that much modern unhappiness comes from attempts to transform women into "pseudo-men." Many sex differences that are "nowadays attributed to oppression, discrimination, and telling fairy stories to children are really just an expression of innate differences," Levin says. "Nobody sits down to choose his personality. That's an idiotic way of putting it. You are given your personality for the most part when you're born."

Levin or no Levin, experiments to undermine the stereotypes are ongoing.

Sandra Bern, a Cornell University psychologist, has explored ways of creating genderless environments. On a personal level she has attempted to raise her own children "gender a-schematically." For Bern, androgyny is the model. "For many people confused about how to behave as a man or woman, androgyny provides both a vision of Utopia and a model of mental health," says the slight, plainly dressed Bern in a tumultuous rush of ideas. "Androgyny does not require the individual to banish from the self whatever attributes and behaviors the culture may have stereotypically defined as inappropriate for his or her sex."

Bem and her husband tried to eliminate sex stereotyping from their own behavior by sharing household chores, bathing the children, making dinner together, and giving them trucks and dolls irrespective of their sex. In reading material they looked for nonstereotypical stories. They even doctored books, drawing beards on waitresses and giving truck drivers "female" hairstyles. Men and women were defined as such in stories only if they had a vagina or penis to determine their sex. The couple censored television programs.

At age four, Bem's son, Jeremy, wore barrettes to nursery school. One day a boy repeatedly told him that "only girls wear barrettes." Jeremy tried to explain that wearing barrettes didn't make one a boy or girl: Only genitalia did. Finally, in frustration, he pulled down his pants to show the boy that having a penis made him a boy. The boy responded, "Everybody has a penis; only girls wear barrettes." At the moment,

Bem refuses to discuss the results of this "experiment": She's writing a book about it.

Focusing on the gender baggage that people carry around in their heads, Bem embarked on a plan to dislodge sex stereotypes—which she considers "immoral"—and liberate the individual's unique abilities and interests. Because she perceived no suitable yardstick for measuring "masculine" and "feminine," she developed her own. The Bem Sex-Role Inventory (BSRI) is designed to measure a person's ability to integrate masculine and feminine traits. Bem and her students collected a list of 200 personality characteristics they thought defined masculine, neuter, and feminine values. A sample of the BSRI's stereotypical masculine qualities includes "forceful" and "risk-taking." Some feminine stereotypical characteristics are "cheerful" and "loyal." An initial group of 100 Stanford undergraduates—half male, half female—judged these characteristics on a scale ranging from "not at all desirable" to "extremely desirable."

If a person scores high on the BSRI in masculine characteristics and low in feminine characteristics, he is said to have a masculine sex role; if high in feminine and low in masculine traits, a feminine sex role. If a person's masculinity and femininity scores are approximately equal, that person is said to have an androgynous sex role. Cross-sexed, or "undifferentiated," individuals are men or women with both low masculinity and femininity scores.

Investigators have used the BSRI to assess changing—or static—notions of gender. Stanford's Sherri Matteo used it to investigate why college students choose to participate in certain sports. She found many picked athletic events that conformed to cultural norms of masculinity and femininity and avoided sports associated with the opposite sex. Sex-typed individuals, those with the strongest identification with their sex, chose their sport solely in this way.

Other studies using the BSRI have found that sex-typed individuals attend more to a person's sex when judging physical attractiveness and differentiate between male and female speakers when asked to recall "who said what" in a group discussion. In another study by Bem, subjects were offered choices to test their willingness to perform sex-inappropriate tasks—such as men ironing clothes. Sex-typed people rejected these tasks and harbored more negative emotions about them.

Today, says Bernd Schmitt of the Graduate School of Business at Columbia University, the BSRI remains an accurate measure in studying degrees of sex typing and androgyny.

Yet androgyny, too, is controversial. In the nineteenth century, writers such as Wilde and Proust exemplified the androgynous male as an artistic ideal necessary to the highest creations; rooted in the vision of a perfect man, androgyny made a man whole by recognizing his female aspects. Bourgeois conventionality, however, deemed it a code name for homosexuality. After being reintroduced in the Seventies, androgyny immediately became politically incorrect. Feminist critics said androgyny overlooked women's inequality and focused too much attention on personalities rather than on class and power distinctions.

But at a time when one can be gay or lesbian, transsexual, a cross dresser, a caring man, or a dominant woman and still be accepted in some part of our social landscape, androgyny seems to be moving to the center. At the century's beginning, Virginia Woolf believed that everyone is partly male and partly female. She saw the mind as a taxi that could be boarded by a man or woman, with the male brain predominating in men and the female in women. Another way of looking at androgyny "would not entail some merging of the sexes into an androgynous mutant, nor would it produce a hermaphroditic creature with male and female genitalia or beards and breasts," says Marilyn Yalom of Stanford. "I have in my mind's eye the image of a piano with its eighty-eight keys. Everyone would have access to a full keyboard. Women would not be limited to the higher-pitched notes, nor the men to the lower scales."

Androgynous images have long existed among performers. Rudolph Valentino unmasked transvestism by appearing at once feminine and masculine in robes, eyebrow pencil, and lipstick. Elvis shocked the Grand Ole Opry when he wore eye shadow, a precursor to his rhinestone-studded jumpsuits and sequins. Liberace, who single-handedly supported the Australian rhinestone industry and taught androgynous fantasy to the rock stars of the Eighties, may have hit the apex of his career when he hooked himself up to piano wires to fly across the stage as Peter Pan: a middle-aged man, dressing like a woman, playing a young boy. By 1984 Boy George could blithely address national TV saying, "I want to thank America for knowing a good drag queen when they see one." And Grace Jones can ponder her

Janus-faced dual image as supermacho superwoman. "When I put on a wig with long hair, I look like a hooker or drag queen. So I actually look more feminine when I dress like a man."

Today men look like women; women, men. You see it in Calvin Klein ads, in pitches for Solo-Flex machines, and in deodorant commercials, observes the University of Southern California's Nancy Vickers. Just as female bodies were once draped around spark plugs and bottles of scotch, the male body today is sexualized with erotic images. *Top Gun,* says Vickers, contains an undertone of gay relationships between men. Vickers isn't sure where this will lead in the next 20 years. "What I do think is breaking down is a set of binary oppositions between the sexes."

Yet even as these binaries diffuse into a rainbow of gender orientations, a counterforce is mounting to "recapture" masculinity. The poet Robert Bly has achieved renown conducting workshops to help men get in tune with "the wild man inside." For Bly, the wild man is an essential mythic connection to the earth and other men and not the macho or savage man, who has developed what Bly calls the second-rate, domineering side of his identity. Despite teaching workshops where attendees are encouraged to crawl on all fours, butt heads, snort, and engage in flatulence, Bly recognizes the evils of patriarchy. "*Masculine* is not synonymous with *men,* and *feminine* with *women,*" he explains. "A man needs to develop both his feminine and masculine sides as strongly as he can, then distinguish between them and live in the resonating space between. Yet," he adds, "a man who is ashamed of his masculinity will not be a good citizen or a good husband."

A recent "Theater of Virility," conducted by Montreal Jungian analyst Guy Corneau, was devoted to coming to grips with "image," "aggression," and "intimacy." "Whether it is Adrien-the-Hero, Gaétan-the-Homosexual, Narcissus-the-Unloved, Valentine-the-Seducer, Christian-the-Macho..." or others, claimed the brochure, "their portraits are timeless; they represent the forms that masculinity has been taking for centuries." With these identities under siege, it's no wonder men join such groups. Others respond by becoming armchair Rambos. Most are aware the old rules no longer apply, and they don't know what the new rules are. Why do macho men behave the way they do? I asked Matteo. The tall, slender instructor, who could be mistaken for a business executive, admitted she "doesn't have much insight there." She simply avoids this type of male, Matteo says,

recognizing that her position affords her this luxury.

At the Stanford conference, it became obvious that the international participants had viewpoints that varied along cultural lines. According to Frankfurt psychoanalyst Margarete Mitscherlich-Nielson, author of *The Peaceable Sex: On Aggression in Women and Men,* German women generally feel they have the legal structures to ensure equal treatment, but more needs to be done on a personal level. In Germany, she contends, "men traditionally have had the tenderness stripped from their personalities at an early age. Fear instills the father as an idealized authority figure." By addressing gender differences with men, she thinks, women can begin to change society toward more gender-equal relations.

With the rise of a new German national identity, however, she worries that the old myths might rise again. "Those myths usually involve ideal roles for men and women. In Hitler's time it was the myth of the good soldier, the good mother. The notion of identity based on bodily identity," she says, "is always connected with ideology."

Because the French thinkers placed more emphasis on the differences between the sexes than did the American theorists, with their priority on similarity and equality, some U.S. academicians at the conference claimed the French were ten years behind the times. Throughout the meetings, Bem, for example, reiterated the idea that one needs to be a man or woman only when reproducing; otherwise there are no traits in masculinity or femininity worth preserving.

The French researchers emphasized the equality *in* difference: aesthetic, sexual, cultural, and erotic. Élisabeth Badinter, a French philosopher and author of *The Unopposite Sex,* claims that there are opportunities for each sex to "express the other half of themselves without losing their identities." Women especially, she thinks, have been able to adopt male characteristics without losing their basic femininity. Men have not fared so well, "being caught between an outdated model that women reject and a model with less power and a gentleness they fear." Parents should allow little children to distinguish themselves as male and female. Only by feeling secure in their virility and femininity will they be able to display both sides of their personalities. "We are born androgynous, then we assert our sex. And then if we are secure in our identities, we become androgynous again. It's unrealistic to think that paradise can be achieved on Earth," Badinter acknowledges. "We need several generations."

Mind Over Illness

Do Optimists Live Longer?

To stay healthy, think positive—don't let tough situations weigh you down.

Nan Silver

Nan Silver, *a Senior Editor of* American Health, *is converting to optimism.*

"Giving orders was sometimes very hard, if not impossible, because I always had this problem of dealing with men under me, even later in the war and when I had the appropriate rank."—Frank

"During the war I was occasionally bored, because anyone who's ever been aboard ship is bored to tears."—Joe

Frank and Joe are pseudonyms for Harvard University graduates from the early '40s. Both survived World War II. And both were young and healthy veterans when they wrote these lines about their wartime troubles in a 1946 survey. They had similar backgrounds, similar experiences, and neither had glowing memories of the war. Yet their fates would be dramatically different. In the years since, Joe has lived a healthy, robust life, and Frank has been chronically ill.

What's the key reason? Most of us would probably shrug and say luck, or perhaps genetics. But not University of Pennsylvania psychologist Martin E.P. Seligman. At the recent annual meeting of the American Psychological Association (APA) in Washington, DC, he offered a far more surprising—

and controversial—theory, based on research done with psychologist Christopher Peterson of the University of Michigan and Dartmouth College psychiatrist George Vaillant.

After analyzing the words of 99 such Harvard vets, the researchers believe the men's future may have been there, waiting to be discovered, in the very words they used 40 years ago to describe their war experiences. Based on complex analytic measures, Seligman and his colleagues have pegged Frank as a pessimist and Joe as an optimist. That difference may be crucial to mental and physical health, says Seligman. The latest studies even suggest that people like Joe may be more resilient in the face of cancer.

The Harvard study is a recent addition to a growing body of research that suggests a rosy way of thinking and speaking may help protect body and mind from harm. It may also do wonders for your career (see "Stress or Success?"). These studies are adding scientific credence to the old sayings about the power of positive thinking. By changing the way we think about the bad things that happen to us, says Seligman, we may be able to boost our moods—and our physical vitality.

What's Wrong With Frank?

Although both Frank and Joe have

negative memories of military life, Seligman's analysis reveals they differ tremendously in what he calls *explanatory* or *attributional* style. The term refers to how people explain the events in their lives—anything from winning at poker to being bored on ship.

Through explanatory style, Frank and other pessimists (as Seligman defines the term) are identified by three elements in their speech. First (and, Seligman believes, most disastrously), pessimists assume the problem is never-ending, or *stable*. Says Frank: "I always had this problem. . . ." Next, they believe the cause of their problem is *global* rather than specific—it will ruin every aspect of their lives. Frank does a little better here. He's not completely global, because he relates his difficulty with giving orders only to the war. Finally, pessimists blame themselves when trouble arises. Seligman calls this being *internal*. Frank assumes *he's* the cause of his problem, not the sullen privates who refuse to listen.

In general, then, Frank's a far cry from his buddy Joe, whom Seligman considers an optimist. Joe is bored only "occasionally." He thinks his hardship is temporary (unstable), and entirely specific (only on the ship) rather than global. And, for Joe, problems are caused by *external* circumstances. His boredom isn't his fault;

anyone aboard ship feels that way. (To test *your* explanatory style, see "How Optimistic Are You?")

The evidence is mounting that people tend to stick to one explanatory style throughout their lives. At the APA meeting, Seligman reported on a study by University of Pennsylvania psychologist Melanie Burns. She compared the teenage diaries of 30 people now in their 70s with current writing samples. Their styles had remained the same.

And in their study of Harvard vets, Seligman and colleagues found that the statements Joe, Frank and the others had made when young and fit told much about their futures. Seligman's theory: "If you always go around thinking, 'It's my fault, it's going to last forever, and it's going to undermine everything I do,' then when you do run into further bad events, you become at risk for poor health."

More evidence comes from a study by Christopher Peterson. While at Virginia Polytechnic Institute and State University in Blacksburg, he measured the way 172 college students reacted to bad events. He also checked their health and moods. One month later he found that, whatever the initial health status, pessimists had become ill more often. "And," he adds, "a year later, they had made significantly more visits to the doctor."

Most research suggests that pessimism is much more dangerous in the face of bad events than when the going's good, says Seligman. But in one study, he did find that consistently pooh-poohing success *can* do long-term damage—at least to famous baseball players.

A pessimistic response to *good* news is unstable, specific and external—"It won't last, it won't change my life, I was just lucky." So far, Seligman's research team has analyzed the sports-page quotes of 34 Baseball Hall of Famers who played between 1900 and 1950. Result: Pessimists, who said their ballpark victories were short-lived and due to "luck," lived significantly shorter lives than extreme optimists like Rube Marquard (who died at age 90).

How Optimistic Are You?

The scene: Your mate has just walked out on you. Which of the eight reasons below do you think best represents the way you'd honestly react?

It's good news if you chose an unstable reason (Nos. 5 through 8)—you don't tend to think bad times last forever. The healthiest choice: No. 8; it's

also external (your mate's problem caused the breakup) and specific (not all men or women are moody). If you chose a stable reason (Nos. 1 through 4), you may want to work on being more optimistic. No. 1's the least healthy: It's self-blaming and all-encompassing.

		Global	*Specific*
STABLE	Internal	1. I'm completely unlovable.	3. I'm unlovable because I'm so moody (picky, boring, unattractive).
	External	2. My mate and *all* men (women) are jerks.	4. My mate is a jerk.
UNSTABLE	Internal	5. Sometimes I just get so moody.	7. Sometimes I get so moody toward my mate.
	External	6. Sometimes, my mate and *all* men (women) get into terrible moods.	8. Sometimes my mate gets into terrible moods.

Stress or Success?

Optimism doesn't just help keep you healthy and in high spirits—it's also linked to greater activity and risk-taking. The reason: Quitting often stems from helplessness, says psychologist Martin E.P. Seligman. And your explanatory style may determine how active or helpless you are.

One of Seligman's favorite examples: Lyndon Baines Johnson. Normally he had "an average explanatory style for an American man," says Seligman. But before making certain crucial and controversial decisions as President—such as doubling the troop commitment in Vietnam—his words (measured from transcripts of press conferences) suddenly became wildly optimistic. And, right before his decision not to run for re-election, his style swung the other way—a cue that he would soon make a passive decision.

LBJ, of course, was overly optimis-

tic and took risks that harmed others. But for many people, an optimistic style is linked to *true* success.

In fact, explanatory style may be better than more standard measures at predicting achievement in certain situations.

In one of Seligman's studies, a "special force" of 100 insurance salesmen who failed Metropolitan Life's traditional entrance exam—but scored as high optimists on Seligman's explanatory-style questionnaire—is outselling Met's regular recruits by 20% to 25%.

Studies of students have brought similar results. At the University of Pennsylvania, psychologist Leslie Kamen found that optimistic freshmen did better in their first-semester grades than the admissions committee had predicted from high-school scores and averages. Pessimists did worse.

The Talking Blues

Baseball players, war veterans, students. In every case, chronic negative thinking has been linked to poorer health. What makes doom and gloom so dangerous? Years of research by Seligman and other psychologists into *depression* offers an explanation.

These "cognitive" psychologists have long believed our thoughts—written, spoken or silent—may play a determining role in behavior and health. But at first their work focused not on physical health but on the link between low moods and feelings of helplessness. A key to their theories: studies by Seligman and others showing that animals faced with unavoidable electric shocks eventually stop trying to escape. They become helpless—and depressed—and may continue to behave passively ever after. In extreme cases they succumb to what Seligman calls "submissive death."

Many psychologists believe that in humans, too, helplessness can lead to low mood. But Seligman, for one, doesn't think it's helpless *situations* that cause the problem, but *thoughts* of helplessness—the negative explanatory style—that those situations may generate.

Why? Thoughts triggered by a specific event—say a failure at work—can build a power all their own, Seligman believes: "If you consistently respond to such events pessimistically, that negative style can actually *amplify* your feelings of helplessness and spread to other areas of your life."

Psychologists have already studied the explanatory style of all types of people—children, students, the elderly, even prisoners—and found evidence that a pessimistic style may indeed cause depression.

In one series of studies, psychologists Susan Nolen-Hoeksema (now at Stanford University) and Joan Girgus of Princeton University repeatedly tested the mood and explanatory style of 168 third, fourth and fifth-graders. Those who had an optimistic style, but were depressed for some reason in the first month, tended to feel upbeat three months later. And those who started out momentarily happy, but spoke like pessimists, later became blue.

The Dangerous Difference

How does pessimism lead to poor *health*? For one thing, people who develop an "I surrender" attitude are less likely to take good care of themselves, eat right, see doctors or seek support from family and friends, says Seligman.

But the latest research also suggests a far more direct route to harm: Pessimistic thinking may actually hamper your immune system. When laboratory rats were made helpless, their immune systems were often slower and less successful in battling implanted tumor cells, according to research by Hymie Anisman of Carleton University in Ottawa and Steven Maier of the University of Colorado in Boulder. More of these rats died than others who hadn't been made helpless but were fighting the same cancer (see "The Hope Factor," *AH*, July/August, '83).

Now psychologists are finding similar results in people faced with illness. In a pilot study of 13 cancer patients with advanced melanoma, Sandra Levy at the University of Rochester reports that an optimistic style was the *number one* psychological predictor of who would live longest. The study was so small that Levy believes the results are only "suggestive." Yet at the recent APA meeting, she announced the latest results of a study of recurring breast cancer. Again, a connection: Optimism was linked to a longer cancer-free period before the disease returned.

On the basis of these findings, Levy believes that "joy," as opposed to helplessness, may help cancer patients by giving them more stamina to withstand the disease's onslaught. Levy is now collaborating with Seligman on further studies of breast cancer patients.

As part of yet another continuing research project, University of Pennsylvania psychologist Leslie Kamen, along with Seligman and psychologist Judith Rodin of Yale, is studying the explanatory style of 58 healthy people ages 60 to 90. No matter how healthy they seemed, those elderly people who began the study with a pessimistic style had lower levels of certain immune system cells than the optimists.

Psychologists are still debating whether pessimism has to be long-lasting and pervasive in order to harm. Seligman believes it does. Others think it can cause trouble even if it crops up in just one situation—say, when you're battling cancer.

In either case, the latest research offers compelling evidence of the rich rewards positive thinking can bring—and the damage negative thoughts can cause. Says Seligman: "It's not reality itself that's producing this risk factor, but what you do with reality and the way you think about it."

Detoxing Your Thoughts

Whatever causes pessimistic thinking, it *can* be changed, says psychologist Martin E.P. Seligman. The tool: cognitive therapy, in which the therapist helps the patient examine—and alter—erroneous and pessimistic thinking patterns. Studies have shown that cognitive therapy is as successful as drug therapy in alleviating depression. And research by psychologist Robert DeRubeis of the University of Pennsylvania and Mark Evans of the University of Minnesota suggests it may work by changing your explanatory style.

Now psychologists are studying whether cognitive therapy can do for the immune system what it seems to do for mood. In a joint project, psychologists Seligman, Judith Rodin and Sandra Levy are giving 12 weeks of cognitive therapy to cancer patients.

Will this treatment help battle the disease? "I think it's kind of a long shot," Seligman admits. "If, for example, it's a small tumor load, then I think what goes on in our heads can make a difference—maybe even a life-saving one. But if a crane falls on you, it doesn't much matter whether you're an optimist."

In the future, Seligman hopes that short-term cognitive therapy will be used as prevention—before illness or depression strikes. If you want to try the treatment, look for a therapist specifically trained in *cognitive* techniques, as developed by University of Pennsylvania psychiatrist Aaron T. Beck or New York psychologist Albert Ellis (his brand is called Rational Emotive Therapy). Also check for membership in professional organizations, such as the APA.

Dr. Beck's group, the Center for Cognitive Therapy (133 S. 36th St., Suite 602, Philadelphia, PA 19104, 215-898-4100), offers a nationwide referral service that can match you with a therapist in your area.

HEALTH'S CHARACTER

Hans J. Eysenck

Hans J. Eysenck, Ph.D., D.Sc., is one of the world's most cited psychologists. He is a professor at the Institute of Psychiatry of the University of London, where he started the discipline of clinical psychology in Great Britian. He is a pioneer in the use of behavior therapy as well as research in personality theory and measurements.

Imagine this: A simple, six-question test predicts whether you are likely to get cancer or heart disease or to stay healthy. These predictions would not be based on traditional medical risks such as smoking or obesity but on your personality.

If the test indicates that you have a disease-prone personality, there would be some short-term behavior therapies (no radiation treatments, no surgery, no drugs) that protect you against cancer or a heart attack or help you live longer if you are already sick.

It sounds too good to be true, but it just might be. Dramatic results from studies completed in Europe over the past several years point to a very strong connection between certain personalities and specific illnesses. If the research I am about to describe holds up under ongoing scrutiny, we will be entering a new era of health care and disease prevention.

Theories about disease-prone personalities usually draw loud protests from the medical community, but such ideas are hardly new. The notion that people with certain personality characteristics are likely to develop coronary heart disease dates back more than 2,000 years to Hippocrates. The idea that people of a different personality type are more likely to develop cancer has also been around for a long time. These ideas are based on centuries of observations made by keen-

---

The world's most-quoted psychologist contends that a Yugoslav's controversial experiments prove that certain personalities are prone to cancer, others to heart disease. But you can learn to be prone to health.

---

eyed physicians; they should not be rejected simply because they were made without modern methodological and statistical expertise.

The type of personality often ascribed to the cancer-prone individual combines two major features. One is an inability to express emotions such as anger, fear and anxiety; the other is an inability to cope with stress and a tendency to develop feelings of hopelessness, helplessness and

finally depression. In the late 1950s, a Scottish oncologist, David Kissen, and I tried to test some of these ideas. We administered psychological questionnaires to patients coming to Kissen's lung cancer clinic before they were diagnosed as having cancer. We wanted to find out how readily these people expressed their emotions. We then compared those with a diagnosis of lung cancer to those with a non-malignant diagnosis. People who found it easier to express their emotions seemed to be protected from cancer, while those who could not suffered from cancer much more than chance would have predicted.

These results have been replicated by other researchers studying lung cancer in men and breast cancer in women. In general, the more recent studies characterized the cancer-prone person as un-assertive, over-patient, avoiding conflict and failing to express negative emotions. However, many of these studies were small and had some technical problems with methodology, and other studies found no association between cancer and personality traits (see "Fighting Cancerous Feelings," *Psychology Today*, May 1988).

Coronary heart disease has also been linked to certain personality types, most often to the so-called "Type A" personality or behavior pattern, which was summarized by its discoverers in the late 1950s as "excessive and competitive drive, and an enhanced sense of time urgency". Later research in the '70s and '80s has shown that Type A behavior is actually composed of several different components and that many of them do not in fact predict coronary heart disease. The only components that seem to stand up to the test are tendencies towards anger, hostility and aggression.

But many studies of heart disease and behavior focused on people who were already ill, and it is possible that the disease caused the personality pattern, rather than the other way around. And several studies of healthy people using the Type A behavior scales and interviewing methods found a very weak link to heart disease or no link at all (see "Type A On Trial," *Psychology Today*, February 1987).

So the whole question of personality and disease has been shrouded in uncertainty, due to the absence of large-scale studies in which personality traits are determined first and the people under investigation are then observed for many years to see who dies and of what disease.

Three such studies have recently been completed and published, all of them carried out by Ronald Grossarth-Maticek, a Yugoslav psychologist who carried out his original research in the 1960s in his home country and then went to West Germany to work in Heidelberg. He took large random samples of people, measured their personality traits, smoking and drinking habits, physical health and other characteristics. He then checked on them for periods of 10 or more years to learn whether aspects of personality could be linked to death from cancer or heart disease or to a long and healthy life. Several American and British psychologists, including myself, have collaborated with him in recent years.

Grossarth-Maticek measured personality in two ways. He used a series of short questionnaires to look at various aspects of the cancer-prone personality and the heart disease-prone personality, as he conceptualized them. The most important questions measured tendencies toward hopelessness and helplessness, rational and anti-emotional behavior and a lack of angry responses to traumatic life events (it is a testament to Grossarth-Maticek's astuteness that his ideas in the early 1960s agree almost perfectly with the most recent results of American and British research in this field).

An alternative method of ascertaining personality involved lengthy interviews in which the subjects were allocated to one of four types: Type 1, cancer-prone; Type 2, coronary heart disease-prone; Types 3 and

4, relatively healthy people who could deal with stress in a non-self-destructive fashion. Grossarth-Maticek has also developed a short questionnaire that distinguishes these four personality types (see "The Health Personality Test"). You can take it and score yourself to find out your health personality.

Based on these personality types, Grossarth-Maticek was able to predict death from cancer among these people with an accuracy of 50 percent, which is six times higher than a prediction from cigarette smoking. Of the Type 1 people who died, almost half died from cancer, while fewer than one-tenth died from heart disease. About one-third of the Type 2 people died of heart disease, but only about one-fifth died from cancer. Type 3 and Type 4 showed relatively few deaths.

In the Yugoslav study, the people were

Until recently, no large studies have determined personality first, then followed people for years to see who dies of what disease. A few years ago, Grossarth-Maticek completed three such studies.

---

for the most part the oldest inhabitant in every second house in a small town; however, Grossarth-Maticek also included a number of people who were suggested as being in a state of high stress. It is unscientific to throw together two different populations in one study, and adding stressed individuals to the study has been criticized, since it might have artificially strengthened the connection between the death rates and the disease-prone personality groups. But a recent reanalysis has shown that the connection is actually stronger without the stressed people.

Later, in Heidelberg, Grossarth-Maticek studied a random group of men and women between 40 and 60 years of age (see "Mind-Body Connections"). The overall number of deaths in this study was much smaller than it was in the Yugoslav study because the people in Heidelberg were much younger on average. However, as before, Type 1 people tended to die of cancer and Type 2 people tended to die of heart disease.

In Heidelberg, Grossarth-Maticek also examined a second group, closely resembling the first in age, sex and smoking habits. However, this second group of

people was nominated as people suffering from severe stress. If stress plays an important part in causing death from cancer and heart disease, far more people in this group should have died of these illnesses. This was indeed so: Approximately 40 percent more people in the stressed group died of these diseases. These data are for a 10-year follow-up, and there was little change when a 13-year follow-up was completed.

These dramatic results, indicating a powerful role for personality and behavior in cancer and heart disease, lead to an all-important question: Can we prevent these deaths by changing people's personalities?

Grossarth-Maticek and I tried to use behavior therapy to teach cancer- and heart disease-prone people to express their emotions more readily, to cope with stress, to wean them of their emotional dependencies and to make them more self-reliant. In other words, we taught them to behave more like the healthier personality types. We used relaxation, desensitization, modeling, suggestion and hypnosis and other standard behavioral techniques (see "Steps To A Healthier Self"). The results were astonishing.

100 people with cancer-prone personalities were divided into two groups: 50 who received no therapy and 50 who did receive it. Far more people died of cancer (and of other causes) in the no-therapy group than in the therapy group. After 13 years, 45 people who got therapy were still alive. Only 19 were alive in the no-therapy group.

We tried a similar experiment with 92 heart disease-prone people, divided into therapy and no-therapy groups. Here too there were marked differences 13 years later, with 37 people surviving with therapy and 17 surviving without it.

These results were encouraging, to say the least; however, the therapy in these studies consisted of about 30 hours of individual treatment, which is fairly lengthy and expensive. We decided to look for ways to reduce the treatment time and expense.

We tried using group therapy, in which groups of some 20 people met for about six hours in all, on two or three occasions. Here too we found a marked difference in the number of people who died of cancer and coronary heart disease, again favoring the therapy group. In a third study, we tried short-term therapy on an individual basis, again with favorable results.

There is also evidence that similar treatment can prolong life in people who

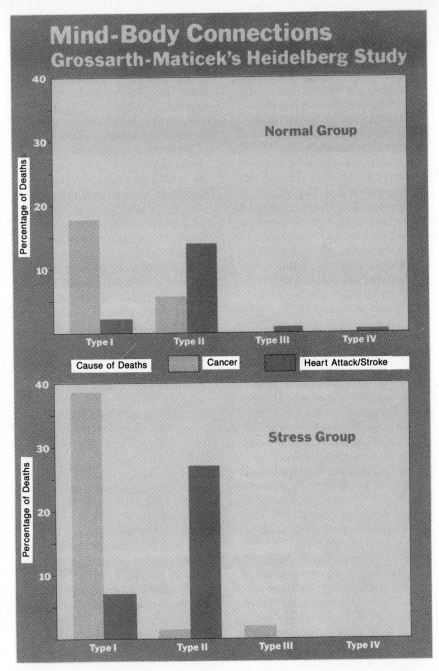

Mind-Body Connections
Grossarth-Maticek's Heidelberg Study

Normal Group

Cause of Deaths — Cancer — Heart Attack/Stroke

Stress Group

Top: More of the Type 1 (cancer-prone personality) people who died during a 10-year period in Heidelberg, West Germany, succumbed to cancer than died of heart disease. More of the Type 2 (heart disease-prone personality) people died of heart-related problems. These two diseases claimed only a small percentage of Types 3 and 4 (healthy personalities). Bottom: This mind-body pattern showed up to a much greater degree among people living under a lot of stress, indicating that stress can exacerbate these illnesses.

Half of each group also received behavior therapy. Survival rates were 11 months for those who received no type of therapy, 14 months for those who received only chemotherapy, 15 months for those who received only behavior therapy and 22 months for those who received both. The combined effect of both types of therapy is stronger than simply adding the individual effects of chemotherapy and behavior therapy.

The names and addresses of all participants in the preventive therapy studies were given to two independent research organizations, which were responsible for ascertaining death and cause of death. Thus there was reasonable control over the procedures.

Similar results, although using somewhat different methods and populations, have been obtained independently in the United States. In one study, psychiatrist David Spiegel and his colleagues at the Stanford University School of Medicine have reported on the effects of a psychotherapy group treatment for breast cancer patients. The average survival rate during the study was 35 months for the group in therapy, as opposed to just 19 months for the group that was not — a difference even greater than that reported by Grossarth-Maticek.

Psychologist Judith Rodin at Yale University Medical School has also found that a similar type of therapy can lower the cortisol levels of elderly women in a nursing home and prolong their lives. This is very important: Cortisol may be the link between personality and stress, on the one hand, and cancer on the other. Cortisol has often been linked with depression and feelings of hopelessness and helplessness; also, cortisol weakens the immune system, thus rendering it less capable of dealing with menaces such as cancer cells. This may be one way in which personality, stress and disease interact.

These results are impressive and suggest a revolution in medical practice. The type of therapy I've described would go a long way toward preventing early deaths from cancer and coronary heart disease. It would also significantly decrease the enormous health budget which has to pay for diagnosis and treatment, hospital care and operations, and so much else entailed by high rates of cancer and heart disease. Equally important, life prolonged through behavior therapy might not entail the very severe side effects of chemotherapy and other types of medical intervention.

I am not suggesting that we should completely reorganize modern medicine

already have cancer. Grossarth-Maticek formed 24 pairs of cancer patients, each pair equal in age, sex, social background, type and extent of cancer and medical treatment. One person in each pair was allocated by chance to behavior therapy, one to a no-therapy group. Survival on the average was about five years for the

therapy group and only three years for the other group.

In another study, we compared the effectiveness of behavior therapy as an adjunct to chemotherapy. Of 100 woman, all with terminal breast cancer, 50 elected to have chemotherapy and 50 rejected it.

Steps to a Healthier Self

KATARINA KOLB loved her married boyfriend, but he seemed to be much more concerned about his wife than he was about her. Katarina, a 38-year-old German woman, also felt rejected by her father but could not speak to him about it. And she had breast cancer.

Katarina—not her real name—felt depressed and hopeless. According to psychologists Ronald Grossarth-Maticek and Hans Eysenck, she had the classic personality traits of a person vulnerable to cancer. She repressed her anger and anxiety, and felt helpless to find ways to solve her problems.

To change this disease-prone behavior, Katarina took a course of treatment that Grossarth-Maticek and Eysenck call "autonomy training." During either individual or group sessions, therapists explain the difference between the healthy and disease-prone personalities and use relaxation methods, coping techniques and desensitization to help patients move toward the healthy personality style. Grossarth-Maticek and Eysenck use this approach with both cancer-prone and heart-disease-prone people. Individuals susceptible to heart disease learn to abandon the tendencies toward hostility and aggression that the researchers say put them at risk. The key change for cancer-prone people is to stop being overly passive.

Cancer-prone personality types often believe that they are incapable of meeting their needs on their own and depend on another person, job or institution to enhance their sense of self. Katarina, for example, could not get the support she longed for from her married boyfriend but felt she couldn't get along without him. Her feelings of helplessness and anxiety led to passive acceptance of the situation.

When the therapist asked Katarina to explain her behavior, she gained a sense of perspective on herself for the first time. "I've never really thought about this, but it's very destructive, really. Every time I get rejected I get depressed." At her therapist's suggestion, she began to write down ways to get rid of self-defeating behavior.

Her first step was to avoid confrontations with her father in which she knew she would end up feeling rejected. "I won't make demands on him, because when I do, I usually lose and I find that difficult to bear." The therapist helped her use mental imagery to picture several situations involving her father in which she had no expectations and did not need to make any demands.

Katarina reported success at her next session and said she was beginning to like and value herself. She was becoming less dependent on her father and boyfriend and wanted to find new, interesting activities to take her mind off her illness. "I will call up my girlfriend and ask her to go for a walk with me every day, and I will ask my old tennis partner whether he would like to come and have a game with me," she decided.

By the next session, Katarina had gone for several walks and had found three new tennis partners. She told her therapist that she wanted to be more relaxed; she wanted "a state in which inner inhibitions and fears are reduced, in which I believe in myself, trust myself and think I am doing the right thing." The therapist put her into a state of deep hypnosis and repeated some suggestions, created by Katarina herself: "I become more relaxed, happier and happier, and find myself in a wonderful landscape near the sea. I am at one with nature and free of all inhibitions. At the same time I can believe in myself and the success of all my wishes."

Eventually, Katarina sought ways to change her relationship with her boyfriend. He usually visited her once a day, promising to stay for a long visit but always left after only a short time. "Such behavior I will not tolerate any more!" she decided. Again, she used mental imagery, picturing unfulfilling moments in the relationship, and soon she had little desire to see her boyfriend again.

Mental imagery is also used to help other cancer patients combat their disease. Patients visualize white blood cells conquering a malignancy, and by doing so begin to feel some mastery over the illness, while also learning to release anger and resentment.

Autonomy training emphasizes avoiding behavior that leads to short-term solutions, such as escaping a personal rejection, but has long-term negative effects, such as an overall sense of helplessness. And Katarina had clearly reached a new level of autonomy. By ending her relationship with her boyfriend she chose long-term independence over the short-term goal of having some of her boyfriend's attention.

Grossarth-Maticek and Eysenck have found that the patients who succeed in changing their behavior in this way become more self-reliant, less demanding and less rigid than those who don't learn to make these changes. And for those who make the changes, Grossarth-Maticek and Eysenck's research shows that chances of getting cancer are greatly reduced. If they already have the disease, their lives should be prolonged by several years. While Katarina still had some self-doubts at the end of her therapy, she also had learned coping skills to deal with her problems. "I have experienced the negative consequences from putting one's self second," she said. "I shall always keep these consequences in my thoughts, act accordingly and feel good about myself."

—MIA ADESSA

on the basis of these results; obviously as in all such studies, there are faults and possible errors which make it imperative that an independent replication be carried out. No study is perfect, and science demands replication, particularly where life-and-death consequences are so strongly involved.

We obviously are only at the beginning of understanding the apparent interaction between body and mind, but as the Indian sage, Mahābhārata, said 4,000 years ago, "There are two classes of disease—bodily and mental. Each arises from the other, and neither exists without the other. Mental disorders arise from physical ones, and likewise physical disorders arise from mental ones." As the physicist has given up contrasting time and space and now deals with a space-time continuum, so we should stop talking about body and mind as separate entities and rather speak of a body-mind continuum. The study of this continuum will have vital consequences for our understanding of the human condition and may revolutionize our conception of disease, prevention and cure.

The Health Personality Test

THIS IS a short scale for rating yourself according to the four health personality types. This test is intended to illustrate the differences among the personality types. Indicate how closely the description in each question fits you by circling a number from **1** to **10** that best describes you or your situation. **1** means "Not at all" and **10** means "Very much."

1) Have you been repeatedly hopeless and helpless during the last 10 years of your life, either because of the withdrawal of persons who were very important to you and/or your failure to achieve particularly important aims in life? This hopelessness and depression was caused because these events made it impossible for you to satisfy your most important emotional needs, such as those for love, nearness, understanding and recognition. The cause might be the death of or separation from some particularly important person, causing disappointment and difficulties. How closely does this description fit your own case?

Not at all 1   2   3   4   5   6   7   8   9   10 Very much

2) Have you been repeatedly excited, annoyed and resigned in the last 10 years because people disturbed you and interfered with your plans? This excitement and annoyance was caused by your failure, in spite of constant effort to change the situation, allowing some person or persons to prevent the satisfaction of your all-important needs or the achievement of an all-important goal, such as happiness with a sexual partner or advancement at work. How closely does this description fit your own case?

Not at all 1   2   3   4   5   6   7   8   9   10 Very much

3) Considering the past 10 years, particularly your relations with people who were particularly important to you from an emotional point of view (either positively or negatively), which of the four reactions described below would be most descriptive of you and to what extent?

A) I seek and long for closeness and emotional contact with a person or persons who are at the moment too distant from me because of a death, a separation, lack of understanding on the part of my partner, or some shocking or too-demanding events. I would be willing to do anything to diminish this distance, but I do not succeed in reaching the wished-for intimacy. How closely does this description fit your own case?

Not at all 1   2   3   4   5   6   7   8   9   10 Very much

B) I seek distance or separation from one person or persons whose closeness to me (as a partner, in a work or other situation) I experience as crushing. In spite of my efforts I fail to achieve this distancing or separation, largely because of fear of the consequences, such as fear of financial difficulties. How closely does this description fit your own case?

Not at all 1   2   3   4   5   6   7   8   9   10 Very much

C) I alternate between great emotional closeness to a person who is important to me and great emotional distancing and separation. My actions only achieve a regular alteration of too-great closeness and too-great distance interspersed with moments in which distance and nearness are optimal. How closely does this description fit your own case?

Not at all 1   2   3   4   5   6   7   8   9   10 Very much

D) My relations with people who are important to me are neither crushingly close nor too-distant emotionally. Nearness and distance are for the most part optimal and regulated appropriately. I increase the distance from people who annoy me and decrease the distance to people with whom I interact positively. How closely does this description fit your own case?

Not at all 1   2   3   4   5   6   7   8   9   10 Very much

4) During the past 10 years, have you always been in a position to enjoy relaxation in various bodily activities, such as sports, work and sex, using these activities as a pleasant alternative to mental relaxation and activity? Yes/No
If the answer is No, were you prevented from doing so:
A) By the sudden or gradual change due to persons distancing themselves from you or by the loss of a position in a work situation?
B) Because of people or conditions disturbing or annoying you without your having the power to change them according to your desires, or to leave them?
C) Through people who alternated and made emotionally unacceptable demands on you while at other times distancing themselves from you.

5) In the past 10 years, have you repeatedly acted in such a way that emotionally negative (undesirable) consequences occurred? Were you unable to find ways of acting that led to more positive and desirable consequences, such as better interaction between you and emotionally important persons? How closely does this description fit your own case?

Not at all 1   2   3   4   5   6   7   8   9   10 Very much

6) Do you have frequent feelings of fear and anxiety (a general state of anxiety, a syndrome of anxiety, periods during which you suffer from anxiety, fears of being threatened or persecuted, fear of not being able to cope with life and its problems, fear of specific situations)? These fears should be relatively unrealistic, in the sense that you are in the position to avoid them if need be. How strong is this anxiety?

Not at all 1   2   3   4   5   6   7   8   9   10 Very much

HOW TO SCORE THE TEST. You get four scores on this test, not just one; each score corresponds to a health personality type. Type 1 is cancer-prone, Type 2 is heart-disease-prone, Type 3 is healthy with a tendency to act unconventionally and Type 4 is also healthy. You compare your four scores with one another, not to the scores of other people. The highest of your scores indicates your health personality.

Type 1 Add the ratings for question 1 and question 3A. If the answer to question 4 is "No" and the reason is A, add 10 more points. Add on the ratings for question 5 and question 6. Sum up the total.

Type 2 Add the ratings for question 2 and question 3B. If the answer to question 4 is "No" and the reason is B, add 10 more points. Add on the ratings for question 5 and question 6. Sum up the total.

Type 3 Add the rating on any part of question 3 to the rating on question 3C. If the answer to question 4 is "no" and the reason is C, add 10 more points. Add on the ratings for question 5 and question 6. Sum up the total.

Type 4 If your total score on questions 1, 2 and 3 was less than 15, give yourself 10 points. Add the rating on question 3D. If the answer to question 4 is "Yes," add 10 more points. If your rating on either question 5 or question 6 was less than 5 points, give yourself 10 points for that question. Sum up the total.

Social Processes

Most psychologists focus their work on the level of the individual person. However, people do not live in social vacuums, but rather interact frequently. If you ask someone to list some of the important aspects of her or his life, you will probably hear several having to do with relationships. The study of how individuals behave in interpersonal relationships has been largely the province of social psychology, although clinical psychology certainly has much to offer as well.

One of the primary focuses of social psychological research has been aggression. As the number of prisoners continues to rise and new prisons are required, the questions about the causes of aggression become more common and urgent. Richard Herrnstein and James Wilson examine the traditional wisdom about criminal behavior running in families, and look specifically at the heritability component.

A very specific and worrisome form of criminal aggression is terrorism, which seems to spring from an authoritarian outlook on life. As Bob Altemeyer tells us, prejudice may be dangerous in more ways than we ever thought.

Social psychology has long been interested in the study of social interaction, but has only recently delved into that most intimate language: touch. Clearly, we touch for a variety of reasons, in varying contexts, and in many different patterns and styles. What forces determine the nature and meaning of touching, and are touches easily discriminated and correctly interpreted? Stephen Thayer's article will fascinate you with the answers to these questions and more.

One social phenomenon growing rapidly in the United States is the self-help group. Whether aimed at personal growth, the learning of new skills, or the conquering of an addiction, self-help groups are widely claimed to be effective and affordable alternatives or adjuncts to traditional therapy. How do they work? When do they work? Do they sometimes not work at all?

Looking Ahead: Challenge Questions

How convincing is the evidence for a genetic component in criminal behavior? In the best interests of a noncriminal majority, should the reproduction of criminals be prevented?

What should authoritarian leaders, parents, and supervisors expect from the people they interact with? What clues do we get from studies on authoritarianism that might help us to deal with international terrorists?

What factors determine the frequency, intimacy, and meaning of a human touch? Do men and women interpret touch differently?

Under what circumstances should a person be encouraged to participate in a self-help group? Are there any circumstances when you might suggest to a friend that she or he not participate?

Unit 9

ARE CRIMINALS MADE OR BORN?

Evidence indicates that both biological and sociological factors play roles.

**Richard J. Herrnstein and
James Q. Wilson**

*Richard J. Herrnstein is a professor of psychology
and James Q. Wilson a professor of government at
Harvard.*

A revolution in our understanding of crime is quietly overthrowing some established doctrines. Until recently, criminologists looked for the causes of crime almost entirely in the offenders' social circumstances. There seemed to be no shortage of circumstances to blame: weakened, chaotic or broken families, ineffective schools, antisocial gangs, racism, poverty, unemployment. Criminologists took seriously, more so than many other students of social behavior, the famous dictum of the French sociologist Emile Durkheim: Social facts must have social explanations. The sociological theory of crime had the unquestioned support of prominent

editorialists, commentators, politicians and most thoughtful people.

Today, many learned journals and scholarly works draw a different picture. Sociological factors have not been abandoned, but increasingly it is becoming clear to many scholars that crime is the outcome of an interaction between social factors and certain biological factors, particularly for the offenders who, by repeated crimes, have made public places dangerous. The idea is still controversial, but increasingly, to the old question "Are criminals born or made?" the answer seems to be: both. The causes of crime lie in a combination of predisposing biological traits channeled by social

circumstance into criminal behavior. The traits alone, do not inevitably lead to crime; the circumstances do not make criminals of everyone; but together they create a population responsible for a large fraction of America's problem of crime in the streets.

Evidence that criminal behavior has deeper roots than social circumstances has always been right at hand, but social science has, until recent years, overlooked its implications. As far as the records show, crime everywhere and throughout history is disproportionately a young man's pursuit. Whether men are 20 or more times as likely to be arrested as women, as is the case in Malawi or

Brunei, or only four to six times as likely, as in the United States or France, the sex difference in crime statistics is universal. Similarly, 18-year-olds may sometimes be four times as likely to be criminal as 40-year-olds, while at other times only twice as likely. In the United States, more than half of all arrests for serious property crimes are of 20-year-olds or younger. Nowhere have older persons been as criminal as younger ones.

It is easy to imagine purely social explanations for the effects of age and sex on crime. Boys in many societies are trained by their parents and the society itself to play more roughly and aggressively than girls. Boys are expected to fight back, not to cry,

Intelligence and temperament have heritable bases and influence behavior.

and to play to win. Likewise, boys in many cultures are denied adult responsibilities, kept in a state of prolonged dependence and confined too long in schools that many of them find unrewarding. For a long time, these factors were thought to be the whole story.

Ultimately, however, the very universality of the age and sex differences in crime have alerted some social scientists to the implausibility of a theory that does not look beyond the accidents of particular societies. If cultures as different as Japan's and Sweden's, England's and Mexico's, have sex and age differences in crime, then perhaps we should have suspected from the start that there was something more fundamental going on than parents happening to decide to raise their boys and girls differently. What is it about boys, girls and their parents, in societies of all sorts, that leads them to emphasize, rather than overcome, sex differences? Moreover, even if we believed that every society has arbitrarily decided to inculcate aggressiveness in males, there would still be the greater criminality among *young* males to explain. After all, in some cultures, young boys are not denied adult responsibilities but are kept out of school, put to work tilling the land and made to accept obligations to the society.

But it is no longer necessary to approach questions about the sources of criminal behavior merely with argument and supposition. There is evidence. Much crime, it is agreed, has an aggressive component, and Eleanor Emmons Maccoby, a professor of psychology at Stanford University, and Carol Nagy Jacklin, a psychologist now at the University of Southern California, after reviewing the evidence on sex differences in aggression, concluded that it has a foundation that is at least in part biological. Only that conclusion can be drawn, they said, from data that show that the average man is more aggressive than the average woman in all known

societies, that the sex difference is present in infancy well before evidence of sex-role socialization by adults, that similar sex differences turn up in many of our biological relatives—monkeys and apes. Human aggression has been directly tied to sex hormones, particularly male sex hormones, in experiments on athletes engaging in competitive sports and on prisoners known for violent or domineering behavior. No single line of evidence is decisive and each can be challenged, but all together they convinced Drs. Maccoby and Jacklin, as well as most specialists on the biology of sex differences, that the sexual conventions that assign males the aggressive roles have biological roots.

That is also the conclusion of most researchers about the developmental forces that make adolescence and young adulthood a time of risk for criminal and other nonconventional behavior. This is when powerful new drives awaken, leading to frustrations that foster behavior unchecked by the internalized prohibitions of adulthood. The result is usually just youthful rowdiness, but, in a minority of cases, it passes over the line into crime.

The most compelling evidence of biological factors for criminality comes from two studies—one of twins, the other of adopted boys. Since the 1920's it has been understood that twins may develop from a single fertilized egg, resulting in identical genetic endowments—identical twins—or from a pair of separately fertilized eggs that have about half their genes in common—fraternal twins. A standard procedure for estimating how important genes are to a trait is to compare the similarity between identical twins with that between fraternal twins. When identical twins are clearly more similar in a trait than fraternal twins, the trait probably has high heritability.

There have been about a dozen studies of criminality using twins. More than 1,500 pairs of twins have been studied in the

United States, the Scandinavian countries, Japan, West Germany, Britain and elsewhere, and the result is qualitatively the same everywhere. Identical twins are more likely to have similar criminal records than fraternal twins. For example, the late Karl O. Christiansen, a Danish criminologist, using the Danish Twin Register, searched police, court and prison records for entries regarding twins born in a certain region of Denmark between 1881 and 1910. When an identical twin had a criminal record, Christiansen found, his or her co-twin was more than twice as likely to have one also than when a fraternal twin had a criminal record.

In the United States, a similar result has recently been reported by David Rowe, a psychologist at the University of Oklahoma, using questionnaires instead of official records to measure criminality. Twins in high school in almost all the school districts of Ohio received questionnaires by mail, with a promise of confidentiality as well as a small payment if the questionnaires were filled out and returned. The twins were asked about their activities, including their delinquent behavior, about their friends and about their co-twins. The identical twins were more similar in delinquency than the fraternal twins. In addition, the twins who shared more activities with each other were no more likely to be similar in delinquency than those who shared fewer activities.

No single method of inquiry should be regarded as conclusive. But essentially the same results are found in studies of adopted children. The idea behind such studies is to find a sample of children adopted early in life, cases in which the criminal histories of both adopting and biological parents are known. Then, as the children grow up, researchers can discover how predictive of their criminality are the family histories of their adopting and biological parents. Recent studies show that the biological family his-

tory contributes substantially to the adoptees' likelihood of breaking the law.

For example, Sarnoff Mednick, a psychologist at the University of Southern California, and his associates in the United States and Denmark have followed a sample of several thousand boys adopted in Denmark between 1927 and 1947. Boys with criminal biological parents and noncriminal adopting parents were more likely to have criminal records than those with noncriminal biological parents and criminal adopting parents. The more criminal convictions a boy's natural parents had, the greater the risk of criminality for boys being raised by adopting parents who had no records. The risk was unrelated to whether the boy or his adopting parents knew about the natural parents' criminal records, whether the natural parents committed their crimes before or after the boy was given up for adoption, or whether the boy was adopted immediately after birth or a year or two later. The results of this study have been confirmed in Swedish and American samples of adopted children.

Because of studies like these, many sociologists and criminologists now accept the existence of genetic factors contributing to criminality. When there is disagreement, it is about how large the genetic contribution to crime is and about how the criminality of biological parents is transmitted to their children.

Both the twin and adoption studies show that genetic contributions are not alone responsible for crime — there is, for example, some increase in criminality among boys if their adopted fathers are criminal even when their biological parents are not, and not every co-twin of a criminal identical twin becomes criminal himself. Although it appears, on average, to be substantial, the

precise size of the genetic contribution to crime is probably unknowable, particularly since the measures of criminality itself are now so crude.

We have a bit more to go on with respect to the link that transmits a predisposition toward crime from parents to children. No one believes there are "crime genes," but there are two major attributes that have, to some degree, a heritable base and that appear to influence criminal behavior. These are intelligence and temperament. Hundreds of studies have found that the more genes people share, the more likely they are to resemble each other intellectually and temperamentally.

Starting with studies in the 1930's, the average offender in broad samples has consistently scored 91 to 93 on I.Q. tests for which the general population's average is 100. The typical offender does worse on the verbal items of intelligence tests than on the nonverbal items but is usually below average on both.

Criminologists have long known about the correlation between criminal behavior and I.Q., but many of them have discounted it for various reasons. Some have suggested that the correlation can be explained away by the association between low socioeconomic status and crime, on the one hand, and that between low I.Q. and low socioeconomic status, on the other. These criminologists say it is low socioeconomic status, rather than low I.Q., that fosters crime. Others have questioned whether I.Q. tests really measure intelligence for the populations that are at greater risk for breaking the law. The low scores of offenders, the argument goes, betray a culturally deprived background or alienation from our society's values rather than low intelligence. Finally, it is often noted that the offenders in some studies have been caught for their crimes. Perhaps the ones who got away have higher I.Q.s.

But these objections have proved to be less telling than they once seemed to be. There are, for example, many poor law-abiding people living in deprived environments, and one of their more salient characteristics is that they have higher I.Q. scores than those in the same environment who break the law.

Then, too, it is a common misconception that I.Q. tests are invalid for people from disadvantaged backgrounds. If what is implied by this criticism is that scores predict academic potential or job performance differently for different groups, then the criticism is wrong. A comprehensive recent survey sponsored by the National Academy of Sciences concluded that "tests predict about as well for one group as for another." And that some highly intelligent criminals may well be good at eluding capture is fully consistent with the belief that offenders, in general, have lower scores than nonoffenders.

If I.Q. and criminality are linked, what may explain the link? There are several possibilities. One is that low scores on I.Q. tests signify greater difficulty in grasping the likely consequences of action or in learning the meaning and significance of moral codes. Another is that low scores, especially on the verbal component of the tests, mean trouble in school, which leads to frustration, thence to resentment, anger and delinquency. Still another is that persons who are not as skillful as others in expressing themselves verbally may find it more rewarding to express themselves in ways in which they will do better, such as physical threat or force.

For some repeat offenders, the predisposition to criminality may be more a matter of temperament than intelligence. Impulsiveness, insensitivity to social mores, a lack of deep and enduring emotional attachments to others and an appetite for danger are among the temperamental characteristics of high-rate offenders. Temperament

is, to a degree, heritable, though not as much so as intelligence. All parents know that their children, shortly after birth, begin to exhibit certain characteristic ways of behaving — they are placid or fussy, shy or bold. Some of the traits endure, among them aggressiveness and hyperactivity, although they change in form as the child develops. As the child grows up, these traits, among others, may gradually unfold into a disposition toward unconventional, defiant or antisocial behavior.

Lee Robins, a sociologist at Washington University School of Medicine in St. Louis, reconstructed 30 years of the lives of more than 500 children who were patients in the 1920's at a child guidance clinic in St. Louis. She was interested in the early precursors of chronic sociopathy, a condition of antisocial personality that often includes criminal behavior as one of its symptoms. Adult sociopaths in her sample who did not suffer from psychosis, mental retardation or addiction, were, without exception, antisocial before they were 18. More than half of the male sociopaths had serious symptoms before they were 11. The main childhood precursors were truancy, poor school performance, theft, running away, recklessness, slovenliness, impulsiveness and guiltlessness. The more symptoms in childhood, the greater the risk of sociopathy in adulthood.

Other studies confirm and extend Dr. Robins's conclusions. For example, two psychologists, John J. Conger of the University of Colorado and Wilbur Miller of Drake University in Des Moines, searching back over the histories of a sample of delinquent boys in Denver, found that "by the end of the third grade, future delinquents were already seen by their teachers as more poorly adapted than their classmates. They appeared to have less regard for the rights and feelings of their peers; less awareness of the

need to accept responsibility for their obligations, both as individuals and as members of a group, and poorer attitudes toward authority."

Traits that foreshadow serious, recurrent criminal behavior have been traced all the way back to behavior patterns such as hyperactivity and unusual fussiness, and neurological signs such as atypical brain waves or reflexes. In at least a minority of cases, these are detectable in the first few years of life. Some of the characteristics are sex-linked. There is evidence that newborn females are more likely than newborn males to smile, to cling to their mothers, to be receptive to touching and talking, to be sensitive to certain stimuli, such as being touched by a cloth, and to have less upper-body strength. Mothers certainly treat girls and boys differently, but the differences are not simply a matter of the mother's choice — female babies are more responsive than male babies to precisely the kind of treatment that is regarded as "feminine." When adults are asked to play with infants, they play with them in ways they think are appropriate to the infants' sexes. But there is also some evidence that when the sex of the infant is concealed, the behavior of the adults is influenced by the conduct of the child.

Premature infants or those born with low birth weights have a special problem. These children are vulnerable to any adverse circumstances in their environment — including child abuse — that may foster crime. Although nurturing parents can compensate for adversity, cold or inconsistent parents may exacerbate it. Prematurity and low birth weight may result from poor prenatal care, a bad diet or excessive use of alcohol or drugs. Whether the bad care is due to poverty, ignorance or anything else, here we see criminality arising from biological, though not necessarily genetic, factors. It is now known that these babies are more likely than normal babies to be the victims of child abuse.

We do not mean to blame child abuse on the victim by saying that premature and low-birth-weight infants are more difficult to care for and thus place a great strain on the parents. But unless parents are emotionally prepared for the task of caring for such children, they may vent their frustration at the infant's unresponsiveness by hitting or neglecting it. Whatever it is in parent and child that leads to prematurity or low birth weight is compounded by the subsequent interaction between them. Similarly, children with low I.Q.s may have difficulty in understanding rules, but if their parents also have poor verbal skills, they may have difficulty in communicating rules, and so each party to the conflict exacerbates the defects of the other.

THE STATEMENT that biology plays a role in explaining human behavior, especially criminal behavior, sometimes elicits a powerful political or ideological reaction. Fearful that what is being proposed is a crude biological determinism, some critics deny the evidence while others wish the evidence to be confined to scientific journals. Scientists who have merely proposed studying the possible effects of chromosomal abnormalities on behavior have been ruthlessly attacked by other scientists, as have those who have made public the voluminous data showing the heritability of intelligence and temperament.

Some people worry that any claim that biological factors influence criminality is tantamount to saying that the higher crime rate of black

compared to white Americans has a genetic basis. But no responsible work in the field leads to any such conclusion. The data show that of all the reasons people vary in their crime rates, race is far less important than age, sex, intelligence and the other individual factors that vary within races. Any study of the causes of crime must therefore first consider the individual factors. Differences among races may have many explanations, most of them having nothing to do with biology.

The intense reaction to the study of biological factors in crime, we believe, is utterly misguided. In fact, these discoveries, far from implying that "criminals are born" and should be locked up forever, suggest new and imaginative ways of reducing criminality by benign treatment. The opportunity we have is precisely analogous to that which we had when the biological bases of other disorders were established. Mental as well as physical illness — alcoholism, learning disabilities of various sorts, and perhaps even susceptibilities to drug addiction — now seem to have genetic components. In each case, new understanding energized the search for treatment and gave it new direction. Now we know that many forms of depression can be successfully treated with drugs; in time we may learn the same of Alzheimer's disease. Alcoholics are helped when they understand that some persons, because of their predisposition toward addiction to alcohol, should probably never consume it at all. A chemical treatment of the predisposition is a realistic possibility. Certain types of slow learners can already be helped by spe-

cial programs. In time, others will be also.

Crime, admittedly, may be a more difficult program. So many different acts are criminal that it is only with considerable poetic license that we can speak of "criminality" at all. The bank teller who embezzles $500 to pay off a gambling debt is not engaging in the same behavior as a person who takes $500 from a liquor store at the point of a gun or one who causes $500 worth of damage by drunkenly driving his car into a parked vehicle. Moreover, crime, unlike alcoholism or dyslexia, exposes a person to the formal condemnation of society and the possibility of imprisonment. We naturally and rightly worry about treating all "criminals" alike, or stigmatizing persons whom we think might become criminal by placing them in special programs designed to prevent criminality.

But these problems are not insurmountable barriers to better ways of thinking about crime prevention. Though criminals are of all sorts, we know that a very small fraction of all young males commit so large a fraction of serious street crime that we can properly blame these chronic offenders for most such crime. We also know that chronic offenders typically begin their misconduct at an early age. Early family and preschool programs may be far better repositories for the crime-prevention dollar than rehabilitation programs aimed — usually futilely — at the 19- or 20-year-old veteran offender. Prevention programs risk stigmatizing children, but this may be less of a risk than is neglect. If stigma were a problem to be avoided at all costs, we would have to dismantle most special-needs education programs.

Having said all this, we must acknowledge that there is at present little hard evidence that we know how to inhibit the development of delinquent tendencies in children. There are some leads, such as family training programs of the sort pioneered at the Oregon Social Learning Center, where parents are taught how to use small rewards and penalties to alter the behavior of misbehaving children. There is also evidence from David Weikart and Lawrence Schweinhart of the High/Scope Educational Research Foundation at Ypsilanti, Mich., that preschool education programs akin to Project Head Start may reduce later deliquency. There is nothing yet to build a national policy on, but there are ideas worth exploring by carefully repeating and refining these pioneering experimental efforts.

Above all, there is a case for redirecting research into the causes of crime in ways that take into account the interaction of biological and social factors. Some scholars, such as the criminologist Marvin E. Wolfgang and his colleagues at the University of Pennsylvania, are already exploring these issues by analyzing social and biological information from large groups as they age from infancy to adulthood and linking the data to criminal behavior. But much more needs to be done.

It took years of patiently following the life histories of many men and women to establish the linkages between smoking or diet and disease; it will also take years to unravel the complex and subtle ways in which intelligence, temperament, hormonal levels and other traits combine with family circumstances and later experiences in school and elsewhere to produce human character.

MARCHING IN STEP

A Psychological Explanation of State Terror

BOB ALTEMEYER

BOB ALTEMEYER, an associate professor of psychology at the University of Manitoba, in Winnipeg, is the author of RIGHT-WING AUTHORITARIANISM, *published in 1981, and of the forthcoming* UNDERSTANDING RIGHT-WING AUTHORITARIANISM, *to be published by Jossey-Bass. The research described in this article was awarded the American Association for the Advancement of Science's Prize for Behavioral Science Research in 1986.*

DURING THE SECOND WORLD WAR, as the persecution of European Jews was reaching its terrible, final savagery, a team of social scientists at the University of California at Berkeley embarked on a research project of rare urgency: they set out to uncover the psychological roots of anti-Semitism—a prejudice that had proved virulent enough not only to place innocent people on trains to Auschwitz and Buchenwald but to turn millions of their neighbors into indifferent spectators. In a series of attitude surveys, conducted with American subjects, the Berkeley researchers found that people who were hostile toward Jews often expressed similar feelings toward other minorities as well, including blacks, Hispanics, and Filipinos. In addition, these highly prejudiced people seemed to share a great reverence for their own ingroup (a sentiment reminiscent of the Nazis' belief in Aryan supremacy) and an extreme willingness to prostrate themselves before established authorities. All of this led the researchers to conclude that anti-Semitism was not a self-contained phenomenon but a symptom of what they dubbed the prefascist, or authoritarian, personality. Drawing on psychoanalytic theory to describe this odd combination of hostility and submissiveness, they defined the authoritarian as a person whose conscious, rational ego had been overpowered by an overzealous superego and by a seething id.

Starting from the Freudian assumption that the way a person responds to the world is determined largely by early experiences within the family, the Berkeley researchers speculated that authoritarianism is a disguised and delayed expression of the anger felt by children toward cold, harsh, punitive parents. In a 1950 book entitled *The Authoritarian Personality*, the group theorized that, to avoid retaliation, the enraged child learns to conceal these hostile feelings both from his parents and from himself and to direct them instead at society's traditional scapegoats. By belittling and brutalizing social outcasts, the authoritarian could vent his fury at his parents and other dominating authorities without ever appearing defiant. Such behavior would meet the demands of the superego (to be an obedient child or citizen) while at once satisfying the id's urge to attack someone.

From this general idea, the Berkeley group eventually developed a more detailed model, which defined the authoritarian personality in terms of nine distinctive character traits, and designed a test—the F, or Fascism, scale—to measure those traits in people. The F scale consisted of statements, such as "No weakness or difficulty can hold us back if we have enough will power" and "Someday it will probably be shown that astrology can explain a lot of things," with which subjects could agree or disagree to varying extents. A person's response to any given statement was considered a sign of his predisposition toward one of the nine telltale traits: submissiveness; conventionalism; aggressiveness; a concern with power and toughness; a reliance on superstitions and stereotypes; a preoccupation with sex; a projection of one's own undesirable qualities onto others; a lack of introspection; or destructiveness and cynicism. Since people who scored high on the F scale tended also to be extremely prejudiced, the theory appeared valid, and it eventually permeated the culture at large. Anyone who has heard that Hitler's hatred of Jews was rooted in repressed hostility toward his stern father has encountered the popular version of the Berkeley theory.

But there were doubts from the outset about the scientists' methods and conclusions. For one thing, the research was not based on a representative sample of Americans; indeed, forty percent of the highly prejudiced men interviewed for one key study were inmates at the San Quentin penitentiary. Nor had the interviews been conducted by "blind" interrogators (people ignorant of the hypothesis being tested), to guard against biased results. But the loudest criticisms were directed at the F scale itself. Responses to the items in the survey simply did not indicate that highly prejudiced people share all nine character traits. Many respondents who seemed highly superstitious, for example, showed little concern with power and toughness. Similarly, subjects might appear preoccupied with sex but not seem destructive or cynical. And even when relationships were apparent between people's responses to particular survey items, one could not be sure there were similar relationships between the traits supposedly measured by those items. Because the authoritarian response was always to *agree* with a particular statement, it was possible that subjects who seemed to exhibit all nine traits were just engaged in yea-saying—the tendency of test subjects to respond affirmatively to survey items when they have no real opinion.

Because the F scale, for all its shortcomings, served as a general predictor of prejudice, studies based on the test continued for some time to appear in the journals. In the long run, though, these findings showed an uncanny ability to contradict one another, and by the end of the sixties the literature on authoritarianism was such a tangled web that researchers turned to more promising endeavors. The quest to understand the authoritarian personality, instead of being successfully concluded, was merely abandoned.

There was, however, an underlying pattern in the web. During the late 1960s, I noticed that although F-scale studies had not produced a rigorous definition, much less a convincing explanation, of the authoritarian personality, three of the scale's nine target traits had turned up more regularly than the others. Specifically, the data suggested that people who are highly submissive to established authority (readier than others to accept its judgments and trust its words) tend also to be conventional (clinging to orthodox notions of proper behavior) and to become highly aggressive when they think established authorities will approve.

To test this interpretation, I spent several years analyzing people's responses to hundreds of survey statements taken from the F scale and various other attitude tests. My objective was to determine which traits, of all those that had been deemed relevant to authoritarianism, actually ran together. Consistently, the data suggested that submissiveness, conventionalism, and aggressiveness did but that other traits, including superstition and dogmatism, did not. So, to get a clearer view of the relevant traits, I developed an alternative to the F scale, an attitude survey called the Right-Wing Authoritarianism (RWA) scale. Unlike the old test, the RWA scale has demonstrated consistent statistical links between the traits it measures and has thus provided a reliable overall index of people's authoritarian leanings. And it is now beginning to *explain* particular aspects of the authoritarian's personality, including his propensity to behave so aggressively.

It has been evident, ever since the psychologist Stanley Milgram conducted his famous electric shock experiments during the 1960s, that ordinary people can easily be induced to hurt an innocent victim if commanded by someone (even a scientist in a lab coat) who is perceived as a legitimate authority. But some people seem far readier than others to attack on command. The question of what motivates such behavior in the name of higher authorities is hardly an idle curiosity; some of the most horrifying events of our time—from the Holocaust to the My Lai massacre; from the persecution of dissidents in Chile to the deaths by torture in South African prisons—have been acts of authoritarian aggression. Such atrocities are not unique to any political or economic system; Communist and anti-Communist dictatorships seem equally capable of violent repression. But to the degree that such violence is committed in behalf of a society's established traditions and authorities, it can be called right-wing. In this sense, the mistreatment of Soviet dissidents is no less right-wing than is Guatemalan repression. Understanding the causes and dynamics of such behavior could be a first step toward stopping it—and stopping it surely ranks among the world's more urgent political tasks.

BECAUSE PEOPLE are not necessarily aware of their authoritarian tendencies, let alone prepared to admit them to others, the RWA test does not ask subjects to assess themselves directly. It is presented as a public opinion poll, with each of its thirty statements designed to gauge the respondent's submissiveness ("It is always better to trust the judgment of the proper authorities in government and religion") or conventionalism ("It may be considered old-fashioned by some, but having a decent, respectable appearance is still the mark of a gentleman and, especially, a lady") or aggressiveness ("Once our government leaders and the authorities condemn the dangerous elements in our society, it will be the duty of every patriotic citizen to help stomp out the rot that is poisoning our country from within"). There are nine possible responses to each statement, ranging from "very strongly disagree" (-4) to "very strongly agree" ($+4$), and half the items are worded in such a way that the authoritarian response is to disagree, as with "It is important to protect fully the rights of radicals and deviants." Taken together, a subject's responses provide a numerical measure of his authoritarian leanings.

Since the RWA scale was developed, in 1973, it has been administered to groups throughout North America and in other parts of the world, and those who have scored high on it have been found to share a wide range of attitudes and behavioral patterns. For example, high scorers are more tolerant than others of abuses by government officials (Americans with high RWA scores supported Richard Nixon the longest during the Watergate crisis); they tend, in hypothetical situations, to impose harsher sentences on most lawbreakers; and they are more likely than others to express contempt for various minorities, including Jews, blacks, Asians, Africans, Native Americans, homosexuals, and people with "strange" religions.

Perhaps the most chilling finding of all came from an attitude survey devised in 1982 to see how far people with high RWA scores would go toward supporting state-sanctioned persecution of some group. The survey, known as Posse, was administered to roughly six hundred Canadian college students and several hundred of their parents. It began with this scenario:

Suppose the Canadian government, sometime in the future, passed a law outlawing the Communist Party in Canada. Government officials then stated that the law would be effective only if it were vigorously enforced at the local level, and appealed to every Canadian to aid in the fight against Communism.

This was followed by six statements, and the subjects were asked to indicate on a scale of -4 to $+4$ how well each statement applied to them. Would they tell their friends it was a good law? Identify any Communists they happened to know? Help the police hunt them down? Participate in an attack on the Communist headquarters if it were organized by "the proper authorities"? Endorse the use of "physical force" to make captured Communists reveal the identities of others? Support the execution of Communist leaders?

Most of the subjects said they were unlikely to do these things. But whereas people with low RWA scores considered themselves extremely unlikely to participate, those with high scores said they were only moderately unlikely. These people would presumably be the first to change their minds if the government launched a campaign of propaganda or pressure, as the Nazis did against Jews in Germany. And one could, of course, assemble a fair-sized posse from the respondents who were ready to saddle up today if the authorities would only give the word.

Similar studies have shown that high scorers are more likely than others not only to hunt down and kill Communists but to help persecute others, as well. One might expect low scorers to be more aggressive than highs toward, say, the Ku Klux Klan; yet when the Klan was hypothetically outlawed, high scorers remained the least reluctant of five hundred and twenty-six respondents to accept and act on the edict. The same pattern held when Canada's Progressive Conservative Party—a party for which high scorers had, in other surveys, voiced strong support—was banned. Though reluctant to persecute such a respectable group, people with high RWA scores were once again more likely than others to accept the "necessity" of destroying the party. It seems, in short, that they would be the first to attack almost *any* target—left-wing or right-wing, respectable or unsavory—as long as their behavior was sanctioned by some established authority. They themselves surely would feel more hostile toward Communists than toward Progressive Conservatives, but, as these tests make clear, it is not just an authoritarian's hostility that sets him apart. It is his submissiveness—his readiness to substitute an authority's judgment, however depraved, for his own.

WHAT MIGHT ACCOUNT for the authoritarian's hostile tendencies? Of the three classic models of aggression—those defining it broadly as a product of repressed instinctual drives, of frustration, and of social learning—two seem to have little bearing on the authoritarian syndrome.

The repressed-drive explanation advanced by the Berkeley theorists in 1950 has proved difficult to test. When authoritarians are asked to describe their childhoods, or their parents are asked to talk about how they raised their children, there is little evidence of a cold, harsh upbringing. In a sense, this is exactly what the theory predicts—that the authoritarian will conceal his resentment against his parents, even from himself. But, regardless of how well the authoritarian has succeeded at repressing such feelings, they should, according to psychoanalytic theory, be discernible in his dreams, fantasies, and slips of the tongue. Yet when students, identified only by their RWA scores, are encouraged to record their daydreams and fantasies, their journal entries and those of nonauthoritarians are largely indistinguishable. Thus, there is still no sign that authoritarians are motivated by the repressed destructive drives postulated by psychoanalytic theory.

The second classic theory—which says aggression is usually the result of some frustration in life—was first advanced by John Dollard and Neal E. Miller, both of Yale University, in 1939. To support this idea, Dollard and Miller cited, among other things, an inverse relationship between the annual per-acre value of cotton and the number of blacks lynched in fourteen southern states each year. (Low prices, presumably, increased economic frustration among whites, prompting aggression against the scapegoat minority.)

The frustration–aggression hypothesis was taken a step further in 1962 by Leonard Berkowitz, of the University of Wisconsin at Madison, who argued that angry people are especially likely to attack someone if there are cues in their environment that carry violent connotations. In Berkowitz's most celebrated study, students participating in a bogus behavioral experiment were insulted by a confederate whom Berkowitz had instructed to pose as a fellow volunteer. Shortly thereafter, the subjects got a chance to administer what they thought were electric shocks to the confederate—but whereas some of the angry subjects did their shocking at a table strewn with badminton equipment ("for another experiment"), others administered shocks in a room where there were guns on the table. As Berkowitz had predicted, the frustration elicited more aggression from angry subjects with guns in their midst than from those eyeing implements of backyard leisure. Since the two environments were identical in every other respect, the guns seemed to be decisive.

If the frustration model were applicable to *authoritarian* aggression, authoritarians would typically be highly frustrated people—sexually frustrated, perhaps, or financially disappointed, or angry about a lack of social esteem. The reason criminals, minorities, and social outcasts would so easily elicit the authoritarian's hostility is that they are often associated, either as perpetrators or as victims, with violence. The problem is that authoritarians do not seem, as a group, to be any more frustrated than the rest of us. When subjects are surveyed, anonymously, on whether they get as much sex as they want or expect, males typically voice more frustration than females, but this is true regardless of whether the men score high or low on the RWA scale. Nor does frustration over money, social standing, or self-esteem seem to vary in proportion to RWA scores. Such discontent is the fate of authoritarians and nonauthoritarians alike.

THE THIRD CLASSIC THEORY of aggression is somewhat more useful for our purposes. As formulated by the Stanford University psychologist Albert Bandura, during the 1960s and 1970s, it stresses the social-learning experiences of the individual—in particular, his capacity for learning aggression from such models as parents and television personalities. Once learned, aggression is said to be triggered by various "instigators"—including not only frustration but also anxiety, threats and insults, physical pain, and the anticipation of rewards. Bandura does not assume that instigation leads automatically to aggressive responses, however. At the same time that children are learning aggressive responses from parents and others, he believes, they are being taught that it is not acceptable to act aggressively. These learned inhibitions against attacking must, according to Bandura, be breached before people will strike out at others.

A social-learning theorist might propose that the authoritarian's tendencies have been copied from hostile, bigoted parents. As it turns out, though, there is no strong correlation between the prejudices of university students and those of their folks. Authoritarian aggression seems to have deeper roots; it is not simply grafted by one generation onto the next.

Another possibility consistent with Bandura's model is that the authoritarian's hostility is rooted in the guilt he feels at falling short of the demands made by parents and other authorities. People with high RWA scores tend to come from highly religious backgrounds and often recall being expected to live up to a stricter moral code than others. Such circumstances create rich opportunities for feeling sinful, and, as Bandura has pointed out, "there is no more devastating punishment than self-contempt." It follows that, just as threats or physical pain may instigate attacks on others, so might feelings of guilt.

Still another possibility consistent with the social-learning model is that the authoritarian is motivated by the envy he feels toward those who are not so burdened by restrictive moral conventions. Indeed, college students with high RWA scores are more likely than their peers to report that they missed out on "fun times" during high school by adhering to a strict code of conduct. Feeling thus deprived, might they not take consolation in seeing sinners punished for their transgressions? Apparently so. For the same students are the most likely, when asked how they feel about schoolmates who got into trouble by way of sex, drugs, or alcohol, to agree that it "serves them right."

Fear is another aversive stimulus that could have special relevance to authoritarian aggression. It may be that people who are especially submissive to authorities, and who cling to conventional notions of proper behavior, are especially fearful of social change and disorder. When questioned about their upbringings, people with high RWA scores typically recall receiving relatively stern warnings during childhood about kidnappers, molesters, tramps, winos, and other potentially dangerous people. The world, in short, was presented to them as a dangerous place. So it is not surprising to find that, as adults, authoritarians are more anxious than others about terrorist attacks and highway accidents, and more likely to worry about catching AIDS from drinking fountains, nor that they tend to agree with such statements as "It seems that every year there are fewer and fewer truly respectable people" and "Any day now, chaos and anarchy could erupt around us."

Any of these aversive stimuli—guilt or envy or fear—might, by the logic of Bandura's theory, instigate aggressive impulses. But if those impulses are normally kept in check by learned inhibitions, what might serve to unleash them? One strong candidate would be a sense of self-righteousness. There is compelling evidence that authoritarians consider themselves morally superior. They are not unique in this regard; almost anyone will, if asked, report that he is more moral than other people, not to mention a better driver, lover, friend, or worker. But this self-serving bias is especially pronounced in authoritarians. They may not actually conduct themselves any more virtuously than other people—studies have shown that students with high RWA scores are no more willing than others to donate blood during a campus drive, and no less likely to cheat on exams—but they perceive themselves as being far more virtuous. When high scorers are asked to evaluate a fictitious person whose responses to the statements on the RWA test are opposite their own, they are more likely than low scorers to agree that the person has not "thought carefully" about the issues, that he is not particularly "good or moral," and that his ideas may be "dangerous to our society."

It seems clear, then, that authoritarians are more prone than others both to feelings that might produce aggressive impulses and to a sense of self-righteousness, which might weaken their inhibitions against attacking others. The question is: In what measure do these qualities contribute to authoritarian aggression?

IT STANDS TO REASON THAT, if any one of these factors—guilt, envy, fear, or self-righteousness—helps make authoritarians aggressive, then eliminating that factor should make them less so. We cannot work such magic on real people, unfortunately, but we *can* do something mathematically akin to it—by testing subjects for authoritarianism and for aggressiveness, then determining how each measurement correlates with a measure of one of the contributing factors under investigation. To the extent that any third factor correlates with both of the first two, it can be said to account for part of the relationship between them. In other words, if people who score high on tests that measure authoritarianism and aggressiveness also score high on a test that measures, say, their fear of a dangerous world, then fear can be said to account, statistically, for part of the correlation. Exactly how great a part can be determined through a technique known as partial correlation analysis.

The correlation between two sets of numbers (a statistic that can range in absolute value from 0.00 to 1.00) is the square root of another value known as the index of codetermination. That is to say, it reveals, when multiplied by itself, just how much of the variation within one set can be attributed to variation within the other. If we compare the adult heights of several hundred parents and several hundred offspring, the statistical correlation is usually about 0.50, indicating (when squared) that parents' heights account for 0.25, or a quarter, of the variation in the adult heights of their children. The remaining seventy-five percent presumably reflects other factors.

Because human behavior is shaped by so many variables, a measure of just one personality trait rarely accounts for more than about ten percent of the variation in a particular form of behavior. But the RWA scale often correlates 0.50 or more with measures of authoritarian aggression, which is to say, RWA scores typically explain about twenty-five percent of the variation in certain forms of hostility. It is this statistical relationship between authoritarianism and hostility that we are trying to explain in terms of possible instigators and disinhibitors.

The relationship is particularly well captured by a tool called the Attitudes Toward Homosexuals (ATH) scale, a survey, scored in the same manner as the RWA scale, that consists of such statements as "Homosexuals should be locked up to protect society" and "In many ways, the AIDS disease currently killing homosexuals is just what they deserve." An experiment conducted at the University of Manitoba found a correlation of 0.54 between subjects' RWA scores and their ATH scores. Authoritarianism, then, accounted for fully twenty-nine percent of the variation in the subjects' aggressiveness toward homosexuals.

The question is: What makes authoritarians so hostile toward gays? To find out, I asked the same subjects who had been given the RWA and ATH tests to complete sixteen other measures, as well. These assessed not only the hypotheses about guilt, fear, envy, and self-righteousness but also a number of other possible contributors, including the influence of parents, teachers, peers, religious authorities, the media, even the subjects' own experiences with homosexuals. The answers to the vast majority of these tests failed to correlate strongly with the RWA and ATH scores, suggesting that most of the factors had little to do with the authoritarians' aggressiveness. But there were two notable exceptions: fear and self-righteousness. When the students completed a Fear of a Dangerous World survey (composed of such statements as "The world is full of dangerous people who will attack you for no reason at all"), the scores correlated appreciably with both the RWA results and the ATH responses. And when the subjects were given a test designed to measure self-righteousness (the one that invited them to pass judgment on people whose RWA responses were opposite their own), the correlations were even stronger.

If authoritarians are aggressive partly because they associate their targets (homosexuals, in this case) with a disintegrating, threatening world, then mathematically eliminating the part of the RWA–ATH relationship that consists of the correlation of those two scores with fear of a dangerous world should make a noticeable difference. And it does. When the fear factor is "partialed out," the 0.54 correlation between RWA and ATH scores drops to 0.46, and the amount of ATH variation that can be predicted on the basis of RWA scores drops from twenty-nine percent (0.54 squared) to just twenty-one (0.46 squared), or about seventy-two percent of its original value. Self-righteousness seems to be an even more important factor; mathematically eliminating it reduces the authoritarianism–aggressiveness relationship to just sixty-two percent of its original value.

None of this would be very impressive if fear and self-righteousness were two competing explanations for the authoritarian's aggressiveness, for neither one accounts for the majority of it. But the two factors are highly compatible, with fear of a dangerous world serving as the instigator that arouses the authoritarian's hostility and self-righteousness serving as the disinhibitor that unleashes it. If we partial out their *combined* effect, the RWA–aggressiveness correlation drops from 0.54 to 0.35, and the original twenty-nine-percent overlap between the two shrinks to a mere twelve percent, or about forty-one percent of its original value. In short, most of the relationship disappears. With just two variables, more than half the authoritarian's aggressiveness has been explained. Fear's fingerprints seem to be all over the trigger of the weapon, and those of self-righteousness all over the unlocked safety.

Hostility toward homosexuals is not the only form of authoritarian aggression that fear and self-righteousness seem to account for; similar experiments, involving other authoritarian tendencies,

have produced similar results. When, for example, fear and self-righteousness are partialed out of the correlation between RWA scores and scores on a test in which subjects impose prison sentences on hypothetical criminals, they account for nearly three-quarters of the RWA–harshness correlation. No other variable tested explains as much, alone or in combination with anything else. In another experiment, subjects were asked to complete a booklet containing the RWA test and five indexes of aggressiveness: the ATH scale, a criminal-sentencing scale, a general prejudice scale, and two posse scales (one in which the government bans Communism and one in which it outlaws "weird" religions). In every case, fear and self-righteousness, when partialed out in tandem, accounted for most of the relationship between RWA scores and aggressiveness. The pattern held whether the subjects were college students or their parents.

Together, these results suggest an answer to the question that posed itself so grotesquely in Nazi-occupied Europe, an answer more compatible with Bandura's social-learning theory than with Berkowitz's frustration hypothesis or the psychoanalytic explanation ventured by the Berkeley theorists. It seems that highly submissive, conventional people easily come to feel gravely threatened by social change or disorder. This fear seems to originate with their parents' warnings that the world is a dangerous and hostile place, though it may be reinforced by the mass media's emphasis on crime and violence in our society. Other emotions, such as envy, may feed the authoritarian's hostility, but not to nearly as great an extent.

Fear will not produce aggression if one's learned inhibitions are strong; people with low RWA scores may want to lash out at times and yet not feel entitled to do so. But authoritarians, because they identify so strongly with established authorities (including, in many cases, God), perceive themselves as morally superior, and this moral certainty impels them toward brutality.

This research, for reasons that should be obvious, is conducted at one remove from reality. No one has taken a group of subjects, made them fearful and self-righteous, and then handed them a whip and a scapegoat to see how they behave. Instead, we have examined relationships between the attitudes that people express on questionnaires. This sort of analysis never actually proves the hypotheses it supports; it is not known, empirically, that fear and self-righteousness *cause* authoritarian aggression, only that particular forms of authoritarian aggression vary in proportion to certain measurable attitudes. But that in itself could be powerful knowledge. If authoritarian aggression is often accompanied by fear and self-righteousness, then finding ways of freeing authoritarians from that explosive combination of feelings may not only improve their lives but help shelter their neighbors from their wrath.

CLOSE ENCOUNTERS

Silent but powerful, a touch can comfort, greet, persuade, inflame.
Small wonder societies keep our contacts under tight control.

STEPHEN THAYER

*Stephen Thayer, Ph.D., is a professor of psychology at City College
and the Graduate Center of the City University of New York.*

IN MAY 1985, Brigitte Gerney was trapped beneath a 35-ton collapsed construction crane in New York City for six hours. Throughout her ordeal, she held the hand of rescue officer Paul Ragonese, who stayed by her side as heavy machinery moved the tons of twisted steel from her crushed legs. A stranger's touch gave her hope and the will to live.

Other means of communication can take place at a distance, but touch is the language of physical intimacy. And because it is, touch is the most powerful of all the communication channels— and the most carefully guarded and regulated.

From a mother's cradling embrace to a friend's comforting hug, or a lover's caress, touch has the special power to send messages of union and communion. Among strangers, that power is ordinarily held in check. Whether offering a handshake or a guiding arm, the toucher is careful to stay within the culture's narrowly prescribed limits lest the touch be misinterpreted. Touching between people with more personal relationships is also governed by silent cultural rules and restraints.

The rules of touch may be unspoken, but they're visible to anyone who takes the trouble to watch. Psychologist Richard Heslin at Purdue University, for instance, has proposed five categories of touch based on people's roles and relationships. Each category includes a special range of touches, best described by the quality of touch, the body areas touched and whether the touch is reciprocated.

FUNCTIONAL-PROFESSIONAL touches are performed while the toucher fulfills a special role, such as that of doctor, barber or tailor. For people in these occupations, touch must be devoid of personal messages.

SOCIAL-POLITE touches are formal, limited to greeting and separating and to expressing appreciation among business associates and among strangers and acquaintances. The typical handshake reflects cordiality more than intimacy.

FRIENDSHIP-WARMTH touches occur in the context of personal concern and caring, such as the relationships between extended-family members, friendly neighbors and close work mates. This category straddles the line between warmth and deep affection, a line where friendly touches move over into love touches.

LOVE-INTIMACY touches occur between close family members and friends in relationships where there is affection and caring.

SEXUAL-AROUSAL touches occur in erotic-sexual contexts.

These categories are not hard and fast, since in various cultures and subcultures the rules differ about who can touch whom, in what contexts and what forms the touch may take. In the Northern European "noncontact cultures," overall touch rates are usually quite low. People from these cultures can seem very cold, especially to people from "contact cultures" such as those in the Mediterranean area, where there are much higher rates of touching, even between strangers.

In the United States, a particularly low-touch culture, we rarely see people touch one another in public. Other than in sports and children's play, the most we see of it is when people hold hands in the street, fondle babies or say hello and goodbye. Even on television shows, with the odd exceptions of hitting and kissing, there is little touching.

The cultural differences in contact can be quite dramatic, as researcher Sidney Jourard found in the 1960s when he studied touch between pairs of people in coffee shops around the world. There was more touch in certain cities (180 times an hour between couples in San Juan, Puerto Rico, and 110 times an hour in Paris, France) than in others (2 times an hour between couples in Gainesville, Florida, and 0 times an hour in London, England).

Those cultural contact patterns are embedded early, through child-rearing practices. Psychologist Janice Gibson and her colleagues at the University of Pittsburgh took to the playgrounds and beaches of Greece, the Soviet Union and the United States and compared the frequency and nature of touch between caregivers and children 2 to 5 years old. When it came to retrieving or punishing the children, touching rates were similar in all three countries. But on touches for soothing, holding and play, American children had significantly less contact than those from the other cultures. (Is that why we need bumper stickers to remind us: "Have you hugged your child today?")

Greek and Soviet kids are held, soothed and touched playfully much more than American kids.

Men greet people with fewer lip kisses, embraces and kinds of touch than women do.

Generalizations about different national or ethnic groups can be tricky, however. For example, despite widespread beliefs that Latin Americans are highly contact-oriented, when researcher Robert Shuter at Marquette University compared public contact between couples in Costa Rica, Colombia and Panama, he found that the Costa Ricans both touched and held their partners noticeably more than the couples did in the other two countries.

Within most cultures the rules and meanings of touch are different for men and women, as one recent study in the United States illustrates. Imagine yourself in a hospital bed, about to have major surgery. The nurse comes in to tell you what your operation and after-care will be like. She touches you briefly twice, once on the hand for a few seconds after she introduces herself and again on the arm for a full minute during the instruction period. As she leaves she shakes your hand.

Does this kind of brief reassuring touch add anything to her talk? Does it have any kind of impact on your nervousness or how you respond to the operation? Your reaction is likely to depend upon your gender.

Psychologist Sheryle Whitcher, while working as a graduate student with psychologist Jeffrey Fisher of the University of Connecticut, arranged for a group of surgery patients to be touched in the way described above during their preoperative information session, while other patients got only the information. Women had strikingly positive reactions to being touched; it lowered their blood pressure and anxiety both before surgery and for more than an hour afterwards. But men found the experience upsetting; both their blood pressure and their anxiety rose and stayed elevated in response to being touched.

Why did touch produce such strikingly different responses? Part of the answer may lie in the fact that men in the United States often find it harder to acknowledge dependency and fear than women do; thus, for men, a well-intentioned touch may be a threatening reminder of their vulnerability.

These gender differences are fostered by early experiences, particularly in handling and caretaking. Differences in parents' use of touch with their infant children help to shape and model "male" and "female" touch patterns: Fathers use touch more for play, while mothers use it more for soothing and grooming. The children's gender also affects the kinds of touches they receive. In the United States, for example, girls receive more affectionate touches (kissing, cuddling, holding) than boys do.

By puberty, tactile experiences with parents and peers have already programmed differences in boys' and girls' touching behavior and their use of personal space (see "Body Mapping," this article). Some results of this training are evident when men and women greet people. In one study, psychologists Paul Greenbaum and Howard Rosenfeld of the University of Kansas watched how travelers at the Kansas City International Airport touched people who greeted them. Women greeted women and men more physically, with mutual lip kisses, embraces and more kinds of touch and holding for longer periods of time. In contrast, when men greeted men, most just shook hands and left it at that.

How do you feel about touching and being touched? Are you relaxed and comfortable, or does such contact make you feel awkward and tense? Your comfort with touch may be linked to your personality. Psychologist Knud Larsen and student Jeff LeRoux at Oregon State University looked at how people's personality traits are related to their attitudes toward touching between people of the same sex. The researchers measured touch attitudes through questions such as, "I enjoy persons of my sex who are comfortable with touching," "I sometimes enjoy hugging friends of the same sex" and "Physical expression of affection between persons of the same sex is healthy." Even though men were generally less comfortable about same-sex touching than women were, the more authoritarian and rigid people of both sexes were the least comfortable.

A related study by researchers John Deethardt and Debbie Hines at Texas Tech University in Lubbock, Texas, examined personality and attitudes toward being touched by opposite-sex friends and lovers and by same-sex friends. Touch attitudes were tapped with such questions as, "When I am with my girl-/boyfriend I really like to touch that person to show affection," "When I tell a same-sex intimate friend that I have just gotten a divorce, I want that person to touch me" and "I enjoy an opposite-sex acquaintance touching me when we greet each other." Regardless of gender, people who were comfortable with touching were also more talkative, cheerful, socially dominant and nonconforming; those discomforted by touch tended to be more emotionally unstable and socially withdrawn.

A recent survey of nearly 4,000 undergraduates by researchers Janis Andersen, Peter Andersen and Myron Lustig of San Diego State University revealed that, regardless of gender, people who were less comfortable about touching were also more apprehensive about communicating and had lower self-esteem. Several other studies have shown that people who are more comfortable with touch are less afraid and suspicious of other people's motives and intentions and have less anxiety and tension in their everyday lives. Not surprisingly, another study showed they are also likely to be more satisfied with their bodies and physical appearance.

These different personality factors play themselves out most revealingly in the intimacy of love relationships. Couples stay together and break apart for many reasons, including the way each partner expresses and reacts to affection and intimacy. For some, feelings and words are enough; for others, touch and physical intimacy are more critical.

In the film *Annie Hall*, Woody Allen and Diane Keaton are shown split-screen as each talks to an analyst about their sexual relationship. When the analyst asks how often they have sex, he answers, "Hardly ever, maybe three times a week," while she describes it as "constantly, three times a week."

How important is physical intimacy in close relationships? What role does touch play in marital satisfaction? Psychologists Betsy Tolstedt and Joseph Stokes of the University of Illinois at Chicago tried to find out by interviewing and observing couples. They used three measures of intimacy: emotional intimacy (feelings of closeness, support, tolerance); verbal intimacy (disclosure of emotions, feelings, opinions); and physical intimacy (satisfaction with "companionate" and sexual touch). The

Body Mapping: The Sexual Revolution

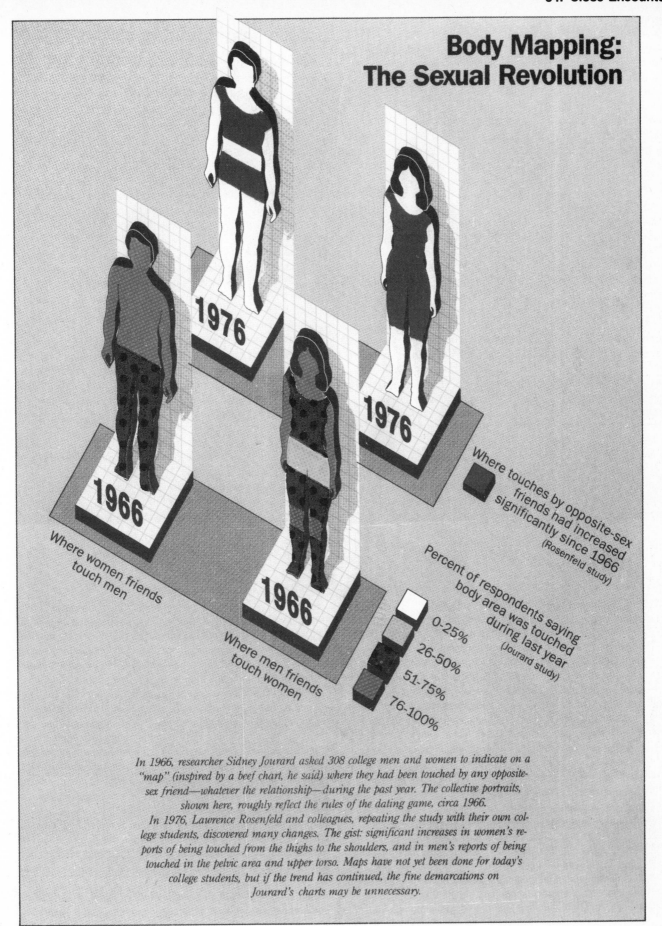

1976

1966

Where women friends touch men

1976

1966

Where men friends touch women

Where touches by opposite-sex friends had increased significantly since 1966
(Rosenfeld study)

Percent of respondents saying body area was touched during last year
(Jourard study)

0-25%

26-50%

51-75%

76-100%

In 1966, researcher Sidney Jourard asked 308 college men and women to indicate on a "map" (inspired by a beef chart, he said) where they had been touched by any opposite-sex friend—whatever the relationship—during the past year. The collective portraits, shown here, roughly reflect the rules of the dating game, circa 1966.

In 1976, Lawrence Rosenfeld and colleagues, repeating the study with their own college students, discovered many changes. The gist: significant increases in women's reports of being touched from the thighs to the shoulders, and in men's reports of being touched in the pelvic area and upper torso. Maps have not yet been done for today's college students, but if the trend has continued, the fine demarcations on Jourard's charts may be unnecessary.

researchers also measured marital satisfaction and happiness, along with conflicts and actual separations and legal actions.

They found that each form of intimacy made its own contribution to marital satisfaction, but—perhaps surprisingly to some—physical intimacy mattered the least of the three. Conflict and divorce potential were most connected to dissatisfaction with emotional and verbal intimacy.

Touch intimacy may not usually have the power to make or break marriages, but it can sway strangers and even people close to you, often without their knowledge. The expressions "to put the touch on someone" and "that person is an easy touch" refer to the persuasive power of touch. Indeed, research shows that it is harder to say no to someone who makes a request when it is accompanied by a touch.

Politicians know this well. Ignoring security concerns, political candidates plunge into the crowd to kiss babies and "press the flesh." Even a quick handshake leaves a lasting impression—a personal touch—that can pay off later at election time.

A momentary and seemingly incidental touch can establish a positive, temporary bond between strangers, making them more helpful, compliant, generous and positive. In one experiment in a library, a slight hand brush in the course of returning library cards to patrons was enough to influence patrons' positive attitudes toward the library and its staff. In another study, conducted in restaurants, a fleeting touch paid off in hard cash. Waitresses who touched their customers on the hand or shoulder as they returned change received a larger percentage of the bill as their tip. Even though they risked crossing role boundaries by touching customers in such familiar ways, their ingratiating service demeanor offset any threat.

In certain situations, touch can be discomforting because it signals power. Psychologist Nancy Henley of the University of California, Los Angeles, after observing the touch behavior of people as they went about their daily lives, has suggested that higher-status individuals enjoy more touch liberties with their lower-status associates. To Henley, who has noted how touch signals one's place in the status-dominance hierarchy, there is even a sexist "politics of touch." She has found that women generally rank lower than men in the touch hierarchy, very much like the secretary-boss, student-teacher and worker-foreman relationships. In all of these, it is considered unseemly for lower-status individuals to put their hands on superiors. Rank does have its touching privileges.

The rules of the status hierarchy are so powerful that people can infer status differences from watching other people's touch behavior. In one experiment by psychologists Brenda Major and Richard Heslin of Purdue University, observers could see only the silhouettes of pairs of people facing each other, with one touching the other on the shoulder. They judged the toucher to be more assertive and of a higher status than the person touched. Had the touch been reciprocal, status differences would have disappeared.

Psychologist Alvin G. Goldstein and student Judy Jeffords at the University of Missouri have sharpened our understanding of touch and status through their field study of touch among legislators during a Missouri state legislative session. Observers positioned themselves in the gallery and systematically recorded who initiated touch during the many floor conversations. Based on a status formula that included committee leadership and membership, they discovered that among these male peers, the lower-status men were the ones most likely to initiate touch.

When roles are clearly different, so that one individual has

TOUCHY ISSUES

TOUCH IS A GESTURE of warmth and concern, but it can also be seen as intrusive, demeaning or seductive. Because of these ambiguous meanings, touch can sometimes be problematic for therapists, who must be careful to monitor their touch behavior with clients. Because difficult legal and ethical issues surround possible misinterpretation of touch, many therapists avoid physical contact of any sort with their clients, except for a formal handshake at the first and last sessions. But in a number of body-oriented psychotherapies, such as Wilhelm Reich's character analysis and Alexander Lowen's bioenergetic therapy, touch is used deliberately as part of the treatment process; it is meant to stir emotions and memories through the body and not just the mind.

Imagine meeting your therapist for the first time. You are greeted in the waiting room and guided into the consultation room. You have the therapist's full attention as you speak about what brings you to therapy. Twice during the session the therapist briefly touches you on the arm. Before you leave, you make an appointment to meet again.

How are you likely to evaluate your first session? Do you think the therapist's touch might affect your reactions to therapy or to the therapist? Could it affect the process of therapy?

Sessions like the one just described have been studied by psychologist Mark A. Hubble of Harding Hospital in Worthington, Ohio, and colleagues, using therapists specially trained to touch their clients in consistent ways during their first counseling session. Results show that, compared with clients who were not touched, those who were touched judged the therapist as more expert. In an earlier, similar study by researcher Joyce Pattison, trained judges rated clients who had been touched as deeper in their self-exploration.

Although there are clearly some risks, perhaps more therapists should consider "getting in touch" with their clients by adding such small tactile gestures to their therapeutic repertoire.

control or power over the other, such as a boss and a secretary, then touch usually reflects major dominance or status differences in the relationship. But when roles are more diffuse and overlapping, so that people are almost equal in power—as the legislators were—then lower-status people may try to establish more intimate connections with their more powerful and higher-status colleagues by making physical contact with them.

Touching has a subtle and often ambivalent role in most settings. But there is one special circumstance in which touch is permitted and universally positive: In sports, teammates encourage, applaud and console each other generously through touch. In Western cultures, for men especially, hugs and slaps on the behind are permitted among athletes, even though they are very rarely seen between heterosexual men outside the sports arena. The intense enthusiasm legitimizes tactile expressions of emotion that would otherwise be seen as homosexually threatening.

Graduate student Charles Anderton and psychologist Robert Heckel of the University of South Carolina studied touch in the competitive context of all-male or all-female championship swim meets by recording each instance of touch after success and failure. Regardless of sex, winners were touched similarly, on aver-

At swim meets, winners were touched six times more than losers were.

age six times more than losers, with most of the touches to the hand and some to the back or shoulders; only a small percent were to the head or buttocks.

This swimming study only looked at touch between same-sex teammates, since swim meets have separate races for men and women. Would touch patterns be the same for mixed-gender teams, or would men and women be inhibited about initiating and receiving touches, as they are in settings outside of sports? Psychologists David Smith, Frank Willis and Joseph Gier at the University of Missouri studied touching behavior of men and women in bowling alleys in Kansas City, Missouri, during mixed-league competition. They found almost no differences between men and women in initiating or receiving touches.

Without the social vocabulary of touch, life would be cold, mechanical, distant, rational, verbal. We are created in the intimate union of two bodies and stay connected to the body of one until the cord is cut. Even after birth, we need touch for survival. Healthy human infants deprived of touch and handling for long periods develop a kind of infant depression that leads to withdrawal and apathy and, in extreme cases, wasting away to death.

As people develop, touch assumes symbolic meaning as the primary system for expressing and experiencing affection, inclusion and control. Deprived of those gestures and their meanings, the world might be more egalitarian, but it would also be far more frightening, hostile and chilly. And who would understand why a stranger's touch meant life to Brigitte Gerney?

GETTING HELP FROM HELPING

As self-help groups proliferate, psychologists and other professionals are trying to figure out what they are and just how they work.

DAN HURLEY

Dan Hurley, a New York writer, is a frequent contributor to Psychology Today.

It's the Tuesday night meeting of the Staten Island chapter of Recovery Inc. Mac, speaking in the West Indies accent of his native St. Vincent, tells the 17 men and women seated around a table in a local church how he handles the severe anxiety that once kept him from working as a construction foreman. Frank, a New Jersey electrician in his 50s, explains how he keeps himself from relapsing into the paranoid schizophrenia that less than three years ago had him growing a long beard, wearing a rope belt and rusty knife and believing that he was the greatest saint of all time. Finally, Bettyann, a gray-haired housekeeper and mother of four, tells of the 24 years she spent inside her home, a hostage of agoraphobia.

"I couldn't go out to the garbage can at the curb," Bettyann says. "I couldn't go to church. Then, six months after I started coming to Recovery, I was able to drive all the way down to Florida with my husband. I'm not saying I don't have the anxiety anymore, but I am able to overcome it. Recovery made me feel like I'm not singled out. Somebody else is in the same boat."

An estimated 12 million people now help themselves and their neighbors by participating in roughly 500,000 self-help groups. These groups range from such nationally established organizations as Recovery Inc., founded 50 years ago by psychiatrist Abraham A. Low to help people with debilitating psychological problems, to Mistresses Anonymous, Bald-Headed Men of America and Fundamentalists Anonymous (see "Leaving the Fold," this article).

"Self-help gives you control of your own life," says Frank Riessman, a psychologist at the City University of New York and founding director of the National Self-Help Clearinghouse. "It's being accepted far more than it used to be. It's very populist, very participatory."

Fifteen years ago, not one clearinghouse existed to provide information on self-help groups or encourage the development of new ones. The creation of more than 40 clearinghouses since then "is an important social phenomenon," says Fran Dory, executive director of the New York City Self-Help Clearinghouse. In 1985, Riessman and Dory led the first national meeting of local clearinghouses; the International Network for Mutual Help Centers was formed that year. And in September 1987, Surgeon General C. Everett Koop sponsored a workshop to create a national agenda of policies, programs and activities to promote self-help.

Although people have joined together to find strength in groups for thousands of years, the modern self-help group composed of people facing a single problem can be traced back to June 10, 1935, when two men known to the public as Bill W. and Doctor Bob first met to help each other stay sober. They eventually founded Alcoholics Anonymous (AA). By 1986, AA membership totaled an estimated 804,000 in the United States and Canada, with 41,000 registered groups meeting regularly. Worldwide membership is estimated at 1.5 million, making AA by far the largest self-help group in the world. In the 1970s, it spawned similar groups for people closely involved with alcoholics (Al-Anon), teenage children living with alcoholic parents (Alateen), Gamblers Anonymous and Overeaters Anonymous. Today, at least 14 organizations follow the AA format.

As self-help, or, more accurately, mutual-help groups proliferate, psychologists and other professionals are trying to define exactly what a self-help group is. The California Self-Help Center, located at the psychology department at the University of California, Los Angeles, has created 198 categories to cover the state's 3,300 groups and broken them into four broad types: those for physical and mental illness, those for reforming addictive behavior, those for coping with a crisis of transition and those for friends and relatives of the person with the problem.

Uniting all types of self-help groups is what Riessman calls the "self-help ethos. It's the spirit of the movement: getting help from helping. It's very democratic and destigmatizing. Any type of behavior or condition can be accepted. You don't have to hide that you're a drug abuser or that you have cancer. You share it with other people and help each other."

Yet within the common philosophy, "you get a million and one formats," says psychologist Morton A. Lieberman, of the University of California, San Francisco. Recovery Inc., for example, follows a rigid format beginning with a reading from *Mental Health Through Will-Training,* written by the group's founder. Then, five or six members give examples of upsetting events and how they dealt with them in light of the group's teachings. Other groups that try to change members' behavior usually use a similarly rigid format. Groups that focus on facing a painful situation, such as bereavement, tend to have a more loosely structured "care and share" style.

Some groups do not even hold meetings. Mended Hearts, for heart-disease patients and their families, visits hospital patients to offer reassurance. Eight years ago, Sam Fixman was visited just after his open-heart surgery, and today he is president of the Brooklyn chapter of Mended Hearts. Each week a local hospital provides him with the names of new patients, and he and other group members make the rounds.

"About a month ago I had the most incredible emotional experience of my life," says Fixman, a 55-year-old account executive at a subscription agency. He visited a man who had just come out of surgery and was still under anesthesia, with tubes attached to his chest and in his mouth. "Listen, I've been through this before," Fixman told him. "You're coming off the anesthesia now." The man grabbed Fixman's arm tightly and began to cry. Barely fighting off tears himself—"I needed to be strong for him"—Fixman promised to return that night and again the next day. "And I did. He just wanted someone to reassure him that he was going to be OK. I got help and I made it, and I've got to see that someone else gets the same help. For me it's a must thing to do."

Other groups actively reach out to people not likely to form self-help groups on their own. Roger Williams, of the health and human issues outreach department at the University of Wisconsin-Madison, for example, has helped form many of the 30 self-help groups for Wisconsin farm families in the past two years. The Sisterhood of Black Single Mothers, founded 14 years ago by Daphne Busby in Brooklyn's devastated Bedford-Stuyvesant neighborhood, offers more than support groups to its nearly 1,000 members. "It has to be more than just sitting around talking," Busby says. "We provide courses in basic literacy and life management, we do peer counseling and

we're preparing to offer housing. Our job is to empower women, to connect them to a network."

Perhaps the newest type of self-help group is one held via computer networks. "One member is in Oregon, another is in Minnesota, another is in Florida, but they're all together," says Edward Madara, who as director of New Jersey's Self-Help Clearinghouse has helped form four computer-linked groups so far.

What makes self-help groups work is still a puzzle to psychologists, but they have a few clues. One key process that psychologist Stephen B. Fawcett sees at work in self-help groups is that members learn about common aspects of their problem. Fawcett and his colleagues at the University of Kansas have audiotaped several groups' meetings "to get a sense of the anatomy of self-help groups," he says. "To our surprise, the predominant activity seems to be information-giving; especially important are personal disclosures. We find relatively few statements of support and sympathy."

A second factor is that members often come to accept an ideology that allows them to reattribute the cause of their problem and thereby change their behavior. Alcoholics are told in AA that they are not in control of their drinking and must turn their lives over to a Higher Power; parents of schizophrenic children are told in the National Alliance for the Mentally Ill that biochemistry, not their child rearing, is the primary culprit. Some psychologists may dispute these claims, but few would deny the improvements in behavior they permit. To researcher Paul Antze, such ideologies offer a "cognitive antidote" to the problem.

Strong group acceptance and shared understanding of what was previously a hidden problem are other keys to making self-help groups effective. "Homogeneity among the members seems to be one of the critical and distinguishing factors in what makes many self-help groups powerful," says Marion Jacobs, codirector of the California Self-Help Center and adjunct professor of psychology at UCLA.

The power of meeting with other alcoholics through AA changed the life of Ellen M. After starting with glue-sniffing in sixth grade, Ellen reached the point three years ago, at the age of 27, where she was shooting heroin, drinking daily, having repeated blackouts and at times working as a prostitute. She credits an intensive treatment program with helping her quit drugs and alcohol. "But quitting is easy," she says. "I quit a thousand times. AA has taught me constant abstinence. What did it for me at the beginning was that I was not alone, that there was a roomful of people working toward what I was working toward. Normies [the term she uses for nonaddicts] don't understand. AA showed me that I wasn't so different. I had always thought I was dropped here by aliens. Until AA, nobody understood how I felt at 3 a.m. sitting by myself with a bottle."

The sense of normalization that grows from being with people who share a problem leads to development of a social support network. An important ingredient in AA's success, for instance, is the use of spon-

LEAVING THE FOLD

In April of 1985, Wall Street lawyer Richard Yao and banker James Luce placed a two-line classified ad in the *Village Voice* to announce the formation of a new group, Fundamentalists Anonymous (FA). The pair hoped to get a few encouraging responses. Instead, they received 500 calls from around the country and within three weeks found themselves on the *Phil Donahue Show*. Less than three years later, they have 46 chapters, 40,000 members and a national office in New York City, for which Yao has left his legal career to become executive director.

"There's obviously an incredible need out there," says Yao, whose only training in psychology was a few courses while attending Yale Divinity School. The need, he says, comes from the "fundamentalist mindset," a tendency to be authoritarian, intolerant and compulsive about control. Yao claims that this mindset often causes intense fear and guilt, inability to talk about the fundamentalist experience, depression, loneliness, low self-esteem, aversion to authority and anger over the time lost while in the fold. The cure, as he sees it, is support from other former fundamentalists. FA also makes referrals to licensed psychologists for any member who needs one, and psychologists likewise have referred many clients to FA.

Psychologist Marlene Winell of Fort Collins, Colorado, has treated about 40 former fundamentalists in her private practice, and she finds great support for Yao's claims. "I was a zealous fundamentalist myself," says Winell, who was reared by missionary parents in Taiwan and spent much of her youth proselytizing door-to-door. "If you stay inside the fundamentalist system, you're fine. But if you try to get away from it, it's like having the ground pulled out from beneath your feet. You have to restructure your entire world."

Other psychologists agree that while fundamentalism itself does not seem pathological, the experience of leaving it behind can cause a transition crisis similar to divorce or the death of a loved one. "FA helped me go back and look at my resentment," says Gary W. Hartz, a psychologist with the Veterans Administration in Los Angeles. "I felt bitter about the time I lost," he says, "and ashamed about some of the things I did, like evangelizing students at Daytona Beach during spring break to give up two of the Five S's—sex and suds—and stick to the sun, surf and sand."

Another person who seems to have gone through many of the typical problems of erstwhile fundamentalists is former presidential candidate Gary Hart, who was reared in the Church of the Nazarene. "He did not get a chance to party or date or drink like a normal teenager," Yao says. "In my opinion he's trying to make up for lost time."

Despite Yao's claims and the popular reception FA has received, "There are not enough data to support the idea that fundamentalism in general is bad for people, based exclusively on the claims of former fundamentalists," says Lee A. Kirkpatrick, a doctoral candidate in psychology at the University of Denver. "Saying that personality characteristics associated with fundamentalism are 'pathological' is merely a value judgment." In fact, studies by psychiatrist Marc Galanter have found that while 36 percent of Unification Church dropouts had "serious emotional problems," most new members showed a dramatic decrease in neurotic distress. Noting that all of Yao's members are fundamentalist dropouts, Kirkpatrick says psychologists should find out if Yao's claims are valid for current fundamentalists. Yao admits, "I'm not an academic. All I know is it works."

sors, members who are already sober and who serve as guides to new members. In Ellen's case, her sponsor would come to her house in the middle of the night when Ellen was drunk and violent. "She could talk to me heart-to-heart, not down to me like some nurse in an addiction ward," Ellen says. "We're human beings. We have to be connected, to have a social core. AA is my social core." Today, Ellen has been sober for more than two years, lives with her husband again and works as a service coordinator at a community alcoholism program in Los Angeles.

Not all the results of the self-help process are positive. To psychologist Stanton Peele, author of *The Meaning of Addiction*, AA's cognitive antidote is "essentially a religious conversion experience. There's a very heavy group socialization process that goes on,

a kind of brainwashing. You're not allowed to say you used alcohol socially and under control. You have to say you've lost total control. In fact the research shows that people go through cycles in which they manage it, and then go off the deep end."

The social support that a newcomer gets from a sponsor can also be dangerous, says psychologist Linda W. Scheffler, author of *Help Thy Neighbor*. In her experience with members of Overeaters Anonymous, "I've seen at least one person who has been damaged in a relationship with a sponsor. There is a real danger in the intimate pairing and counseling that goes on. I found it a malevolent influence in some patients' lives." Counseling is hard for professionals, she says, but harder still for untrained group members.

At best, the concept of social support remains

fuzzy, and Lieberman stresses that "to generalize that all self-help groups work because of social support would be utter nonsense." In a study of widows and widowers Lieberman found that those who had established give-and-take personal relationships with other members benefited from their self-help group far more than those who hadn't; yet a similar study of bereaved parents found no added benefits with such relationships. Lieberman has also studied groups in which no members showed any psychological improvement whatsoever. "By no means are all self-help groups successful," he says. "We do have studies that are encouraging, but as to how they work in general and why they work and for whom, we just don't know."

Until more is known about self-help groups in general and AA in particular, some psychologists worry about the increasingly popular view that AA is the only way for alcoholics to achieve long-term sobriety. "AA is obviously very popular and still growing, but there are no data showing it's the best approach," says psychologist William R. Miller of the University of New Mexico. The only two experimental studies that exist compared people who were ordered by the courts to attend AA with others who were not; the studies found no significant impact for AA, Miller says.

With the courts routinely requiring convicted drunk drivers to attend AA, and most treatment centers doing the same, "AA is no longer real self-help," says Peele. "It's been medicalized. Self-help is a great tradition, but it can't be forced upon people. We're being held hostage by the groups now."

The tension between academics and self-helpers is

acknowledged by Riessman, the national clearinghouse director who has written three books on self-help and served on President Carter's Mental Health Commission. When speaking to self-help groups, he says he has to emphasize his own involvement in groups or else his audience will reject him as "just an observer." Even so, Riessman admits that an important factor in the current growth of self-help groups is the increasing number of referrals by psychologists, physicians and social agencies.

Psychologists such as Fawcett, however, offer self-help groups more than referrals. Fawcett hopes to translate his research on what makes groups tick into training materials for group leaders. And the California Self-Help Center has recently created a taped instruction program called Common Concern that leads groups through basic lessons in communication, running a group effectively and troubleshooting typical problems, such as giving premature advice and dealing with people who monopolize sessions.

UCLA's Jacobs believes that prominent professionals, such as Surgeon General Koop, can raise self-help from a provincial and spontaneous phenomenon to an effective movement. And the role of psychologists, she suggests, should be to give "tools and consultations" to help groups get started and maintain themselves when they get bogged down or have other problems. Sweeping her hand toward a window overlooking downtown Brooklyn, where she recently visited, Jacobs says, "I promise you, there are self-help groups all around this neighborhood. But right now they blend into the local scenery, like the PTA and the Elks. In coming years they may stand out as a legitimate way to deliver mental-health services."

Psychological Disorders

The history of mental and emotional disorders is sharply punctuated by changes in perspective. At various times, those who suffered from these disorders were persecuted as witches, tortured to drive out possessing spirits, punished as sinners, jailed as dangerous to society, confined to asylums as insane, and hospitalized as suffering from an illness. Today, psychologists propose that the view of disorders as "illnesses" has outlived its usefulness. We should think of them as either biochemical disturbances or disorders of learning, in which the person develops a maladaptive pattern of behavior that is then maintained by an inappropriate environment. At the same time, we need to recognize that these reactions to stressors in the environment, or to inappropriate learning situations, may be genetically predisposed, that is, some people may more easily develop the disorders than others.

Nonetheless, serious disorders are serious problems, and not just for the individual who is the patient or client. The impact of mental illness on the family and friends of the afflicted person has often been overlooked, but deserves our full attention. The search for answers and the placing of blame are just two of the problems therapists must be alert to in dealing with families.

Dementia has always been a problem of grave concern. Difficulty in diagnosis, particularly early in its course, often confined the victim to a state of hopelessness. Better diagnostic procedures have made Alzheimer's disease a household term, yet many questions about its course and cause remain unanswered.

The most common diagnostic term applied to outpatients today is depression. This category undoubtedly covers a wide range of patterns of response. Recently, scientists and clinicians have become aware of a specific low-grade form of depression that is now called dysthymic disorder. Once discovered, it's very easy to treat.

While diagnostic labels have changed in the past decade, the underlying element of most maladaptive patterns of behavior continues to be anxiety. In "Anxiety and Panic: Their Cause and Treatment," we learn that a biochemical as well as a learning approach can best serve the diagnostician who deals with people beset by this most troubling condition.

Looking Ahead: Challenge Questions

What support systems do we need to provide to families of those who suffer from emotional problems and particularly from severe forms of mental disorders?

Considering our current knowledge about Alzheimer's disease, what would be the next logical steps in the search for the specific cause and the development of a reasonable treatment?

If a friend appears to have a dysthymic disorder, how would you explain or describe it to him or her, and what would you encourage him or her to do about it?

How can we determine the specific cause of a given anxiety or panic attack? Based on whether the cause is chemical or learned, what can be done to eliminate these uncomfortable experiences?

Unit 10

WHEN MENTAL ILLNESS HITS HOME

Sometimes after months of silence the telephone would ring in the darkness, startling Mary Alexander from sleep. "Do you have a daughter . . . ?" The voice blandly official, the caller in some other town or state, in Minneapolis this time, or Pittsburgh, "Mrs. Alexander, do you have a daughter . . . ?" She would close her eyes, waiting for the next words, bracing for them. "Mrs. Alexander, do you have a daughter who is living on the golf course and disturbing neighbors?" Who is walking down the street in mid-December with no clothes on. . . . Who tried to throw herself in front of a bus. . . . "Mrs. Alexander, we have your daughter here in the hospital. . . ." In her mind are images of Janet years ago, building a fort with her three younger sisters, her blond hair in long straight locks. Janet on the chairlift with her father in Aspen, or reading, curled in the window seat of the big New England farmhouse, white chenille bedspreads, a framed picture of blue mountains and open fields. "I swear to God, I would rather my child had cancer than this agony of a disease. . . ."

"Deinstitutionalization has failed." It is the mental-health mantra of the '80s, a popular slogan, borrowed by politicians and pundits. On our streets, severely disturbed people are among the homeless, living without treatment or community resources, eating out of garbage cans, filing through revolving doors to hospitals and jail cells. Yet those who are homeless are only the most visible subplot of a larger story. In fact, 60 percent of the 2 million Americans with disabling mental illness live with their families at least part of the time, and hundreds of thousands more reside in nursing homes and privately run "board and cares." In quiet suburban neighborhoods and in Park Avenue apartments, parents take out second mortgages to pay for the care of mentally ill sons and daughters. Husbands, aunts, brothers offer prayers for a cure. Over the years, families shepherd those they love through a torturous labyrinth of mental-health services, often to no obvious benefit.

"More money" is the familiar cry of those who work within an overburdened system. But it is not just a problem of money. "There is a kind of Russian distribution system, where the food never reaches the shelves. It rots in the countryside," says Dr. John Talbott, chairman of psychiatry at the University of Maryland, who has long pondered these

problems. There is a constant shortage of hospital beds, but no long-term plan for building the community services that could keep patients out of hospitals to begin with. There are outpatient clinics, but no one to make sure patients arrive there to be treated. There are model programs, but they reach only a fraction of those who are in need. There is a two-tiered network of care, public and private, rich and poor. But even wealth does not ensure good treatment.

In this fragmented and sublimely ineffective system, cities, states and the federal government play "chicken" to see which will shoulder the financial burden of the mentally ill. Mental-health workers squabble over priorities and semantics. Everyone is affected by the deeply cynical decision society seems to have made collectively, if unconsciously: We will do nothing.

In the face of this national tragedy, it is the families of the mentally disturbed who are finally forcing change. A coalition of families, the National Alliance for the Mentally Ill, almost singlehandedly persuaded the National Institute of Mental Health to shift its $345 million research program away from more sociological studies, toward research on the cause and treatment of schizophrenia and other serious disorders. In Chicago, St. Louis and New Orleans, when parents found rehabilitation centers or

housing projects for the mentally ill nonexistent, they went out and created them. In Massachusetts, a state that has inspired its share of mental-hospital exposés, the Department of Mental Health two years ago decided to bring both families and former patients into the equation: In a unique collaborative arrangement, citizen monitors conduct unannounced inspections of all public psychiatric institutions. The involvement of families, says Dr. Herbert Pardes, president-elect of the American Psychiatric Association and a former NIMH director, "is one of the most important things to happen in the history of mental health."

Families, and patients themselves, want to change more than just programs and services; they are struggling to eliminate the entrenched stereotypes and age-old misconceptions still governing society's attitudes toward mental illness. It was not that long ago that insanity was a family secret, that a schizophrenic aunt or daughter was chained in the attic. And still, today, a qualified engineer is denied a job because three years ago he was treated for depression, a psychiatrist is disqualified as an expert witness because while in training she received psychotherapy, and a presidential candidate must act quickly to squelch rumors that he might have sought counseling after his brother's death.

The myths have to be debunked through constant repetition: Schizophrenia is not the same as "split personality"; mental illness is not the result of weak character or moral failure; most mental patients are not violent; serious mental disorders are not "hopeless," and patients can get better, with the right treatment.

"Progress is more often illusion than reality," says Dr. John Nemiah, editor of the *American Journal of Psychiatry,* writing about society's management of chronic mental illness. "We are perhaps no further along than we were 200 years ago—indeed, we may have been traveling in circles."

Mental illness has always baffled and disturbed. Anyone who has seen up close the disintegration of a mind by schizophrenia, the laceration of consciousness, the shredding of thought that is paired with deep apathy and withdrawal, must wonder how such a thing occurs. No less puzzling are the violently distorted moods of manic-depression, highs that send the sufferer into an unstoppable frenzy of words and wild ideas, lows that plunge him into such a state of despair that "one's only wish is for silence and solitude and the oblivion of sleep," as composer Hector Berlioz described it. "For anyone possessed by this," wrote Berlioz, who during his youth fell victim to crippling emotional swings, "nothing has meaning, the destruction of a world would hardly move him."

The musician's eloquence conveys the texture of psychic torment but not its prevalence. At any moment, 25 percent of hospital beds in the U.S. are filled by mental patients, more than the total for cancer, heart disease and respiratory illness patients combined. Insanity appears to have been common in past centuries as well; it is only society's response to it that has changed.

The Puritans believed "distraction," as they called it, was possession by the Devil, or else punishment for sins. Yet the strange behavior of those afflicted was looked upon with tolerance. The Puritans were certain of the moral order and could view departure from the rational without themselves becoming unsettled by it.

Through much of the 1700s, family or friends were expected to take care of the mentally ill. Thus James Otis, Jr., a prominent politician in prerevolutionary Massachusetts, was remanded to his father's house or taken to the country by colleagues when he periodically went mad, once smashing all the windows in Boston's town hall. When no family was present, community leaders took over, sometimes "auctioning out" the person to a foster family.

By the 19th century, this early version of a community mental-health system was breaking down. "What worked in small villages didn't work with urbanization," says Gerald Grob, professor of history at Rutgers University. Immigrants poured into American cities, and persons suffering from schizophrenia or other mental disorders wandered the streets or were sent to almshouses or jail cells. Dorothea Dix, the crusading schoolteacher who took up the cause of the mentally ill in the mid-1800s, found disturbed individuals living in sordid conditions, "confined in cages, closets, cellars, stalls, pens: Chained, naked, beaten with rods and lashed into obedience."

Humane treatment in mental hospitals, Dix felt, was the solution, and by the time of her death in 1887 every state had at least one public mental hospital. There, doctors practiced a treatment called "moral therapy," because insanity was, they believed, caused by a childhood spent in an improper environment. The hospitals were proud of their "cures" for mental illness, often discharging patients within a year. They kept meticulous—if peculiar—statistics. From the 1843 annual report of Utica State Asylum:

"Total weight on admission of
276 patients   34,856 lb.
Total weight of those
discharged and remaining,
December 1st   35,825 lb.
Increase in weight of all
received   1,029 lb."

Towns and cities initially paid for the care of their residents at the state hospital. But by the 1890s, in an effort to discourage communities from cutting costs by keeping the afflicted in local almshouses, mental patients were declared wards of the state. So began the warehousing that in this century was the function of state hospitals. Seizing the opportunity to shift the economic burden onto the state, local officials began to redefine senility as "psychiatric illness," sending thousands of elderly men and women, demented and physically fragile, to state institutions. Between 1900 and World War II, more than half of patients admitted to state hospitals were over 65 years of age.

From there, the story is all too familiar. There were exposés, *The Snake Pit, The Shame of the States.* New studies showed that patients could be treated effectively, humanely and less expensively, in the community, and the serendipitous development of antipsychotic drugs in the 1950s made this a viable alternative. Then, in the 1960s, the Great Society initiated a wholesale policy of deinstitutionalization. State hospitals emptied their wards, from 558,000 patients in 1955 to fewer than 130,000,

mostly short-term patients, today. At the same time, the Community Mental Health Centers Act of 1963 called for the opening of 2,000 community treatment centers around the nation, and the federal government poured millions of mental-health dollars into counties and cities. But the dream was never realized. Fewer than half the projected centers actually came into being. The bulk of federal funds was spent on mental-health "prevention," on therapy for divorced mothers and low-income families, not on care for the chronically ill.

Toward the end of his life, the painter Vincent van Gogh wrote to his brother, Theodore, "What consoles me is that I am beginning to consider madness as an illness like any other, and I accept it as such." Were there a credo for the family movement, it might well be van Gogh's words. "The evidence that serious mental illnesses are diseases is now overwhelming," says Dr. E. Fuller Torrey, a psychiatrist whose sister is schizophrenic and who recently published *Nowhere to Go: The Tragic Odyssey of the Homeless Mentally Ill.* "Why should we treat them any differently than Parkinson's or Alzheimer's or multiple sclerosis?"

But old attitudes die hard. With the rise of psychoanalysis in the United States in the mid-20th century came a view of mental illness that held mothers and fathers responsible. Freud himself doubted that schizophrenia and other psychotic disorders could be ameliorated through his "talking cure." But he talked of conflicts and drives and the role of early-childhood experiences, and others picked up the theme, adding the term "schizophrenogenic mother."

The family movement prefers to call mental illnesses "brain diseases" and speaks of Freud with disdain. It is more than a quibble over words. The notion that the patient or his family is somehow to blame has persisted in the public mind, affecting in a very real way the fate of those afflicted. Most private insurers require larger co-payments and set lower reimbursement ceilings for psychiatric disorders. To many families, this seems just another bitter legacy of an emphasis on mental "health" instead of mental illness, a focus that blurred distinctions between the "worried well" and the "walking wounded." And some argue that the former—those suffering from life dissatisfaction or other mild ills—should pay more for counseling out of pocket. The latter, those with more-serious disorders that require extended hospitalization or drug therapy, ought to be fully covered.

Deinstitutionalization has created other agonizing dilemmas, among them those of people who are desperately ill but don't want treatment. Family advocates are attempting to reshape policy

EXPLAINING THE INEXPLICABLE

Scientists are finding that a genetic predisposition may be triggered by stress

Over the centuries, everything from "an excess of passions" to the malevolent influence of the moon has been proposed as a scientific explanation for mental illness. But modern psychiatry, trading on technological advances in neuroscience and molecular genetics, is beginning to confirm what many suspected. The extreme changes in perception, behavior and mood that occur in serious mental disorders are, at least in part, biological.

Psychiatrists have always recognized that schizophrenia and manic-depression differ markedly from less severe complaints. Unlike "the blues," or mild anxiety, these illnesses can make it impossible for those afflicted to hold jobs or negotiate daily routines. While the emotional swings of manic-depression begin in adulthood, schizophrenia most often develops in adolescence or early adulthood. Many experts believe it will prove to be a family of illnesses rather than a single disorder, but there are common characteristics: Thought patterns become peculiar and convoluted. Hallucinations and delusions often mix with withdrawal and apathy.

Early evidence that changes in brain chemistry might be involved in schizophrenia and manic-depression came from the development of drugs to treat them. Researchers discovered that antipsychotic drugs, which help about 60 percent of schizophrenics, change the levels of a substance called dopamine, one of many chemicals that transmit nerve impulses in the brain. Antidepressants and drugs like lithium carbonate, used to treat mania, alter the balance of other neurotransmitters and bring relief to the vast majority of sufferers. But though scientists reason that these chemicals are involved in mental illnesses, their role is still unproved.

Window to the brain. The case for brain irregularities has been strengthened with the development of imaging devices that can take readings of brain structure and function. In schizophrenic patients, brain scans indicate that the frontal lobe—intimately tied up with high-order abilities such as future planning—shows lower-than-normal levels of blood flow during the performance of a simple cognitive task. Other studies have found that some schizophrenics have enlarged brain ventricles—the fluid-filled spaces within the brain—indicating that brain tissue has shrunk or developed abnormally.

At the same time, psychiatrists are building evidence for heredity's contribution to mental illness. Researchers have known for years that schizophrenia and manic-depressive illness tend to run in families. But only recently have they been able to start tracking down the specific gene or genes that may predispose someone to fall ill. Last fall, an international team of scientists reported finding an abnormality on chromosome 5 in 39 schizophrenic members of five families. An earlier, 11-year study of a Pennsylvania Amish family with a history of manic-depression found that afflicted individuals shared an abnormal gene on another chromosome, No. 11.

Yet this work is only the barest blush of a beginning. No one so far has succeeded in replicating the studies. And because all mental illnesses involve complex human behaviors, most experts believe genetic predisposition will not turn out to be as simple as a single abnormal gene.

The nature of nurture. Even without the specifics of inheritance, however, scientists have been able to estimate an individual's risk of developing severe mental illness. In schizophrenia, for example, a child with one schizophrenic parent runs an 8-to-18-percent likelihood of being afflicted. If both parents are schizophrenic, that figure jumps to between 15 and 50 percent. But unlike diseases such as Down syndrome, mental disorders are only in part genetic, as studies of identical twins have shown. Even when one twin is schizophrenic, the other has only a 50-to-60-percent chance of developing the disease.

However strong the influence of heredity, researchers believe that severe mental illness has a substantial nurture component as well. "The question is not nature vs. nurture, but the nature of nurture," says Dr. Jack Grebb, of New York University Medical Center. One theory suggests schizophrenia may result from prenatal events—infection by a virus, perhaps—that affect a fetus genetically susceptible to the illness. Another theory proposes stress as the triggering factor. There is some evidence that a high degree of emotional tumult in a family, good or bad, may make schizophrenic patients more prone to relapse. "But this doesn't suggest that the families of schizophrenics are any different from other families," says Dr. William Carpenter, director of the Maryland Psychiatric Institute. "It suggests that within family life there are things that patients may have a hard time dealing with." In a field filled with many more questions than answers, the fact that bad parenting is not likely to cause schizophrenia may be the one thing scientists are increasingly sure of.

here as well. The problem was dramatized last year in the courtroom battle of Joyce Brown, a k a Billie Boggs. Living on the streets of Manhattan, Brown was hospitalized against her will as part of an attempt by New York Mayor Ed Koch to widen the scope of his state's commitment law. When a trial judge concluded that Brown—who shouted at passers-by, ripped dollar bills into shreds and used the sidewalk as a commode—was sane, it triggered a storm of editorials. "We have condemned the homeless mentally ill to die with their rights on," protested columnist Charles Krauthammer.

Many families now are pressing for lawmakers to make it easier to force very ill patients into treatment, even if they do not pose a danger to themselves or others. As it now stands, lawyers, not doctors, decide when someone should be hospitalized, families say. In some urban areas, a patient must literally be slashing his wrists or brandishing a weapon before he can be held in a hospital. At least 15 states have rewritten their commitment laws to reflect this view. Yet civil libertarians and most former patients deeply oppose such legal reforms. A person who has committed no crime and who is not dangerous should not be incarcerated against his will, they say. At least one study suggests that changing laws only makes things worse, that it leads to even greater over-crowding in crisis clinics and amplifies the already dire shortage of hospital beds.

These are signs of a deeply ailing system, one that no simple wave of a legislator's pen will heal. "No matter where you look, something is broken and needs to be fixed," says Laurie Flynn, NAMI's executive director. Of the $17 billion plus spent annually in the U.S. on mental-health care, more must be funneled toward those who most need it, in the form of coordinated community services, networks of halfway and three-quarterway houses, crisis centers, outreach teams, housing, job training programs.

Innovative programs, programs that *work*, already exist in small pockets across the country, in Madison, Wis., in Tucson, Ariz., in Toledo, Ohio. The Robert Wood Johnson Foundation has awarded a total of $29 million to nine cities to redesign their mental-health systems. Even in New York City, where thousands are homeless or on the brink of homelessness and the bleak interior of the Bellevue Hospital crisis clinic is almost always crowded, there are islands of sanity. The solution is not, as Koch recently concluded, to take patients out of hospitals and place them in homeless shelters, even if the shelters offer mental-health services. Rather, there are places where mental patients live with dignity: The St. Francis residences, a program run by three Franciscan friars; Fountain House, where 4,000 mentally disable club members learn skills and function as capable members of a community, many living on their own in subsidized apartments.

The reign of the state hospitals ended in a flurry of exposés, accounts of patients chained to beds, lying in their own feces. A return to warehousing mental patients in large state institutions is not the answer. "It's not economically, legally, morally, ethically or clinically feasible," says Steven Schnee, superintendent of San Antonio State Hospital. "It's not necessary. It's not appropriate. Mentally ill people deserve the opportunity to make a contribution."

Until there is a cure for schizophrenia, there will be a need for long-term care for the small group of patients who cannot function even with medication, or who are continuously violent or suicidal. "Some patients require intensive treatment," says Leona Bachrach, of the University of Maryland. "It can be done in the community. We know that

because in a few places it has been done. But there is a lag between knowing and doing it, and into this gap many disabled people fall." In the meantime, state hospitals, most of which are themselves overcrowded, try to fill this role.

Yet the most basic obstacle to treating mental illness is neither lack of knowledge nor lack of money. It is a question of values. The values of a psychiatric profession that rewards private practice and economically penalizes those who choose to work with the severely ill in the public sector; a society that takes cancer and heart disease seriously but largely ignores mental illness; the values of citizens who don't want halfway houses in *their* neighborhoods and often forget that the homeless man they see on the television screen is also someone's son, someone's brother.

PATIENTS FOR SALE: SUPPLY IS UP, DEMAND DOWN

In overcrowded psychiatric emergency rooms, healers become auctioneers

In a strained mental-health system, beds are scarce and indigent patients unpopular, a reality captured by the title of a recent journal article: "The Hospitalizable Patient as Commodity: Selling in a Bear Market." Inner-city psychiatric emergency rooms from New York to San Francisco are battlegrounds in a war between the private and public sectors as workers struggle to secure beds for their patients. These crisis clinics are a microcosm of the larger system, a showcase for forces that crush idealism and make good care all but impossible.

Police bring in a flood of patients, the psychic casualties of downtown streets and welfare hotels. Overwhelmed emergency rooms try to stem the tide. Public hospitals must treat anyone who comes in, so their emergency rooms devise subtle ways to discourage customers. In one Manhattan crisis clinic, administrators require police to stay until a disposition is reached for any patient they bring in. The process can take hours.

Psychiatric emergency rooms are supposed to provide brief treatment and, if necessary, find patients beds in hospitals

or halfway houses. But this task is more difficult to do for some patients than for others, forcing even the most dedicated care provider into the role of salesman. Emergency-room workers must coax and cajole, cutting through the skepticism of an admissions nurse at the other end of a telephone line. Private hospitals and nursing homes are picky about whom they will take. State hospitals often have quotas for how many patients they accept from a given city or county.

Creative excuses. For hospitals on the receiving end, the cardinal rule is to find an excuse for keeping out undesirable patients. "We only admit medicaid patients one day a week" was one creative explanation given doctors at a Bronx emergency room by a hospital that would not take a 16-year-old suicidal patient. It took 13 days and negotiations with 10 hospitals before the girl was finally placed in a locked psychiatric ward.

The sellers have their techniques, too. "If you make a patient sound too bad, hospitals won't take him," says Joe Larson, a psychiatric nurse at San Francisco General Hospital's psychiatric emergency room. "If he doesn't sound bad enough, they're afraid his medicaid will be cut off and they'll be stuck with the bill."

The hardest patients to sell are the repeaters with bad reputations, the fire set-

ters and those who are potentially violent. Drug abuse is a negative selling point. So is no health insurance, AIDS, incontinence or a need for long-term care or constant observation.

More often than not, the emergency-room workers fail, and their unfortunate charges spend as long as a week sleeping on foldout armchairs, watching television and pacing in cramped quarters beneath blue-white fluorescent lights. In Northern California, four psychiatric emergency rooms were recently issued citations by state officials for keeping patients longer than the mandated 24-hour limit. But they have no choice. If a patient is dangerous to himself or others, the hospital cannot let him go.

Ultimately, difficult patients often end their emergency-room stay by being sent to the overcrowded wards of the same city hospitals—dumping grounds for the poor and the uninsured, for patients no one else will take. "We enter the field with the best of intentions, to comfort, aid and assist," writes Stephen Goldfinger, M.D., of Harvard University Medical School. "And yet how easy it becomes to lose these lofty motivations when confronted with the daily realities. . . . We are all—patients, planners and practitioners—diminished by this process."

THE CLOUDED MIND

When a key brain enzyme disappears, so does memory.

Michael Shodell

Michael Shodell is a contributing editor of Science 84.

Old age, even in cultures where it is venerated, is often viewed with ambivalence. And as living standards and medicine continue to improve, more and more of us will be the butts of Fan Ch'eng-ta's fine joke. For with an increased life-span, afflictions that once were rare have become common. Among the gravest of these is Alzheimer's disease, an illness that destroys the mind, leaving the body behind as a grim reminder of the person who once was there. As cancer, another all-too-familiar companion of the later decades, has become a relentless reminder of the urgency in seeking the secrets of the cell, so Alzheimer's disease has left us with another pressing challenge—uncovering the mysteries of the mind.

Alzheimer's disease is one of the most fearsome and devastating aspects of aging: It has no known cause, no prevention, no cure. It afflicts about a million people, roughly five percent of the population over 65. By the year 2000 an estimated three to four million Americans, or one of every 10 adults over 65, will be a victim. Hundreds of scientists around the world are dedicated to understanding this affliction. Some are isolating Alzheimer's biochemical defects in the brains of victims, others are comparing these to similar ones in other dementias, while still others are looking at rare dementia-causing diseases from distant parts of the globe.

In this way, they hope to pin down Alzheimer's cause, which is as elusive today as it was in 1906 when the German neurologist Alois Alzheimer first described the disease in a report entitled "Concerning a unique illness of the brain cortex." Alzheimer was the first to show that senile dementia was not just a natural wearing out of the mind, a belief common then as it had been through the centuries. Shakespeare reflected that conviction when he described the last age of man as "second childishness and mere oblivion." While severe dementia may be caused by a number of illnesses, such as brain tumors, alcoholism, or arteriosclerosis of brain blood vessels, Alzheimer's disease is by far the single most prevalent cause of mental deterioration in the elderly.

Victims initially have trouble remembering recent events. Gradually, as their minds deteriorate, they become more confused and forgetful, repeating questions asked moments before, for example, or getting hopelessly lost while traveling to previously familiar places. Disorientation grows, and memories of the past disappear, sometimes accompanied by paranoia, hallucinations, and violent mood swings. Patients can no longer cook, drive, or use tools. Later, they lose their ability to read, write, eat, walk, or talk. Finally the disease culminates in a full dementia, the undoing of the mind.

In his seminal paper Alzheimer first described one of the two physical characteristics of the disease: the clumping of fibers within nerve cells, called neurofibrillary tangles. The other—the so-called senile plaques—are filled with knobby, abnormal nerve axons and terminals wreathed around amyloid, a waxy, translucent protein that looks like rippled pasta. These structures nest among the mass of normal brain cells and fibers in the cerebral cortex, the outer layer of the brain in which higher thought processes and abilities originate, and the hippocampus, which seems to play a special role in learning and memory. The plaques and tangles can easily be seen with a low-power microscope.

In examining his deceased patient's brain, Alzheimer was following a medical tradition begun in the mid-18th century by the Italian anatomist Giovanni Battista Morgagni, whose studies of more than 700 autopsies demonstrated for the first time, among other things, that hemorrhaging of the brain produced paralysis on the opposite side of the body, perhaps the first time anyone connected stroke with the rupturing of brain vessels.

Today, autopsy is still a major source of medical information that can be obtained in no other way. In Alzheimer's victims, for instance, autopsy reveals the presence of the plaques and tangles essential for a final diagnosis of the disease. Diagnosis while the patient is alive can only be made provisionally, based on psychological and performance tests and the patient's family and case histories. Moreover, since old animals do not get Alzheimer's, autopsies provide the only way to perform research on actual brains.

The first autopsies of Alzheimer's patients clearly revealed that plaques and tangles were the disease's signature upon the brain. The structures correlated well with the disease; the sicker the person, the more he had. But the plaques and tangles also appeared in the brains of apparently healthy older people, although to a considerably lesser extent, perhaps because of their age or because of some environmental injury. In the mid-1970s, researchers found to their surprise that the signature of Alzheimer's was indeed writ upon the cortex, but the hand that did the writing was located in another region of the brain altogether.

One of the first indications of what was actually going on came from Peter Davies, then at the Institute of Neurology in London and now at Albert Einstein College of Medicine in New York City. He showed that the cortices and hippocampi of Alzheimer's sufferers had a tremendously reduced level—from 60 to 90 percent compared to age-matched controls—of an enzyme called choline acetyltransferase, or CAT, needed for making the chemical acetylcholine.

Acetylcholine is one of the essential brain substances known as neurotransmitters, specialized chemicals that carry messages between neurons. Within the brain's three-pound gelatinous mass are more than one trillion neuron cells, each having on average about 50,000 different connections to other neurons. Just one cubic centimeter of cerebral cortex contains approximately one trillion such neuron-to-neuron connections. And it is within this extraordinary labyrinthine network that the mind and memory are located, as well as the terrible defects that are the cause of degenerative illnesses like Alzheimer's disease.

Neurotransmitters such as acetylcholine are at the heart of the functioning of that network. Without them the neuronal wires of communication would still be in place, but the lines would be dead. Although dozens of neurotransmitters are now known, and more are discovered every year, any particular neuron usually stores enzymes that make predominantly just one neurotransmitter. Moreover, groups of neurons that generally make the same transmitter are often found clustered together in defined areas of the brain known as nuclei. The neurons themselves may have very long projections, or axons, for carrying their chemicals to distant regions of the brain. Thus, a deficiency of acetylcholine in one part of the brain could be caused by the lack of enzymes in some distant nucleus of the brain.

In the late 1970s and early 1980s, Joseph T. Coyle, Donald Price, and Mahlon DeLong at the Johns Hopkins University School of Medicine demonstrated that this scenario exactly captures Alzheimer's fatal process: The deficit of the enzyme and its neurotransmitter appears in the cortex, but the actual source of the problem lies some distance away in a small region known as the nucleus

basalis, lying just above the site where the optic nerves meet and cross. Moreover, autopsies revealed shrunken and abnormal cells or an unmistakable and dramatic loss of neurons from the nucleus basalis in Alzheimer's sufferers— up to 75 percent in some cases—but not in most age-matched controls, which explained why there was so little enzyme being manufactured.

Alzheimer's disease began to look, at least to some researchers, like a neurotransmitter-specific disease. The classic example of this sort of ailment is Parkinson's disease, typically appearing in the middle years of life. Its symptoms include tremors and severe problems of muscular control, sometimes complicated by dementia. The disease is caused by a loss of neurons in the base of the brain, which actually depletes dopamine in the cortex. Drugs can increase the levels of dopamine in the brain, at least for awhile, and temporarily bring the Parkinson symptoms under control, but the progressive brain cell loss continues, compounding the disease effects and making the drugs less and less effective as the illness progresses. Similar approaches to Alzheimer's disease, using drugs that should increase or otherwise enhance brain acetylcholine activity, have not proven equally effective even in the short term, perhaps because other neurotransmitters are involved in Alzheimer's or because the drugs available now don't increase acetylcholine activity enough.

One still highly experimental approach that might accomplish this sort of goal has recently been attempted in Parkinson's disease. Functioning cells from the adrenal glands, which produce a chemical closely related to dopamine, have been transplanted to the deteriorating brains of two Parkinson's disease patients at the Karolinska Institute in Stockholm, but it is still too soon to tell if the technique will have any value in the long run for Parkinson's—or Alzheimer's.

Other researchers are trying a different tack by relating a lack of acetylcholine to memory loss. Folklorists wrote about how jimson or devil weed could erase memories for as much as a week or more. Scopolamine, the active ingredient, produces the same effect but for short intervals when given in small doses. It was once used regularly, for example, to reduce the perceived pain of labor, by erasing the mother's recollections of the birth of her child. Experiments with young adult volunteers have shown that scopolamine, by blocking acetylcholine receptors, affects memory. Intrigued with the ability of this drug to interfere with the normal functioning of a specific neurotransmitter, researchers attempted to examine its exact relation to memory and other cognitive functions. When David Drachman of the University of Massachusetts Medical Center administered scopolamine to healthy young volunteers, a temporary state of memory loss and confusion resulted that was, at least under the restricted testing procedures used, virtually indistinguishable from the responses of old people and similar to those of Alzheimer's patients.

The best approach to Alzheimer's, of course, would be to learn how to prevent the terrible symptoms from arising in the first place. And that means finding the cause. One possibility is that Alzheimer's disease lies in the genes. One such disease in which the faulty genes are clearly hereditary—all children with the fatal illness have an affected parent—is Huntington's disease or Huntington's chorea, from the same Greek root as choreography, referring to the jerky spasmodic movements of the head, limbs, and body. Researchers have recently isolated a marker for the disease on a particular region of chromosome number four.

Similar hereditary connections have been found in Alzheimer's disease, although they are much less conclusive than in Huntington's disease. Several family trees have been described in which the incidence of Alzheimer's disease can be traced back for up to seven and even eight generations, but the more common pattern appears not to be hereditary at all. These differing patterns could suggest instead that there are nongenetic varieties of the disease and types that are hereditary as well. There might even be a genetic component in all forms of Alzheimer's disease, but the hereditary trait shows up clearly only when there is reliable medical data going back several generations or a sufficient number of older people represented on the receding branches of any given family tree. There might be still another type of Alzheimer's in which genes control the susceptibility to the disease, but the environment triggers the ailment.

The distinction between hereditary and nonhereditary diseases began to break down in the 1960s, largely because of the demonstration of what are known as slow virus diseases. These sorts of infections originally came to light through study of a strange illness at first apparently of interest only to the isolated Fore tribe of the forested highlands of New Guinea—the only people in the world known to get the disease of kuru, which means fear or trembling. Through a combination of anthropological, medical, and epidemiological creativity and tenacity, D. Carleton Gajdusek of the U.S. National Institutes of Health was able to show that this illness, which appeared to be a classic chronic degenerative disorder, was actually caused by an infectious agent. The kuru agent was not passed from person to person, but rather from the dead to the living as the mothers and children handled the infected brains of the deceased as part of their mourning ritual. The disease progressively attacks the brain and nervous system of its victims, who first shiver, stagger, slur their speech, eventually can neither walk nor sit up without assistance, and, finally unable to chew or swallow, die.

The discovery of this agent, and the establishment of its ability to have infected years or even decades before its devasting effects have become unleashed upon the brains of its victims—effects that include dementia and probably the senile plaques in the victims' brains as well—brought a new perspective to the consideration of degenerative neurological disease. Such kurulike agents are now known to occur in a variety of species, including the widespread scrapie disease of sheep, and another human affliction known as Creutzfeldt-Jakob syndrome that occurs virtually worldwide. Named after the German scientists who discovered it in 1920, Creutzfeldt-Jakob syndrome causes a severe form of senility that strikes people in their middle to later decades and progresses far more rapidly than

Alzheimer's. It is also a disease, although far rarer than Alzheimer's, for which family inheritance patterns have been demonstrated in some instances. But even in these cases, infectious slow viruses—similar to the kuru and sheep scrapie viruses—are the actual cause.

Another seemingly isolated incidence of disease on a remote Pacific island offers yet another possible candidate as the cause of Alzheimer's—the environment. A tribe known as the Chamorros, living in a relatively underdeveloped region on Guam, develop extremely high incidences of Lou Gehrig's disease (amyotrophic lateral sclerosis or ALS)—the progressive wasting of muscles that killed baseball's "iron man"—as well as Parkinsonlike ailments and dementia accompanied by Alzheimerlike neurofibrillary tangles. It turns out that the region of Guam where the tribe lives is almost entirely devoid of such essential minerals as calcium and magnesium. Neuropathologist Daniel Perl of the University of Vermont believes that these deficits combined with and possibly leading to unusually high accumulations of heavy metals, especially aluminum, seem to play a role in the genesis of the illnesses of the Chamorros. In addition, Perl has shown that the tangles in the brains of victims of Alzheimer's disease also contain aluminum and that this metal, when injected into the brains of experimental animals, can also lead to the formation of similar, although not identical, tangles.

This discovery has caused people to worry about using aluminum pots, pans, foil, deodorants, and Rolaids for fear the metal will accumulate in the brain. Perl says that the evidence available is not sufficient to warrant these concerns. Aluminum is the most ubiquitous metal on Earth, and it is impossible to avoid it. Although it is definitely toxic to the nervous system, most people luckily have efficient barriers to prevent aluminum from getting into the brain. Perl says he is now trying to find out what the barrier mechanisms are that keep aluminum out. He is also studying the potential effects of advancing age, slow viruses, and other factors on the integrity of the barrier system.

The list of suspects implicated in Alzheimer's disease, then, is distressingly broad: genetics, infectious agents, and environment—either acting alone or in concert. Should the cause be infectious or environmental, researchers might be able to eliminate or inactivate it. But what if it should be something more fundamental and far-reaching—a genetic program for senility that is part of the aging process—one of the seven stages of man? Were that so, Alzheimer's would not be a disease at all. There would be no cure. Doctors could only make the affliction more bearable.

By comparing Alzheimer's to known diseases such as Parkinson's, kuru, and Creutzfeldt-Jakob, however, it seems likely that Alzheimer's is a true disease. As such there is hope for seeking its causes and its possible cures. Then aging need not portend Shakespeare's "mere oblivion" after all, but rather a stage of life to be appreciated for its own strengths as well as for its weaknesses—a stage as legitimate and no more pathological than any other.

Dysthymic Disorder

The DD's

BLUES WITHOUT END

When you say, "Have a nice day,"
five million Americans don't know what
you're talking about.

Winifred Gallagher

Winifred Gallagher *is a Senior Editor at* American Health.

The psychiatrist asked his patient how long she'd been in poor spirits. "Since the sperm hit the egg," she said. "I can tell by the way other people act that they're happy, but I don't know what that's like. I never have a happy day."

Research now shows that her melancholy description may not be just a colorful exaggeration. About five million Americans—twice as many women as men—suffer from a chronic, sometimes lifelong, low-grade depression called "dysthymic disorder" (DD). The typical DD victim is in her late 30s to 40s, but epidemiologists are alarmed by DD's increasing prevalence in younger people, particularly children.

Considering the long, grey shadow DD casts, it's unfortunate that the af-flicted—and their families and friends—often have no idea that this unhappiness is caused by a very treatable disease. Often, the sufferer has repeatedly sought help from physicians and psychotherapists for secondary symptoms such as fatigue, or personality problems like low self-esteem. In fact, until recently, a DD victim was said to be suffering from a

Sadness gradually seems normal—"the way life is."

DD rates are twice as high for women as for men . . . High-risk ages: 30s and 40s . . .

"depressive personality." Now health professionals are learning that until the patient's depression itself is identified and treated, she's not very likely to get better.

Psychologists used to focus on a more obvious form of the blues known as a "major depressive episode." A major depression profoundly upsets a person's mental and physical equilibrium, but its symptoms generally subside in six to nine months—or, with treatment, within weeks.

In contrast, the symptoms of DD, which persist for at least two years, are mild enough to permit a victim to go through the motions of life at home and work. As the months go by, sadness gradually seems normal, at least for her—"the way life is" or "the way I am." She and her circle forget what she was like before the blues descended. This confusion of illness with personality or the circumstances of life often keeps DD sufferers from finding the right help.

Once DD is diagnosed, treatment can bring prompt, dramatic relief. Many patients are helped by newer, short-term psychotherapies that teach practical ways to correct the intellectual and emotional distortions caused by the blues. A growing body of research is prompting more doctors to prescribe aerobic exercise for both depressed and anxious patients. But the latest advance is the use of an old remedy in a new way.

Antidepressant medicines were previously prescribed only for shorter, severe "biological" depressions. Recently James Kocsis and Allen Frances, professors of psychiatry at New York Hospital-Cornell Medical Center, have shown that antidepressants can often relieve mild chronic melancholy. One patient summed up the results of drug treatment this way: "For the first time in my life, I feel like I'm not walking waist-deep in mud."

"DD is a very substantial public health problem that has been vastly overlooked and unrecognized," says Dr. Robert Hirschfeld, a psychiatrist who directs off-site research sponsored by the National Institute of Mental Health in Rockville, MD. This year, the NIMH is sponsoring a major outreach program—Project D/ART, for Depression Awareness, Recognition and Treatment—to teach the public and health professionals about DD and other forms of depression.

Whiny, Moody, Guilt-Ridden

Just about everyone gets mildly depressed on occasion—you'd almost have to be crazy not to, according to Dr. Gerald L. Klerman, a leading depression researcher and professor of psychiatry at New York Hospital-Cornell. On any given day, 10% of Americans say they're melancholy. About 40% claim they've had five to 10 blue days in a year. "A friend might say, 'What's the matter? You don't seem like yourself lately,' " says Klerman. "This type of brief, mild depression is the psychological equivalent of the common cold, and there's a lot of it going around."

Like these "normal" depressions, DD often starts out as an understandable reaction to a dispiriting event. But in DD, the symptoms, though mild, drag on and on. "It's normal to be upset about a friend's death or getting fired, but not to say 'I'll never have another friend' or 'I'm worthless,' " says Dr. Kocsis. "When the person's ideas about what's going on are unrealistic, and melancholic symptoms persist, he or she is heading toward a psychiatric disorder."

Like other sick people, victims of DD feel poorly. Their physical symptoms—often fatigue or aches and pains—are troublesome. Their psychological ones are worse: dysphoria (unhappiness) and anhedonia (the inability to feel pleasure). Dysthymics tend to be pessimistic, whiny, moody and guilt-ridden, as well as sad. They're bored, and sometimes boring. They feel helpless and hopeless. If something good happens, they think it's a fluke; if something bad happens, they know it's their fault. "You can recognize dysthymics by their unhappy yet functional lives," says Dr. Frances. "They suffer."

Dysthymics suffer most in those aspects of life that call for spontaneity, fun, intimacy and sensitivity toward others. They usually do better at work than at love or play—Abraham Lincoln was a depressed superachiever. Often, pessimism and poor self-esteem prevent a victim from developing either her public or private potential. "Dysthymics tend to have a job, but not a great job, and a marriage, but not a great marriage," says Kocsis. "Just as they're chronically depressed, they can end up 'chronically wed'—stuck in a bad relationship they can't get themselves out of."

A bout of DD, like a struggle with major depression, can be almost as grueling for close associates as for the victim. The toll it takes on relationships is one reason that prompt treatment is important, says Klerman: "Studies show that most people first respond to a depressed person with sympathy and support. But if the sadness and complaints persist, that sympathy gives way to irritability and avoidance. This is a normal reaction that ends up isolating the patient even more. She feels that nobody likes her—and sometimes she's right."

"To me, the question is not why people get depressed. After all, human life is stressful," says Klerman. "The question is why some people

For many people, depression seems to run in the family.

Increasing risk in kids . . . Symptoms last at least two years . . . Often goes untreated . . .

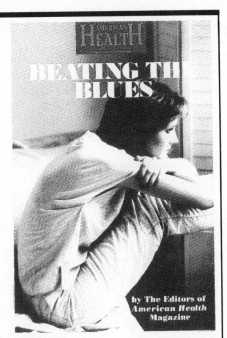
Researchers are more puzzled by cases of DD that begin early in life. (Until quite recently, it was believed that children didn't suffer from true depression.) Many juvenile depressions—usually responses to traumas like divorce or the death of a parent—do seem to disappear on their own in time. But a substantial number of DD patients have been depressed for no discernible reason since an undetermined point in childhood. Interviews with their families back up their accounts—they were indeed sad kids. They often have depressed relatives, suggesting that depression may be a family trait.

Determining DD's cause—whether biological or psychological—is not a prerequisite for effective treatment. "Everything in life is biological as well as psychological—look at the biological way the brain responds to hope in placebo experiments!" says Frances. "The brain is constantly influenced both by one's experiences and its own chemistry. So it's not surprising that there are biological and psychological ways to break up the cycle of depressed neurochemistry, thoughts and experiences. The right intervention in any one of these areas—with drugs, psychotherapy, behavioral changes—could turn the vicious cycle into a benign one."

Drugs: An Old Innovation

Just as many factors can contribute to a headache, many influences combine to produce an individual's depression. Once DD has been diagnosed, the victim's treatment has to be tailored to his psyche, chemistry or both—a painstaking process that can take some time. "Patients get demoralized if one approach doesn't work. But not to despair! Almost everyone

stay depressed. Most people can turn it off after five or 10 days and cope, while others get hung up for years on end, and make everyone miserable."

Biochemistry of the Blues

Today, biological psychiatrists think that DD is often caused by the same unfortunate conjunction of external stress and biological predisposition that triggers more severe depressions. Along with his genes, a victim inherits a tendency to have unbalanced levels of neurotransmitters, the chemicals that govern the electrical transmission of information throughout the brain. When this communication sys-

tem malfunctions, so does the ability to think and feel appropriately.

Studies show that lots of DD patients and their relatives have had—or will have—episodes of major depression as well. Klerman suspects that many dysthymics—with the exception of those who've had DD since they were kids—had an acute episode of major depression that they never really recovered from. He points out that while most of those who suffer a major depressive episode are over it in a year, 15% aren't; three years later, about 5% of them still feel blue. These people may be "left with a residual anhedonia, pessimism and fatigue," says Klerman.

Drug therapy helped a depressed lawyer finally begin her practice.

On any day, 10% of Americans are blue . . . 40% have 5 to 10 blue days a year . . .

will benefit from one of a combination of treatments," says Frances. "You can be a nonresponder to one, and do very well on another."

Frances' point was made plain in the controlled drug study of dysthymics Kocsis and he completed in 1986. Most of their 53 patients, who had been depressed for an average of 19 years, had previously tried psychotherapy without success. 28 of these patients were then given the antidepressant Tofranil, without accompanying talk therapy. Six weeks after they started to take the drug, about 60% of the subjects who stuck with the treatment had recovered. Even the researchers were somewhat surprised by how well the antidepressant worked.

The major hitch in antidepressant treatment is that the drugs don't start working until three weeks after they're first prescribed. The patient usually takes several capsules daily for six to 12 months; when they're no longer needed, the dosage is tapered off under careful medical supervision. Side effects are usually mild—for example, dry mouth, constipation and brief memory lapses. While psychiatrists often supervise antidepressant treatment, the drugs can be prescribed and successfully monitored by general practitioners—the doctors that most victims of DD consult first.

Unfortunately, a longstanding bias against psychiatric drugs can lead doctors and patients to regard medication as a "defeat," instead of as part of a systematic approach to finding the right treatment. "Until recently, no one would have thought of giving medication to a mildly depressed patient, because his was considered a 'psychological' disorder that needed psychotherapy," says Kocsis. He and Frances suggest that a patient try psychotherapy first; if symptoms persist

after six months, an antidepressant should be considered, or even a combination of drugs and talk.

"The patients in our study really got better," says Frances. "We're not just talking about taking the edge off the latest blip in their depression, but about feeling better than they'd ever felt before." One subject, in her mid-30s, had been so demoralized by the

blues that she'd been working as a secretary even though she had a law degree. Shortly after starting on the antidepressant, she began a successful career as a lawyer.

Traditional psychodynamic therapists believe that depression is caused by guilt, anger, dependency and excessive need for approval. They try to help the patient gain control over the

DOES SOMEONE YOU KNOW HAVE DD?

"We don't have a blood test to determine whether someone is a latent dysthymic," says Dr. Gerald Klerman of New York Hospital-Cornell. "The diagnosis must be based on the individual's report of his symptoms and functioning." How does a doctor or friend tell if someone is depressed? "He should ask," says Klerman, "and he often doesn't."

Three or four "Yes" answers to the following questions could mean that someone you know is suffering from DD. Has the person been:

■ In a blue mood for most of the day, more days than not, for at least two years? (Children and teens may seem irritable rather than depressed; they need to have symptoms for only a year to fit the DD criteria.)

■ Free of the blues only for periods of less than two months at a time during the past two years?

■ Eating too much or not enough?

■ Sleeping too much or not enough?

■ Complaining of low energy?

■ Demonstrating poor self-esteem?

■ Having difficulty concentrating or making decisions?

■ Showing signs of desperation or hopelessness?

In addition, these symptoms must

not be the result of psychosis, depressive disorders besides DD, or physical influences on mood, such as antihypertension drugs.

Many victims of DD bear other emotional burdens as well—often anxiety and alcohol or drug abuse. Some of their symptoms overlap with those of other psychiatric disorders.

For information on how to find a health professional qualified to diagnose and treat DD, contact:

■ National Depressive and Manic-Depressive Association (NDMDA), Merchandise Mart, PO Box 3395, Chicago, IL 60654. Patient-run educational support and a referral network for patients and their families. Send an SASE with 56¢ postage on it.

■ National Alliance for the Mentally Ill (NAMI), 1901 N. Fort Myer Drive, Suite 500, Arlington, VA 22209. Support and education for patients and families; 800 affiliates nationwide.

■ The National Mental Health Association (NMHA), 1021 Prince St., Alexandria, VA 22314-2971; 703-684-7722. The nation's oldest organization concerned with all aspects of mental health; 600 affiliates nationwide.

■ Depression Awareness, Recognition and Treatment Program (D/ART), National Institute of Mental Health, 5600 Fishers Lane, Rockville, MD 20857; Attn: D/ART Public Inquiries. Health care providers and the public can request information.

People with DD need short-term therapy—not endless analysis.

5% of those with major depression still suffer after 3 years . . . Drug therapy brings relief to 60% . . .

unconscious conflicts that underlie those emotions. Some are undoubtedly helped, but the results are unpredictable and the treatment is lengthy and expensive.

Today, a second generation of eclectic psychotherapists is attacking depression with "psychoeducation," rather than introspection and reflection on the past. As far as they're concerned, the blues come from "depressed" patterns of thinking, feeling, acting, and dealing with others. But if that's true, learning new, positive patterns can be the cure.

Talk Therapy vs. Drugs

Studies have shown these new talk therapies work: Their overall results are comparable to those of antidepressants. *Cognitive therapy* corrects the depressed person's typically negative, distorted thoughts, which inspire the self-destructive behavior that worsens their depression. *Interpersonal psychotherapy* (IPT) uses the patient's ability to function in relationships as a gauge of his emotional health; by strengthening his coping and communication skills, social bonds also become the means of relieving his depression. *Behavioral therapy* combines aspects of these two approaches and adds a third focus: learning to balance life's pluses and minuses.

According to behaviorist Robert Becker, associate professor of psychiatry at the Medical College of Pennsylvania in Philadelphia, each person has a "set point" beyond which he can't neutralize stresses with rewards. When a negative event—say, divorce—pushes him beyond that point,

he feels upset. If his life has revolved around his wife for a decade, his skills at forming new relationships are rusty, or nonexistent. Feeling isolated and out of synch, he may become seriously depressed.

Along with negative thinking, poor social interactions and diminished capacity for pleasure, the depressed often have difficulty managing their time, says Peter Lewinsohn, a behavioral psychologist at the University of Oregon and the Oregon Research Institute. "Because they have trouble balancing the positive and negative— say, work and play—they often need to learn how to structure the kind of productive day that will decrease their depression," he says. "They need to learn to work for four hours, *then* fool around with the dog."

In a course of 15 weekly sessions of behavioral therapy ($60 to $90 each), the patient/student and his therapist/ teacher attack depression with carefully planned lessons, demonstrations and homework assignments that increase social skills and maximize life's pleasures. Soon, changes in behavior lead to changes in thoughts and feelings—a process that eventually vanquishes depression in about 70% of patients, according to Dr. Becker. He recalls one depressed subject, a young woman who longed to marry:

"Her method of bringing about her goal was to fantasize about a particular man, then, one day, blurt out that she loved him. When the guy withdrew in shock, she decided that men always rejected her and she'd better give up. During therapy, she learned that relationships happen in stages—something she really hadn't understood before. Her first assignment was to

say hello and introduce herself to a man. The next week, she had to have a chat with him.

"Slowly, she learned that there are gradual stages to intimacy—that she needed to be friends with a man before marrying him. Before long, her social activity increased and she began dating. Her depressed mood disappeared. And the therapy also transferred over into other areas, so her relationships with her parents and co-workers became better as well."

Science is progressing in its search for the causes and cures of DD's unremitting sadness—happily, a state that most people can't even imagine. "A healthy person will say to a dysthymic, 'Pull yourself together! This trouble is all in your mind!'" says Klerman. "Remember that just as the healthy person can't grasp chronic blues, the dysthymic can't understand—or has forgotten—what it is to be spontaneous or joyful."

Now, several effective treatments mean that the good spirits of most victims of DD can be restored. "In the process of rethinking depression, we've begun to treat many more 'normal people,'" says Klerman. "In an earlier era, dysthymics would have said their suffering was God's will and resigned themselves to it. These days, they can say it's caused by catecholamines or stress!"

Opinions may differ about the causes and cures of DD, but on one point, all the experts agree. "People who come in for treatment do well," says Dr. Lewinsohn. "Our problem now is getting the majority of the depressed to take advantage of the help that's available."

Anxiety and Panic: Their Cause and Treatment

UNCOVERING THE BIOLOGICAL ROOTS OF THE TERRIFYING ANXIETY THAT STRIKES MILLIONS WITHOUT WARNING.

Scott M. Fishman and David V. Sheehan

Scott M. Fishman is a research associate with the endocrine unit at Massachusetts General Hospital. David V. Sheehan is professor of psychiatry and director of clinical research, University of South Florida School of Medicine.

Susan, a 25-year-old legal secretary, was about to leave her office one night when she was suddenly overwhelmed by anxiety she had never experienced before—an intense panicky sensation that something dreadful and frightening was going to happen to her. She became flushed and found breathing difficult, almost as though she were choking.

She struggled to maintain her composure, but within seconds she felt dizzy and lightheaded. Waves of fear coursed through Susan. The sound of her heart beating fast and strong and the sensation of blood rushing through her body at great pressure made her think that she might be dying. Her legs were rubbery, but she managed to make it outside for some fresh air. Gradually the feeling subsided. Relieved but still shaky, she made her way home.

Susan had suffered a panic attack. For many people around the world—4 million to 10 million in the United States alone—such attacks strike with little warning and for no apparent reason. Most of the victims are women, usually in their childbearing years. What they experience is unlike ordinary anxiety, the nervousness most people experience before giving a speech or being interviewed for a job. As Susan described the terror of her attack, "It could not be worse if I were hanging by my fingertips from the wing of a plane in flight. The feeling of impending doom was just as real and frightening."

In the months that followed, the attacks grew more frequent. Occasionally there would be only a few symptoms. Other times the fierce anxiety would strike with multiple symptoms and terrifying force. Lightheadedness; dizziness; rubbery legs; difficulty breathing; a racing, palpitating heart; choking and tingling sensations; changes in mental perception—any or all might be involved.

As the attacks continued, Susan feared that one might occur while she was driving her car, so she gave up driving. She began to avoid situations and places in which attacks occurred. Gradually the phobias grew so numerous that she could no longer work at her job and was terrified even to spend time with others. Finally, the paralyzing fear confined her to her home.

The array of symptoms that characterize panic disorder can be so confusing and numerous that accurate diagnosis is difficult. In Susan's case, she saw firsthand how the disorder can disguise itself as many other conditions. In several months, Susan saw a cardiologist, a neurologist, an ear, nose and throat specialist, a gastroenterologist and an endocrinologist, none of whom uncovered any physical disorder. Finally, she saw a psychiatrist who specialized in anxiety disorders, and she started on an effective treatment plan. After the attacks were blocked with an anti-panic drug, Susan worked with a psychologist to overcome the debilitating phobias that she had learned in reaction to the attacks.

The fact that certain drugs block or relieve panic attacks suggests that the

T HE FACT THAT CERTAIN DRUGS BLOCK OR RELIEVE PANIC SUGGESTS THAT THE DISORDER HAS A BIOCHEMICAL BASIS. BUT AT THE MOMENT WE KNOW MORE ABOUT WHAT DRUGS WORK THAN WHY THEY WORK.

disorder has a biochemical basis. But at the moment we know more about what drugs work than why they work.

Before researchers could study panic disorder in an organized way, they needed a technique—what scientists call a research model—to cause panic attacks in the laboratory so that biochemical changes could be studied as they occurred. Without this, researchers and patients would have to wait together for a spontaneous attack, a method that is clearly impractical. A look back into research provided a better answer.

During the 1940s, several researchers had observed that strenuous exercise intensified the symptoms of peo-

ple with chronic anxiety. These patients also had higher levels of lactic acid in their blood when they worked out than did normal individuals who did the same amount of exercise. The anxiety of the former group increased as the levels of lactic acid rose in their blood, while people in the normal group experienced no such anxiety.

Psychiatrist Ferris Pitts of the University of Southern California School of Medicine used these findings as the basis for research in which he injected chronic-anxiety patients with sodium lactate. The injections produced panic similar to their usual attacks, while normal people had no such responses to the lactate. When he gave lactate to

anxiety sufferers in the form of an infusion (a constant flow of sodium lactate), he found he could stop their panic simply by turning off the flow. This discovery gave researchers the tool they needed for monitoring panic attacks and comparing the biochemical reactions of patients with those of others.

Whatever its cause, a panic attack ultimately must involve the brain. To explain this involvement, Daniel Carr, an endocrinologist at Massachusetts General Hospital, has developed a theory that integrates information from a number of studies in which panic attacks were provoked. He notes that inhaling modest amounts of carbon dioxide has the same effect as lactate infusion: It produces attacks in nearly all predisposed patients but rarely in normal men and women. This explains a phenomenon doctors in the armed forces have observed: People with chronic anxiety cannot tolerate wearing gas masks, apparently because the masks make them breathe in some of their own exhaled carbon dioxide.

Carr states that lactate and carbon dioxide act on sensors, called chemoceptors, that work like smoke

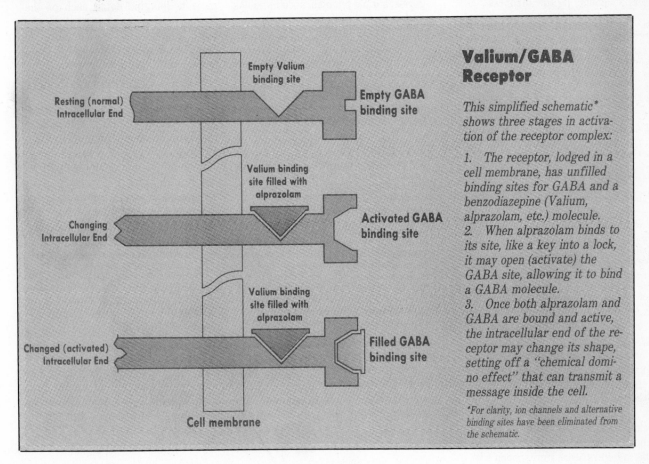

Valium/GABA Receptor

This simplified schematic* shows three stages in activation of the receptor complex:

1. The receptor, lodged in a cell membrane, has unfilled binding sites for GABA and a benzodiazepine (Valium, alprazolam, etc.) molecule.
2. When alprazolam binds to its site, like a key into a lock, it may open (activate) the GABA site, allowing it to bind a GABA molecule.
3. Once both alprazolam and GABA are bound and active, the intracellular end of the receptor may change its shape, setting off a "chemical domino effect" that can transmit a message inside the cell.

*For clarity, ion channels and alternative binding sites have been eliminated from the schematic.

Labels within figure: Empty Valium binding site; Empty GABA binding site; Resting (normal) Intracellular End; Valium binding site filled with alprazolam; Activated GABA binding site; Changing Intracellular End; Valium binding site filled with alprazolam; Filled GABA binding site; Changed (activated) Intracellular End; Cell membrane alarms to monitor the acidity in blood. In normal individuals, the alarm signals that serious changes have occurred, such as a buildup of carbon dioxide, which may indicate that oxygen is not reaching the body's organs. When this happens, panic may be a useful reaction, pushing people to take appropriate action before they suffocate. But in someone who suffers from panic disorder, Carr suspects that faulty or oversensitive chemoceptors create terror when there is no reason for it.

One test of Carr's theory is to see if drugs known to enhance the sensitivity of chemoceptors worsen panic symptoms. Caffeine and progesterone, both of which stimulate chemoceptors, have yet to be tested in panic patients. But since we know that progesterone is secreted during the luteal phase of the menstrual cycle, this may be one reason that more women than men have panic attacks and why some women suffer most from anxiety prior to menstruation. The same factors may help explain premenstrual syndrome, a condition characterized by many of the symptoms exhibited during panic attacks: anxiety, irritability, nausea, headache, lightheadedness.

*I*N SOMEONE WHO SUFFERS FROM PANIC DISORDER, FAULTY OR OVERSENSITIVE CHEMOCEPTORS MAY CREATE TERROR WHEN THERE IS NO REASON FOR IT.

Neuroscientist Eugene Redmond of Yale University studied the relationship between brain activity and anxiety attacks by implanting electrodes in the brains of stumptailed monkeys. When he electrically stimulated the locus ceruleus, a region that has a diminished blood-brain barrier, the monkeys behaved as if they were panicked, anxious or fearful. When Redmond damaged the area surgically, the monkeys were unresponsive to

PHOBIA THERAPY: LEARNING HOW TO

Everyone experiences anxiety at times—a troubled uneasiness of mind mixed with uncertainty and doubt. But when the feeling is persistent, with an intensity out of proportion to the object or situation that caused it, therapists call the condition phobia.

Phobias can develop in several ways. They can result from anxiety attacks, as people associate their feelings of panic with the places and situations in which they occur. They can grow out of specific experiences—a dog bite received in childhood, for example. Or they can be learned from others, such as by observing parents who fear lightning or bugs. In some cases the fear is displaced from its original source to a different place or situation.

The *Diagnostic and Statistical Manual of Mental Disorders* of the American Psychiatric Association divides phobias into three broad categories: simple phobias, social phobias and agoraphobia. Simple, monosymptomatic phobias are most commonly triggered by specific objects, animals or situations—irrational, consuming fear of heights, cats or enclosed spaces, for example. Social phobias are brought on by the presence of other people. They may prevent sufferers from speaking before an audience, eating in restaurants or writing their names when someone else is around.

Agoraphobia (fear of open spaces) is more complex and harder to treat. Psychologist Alan Goldstein of Temple University, who runs a phobia program in Bala Cynwyd, Pennsylvania, calls it "a fear of fear." Agoraphobia can completely incapacitate otherwise normal individuals, eventually making them afraid even to leave their houses.

Phobias are treated today with psychotherapy, behavioral therapy, cognitive therapy, drug therapy or a combination of these. In psychotherapy, the objective is to help patients understand the roots of their disorder. Today, most psychologists believe that psychotherapy is not very effective by itself in helping the phobic patient. Simple phobias and social phobias are most commonly treated today with behavior therapy—getting patients to learn new, more appropriate responses to whatever it is they fear. "The key to behavioral treatment is exposure to the stimulus," says Stephen Garber, a psychologist from Atlanta who specializes in treating phobia and anxiety. There are at least three behavioral techniques to accomplish this.

Systematic desensitization, developed in the 1950s, is still widely used. The therapist discusses the phobia with the patient and constructs a hierarchy of fears. For someone who fears driving, for example, the hierarchy might consist of opening the car door, sitting inside, placing the key in the ignition, turning the key and, finally, stepping on the accelerator pedal. As the therapy proceeds, patients imagine doing each of the feared actions and progress to the point where they can actually do them. The therapist teaches them how to relax during each step, using meditation, deep breathing or other techniques.

In "implosive" or "flooding" therapy, the therapist guides the patient through the entire feared situation all at once, either by imagining it ("implosive") or actually experiencing it ("flooding"). The idea is to have patients experience the fear for as long as possible, so that they emerge tired and mentally fatigued but no longer fearful.

A third behavioral approach, modeling, was spearheaded by psychologist Albert Bandura of Stanford University. He suggests that one possible cause of phobias is inappropriate responses that are learned in early life from parents, relatives and friends. A child who sees his mother recoil from a harmless snake, for example, may develop a persistent fear of all snakes in later life. Bandura adds that the media can often heighten various fears—of sharks, for in-

DEAL WITH FEAR AND THE FEAR OF FEAR

JOHN GOODMAN

*A*GORAPHOBIA
CAN COMPLETELY
INCAPACITATE OTHERWISE
NORMAL INDIVIDUALS,
EVENTUALLY MAKING THEM
AFRAID EVEN TO LEAVE
THEIR HOUSES.

stance. Modeling consists of watching someone else (usually the therapist) go through the feared situation and react appropriately. An ophidiophobe (one who fears snakes) might watch the therapist calmly handle a harmless snake.

Cognitive therapy, typified by Albert Ellis's Rational-Emotive Therapy, focuses on altering patients' self-perceptions, teaching them to deal with situations rather than avoid them. Patients learn to monitor their fearful thoughts during an attack and substitute more rational responses to the situation.

Whatever approach therapists use,

they must help their patients deal with immediate anxiety each time the feared situation arises. Until recently, minor tranquilizers such as Valium and Librium were often prescribed to make patients comfortable enough to continue therapy. Now, Goldstein says, "Most psychologists stay away from drug therapy for monosymptomatic phobias, because while there is some evidence that tranquilizers ease anxiety, they may block the recovery process as a whole." It is important for phobia sufferers to experience and control the fear, not to avoid it. Instead of prescribing drugs, psychologists teach their patients relaxation, deep breathing and, less often, self-hypnosis and biofeedback techniques to deal with anxiety.

Panic attacks create especially difficult problems. People who suffer such attacks suddenly become frightened, experience heart palpitations, chest pains, trembling, nausea, feelings of suffocation and a variety of other unpleasant sensations—all with no apparent cause. The fear remains even after the attack itself is over, and the victims start to feel panicky everywhere. When the fear becomes so pervasive that they feel safe only at home, the victims are suffering from agoraphobia.

"A person who had her first panic attack in a French restaurant might initially avoid the restaurant," Garber says, but the trail of illogic can spread like wildfire. "A series of attacks can lead to a more generalized fear. In a period of months, she might avoid all French restaurants, then avoid eating out at all, then avoid driving near a restaurant and finally avoid driving altogether."

Many of the same approaches used for treating the simpler phobias have been used for agoraphobia, with less success. The TERRAP program, developed by psychiatrist Arthur Hardy in Menlo Park, California, has treated thousands of agoraphobic patients since 1975 with a combination of behavioral, cognitive and experi-

ential techniques. At Temple University, Goldstein runs several treatment programs with a four-point attack. "We teach agoraphobic patients to relax, to use breath control and to stop their panicking thoughts and focus on the 'here and now' to help them deal with panic attacks," he says. "To deal with the avoidant behavior, we use behavioral therapy and exposure techniques to build coping skills. We help them to identify their feelings and get in touch with them. We determine whether there are unresolved grief issues and help them come to grips with them if there are." Finally, Goldstein examines the family environment for clues as to what at home might be reinforcing the disorder.

Some therapists argue that drug therapy is no more useful for agoraphobics than for those with simple phobias. But there are others who see drugs as useful for treating the panic aspect of the disorder. "We are coming to realize that some people respond well to the drugs while others do not," says psychiatrist Robert DuPont, founding president of the Phobia Society of America. "Still others respond to behavioral or cognitive treatment but don't respond to the drugs, and some respond to both."

DuPont calls phobias "the most treatable of psychiatric disorders." Some 70 or 80 percent of all patients with simple or social phobias can be cured. And with recent advances in understanding the biological bases of panic attacks, even agoraphobia and panic disorder soon may be reliably treated.

To receive a free fact sheet on phobia treatments and advice on how to find effective treatment in your area, send a stamped, self-addressed envelope to: The Phobia Society of America, Department PT, 5820 Hubbard Drive, Rockville, Maryland 20852. For $2.50, the center will send a list of more than 250 treatment centers around the country.

—Jeff Meer

threats and didn't show normal fear when approached by humans or dominant monkeys. Since the locus ceruleus is rich in cells that contain the neurotransmitter norepinephrine, Redmond concluded that panic, anxiety and fear may be controlled by changes in norepinephrine metabolism in this brain region. Finding an isolated area such as this—one vulnerable to the influence of substances in the blood due to its lack of a protective blood-brain barrier—gives us valuable information about the physiological roots of panic attacks.

Three distinct classes of drugs are known to relieve panic attacks: the monoamine oxidase (MAO) inhibitors and the tricyclics (both antidepressants) and a newly available drug, alprazolam (a benzodiazepine). Researchers also know that patients who suffer from panic attacks experience less fear if they receive these drugs before they receive lactate infusions. It seems that the drugs change the patients' metabolism, eliminating their abnormal sensitivity to lactate.

While the anti-panic drugs relieve anxiety symptoms, they have undesirable side effects, including drowsiness or high blood pressure. To find other useful drugs that don't have these effects, researchers must understand precisely how and in what parts of the body the anti-panic drugs work. Since the MAO inhibitors and the tricyclics act on norepinephrine, it may be that norepinephrine affects anxiety by transmitting a nerve signal through the locus ceruleus. But we don't know how the antidepressant properties of these drugs relate to their anti-panic effects.

Alprazolam has fewer side effects than do the other anti-panic drugs and provides faster relief, but researchers are even less certain how it works, except that it seems to operate differently from the antidepressants. We know that alprazolam binds to the same receptor molecules in the brain that bind Valium, a benzodiazepine drug that has a chemical structure in common with alprazolam. (A drug or neurotransmitter "binds" to chemical receptors that are shaped to receive and use it rather than other chemicals.)

We know that when taken in therapeutic doses, both Valium, which is ineffective in treating panic attacks, and alprazolam change the shape of the re-

THE ANXIOUS BRAIN

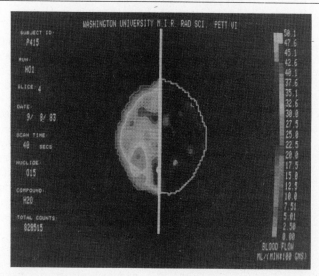

PET scan shows blood flow in the parahippocampal gyrus of a person susceptible to panic attacks. The lighter area at right indicates higher blood flow in that hemisphere.

A research team at the Washington University School of Medicine in St. Louis has discovered an interesting difference in blood flow in the brains of people who suffer panic attacks and of those who don't. They examined seven individuals who had such attacks in response to injections of lactate, three who were not lactate sensitive and six with no history of the disorder. Using positron emission tomography (PET scans), the researchers measured blood flow in seven areas of the brain that are thought to control panic and anxiety reactions. In one of these areas, the parahippocampal gyrus, the researchers observed a startling difference between the lactate-sensitive patients and the others.

In every lactate-sensitive patient, the blood flow on the right side of the gyrus was much higher than on the left side (see illustration). This difference was not seen in the other two groups. "There is usually a great degree of symmetry in the brain," explains neurologist Marcus Raichle, a member of the research team, "but this difference went well beyond the normal range of that symmetry. In every instance the pattern of blood flow was different than normal, and the flow on the right side was higher than the left."

Neither the high flow on the right side nor the low flow on the left was outside the normal range for those regions. It was the large difference between the two that was significant. To confirm their finding, the researchers gave PET scans to 20 additional volunteers, and they found this distinctive pattern in only one, a 34-year-old woman. Her psychiatric history showed symptoms of panic attacks, and when the researchers gave her a lactate injection, she had an attack. None of the other 19 volunteers reported any history of psychiatric illness.

It appears that this brain abnormality consistently distinguishes lactate-sensitive panic sufferers from other people. The researchers say it may reflect an exaggeration of the normal hemispheric specialization in part of the brain important to the expression of anxiety. "The difference in blood flow between hemispheres probably is connected with difference in metabolic rate," Raichle explains. "Any changes in blood flow reflect differences in the activity of nerve cells on the two sides."

—*Joshua Fischman*

THE DISCOVERY OF RECEPTORS IN THE BRAIN FOR VALIUM, A MANMADE SUBSTANCE, HAS STIMULATED A SEARCH FOR A NATURALLY OCCURRING HORMONE THAT REGULATES ANXIETY THROUGH THE SAME RECEPTORS.

ceptor molecule they share. Further changes may then occur at the receptor molecule for a neurotransmitter known as gamma-amino butyric acid (GABA). The GABA receptor is closely associated with the Valium receptor, as shown in the diagram on a previous page. Perhaps the chemical interaction between alprazolam and the Valium receptor changes the metabolism of GABA, which in turn produces a series of changes in the biochemistry of the cell and thus lessens anxiety.

The fact that there are receptors in the brain for Valium, a manmade substance, has stimulated a search for a naturally occurring hormone that regulates anxiety through the same receptors. The body might not have a receptor for Valium if it did not naturally produce a substance that binds with it.

The body's natural opiates were discovered through this same reasoning. Researchers found receptors for narcotics such as morphine and heroin before they knew that the body produces its own opiate hormones and neurotransmitter inhibitors (beta endorphin and the enkephalins) that bind to the same receptors. It may be that panic disorder is a deficiency disease much like diabetes. Diabetes occurs when the body does not produce enough insulin. Perhaps panic disorder results when a hormone or neurotransmitter that normally regulates anxiety is missing or deficient in some way.

Studies of panic disorder in families and among twins suggest that it has a genetic basis. Individuals who have relatives with panic anxiety are more likely to suffer similar attacks than are those with no family history of such attacks. Furthermore, identical twins, who have exactly the same genetic makeup, are more likely to both suffer from panic attacks than are fraternal twins, who share the same environment but only half the genes.

As in many scientific pursuits, new answers lead to new questions. Although we have much more to learn about panic disorder, its biological basis seems clear. As our understanding increases, we hope to develop accurate diagnostic tests to identify people who are susceptible to panic disorder, give them proper treatment earlier and prevent or lessen the development of the phobias and other problems that result from such attacks.

Psychological Treatments

A major problem long confronting psychology has been the definition of therapeutic interventions—psychotherapy. As new theories and models have emerged from research on a variety of fronts, new applications in therapy have followed. The result has been an increasingly complex, and increasingly confusing, array of helping efforts. In this section you will read several articles in which more than one method is applied. Perhaps what is really needed is not new methods, or even comparisons among methods. Perhaps a new way of focusing on the therapeutic paradigm will reduce our focus or emphasis on methods, procedures, and underlying theories. In the meantime, the plethora of procedures continues to grow.

Most of the recent developments have involved attempts to ensure that psychotherapy provides the help it promises, and the first two articles in this section deal with that issue. The first article, by Daniel Goleman, focuses on the responsibility of the client during treatment, while the second, by Paul Quinnett, emphasizes both the essential features of successful therapeutic methods and the shared responsibility for making the therapeutic relationship work well.

In recent years, the most common diagnostic label used in outpatient settings is depression, yet the causes and cures of this condition remain undiscovered. In "Beating Depression," Erica Goode points out that depression is a catch-all term for a host of mood disorders. Significant and positive new findings on the efficacy of drugs and other therapies for this debilitating condition are reported.

When we think of psychotherapy, we generally envision adults as clients, or perhaps school-aged children. But as we become more alert to the development of emotional problems, we find the roots extending into very early infancy. It seems only natural, then, to read an article describing infant psychotherapy and the early signs and symptoms that prompt parents to bring their infants to the clinician.

Not all people who suffer from emotional distress receive or benefit from professional intervention. Rapidly growing in popularity and availability, self-help groups are the major (or only) source of support and encouragement many people get as they shed maladaptive habits and develop new strengths and skills. As Neshama Franklin points out, these groups deal with a wide range of problems, but share certain characteristics and strategies.

Throughout this section, we see the direct application of principles derived from psychological research to the understanding and treatment of disordered and inappropriate behavior. This is the ultimate goal of psychology: to improve the human condition. It is a goal well worth seeking, both personally and professionally.

Looking Ahead: Challenge Questions

One of the most serious challenges facing psychologists today is the need to demonstrate that psychotherapy is effective. How can both client and therapist assume or share responsibility for monitoring the progress of therapy?

How can we have more than one theory and more than one effective treatment for depression? Is depression not one disorder? If you were conducting research into the causes of depression, what type of study would you design next?

Is it fair to compare different treatments, when people who really need help are assigned at random to control conditions? Is it reasonable to believe that we will find a single best treatment for depression? According to current research knowledge, what treatment method works best?

How can a parent or other concerned adult know that an infant needs psychotherapy? What types of therapy work with infants? How could we tell if the therapy is working?

Under what conditions should a person seek support from a self-help group? Are such groups likely to produce as much benefit as working with a professional therapist?

When to Challenge The Therapist–and Why

Daniel Goleman

Daniel Goleman writes about psychology for The New York Times.

How patients should evaluate their own treatment–and what they should do about it.

FOR ANYONE UNDERGOING PSY-chotherapy, the question is inevitable. Is it working? When symptoms linger, or problems that seemed gone reappear, or doubts arise about the therapist, it's natural to wonder. Is it time to switch therapists? Or is the treatment, in fact, working to the extent it can? And is the pain that persists essentially what everyone must suffer from time to time?

Until recently, there have been no sure standards by which patients could assess the effectiveness of therapy. But new research has shed light on what actually happens in the course of treatment and has spelled out what progress patients can expect.

Moreover, psychotherapy researchers are now encouraging patients who have doubts about their treatment or their progress to take up those doubts forthrightly with their therapists. According to the orthodox Freudian view, patient complaints indicate a problem not with the therapy, but with the patient, a result of negative transference, in which childhood conflicts with parents are projected onto the therapist. But most experts now agree that such doubts can signify real problems with the therapy and need to be carefully examined.

Research by Lester Luborsky, a clinical psychologist at the University of Pennsylvania and author of "Who Will Benefit from Psychotherapy?" published this fall, provides more reason to treat the matter with some urgency. He has found that up to a tenth of all patients may actually be harmed by therapy — their problems get worse or they end up frustrated or unhappy with the course of treatment.

IN THE PAST, THE LACK OF OBJECTIVE guidelines made it difficult for patients to know what should happen at what point in therapy. While there can be no universal timetable, recent studies have shown that the most noticeable improvements tend to occur toward the beginning of treatment. As therapy continues, it takes longer for changes to occur, because the problems being dealt with are more deep-seated. The most profound changes, which affect longstanding personality characteristics, are the slowest.

These conclusions are based on studies involving 2,431 patients done by a research team led by Kenneth I. Howard, head of clinical psychology at Northwestern University. Howard found that for people in once-a-week therapy (the frequency of visits for 90 percent of patients), there is a striking pattern of improvement: a negatively accelerating curve.

Using statistical methods to describe the overall improvement of patients (rather than improvements in any one symptom), the researchers developed a way to predict their recovery: 10 percent of patients improve before the 1st session; 20 percent have improved after the 1st session; 30 percent after the 2d session; 40 percent after the 4th session; 50 percent after the 8th session; 60 percent after the 13th session; 70 percent after the 26th session; 80 percent after the 52d session, and 90 percent after the 104th session.

That final 90 percent figure is considered a "ceiling effect" beyond which little additional improvement can be expected. The reason: psychotherapy does not help everyone, and those who are going to improve will almost certainly have shown at least some progress within two years.

The study found that 10 percent of patients show improvement after making an appointment, even before seeing a therapist. This may simply be relief at having done something concrete about getting help. Or it may reflect a spontaneous remission, the clearing up of problems without outside help.

Another recent study, by Howard and Marc A. Zola, a psychologist at the Institute of Living in Hartford, examined which of 90 common patient complaints clear up, on average, at what point in treatment. Their findings, reported at a meeting of the Society for Psychotherapy Research, are based on checklists filled out by 351 patients, in which they noted their symptoms before starting treatment and at various stages in therapy.

The first eight sessions of therapy mark a "remoralization phase," in which acute symptoms of distress tend to dissipate rapidly and the patient regains at least a guarded sense of optimism. Many symptoms clear up in these first sessions, changing little more, if at all, throughout the rest of treatment. These problems include difficulty controlling impulses, such as the urge to smash things or getting into frequent arguments; trouble thinking straight, concentrat-

ing or making decisions, or feeling "blocked" in finishing things; being demoralized, feeling inferior or being lonely, even when with friends.

During this phase, the therapist "helps the patient settle down and establish a working relationship," says Howard. "The patient should get the message that he's not alone with his troubles, that there is some hope, that he's found someone to help."

In the next phase, which lasts roughly from the second month of treatment to the sixth, there is a "remobilization" of the patient's ability to handle life. At this point many symptoms of anxiety and depression tend to abate, such as lack of energy, hope or interest in life and feelings of fearfulness or nervousness.

The last phase, from six months onward, is largely "preventive," according to Howard. In this stage therapy focuses on habitual personality patterns that cause self-defeating reactions to life, such as feelings of worthlessness, mistrust and self-blame. Therapy during this phase is intended to help the patient find ways to prevent a recurrence of his or her symptoms.

"This is the phase in therapy where patients are trying to understand themselves better, not just looking for the relief of some troubling problems," says Howard. "The focus shifts to the recurrent patterns in a person's life — the failed relationships, for example."

ALTHOUGH THESE FINDings are not meant as a standard for measuring progress in any specific case, they may reassure some people who are impatient with the pace of therapy, and may raise doubts in others. Doubts — about the therapist or the therapy itself — can arise at any time in the course of treatment. Even though such feelings are common, patients are often reluctant to discuss them for fear of sabotaging the experience, especially in short-term therapy, which can be fewer than 12 sessions. "There's a wish to keep things happy, because if it got too negative, therapy might end before the negativity is resolved," Lester Luborsky says of shorter therapy.

"Patient misgivings represent one of the most thorny problems for patient and therapist alike," says Dr. Robert S. Wallerstein, a psychiatrist at the University of California, San Francisco School of Medicine and president of the International Psychoanalytical Association. "Sometimes it means that these two people just don't work well together," he says.

If doubts occur at the first meeting of patient and therapist, experts say that it's wise to shop

The key to productive therapy is the formation of a good working alliance. Candor and respect between patient and therapist increases the likelihood that treatment will be successful.

around, and advise consulting two or three therapists before settling on one. Howard has found that a patient's first impression of a therapist is usually accurate. If at the first session the patient feels that the therapist is apprehensive, unsure of himself or inattentive, it is a good indication that the treatment won't be productive. "If the therapist strikes you from the start as not connected to you, it's a warning you'll have to spend lots of time and energy forming a good working relationship, as opposed to finding a therapist where you click," Howard says.

That is not to say that for therapy to work patient and therapist must immediately feel perfectly attuned to each other. Sometimes when a first session seems "virtually perfect," Kenneth Howard notes, the following sessions are a letdown by comparison.

In a study by Howard in which patients evaluated their therapy after each session, in those cases where a therapist struck a patient as "off" from the beginning and where that perception stuck, the results of the treatment were generally poor. When patient and therapist became more attuned to each other as time went on, the outcome tended to be positive, even if the patient's first impression was not favorable.

The key to productive therapy, according to Lester Luborsky, is the formation of a good working alliance. If the patient feels understood by the therapist, has confidence that the therapist can help and feels that they have similar ideas about how treatment should proceed, the relationship has a good chance of yielding positive results.

Even in successful therapy, however, patients sometimes have misgivings. In such cases, Dr.

Wallerstein says, "the feelings may be a symptom of precisely what the patient is in therapy to resolve." These feelings frequently emerge after six months or so, once the problem that brought the patient to treatment has receded. In the foreground at this time are issues between patient and therapist that represent patterns of conflict that sometimes go back to the patient's childhood.

"The issues are the same ones that have to be negotiated in any intimate relationship: hostility, trust, dependency and sexuality," says Howard. "When they emerge, they are expressed as a conflict with the therapist. Whether therapy ends at this point depends on the willingness of client and therapist to confront what's going on. Some patients suddenly see their therapist as a malevolent force trying to keep them dependent, or as being angry or disappointed with them."

Candor between patient and therapist increases the likelihood that treatment will be successful. It's crucial that the patient discuss negative feelings with the therapist, and work toward a resolution. If that doesn't happen, the therapy can founder. Dr. Wallerstein says that "many abrupt endings the therapist can't account for are due to the patient having deep misgivings he could not bring himself to mention."

What happens after doubts are raised is a telling sign of whether the working relationship is a sound one. While some therapists welcome a patient's expression of doubts, others feel threatened, which is likely to inhibit future communication. "If a therapist gets defensive about a patient's misgivings, that puts a sharp limit on the treatment," says Dr. Wallerstein. "You want to be free to say whatever is on your mind to your therapist."

If things don't improve once doubts are aired, it's probably better for the patient to find another therapist. Researchers at Payne Whitney Clinic in New York found that dissatisfied patients made more progress when they switched therapists rather than staying with one with whom they felt unhappy. "Too many patients feel that if they don't do well, they're failures as patients, rather than

seeing that the particular match just did not work out," says Luborsky. Few patients realize that they are free to consult with another therapist if they have serious doubts about their treatment.

Most consulting therapists insist that the patient first discuss his doubts with the current therapist. Then the consulting therapist will meet separately with the patient and the therapist, and recommend either that therapy continue or that it be stopped.

When to terminate therapy can be a point of disagreement between patient and therapist. Early in treatment most patients feel better before they seem better to their therapists, according to Howard's research. He found that, in general, patients rated themselves as more improved than their therapists did. It was not until after six months of treatment that patients' and therapists' ratings of progress dove-tailed more often than not.

How, then, can a patient know when therapy is completed? Luborsky advises that if the patient feels that the problems that brought him to treatment are under control, and if he believes that the gains can be maintained without the therapist, then it's time to discuss terminating the treatment. The patient should review his original goals with the therapist and decide if they have been met.

Often, however, the prospect of ending therapy raises insecurities about being on one's own. Therapists say that it is quite common for symptoms to recur as a patient faces the end of treatment. If they do, the patient and therapist should discuss why the problems have reappeared, and usually they will wane.

Therapy is as much an art as a science. Unlike surgery, where success is clearly defined, the results of psychotherapy are highly subjective. Although studies have yielded general guidelines with which to gauge the progress of treatment, therapy is still an individual experience with periods of both rapid and barely discernible change, and with times of confidence in the process and of doubts.

"Patients need to be reminded over and over that when therapy is working, there will be times they don't feel it is helping them at all," says Luborsky. "It is those times that can be very fruitful, if you talk them over with your therapist. What may seem like the low point in therapy may actually turn out to be the most productive."

The Key to Successful Therapy

PAUL G. QUINNETT

Paul G. Quinnett, Ph.D., is director of adult services at the Spokane Community Mental Health Center and has a private practice. He is the author of two books, The Troubled People Book *and* Suicide: The Forever Decision, *both published by Continuum.*

anxiety, depression, headaches, panic attacks, anger, loneliness—these and other signs of distress are what prompt most people to seek out therapy. And while they're usually unsure about what's causing the problem, they hope the therapist will relieve it directly—or at least help them find relief for themselves.

This pain is the first thing I see when someone comes into my office, and it becomes the first order of business: Relieve the person's distress as quickly as possible. But although symptoms usually bring people to therapy, simply relieving distress won't produce lasting benefits. This requires goal-setting, a task I consider the heart of successful therapy. This usually happens in two stages: early, short-term objectives followed by later, long-term goals.

To get the most out of therapy, it's important to understand how the process operates. Therapists generally start with what we call our working hypothesis—a best-guess answer to the age-old therapy question: Why now? What, we ask ourselves, tipped the scales? What happened that brought this man or woman to this particular office at this particular time?

We try to come up with some sort of answer by the end of the first interview. Doing so helps us make a better diagnosis of what's wrong, which in turn often suggests a specific treatment. Moreover, as we accumulate more and more research, better diagnoses should lead to more effective therapies. The answer to "why now" also makes it more apparent exactly what the client needs and expects from us.

If the answer is simple, the goals we set later can usually be simple. If the client says, "I want you to teach me to be strong enough to ask my boss for a raise," the therapist can say yes he can or no he can't. "I want to lose 30 pounds" or "I'm afraid of heights and I'd like to fly to Chicago to see my mother" are equally clear.

It is the rare client, however, who comes to a first appointment with such specific, measurable goals. Most are much less sure what it is they hope therapy will accomplish, beyond giving them some immediate relief. But unless goals are set as soon as possible, clients may waste time and money looking for help that doesn't exist, and therapists may waste the clients' time working on problems the clients don't consider problems.

Stage One: Setting Early Goals

Here's how to start deciding what you want your therapy to accomplish:

1. As best you can, jot down what you think is causing you distress. This list of events, relationships or stresses can be long or short, but simply writing them down can help you understand better what has been going on, and going wrong.

Bringing this information to your first session will help the therapist understand you better from the start, and the process of preparing it may help you collect your thoughts for the first appointment. Your insight reveals a lot about how you think and how you understand the way life works. Left to their own devices and theories, therapists may come up with all sorts of reasons their clients are suffering. They can be dead wrong and start therapy off on the wrong track, heading in the wrong direction.

2. After the first visit, consider carefully how comfortable you felt. Will you and the therapist be able to work together week after week? Since a good relationship is so important in successful therapy, you should feel a satisfying level of trust and understanding early on.

If you didn't like her, or felt he talked down to you, or found yourself drawing away and losing hope, look for another therapist. Research suggests that patient-therapist compatibility is the best predictor of how well therapy will go. It's important, however, not to give up on therapy itself just because you don't click with the first person you see.

3. As you work with your chosen therapist in setting early goals, try to make them measurable in some way. This isn't always easy, but when the changes you want can be measured, it's a lot easier to tell, down the road, how well the therapy is working.

For example, if you and your mother have a disastrous relationship, one goal might be to carry on a telephone conversation with her without losing your temper. After you've done this three or four times, you'll know you've made progress.

Sleeping through the night without nightmares, raising your grade-point average, gaining or losing weight, giving a speech without your knees knocking together—all are measurable goals that will let you know how the therapy is going. Goals that are broad, vague or built on psychobabble ("I want to get my head together," or "I want to be a fully realized human being") are neither helpful to you or your therapist nor are they easily achievable.

It's best to help set your own goals. But if you like leaving difficult questions to the experts or find this goal-setting business confusing, don't worry about it. A big part of any therapist's job is to help you clarify exactly what it is you want to change and to help you agree on what the two of you will do together to achieve it.

Long-Term Goals:
The Important Next Step

While agreeing on early, measurable goals is vital, I often spend much of my time helping a client clarify longer-term goals for change that are really goals for life: success, rewarding relationships, creative expression, a sense of competence and confidence in handling conflict—the ability, in Freud's words, "to love and work."

Because determining what you'd like to do with the rest of your life involves your personality, beliefs, values, dreams, ambitions and imagination, there is no easy way to go about it. But successful therapy demands precisely this sort of self-exploration: looking into your future after carefully examining your past and, in the process, preparing you to set a fresh course for the life you want.

One recent client—I'll call her Sandra—is a good example of how the process works. She had come through her divorce successfully, moved to a new apartment and was thinking of changing her job. After 20-some sessions, we were sorting out the kind of future she wanted. It was the first time in her life, Sandra told me, that she felt truly responsible for her own future. The experience was both heady and frightening.

"Ted always made the big decisions," she explained. "I guess I just came to rely on him. In a way, I can feel myself wanting you to tell me what to do next."

But Sandra had learned the therapist's Prime Directive: We help people grow; we don't tell them where and how. She had also learned that excessive dependency could be destructive. As we entered the final stages of therapy, Sandra was doing the hard work, setting goals for herself, her future.

"It's scary," she admitted, "this taking charge of my life. But then again, it feels pretty good."

Three Issues to Settle
Before You Choose a Therapist

✱ **Do you agree on methods?** Even after you and your therapist see eye-to-eye on the goals of therapy, you may not agree on just how to achieve them. Therapists use particular methods because they believe in them. But it's your mind and your body. If you believe, based on what you've heard, that hypnosis will work better than biofeedback for your tension headaches, then you'd best start with someone who practices hypnosis.

✱ **Does your therapist believe in partnership?** Most therapists now feel clients have every right to be closely involved in all phases of their therapy, from the setting of goals to agreeing on the type and length of therapy. If the first therapist objects to such a shared approach, consider taking your business elsewhere.

✱ **Are you looking for an evaluation or therapy?** If you want a professional opinion in a dispute over child custody, say, or would like to know whether Uncle Harry is competent to manage his millions, what you are asking for is an evaluation. If your aim is treatment for a personal problem, or for someone else's problem, it's therapy you're after.

An evaluation generally implies that the therapist's findings or opinions will be used later for some purpose other than therapy. Beware of a therapist who is willing to give his professional opinion but isn't really competent in that area.

To avoid such problems, try to talk to a therapist by phone before you set up a formal interview. That way, you both understand just what you are meeting about, what you want done and whether this person is the one to do it.   —P.G.Q.

BEATING DEPRESSION

Treatment of mood disorders is psychiatry's greatest success story. As the biological roots of the illness become better understood, the stigma is subsiding

It is as if the person Dr. Peter Kent used to be is now buried somewhere inside this man who cannot summon the energy to get out of bed, who lies for hours staring blankly, sighing, his thoughts traveling in bleak circles. Kent's colleagues at the hospital have been told by his secretary that the 41-year-old cardiologist is on "personal leave," nothing more. They have not been told about the psychiatric ward that resembles an exclusive college dormitory, about the faint institutional smell, Monet's vision of Giverny on the wall, the living room where patients play pool or sit smoking cigarettes. They do not know that Kent is, for the moment, spending his afternoons in group therapy and watching the "Oprah Winfrey Show."

Kent's secretary is protecting him from what people—his patients, other doctors, the public—might think. It is very hush-hush, his illness. Indeed, this magazine is protecting him, too. We have changed his name in order to write about him, creating a new identity for this altered, sluggish self, the ailing Dr. Kent who finds it painfully difficult to string words into a sentence, who yawns every few minutes and shifts his gaze away, up to the ceiling, over to the daffodils on the table. "It's like being in quicksand," he says. "There's a sense of doom, of sadness."

The need for secrecy is troubling. Kent has not embezzled money, cheated on his income tax or seduced 16-year-old girls. He is not a bad person; on the contrary, his gentleness and quiet concern must be reassuring to patients who are recovering from heart attacks or facing bypass surgery. He is guilty only of having fallen victim to an illness that, because it affects the mind and the personality, is still tinged with shame, as if to suffer from it were somehow an admission of poor character, or weak will.

Though it is more common than diabetes, serious depression—the kind that can lead to suicide or land one in a mental hospital—remains an issue that can unhorse presidential candidates or bind a family in embarrassed silence. There are signs, however, that this view is shifting, that science is at last making headway against fear. Those who have sampled depression's dark offerings are speaking out, describing both the depth and harrowing intensity of their ordeal. Some of their faces are familiar: An actress, a prominent attorney, a talk-show host, a businesswoman. Most recently, author William Styron, writing in *Vanity Fair,* has described his own plunge into despondency, "a veritable howling tempest in the brain," that nearly cost him his life. With each declaration the cur-

tain is drawn back a little further, a kind of mental *glasnost* reminiscent of the thaw that followed Betty Ford's public discussion of her struggle with breast cancer.

There are wider reflections of the changing climate. Large corporations, once oblivious to the impact of psychological factors, are beginning to pay more attention to their employes' state of mind, realizing that mental well-being is essential for high productivity and lower medical costs. They have reason for concern: A recent study by the Rand Corporation found that depression can be as disabling as coronary-artery disease or arthritis, with depressed individuals spending more days in bed than those with chronic lung or gastrointestinal problems. And, perhaps sensing growing interest in the subject, the media, too, have become expansive when it comes to mental illness. Public television this winter launched a new series, "Moods & Music," spotlighting the link between creativity and mood disorders (see next page). Says Dr. Robert Hirschfeld, chief of the Mood, Anxiety, and Personality Disorders Research Branch of the National Institute of Mental Health (NIMH): "People are now recognizing depression as an illness and not a character flaw."

1 In 12 Americans

In part, this new-fledged openness

rests upon an expanding body of research that in the last three decades has given scientists a much greater understanding of mood disorders—illnesses that will afflict more than 20 million Americans at some point in their lifetime. The treatment of depression and manic depression is "psychiatry's No. 1 success story," says Dr. Frederick Goodwin, administrator of the U.S. Alcohol, Drug Abuse and Mental Health Administration and co-author of *Manic Depressive Illness,* to be published by Oxford University Press this spring.

A new generation of drugs allows a sophistication and flexibility in treatment that was not possible in the past. One such antidepressant, Anafranil, also used to treat obsessive-compulsive disorder, won final approval from the Food and Drug Administration last month. Other medications are in the pipeline. For the first time, studies are also beginning to reveal how and where psychoactive drugs exert their action on the brain. Further, scientists have taken the initial steps toward solving the difficult problem of which pharmacological treatments work most reliably for different manifestations of the illness. Experts know more, too, about the types of psychotherapy best suited to defeating the feelings of hopelessness and paralysis that infuse the depressive state.

By far the most powerful lever for changing public attitudes comes from the growing body of work that establishes depression as a disease that is biologically based, at least in its most disabling forms. Both severe depression and manic depression involve dramatic physiological changes, and the evidence points to a hereditary vulnerability that is then triggered by environmental stress. Using high-tech scanners, chemical probes and genetic mapping techniques—the newest tools of a rapidly developing science— researchers are starting to fill in the unknowns of an immensely complicated equation, one capable of leaving the brain, as Lord Byron imagined it in *Childe Harold,* "In its own eddy boiling and o'erwrought, A whirling gulf of phantasy and flame."

Mood disorders take many forms, and researchers historically have been hard pressed to draw iron-clad distinctions among types, or even to differentiate reliably between "normal" dips in mood and the psychic transformation that constitutes depressive illness. Confusing the issue further is the colloquial use of the word *depression* to describe a range of unpleasant, but inevitable, consequences of living. One is "depressed" after a bad day at the office, or the breakup of a love relationship.

Clinical depression is at once more

intense and longer lasting than the brooding funks that seize everyone from time to time. Of patients hospitalized for depression, 40 to 60 percent suffer from the disease in its classical form, once referred to as "melancholia." Submerged in recrimination and self-doubt, these patients lose their appetite, suffer an array of bodily aches, show little interest in sex and awaken in the early-morning hours. They may pace the floor in agitation, or their speech and movement may be drastically slowed, almost as if they had suddenly developed a peculiar and sudden form of brain damage. Yet this facade of lethargy is deceptive. In fact, says Dr. Philip Gold, chief of the NIMH Clinical Neuroendocrinology Branch, severe depression may be a state of hypervigilance and intense arousal: "Such patients are so overwhelmed and overstimulated," says Gold, "that they just kind of sit still."

Winter's discontent

Less common than melancholia is a pattern in which the symptoms are reversed. Patients eat more than usual and sleep for long hours, only reluctantly emerging into wakefulness. In recent years, more and more patients have also been reporting to clinics with still other forms of depression that researchers are only beginning to categorize. In seasonal affective disorder (SAD), despair sets in

MELANCHOLY'S CREATIVE SIDE

"As an experience, madness is terrific I can assure you, and not to be sniffed at," British novelist Virginia Woolf once wrote in a letter to a composer friend. Woolf, author of *To The Lighthouse* and *Orlando,* among other works, careened from feverish periods of writing to weeks immersed in bottomless gloom, according to the memoirs of her husband Leonard Woolf.

Neither the novelist's mood swings nor the conviction that her work was enhanced by them is unusual in creative individuals. Indeed, mood disorders seem to have a predilection for artistic victims, and the list of painters, composers and writers who suffered from depression—or, even more commonly, manic depression—is a long one. "Creativity involves making associations between unrelated ideas," says Kay Jamison, associate professor of psychiatry at Johns Hopkins University School of Medicine and executive producer of the PBS series "Moods & Music." "In a

slightly manic phase, you can link things that before were just isolated ideas."

George Frideric Handel, who scholars believe may have been manic depressive, composed his "Messiah," a work that takes almost 4 hours to perform, in a mere three weeks—presumably riding on the frenetic high of his illness. Gustav Mahler, in a letter to a friend, described with uncanny precision a type of "rapid cycling" manic depression in which moods shift precipitously, sometimes within weeks or even days. "The fires of a supreme zest for living and the most gnawing desire for death alternate in my heart, sometimes in the course of a single hour," Mahler wrote.

Poets Anne Sexton and Robert Lowell, Vincent van Gogh and photographer Diane Arbus all fought the demons of mental disintegration, and all managed to turn the battle to their creative advantage. Far too often, however, artists also pay with their lives, choosing suicide as a balm for their psychic wounds.

The link between creativity and mood

disorders is validated by research. Harvard University researchers Dr. Ruth Richards and Dennis Kinney gave creativity tests to 33 Danish patients diagnosed with manic depression or a milder form of the illness. The same tests were given to their relatives. The scientists found that both patients and relatives scored higher than normal subjects. Similarly, in a study of creative writers enrolled in the prestigious University of Iowa Writers' Workshop, psychiatrist Nancy Andreasen discovered that 80 percent of the writers had suffered at least one episode of depression or mania in their lifetime, compared with 30 percent in a control group of lawyers, hospital administrators and social workers. The writers also showed a significantly higher incidence of alcoholism than the other subjects. It is possible, suggests Andreasen, that the sensitivity, openness, adventuresome nature and independent character of creative individuals in some way makes them more vulnerable to mental illness, in particular mood disorders.

with the disappearance of the lingering daylight hours of summer and persists for as long as short days and the cold winter sun remain. As spring returns, however, patients with SAD feel their energy return. Their desolation lifts, and their lives return to normal. "Dysthymia," on the other hand, is a chronic, if milder, form of depression that can last for months or even years. Researchers estimate that nearly 9 million Americans are locked in dysthymia's dispiriting grip. "It's like a low-grade infection," says Virginia Commonwealth University clinical psychologist James McCullough. "Dysthymics never really feel good."

At the most extreme end of the spectrum, a depressed patient can cross the border into psychosis. "I heard a voice, a male voice; it was the voice of death," says a 31-year-old entertainer, hospitalized for severe depression after she told friends she was afraid she might hurt herself or someone else. "The voice said, 'Hey, kiddo, you know I'm waiting right on the horizon for you.' It was telling me how my body was going to die, trying to catch me off guard. 'Jump in front of that car,' it told me."

Mania shares this departure from reality. Possessed of limitless energy, thoughts racing, manic-depressive patients in the elated phase of the illness may stay up all night, insist they are in touch with creatures from outer space, become uncharacteristically promiscuous or run up thousands of dollars in credit-card bills. One woman, a West Coast business executive, packed her briefcase, put on her best tailored suit and flew to Washington, D.C. Her mission: To convince the Federal Bureau of Investigation that a dangerous conspiracy threatened national security. The FBI agents were perplexed. Should they heed the woman's conservative attire and articulate manner or their hunch that something about her tale was not quite right?

The demographics of depression have changed dramatically in the last half-century. Cornell University psychiatrist Gerald Klerman and Columbia University epidemiologist Myrna Weissman, reviewing studies tracking fluctuating patterns of illness in 10 countries, have found that in developed nations, including the U.S., rates of depression increased markedly for postwar baby-boomers—those born in the period between 1945 and 1955—with the incidence peaking between 1975 and 1980. This upward trend seems to have been only temporary, however. Klerman's newest data, still unpublished, suggest that as the baby-boom generation turns 40, "the turmoil is subsiding," the curve sloping downward again. Suicides also declined in the '80s for baby-boomers,

Klerman says, and rates of depression for those born in succeeding decades show a similar downward trend.

A host of theories

What accounts for these shifts? Researchers can only speculate. Fiercer competition in the labor force during the 1960s and '70s, a greater gap between expectations and fulfillment than in previous generations, increased drug use and greater mobility all have been proposed as possible reasons for the increases in the 1970s. Some even suggest that a change in biological factors is at work, but conclusive evidence for any of these theories is not yet in hand. Nor can experts at present convincingly account for changes in the male-to-female ratio among depressed patients. Women with "unipolar" depression—that is, without manic swings—have traditionally outnumbered men 3 to 1. But Weissman has found indications that men are catching up, with women now diagnosed with the illness at rates only twice those of men.

I should have done things differently.

This is one of the thoughts that Peter Kent cannot stop thinking as he eats chicken teriyaki for lunch in the psychiatric ward's dining room, or walks down the long, gray-carpeted hallway. He has a mental image of himself talking on the telephone, listening to his fiancée tell him it is over. He can see himself calling a few weeks later, hearing the metallic whir of her answering machine, her voice saying (impossibly, astoundingly), "You have reached the residence of Mr. and Mrs. . . . ."

There were other things—events that, though he did not know it at the time, were leading him toward this spinning descent. Problems in his medical practice. Arguments with a friend. Indeed, there is the matter of his illness seven years ago, an episode of mania that lasted for several weeks, causing him to believe that a stranger was, in fact, his father in disguise. Yet none of these things is, in itself, an explanation, a solution to the riddle of "Why here, why now?"

Tracing the origins of mood disorders, illnesses that affect not only behavior and physiology but our very sense of ourselves, is a formidable task. For mind and body are inextricably joined, and everything we imagine, dream, experience or fear is ultimately translated into the firing of nerve cells and the ebb and flow of chemicals in the brain. How do we sort out the events that began internally, in a strip of DNA or a malfunctioning neuron, from those that have their roots in external events: A broken love affair, the death of a friend, the loss of a job? It is with this conundrum that scientists who would

understand mental illness struggle. The answers that emerge are always somewhat murky, always two-sided, always a compromise of nature and nurture—which, after all, work hand in hand.

Yet there are some certainties. Researchers now know, for example, that certain forms of mood disorder—specifically manic depression and severe, recurrent, unipolar depression—run in families. This fact is demonstrated by dozens of research projects, including a 1986 study that examined the family pedigrees of depressed adults adopted as children and found an increased incidence of mood disorders in biological, as opposed to adoptive, relatives. As Columbia University's Weissman puts it: "Depression is a family affair."

Both depression and mania are also accompanied by changes in brain chemistry, though these changes are not fully understood. In the early days of research, scientists thought in terms of relatively simple models of chemical imbalance: Depression, for example, was thought to stem from an insufficiency of norepinephrine, one of many substances mediating the transmission of nerve impulses in the brain. Now, few experts talk about "too much" or "too little" of a single chemical. Instead, they believe mood disorders are the result of a complex interplay among a variety of chemicals, including neurotransmitters and hormones.

Genetic legacy

How much of this is influenced by heredity? The consensus is that genetic factors are at work, and in the last few years, laboratories all over the world have set out to track down the gene, or multiple genes acting in concert, that predispose an individual to depression or manic depression. This search has proceeded in fits and starts. Discoveries are announced, only to be called into question when other scientists fail to duplicate the findings. Most recently, the highly publicized results of a 1987 study of manic depression in the Amish—results that seemed to locate the gene for the illness on the short arm of chromosome 11—fell through when a research team re-analyzed the Amish pedigree, adding new subjects.

The team, which included some of the original researchers, concluded in an article published in *Nature* last November that while the evidence for a genetic marker in the Amish is still strong, the chances are slim that it is on chromosome 11. Another study, this one of an Israeli family, linked the gene for manic depression to the X chromosome. But so far, attempts to replicate this association have also been unsuccessful. Nonetheless, few researchers doubt that genetic studies will eventually yield results.

Even when they do, however, heredity will not tell the whole story. Depression and manic depression appear to be triggered by stress. And in some milder forms of mood disorder, experience—rather than genetics—may play the starring role. Traumatic events clearly are capable of precipitating changes in mood and behavior. In particular, scientists consistently find that being the child of a depressed parent may double or even triple the risk of depression in later life. Parents who suffer from depressive illnesses, these studies indicate, are more likely to be withdrawn, critical, inconsistent and irritable in child-rearing. Their own pain, expressed in this way, may thus become a burden for their offspring. According to a new report published last month, some children in this difficult atmosphere develop intense, exaggerated feelings of guilt—states of mind that then pave the way for depression and other emotional problems.

Losses in childhood

Perhaps most devastating is the loss of a parent in childhood, either through death or abandonment. The evidence suggests, according to British psychoanalyst John Bowlby, that those who have lost a parent, especially the mother, are more likely to develop serious psychiatric problems and, more specifically, to become psychotically depressed and suicidal. Work by University of London researchers George Brown and Tirril Harris demonstrates that women who lose their mothers before the age of 17 are significantly more prone to depression as adults. The crucial factor, Brown and Harris say, is how the father, or parental surrogate, provides for the child: "Inadequate care . . . roughly doubled the risk of depression in adulthood."

Any true understanding of mood disorders must take into account this intricate interplay between psychology and biology. NIMH psychiatrist Dr. Robert Post and others have done just that in the theory of "kindling," an attempt to explain the fact that episodes of mania

---

RESOURCES AND INFORMATION ON DEPRESSION

Help is readily available for the millions who suffer

The warning signs of depression:

- Persistent sad, anxious or empty mood
- Feeling hopeless or worthless
- Loss of interest or pleasure in activities, including sex
- Sleep disturbances (early-morning waking or oversleeping)
- Decreased appetite, losing weight or eating more than usual
- Recurrent thoughts of death or suicide
- Difficulty concentrating, remembering, making decisions
- Irritability, excessive crying
- Physical symptoms such as headaches, digestive disorders, nausea or chronic pain

The warning signs of mania:

- Increased energy and decreased need for sleep
- Unrealistic or exaggerated beliefs in abilities
- Inappropriate elation
- Increased talking, moving and sexual activity
- Racing thoughts
- Impulsive behavior without regard to consequences

Where to go for help:

- See your family doctor to rule out other illnesses
- Medical-school psychiatry department
- Community mental-health center
- Local mental-health association

The National Alliance for the Mentally Ill (NAMI)

P.O. Box NAMI-Depression
Arlington, Va. 22216

DEPRESSION/Awareness, Recognition, Treatment (D/ART)
National Institute of Mental Health
Rockville, Md. 20857

National Depressive and Manic Depressive Association
53 West Jackson Blvd.
Box USN
Chicago, Ill. 60604

National Mental Health Association
Information Center
1021 Prince Street
Alexandria, Va. 22314

The National Foundation for Depressive Illness
P.O. Box 2257

New York, N.Y. 10116
Include $5 and a self-addressed, stamped envelope for literature

American Psychiatric Association
1400 K Street, N.W.
Suite 501—Dept. USN
Washington, D.C. 20005
Include a self-addressed, stamped envelope for literature

National Association for Research on Schizophrenia and Depression
60 Cutter Mill Road, Suite 200
Great Neck, N.Y. 11021

Books

Depression and Its Treatment: Help for the Nation's #1 Mental Problem, by John H. Greist, M.D., and James W. Jefferson, M.D. (American Psychiatric Press, Washington, D.C., 1984; $7.95).

Overcoming Depression, by Demitri F. Papolos, M.D., and Janice Papolos (Harper & Row, New York, 1987; $9.95).

Control Your Depression, by Peter M. Lewinsohn et al. (Prentice Hall Press, New York, 1986; $9.95).

Feeling Good: The New Mood Therapy, by David D. Burns, M.D. (New American Library, New York, 1980; $4.95).

Do You Have a Depressive Illness? by Donald F. Klein, M.D., and Paul H. Wender, M.D. (New American Library, New York, 1988; $7.95).

Is Your Child Depressed? by Joel Herskowitz, M.D. (Pharos Books, New York, 1988; $14.95).

and depression appear initially in response to some external stress, but later seem to acquire a momentum of their own. Repeated low-level stresses, Post suggests, might build up until they trigger a manic swing in mood, much as experimenters can "kindle" seizures in the brain by delivering low-level electrical shocks to cells deep in its interior. Or conversely, the brain may become progressively "sensitized" to the effect of environmental stress. Eventually, bouts of illness may occur with no help from outside events.

Such analogies are approximations, hypothetical road maps for an as yet uncharted territory. Yet those who suffer in depression's depths or negotiate mania's precarious heights may count themselves fortunate. Emerging from their illness is not dependent upon perfect scientific knowledge, and tools for treatment are already in hand.

What will happen when he goes home?

Peter Kent's psychiatrist at the hospital asks him this. The nurses who monitor his mood, who cajole and counsel him, who keep track of how much he eats and whether he wakes up at night, ask him this as well. His chances of full recovery are good, but not assured. Perhaps 30 percent of severely depressed patients "get better on antidepressants but do not get completely well," says Dr. Jan Fawcett, chairman of psychiatry at Rush Presbyterian–St. Luke's Medical Center in Chicago.

Leaving the hospital, Kent will rest for a while, filling his time with volunteer work before returning to his medical practice. In part, how the cardiologist fares will be determined by other people. His colleagues. His friends. Can they accept a doctor who has become a patient? He has his doubts: "They would look at it negatively," he says. "It's best if they don't find out." Yet it is possible, though far from certain, that Kent is mistaken and that he will find good will where he expects ostracism or disdain. It is possible that the time for secrecy is nearly over, that what Styron has called "Darkness Visible" is, at last, an illness like any other.

---

by Erica E. Goode
with Nancy Linnon and Sarah Burke

Infants in Need of Psychotherapy?
A Fledgling Field Is Growing Fast

DANIEL GOLEMAN

'Therapy for minor problems in infancy can prevent major problems later in life.'

Baby blocks are the latest accessories in some psychiatrists' offices, as a new idea is gaining popularity: psychotherapy for infants.

The fledgling field, virtually nonexistent a dozen years ago, is growing rapidly. No one knows how many children have been treated or need treatment because the Government does not keep statistics on it, but as many as 10,000 professionals are now offering such therapy. In addition to psychiatrists and psychologists, the practitioners include pediatricians, social workers and nurses.

For parents, this means that there is somewhere to turn for expert advice on the emotional ups and downs of babies, and to lay to rest fears, often ungrounded, that something is awry. And, if a baby is found to have an emotional problem, a psychotherapist stands ready to help.

'Window of Opportunity'

The field's fundamental assumption is, in essence, that an ounce of prevention is worth a pound of cure.

"Therapy for minor problems in infancy can prevent major problems later in life," said Dr. Robert Emde, a psychiatrist at the University of Colorado Medical School. "This is a prime window of opportunity." Dr. Emde is also president of the World Association for Infant Psychiatry, the main professional group in the field.

In extreme cases, when the parent is inadequate or absent, therapy involves a team of caretakers who substitute for the parents. For children who are less disturbed, therapy focuses on evaluating what is wrong in the relationship between the parent and child and then coaching the parent to better respond to the child's needs.

In part, the rise of infant psychiatry is traced to recent research into emotional development in infants. While the benchmarks of biological growth have long been known, those of emotional growth have only recently been charted, allowing clear guidelines for spotting troubled infants for the first time.

"We now know much more than ever before about the emotional, social and behavioral development of normal infants," said Dr. Justin D. Call, chief of Child and Adolescent Psychiatry at the University of California at Irvine, a founder of the field. "It makes the recognition of problems clearer much earlier in life than had been possible."

Putting Infancy on the Map

"It put infancy on the psychiatric map," he said. "We saw that we should be intervening before the age of 3." Infancy is reckoned to end at that age.

Dr. Eleanor Szanton, director of the National Center for Clinical Infant Programs in Washington, said 20 times more infants were being seen for emotional difficulties and related problems than were seen 10 years ago because professionals now knew what to look for. Most parents, though, do not yet know to ask for help, she said.

A separate trend has also contributed to the interest in infant psychotherapy. In the last two decades, Dr. Call noted, there has been a steady increase in the number of infants born to mothers who take drugs or mothers in their early teens. Rates of infant abuse and neglect have also gone up. All these factors are tied to the likelihood of serious emotional problems in infants.

For some parents, the mere list of troubles the field treats is likely to stir concern. Much of it is unwarranted, therapists say, noting that parents have muddled through for ages without the help of infant psychiatry.

Still, various studies are showing there is a genuine need for infant psychiatry. Surveys of infants brought to pediatricians' offices in various cities have found that from 10 percent to 15 percent have a severe emotional problem, such as depression or an inability to respond to people, Dr. Call said.

Ten to 15 percent more have mild problems, like being withdrawn, that would benefit from short-term treatment, said Dr. Call.

Dr. Szanton said, "Perhaps the saddest problem of all in infants is failure to thrive, where a baby gains no weight, becomes indifferent to the world, and withers."

For practioners of infant psychotherapy, there are only a few formal training programs in departments of psychiatry or pediatrics. Some social work and nursing programs also offer courses.

The majority of those now working in the field have attended short-term training programs. The first of these postgraduate training institutes was held in 1978 with 400 participants; the most recent was held two years ago and attendance jumped to 1,200.

For a child needing psychotherapy, insurance policies that pay for psychiatric care will usually cover the costs of treating an infant. But therapists say the policies often require formal diagnosis of a specific psychological problem, which can alarm parents when expressed clinically.

The most serious psychological dis-

Benchmarks of emotional growth have only recently been charted.

Infant Behavior: When to Be Concerned

Many things that distress parents of babies are not signs of serious problems, but certain behaviors and traits may indicate an underlying problem and should be brought to the attention of a pediatrician.

Usually Not Problems	Possibly Signs of Psychological Disturbance

BIRTH TO ONE MONTH

Usually Not Problems	Possibly Signs of Psychological Disturbance
Preference for eating every two hours. Prickly heat rash. "Not satisfied" with feeding. Wanting to be held "all the time." Grunting and red face with bowel movements. Sucking finger or thumb.	Failure to gain weight. Excessive spitting up. Absence of eye contact. Failure to hold head up. Failure to show anticipatory behavior at feeding. Failure to hold on with hands. Ticlike movements of face and head.

2 TO 3 MONTHS

Usually Not Problems	Possibly Signs of Psychological Disturbance
Irritable crying. Colic. Constipation. Not sleeping through the night.	Failure to thrive. Indifference to human face, voice and play overtures. Persistent hyperactivity. Persistent sleep disturbance. Vomiting and diarrhea without physical illness. Hyperresponsiveness or hyporesponsiveness.

4 TO 6 MONTHS

Usually Not Problems	Possibly Signs of Psychological Disturbance
Demands for attention. Preference for being propped up. "Spoiled." Teething or biting problems.	Wheezing without infection. Failure to enjoy upright position. Indifference toward feeding. Excessive rocking, except at night or when alone. Rumination (swallowing regurgitated food).

7 TO 9 MONTHS

Usually Not Problems	Possibly Signs of Psychological Disturbance
Dropping things. Messy feeding. Disrupted sleep associated with teething, move to new home or illness. "Temper."	Unpatterned sleeping and eating. Eating problems like refusing to use hands or to hold glass or a very limited diet. Failure to imitate simple sounds and gestures. Lack of distress with strangers. Failure to show and respond to recognizable signals, like joy, surprise or fear. Self-destructive behavior. Withholding of bowel movements. Apathy.

10 TO 16 MONTHS

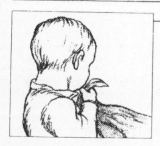

Usually Not Problems	Possibly Signs of Psychological Disturbance
Getting into things; climbing. Declining appetite. Problems with self-feeding and being fed. Screaming. Mild tantrums. Attachment to "security blanket."	Absence of words. Withdrawn behavior. Excessive rocking and posturing. Absence of distress at separation. Night wandering. Excessive distractibility.

Source: adapted from J. D. Call in "Practice of Pediatrics." Harper & Row

The New York Times/March 23, 1989; illustrations by Giora Carmi

turbances in infants are usually attributed to parental abuse or neglect of a baby's basic needs, like warmth or regular meals. Doctors say neglect, including of an infant's emotional needs, can slow intellectual growth.

Variety of Symptoms

Doctors who treat infants with severe problems say they display a variety of symptoms, including continuous inconsolable crying and frantic shaking, a tendency to shrink from touch, extreme sadness, lethargy, and indiscriminate rage.

Much of the work in infant psychiatry is with milder problems. Among the more common varieties are "attachment disorders," in which infants have difficulty forming a trusting bond with parents. The child, for instance, may shrink from parents or not respond. While the attachment problems can sometimes be severe, they are often mild, reflecting minor idiosyncrasies in how parents treat an infant.

One such baby was treated by Dr. Stanley Greenspan, a professor of child health and development at George Washington University medical center.

"He was just 9 months," Dr. Greenspan said. "He was highly irritable and would cry for an hour at the slightest irritant. Whenever his mother would leave the room, he'd throw a tantrum. But while she was with him, he's just lie there passively."

In evaluating the infant, Dr. Greenspan discovered he was hypersensitive to touch, so that a normally enjoyable cuddle would irritate him. His mother had responded to his extreme irritability by becoming overprotective. If he began to reach for something, she would get it for him before he could complete the motion.

"She was making him passive by hovering and anticipating his every move," Dr. Greenspan said. In a few sessions, Dr. Greenspan got her to delay her impulse to intervene. At the same time, he encouraged the parents to handle their baby more gingerly, so as not to irritate his skin.

"A new focus of therapy in infant psychiatry is on treating disturbances in relations between parents and infant," Dr. Call said.

Typical of these problems are lonely parents who become excessively dependent on their infants, and who keep the infant from developing the normal independence of a 2-year-old. Another common pattern is seen when parents discipline an infant with stiff corporal punishment.

"Corporal punishment, especially when the child is too young to understand it, can lead the child to become defiant, even start provoking punishment, and, finally, estranged from his parents," Dr. Call said.

Then there are the problems that worry parents, but are only part of the normal travails of infancy.

"There are a fair number of kids who by temperament are hypersensitive to stimulation, irritable and sleep poorly," said Dr. Emde. "It's one of the most common complaints from parents. When we evaluate the child, we let the parents know it's common and doesn't go on forever."

He added: "There are some practical steps parents can take, such as keeping things quiet and calm around the infant. But when parents are far more anxious than they need to be, it just makes matters worse."

Help yourself: self-care for emotional problems

NESHAMA FRANKLIN

I had no choice," Kirsten Nielsen says. "I just had to gut it out." That's how this 42-year-old mother of two sons describes her successful two-year effort to manage her manic-depression without lithium. Nielsen, of Santa Cruz, California, elimi-

> **Support groups are comforting, non-judgmental, and inexpensive.**

What's wrong with therapy?

It is estimated that almost one-third of the population receives professional therapy sometime in their lives. At an average cost of about $65 an hour, psychotherapy is a big business. Although there is no doubt that it is beneficial to many, there is a great deal wrong with it—both the way it is presented to the public and the way it is practiced.

The abuses can be grouped into four categories: misleading promises about its scope and effects; use of one kind of therapy when another is more effective; use of psychotherapy when alternative treatments are superior in results or cost; and too-lengthy terms of treatment.

Promises, promises

Psychotherapy is promoted as useful for all the traditional psychological problems, as well as new problems discovered almost daily: midlife crisis, computer phobia, and conversion to unpopular religious beliefs. Of 500 people who came to one large New York psychiatric clinic for evaluation, therapy was recommended for all but four. Imagine the outcry if surgery were recommended for 99 percent of patients coming to a medical clinic. Whenever a method is universally prescribed, one of two things must be true: The Millennium has arrived or something is seriously wrong.

Another promise of therapy is overwhelming change of personality. Fringe therapies such as primal scream and est are not alone in claiming dramatic change. Psychoanalysis, the oldest and in many people's eyes the most respectable therapy, produces, in the words of Anna Freud, "thoroughgoing personality changes," and some therapists talk about reorganizing or remaking personalities. But as New York psychologist Albert Ellis notes, ther-

apists talk and write about their most spectacular successes; "the poor, partial, or later-relapsing 'successful' cases are much less often published." Only a small percentage of clients are changed to a degree that justifies using terms like "recovery" or "cure."

Which therapy?

The second abuse of therapy is in using a form that is less effective or efficient than another. We now know that certain methods work better for certain problems. Brief sex therapy has demonstrated its superiority for problems like lack of orgasm, premature ejaculation, and erection complaints. Behavioral methods have proven best for phobias, obsessive-compulsive problems, and some social skill deficiencies. Depression can be successfully attacked using specialized short-term therapies. Finally, hypnosis, relaxation training, and cognitive therapy have shown promise in the control of pain.

Since the majority of therapists do not practice behavioral or sex therapy, many problems undoubtedly are being treated with inferior methods. And worse, the patients are not informed of choices.

Alternatives

The third category of abuse is using psychotherapy when alternative treatments are more effective or less costly. Many people who find their way into a therapist's office would benefit from drugs they are not offered. If the therapist is a psychologist, clinical social worker, psychiatric nurse, or marriage counselor, he or she cannot prescribe drugs.

Medication is not the only alternative to psychological therapy. There is considerable evidence that professional therapy is no more beneficial for a number of problems than attending self-help groups (many of which are free or relatively inexpensive), or just talking to nated lithium using a unique self-management regimen she developed in partnership with San Francisco psychiatrist Dr. Jeffry Ordover. Ordover warned her that living without lithium would be "the hardest thing she would ever do." Nielsen learned that he was right. Since its introduction in the early 1970s, lithium carbonate has become much more than simply the "drug of choice" to control the debilitating mood swings of manic-depression. Many psychiatrists consider it a "miracle drug."

Nielsen and Ordover are quiet pioneers on the frontiers of the mental health system. They are breaking new ground beyond traditional psychotherapy and drug treatments. The trail is rocky, but they are not alone. Growing numbers of ex-mental patients and people troubled by serious emotional problems are coping successfully with their conditions using alternative therapies based on support groups and other self-care practices.

Numerous self-help and support groups around North America help participants deal with a whole range of personal problems, often as adjuncts to professional therapy and/or medical treatment. Many focus on mental health problems—phobias, compulsions, coping with traumatic events or chronic problems, or just dealing with emotional stress in general. Some ex-mental patients have formed groups that

an interested but untrained person.

Psychologists at Vanderbilt University assigned young men with garden variety neuroses to one of two groups of therapists. The first consisted of the best professional psychotherapists in the area, with an average 23 years of experience; the second group was made up of college professors with reputations of being good people to talk to but with no training in psychotherapy. Therapists and professors saw their clients for no more than 25 hours. The results: "Patients undergoing psychotherapy with college professors showed . . . quantitatively as much improvement as patients treated by experienced professional psychotherapists."

Research indicates that Alcoholics Anonymous is as useful as professional therapy for treating alcoholics. The cure rate isn't high—addictions being resistant to change—but therapy doesn't work any better. Likewise, when it comes to weight problems and drug abuse, no data support the contention that professional therapy is more effective than groups like Weight Watchers. Why induct drinkers, smokers, overweight people, and drug abusers into lengthy, often expensive, and usually fruitless therapy?

How long has this been going on?

The fourth abuse of psychotherapy is carrying it on interminably. Although a good deal of therapy consists of fewer than 20 sessions, much of the brief work is done in clinics and agencies where time limits are enforced. In private practice, where therapists are free to do as they choose, lengthy therapy is often the rule.

What's wrong with therapy taking two, four, or more years? Only one thing: Although for decades the bias among therapists has been that lengthy therapy is best, there is no evidence that longer is better. The few therapies

At an average cost of $65 an hour, psychotherapy is big business. And as is often the case with big business, consumers must be wary.

that have demonstrated effectiveness—behavioral therapy, cognitive therapy, and sex therapy—are all typically brief. Not one of the longer psychotherapies has demonstrated its superiority to briefer treatment for any problem. In the last two decades a small but vocal group of psychoanalysts have called lengthy therapy unnecessary and have offered evidence that changes can be brought about in fewer than 25 sessions.

—Bernie Zilbergeld
Science 86

Excerpted with permission from Science 86 *(June 1986). Time, Inc. has since acquired Science 86 and merged it with* Discover *magazine. Subscriptions: $24/yr. (12 issues) from Discover, Time-Life Bldg., 541 N. Franklin Court, Chicago, IL 60611.*

Got a problem? See a friend.

For far too long people have been led to believe that the person suffering from an excess of life's problems needs "expert" medical and psychotherapeutic intervention (thus allowing the "patient" to qualify for "illness") to the ultimate detriment of his mental equilibrium and often at considerable financial cost. Such a view is dangerous nonsense. Clearly there are differences between real psychiatric disease such as schizophrenia and manic-depressive illness and those normal but unpleasant mental states that are an inescapable and often valuable part of everyday living.

I believe we need a redefinition of the proper boundaries of psychological illness. We need a tougher, more rigorous and uncompromising attitude toward what does and what does not constitute disease. Therapists have mistakenly categorized millions of people mentally ill when their chief deficiency is an inadequate approach to problems and unrealistic expectations of what life should give them. A huge therapy industry has created itself to minister to, and profit from, the plight of these "neurotics."

For the therapists to take money for mere talk is, I would argue, in many cases both negligent and, despite the purest of motives, irresponsible. They harm the individual in his pursuit of mental health and encourage dependency and sterile introversion. Above all, they delay interminably that brave confronta-tion of life's problems in which alone salvation lies. The widespread popularity of such an approach comes on the fact that talking about ourselves is strongly pleasurable, that we all like to be the center of attention. In pandering to this mildly unworthy desire, these people do us more than a disservice. For, to the extent that such talk-therapy is pleasant, and its withdrawal difficult and traumatic, I would argue that, like Valium and cocaine, it is psychologically addictive. In the short term it may make us feel better—a quick fix of confidence—but over the years we will pay a considerable price in terms of dependency and lowered self-esteem.

Ostensibly opposed to talk-therapists, but in fact sharing their expert/patient approach, are the medico-biologists. Instead of intellectual insights and exotic theories, their stock-in-trade is chemical panaceas that they dish out like candy to individuals who are not ill. In both cases the end result is the same: a passive "patient" prostrate at the feet of the "healer," suffering the psychological pain of guilt as he learns to like himself less.

Talk therapy and Valium offer no solutions in the absence of real illness. They must be replaced by something of value. I offer Moral Therapy, a philosophy based not on fantasies, pseudo-intellectual gymnastics, or chemistry, but on common sense, on what we know in our hearts. Nobody gets paid for prac-

combine mutual support with political advocacy.

At a time when U.S. government agencies have cut back on mental health programs, and when traditional networks such as extended families and neighborhood and religious groups may be unavailable, mutual aid groups can provide crucial support for people who feel stigmatized, ignored, or isolated. They offer welcome relief from the waiting lists and bureaucracies that typify what Ralph Nader's Health Research Group called "the mental health maze." Support

The self-help approach and professional services need not be mutually exclusive nor antagonistic.

groups are comforting, non-judgmental, and inexpensive. Sharing insights and down-to-earth techniques for surmounting serious problems inspire those in the group to "keep on keeping on."

Unfortunately, there has been considerable resistance to—and ignorance about—the self-help/support-group movement from the professional community. Physicians and psychotherapists sometimes have difficulty reconciling them with their own clinical, analytical, illness-oriented model. Some professionals criticize support groups for operating with limited knowledge apart from professional guidance, or for basing their approach on "emotion" rather than "science."

The self-help/support-group approach and professional services need not be mutually exclusive nor antagonistic. In fact, if more mental health workers got involved in support-group work, they might find welcome relief from the burn-out that plagues their profession.

ticing Moral Therapy. Nobody profits from solving the problems of others except in feeling that natural satisfaction we all experience when we have been of service. There are no experts, no training institutes, no degrees or examinations, no gurus. There is nothing but us, our experience of life, our warmth and empathy, the voice of our conscience.

In the absence of psychological illness, we can practice the principles of Moral Therapy on ourselves and on others. Contentedness can exist only if self-respect is high. Only if we like ourselves can we be happy. At all times and in all situations we must obey our own moral codes. Only by doing what we ourselves consider to be right and good can we travel the road to self-respect. Insofar as we disregard our moral imperatives we must suffer the psychological pain of guilt. If we use the guilt mechanism properly and recoil from those actions that cause it to operate, it will serve us well. In the absence of disease, then, guilt is good for us.

With the right help from friends and loved ones, we can all learn to like ourselves more. As concerned and forceful friends, we can become the practitioners of a new Moral Therapy. Into the vacuum created by the disappearance of the paid "expert" will step family, friends, priests, neighbors, husbands, wives, and children. For too long their rightful role has been wrongfully usurped by impostors. The time has come for them to reclaim it.

In particular we should realize and encourage others to realize that self-respect is increased by searching out and achieving more difficult rather than easier objectives. By seeking difficulty and avoiding the easy way in pursuit of what we consider to be worthy ambitions, we will like ourselves more.

—Garth Wood

Excerpted with permission from the book The Myth of Neurosis *(1986, $15.96, $7.95 paperback, Harper & Row, 10 E. 53rd St., New York, NY 10022). ©1983, 1986 by Dr. Garth Wood.*

Many support groups deal with serious mental health problems. Two of the largest are Recovery, Inc., and Emotions Anonymous, which sponsor groups throughout North America. Recovery, Inc., was founded in 1937 by Abraham Low, M.D., a Vienna-trained non-Freudian psychiatrist, to supplement after-care services for ex-mental patients. The organization is now open to anyone. Today Recovery, Inc., sponsors about 1,000 support groups that meet weekly throughout North America and abroad.

The groups are led by members who have attended consistently for at least six months, and who have used the techniques successfully themselves. The organization sees itself as a supplement to—not a replacement for—professional therapy and enjoys broad support among psychiatrists and other therapists. Many participants are referred by a therapist.

The presentations at a typical Recovery meeting follow a strict formula: first a brief description of the traumatic incident, then the symptom(s) it provoked. Recovery calls this "spotting," recognizing problems and the reactions they cause. Next comes "coping," a brief rundown of how the person dealt with the incident using either will power or muscle control. Participants also describe the way they would have reacted before their Recovery training. Finally, they "endorse" themselves, pat themselves on the back for their insights and coping actions. Endorsement is often difficult because most people with emotional problems—for that matter, most people in general—tend to negate their accomplishments.

A young man, who seemed markedly nervous and withdrawn, said he'd been to a party where he felt everyone acted cold toward him. He "spotted" this as "fearful temper." ("Fearful temper" and "angry temper" are two sides of the same coin. The former is self-blame, which leads to depression; the latter is blaming others, which leads to acting out.) He started to shake and in

Most people with emotional problems tend to negate their accomplishments.

pre-Recovery days would have screamed and made a scene, but he was able to control the impulse. The group endorsed him for going to the party in the first place. "It's strengthening to do the things you fear." "It's good that you were 'self-led' and not 'symptom-led'." "It's average to feel uncomfortable when you don't know people." (The concept of "being average" comes up frequently in Recovery groups. It's the recognition that one's symptoms are normal, not pathological.) The phrases in quotes came up frequently. At first they sounded like jargon, but I gradually came to appreciate their value as code words that helped the members recognize their hard-won victories over fears and former habits.

Founded in 1971, Emotions Anonymous (EA) is patterned after the original self-help group, Alcoholics Anonymous (AA). EA adapted the AA program of confession, mutual aid, and 24-hour-a-day telephone support among members.

All the "Anonymous" organizations share a simple, homespun, non-religious spirituality. Weekly meetings open with a prayer: "God grant me the serenity to accept the things I cannot change, the courage to change the things I can, and the wisdom to know the difference." Speakers at EA meetings first admit that by themselves they are powerless over their emotions, then say they could be restored to sanity by a power greater than themselves. This power is open to individual interpretation. For some, it's "The Man Upstairs"; for others it's "Life Itself." The focus is on coping, on learning to live in relative peace despite unsolved problems, and on living life "one day at a time."

Although Recovery, Inc., and Emotions Anonymous deal with a broad range of emo-

tional problems, there are also a host of problem-specific groups and support networks. To find one that meets your individual needs, contact your local community mental health center, or the National Self-Help Clearinghouse (33 W. 42nd St., Room 1227, New York, NY 10036).

Co-Counseling is an approach that trains people to give and accept reciprocal emotional support. Co-Counseling classes themselves serve as support groups, and after the training period, each member gets a list of local members available for counseling sessions.

The National Alliance for the Mentally Ill (NAMI) is a grassroots coalition of friends and relatives of those with serious mental health problems. The organization advocates for the mentally ill by promoting improved services.

The American Schizophrenia Association sponsors support groups for the families of schizophrenics, and explores such issues as residential treatment, relaxation training to reduce the side effects of medications, and orthomolecular therapy with vitamin and mineral supplements.

Studies have shown that success of therapy has less to do with methodology than the mere fact of recognizing a problem and deciding to do something about it. If the process of trying to cope with "the slings and arrows of outrageous fortune" seems beyond your strength, take heart. Whatever your situation, others who face similar challenges are eager to help.

Excerpted with permission from Medical Self-Care *(Winter 1984). Subscriptions: $15/yr. (6 issues) from Medical Self-Care, Box 1000, Point Reyes, CA 94956. Back issues: $2.50 from same address.*

The concept of "being average" comes up frequently in recovery groups.

Glossary

This glossary of psychology terms is included to provide you with a convenient and ready reference as you encounter general terms in your study of psychology and personal growth and behavior that are unfamiliar or require a review. It is not intended to be comprehensive, but taken together with the many definitions included in the articles themselves, it should prove to be quite useful.

Abnormal Irregular, deviating from the norm or average. Abnormal implies the presence of a mental disorder that leads to behavior that society labels as deviant. There is a continuum between normal and abnormal. These are relative terms in that they imply a social judgment. *See* Normal.

Accommodation Process in cognitive development; involves altering or reorganizing the mental picture to make room for a new experience or idea.

Acetylcholine A neurotransmitter involved in memory.

Achievement Drive The need to attain self-esteem, success, or status. Society's expectations strongly influence the achievement motive.

ACTH (Adrenocorticotropic Hormone) The part of the brain called the hypothalamus activates the release of the hormone ACTH from the pituitary gland when a stressful condition exists. ACTH in turn activates the release of adrenal corticoids from the cortex of the adrenal gland.

Action Therapy A general classification of therapy (as opposed to insight therapy) in which the therapist focuses on symptoms rather than on underlying emotional states. Treatment aims at teaching new behavioral patterns rather than at self-understanding. *See* Insight Therapy.

Actor-Observer Attribution The tendency to attribute the behavior of other people to internal causes and the behavior of yourself to external causes.

Acupuncture The technique for curing certain diseases and anesthetizing by inserting needles at certain points of the body, developed in China and now being studied and applied in the West.

Adaptation The process of responding to changes in the environment by altering one's responses to keep one's behavior appropriate to environmental demands.

Addiction Physical dependence on a drug. When a drug causes biochemical changes that are uncomfortable when the drug is discontinued, when one must take ever larger doses to maintain the intensity of the drug's effects, and when desire to continue the drug is strong, one is said to be addicted.

Adjustment How we react to stress; some change that we make in response to the demands placed upon us.

Adrenal Glands Endocrine glands involved in stress and energy regulation.

Affective Disorder Affect means feeling or emotion. An affective disorder is mental illness marked by a disturbance of mood (e.g. manic depression.)

Afferent Neuron (Sensory) A neuron that carries messages from the sense organs toward the central nervous system.

Aggression Any act that causes pain or suffering to another. Some psychologists believe that aggressive behavior is instinctual to all species, including man, while others believe that it is learned through the processes of observation and imitation.

Alienation Indifference to or loss of personal relationships. An individual may feel estranged from family members, or, on a broader scale, from society.

All-or-None Law The principle that states that a neuron only fires when a stimulus is above a certain minimum strength (threshold), and when it fires, it does so at full strength.

Altered State of Consciousness (ASC) A mental state qualitatively different from a person's normal, alert, waking consciousness.

Altruism Behavior motivated by a desire to benefit another person. Altruistic behavior is aided by empathy and is usually motivated internally, not by observable threats or rewards.

Amphetamine A psychoactive drug that is a stimulant. Although used in treating mild depressions or, in children, hyperactivity, its medical uses are doubtful, and amphetamines are often abused. *See* Psychoactive Drug.

Anal Stage Psychosexual stage, during which, according to Freud, the child experiences the first restrictions on his impulses.

Animism The quality of believing life exists in inanimate objects. According to Piaget, animism is characteristic of children's thinking until about age two.

Antisocial Personality Disorder Personality disorder in which individuals who engage in antisocial behavior experience no guilt or anxiety about their actions; sometimes called sociopathy or psychopathy.

Anxiety An important term that has different meanings for different theories (psychoanalysis, behavior theory); a feeling state of apprehension, dread, or uneasiness. The state may be aroused by an objectively dangerous situation or by a situation that is not objectively dangerous. It may be mild or severe.

Anxiety Disorder Fairly long-lasting disruptions of the person's ability to deal with stress; often accompanied by feelings of fear and apprehension.

Applied Psychology The area of psychology that is most immediately concerned with helping to solve practical problems; includes clinical and counseling psychology, and industrial, environmental, and legal psychology.

Aptitude Tests Tests which are designed to predict what can be accomplished by a person in the future with the proper training.

Arousal A measure of responsiveness or activity; a state of excitement or wakefulness ranging from deepest coma to intense excitement.

Aspiration Level The level of achievement a person strives for. Studies suggest that people can use internal or external standards of performance.

Assertiveness Training Training which helps individuals stand up for their rights while not denying rights of other people.

Assimilation Process in cognitive development; occurs when something new is taken into the child's mental picture of the world.

Association Has separate meanings for different branches of psychology. Theory in cognitive psychology suggests that we organize information so that we can find our memories systematically, that one idea will bring another to mind. In psychoanalysis, the patient is asked to free associate (speak aloud all consecutive thoughts until random associations tend of themselves to form a meaningful whole). *See* Cognitive Psychology, Psychoanalysis.

Associationism A theory of learning suggesting that once two stimuli are presented together, one of them will remind a person of the other.

Ideas are learned by association with sensory experiences and are not innate. Among the principles of associationism are contiguity (stimuli that occur close together are more likely to be associated than stimuli far apart), and repetition (the more frequently stimuli occur together, the more strongly they become associated).

Association Neurons Neurons that connect with other neurons.

Attachment Process in which the individual shows behaviors that promote the proximity or contact with a specific object or person.

Attention The tendency to focus activity in a particular direction and to select certain stimuli for further analysis while ignoring or possibly storing for further analysis all other inputs.

Attitude An overall tendency to respond positively or negatively to particular people or objects in a way that is learned through experience and that is made up of feelings (affects,) thoughts (evaluations,) and actions (conation.)

Attribution The process of determining the causes of behavior in a given individual.

Autism A personality disorder in which ae child does not respond socially to people.

Autonomic Nervous System The part of the central nervous system (The other part is the central nervous system) that is for emergency functions and release of large amounts of energy (sympathetic division) and regulating functions such as digestion and sleep (parasympathetic division.) *See* Biofeedback.

Aversion Therapy A counterconditioning therapy in which unwanted responses are paired with unpleasant consequences.

Avoidance Conditioning Situation in which a subject learns to avoid an aversive stimulus by responding appropriately before it begins.

Barbiturates Sedative-hypnotic, psychoactive drugs widely used to induce sleep and to reduce tension. Overuse can lead to addiction. *See* Addiction.

Behavior Any observable activity of an organism, including mental processes.

Behaviorism A school of psychology stressing an objective approach to psychological questions, proposing that psychology be limited to observable behavior and that the subjectiveness of consciousness places it beyond the limits of scientific psychology.

Behavior Therapy The use of conditioning processes to treat mental disorders. Various techniques may be used, including positive reinforcement in which rewards (verbal or tangible) are given to the patient for appropriate behavior, modeling in which patients unlearn fears by watching models exhibit fearlessness, and systematic desensitization in which the patient is taught to relax and visualize anxiety-producing items at the same time. *See* Insight Therapy, Systematic Desensitization.

Biofeedback The voluntary control of physiological processes by receiving information about those processes as they occur, through instruments that pick up these changes and display them to the subject in the form of a signal. Blood pressure, skin temperature, etc. can be controlled.

Biological (Primary) Motives Motives which have a physiological basis; include hunger, thirst, body temperature regulation, avoidance of pain, and sex.

Biological Response System System of the body that is particularly important in behavioral responding; includes the senses, endocrines, muscles, and the nervous system.

233

Biological Therapy Treatment of behavior problems through biological techniques; major biological therapies include drug therapy, psychosurgery, and electroconvulsive therapy.

Bipolar Disorder Affective disorder which is characterized by extreme mood swings from sad depression to joyful mania; sometimes called manic-depression.

Body Language Communication through position and movement of the body.

Brain Mapping A procedure for identifying the function of various areas of the brain; the surgeon gives tiny electrical stimulation to a specific area and notes patient's reaction.

Brain Stimulation The introduction of chemical or electrical stimuli directly into the brain.

Brain Waves Electrical responses produced by brain activity that can be recorded directly from any portion of the brain or from the scalp with special electrodes. Brain waves are measured by an electroencephalograph (EEG). Alpha waves occur during relaxed wakefulness and beta waves during active behavior. Theta waves are associated with drowsiness and vivid visual imagery, delta waves with deep sleep.

Bystander Effect Phenomenon in which a single person is more likely to help in an emergency situation than a group of people.

Cannon-Bard Theory of Emotion Theory of emotion which states that the emotional feeling and the physiological arousal occur at the same time.

Catatonic Schizophrenia A type of schizophrenia which is characterized by periods of complete immobility and the apparent absence of will to move or speak.

Causal Attribution Process of determining whether a person's behavior is due to internal or external motives.

Cautious Shift Research suggests that the decisions of a group will be more conservative than that of the average individual member when dealing with areas for which there are widely held values favoring caution (e.g. physical danger or family responsibility). *See* Risky Shift.

Central Nervous System The part of the human nervous system which interprets and stores messages from the sense organs, decides what behavior to exhibit, and sends appropriate messages to the muscles and glands; includes the brain and spinal cord.

Central Tendency In statistics, measures of central tendency give a number that represents the entire group or sample.

Cerebellum The part of the brain responsible for muscle and movement control and coordination of eye-body movement.

Cerebral Cortex The part of the brain consisting of the outer layer of cerebral cells. The cortex can be divided into specific regions: sensory, motor, and associative.

Chaining Behavior theory suggests that behavior patterns are built up of component parts by stringing together a number of simpler responses.

Character Disorder (or Personality Disorder) A classification of psychological disorders (as distinguished from neurosis or psychosis). The disorder has become part of the individual's personality and does not cause him discomfort, making that disorder more difficult to treat psychotherapeutically.

Chromosome *See* Gene.

Chunking The tendency to code memories so that there are fewer bits to store.

Classical Conditioning See Pavlovian Conditioning.

Client-Centered Therapy A nondirective form of psychotherapy developed by Carl Rogers in which the counselor attempts to create an atmosphere in which the client can freely explore himself and his problems. The client-centered therapist reflects what the client says back to him, usually without interpreting it.

Clinical Psychology The branch of psychology concerned with testing, diagnosing, interviewing, conducting research and treating (often by psychotherapy) mental disorders and personality problems.

Cognitive Appraisal Intellectual evaluation of situations or stimuli. Experiments suggest that emotional arousal is produced not simply by a stimulus but by how one evaluates and interprets the arousal. The appropriate physical response follows this cognitive appraisal.

Cognitive Behavior Therapy A form of behavior therapy which identifies self-defeating attitudes and thoughts in a subject, and then helps the subject to replace these with positive, supportive thoughts.

Cognitive Dissonance People are very uncomfortable if they perceive that their beliefs, feelings, or acts are not consistent with one another, and they will try to reduce the discomfort of this dissonance.

Cognitive Psychology The study of how individuals gain knowledge of their environments. Cognitive psychologists believe that the organism actively participates in constructing the meaningful stimuli that it selectively organizes and to which it selectively responds.

Comparative Psychology The study of similarities and differences in the behavior of different species.

Compulsive Personality Personality disorder in which an individual is preoccupied with details and rules.

Concept Learning The acquisition of the ability to identify and use the qualities that objects or situations have in common. A class concept refers to any quality that breaks objects or situations into separate groupings.

Concrete-Operational Stage A stage in intellectual development according to Piaget. The child at approximately seven years begins to apply logic. His thinking is less egocentric, reversible, and the child develops conservation abilities and the ability to classify. *See* Conservation.

Conditioned Reinforcer Reinforcement that is effective because it has been associated with other reinforcers. Conditioned reinforcers are involved in higher order conditioning.

Conditioned Response (CR) The response or behavior that occurs when the conditioned stimulus is presented (after the CS has been associated with the US).

Conditioned Stimulus (CS) An originally neutral stimulus that is associated with an unconditioned stimulus and takes on its capability of eliciting a particular reaction.

Conditioned Taste Aversion (CTA) Learning an aversion to particular tastes by associating them with stomach distress; usually considered a unique form of classical conditioning because of the extremely long interstimulus intervals involved.

Conduction The ability of a neuron to carry a message (an electrical stimulus) along its length.

Conflict Situation which occurs when we experience incompatible demands or desires.

Conformity The tendency of an individual to act like others regardless of personal belief.

Conscience A person's sense of the moral rightness or wrongness of behavior.

Consciousness Awareness of experienced sensations, thoughts, and feelings at any given point in time.

Consensus In causal attribution, the extent to which other people react the same way the subject does in a particular situation.

Conservation Refers to the child's ability to understand laws of length, mass, and volume. Before the development of this ability, a child will not understand that a particular property of an object (e.g. the quantity of water in a glass) does not change even though other perceivable features change.

Consistency In causal attribution, the extent to which the subject always behaves in the same way in a particular situation.

Consolidation The biological neural process of making memories permanent; possibly short-term memory is electrically coded and long-term memory is chemically coded.

Continuum of Preparedness Seligman's proposal that animals are biologically prepared to learn certain responses more readily than others.

Control Group A group used for comparison with an experimental group. All conditions must be identical for each group with the exception of the one variable (independent) that is manipulated. *See* Experimental Group.

Convergence Binocular depth cue in which we detect distance by interpreting the kinesthetic sensations produced by the muscles of the eyeballs.

Convergent Thinking The kind of thinking that is used to solve problems having only one correct answer. *See* Divergent Thinking.

Conversion Disorder Somatoform disorder in which a person displays obvious disturbance in the nervous system, however, a medical examination reveals no physical basis for the problem; often includes paralysis, loss of sensation, or blindness.

Corpus Callosum Nerve fibers that connect the two halves of the brain in humans. If cut, the halves continue to function although some functions are affected.

Correlation A measurement in which two or more sets of variables are compared and the extent to which they are related is calculated.

Correlation Coefficient The measure, in number form, of how two variables vary together. They extend from -1 (perfect negative correlation) to $+1$ (perfect positive correlation).

Counterconditioning A behavior therapy in which an unwanted response is replaced by conditioning a new response that is incompatible with it.

Creativity The ability to discover or produce new solutions to problems, new inventions, or new works of art. Creativity is an ability independent of IQ and is open-ended in that solutions are not predefined in their scope or appropriateness. *See* Problem-Solving.

Critical Period A specific stage in an organism's development during which the acquisition of a particular type of behavior depends on exposure to a particular type of stimulation.

Cross-Sectional Study A research technique that focuses on a factor in a group of subjects as they are at one time, as in a study of fantasy play in subjects of three different age groups. *See* Longitudinal Study.

Culture-Bound The idea that a test's usefulness is limited to the culture in which it was written and utilized.

Curiosity Motive Motive which causes the individual to seek out a certain amount of novelty.

Cutaneous Sensitivity The skin senses: touch, pain, pressure and temperature. Skin receptors respond in different ways and with varying degrees of sensitivity.

Decay Theory of forgetting in which sensory impressions leave memory traces that fade away with time.

Defense Mechanism A way of reducing anxiety that does not directly cope with the threat. There are many types, denial, repression, etc., all of which are used in normal function. Only when use is habitual or they impede effective solutions are they considered pathological.

Delusion A false belief that persists despite evidence showing it to be irrational. Delusions are often symptoms of mental illness.

Dependent Variable Those conditions that an experimenter observes and measures. Called "dependent" because they depend on the experimental manipulations.

Depersonalization Disorder Dissociative disorder in which individuals escape from their own personalities by believing that they don't exist or that their environment is not real.

Depression A temporary emotional state that normal individuals experience or a persistent state that may be considered a psychological disorder. Characterized by sadness and low self-esteem. *See* Self-Esteem.

Descriptive Statistics Techniques that help summarize large amounts of data information.

Developmental Norms The average time at which developmental changes occur in the normal individual.

Developmental Psychology The study of changes in behavior and thinking as the organism grows from the prenatal stage to death.

Deviation, Standard and Average Average deviation is determined by measuring the deviation of each score in a distribution from the mean and calculating the average of the deviations. The standard deviation is used to determine how representative the mean of a distribution is. *See* Mean.

Diagnostic and Statistical Manual of Mental Disorders (DSM) DSM-III was published in 1980 by the American Psychiatric Association.

Diffusion of Responsibility As the number of witnesses to a help-requiring situation—and thus the degree of anonymity—increases, the amount of helping decreases and the amount of time before help is offered increases. *See* Anonymity.

Discrimination The ability to tell whether stimuli are different when presented together or that one situation is different from a past one.

Disorganized Schizophrenia A type of schizophrenia which is characterized by a severe personality disintegration; the individual often displays bizarre behavior.

Displacement The process by which an emotion originally attached to a particular person, object, or situation is transferred to something else.

Dissociative Disorders Disorders in which individuals forget who they are.

Distal Stimuli Physical events in the environment that affect perception. *See also* Proximal Stimuli.

Distinctiveness In causal attribution, the extent to which the subject reacts the same way in other situations.

Divergent Thinking The kind of thinking that characterizes creativity (as contrasted with convergent thinking) and involves the development of novel resolutions of a task or the generation of totally new ideas. *See* Convergent Thinking.

DNA *See* Gene.

Double Bind A situation in which a person is subjected to two conflicting, contradictory demands at the same time.

Down's Syndrome Form of mental retardation caused by having three number 21 chromosomes (trisomy 21).

Dreams The thoughts, images, and emotions that occur during sleep. Dreams occur periodically during the sleep cycle and are usually marked by rapid movements of the eyes (REM sleep). The content of dreams tends to reflect emotions (sexual feelings, according to Freud) and experiences of the previous day. Nightmares are qualitatively different from other dreams, often occuring during deep or Stage 4 sleep.

Drive A need or urge that motivates behavior. Some drives may be explained as responses to bodily needs, such as hunger or sex. Others derive from social pressures and complex forms of learning, for example, competition, curiosity, achievement. *See* Motivation.

Drive Reduction Theory Theory of motivation that states that the individual is pushed by inner forces toward reducing the drive and restoring homeostasis.

Drug Dependence A state of mental or physical dependence on a drug, or both. Psychoactive drugs are capable of creating psychological dependence (anxiety when the drug is unavailable,) although the relationship of some, such as marijuana and LSD, to physical dependence or addiction is still under study. *See* Psychoactive Drugs, Addiction.

Drug Tolerance A state produced by certain psychoactive drugs in which increasing amounts of the substance are required to produce the desired effect. Some drugs produce tolerance but not withdrawal symptoms, and these drugs are not regarded as physically addicting.

Effectance Motive The striving for effectiveness in dealing with the environment. The effectance motive differs from the need for achievement in that effectance depends on internal feelings of satisfaction while the need for achievement is geared more to meeting others' standards.

Efferent Neuron (Motor) A neuron that carries messages from the central nervous system to the muscles and glands.

Ego A construct to account for the organization in a person's life and for making the person's behavior correspond to physical and social realities. According to Freud, the ego is the "reality principle" that is responsible for holding the id or "pleasure principle" in check. *See* Id.

Egocentrism Seeing things from only one's own point of view; also, the quality of a child's thought that prevents him from understanding that different people perceive the world differently. Egocentrism is characteristic of a stage that all children go through.

Electroshock Therapy A form of therapy used to relieve severe depression. The patient receives electric current across the forehead, loses consciousness, and undergoes a short convulsion. When the patient regains consciousness, his mood is lifted.

Emotion A complex feeling-state that involves physiological arousal; a subjective feeling which might involve a cognitive appraisal of the situation and overt behavior in response to a stimulus.

Empathy The ability to appreciate how someone else feels by putting yourself in his position and experiencing his feelings. Empathy is acquired normally by children during intellectual growth.

Empiricism The view that behavior is learned through experience.

Encounter Groups Groups of individuals who meet to change their personal lives by confronting each other, discussing personal problems, and talking more honestly and openly than in everyday life.

Endocrine Glands Ductless glands that secrete chemicals called hormones into the blood stream.

Equilibration According to Piaget, the child constructs his understanding of the world through equilibration. Equilibration consists of the interaction of two complementary processes, assimilation (taking in input within the existing structures of the mind, e.g. putting it into mental categories that already exist) with accommodation (the changing of mental categories to fit new input that cannot be taken into existing categories) and is the process by which knowing occurs. One's developmental stage affects how one equilibrates.

Ethnocentrism The belief that one's own ethnic or racial group is superior to others.

Experiment Procedures executed under a controlled situation in order to test a hypothesis and discover relationships between independent and dependent variables.

Experimental Control The predetermined conditions, procedures, and checks built into the design of an experiment to ensure scientific control; as opposed to "control" in common usage, which implies manipulation.

Experimental Group In a scientific experiment, the group of subjects that is usually treated specially, as opposed to the control group, in order to isolate just the variable under investigation. *See* Control Group.

Experimental Psychology The branch of psychology concerned with the laboratory study of basic psychological laws and principles as demonstrated in the behavior of animals.

Experimenter Bias How the expectations of the person running an experiment can influence what comes out of the experiment. Experimenter bias can affect the way the experimenter sees the subjects' behavior, causing distortions of fact, and can also affect the way the experimenter reads data, also leading to distortions.

Extinction The elimination of behavior by, in classical conditioning, the withholding of the US, and in operant conditioning, the withholding of the reinforcement.

Extrasensory Perception (ESP) The range of perceptions that are "paranormal," (such as the ability to predict events, reproduce drawings sealed in envelopes, etc.).

Fixed-Action Pattern Movement that is characteristic of a species and does not have to be learned.

Fixed Interval (FI) Schedule Schedule of reinforcement in which the subject receives reinforcement for the first correct response given after a specified time interval.

Fixed Ratio (FR) Schedule Schedule of reinforcement in which the subject is reinforced after a certain number of responses.

Forgetting The process by which material that once was available is no longer available. Theory exists that forgetting occurs because memories interfere with one another, either retroactively (new memories block old) or proactively (old memories block new); that forgetting occurs when the cues necessary to recall the information are not supplied, or when memories are too unpleasant to remain in consciousness. *See* Repression.

Formal Operational Stage According to Piaget, the stage at which the child develops adult powers of reasoning, abstraction, and symbolizing. The child can grasp scientific, religious, and political concepts and deduce their consequences as well as reason hypothetically ("what if. . . .").

Frequency Theory of Hearing Theory of hearing that states that the frequency of vibrations at the basilar membrane determines the frequency of firing of neurons that carry impulses to the brain.

Frustration A feeling of discomfort or insecurity aroused by a blocking of gratification or by unresolved problems. Several theories hold that frustration arouses aggression. *See* Aggression.

Functionalism An early school of psychology stressing the ways behavior helps one adapt to the environment and the role that learning plays in this adaptive process.

Gene The unit of heredity that determines particular characteristics; a part of a molecule of DNA. DNA (dioxyribonucleic acid) is found mainly in the nucleus of living cells where it occurs in threadlike structures called chromosomes. Within the chromosomes each DNA molecule is organized into specific units that carry the genetic information necessary for the development of a particular trait. These units are the genes. A gene can reproduce itself exactly, and this is how traits are carried between generations. The genotype is the entire structure of genes that are inherited by an organism from its parents. The environment interacts with this genotype to determine how the genetic potential will develop.

General Adaptation Syndrome (GAS) The way the body responds to stress, as described by Hans Selye. In the first stage, an alarm reaction, a person responds by efforts at self-control and shows signs of nervous depression (defense mechanisms, fear, anger, etc.) followed by a release of ACTH. In stage 2, the subject shows increased resistance to the specific source of stress and less resistance to other sources. Defense mechanisms may become neurotic. With stage 3 come exhaustion, stupor, even death.

Generalization The process by which learning in one situation is transferred to another, similar situation. It is a key term in behavioral modification and classical conditioning. *See* Classical Conditioning.

Generalized Anxiety Disorder Disorder in which the individual lives in a state of constant severe tension; continuous fear and apprehension experienced by an individual.

Genetics The study of the transfer of the inheritance of characteristics from one generation to another.

Genotype The underlying genetic structure that an individual has inherited and will send on to descendants. The actual appearance of a trait (phenotype) is due to the interaction of the genotype and the environment.

Gestalt Psychology A movement in psychology begun in the 1920s, stressing the wholeness of a person's experience and proposing that perceiving is an active, dynamic process that takes into account the entire pattern ("gestalt") of the perceptual field. *See* Behaviorism, Associationism.

Glia Cells in the central nervous system that regulate the chemical environment of the nerve cells. RNA is stored in glial cells.

Grammar The set of rules for combining units of a language.

Group Therapy A form of psychotherapy aimed at treating mental disorders in which interaction among group members is the main therapeutic mode. Group therapy takes many forms but essentially requires a sense of community, support, increased personal responsibility, and a professionally trained leader.

Growth The normal quantitative changes that occur in the physical and psychological aspects of a healthy child with the passage of time.

Gustation The sense of taste. Theory suggests that the transmission of sense information from tongue to brain occurs through patterns of cell activity and not just the firing of single nerve fibers. Also, it is believed that specific spatial patterns or places on the tongue correspond to taste qualities.

Habit Formation The tendency to make a response to a stimulus less variable, especially if it produced successful adaptation.

Hallucination A sensory impression reported by a person when no external stimulus exists to justify the report. Hallucinations are serious symptoms and may be produced by psychoses. *See* Psychoses.

Hallucinogen A substance that produces hallucinations, such as LSD, mescaline, etc.

Hierarchy of Needs Maslow's list of motives in humans, arranged from the biological to the uniquely human.

Higher Order Conditioning Learning to make associations with stimuli that have been previously learned (CSs).

Hippocampus Part of the cortex of the brain governing memory storage, smell, and visceral functions.

Homeostasis A set of processes maintaining the constancy of the body's internal state, a series of dynamic compensations of the nervous system. Many processes such as appetite, body temperature, water balance, heart rate are controlled by homeostasis.

Hormones Chemical secretions of the endocrine glands that regulate various body processes (e.g. growth, sexual traits, reproductive processes, etc.)

Humanism Branch of psychology dealing with those qualities distinguishing humans from other animals.

Hypnosis A trancelike state marked by heightened suggestibility and a narrowing of attention which can be induced in a number of ways. Debate exists over whether hypnosis is a true altered state of consciousness and over to what extent strong motivating instructions can duplicate so-called hypnosis.

Hypothalamus A part of the brain that acts as a channel that carries information from the cortex and the thalamus to the spinal cord and ultimately to the motor nerves or to the autonomic nervous system, where it is transmitted to specific target organs. These target organs release into the bloodstream specific hormones that alter bodily functions. *See* Autonomic Nervous System.

Hypothesis A hypothesis can be called an educated guess, similar to a hunch. When a hunch is stated in a way that allows for further testing, it becomes a hypothesis.

Iconic Memory A visual memory. Experiments suggest that in order to be remembered and included in long-term memory, information must pass through a brief sensory stage.

Theory further suggests that verbal information is subject to forgetting but that memorized sensory images are relatively permanent.

Id According to Freud, a component of the psyche present at birth that is the storehouse of psychosexual energy called *libido*, and also of primitive urges to fight, dominate, destroy.

Identification The taking on of attributes that one sees in another person. Children tend to identify with their parents or other important adults and thereby take on certain traits that are important to their development.

Illusion A mistaken perception of an actual stimulus.

Imitation The copying of another's behavior; learned through the process of observation. *See* Modeling.

Impression Formation The process of developing an evaluation of another person from your perceptions; first, or initial impressions are often very important.

Imprinting The rapid, permanent acquisition by an organism of a strong attachment to an object (usually the parent). Imprinting occurs shortly after birth.

Independent Variable The condition in an experiment which is controlled and manipulated by the experimenter; it is a stimulus that will cause a response.

Inferential Statistics Techniques that help researchers make generalizations about a finding based on a limited number of subjects.

Inhibition Restraint of an impulse, desire, activity, or drive. People are taught to inhibit full expression of many drives (for example, aggression or sexuality) and to apply checks either consciously or unconsciously. In Freudian terminology, an inhibition is an unconsciously motivated blocking of sexual energy. In Pavlovian conditioning, inhibition is the theoretical process that operates during extinction, acting to block a conditioned response. *See* Pavlovian Conditioning.

Insight A sudden perception of useful or proper relations among objects necessary to solve the problem.

Insight Therapy A general classification of therapy in which the therapist focuses on the patient's underlying feelings and motivations and devotes most effort to increasing the patient's self-awareness or insight into his behavior. The other major class of therapy is action therapy. *See* Action Therapy.

Instinct An inborn pattern of behavior, relatively independent of environmental influence. An instinct may need to be triggered by a particular stimulus in the environment, but then it proceeds in a fixed pattern. The combination of taxis (orienting movement in response to a particular stimulus) and fixed-action pattern (inherited coordination) is the basis for instinctual activity. *See* Fixed-Action Pattern.

Instrumental Learning *See* Operant Conditioning.

Intelligence A capacity for knowledge about the world. This is an enormous and controversial field of study, and there is not agreement on a precise definition. However, intelligence has come to refer to higher-level abstract processes and may be said to comprise the ability to deal effectively with abstract concepts, the ability to learn, and the ability to adapt and deal with new situations. Piaget defines intelligence as the construction of an understanding. Both biological inheritance and environmental factors contribute to general intelligence. Children proceed through a sequence of identifiable stages in the development of conceptual thinking (Piaget). The degree to which factors such as race, sex, and social class affect intelligence is not known.

Intelligence Quotient (IQ) A measurement of intelligence originally based on tests devised by Binet and now widely applied. Genetic inheritance and environment affect IQ, although their relative contributions are not known. IQ can be defined in different ways; classically it is defined as a relation between chronological and mental ages.

Interference Theory of forgetting in which information that was learned before (proactive interference) or after (retroactive interference) the material of interest causes the learner to be unable to remember the material.

Interstimulus Interval The time between the start of the conditioned stimulus and the start of the unconditioned stimulus in Pavlovian conditioning. *See* Pavlovian Conditioning.

Intra-Uterine Environment The environment in the uterus during pregnancy can affect the physical development of the organism and its behavior after birth. Factors such as the mother's nutrition, emotional and physical state significantly influence offspring. The mother's diseases, medications, hormones, stress level all effect the pre- and post-natal development of her young.

Intrinsic Motivation Motivation inside of the individual; we do something because we receive satisfaction from it.

Introspection Reporting one's internal, subjective mental contents for the purpose of further study and analysis. *See* Structuralism.

James-Lange Theory of Emotion Theory of emotion which states that the physiological arousal and behavior come before the subjective experience of an emotion.

Labeling-of-Arousal Experiments suggest that an individual experiencing physical arousal that he cannot explain will interpret his feelings in terms of the situation he is in and will use environmental and contextual cues.

Language A set of abstract symbols used to communicate meaning. Language includes vocalized sounds or semantic units (words, usually) and rules for combining the units (grammar). There is some inborn basis for language acquisition, and there are identifiable stages in its development that are universal.

Language Acquisition Linguists debate how children acquire language. Some believe in environmental shaping, a gradual system of reward and punishment. Others emphasize the unfolding of capacities inborn in the brain that are relatively independent of the environment and its rewards.

Latency Period According to Freud, the psychosexual stage of development during which sexual interest has been repressed and thus is low or "latent" (dormant).

Law of Effect Thorndike's proposal that when a response produces satisfaction, it will be repeated; reinforcement.

Leadership The quality of exerting more influence than other group members. Research suggests that certain characteristics are generally considered essential to leadership: consideration, sensitivity, ability to initiate and structure, and emphasis on production. However, environmental factors may thrust authority on a person without regard to personal characteristics.

Learned Helplessness Theory suggests that living in an environment of uncontrolled stress reduces the ability to cope with future stress that *is* controllable.

Learned Social Motives Motives in the human which are learned; include achievement, affiliation, and autonomy.

Learning The establishment of connections between stimulus and response, resulting from observation, special training, or previous activity. Learning is relatively permanent.

Lifespan Span of time from conception to death; in developmental psychology, a lifespan approach looks at development throughout an individual's life.

Linguistic Relativity Hypothesis Proposal by Whorf that the perception of reality differs according to the language of the observer.

Linguistics The study of language, its nature, structure, and components.

Locus of Control The perceived place from which come determining forces in one's life. A person who feels that he has some control over his fate and tends to feel more likely to succeed has an internal locus of control. A person with an external locus of control feels that it is outside himself and therefore that his attempts to control his fate are less assured.

Longitudinal Study A research method that involves following subjects over a considerable period of time (as compared with a cross-sectional approach); as in a study of fantasy play in children observed several times at intervals of two years. *See* Cross-Sectional Study.

Love Affectionate behavior between people, often in combination with interpersonal attraction. The mother-infant love relationship strongly influences the later capacity for developing satisfying love relationships.

Manic-Depressive Reaction A form of mental illness marked by alternations of extreme phases of elation (manic phase) and depression.

Maternalism Refers to the mother's reaction to her young. It is believed that the female is biologically determined to exhibit behavior more favorable to the care and feeding of the young than the male, although in humans maternalism is probably determined as much by cultural factors as by biological predisposition.

Maturation The genetically-controlled process of physical and physiological growth.

Mean The measure of central tendency, or mathematical average, computed by adding all scores in a set and dividing by the number of scores.

Meaning The concept or idea conveyed to the mind, by any method. In reference to memory, meaningful terms are easier to learn than less meaningful, unconnected, or nonsense terms. Meaningfulness is not the same as the word's meaning.

Median In a set of scores, the median is that middle score that divides the set into equal halves.

Memory Involves the encoding, storing of information in the brain, and its retrieval. Several theories exist to explain memory. One proposes that we have both a short-term (STM) and a long-term memory (LTM) and that information must pass briefly through the STM to be stored in the LTM. Also suggested is that verbal information is subject to forgetting, while memorized sensory images are relatively permanent. Others see memory as a function of association—information processed systematically and the meaningfulness of the items. Debate exists over whether memory retrieval is actually a process of reappearance or reconstruction.

Mental Disorder A mental condition that deviates from what society considers to be normal.

Minnesota Multiphasic Personality Inventory (MMPI) An objective personality test which was originally devised to identify personality disorders.

Mode In a set of scores, the measurement at which the largest number of subjects fall.

Modeling The imitation or copying of another's behavior. As an important process in personality development, modeling may be based on parents. In therapy, the therapist may serve as a model for the patient.

Morality The standards of right and wrong of a society and their adoption by members of that society. Some researchers believe that morality develops in successive stages, with each stage representing a specific level of moral thinking (Kohlberg). Others see morality as the result of experiences in which the child learns through punishment and reward from models such as parents and teachers.

Motivation All factors that cause and regulate behavior that is directed toward achieving goals and satisfying needs. Motivation is what moves an organism to action.

Motor Unit One spinal motoneuron (motor nerve cell) and the muscle fibers it activates. The contraction of a muscle involves the activity of many motoneurons and muscle fibers. Normally we are aware only of our muscles contracting and not of the process producing the contraction, although biofeedback can train people to control individual motor units. *See* Biofeedback.

Narcotic A drug that relieves pain. Heroin, morphine, and opium are narcotics. Narcotics are often addicting.

Naturalistic Observation Research method in which behavior of people or animals in the normal environment is accurately recorded.

Negative Reinforcement Any event that upon termination, strengthens the preceding behavior; taking from subject something bad will increase the probability that the preceding behavior will be repeated. Involves aversive stimulus.

Neuron A nerve cell. There are billions of neurons in the brain and spinal cord. Neurons interact at synapses or points of contact. Information passage between neurons is electrical and biochemical. It takes the activity of many neurons to produce a behavior.

Neurosis Any one of a wide range of psychological difficulties, accompanied by excessive anxiety (as contrasted with psychosis). Psychoanalytic theory states that neurosis is an expression of unresolved conflicts in the form of tension and impaired functioning. Most neurotics are in much closer contact with reality than most psychotics. Term has been largely eliminated from DSM-III.

Nonverbal Behaviors Gestures, facial expressions, and other body movements. They are important because they tend to convey emotion. Debate exists over whether they are inborn or learned.

Norm An empirically set pattern of belief or behavior. Social norm refers to widely accepted social or cultural behavior to which a person tends to or is expected to conform.

Normal Sane, or free from mental disorder. Normal behavior is the behavior typical of most people in a given group, and "normality" implies a social judgment.

Normal Curve When scores of a large number of random cases are plotted on a graph, they often fall into a bell-shaped curve; there are as many cases above the mean as below on the curve.

Object Permanence According to Piaget, the stage in cognitive development when a child begins to conceive of objects as having an existence even when out of sight or touch and to conceive of space as extending beyond his own perception.

Oedipus Complex The conflicts of a child in triangular relationship with his mother and father. According to Freud, a boy must resolve his unconscious sexual desire for his mother and the accompanying wish to kill his father and fear of his father's revenge in order that he proceed in his moral development. The analogous problem for girls is called the Electra complex.

Olfaction The sense of smell. No general agreement exists on how olfaction works though theories exist to explain it. One suggests that the size and shape of molecules of what is smelled is a crucial cue. The brain processes involved in smell are located in a different and evolutionarily older part of the brain than the other senses.

Operant Conditioning The process of changing, maintaining, or eliminating voluntary behavior through the consequences of that behavior. Operant conditioning uses many of the techniques of Pavlovian conditioning but differs in that it deals with voluntary rather than reflex behaviors. The frequency with which a behavior is emitted can be increased if it is rewarded (reinforced) and decreased if it is not reinforced, or punished. Some psychologists believe that all behavior is learned through conditioning while others believe that intellectual and motivational processes play a crucial role. *See* Pavlovian Conditioning.

Operational Definitions If an event is not directly observable, then the variables must be defined by the operations by which they will be measured. These definitions are called operational definitions.

Organism Any living animal, human or subhuman.

Orienting Response A relatively automatic, "what's that?" response that puts the organism in a better position to attend to and deal with a new stimulus. When a stimulus attracts our attention, our body responds with movements of head and body toward the stimulus, changes in muscle tone, heart rate, blood flow, breathing, and changes in the brain's electrical activity.

Pavlovian Conditioning Also called classical conditioning, Pavlovian conditioning can be demonstrated as follows: In the first step, an *unconditioned stimulus* (UCS) such as food, loud sounds, or pain is paired with a neutral *conditioned stimulus* (CS) that causes no direct effect, such as a click, tone, or a dim light. The response elicited by the UCS is called the *unconditioned response* (UCR) and is a biological reflex of the nervous system (for example, eyeblinks or salivation). The combination of the neutral CS, the response-causing UCS, and the unlearned UCR is usually presented to the subject several times during conditioning. Eventually, the UCS is dropped from the sequence in the second step of the process, and the previously neutral CS comes to elicit a response. When conditioning is complete, presentation of the CS alone will result in a *conditioned response* (CR) similar but not always the same as the UCR.

Perception The field of psychology studying ways in which the experience of objects in the world is based upon stimulation of the sense organs. In psychology, the field of perception studies what determines sensory impressions, such as size, shape, distance, direction, etc. Physical events in the environment are called distal stimuli while the activity at the sense organ itself is called a proximal stimulus. The study of perceiving tries to determine how an organism knows what distal stimuli are like since proximal stimuli are its only source of information. Perception of objects remains more or less constant despite changes in distal stimuli and is therefore believed to depend on relationships within stimuli (size *and* distance, for example). Perceptual processes are able to adjust and adapt to changes in the perceptual field.

Performance The actual behavior of an individual that is observed. We often infer learning from observing performance.

Peripheral Nervous System The part of the human nervous system which receives messages from the sense organs and carries messages to the muscles and glands; everything outside of the brain and spinal cord.

Persuasion The process of changing a person's attitudes, beliefs, or actions. A person's susceptibility to persuasion depends on the persuader's credibility, subtlety and whether both sides of an argument are presented.

Phenotype The physical features or behavior patterns by which we recognize an organism. Phenotype is the result of interaction between genotype (total of inherited genes) and environment. *See* Genotype.

Phobia A neurosis consisting of an irrationally intense fear of specific persons, objects, or situations and a wish to avoid them. A phobic person feels intense and incapacitating anxiety. The person may be aware that his fear is irrational, but this knowledge does not help.

Pituitary Gland Is located at the base of the brain and controls secretion of several hormones: the antidiuretic hormone that maintains water balance, oxytocin which controls blood pressure and milk production and ACTH which is produced in response to stress, etc. *See* ACTH.

Placebo A substance which in and of itself has no real effect but which may produce an effect in a subject because the subject expects or believes that it will.

Positive Reinforcement Any event, that upon presentation, strengthens the preceding behavior; giving a subject something good will increase the probability that the preceding behavior will be repeated.

Prejudice An attitude in which one holds a negative belief about members of a group to which he does not belong. Prejudice is often directed at minority ethnic or racial groups and may be reduced by contact with these perceived "others."

Premack Principle Principle that states that of any two responses, the one that is more likely to occur can be used to reinforce the response that is less likely to occur.

Prenatal Development Development from conception to birth. It includes the physical development of the fetus as well as certain of its intellectual and emotional processes.

Preoperational Stage The development stage at which, according to Piaget, come the start of language, the ability to imitate actions, to symbolize, and to play make-believe games. Thinking is egocentric in that a child cannot understand that others perceive things differently.

Primary Reinforcement Reinforcement that is effective without having been associated with other reinforcers; sometimes called unconditioned reinforcement.

Probability (p) In inferential statistics, the likelihood that the difference between the experimental and control groups is due to the independent variable.

Problem Solving A self-directed activity in which an individual uses information to develop answers to problems, to generate new problems, and sometimes to transform the process by creating a unique, new system. Problem solving involves learning, insight and creativity.

Projective Test A type of test in which people respond to ambiguous, loosely structured stimuli. It is assumed that people will reveal themselves by putting themselves into the stimuli they see. The validity of these tests for diagnosis and personality assessment is still at issue.

Propaganda Information deliberately spread to aid a cause. Propaganda's main function is persuasion.

Prosocial Behavior Behavior which is directed toward helping others.

Proximal Stimulus Activity at the sense organ.

Psychoactive Drug A substance that affects mental activities, perceptions, consciousness, or mood. This group of drugs has its effects through strictly physical effects and through expectations.

Psychoanalysis There are two meanings to this word: it is a theory of personality development based on Freud and a method of treatment also based on Freud. Psychoanalytic therapy uses techniques of free association, dream analysis, and analysis of the patient's relationship (the "transference") to the analyst. Psychoanalytic theory maintains that the personality develops through a series of psychosexual stages and that the personality consists of specific components energized by the life and death instincts.

Psychogenic Pain Disorder Somatoform disorder in which the person complains of severe, long-lasting pain for which there is no organic cause.

Psycholinguistics The study of the process of language acquisition as part of psychological development and of language as an aspect of behavior. Thinking may obviously depend on language, but their precise relationship still puzzles psycholinguists, and several different views exist.

Psychological Dependence Situation when a person craves a drug even though it is not biologically necessary for his body.

Psychophysiological Disorders Real medical problems (such as ulcers, migraine headaches, and high blood pressure) which are caused or aggravated by psychological stress.

Psychosexual Stages According to Freud, an individual's personality develops through several stages. Each stage is associated with a particular bodily source of gratification (pleasure). First comes the oral stage when most pleasures come from the mouth. Then comes the anal stage when the infant derives pleasure from holding and releasing while learning bowel control. The phallic stage brings pleasure from the genitals, and a crisis (Oedipal) occurs in which the child gradually suppresses sexual desire for the opposite-sex parent, identifies with the same-sex parent and begins to be interested in the outside world. This latency period lasts until puberty, after which the genital stage begins and mature sexual relationships develop. There is no strict timetable, but according to Freudians, the stages do come in a definite order. Conflicts experienced and not adequately dealt with remain with the individual.

Psychosis The most severe of mental disorders, distinguished by a person being seriously out of touch with objective reality. Psychoses may result from physical factors (organic) or may have no known physical cause (functional). Psychoses take many forms of which the most common are schizophrenia and psychotic depressive reactions, but all are marked by personality disorganization and a severely reduced ability to perceive reality. Both biological and environmental factors are believed to influence the development of psychosis, although the precise effect of each is not presently known. *See* Neurosis.

Psychosomatic Disorders A variety of body reactions that are closely related to psychological events. Stress, for example, brings on many physical changes and can result in illness or even death if prolonged and severe. Psychosomatic disorders can affect any part of the body.

Psychotherapy Treatment involving interpersonal contacts between a trained therapist and a patient in which the therapist tries to produce beneficial changes in the patient's emotional state, attitudes, and behavior.

Punishment Any event that decreases the probability of the preceding behavior being repeated. You can give something bad (positive punishment) to decrease the preceding behavior.

Rational-Emotive Therapy A cognitive behavior modification technique in which a person is taught to identify irrational, self-defeating beliefs and then to overcome them.

Rationalization Defense mechanism in which individuals make up logical excuses to justify their behavior rather than exposing their true motives.

Reaction Formation Defense mechanism in which a person masks an unconsciously distressing or unacceptable trait by assuming an opposite attitude or behavior pattern.

Reactive Schizophrenia A type of schizophrenia in which the disorder appears as a reaction to some major trauma or terribly stressful encounter; sometimes called acute schizophrenia.

Reality Therapy A form of treatment of mental disorders pioneered by William Glasser in which the origins of the patient's problems are considered irrelevant and emphasis is on a close, judgmental bond between patient and therapist aimed to improve the patient's present and future life.

Reflex An automatic movement that occurs in direct response to a stimulus.

Rehearsal The repeating of an item to oneself and the means by which information is stored in the short-term memory (STM). Theory suggests that rehearsal is necessary for remembering and storage in the long-term memory (LTM).

Reinforcement The process of affecting the frequency with which a behavior is emitted. A reinforcer can reward and thus increase the behavior or punish and thus decrease its frequency. Reinforcers can also be primary, satisfying basic needs such as hunger or thirst, or secondary, satisfying learned and indirect values, such as money.

Reliability Consistency of measurement. A test is reliable if it repeatedly gives the same results. A person should get nearly the same score if the test is taken on two different occasions.

REM (Rapid-Eye Movement) Type of sleep in which the eyes are rapidly moving around; dreaming occurs in REM sleep.

Repression A defense mechanism in which a person forgets or pushes into the unconscious something that arouses anxiety. *See* Defense Mechanism, Anxiety.

Reticular Formation A system of nerve fibers leading from the spinal column to the cerebral cortex that functions to arouse, alert, and make an organism sensitive to changes in the environment. *See* Cerebral Cortex.

Retina The inside coating of the eye, containing two kinds of cells that react to light: the rods which are sensitive only to dim light and the cones which are sensitive to color and form in brighter light. There are three kinds of cones, each responsive to particular colors in the visible spectrum (range of colors).

Risky Shift Research suggests that decisions made by groups will involve considerably more risk than individuals in the group would be willing to take. This shift in group decision depends heavily on cultural values. *See* Cautious Shift.

Rod Part of the retina involved in seeing in dim light. *See* Retina.

RNA (Ribonucleic Acid) A chemical substance that occurs in chromosomes and that functions in genetic coding. During task-learning, RNA changes occur in the brain.

Role Playing Adopting the role of another person and experiencing the world in a way one is not accustomed to.

Role Taking The ability to imagine oneself in another's place or to understand the consequences of one's actions for another person.

Schachter-Singer Theory of Emotion Theory of emotion which states that we interpret our arousal according to our environment and label our emotions accordingly.

Schizoid Personality Personality disorder characterized by having great trouble developing social relationships.

Schizophrenia The most common and serious form of psychosis in which there exists an imbalance between emotional reactions and the thoughts associated with these feelings. It may be a disorder of the process of thinking. *See* Psychosis.

Scientific Method The process used by psychologists to determine principles of behavior that exist independently of individual experience and that are untouched by unconscious bias. It is based on a prearranged agreement that criteria, external to the individual and communicable to others, must be established for each set of observations referred to as fact.

Secondary Reinforcement Reinforcement that is only effective after it has been associated with a primary reinforcer.

Self-Actualization A term used by humanistic psychologists to describe what they see as a basic human motivation: the development of all aspects of an individual into productive harmony.

Self-Esteem A person's evaluation of himself. If a person "likes himself," feels he can control his actions, that his acts and work are worthy and competent, his self-esteem is high.

Self-Fulfilling Prophecy A preconceived expectation or belief about a situation that evokes behavior resulting in a situation consistent with the preconception.

Senses An organism's physical means of receiving and detecting physical changes in the environment. Sensing is analyzed in terms of reception of the physical stimulus by specialized nerve cells in the sense organs, transduction or converting the stimulus' energy into nerve impulses that the brain can interpret, and transmission of those nerve impulses from the sense organ to the part of the brain that can interpret the information they convey.

Sensitivity Training Aims at helping people to function more effectively in their jobs by increasing their awareness of their own and others' feelings and exchanging "feedback" about styles of interacting. Sensitivity groups are unlike therapy groups in that they are meant to enrich the participants' lives. Participants are not considered patients or ill. Also called T-groups.

Sensorimotor Stage According to Piaget, the stage of development beginning at birth during which perceptions are tied to objects which the child manipulates. Gradually the child learns that objects have permanence even if they are out of sight or touch.

Sensory Adaptation Tendency of the sense organs to adjust to continuous, unchanging stimulation by reducing their functioning; a stimulus that once caused sensation no longer does.

Sensory Deprivation The blocking out of all outside stimulation for a period of time. As studied experimentally, it can produce hallucinations, psychological disturbances, and temporary disorders of the nervous system of the subject.

Sex Role The attitudes, activities, and expectations considered specific to being male or female, determined by both biological and cultural factors.

Shaping A technique of behavior shaping in which behavior is acquired through the reinforcement of successive approximations of the desired behavior. *See* Successive Approximations.

Sleep A periodic state of consciousness marked by four brain-wave patterns. Dreams occur during relatively light Stage 1 sleep. Sleep is a basic need without which one may suffer physical or psychological distress. *See* Brain Waves, Dreams.

Sleeper Effect The delayed impact of persuasive information. People tend to forget the context in which they first heard the information, but they eventually remember the content of the message sufficiently to feel its impact.

Social Comparison Theory proposed by Festinger which states that we have a tendency to compare our behavior to others to ensure that we are conforming.

Social Facilitation Phenomenon in which the presence of others increases dominant behavior patterns in an individual; Zajonc's theory of social facilitation states that the presence of others enhances the emission of the dominant response of the individual.

Social Influence The process by which people form and change the attitudes, opinions, and behavior of others.

Socialization A process by which a child learns the various patterns of behavior expected and accepted by society. Parents are the chief agents of a child's socialization. Many factors have a bearing on the socialization process, such as the child's sex, religion, social class, and parental attitudes.

Social Learning Learning acquired through observation and imitation of others.

Social Psychology The study of individuals as affected by others and of the interaction of individuals in groups.

Sociobiology The study of the genetic basis of social behavior.

Sociophobias Excessive irrational fears and embarrassment when interacting with other people.

Somatic Nervous System The part of the peripheral nervous system that carries messages from the sense organs and relays information that directs the voluntary movements of the skeletal muscles.

Somatoform Disorders Disorders characterized by physical symptoms for which there are no obvious physical causes.

Somesthetic Senses Skin senses; includes pressure, pain, cold, and warmth.

Species-Typical Behavior Behavior patterns common to members of a species. Ethologists state that each species inherits some patterns of behavior (e.g. birdsongs).

Stanford-Binet Intelligence Scale Tests that measure intelligence from two years through adult level. The tests determine one's intelligence quotient by establishing one's chronological and mental ages. *See* Intelligence Quotient.

State-Dependent Learning Situation in which what is learned in one state can only be remembered when the person is in that state.

Statistically Significant In inferential statistics, a finding that the independent variable did influence greatly the outcome of the experimental and control group.

Stereotype The assignment of characteristics to a person mainly on the basis of the group, class, or category to which he belongs. The tendency to categorize and generalize is a basic human way of organizing information. Stereotyping, however, can reinforce misinformation and prejudice. *See* Prejudice.

Stimulus A unit of the environment which causes a response in an individual; more specifically, a physical or chemical agent acting on an appropriate sense receptor.

Stimulus Discrimination Limiting responses to relevant stimuli.

Stimulus Generalization Responses to stimuli similar to the stimulus that had caused the response.

Stress Pressure that puts unusual demands on an organism. Stress may be caused by physical conditions but eventually will involve both. Stimuli that cause stress are called stressors, and an organism's response is the stress reaction. A three-stage general adaptation syndrome is hypothesized involving both emotional and physical changes. *See* General Adaptation System.

Structuralism An early school of psychology that stressed the importance of conscious experience as the subject matter of psychology and maintained that experience should be analyzed into its component parts by use of introspection. *See* Introspection.

Sublimation Defense mechanism in which a person redirects his socially undesirable urges into socially acceptable behavior.

Subliminal Stimuli Stimuli that do not receive conscious attention because they are below sensory thresholds. They may influence behavior, but research is not conclusive on this matter.

Substance-Induced Organic Mental Disorders Organic mental disorders caused by exposure to harmful environmental substances.

Suggestibility The extent to which a person responds to persuasion. Hypnotic susceptibility refers to the degree of suggestibility observed after an attempt to induce hypnosis has been made. *See* Persuasion, Hypnosis.

Superego According to Freud, the superego corresponds roughly to conscience. The superego places restrictions on both ego and id and represents the internalized restrictions and ideals that the child learns from parents and culture. *See* Conscience, Ego, Id.

Sympathetic Nervous System The branch of the autonomic nervous system that is more active in emergencies; it causes a general arousal, increasing breathing, heart rate and blood pressure.

Synapse A "gap" where individual nerve cells (neurons) come together and across which chemical information is passed.

Syndrome A group of symptoms that occur together and mark a particular abnormal pattern.

Systematic Desensitization A technique used in behavior therapy to eliminate a phobia. The symptoms of the phobia are seen as conditioned responses of fear, and the procedure attempts to decondition the fearful response until the patient gradually is able to face the feared situation. *See* Phobia.

TAT (Thematic Apperception Test) Personality and motivation test which requires the subject to devise stories about pictures.

Taxis An orienting movement in response to particular stimuli in the environment. A frog, for example, always turns so its snout points directly at its prey before it flicks its tongue. *See* Orienting Response.

Theory A very general statement that is more useful in generating hypotheses than in generating research. *See* Hypotheses.

Therapeutic Community The organization of a hospital setting so that patients have to take responsibility for helping one another in an attempt to prevent patients from getting worse by being in the hospital.

Token Economy A system for organizing a treatment setting according to behavioristic principles. Patients are encouraged to take greater responsibility for their adjustment by receiving tokens for acceptable behavior and fines for unacceptable behavior. The theory of token economy grew out of operant conditioning techniques. *See* Operant Conditioning.

Traits Distinctive and stable attributes that can be found in all people.

Tranquilizers Psychoactive drugs which reduce anxiety. *See* Psychoactive Drugs.

Trial and Error Learning Trying various behaviors in a situation until the solution is hit upon; past experiences lead us to try different responses until we are successful.

Unconditioned Response (UR) An automatic reaction elicited by a stimulus.

Unconditioned Stimulus (US) Any stimulus that elicits an automatic or reflexive reaction in an individual; it does not have to be learned in the present situation.

Unconscious In Freudian terminology, a concept (not a place) of the mind. The unconscious encompasses certain inborn impulses that never rise into consciousness (awareness) as well as memories and wishes that have been repressed. The chief aim of psychoanalytic therapy is to free repressed material from the unconscious in order to make it susceptible to conscious thought and direction. Behaviorists describe the unconscious as an inability to verbalize. *See* Repression.

Undifferentiated Schizophrenia Type of schizophrenia which does not fit into any particular category, or fits into more than one category.

Validity The extent to which a test actually measures what it is designed to measure.

Variability In statistics, measures of variability communicate how spread out the scores are; the tendency to vary the response to a stimulus, particularly if the response fails to help in adaptation.

Variable Any property of a person, object, or event that can change or take on more than one mathematical value.

Weber's Law States that the difference threshold depends on the ratio of the intensity of one stimulus to another rather than an absolute difference.

Wechsler Adult Intelligence Scale (WAIS) An individually administered test designed to measure adults' intelligence, devised by David Wechsler. The WAIS consists of eleven subtests, of which six measure verbal and five measure performance aspects of intelligence. *See* Wechsler Intelligence Scale for Children.

Wechsler Intelligence Scale for Children (WISC) Similar to the Wechsler Adult Intelligence Scale, except that it is designed for people under fifteen. Wechsler tests can determine strong and weak areas of overall intelligence. *See* Wechsler Adult Intelligence Scale (WAIS).

Whorfian Hypothesis The linguistic relativity hypothesis of Benjamin Whorf; states that language influences thought.

Withdrawal Social or emotional detachment; the removal of oneself from a painful or frustrating situation.

Yerkes-Dodson Law Prediction that the optimum motivation level decreases as the difficulty level of a task increases.

Source for the Glossary:
The majority of terms in this glossary are reprinted from *The Study of Psychology*, Joseph Rubinstein. ©The Dushkin Publishing Group, Inc., Guilford, CT 06437.
The remaining terms were developed by the Annual Editions staff.

Credits/ Acknowledgments

Cover design by Charles Vitelli

1. Science of Psychology
Facing overview—Medical World News.

2. Biological Bases of Behavior
Facing overview—United Nations photo by John Orr.

3. Perceptual Processes
Facing overview—Dr. Peter Hauri, Dartmouth Sleep Clinic.

4. Learning and Memory
Facing overview—United Nations photo by Marta Pinter. 78—United Nations photo by John Isaac.

5. Cognitive Processes
Facing overview—United Nations photo by Margot.

6. Motivation and Emotion
Facing overview—WHO photo by K. Kalisher.

7. Development
Facing overview—United Nations photo by John Isaac.

8. Personality Processes
Facing overview—Harvard University Press, © 1943, 1971.

9. Social Processes
Facing overview—United Nations photo. 185—Chart: Earth Surface Graphics.

10. Psychological Disorders
Facing overview—The Dushkin Publishing Group photo by Cheryl Nicholas.

11. Psychological Treatments
Facing overview—The Dushkin Publishing Group photo. 216—The Dushkin Publishing Group photo by Pamela Carley Petersen.

ANNUAL EDITIONS ARTICLE REVIEW FORM

■ NAME: _____ DATE: _____

■ TITLE AND NUMBER OF ARTICLE: _____

■ BRIEFLY STATE THE MAIN IDEA OF THIS ARTICLE: _____

_____

_____

_____

_____

■ LIST THREE IMPORTANT FACTS THAT THE AUTHOR USES TO SUPPORT THE MAIN IDEA:

_____

_____

_____

_____

_____

_____

■ WHAT INFORMATION OR IDEAS DISCUSSED IN THIS ARTICLE ARE ALSO DISCUSSED IN YOUR
TEXTBOOK OR OTHER READING YOU HAVE DONE? LIST THE TEXTBOOK CHAPTERS AND PAGE
NUMBERS:

_____

_____

_____

_____

_____

_____

■ LIST ANY EXAMPLES OF BIAS OR FAULTY REASONING THAT YOU FOUND IN THE ARTICLE:

_____

_____

_____

_____

_____

■ LIST ANY NEW TERMS/CONCEPTS THAT WERE DISCUSSED IN THE ARTICLE AND WRITE A
SHORT DEFINITION:

_____

_____

_____

_____

_____

*Your instructor may require you to use this Annual Editions Article Review Form in any number of ways:
for articles that are assigned, for extra credit, as a tool to assist in developing assigned papers, or simply
for your own reference. Even if it is not required, we encourage you to photocopy and use this page;
you'll find that reflecting on the articles will greatly enhance the information from your text.

ANNUAL EDITIONS: PSYCHOLOGY 91/92
Article Rating Form

Here is an opportunity for you to have direct input into the next revision of this volume. We would like you to rate each of the 44 articles listed below, using the following scale:

1. **Excellent: should definitely be retained**
2. **Above average: should probably be retained**
3. **Below average: should probably be deleted**
4. **Poor: should definitely be deleted**

Your ratings will play a vital part in the next revision. So please mail this prepaid form to us just as soon as you complete it.
Thanks for your help!

Rating	Article	Rating	Article
	1. Psychology From the Standpoint of a Generalist		23. Managing Stress and Living Longer
	2. Of One Mind		24. Don't Act Your Age
	3. How the Brain Really Works Its Wonders		25. Shattered Innocence
	4. Is It One Clock, or Several, That Cycle Us Through Life?		26. Confident at 11, Confused at 16
	5. What a Child Is Given		27. The Vintage Years
	6. New Connections		28. Why Can't a Man Be More Like a Woman . . . and Vice Versa
	7. A Pleasurable Chemistry		29. Blurring the Lines: Androgyny on Trial
	8. Are We Led by the Nose?		30. Do Optimists Live Longer?
	9. No Simple Slumber		31. Health's Character
	10. What Dreams Are (Really) Made Of		32. Are Criminals Made or Born?
	11. How to Discover What You Have to Say—A Talk to Students		33. Marching in Step
	12. How Kids Learn		34. Close Encounters
	13. Memory Repair		35. Getting Help From Helping
	14. Extraordinary People		36. When Mental Illness Hits Home
	15. A New Perspective on Cognitive Development in Infancy		37. The Clouded Mind
	16. New Views of Human Intelligence		38. Dysthymic Disorder: The DD's Blues Without End
	17. Is the Brain's Mind a Computer Program?		39. Anxiety and Panic: Their Cause and Treatment
	18. Capturing Your Creativity		40. When to Challenge the Therapist—and Why
	19. The Face as Window and Machine for the Emotions		41. The Key to Successful Therapy
	20. Emotions: How They Affect Your Body		42. Beating Depression
	21. Thinking Well: The Chemical Links Between Emotions and Health		43. Infants in Need of Psychotherapy? A Fledgling Field Is Growing Fast
	22. Dangerous Thoughts		44. Help Yourself: Self-Care for Emotional Problems

(Continued on next page)

ABOUT YOU

Name_____ Date_____

Are you a teacher? ☐ Or student? ☐

Your School Name _____

Department _____

Address _____

City _____ State _____ Zip _____

School Telephone # _____

YOUR COMMENTS ARE IMPORTANT TO US!

Please fill in the following information:

For which course did you use this book? _____

Did you use a text with this Annual Edition? ☐ yes ☐ no

The title of the text? _____

What are your general reactions to the Annual Editions concept?

Have you read any particular articles recently that you think should be included in the next edition?

Are there any articles you feel should be replaced in the next edition? Why?

Are there other areas that you feel would utilize an Annual Edition?

May we contact you for editorial input?

May we quote you from above?

ANNUAL EDITIONS: PSYCHOLOGY 91/92

BUSINESS REPLY MAIL

First Class   Permit No. 84   Guilford, CT

Postage will be paid by addressee

The Dushkin Publishing Group, Inc.
Sluice Dock
DPG **Guilford, Connecticut 06437**